Dominion Built of Praise

JEWISH CULTURE AND CONTEXTS

Published in association with the
Herbert D. Katz Center for Advanced Judaic Studies
of the University of Pennsylvania

Series editors: Shaul Magid, Francesca Trivellato, Steven Weitzman

A complete list of books in the series is available from the publisher.

DOMINION BUILT *of* PRAISE

Panegyric and Legitimacy Among Jews
in the Medieval Mediterranean

JONATHAN DECTER

PENN

UNIVERSITY OF PENNSYLVANIA PRESS
PHILADELPHIA

Published by

University of Pennsylvania Press
Philadelphia, Pennsylvania 19104-4112
www.upenn.edu/pennpress

Printed in the United States of America on acid-free paper
10 9 8 7 6 5 4 3 2 1

Library of Congress Cataloging-in-Publication Data
Names: Decter, Jonathan P., 1971– author.
Title: Dominion built of praise : panegyric and legitimacy among Jews in the medieval Mediterranean / Jonathan Decter.
Other titles: Jewish culture and contexts.
Description: 1st edition. | Philadelphia : University of Pennsylvania Press, [2018] | Series: Jewish culture and contexts | Includes bibliographical references and index.
Identifiers: LCCN 2018004265 | ISBN 9780812250411 (hardcover : alk. paper)
Subjects: LCSH: Hebrew poetry, Medieval—Mediterranean Region—History and criticism. | Laudatory poetry—History and criticism. | Praise in literature. | Jews—Mediterranean Region—Social life and customs—History—To 1500. | Leadership—Religious aspects—Judaism—History—To 1500. | Power (Philosophy) in literature.
Classification: LCC PJ5023 .D43 2018 | DDC 892.41/209—dc23
LC record available at https://lccn.loc.gov/2018004265

For Nikki

CONTENTS

INTRODUCTION

I remember once as a graduate student reading in class a long Hebrew poem, "Lekha re'i ve-re'a ha-me'orim" (Come, my friend and friend of the luminaries), by the eleventh-century Andalusian Jewish poet Shelomoh Ibn Gabirol. We began with the poem's exquisite introduction, which describes a palace garden wherein the flowers, statues, and birds engage in a word battle of one-upmanship, each claiming superiority over his rivals. Ultimately, the poet's voice intrudes upon the scene to silence the competitors and declare that none can compare with the addressee of the poem, whose virtues the poet extols for another ten lines. I remember how we read the poem line by line, meticulously parsing each word, appreciating the aesthetic effects, and comparing themes with themes from Arabic poetry. We began with the first line, and, by the time class ended, we had barely reached the *takhalluṣ* (Ar., "escape verse"), in which the poet made a transition from the description of the garden to praise for his addressee.

In the next class, we did not return to read the panegyric section but began with another *qaṣīda* (Ar., formal ode), Yehudah Halevi's "Ereṣ ke-yaldah haytah yoneqet" (The earth nursed like a baby girl), another nature description leading into panegyric. Again, we read to the *takhallus*, and class ended.[1] None of us missed reading the panegyric in detail. Even a cursory glance at the panegyric sections of several poems revealed a rather predictable set of virtues (generosity, wisdom, eloquence) inevitably presented through tropes that were equally as predictable (generous as the rain, wise as Solomon, speech like arrows). Further, the panegyrics seldom offered any personal data that a biographer or historian might find of interest. And most of all, we found the poet's obsequious posturing downright detestable—all of that fawning was laid on so thick and reeked of phoniness, especially since poets seemed to say the same thing about every addressee.

Alas, medieval Hebrew praise poetry did not fit our literary tastes. Surely, we were not alone. Our preference for love poetry, nature poetry, and other genres was something that we shared with the pioneering scholars of the *Wissenschaft des Judentums*, whose Romantic tastes had a lasting impact on the development of the field of medieval Hebrew poetry. Jefim Schirmann, in a classic article of 1954, "The Function of the Poet in Medieval Spain," wrote about the patronage system that he saw as the primary context for Hebrew panegyric in al-Andalus (Islamic Iberia): "Such dependence [on patrons] induced the poets to indulge in exaggerations and sycophancy of the worst kind."[2] Years later, in his posthumous *Toledot ha-shirah ha-'ivrit bi-Sefarad ha-muslemit* (History of Hebrew poetry in Muslim Spain), Schirmann described the patronage system more generously, though he still maintained a sharp division between praise poetry, which he considered a necessary chore, and the other genres, which he believed were closer to the poets' hearts. "Since it was now possible for [the poet] to work under the protection of a patron, he was able to write in his free time poetry for purposes other than making a living—that is for his personal enjoyment—meditative poems, poems on nature, love, and wine, humorous and invective poems, and poems of grief and complaint."[3]

However, we should not be so quick to judge which literary genres held personal meaning for the poets; Schirmann's assessment reflects his own literary tastes more than theirs. Most peculiar is his placement of panegyric in the "chore" category and invective in the "personal enjoyment" category, since classical and medieval critics, including Aristotle, Ibn Rushd, and Mosheh Ibn Ezra, saw them as two sides of the same coin and often treated them together. While Schirmann may well be one of the finest scholars of medieval Hebrew poetry ever to have lived, it is worth critically evaluating his position on panegyric and the cultural assumptions that it entails. His views are reflective of a general devaluation of panegyric in modernity. Already in 1656, an English dictionary by Thomas Blount defined panegyric as "a licentious kind of speaking or oration, in the praise and commendation of Kings, or other great persons, wherein some falsities are joined with many flatteries."[4] J. A. Burrow has argued that, beginning with the late seventeenth century, "[m]any deep seated changes in society, politics, economics and religious belief have contributed to a culture more at home with tin men than with heroes" ("tin men" being a reference to a poem by Ezra Pound).[5]

Panegyric's decline in modern Europe surely had an impact on scholarship's approach to panegyric in non-Western traditions. Jaroslav Stetkevych notes that

German Orientalists first "enthusiastically engaged and assimilated the *qasida*, including panegyric, particularly in adaptations and translations, but then in the mid-nineteenth century, enthusiasm was replaced by a stale technical approach."[6] In 1909, Louis Ginzberg, a leading scholar of rabbinics, blamed Hai Gaon for having gone in panegyric "to an extreme of extravagance unusual *even in an Oriental writer*."[7] S. D. Goitein also wrote that most praise writings preserved in the Cairo Geniza (a great mass of documents discovered in a Cairo synagogue) were "exasperating by their hyperbolic generalities" (though in this context he wrote that a particular poem was an exception).[8]

No medieval Hebrew poet laments that the exigencies of writing praise poetry kept him from pursuing more noble poetic genres. Poets marshaled their skills in panegyric just as much as they did in other areas. Although the panegyrist had to avoid certain ethical pitfalls, I see no evidence that the poets generally regarded panegyric as a lesser genre.[9] In Mosheh Ibn Ezra's review of desirable literary devices in his Judeo-Arabic treatise on Hebrew poetics, *Kitāb al-muḥāḍara wa'l-mudhākara* (The book of conversations and discussions), more than one-third of the Hebrew poetic excerpts are taken from panegyrics, and one section is dedicated to a device particular to panegyric; in addition, he quotes four lines of an Arabic panegyric by Abū Tammām in order to demonstrate how poetic meaning is conveyed.[10]

If we can judge from the sheer prevalence and persistence of Hebrew panegyric across time and space, it is clear that it played a vital function in Jewish society in the medieval Mediterranean. In fact, the ubiquity of praise as a social practice is difficult to overstate. It was a common feature of social interaction across a host of relationships, quite often divorced from the remunerative patronage structure that Schirmann emphasized. Further, we will see that literary panegyric was only one facet of a broader practice of praise, which also included terms of address and titles, greetings and blessings, and simply commending one party to another. Although such practices may seem strange to us, they were clearly very important to medieval Jews.

As mentioned, panegyrics can be frustratingly ungenerous sources for the historian; they offer typology, not biography, as well as hyperbolic and formulaic statements—what the historian of the Jews Jacob Mann sometimes called "verbiage."[11] Yet positivist historians such as Mann also recognized that panegyrics are sometimes the only surviving sources that testify to the existence of particular figures, where and when they lived, with whom they were in contact, how many sons they had, and other precious tidbits of data. In the present book, however, panegyric will be used in other ways in order to illuminate medieval Jews' most essential notions of group cohesion, human virtue, leadership, and politics; in fact, the book will consider how praise intersected with nearly every aspect of Jewish social and intellectual culture in the medieval Mediterranean.

Dominion Built of Praise

This book presents Jews of the medieval Mediterranean through the lens of praise writing. The focus is on Jewish centers in the Islamic Mediterranean between the tenth and thirteenth centuries and includes an extensive chapter on Jews in the Christian Mediterranean through the fifteenth century. The book has two main interrelated purposes. One is to study the phenomenon of praise writing in Mediterranean Jewish culture from several overlapping perspectives: social-historical, ethical, poetic, political, and theological. These interests are reflected in the table of contents, where the reader will notice an arc beginning with social history and moving toward topics more abstract and ethereal, before closing with a chapter on the Christian Mediterranean and another on interreligious panegyric. Studying medieval Jewish society through the lens of praise writing reveals some of that society's social values and political structures. The subject also helps delineate the place of Jews within the Mediterranean, including their interior and interreligious discourses of power. Panegyric addresses not only relationships within Jewish groups (whether these are intellectual circles or an imagined polity) but also, on occasion, relationships between Jews and their non-Jewish rulers.

The second purpose of the book is to study more specifically the nature and changing elements of images of ideal Jewish leadership, images that hark back to earlier Jewish constructions of power while drawing upon contemporary non-Jewish formulations of legitimacy. Like visual portraits, panegyrics operate according to a code of cultural norms that tell us at least as much about the society that produced them as they do about the individuals they portray.[12] I am thus less interested in studying the people behind literary facades than in studying the facades themselves.[13] This book seeks to understand the valences of conventional character traits ascribed to Jewish leaders both diachronically within the "Jewish political tradition" and synchronically within Islamic (and, to a lesser extent, Christian) civilization and political culture. Throughout the book, I place subjects under discussion in dialogue with related phenomena in contemporary non-Jewish culture, especially the poetics of political legitimacy as expressed in Arabic writing. I argue that points of overlap between Jewish and Islamic discourses of power demonstrate more than a surface functional parallel between Muslim and Jewish forms of "statecraft" but also that ideas of Islamic legitimacy profoundly shaped how Jews conceptualized and portrayed their own leadership. At the same time, the book studies shifting representations of Jewish leadership according to social role, political rank, period, and region.

To a certain degree, I use the word "legitimacy," which appears in the book title, in the way that Max Weber did, whereby a power-holder essentially persuades a power-subject of his rightful authority through various means. For Weber, different types of claims undergirded a variety of forms of legitimacy: traditional, whereby power is secured by claims of long-standing, sometimes sacredly inflected, norms; charismatic, whereby the governed submit because of some extraordinary quality of a given person, family, or office, and this, too, can be inflected with the sacred; and rational or legal, which appeals to norms that are established not by mere precedent but by reason.[14] Throughout this book, the reader will encounter many examples of the first two varieties, though the idea of "authority" is applied here in a very loose way, since the powers of the men in question were often quite limited; in some cases, to offer a man loyalty or "obedience" meant only to say that he was deserving of praise. Further, many of the relationships witnessed here are more lateral than hierarchic, and, in some cases, panegyrics were written by the more powerful for the less powerful upon whom they nonetheless relied. Where I part with Weber most significantly regards what has been recognized as his "ruler-centric" vantage point that understands claims of legitimacy solely as a tool for implementing obedience, for I am equally interested in what panegyrics did for power-subjects—that is, their authors and audiences. These topics are taken up in the coming chapters, but we can say that while Weber's conception of authority might not be sufficiently nuanced for the corpus under discussion, his categorization of types of claims remains remarkably apt.[15]

Further, I argue that praise was not only reflective but also constitutive of power among medieval Jews. That is, authority was a result of its own articulation and could not be realized but for the presentation of praise with its attending metaphors and conceptual frameworks of legitimacy. These metaphors could be relational (e.g., the leader is to his people as the head is to the limbs) or even theological (the leader as a sacred object, an angel, or even God). As Esperanza Alfonso has argued with respect to Hebrew panegyric in al-Andalus, such metaphors are not only hyperbolic but also provide the audience a cognitive means for interpreting the world; they are, as Lakoff and Johnson put it, metaphors to "live by."[16] Metaphors of political structure are fundamental for the effective exercise of power in even the most heavily militarized and dictatorial of regimes. In the case of Jewish leadership in the medieval Mediterranean, which had no military, no real territory, and few means of coercion, such metaphors were sometimes all that existed for the constitution and promulgation of power. Thus, at the core of this book is a fundamental argument about rhetoric, that it is not merely an ornamental layer superadded to a type of discourse but is the very substance of that discourse that has the power to construct "reality" for its audience.

In an eleventh-century Hebrew panegyric for the court astronomer Avraham Ibn al-Muhājir, Mosheh Ibn Ezra wrote: "[His] dominion is built out of precious stones while others' is built out of whitewash and plaster."[17] What Ibn Ezra recognized was that dominion, whether legitimate or illegitimate, was a matter of construction. In fact, the words translated here as "precious stones" (*avnei tehilot*, "stones [worthy of] praise") most literally mean "stones of praise." Dominion is built out of stones of praise. Although Ibn Ezra's intent was probably one of comparison and juxtaposition, the verse conveys that dominion is literally built out of praise; without the building blocks of praise, there would be no dominion.

Most studies of Jewish power have focused on the influence of Jews within the court structures of their host cultures, whether or not they carried arms or fought in battle, and the extent of Jewish autonomy.[18] This study, in contrast, is interested in the representation of power, the idealization of attributes as conveyed in panegyric. Like the panegyrics recited before Caesar in the classical world or the literary and artistic portraits of English monarchs, Hebrew panegyrics depict leaders who are at once members of their age—that is, they are born, die, and attain certain accomplishments—and embodiments of ideals of peoplehood, religion, and epochs.

Many figures included in this book held high offices within the Jewish community, with titles such as *gaon* (academy dean), *rosh golah* (exilarch), *nagid* (leader), and *ra'īs al-yahūd* (head of the Jews); lower-ranking but substantial offices such as *qāḍī* (judge) and *kātib* (scribe); or titles of honor bestowed upon them for communal or philanthropic activity, such as *aluf* (captain), *rosh ha-seder* (head of the order), and *rosh kallah* (head of the assembly).[19] At the same time, the book will treat recipients of panegyric who held no official rank for whom "dominion" (*misrah*) was generally not a reality. Such figures—including grammarians, poets, and exegetes—were portrayed according to sets of conventions particular to their social roles; still, political imagery found its way into their representation as well, albeit in metaphoric form (the "king of poetry" and the like). This book therefore offers a series of cross-sections of the overlapping layers of Jewish society in the medieval Mediterranean—from the macrostructures of trans-regional leadership, to what was more regional, even local, in character, to circles of merchants and intellectuals.

The central body of texts includes the many hundreds of panegyrics dedicated to Jews of these numerous ranks, most often in Hebrew, sometimes in Judeo-Arabic, and, in some cases, both languages. The texts have been preserved through various means, from highly prized examples copied over many times, sometimes in luxury editions of books (and then printed in modernity), to collections of epistles copied by court scribes, and the occasional letters, poems, and other documents haphazardly discarded in the Cairo Geniza.[20] Praise is found not only in freestanding "literary" panegyrics, whether in poetry or prose, but also in texts that are usually designated "documentary sources" such as letters or dedications of books or buildings. One methodological point of this book is to recover the original social function of "literary" texts and to discuss the literary features of "documentary" sources, thus closing the assumed gap between the two corpora; a text presented to the modern reader as a prime example of "medieval Hebrew literature," a text that was copied, anthologized, and commented upon, may have begun its life with a social purpose functionally indistinguishable from a scrap serendipitously preserved in the Geniza. Other sources utilized throughout the book in an ancillary manner include biblical exegesis, legal and lexicographic works, Arabic poetry, and treatises on philosophy, theology, and poetics by Jewish and non-Jewish authors.

Although the focus of the book is on praise among Jews, I also address, in the final chapter, the panegyrics written by Jews in honor of non-Jews, with examples ranging from Byzantium, Egypt, Syria, Castile, and Aragon in Arabic, Hebrew, and Castilian. The chapter demonstrates how Jews adopted discourses of Islamic and Christian power, sometimes praising non-Jewish figures as Muslims or Christians might have praised them, but also how Jews remained reticent about certain aspects of legitimacy and perhaps furtively conveyed to a Jewish audience a poetics of political resistance.

A Culture of Praise

My interest in Jewish panegyric follows renewed interest in panegyric among scholars of classical Greek and Latin literature, who had previously concentrated their efforts on epic and tragedy, and among scholars of Arabic literature.[21] The panegyric turn itself was predicated on new academic interests in the nature and articulation of power, ceremonial aspects of verbal acclamation, anthropological models of exchange, and so forth. As in the cases of other panegyric traditions, a study of Hebrew panegyric is part literary study, part social history, and even part theology. As such, this book will cross paths numerous times with fields of scholarship that grew out of seminal works by figures such as Max Weber, Marcel Mauss, Pierre Bourdieu, Ernst Kantorowicz, George Lakoff and Mark Johnson, Judith Butler, and others.

The word "panegyric" reflects its originally public function, being derived from a Greek root meaning "public festival."[22] In the classical world, a panegyric could be delivered in poetic or prose form and was recited publicly in conjunction with an event such as an emperor's birthday, the celebration of a victorious battle, or a religious holiday. Recent studies on panegyric in the classical world have treated the poet-patron relationship, shifting images of model leadership, and the role of panegyric in the propaganda of the state.[23] The purposes of panegyric extended far beyond a poet's offering flattery in the hopes of monetary compensation. Panegyrics afforded leaders the opportunity to fashion their public personae, a central practice of state propaganda. Yet the presenting of ruler images cannot be seen as a top-down process only; leaders also functioned as screens upon which the values and aspirations of a cultural group could be projected.[24] Poets sometimes wielded surprising amounts of power and could even use panegyric (and invective) to sway rulers.

Literary representations of leaders tend to pass over individual characteristics in favor of fairly stable and conventional images. They change slowly and are culturally determined and contingent upon historical circumstances. For this reason, seemingly minor shifts within a highly conventional corpus of praise literature can be of great value—both to literary scholars and to historians—not because they reveal much about the biographies of the actual leaders in question but because they represent shifting ideals of leadership itself. Pliny praises Trajan for his *humanitas* and *civitas*, stressing his ability to understand and interact with everyday citizens despite his divinity. During the Tetrarchic period, the emperor becomes more removed from his people. Eusebius peppered his portrait of Constantine with references to the biblical

Moses, whose combined political and religious leadership made him an apposite paradigm of the Christian emperor.[25] Medieval Byzantine panegyrists were sure to include the emperor's place of origin, his education, his zeal for orthodoxy, and, rather uniquely, as T. Dennis put it, "imperial perspiration" (employing such expressions as "the sweat of virtue").[26]

As in the classical world, panegyric (Ar., *madīḥ*, praise) played a pronounced public function in the medieval Islamic world. Praise was an established genre in pre-Islamic poetry and occupied an ambivalent place when directed toward the Prophet Muḥammad following the advent of Islam. In numerous anecdotes, Muḥammad is portrayed as rebuking, even maiming, a panegyrist who praised him, though composing panegyric in the Prophet's honor was also one of the charges of Ḥassān Ibn Thābit, essentially the poet laureate of the new *umma* (nation); such panegyrics were essential in creating the image of the Prophet in the early Islamic community, which readily recognized poetic praise as a political mode. Poets became famous for their intricate poems dedicated to his honor (known as the *burda*, or "mantle" tradition), and more popular laudatory poems were recited at festivals such as the celebration of the Prophet's birthday.[27]

As Islam expanded to become an imperial presence in the Near East, panegyric took on specific ceremonial functions. As has been noted by numerous scholars of classical Arabic poetry, including Beatrice Gruendler and Suzanne Pinckney Stetkevych, the primary experience of Arabic panegyric was oral/aural such that the written poetic texts that have reached us are memorializations produced subsequent to a public event—usually a religious holiday, a caliph's inauguration or birthday, the celebration of a military victory, or the like. Royal panegyrics, which were often performed in the context of a *majlis ʿām* (Ar., public assembly), had several audiences: the addressee whose favor the poet sought to curry, the circle of competing poets whom the poet tried to best, and a wider public upon whom the poet (and the addressee) sought to impress a model of just and legitimate government. Many anecdotes have reached us concerning such issues as the "blocking" of the performance—the spatial positioning and physical postures of poet and addressee at the time of recitation—rituals of remuneration, the role of the audience, or the shaming of rival poets.[28]

Arabic panegyric played a fundamental role in the promotion of state propaganda and the caliphal image. In addition to possessing general praiseworthy characteristics such as generosity and valor, caliphs and governors were praised for the nobility and purity of their lineage, their suppression of religious dissidents, their power to thwart enemies, and the eloquence of their tongues and pens in classical Arabic. Paramount in the establishment of political legitimacy were the twin values of territorial expansion through military conquest and the safeguarding of territory for the proper observance of Islam. Poets often concluded panegyrics with hopes for the addressee's long life, for it was through him that the best of all political circumstances were sustained.

In addition to the formal presentation of panegyric in a *majlis ʿām*, praise could be encountered in a great many contexts, including written addresses, public processions, and "familiar gatherings" (sing., *majlis uns*) where the caliph or another man of power surrounded himself with favorites in a less public yet highly ritualized setting.[29] Further, as Samer Ali has stressed, a useful distinction can be made between the *majlis*, the "royal salon," and the *mujālasa*, a salon based on the *majlis* but whose participants were of the "middle strata, which included men of overlapping professions, such as merchants, absentee landlords, military personnel, and courtiers, as well as pious and literary scholars."[30] The difference is captured beautifully in the forms of the words: *majlis*, from the *faʿla* form, "to sit," and *mujālasa*, from the *fāʿala*, "to sit *with someone*," suggesting reciprocity, sociability, and a higher degree of egalitarianism.[31] As we will see in Chapter 1, this distinction obtains in the various performative contexts of Jewish panegyric.

When one addressed a man of power—either through writing or in person—one was expected to bless and praise him appropriately. The Arabic roots that occur most often in connection with these practices are *dʿw*—"to invoke with blessings"—and *mdḥ*, "to praise." The praise genre is called *madīḥ* or *madḥ*; the person offering praise, the panegyrist, is called the *mādiḥ*, and his addressee was simply called the *mamdūḥ*, "the one praised." Because of the range of social relationships that used praise as a mediating device, in this book I generally refer to the addressee of a panegyric as its *mamdūḥ*, rather than more restrictive and overdetermined terms such as "patron" or "Maecenas," though I will use "patron" in specific senses.

There is little doubt that Jews had firsthand knowledge of Arabic panegyric practices wherein poems were performed orally, both in the Islamic East (*mashriq*) and in the Islamic West (*maghrib*). We hear occasional anecdotes about Jews appearing within Muslim courts where panegyric could be heard with frequency. In addition to such known Jewish courtiers as Yaʿaqūb Ibn Qillīs (Egypt), Sulaiman Abū al-Munajjā (Egypt), and Ḥasdai Ibn Shaprut (al-Andalus), the great Arab rhetorician al-Jāḥiẓ (d. 869) records Arabic verses of three Iraqi Jewish poets in his *Kitāb al-bayān* that would likely have been transmitted in a courtly setting (though these are not panegyrics themselves).[32] Hai Ben Sherirah Gaon (939–1038) considered a legal question about the permissibility of Jews drinking wine while listening to music in the company of non-Jews and ruled that this is generally a severe offense but is permissible for "those who stand before the ruler and work for the protection of the Jews."[33] Although the responsum does not mention either offering or hearing panegyric for the ruler, the scene described suggests a *majlis uns*, a familiar gathering, where some version of praise might be heard. The small amount of panegyric for Muslim rulers written by Jews reflects intimate knowledge of praise conventions.[34]

We know that the Jewish exilarch (*rosh galut*) in Baghdad, essentially the mundane head of the Jewish Diaspora, was granted audience before ʿAbbasid caliphs. Natan ha-Bavli (tenth century) describes how the exilarch was given entry by the caliph's chamberlain (*ḥājib*; lit., "one who veils") and was allowed to "see [the caliph's] face." In one anecdote reported by Natan, the exilarch Mar ʿUqba appeared before the caliph in a certain garden of the royal compound every day for a year and "blessed him (*wa-daʿāhu*) with sweet words and comely poems." It turned out that the poems were not of Mar ʿUqba's own composition but were plagiarized from the notebook of the caliph's scribe, an infraction that ultimately resulted in the exilarch's banishment to the Islamic West. Although the anecdote is likely apocryphal and meant to vilify Mar ʿUqba, it does speak to Jewish knowledge of the inner workings of the Islamic court and the function of panegyric during the classical era of Islam.[35]

It also seems that Jews had familiarity with poems in honor of Muḥammad. Among the documents in Arabic script that have turned up in the Cairo Geniza is an unpublished fragment (TS NS 294.62v Figure 1) that is just such a poem that calls upon God to "perfume his tomb with exaltation . . . and [pray] for the one who brought us our clear religion in truth." It is written in a low literary register and, while lacking the prestige of the most famous poems of the *burda* tradition, would have been popular (in fact, a nearly identical version can be heard today at celebrations of the Prophet's birthday in the Muslim world).[36]

Regarding al-Andalus, I know of no anecdote wherein a Jew dedicates a panegyric to a Muslim potentate, though Ibn Bassām relates that the Muslim poet ʿAbd al-ʿAzīz Ibn Khayra al-Qurṭubī composed an Arabic panegyric for the Jewish *kātib* (scribe) Shemuel ha-Nagid (aka Ismāʿīl Ibn Naghrīla). Muslim historians relate that Ibn Naghrīla was fully adept at the art of Arabic

Figure 1. Praise for Muḥammad. TS NS 294.62v. Reproduced by kind permission of the Syndics of Cambridge University Library.

epistle writing, including mastery of Islamic formulas of address; he would have possessed mastery over *duʿā* and governmental titulature.[37] It is difficult to imagine that he did not also encounter panegyrics for Zirid kings firsthand.[38] Other Jews likely had knowledge of panegyrics that circulated following specific military campaigns.[39] Further, we know of numerous encounters between Jewish and Muslim poets, including the case of a Jewish student (Ar., *talmīdh*) who studied under a Muslim.[40] Jewish panegyric writing certainly displays deep familiarity with the conventions of courtly Arabic panegyric. It is possible that this could have been acquired through reading rather than performance, but it seems likely that there were dual origins. Mosheh Ibn Ezra, for example, quotes ʿAbbasid panegyrics that he encountered through works of Arabic literary criticism and may have also heard contemporary Arabic panegyrics, given his position as "chief of police" (*ṣāḥib al-shurṭa*) in Granada.

The internalization of practices of praise is reflected in medieval readings of certain biblical passages. When introducing the praise of Saul and David returning from battle, the text in 1 Sm 18:6 reads, "the women in all the towns of Israel came out singing and dancing to greet King Saul with timbrels, joy, and *shalishim.*" This last word was understood in the Targum and in most commentaries as the name of a musical instrument, but Ibn Janāḥ in al-Andalus translated it as "poems (Ar., *ash'ār*); it is called thus because its station compared with other speech is the station of elites (Ar., *ru'asā'*; pl. of *ra'īs*) compared with other men." The word *shalish* can also refer to a confidant of a king (2 Kgs 7:17) or his military officer (2 Kgs 9:25), hence a *ra'īs*.[41]

Abundant familiarity with ruler adulation is even apparent in work of the pietist Baḥya Ibn Paquda, who harbored significant animus toward political culture as an incubator of human hubris. In arguing that one must invest literary skill in composing praises for God, whether orally or in writing, the practice of *madīḥ* is evoked in detail and with the technical vocabulary of the literary arts: "If one were to render one's thanks (*shukr*) and praise (*ḥamd*) toward [a ruler] for a kindness (*ḥasn*) he bestowed or a favor (*faḍl*) he granted, whether in poetry or prose (*bi-naẓm aw bi-nathr*), in writing or in speech (*bi-kitāb aw khiṭāb*), one would not omit anything from his rhetoric (*balāghah*) or eloquence (*faṣāḥa*): simile and metaphor, truth and falsehood, whatever is permitted for [the poet] to describe [the ruler]. . . . Accordingly, it is fitting to do with acts of obedience to God."[42] Similarly, Avraham Maimonides opines that a prayer precentor is required to stand when reciting *pesuqei de-zimra* (a liturgical section consisting of praises for God from the Psalms) because, "if a poet (*shā'ir*) were to praise a leader (*ra'īs min al-ru'asā*) or a flesh and blood king in a seated position, he would anger the one praised (*al-mamdūḥ*) more than he would please him."[43]

Panegyric was offered among Jews in the Islamic Mediterranean within many types of social arrangements and in connection with virtually any occasion. It was written by poets for paying patrons but also between friends of equal or similar social rank, between communal officials and their superiors and inferiors, between teachers and students, and between merchants. It could be addressed to a single *mamdūḥ*, a small group, or an entire community. Panegyrics were exchanged between confidants who knew each other intimately but also between individuals residing at vast distances who knew each other by reputation only. They could be written for a person's appointment to a position of distinction, a marriage, the circumcision of a son, or the death of a relative (i.e., in addition to a lament over the dead, the poet would praise surviving relatives).

One wrote panegyric when endorsing a political candidate, appointing a communal officer, requesting a favor, expressing gratitude, responding to an invitation to a party, assuaging anger, and even, paradoxically enough, when offering rebuke. Yehudah Halevi praised Abū Naṣr Ibn al-Yesh'a of Egypt upon the death of his handmaiden (Heb., *ammah*; quite possibly a concubine); and when a dog bit the foot of a certain Ezra Ben al-Thiqqa, El'azar Ben Ya'aqov ha-Bavli invented the following: "Beasts rushed to kiss his shoe; they bit him for they did not know that princes wrap their heads with the strap of his shoe and the stars on high prostrate themselves before his feet."[44] The disposition to praise thus made up one aspect of the *habitus*, to use Pierre Bourdieu's term, of Mediterranean Jews, "principles which generate and organize practices . . . objectively 'regulated' and 'regular' without being in any way the product of obedience to rules, they can be collectively orchestrated without being the product of the organizing action of a conductor."[45]

Even beyond the formal presentation of panegyric, praise was used as an agent that bound people together within webs of social relations. One might report to an addressee that a third party had uttered words in his praise. Notice the dynamics in the introduction to the *Epistle to Yemen*, in which Maimonides (d. 1204) responded to a letter from Ya'aqov, son of the noted Yemeni scholar Natanel al-Fayyūmī. The introduction was written in Hebrew while the main content of the epistle was in Judeo-Arabic. Maimonides had not met his correspondent previously and addressed him thus: "To the honored, great, and holy master and teacher, Ya'aqov, wise and kind, beloved and respected sage, son of the honored, great, and holy master and teacher, Natanel al-Fayyūmī, distinguished prince of Yemen, leader of its congregations, head of its communities."

In addition to responding to the pressing issues of Ya'aqov's letter, Maimonides' introduction addressed Ya'aqov's report that Jews in Yemen, "praise, aggrandize, and extol me and compare me with the illustrious geonim." Maimonides also responded to the news that "our friend, our student, Rav Shelomoh, deputy of the priests, the wise, the intelligent, who indulges in hyperboles in praise of me and speaks extravagantly in extolling me, exaggerates wildly according to his desire, and waxes enthusiastic out of his love and kindness."[46] In response to all this praise, Maimonides insists upon his modesty, which was expected according to the unwritten social script. There is no reason to think that the praises referenced in the letter involved formal or poetic panegyric, although Maimonides was certainly the recipient of several literary panegyrics. The praise mentioned here belongs to a more general species of which this and formal panegyric were both a part. Interestingly, the cycle of praise involved not only Maimonides and Yaʿaqov but also those who praised Maimonides to Yaʿaqov; Yaʿaqov's report of praise not only served as a kind of praise in itself but also helped bind him and Maimonides within a specific social and intellectual circle (a contemporary comparison might be the "bringing of regards" from a mutual contact when introducing oneself to someone new). Such practices facilitate the formation of bonds between people who do not know each other but imagine themselves as belonging to the same group.[47] An individual could maintain ties simultaneously in several different or overlapping groups, which could be geographically proximate or diffuse or grounded in different types of social alignment (educational, literary, legal, mercantile). Throughout this book, we will witness the appearance and dissolution over five centuries of numerous groups in the Islamic East, the Islamic West, Christian lands, and in trans-Mediterranean contexts. These groups, their memberships and values, become visible to us through the exchange of panegyric.

Jewish Panegyrics Before the Medieval Period

The Bible, unsurprisingly, foregrounds the praise of God over the praise of human beings, though this praise is often modeled after royal panegyric as known in the Ancient Near East. Psalm 45 likely originated as a royal panegyric, specifically for the occasion of a king's wedding; before turning to the bride, the poem extols the king's handsome appearance, military power, and righteousness and evokes emblems of his power (his throne and scepter). The most sustained biblical passage written in praise of a man, though it is not direct praise delivered to the sovereign, is 1 Kings 5, where Solomon is lauded for extending his rule from the Euphrates to the land of the Philistines, for possessing wisdom, for authoring proverbs, and for initiating the building of the Temple. We find other snippets of praise, as when Moses is described as "exceedingly modest" (Nm 12:3), or when Absalom is praised for his beauty (2 Sm 14:20, 25), or when the woman of Tekoa praises David, "My lord is like an angel of God" (2 Sm 14:7). In Ez 28:2–3, we find a sort of anti-panegyric, which God commands the prophet to deliver to the ruler of Tyre: "You have set your mind like the mind of God! Yes, you are wiser than Daniel; in no hidden matter can anyone compare to you. By your shrewd understanding you have gained riches, and amassed gold and silver in treasuries." This "praise," of course, is only a setup to expose the haughtiness of the sovereign who had claimed divine status yet structurally parallels the performance of panegyric in the ancient Near East.[48]

The first Hebrew praise for a man outside the Bible, and here in poetic form, emanates from the Book of Ben Sira, authored by a priest in Jerusalem circa 180 BCE. The book contains a long and well-known section that begins, "Let me now hymn the praises of men of piety (*ḥesed*), of our fathers in their generations." The text selectively rewrites the lives of Israel's biblical heroes and culminates with praise for Simon the Just, the high priest and Ben Sira's contemporary, including a description of his offering of sacrifices in the Temple on Yom Kippur. The work blends the values of Torah-centered Judaism and Greek paideia; in fact, the work bears the imprints of the traditions of classical biography and the encomium.[49] The praise of Simon combines his ritual functions in the Temple with certain municipal king-like functions such as protecting the people from brigands and defending Jerusalem against enemies and also secures his authority as one who receives commandments and teaches statutes and judgments.

The structure of the praise for Simon is abundantly simple. Following mention of the municipal functions, the appearance of the radiance of the high priest exiting the Holy of Holies is elaborated with a series of similes: "How splendid was he looking out from the Tent and leaving the House of the Curtain: like a bright star among clouds, like a full moon on the holidays [Passover, Sukkot], like the sun shining on the king's temple, like a rainbow in a cloud, like a bud on the branches in the days of the holiday [Passover], like a lily by watercourses, like the blossoms of Lebanon in summer, like the fire of frankincense at the offering, like a vessel of beaten gold adorned with precious stones in the house of a powerful man, like a verdant olive tree abundant with fruit, like a tree whose branch runs with oil."

The similes draw primarily upon the semantic fields of heavenly objects and flora with occasional references to sacrifice, covenant, holidays (especially Passover), and powerful men. Although Simon is a man of power, he is not the king; yet the poem is careful to associate him with kingship by portraying him as the source that illuminates the king's Temple, which had been recently rebuilt. Associating his appearance with the priestly office, the covenant, central holidays, and kingship is hardly haphazard; the similes combine to create a full portrait of the high priest as the embodiment of core values of Jewish life and hence as a legitimate political officer.

As was shown by Cecil Roth, Ben Sira's praise for Simon the Just became the template for a host of liturgical poems (*piyyutim*) inserted into the *'avodah* service of the Yom Kippur liturgy, which, as in Ben Sira's poem, describes the rituals of the high priest in the Holy of Holies.[50] These poems utilize the same incipit and follow the structure of presenting similes in a simple list.[51] They enjoyed many expansions during Late Antiquity and the Middle Ages and are key texts for documenting the representation of power through the similes selected by poets. Although many elements of this genre remain stable over time (especially comparisons with heavenly bodies and flowers as well as allusions to Ezekiel's vision), the precise selection of similes varies in different cultural contexts through the adoption of synchronic images of power. In a version attributed to Yosi Ben Yosi (fifth century), the priest is described "like a garland placed on the forehead of a king," which maintains the association with monarchy and reminds us of the practice of Roman officials appearing wreathed in public processions. In the same poem, the priest is likened to Moses, an angel, and a warrior, "like one clad in the garments and helmet of triumph"; the helmet is another key symbol of power from Late Antiquity.[52]

In Islamic al-Andalus during the eleventh century, Mosheh Ibn Ezra depicted the high priest "like the radiance of a king appearing before the masses, before him the land was like the Garden of Eden" and "like a king in his troop among the longing [i.e., Israel], like the wisdom of an angel of God." Yiṣḥaq Ibn Ghiyat wrote: "How wondrous was the high priest . . . when he went about in his vestibule with the splendor of a king, justice went before him; when he tread upon a pavement of marble, a star rose."[53] Although there are obvious references to Temple rituals, the poets also incorporate elements of caliphal pageantry such as his appearing before the masses, surveying his territory, and moving in a military entourage. The Temple, too, is made into a kind of royal palace replete with a marble floor.[54] These fascinating changes in representation within the fairly fixed corpus of the *'avodah* liturgy is a telling measure of shifting cultural ideals about power. The liturgical poems were only about an imagined priest and not a particular person; the high priest was a screen upon which historically contingent and culturally specific images of power were projected.

Rabbinic literature continues the biblical practice of emphasizing God's praise over man's. Praise for God is presented as a contractual requirement, given the great miracles that God had performed for Israel, an idea captured in a famous passage introducing the *hallel* (praise) service of the Passover seder. Immediately after commending God for having freed "our ancestors" and "us" from Egypt in order to "bring us to and give us the land that He swore to our ancestors," the seder participants recite (with an exceptionally long list of verbs): "Because of this, we must thank, praise, honor, glorify, exalt, magnify, bless, elevate, and celebrate the One who performed all these miracles for us and our ancestors."[55] Further, rabbinic Jews set laudation of the ruler as the operative metaphor in treating praise for God. As David Stern notes, following a study by Ignaz Ziegler in the early twentieth century, "features of the king-mashal [allegory] are modeled upon those of the Roman emperor. . . . The many references in the meshalim to the larger world in which the Rabbis lived certainly show how profoundly familiar the sages were with that world and its culture."[56]

There are points in rabbinic literature wherein a man is praised with a short phrase or epithet: a few sages of the Talmud are given the Aramaic sobriquet *gavra rabba* ("great man"); after Rabbi Yoḥanan had made an astute comment, Rabbi Ḥizqiyah exclaims (also in Aramaic) that "he is not a [mere] mortal" (*leit dein bar inash*). It is reported that Yoḥanan Ben Zakkai "used to recount the praises" (*hayah moneh shivḥan*) of five students, but the text merely illustrates ideal types and does not suggest that he praised the students directly.[57] In fact, rabbinic writing expresses reservation toward direct praise and further demonstrates, as Seth Schwartz argues, that the rabbis largely opted out of the euergetic system of their day.[58] An illustrative text is b. Eruvin 18b, wherein Yermiyahu Ben El'azar expounds upon a discrepancy between Gn 6:9 and 7:1. The narrative voice of the Flood story (i.e., God, in Yermiyahu's view) introduces Noah as a "righteous and upright man in his generation; Noah walked with God." However, when God addresses Noah directly, He calls him "righteous" only. From this, Ben El'azar concludes, "one speaks little of a man's praise before him but all of it when not before him." Even in death, the sages warned against excessive praise for the deceased.[59]

The dramatic shift in the place of praise in Jewish society in the medieval period is illustrated with the following text, an unpublished Geniza manuscript (TS 8 J 16.18r; Figure 2), which is an address to a certain Ovadiah. Following a brief wish for success, the text praises the recipient in a mixture of Judeo-Arabic and Hebrew (Hebrew in italics):

> All that reaches a man with respect to praise [*al-madīḥ*] and sincere thanks [*al-shukr al-ṣarīḥ*] falls short with regard to the lofty lord, confidant of the state, security of kingship, *our lord and master Ovadiah the minister, the noble, the wise, the intelligent,* may God extend his grace, elevate his status, and give him abundant fortune *in the eyes of kings and ministers. May he bless his brothers and his sons*

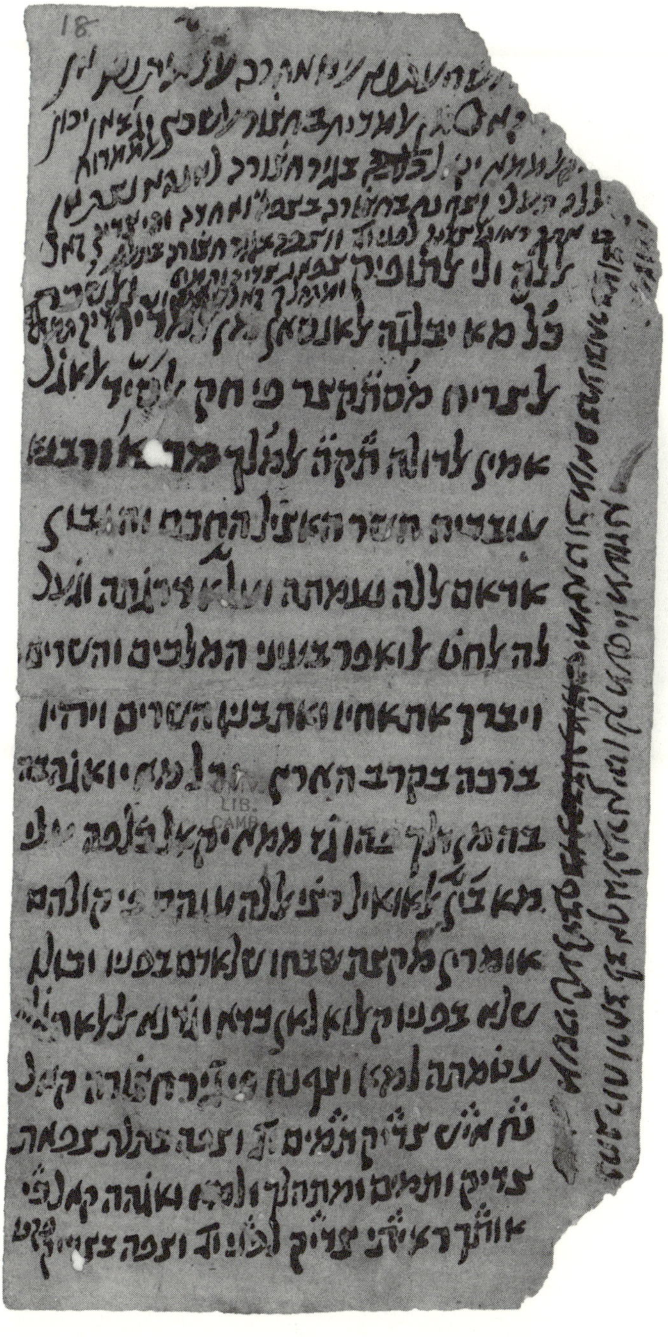

Figure 2. Panegyric for a certain Ovadiah. TS 8 J 16.18r. Reproduced by kind permission of the Syndics of Cambridge University Library.

> *the ministers and may they be a blessing in the midst of the land.* All that they address before him [of praise and thanks] is but a fraction of what is said when he is not present according to what the rabbis [*al-awā'il*], may God be satisfied with them, made clear in their saying, "One says little of a man's praise before him but all of it when not before him." They said this because we have found that God, lofty and exalted, when Noah was not present, described him with three qualities—*righteous, upright, and so on*—but when he addressed him, He said, *"For I have seen you righteous before me" and so on*. He described him as *righteous* only.

The letter suggests that praise had previously been directed to Ovadiah in person, which is not at all surprising, given that he was a man of significant rank. He was called "confidant of the state, security of kingship" (*amīn al-dawla, thiqqat al-mulk*), both of which are titles common in Islamic political discourse that were appropriated within the titulature of the Jewish academies.[60] Most strikingly, the rabbinic warning against direct praise becomes a device exploited *within* panegyric (i.e., all this is said about you in your presence; just imagine what is said when you are not present!). The document also reveals something about the letter's reception and afterlife; the margins bear a text in Judeo-Arabic, composed in a different hand, which explains the content of the letter, including the rabbinic dictum regarding what is "said of praise (*min al-madīḥ*) in the presence of the individual praised (*al-shakhṣ al-mamdūḥ*)" and the references to Noah. The letter was of sufficient value to merit commentary and was interpreted through the contemporary idiom of Arabic praise writing, replete with the terminology of *madīḥ* and *mamdūḥ*. Clearly, a great deal had changed since the rabbinic period.

Why this change? The short answer is Islam, but that is hardly descriptive of a process. It is difficult to identify any single cause that brought Jews into the social practice of offering extensive praise in a manner similar to the practice among Muslims.[61] It would be far too facile to ascribe the Jewish adoption of an Islamic social and political practice to the affinity of Judaism for Islam generally, though perhaps it was of at least some relevance that another aniconic monotheistic community had found a way to accommodate praise for men without usurping God's place as the one true object of praise. Certainly, the Arabization of the Near East is relevant, as are the migration patterns of Jews to cosmopolitan centers of Islamic power and the relocation of the great academies of Sura and Pumbedita from their ancestral homes along the Euphrates to the 'Abbasid capital of Baghdad (late ninth—early tenth century). While the leadership institutions of the geonic period predate the spread of Islam, in the words of Robert Brody: "Under the unifying umbrella of Islam, international trade flourished as never before, and a form of international banking developed as well. Jews played a leading role in both of these areas. . . . [T]he center of this vast empire was transferred from Syria, where the Umayyads had had their capital at Damascus, to Babylonia, where the Abbasids made their capital at Baghdad. The leaders of Babylonian Jewry were thus admirably positioned to influence their coreligionists worldwide, and they made the most of their opportunities."[62]

These transformations aligned the geonim, the leaders of the Baghdad academies (and also their counterparts at the Jerusalem academy), with an imperial perspective, and, in many ways, the administrative functions of the academies mirrored those of the 'Abbasid government whose central preoccupation was to establish and maintain loyalty over a vast region. To these ends, Jewish leaders staged ceremonies of power, political rituals that included laudation and the profession of loyalty; they circulated textual accounts that "re-created" those ceremonies for distant communities; they sent legal opinions (responsa) and epistles on moral themes; and they dispatched emissaries throughout the region to represent them. Further, in comparison with Jews in Late Antiquity, Jews in Islamic empires appeared more often in governmental spaces, either as petitioners before officials or as courtiers, and probably had greater exposure to modes of professing loyalty and acclamation. Still, our knowledge about how these transformations occurred will necessarily remain deficient because of lacunae in the written record.[63]

Inasmuch as satellite Jewish communities in Syria, North Africa, al-Andalus, and Yemen turned to the various academies for legal opinions or expressed loyalty toward them (bonds that could be multiple, shifting, or ephemeral), they also maintained robust local leaderships, including courtiers who enjoyed audience with proximate dynasties of Islamic power, including independent caliphates. The precise interplay between local and central Jewish authority in the Islamic Mediterranean, between hierarchic and horizontal structure, has been and remains a central preoccupation of scholarship.[64] Like responsa literature, panegyrics can help historians create rich pictures of institutional loyalties.

Moreover, bonds among Jews across the region of Islamic aegis were not limited to the hierarchy of religious institutions; Jews participated in smaller and sometimes interrelated groups or social networks that could be oriented toward shared goals of a political, mercantile, or intellectual nature. Inasmuch as a panegyric demonstrates a link, though sometimes an aspirational one, between two men, a full map of panegyric exchanges allows for a kind of representation, however partial, of Jewish social relations in the medieval Mediterranean, both spatially and across ranks. To understand the web of social relations among Jews in the region, we must envision several overlapping maps: (1) academy leaders, their local supporters, emissaries, and adherents in satellite communities; (2) local Jewish authorities and their adherents; (3) merchants, their family members, and partners in enterprise; and (4) intellectuals who had tastes for various types of knowledge.[65] Although not mutually exclusive, the maps for each of these could look quite different, and praise writing is a major resource for marking their contours and characters.[66]

A single author might belong to several social networks simultaneously and address members of each appropriately. Shemuel ha-Nagid of al-Andalus praised his fellow Andalusian Abū Faḍl Ibn Ḥasdai in a pure biblicizing Hebrew for his wisdom, generosity, and eloquence, but, when he lamented Hai Gaon of Baghdad, he wrote in a register described in the manuscript as "like the language of the Mishnah" (*mithl lughat al-mishnah*) and focused on his knowledge of Torah, Mishnah, and Talmud as well as his power of judgment.[67] Here, the linguistic registers themselves, along with the characteristics selected for praise, demarcate the social networks, one a set of Andalusian intellectuals devoted to linguistic purity, the other a group of rabbinic scholars for whom mishnaic Hebrew marked a legal community with ancient roots.[68]

Similarly, Yehudah Halevi praised his fellow Andalusian poet-scholar Yehudah Ibn Ghiyat as one who wears garments of wisdom, fear, integrity, justice, skill, honor, modesty, and kindness, a "tree of knowledge that gives life to those who gather [its fruit], a lion whelp who shepherds ewes."[69] Both Halevi and Ibn Ghiyat belonged to the circle of Andalusian Jews who have sometimes been called "courtier rabbis," though it is preferable to refer to them as they sometimes referred to themselves in Arabic, as *ahl al-adab*, the "people of *adab*," an expansive concept that incorporated wide-ranging knowledge (in poetry, oratory, rhetoric, grammar, exegesis) and a refined, urbane code of etiquette.[70] At the same time, Halevi praised the Nagid Shemuel Ben Ḥananiah of Egypt by dwelling on his power, "A Nagid 'who seeks the good of his people and speaks peace to all its seed,'" a verbatim description of Mordechai, the archetypal Jewish courtier (Est 10:3); "a righteous man who rules over men, who rules with the fear of God," predicated of King David (2 Sm 23:3); "he stood in the counsel of the holy." Moreover, this poem situates the Nagid geographically within the Mediterranean: "Canaan (Palestine) envies Egypt because it is illumined by the light of his face; Shinar (Iraq) studies his ways and beseeches 'Majestic Full of Light' (i.e., God) to see the king who stands above the waters of the Nile. Sefarad (al-Andalus) joins them to measure out his boundary."[71]

Iraq and Palestine, the gravitational centers to which other communities turn, here focus their gaze upon this "king" of Egypt; al-Andalus "joins them" in honoring the Nagid, thus setting the place of al-Andalus within the hierarchy. The representation of Mediterranean geography is taken up in Chapter 4, but a few words are in order here.

The Mediterranean

It should be clear by now that *Dominion Built of Praise* treats a broad geographic expanse that ranges from al-Andalus and North Africa in the Islamic West to Egypt, Palestine, Syria, Yemen, and Iraq in the Islamic East, and then areas along the Mediterranean Sea under Christian control (northern Iberia, southern France, Sicily). This whole region has, with much justification, been called "the Mediterranean," and since I use the term in the title of this book, I will include here a brief discussion of the term's history and my usage of it. At other points, I reflect further on this book as a Mediterranean project.

The idea of the Mediterranean as an object of study enjoyed considerable prestige during the early and mid-twentieth century (with scholars such as Henri Pirenne and Fernand Braudel) and has emerged with renewed force in recent decades.[72] By placing the well-traversed sea at the center of a map rather than segregating Europe, North Africa, and the Middle East according to continent, or the Islamic world from the Christian world according to spheres of religious dominance, scholars have appreciated lines of continuity that emerged across political, religious, or linguistic lines, even *through* war and conflict.[73] Debates over the utility of a Mediterranean orientation have revolved around whether the region (however demarcated) can be analyzed as a unity—a "discriminable whole," in Horden and Purcell's phrasing—or whether the various points around a Mediterranean route remained sufficiently distinct as to resist unified treatment.[74] Should political unity or relative peace be considered a necessary precondition for undertaking the region as a whole? Should continuities such as vocabulary items or culinary influence be considered sufficient for imagining a shared cultural sphere? The harshest critiques of the Mediterranean as an analytic framework have argued that it is essentializing and imperialist, much as Edward Said argued in the case of the Orient.[75]

The first question that might be asked is: Where, exactly, was the Mediterranean—its territorial contours? As Sarah Stroumsa laconically notes in her study of Maimonides as a "Mediterranean thinker," the cultural notion of the Mediterranean world has taken on "impressive dimensions," sometimes reaching as far as the Low Countries and, ironically enough, the Atlantic world.[76] In S. D. Goitein's monumental *A Mediterranean Society*, a study of Jewish (and, to a significant degree, Muslim) society as reflected in the documents of the Cairo Geniza, the Mediterranean meant the areas under Islamic rule that bordered the Mediterranean Sea (Egypt, al-Andalus, the Maghrib, Sicily, Palestine) and included the region termed the Near East, extending toward the Indian Ocean (primarily Syria and Iraq).[77] Although Goitein was well aware that the political and cultural climates of the locales throughout the Mediterranean were diverse, he chose to stress the interconnection and cohesion of Jews in the Arabic-speaking Mediterranean over several centuries, offering the "big picture" according to major categories (economy, family, community) rather than a series of local histories. The further exposure and organization of Geniza documents has allowed Goitein's successors to produce more localized histories, even focusing on fairly small groups of people; but still, the idea of the Mediterranean has not lost meaning.[78]

Throughout most of this book, I use the term "Mediterranean" largely in the way that Goitein used it—an "Islamized Mediterranean," as Fred Astren has termed it.[79] Clearly, figures introduced above, such as Shemuel ha-Nagid of al-Andalus and Yehudah Halevi, can be analyzed simultaneously as members of intimate Andalusian circles and broader trans-Mediterranean networks. In order to document specific phenomena (say, installation to communal office), I bring together examples from Iraq in the tenth century, al-Andalus in the eleventh, and Syria in the twelfth, knowing full well that I am eliding important distinctions. To the extent that "jumping around" is a quality from which *A Mediterranean Society* suffers, the present book will be guilty of the same offense. While I give weight to regional and temporal variation and, at times, strongly emphasize it, I believe that looking at specific locales only would obscure certain elements of Jewish culture across the region.

At the same time, my outlook on the Mediterranean differs from Goitein's in two main respects. First, in Goitein's study, due to the natural pertinence of Geniza materials to Egypt, al-Andalus appears as a remote frontier of the Islamic world (which it undoubtedly was!). Given the focus of the present study on praise writing and the plethora of surviving materials that originated in al-Andalus, this area will loom larger than in *A Mediterranean Society.* Second, whereas the geographic span of Goitein's magnum opus remained more or less within the confines of the Islamic world, this study contains an extended chapter on the Christian Mediterranean, including Christian Iberia, southern France, and Norman Sicily.

One might argue that any segregation between the Islamic and the Christian Mediterranean is artificial and obscures a cultural continuity that was not delimited by language or creed. Thus, the coherence of al-Andalus, Castile, and southern France might be at least as strong as that of Qairawan, Yemen, and Iraq.[80] Not segregating Christian and Islamic domains is further justified when one considers the itineraries of certain individuals. Yehudah Halevi and Yehudah al-Ḥarīzī, the focal characters of Chapter 4, engaged with communities not only in the Islamic East and the Islamic West but also within Christian Iberia and southern France. A Jewish intellectual such as Anatoli Ben Yosef (late twelfth–early thirteenth century) was active in Marseilles, Lunel, Alexandria, and Sicily.[81] Indeed, I consider the movement of people, objects, knowledge, and cultural practices across Islamic and Christian territories to be one of the more interesting and fruitful areas of scholarship today. My segregating the Christian Mediterranean within a single chapter has more to do with chronology than geography and certainly does not reflect an assumption that the Islamic world was at odds with Christendom.

Finally, this book is not an attempt to write a grand history "*of* the Mediterranean," the vast project attempted by Horden and Purcell, but rather a relatively modest history of an identifiable phenomenon "*in* the Mediterranean"—and then largely within the confines of a single religious community.[82] Although social and political dynamics vary substantively over time and space, the basic practice of offering praise remained a constant among Mediterranean Jews. We are not simply witnessing a set of parallel cultures of praise but a coherent, genetically interrelated corpus of texts with shared literary features and tropes; certain continuities exist across Islamic and Christian domains on the level of both literary history and the construction of legitimacy.[83] This project is therefore grounded in a relatively concrete kind of "connectivity," the term given by Horden and Purcell for justifying a Mediterranean study, and demonstrates the coherence, at some minimal level, of Jewish culture throughout the region over the centuries.[84] I therefore see differences among Jewish groups across the regions of the Mediterranean not as differences *between* but rather as differences *within*. At the same time, this is a study in regionalism: for example, distinct features in the representation of Jewish legitimacy emerge in Christian domains due to the different place of Jews and Judaism within Christian theology and the nature of Jewish-Christian debate. Concentrating on the practice of panegyric and the representation of legitimacy over space and time allows for significant, if subtle, changes in Jewish culture to emerge.

Outline of Chapters

Dominion Built of Praise begins with two chapters on the social function of Jewish panegyric in the Islamic Mediterranean. The first, "Performance Matters: Between Oral Acclamation and Epistolary Exchange," studies how Jewish panegyric texts were patronized, received, performed, and circulated. Were they delivered orally, either before small or large audiences, or read privately by their *mamdūḥs*? What relationship exists between the written testimonies and oral/aural experiences? Here I consider the function of panegyric within Jewish political rituals, such as the appointment of a man to office, less formal social gatherings, and within epistolary exchange in which it helped forge and maintain bonds over distances.

Chapter 2, "Poetic Gifts: Maussian Exchange and the Working of Medieval Jewish Culture," reflects upon the metapoetic trope by which medieval Jewish authors referred to their panegyrics as "gifts." Jewish culture in the Islamic Mediterranean may be said to have operated according to a complex "economy of gifts" wherein goods and favors were exchanged among people over distances and at close proximity to one another. The rhetoric of gift giving permeates panegyrics and reveals a great deal about the functions that their authors and readers ascribed them. I argue, based on the theory of gift exchange first advanced by Marcel Mauss (a theory that has already been applied to Greek, Latin, and Arabic panegyric), that portraying panegyrics as gifts constituted them as material objects whose value served as or demanded reciprocation, thus initiating or perpetuating a cycle of loyalty. Toward the end of the chapter, I consider the specific implications of describing gifts through the language of the sacrificial cult of ancient Israel, as though these gifts were offered not for their human recipients but rather for God.

Chapter 3, "'Humble Like the Humble One': The Language of Jewish Political Legitimacy," reviews dominant characteristics ascribed to idealized

Jewish figures and interprets the cultural resonances of these virtues through diachronic and synchronic representations of power and legitimacy. Thus, the chapter considers such elements as associating the *mamdūḥ* with biblical predecessors (e.g., Moses, David, Samuel) and offices (priests, prophets, kings) as well as resonances with contemporary images of Islamic legitimacy. Further, the chapter considers ways in which panegyrists tailored their compositions for *mamdūḥ*s of different rank.

Chapter 4, "'Sefarad Boasts over Shinar': Mediterranean Regionalism in Jewish Panegyric," reflects upon the present study as a "Mediterranean" project. The subject of this book offers an ideal case study for thinking through debates concerning Mediterranean cohesion in that it traces a demonstrable feature of continuity and connectivity—the praise writing of Jews who lived, traveled, and traded around "the sea"—even as it stresses variations and disjunctions among the several subregions. With a focus on the panegyrics of Yehudah Halevi and Yehudah al-Ḥarīzī, I argue that minor fluctuations in the idealization of leadership across the highly conventional and relatively stable corpus of Jewish panegyric provide a telling measure of differences in Jewish political cultures.

Although panegyric writing was clearly more normative and acceptable in the medieval period than it is in our own day, the practice was not without its detractors. The ethical misgivings surrounding the culture of praise were several, from the worldly aspirations of fame-seeking *mamdūḥ*s, to the sincerity of the panegyrist (especially when he received remuneration), the potential falsehood of poetic statements themselves, and the problem of praising men when, theologically speaking, all praise was properly due to God. In Chapter 5, "'A Word Aptly Spoken': The Ethics of Praise," I review comments concerning praise among major Jewish authors (e.g., Sa'adia Gaon, Baḥya Ibn Paquda, Mosheh Ibn Ezra, Maimonides) who expressed qualms about the practice or tried to navigate the ethical concerns implicit. Because these authors did not treat these topics extensively or systematically, their views are gleaned from occasional statements in their biblical exegesis and ethical and poetic writings. I show that, with a few exceptions, praise writing was viewed as ethically sound as long as it was executed within certain parameters.

Chapter 6, "'A Cedar Whose Stature in the Garden of Wisdom . . .': Hyperbole, the Imaginary, and the Art of Magnification," continues with one theme raised in Chapter 5 concerning the potential of panegyric for presenting falsehood. Beyond the suspicion that the conniving panegyrist could simply lie for personal gain was the concern that panegyric, like other poetic genres, relied upon "deception" as its very mode of discourse. This chapter considers the role of hyperbole and metaphor in panegyric composition as well as the prescribed boundaries for these devices, especially with regard to Mosheh Ibn Ezra's Judeo-Arabic treatise on Hebrew poetics within the context of Arabic poetics. I demonstrate that the fundamental mode of panegyric discourse is what Aristotle called *auxesis*, "magnification" (Heb., *giddul*; Ar., *ta'aẓīm*) and that magnifying the qualities of a *mamdūḥ* was not only permitted but was required according to "his due." Although poetic discourse remained a kind of deception, it was a unique quality of poetic speech that it could make statements that were meaningful without any particular claim to truth.

Chapter 7, "In Praise of God, in Praise of Man: Issues in Political Theology," is an exhaustive treatment of the poetic device of praising *mamdūḥ*s with phrases that are predicated of God in the Hebrew Bible. The discussion is situated within classical Arabic literary criticism, in which the practice of interlacing panegyrics with God's praises from the Qur'ān was sometimes labeled contemptible speech and even polytheism (Ar., *shirk*, "attributing partners to God"). Despite such condemnations, Muslim and Jewish poets adopted this poetic practice precisely because it pressed against a perceived boundary between the human and the divine. Not only was sacred hyperbole rhetorically effective, but it provided poets a means of conveying vital aspects of political ideology. Through engagement with the idea of political theology as formulated by Carl Schmitt and Ernst Kantorowicz, I argue that divine association in panegyric did not make *mamdūḥ*s divine so much as it presented a theological structure within politics.

Chapter 8, "'May His Book Be Burnt Even Though It Contains Your Praise!': Jewish Panegyric in the Christian Mediterranean," follows themes developed throughout the book in Christian Iberia, southern France, and Sicily during the later Middle Ages. I stress continuities and disjunctions in patronage relationships, poetic ideals, modes of representation, and political culture. The chapter recognizes new elements that left imprints on the panegyric corpus such as the kabbalah, Jewish-Christian polemics, religious conversion, and Romance vernacular literature.

Chapter 9, "The Other 'Great Eagle': Interreligious Panegyrics and the Limits of Interpretation," treats the several poems penned by Jewish authors in honor of Muslim and Christian addressees (in Hebrew, Judeo-Arabic, Arabic, and Castilian). The chapter studies the discursive strategies through which Jews praised non-Jewish rulers and explores how Jews used panegyric to negotiate their political position within local and imperial structures. Although recognizing the temporal authority of non-Jewish potentates while maintaining traditional Jewish stances on sacred history could certainly be awkward, inter-religious panegyrics reveal various strategies for accommodating these rival claims. Further, the chapter investigates the methodological issues involved in determining whether words of praise should be read subversively as containing a "hidden transcript" that conceals a poetics of Jewish resistance.

A brief afterword revisits some major points of the book.

CHAPTER 1

Performance Matters: Between Public Acclamation and Epistolary Exchange

And my speech I purified, smelted, and cleansed
on balanced scales, marked it out with a stylus. . . .
I worked on it from afternoon to evening. It is sweet like honey. . . .
Recite it every Sabbath like the readings from the Torah and the
Prophets,
write and recall it throughout the generations.

—Hai Gaon

These are verses from the conclusion of a lengthy panegyric (more than two hundred lines, all in quantitative meter and monorhyme) by Hai Ben Sherirah (d. 1038), gaon of the Sura academy in Baghdad, in honor of Rav Yehudah Rosh ha-Seder, a dignitary in Qairawan. After the wedding of Yehudah's son Dunash, Yehudah sent a letter to Hai, along with a monetary gift for the academy. In the panegyric, Hai expresses gratitude for the gift and offers extensive praise for Yehudah, Yehudah's wife,[1] Dunash, and the bride's family. A small portion of the praise for Yehudah is as follows: "Through him nations in Togarmah and Qedar are blessed. His kindness is upon all like rising vapor and incense. All his oils are scented like spiced early rain, aloe, myrrh, and cinnamon, every powder burning (Sg 3:6). His beneficence is great, too vast to measure. Who can seek out his praise and who can count it when he gives without asking, disperses for others to keep. A thousand gold pieces are like a *gerah* in his eyes. Before him a hundred thousand *kikarim* are like an *agorah*. To every patron he is a king upon a throne and seat; before him others are like concubines."[2]

In the poem, Hai also refers to the arrival of Yehudah's letter and gift: "It arrived like lightning reaching Venus, shining and gleaming. I kissed it and fastened it on me like a sash. I set it in my place exposed, not concealed, and showed it to every guest to rejoice with me and sing. My portion from his wedding that was sent as a gift (*ashkarah*) will be considered by God an offering and sacrifice (*minḥah ve-azkarah*). He made it ransom for him for pardoning and atonement. Out of [the gift], I made a holiday [for scholars] and a special day of rejoicing for all the sages of my academy, for lifting spirits and exchanging gifts (*terumiyah ve-liteshurah*)."[3]

We begin this section on the social function of Jewish panegyric with this poem because it captures several aspects of the complex dynamics that we will be discussing in this and the following chapter. It is clear that this panegyric was presupposed by and participated in a broad social and administrative system that involved trans-Mediterranean communal bonds, correspondence, the sending of monetary donations, and hyperbolic address. Yehudah held the title Rosh ha-Seder ("head of the order"), which would have been bestowed upon him by a Baghdadi gaon—likely, in this case, because of philanthropic and scholarly activity.[4] The concluding dedication conveys that Hai composed the poem from noon until night and commands that others learn and recite it on the Sabbath and new moons to be remembered for generations. Following the poem, the letter continues with praise and assures the recipient that "our companions, students, and loved ones" will "learn and teach [the poem] and publicize it far and wide." Those who hear it will "not find all this praise strange or foreign" but rather "a word aptly spoken" (cf. Prv 25:11).[5]

Here we witness the sending of a poem from a gaon, a man of the highest spiritual and intellectual rank, to a prominent donor and communal leader who was nonetheless the gaon's social subordinate in a far-off community. Despite his higher status, the gaon took the posture of a poet praising his *mamdūḥ*, appropriate because the donor was arguably a kind of "patron." The panegyric was part of an epistolary exchange whereby the poem, despite its ornate style, functioned essentially as a letter, one whose value was enhanced by its meter, rhyme, and beauty, and the labor of whose execution was emphasized by the poet-gaon.

This exchange between gaon and communal leader, between the Islamic East and the Islamic West, falls roughly in the middle of the period under discussion in most of this book, c. 950–1250. The poem extends backward in time to a Hebrew panegyric tradition that had been developing for a century and certainly would not be the last such panegyric to be composed. The formal features, including quantitative meter and monorhyme, indicate that Hai was following the Arabized prosodic innovations introduced by Dunash Ben Labrat in al-Andalus during the tenth century (one of Dunash's panegyrics to Ḥasdai Ibn Shaprut likewise emphasizes its being composed in quantitative meter).[6] Finally, the poem illuminates the central subject of the present chapter concerning the performance practices of Jewish panegyric. On the one hand, the poem is clearly part of an epistolary exchange. On the other, Hai's text testifies to the broader circulation of both the initial letter and the poetic response beyond the eyes of their immediate recipients. The gaon set Yehudah's letter out for "guests" and ordered that the panegyric be read publicly.[7]

One set of questions that we must address in determining what Jewish panegyrics were ultimately for—what function they held in the constitution of medieval Jewish society—is how they were received, performed, and circulated. Were they delivered orally, before small or large audiences? Read privately by their addressees? What relationship exists between the written testimonies and oral/aural experiences? We will see that the performance practices of Jewish panegyric in the medieval Islamic Mediterranean were variegated and had written as well as oral dimensions, though the sources elucidate most poignantly the degree to which panegyrics were embedded within epistolary exchange. This is not entirely surprising, since written texts testify to the practices of written culture primarily but to oral culture only serendipitously; it might be the case that the occasional hints that we have of oral recitation are the tip of an iceberg that is largely submerged or has melted away. Still, we do learn that figures were acclaimed aloud, sometimes publicly and even ceremonially, as suggested by Hai's poem. The written text of the panegyric, which was sent over a distance in response to a letter, preceded the oral performance, but we may assume that public acclamation also took place.

* * *

The primary purpose of this chapter is to consider the evidence for oral and written aspects of Jewish panegyric practice in the contexts of the Islamic Mediterranean, including the world of the academies, local political structures, mercantile circles, and other social and intellectual relationships. Although much of the information considered is rather technical—including scribal inscriptions, the layout of manuscript pages, lists of books—the chapter remains focused on broader cultural issues such as the nature of patronage, the place of panegyric in society, the machinery of disseminating images of leadership, and the continuity and disjunction of Jewish regions across the Mediterranean. The chapter also offers close readings of texts with a focus on political vocabulary.

The discussion begins by reviewing the practice of Jewish panegyric in the Islamic East, where the tradition began, and then turns to the practice in the Islamic West, particularly within al-Andalus. I review the relatively scant evidence that we have for the oral performance of Jewish panegyric, whether in public ceremonies—what might be called "political rituals"—or in small gatherings, and the more extensive evidence we possess regarding its place in epistolary exchange. The chapter stresses the epistolary context for Jewish panegyric alongside a performative, sometimes ceremonial, one while also breaking down the dichotomy presumed to exist between the two. I do not propose an austere culture of poetic reading that negated aural experience; as demonstrated, poems that played a primarily epistolary function could be recited publicly subsequent to reception.

In discussing the subject of Jewish regionalism within the Mediterranean, I also offer, inter alia, a critique of what has generally been dubbed the "courtly" Jewish culture of al-Andalus. It has often been asserted that the Jews of al-Andalus imitated the performance practices of Islamic courts where poets lauded caliphs for pay and thus engaged in a kind of miniature Jewish court culture; a key element of this portrayal has been the image of the Jewish patron surrounded by professional poets who recited his praise in exchange for money. Although the courtly image is justified to an extent, it has also been partly misunderstood, a point that has had the effect of distorting our ideas about Andalusian Jewish panegyric and its function. In the Islamic West, as in the Islamic East, Hebrew panegyric practice involved epistolary as well as performative elements, which makes its role more continuous than has been imagined. Further, the performative settings of Jewish panegyric recall both the hierarchic *majlis* as well as the more egalitarian *mujālasa*, as distinguished in the Arabic context by Samer Ali and discussed in the Introduction to this book.[8]

Evidence for the Oral Performance of Panegyric in the Islamic East

Our sources for the oral performance of Jewish panegyric in the Islamic East are fairly sparse.[9] Even more rarely do we find indications of oral performance in connection with an actual political ceremony. Natan ha-Bavli, writing in the tenth century, reports that when a new exilarch was invested on the Sabbath, he stood under a canopy beneath which a cantor also placed his head in order to "bless [the exilarch] with prepared blessings (*berakhot metuqanot*), prepared the previous day or the day before, in a soft voice so that no one could hear them save those sitting around the dais and the young men beneath it. When he blessed him the young men would respond 'Amen!' in a loud voice but all the people remained silent until he had finished his blessings."[10]

Because Natan's text was originally written in Judeo-Arabic and this section survives only in a medieval Hebrew translation, we are left to deduce what Arabic word lay behind the Hebrew *berakhot* (blessings). It seems likely that the word was *du'ā*, "invocations with blessings," which were frequently used when acclaiming men of power in Islamic political ceremonies.[11] On the one hand, the acclamations associated with this installation call to mind the setting of a *majlis 'ām*, a public assembly, and the installation of a caliph. On the other, the fact that the hearing of blessings was limited to a small circle of elites distinguishes the performative context.[12]

The only mention in Natan's account of "praises" comes after the conclusion of the Musaf service, when the exilarch returned to his home amid an entourage of congregants, "and when the exilarch exits all the people go out before him and after him and say before him words of poetry and praise (*omrim lefanav divrei shirot ve-tishbaḥot*) until he arrives at his home." One wonders exactly what these *divrei shirot ve-tishbaḥot* entailed. Were they sung or recited? Were they in Arabic or in Hebrew? Were they specific for the occasion, previously composed, or spontaneous? There may be some parallel here also to the public entourage in Muslim celebrations. As Paula Sanders notes, "popular" festivals in Fatimid Cairo could move from the "streets, to al-Azhar, to the palace" and could involve poets offering "invocations and blessings."[13] As I have argued elsewhere, the ceremony described by Natan "drew simultaneously on the idioms of ancient Jewish rites and contemporary Muslim ceremonial to articulate an image of leadership and political legitimacy that blended Jewish categories . . . with resonances of caliphal power." There I also concluded that "the elites of Babylonian Jewry recognized that presiding over the Jewish world was a type of statecraft and, as Clifford Geertz notes, that 'statecraft is a thespian art.'"[14]

An important text that is highly suggestive of a ceremonial performance is a long panegyric in honor of Daniel Ben 'Azariah (d. 1062), a gaon of the Jerusalem academy who emanated from a family that claimed descent from King David. This gaon was able to bolster the position of the Palestinian academy even unto Iraq and was greatly esteemed by the Palestinian community of Fustat. He seems to have had some difficulty securing loyalty among Jews in the Islamic West, though he was praised in verse by none other than Shemuel ha-Nagid of al-Andalus as a kind of political endorsement.[15]

In 1057, around the time that Ben 'Azariah assumed the position of gaon, the poet 'Eli ha-Kohen composed a panegyric in his honor using a form, structure, and style that were entirely unique.[16] It is clear that the poet saw his poem as related to the Arabic poetic tradition, since he gives it the heading *qaṣīda* (Ar., "formal ode") in the manuscript. Although the poem suggests no clear liturgical context, its form is closer to the style of the classical *piyyut* than the relatively new Arabized poetry of the Andalusian school, despite the fact that this latter form had penetrated Jewish communities throughout the Islamic world by the eleventh century and would have been familiar to Ben 'Azariah. Like the *'avodah* liturgy of Yom Kippur, the poem begins by recounting the creation of the world, leading to a long yet selective review of Israel's history that culminates with praise for Ben 'Azariah.[17] Much of the historical summary dwells on tracing Ben 'Azariah's lineage from King David, which, as Arnold Franklin notes, "dramatically suggests that [Ben 'Azariah's] assumption of the post of gaon be viewed as part of a divine plan extending back to creation itself."[18]

The copy of the poem that survives is an autograph draft that includes alternate versions of verses throughout. Although we have no external testimony that this panegyric was performed, I agree with Ezra Fleischer, who published the poem, that the internal evidence suggests a public performance, quite possibly from the time of the gaon's investiture (alternatively, the poem could simply have been given to the gaon or recited in a small audience). In the section reviewing the history of Israel, the text focuses on the moment of King David's investiture (lines 135–45), in all likelihood alluding to the performative context of the poem.

The poem gives no indication of the setting in which it was recited, but the manuscript does bear a date, the thirteenth of Nissan, just before the festival of Passover. The association with Passover is further corroborated by allusions within the poem itself. Just after recounting the Israelites' enslavement in Egypt, the plagues, and the Exodus, the poet dedicates several lines to the laws of Passover, concluding with Ex 13:10, "You shall keep this ordinance at its set time from year to year" (lines 86–91). Did a ceremony of installation take place on Passover? As discussed in the Introduction, the dedication of Arabic panegyrics often coincided with particular Islamic festivals and hence the recitation of the panegyric for Ben ʿAzariah at Passover might present a Jewish analogue to this practice. Although Fleischer found the link with Passover puzzling, there is a certain logic in associating the festival with a political ceremony. The Exodus from Egypt marks Israel's entry into the realm of the political, becoming in the desert a hierarchically organized camp, a kind of community, polity, or even quasi-state. Even if the poem were not written for an investiture specifically, Passover would have been an appropriate occasion for reiterating—indeed, *representing*—the divine origins of the Jewish "polity" and solidifying bonds of political loyalty. This poem cannot be categorized neatly as "secular" or "sacred"; it demonstrates just how intimately the two were linked such that the elevation of a man's status was integrated within sacred history and the act of praising him was imbued with sacrality.

Although we have no other description of a Jewish ceremony as elaborate as that of the exilarch's investiture as described by Natan ha-Bavli, occasional texts from subsequent centuries refer to political rituals that recount many of the same basic elements. Shemuel Ben ʿEli was a *rosh yeshivah* (head of the academy) in Baghdad who penned a number of epistles to Jewish communities in Iraq, Persia, and Syria between 1184 and 1207.[19] Several of the letters concern a certain Zekhariah Ben Barkhael, a native of Aleppo who wrote to Ben ʿEli in his youth, studied with him in Baghdad, and ultimately became the sage's successor. In 1190, Ben Barkhael was appointed *av bet din* (head of court) and dispatched to communities in Iraq and Syria. His responsibilities included the rendering of judgments, gathering funds, and the appointment of "scribes, cantors, prayer leaders, and community heads." Throughout the letters, Ben Barkhael is presented as an extension of and proxy for the *rosh yeshivah* himself, a "limb of the body," as Ben ʿEli calls him in one instance.[20] Jews should pay homage to the *av bet din* much as they would to the *rosh yeshivah* himself; yet Ben ʿEli is also careful to safeguard his own rank by describing Ben Barkhael's status as derivative and a matter of investiture.

The epistles' aim was to establish the new *av bet din*'s, and hence the *rosh yeshivah*'s, authority and legitimacy in satellite communities. To this end, they recount at length Ben Barkhael's praiseworthy qualities and request that certain rituals be observed concerning his public appearances, including his verbal "magnification" (Heb., *giddul*). The epistles thus refer to ceremonies of power that have already taken place, convey the appointee's praiseworthy qualities through writing, and call for further rituals to be observed in the future. In one of the Hebrew letters, after enumerating Ben Barkhael's merits, Ben ʿEli writes:

> When we saw these precious and honored characteristics in him, including fear of God, love of the commandments, and intelligence and knowledge, we laid hands upon him (*samakhnuhu*) as *av bet din* of the yeshivah and gave him authority to judge, teach, and permit firstborn animals (for slaughter) (cf. b. Sanhedrin 5a), to explicate the Torah in public, to set the pericopes, and to appoint the translator. Before he expounds, "Hear what he holds!"[21] should be said and after he expounds his name should be mentioned in the *qadish*. . . . It is incumbent upon the communities, may they be blessed, when they hear that he is approaching, that they go out to greet him and come before him with cordiality so that he may enter a multitude (*'am rav*) with glory. When he comes to the synagogue, they must call before him and he must sit in glory on a splendid seat and comely couches with a cushion behind him, as is appropriate for *av bet dins*. He also possesses a signet ring to sign documents, rulings, and epistles that are appropriate for him to sign.[22]

The "laying of hands" is a gesture of investiture from one of higher authority to one of lower authority (based on Moses' investiture of Joshua in Dt 34:9), while the signet ring is a standard emblem of political authority throughout Near Eastern cultures.[23] Many of the points in this letter are reiterated in a second epistle, now in Judeo-Arabic with Hebrew phrases interspersed. The *rosh yeshivah* writes that "his presence among you is in place of our presence" and continues (Hebrew in italics): "We conferred distinction upon him, selected him and made it incumbent to treat him with honor and respect. We elevated his station and gave him the title (*talqībuna*) *av bet din of the yeshivah*.[24] It is incumbent upon the *communities of our brethren, may they be blessed*, that, when they hear of his arrival and his appearance before them, they gather to meet him with rejoicing and gladness, exuberance, joy, respect, magnification (*i'ẓām*), abundant offering, and reverence and that his seat be made beautiful."

This text also goes on to mention rituals associated with Ben Barkhael's teaching, pronouncing his name in the *qadish*, the signet ring, and his right to make appointments. Ben 'Eli concludes, lending authority to the appointee while claiming his own jurisdiction: "His speech is our speech and his command is our command. He who brings him near brings us near and he who distances him distances us."[25]

"Magnification" and "reverence" undoubtedly involved praise of some sort, though it is difficult to know whether this included the formal presentation of panegyric. Ben ʿEli certainly saw the enumeration of the judge's virtues a requisite purpose of his letter and recognized that the verbal pronouncement of Ben Barkhael's greatness was essential to constituting his aura of authority and ultimately his effective leadership. Ben ʿEli recognized that dominion was built of praise.

Epistolary Panegyric in the East

In comparison with our knowledge of the oral performance of Jewish panegyric in the Islamic East, our knowledge of the place of panegyric in epistolary exchange is quite extensive. As suggested above and exemplified by the poem that opened this chapter, many panegyric texts functioned essentially as letters or as part of a correspondence in which a poem accompanied a letter proper, itself often written in rhymed prose with extensive literary effects. Hai Gaon's poem to Rav Yehudah was intended for a dual purpose: to function as a letter (in response to another letter) while allowing—indeed, mandating—broader circulation and oral performance.

Over the course of the century prior to Hai's correspondence with Rav Yehudah, Jewish letter writing had undergone a revolution, owed to Jewish knowledge of Arabic epistolary practices and the expanded functions of correspondence in the organization of the Jewish world. Letters were written for any number of reasons: to update a loved one on one's state, to inform a business partner on dealings, to initiate a relationship with someone of higher or lower rank, to ask for or offer a legal opinion, to request money or favors of a recipient, or to offer gratitude for a previous kindness. Most of these epistolary registers would be expected to include praise for their addressees, which could be as simple as a few well-chosen terms of address or as extensive as a rhymed, metered poem spanning hundreds of verses.[26]

Modern readers have sometimes been struck, even puzzled, by the amount of panegyric contained within Jewish letter writing. In fact, some letters seem to be little more than a long series of praises, especially striking since paper was sufficiently precious that letter writers covered every speck of available space, including the margins, with ink. Jacob Mann refers to one Geniza document (TS Loan 203.2), a letter by Sherirah Gaon of Pumbedita to Yaʿaqov b. Nissim of Qairawan, as "the end of a letter consisting merely of verbiage."[27] Yet these documents provide us with an intimate glimpse into the inner logic of medieval Jewish culture, for their rhetoric bespeaks some of its most fundamental conceptions of leadership, friendship, and interpersonal connection.

There has not yet been a comprehensive treatment of Jewish letter writing based on Geniza materials and in light of Arabic epistolary practices that takes into account the full range of stylistic differences across period, location, and social rank, though there have been various localized treatments.[28] Goitein, of course, discussed (especially merchant) Jewish letter writing at many points in *A Mediterranean Society*, and Assaf, already in the early twentieth century, pointed out that epistles of the Baghdad academy from the late twelfth and early thirteenth centuries followed a standard form that included long sections of praises and blessings at the beginning and end.[29] Structural and rhetorical analyses of all types of Jewish letter writing preserved in the Geniza remains an important topic for research, but here I wish only to emphasize praise as a pervasive aspect; it is exchanged among people of all ranks and, especially in the case of more powerful figures, played a constitutive role in the establishment of political legitimacy. In the section below, I present a general overview of Jewish letter writing in the Islamic Mediterranean, including the nodes at which praise was integrated, and argue further for narrowing the presumed gap between written and oral elements of panegyric performance.

On the Art of Medieval Jewish Letter Writing

Jewish letter writing can be dated prior to the geonic period; there are several references to the sending of letters in the Hebrew Bible (e.g., Est 3:13, 8:10), and Jewish letters survive from Late Antiquity (obvious examples include the Bar Kokhba letters and the Pauline epistles, though there are others). Jewish letters by *nasi*s are attested in Late Antiquity through references in the Babylonian and Jerusalem Talmuds as well as in a comment by Eusebius. As Isaiah Gafni points out, within rabbinic literature, excerpts of epistles are quoted in Hebrew even within Aramaic contexts, which may speak to Hebrew's status in formal correspondence either as a "national" or "trans-national" language. As Gafni also points out, it seems that Jews were well acquainted with the epistolary practices of Late Antiquity, illustrated colorfully by an anecdote in which a scribe in the service of Yehudah ha-Nasi drafted a letter to Caesar that the Nasi tore up and revised to make the opening salutation adhere to a more formal standard, "To the lord the king from Yehudah, your servant."[30]

The transformation of the geopolitical landscape brought by the expansion of Islam dramatically changed the organization of the Jewish world. The central administrative preoccupation of the academies at Baghdad and the competing Palestinian academy was the cultivation and preservation of loyalty from satellite communities from the far west to the far east of the Islamic world. Gaons sought to create standards of practice over these vast territories, encouraged adherence to their legal authority, and solicited funds from distant communities to run the academies. The movement of the Babylonian academies to the capital of Baghdad in the late ninth or early tenth century situated the gaons at the center of power, an ideal position for executing their administrative tasks and for cultivating their intellectual tastes.[31] New levels of connection between center and periphery were facilitated by the relative political unity, however fractious, of the ʿAbbasid Empire and the advent of rapid communication.

In many respects, the powers and responsibilities of the Jewish academies mirrored what was taking place administratively within the Islamic political world, whose governments also sought loyalty over vast territories and relied on an efficient system of mail delivery to bind center and periphery.[32] Neither private Jewish nor Muslim citizens had access to this governmental postal system, but the academies were able to use their own emissaries to circulate its letters, likely following similar routes. Other Jewish postal traffic seems to have been maintained through the "serendipitous, although heavy, traffic of Jewish travelers" and a more formalized system that Goitein described as a "commercial mail service" wherein Muslim couriers delivered letters sent among Jews.[33]

Islamic civilization also witnessed the rise of the court scribe (*kātib*), a powerful office that required knowledge of rhetoric, religion, poetry, philosophy, and diplomacy.[34] Letter writing became an art form in its own right that merited the composition of manuals offering advice for scribes including *al-Risāla ilā al-kuttāb* (Epistle to the secretaries), by ʿAbd al-Ḥamīd al-Kātib; *Adab al-kātib* (The etiquette of the secretary), by Ibn Qutaiba; *Adab al-kuttāb* (The etiquette of the secretaries), by al-Ṣūlī; *Tashīl al-sabīl ilā taʿallum al-tarsīl* (Easing the path to learning the art of letter writing), by al-Ḥumaydī; and the late fourteenth-century–early fifteenth-century *Ṣubḥ al-aʿashā' fī ṣināʿat al-inshā'* (Morning light for the night-blind in composing letters), by al-Qalqashandī.[35] As stated by A. Arazi: "Even an administrative letter should be composed according to artistic and literary criteria; in society's view, it belonged to the domain of the fine arts, and accordingly, the *kātib* was considered above all an artist."[36] Members of the *dīwān al-inshā'*, the correspondence bureau or chancery, were expected to gain mastery over literary techniques associated with the composition of poetry; al-Khwārazmī, in reviewing the technical vocabulary utilized within the chancery, defines various types of wordplay and rhetorical devices using works of poetics as his basis.[37]

Epistolographic manuals not only reflect the aesthetic and intellectual ideals of the age but also reveal a great deal about how society was organized and how the relations among various ranks of people were imagined. Al-Ḥumaydī (c. 1028–95), who was born in Córdoba and died in Baghdad, intended his book for "private letter writing" (*ikhwāniyya*) and planned another book that would deal with "letters from rulers dealing with matters of governance" (*sulṭāniyya*).[38] Within the volume on private letters, opening blessings are organized hierarchically according to the ranks and professions of the correspondents (caliphs, governors, scribes, judges, merchants). Although these openings essentially offer the same blessings for long life, for God's kindness and favor, and so on, the precise phrasing encodes social rank and negotiates the status differential between writer and recipient. Some elements also relate to the particular profession, as when a merchant is wished good fortune and even profit in business.[39] The *Ṣubḥ al-aʿashā'* similarly organizes blessings according to social rank, what is appropriate for a superior to send to an inferior (*ra'īs* and *mar'ūs*) and vice versa. One of the most unadorned forms of address occurs when a father writes to his son. When a letter is sent from a subordinate to a superior, the formulas tend to expand and become more elaborate rhetorically—for example, "May God elongate the life of the *qāḍī* (judge) in might (*ʿizz*) and happiness; may He extend his prestige (*karāma*) and execute His kindness (*niʿma*) for him with the broadest well-being (*ʿāfiya*) and the utmost security (*salāma*)."[40] Actual letters discovered in Quseir, which were directed to an elder merchant, follow similar formulas.[41] In short, blessings constitute a form of praise because their wording can mark the relative status of author and addressee.

The Geniza document Oxford e.74 1a–6b is part of a Judeo-Arabic transcription of an Arabic epistolary manual attributed to Aḥmad Ibn Saʿd al-Iṣfahānī; the work was divided into twenty-one chapters, beginning with *taḥmīdāt* (doxology) and *sulṭaniyāt*, and included examples for different genres, occasions, and purposes, including the expression of condolence, gratitude, apology, and, of course, praise (*al-thanā'*).[42] While the section on praise does not survive, it seems likely that it included formulations for figures of different rank. The existence of the text in Hebrew characters, which even preserves specifically Islamic formulations (including qur'ānic verses), indicates that the genre was sufficiently important among Jews to be studied and, in all likelihood, imitated.[43] Further, a book list from the Geniza includes a work titled *adab al-kātib*, possibly the guide for scribes by Ibn Qutaiba.[44]

As Haggai Ben Shammai points out, the Judeo-Arabic correspondence of the academies adopts conventions of Islamic chancery correspondence.[45] With likely precedent from Late Antiquity, numerous Jewish letters from the Islamic milieu open with an introductory formula of blessing, often in three parts, with dimensions of literary play. Examples of mellifluous letter introductions abound in Geniza correspondence. As is the case with the formulas for blessing in Islamic correspondence, the degree of ornament and even length usually correspond with rank. Saʿadia Gaon gives examples of the types of wordplay that "we constantly write in our epistles" (*fī rasāʾilinā*),[46] and, in a fragment from an actual letter by Saʿadia, itself a response to a panegyric, the opening blessings follow the same pattern.[47] Here Saʿadia was writing to a student of one of his disciples and likely invested the blessing with literary effect to demonstrate his skill, to "thank" the inquirer for his query and poem, and to mark them both as members of the same Jewish social and intellectual elite.

Although there are no manuals for Hebrew letter writing on the scale of the Arabic guides for scribes, there do survive Geniza manuscripts that compile Hebrew literary introductions for letters to addressees, both real and hypothetical, of various ranks (gaon, scribe, cantor, even synagogue caretaker), thus following the structural organization of Arabic epistolary manuals.[48] The most significant of these formularies (TS J 3.3; Figure 3) was published by Tova Beeri.[49] Such texts were probably intended to circulate as models for Jewish letter writers, including aspiring scribes. The mere existence of these documents demonstrates that Hebrew letter writing was also considered an art that adhered to conventions. Many of these introductions, and many actual letters dedicated to known recipients, include panegyric sections ranging from a few lines to several manuscript pages. Much of the literary creativity associated with versified panegyrics is observed within epistles, and the execution of literary praise was not dependent upon a "courtly" structure, per se; it was a by-product, or better a means, of human interconnection, whether bureaucratic, intellectual, mercantile, or familial.

There is also ample evidence for the Arabization of Jewish writing in letters exchanged between merchants or family members. Mark Cohen has demonstrated that authors of Hebrew letters found in the Geniza employ loan translations of Arabic locutions; examples include Jewish versions of the

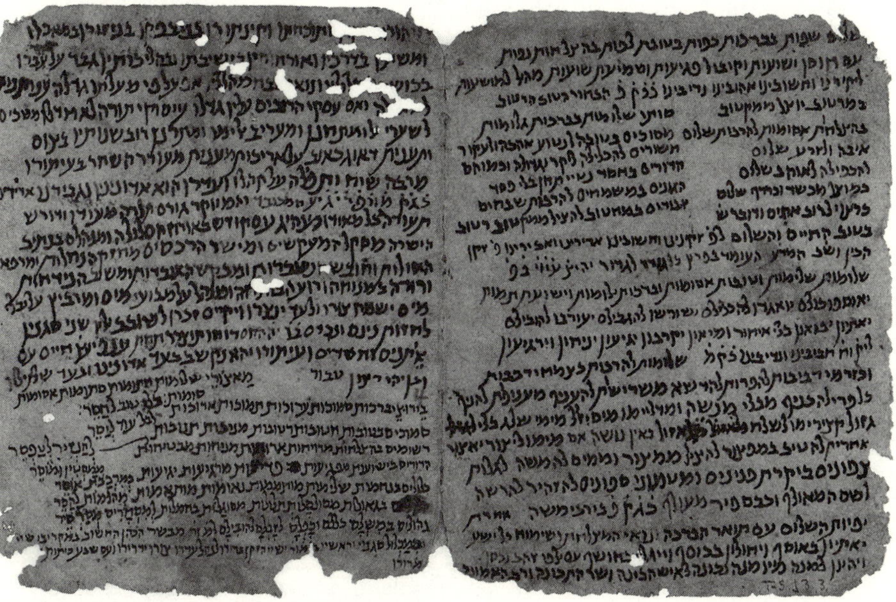

Figure 3. Epistolary formulary. TS J 3.3 (2r). Reproduced by kind permission of the Syndics of Cambridge University Library.

basmallah, certain epithets for God, opening and closing formulas, blessings for the addressee, and wishes that the addressee's enemies be thwarted.[50] In some cases, certain Hebrew words absorb the semantic force of their Arabic equivalents or cognates (*shelomot* = *salāma*; *ne'imot* = *ni'ma*; *haṣlaḥa* = *tawfīq*). Like Arabic letters, Hebrew counterparts sometimes incorporate Hebrew poetry or rhymed prose within the body of the letter.[51] Hebrew held a certain cachet and was used even when both correspondents knew Arabic (as mentioned, this was also the case when Aramaic was the lingua franca of the Near East). The historical Jewish language was important in delineating boundaries for a specific community of learned Jewish men. Still, the spirit of their writing remained that of the Arabic milieu in which they lived.[52]

Titulature

Another hallmark of letters of Arabic-speaking Jews from the Islamic Mediterranean is the addressing of a recipient, whether of higher or lower rank, with a series of appropriate terms and epithets that can be in Hebrew and/or

Judeo-Arabic. This can be as simple as the ubiquitous "Our master and teacher" (*mareinu ve-rabeinu*) or as complicated as several lines of carefully chosen and rhetorically sophisticated phrases. In certain circumstances, the epithets selected represent actual titles that were bestowed upon their bearers in an official sense. In other cases, the epithets evoke the style of formal titles but are actually devoid of official function. It is not always easy to distinguish the official from the unofficial, but in either case, the formulations are telling measures of Jewish notions of power and "statecraft" and bear the stamp of Islamic titulature practices.[53]

Addressing a powerful figure in the medieval Islamic world was a highly ritualized act that adhered to fairly strict conventions. This was the case whether the "encounter" was in person or in writing.[54] Caliphs, *wazīr*s, governors, scribes, and judges all expected to be addressed with strings of titles that marked their elevated status. As Islamic civilization developed an increasingly formalized political structure, the *laqab* (lit., "nickname") was transformed from being a rather nonspecific form of admiration to an official, fixed, and prestigious honorific. Caliphs claimed *laqab*s for themselves as regnal titles and reserved the right to bestow them upon their favorites. Caliphs and other high-ranking officials often signed documents with nothing but their honorary titles, insignia known as *ʿalāma*s specific to the individuals.

Most cynically, Muslim historians quipped that titles were bestowed upon underlings with liberality because the caliphate had nothing real to offer them (such as money, a practice that has been followed well by university administrators). Yet such honorifics were an essential part of the political machinery of Eastern Islamic lands and also enjoyed more limited usage in the Islamic West.[55] The terms selected convey ideals of the state, and the trained eye can glean a tremendous amount from such titles and epithets of address. The types of titles selected changed from one Islamic dynasty to another and were likely formulated in reaction to one another. The tenth century, it has been observed, witnessed the proliferation of compound honorifics, including as their second terms words like *dīn*, "faith"; and *dawla* or *mulk*, "secular power," or less commonly, compounded with *umma*, "nation" and *milla*, "religious community."[56] Kramers argues that titles stressing worldly political affiliation, popular among the Shiʿite Fatimids, were rejected by later Sunni dynasties in favor of titles stressing religious advocacy and fidelity.[57]

Titles of caliphs and other officials from Fatimid and Ayyubid Egypt are preserved in the handful of petitions addressed to powerful men by those of lower rank (including the truly lowly) found in the Cairo Geniza and the archive of Saint Catherine's monastery in the Sinai desert.[58] S. M. Stern published three petitions addressed to Fatimid caliphs or viziers, all of whom seemed to expect a high degree of honorary "verbiage" when addressed. Marina Rustow and Geoffrey Khan are doing more work in this area presently. The formulas of titles in these documents do not merely list flattering praises but reflect fundamental conceptions of the state. The Fatimid caliph is referred to repeatedly with phrases such as "Justice of the prophetic dynasty" (*'adl al-dawla al-nabawiyya*); the *wazīr* Ṭalā'i is "the Most Excellent Lord, the Pious King,[59] Helper of Imams, Averter of Misfortune, Commander of the Armies, Sword of Islam, Succor of Mankind, Protector of the Qadis and the Muslims, Guide of the petitioners among the Believers."[60] And so forth.

Jews followed standard titulature practices when referring to Muslim leaders in Fatimid Egypt.[61] A Jewish petitioner addressed Caliph al-Āmir (1101–30) "our Lord and Master, the Imām al-Āmir bi-Aḥkām Allah, Commander of the Faithful" and "the pure and noble prophetic Presence" (*al-maqām al-nabawī al-ṭāhir al-sharīf*).[62] Similarly, TS NS 110.26r (Figure 4), published by Goitein, is composed in a mixture of Hebrew, Arabic, and Judeo-Arabic (Hebrew in plain font, Judeo-Arabic in italics, Arabic script in bold italics): "leader of the sons of Qedar, *our lord* ***and master the Imām*** . . . the great king, *the Imām al-Āmir bi-Aḥkām Allah, Commander of the Faithful*."[63] During the second half of the twelfth century, the author of a letter offers extensive blessings for the "Place" (i.e., the ruler),[64] modified with a set of adjectives in Judeo-Arabic: "the holy, descended from 'Alī, the Imāmī, belonging to the family of the Prophet, the pure."[65] This formulation, with its focus on pure descent through Muḥammad and 'Alī, is specific to Shi'ite leadership and reflects Jews' full awareness of Fatimid court practices; Jews did not hesitate to refer to the rulers' descent from the "Prophet," thereby glossing over the Jews' complicated relationship with recognizing the legitimacy of Muḥammad's prophetic claim.[66]

Addresses to Jewish dignitaries, whether sent from lower rank to higher or vice versa, also include lengthy lists of honorifics, a practice undoubtedly derived from the use of *laqab*s within Islamic society.[67] In some cases, Jewish leaders signed documents with *'alāma*s, which claimed status in the same manner as Muslim leaders.[68] Further, the recipient of a letter could expect to be addressed with a string of terms specific to his rank, mode of leadership (spiritual/mundane), and relationship to the author.

In many cases, honorifics served as official titles.[69] Gaons bestowed titles upon subordinate representatives of the yeshivah when appointing them. As mentioned above, when Shemuel Ben 'Eli appointed Zekhariah Ben Barkhael

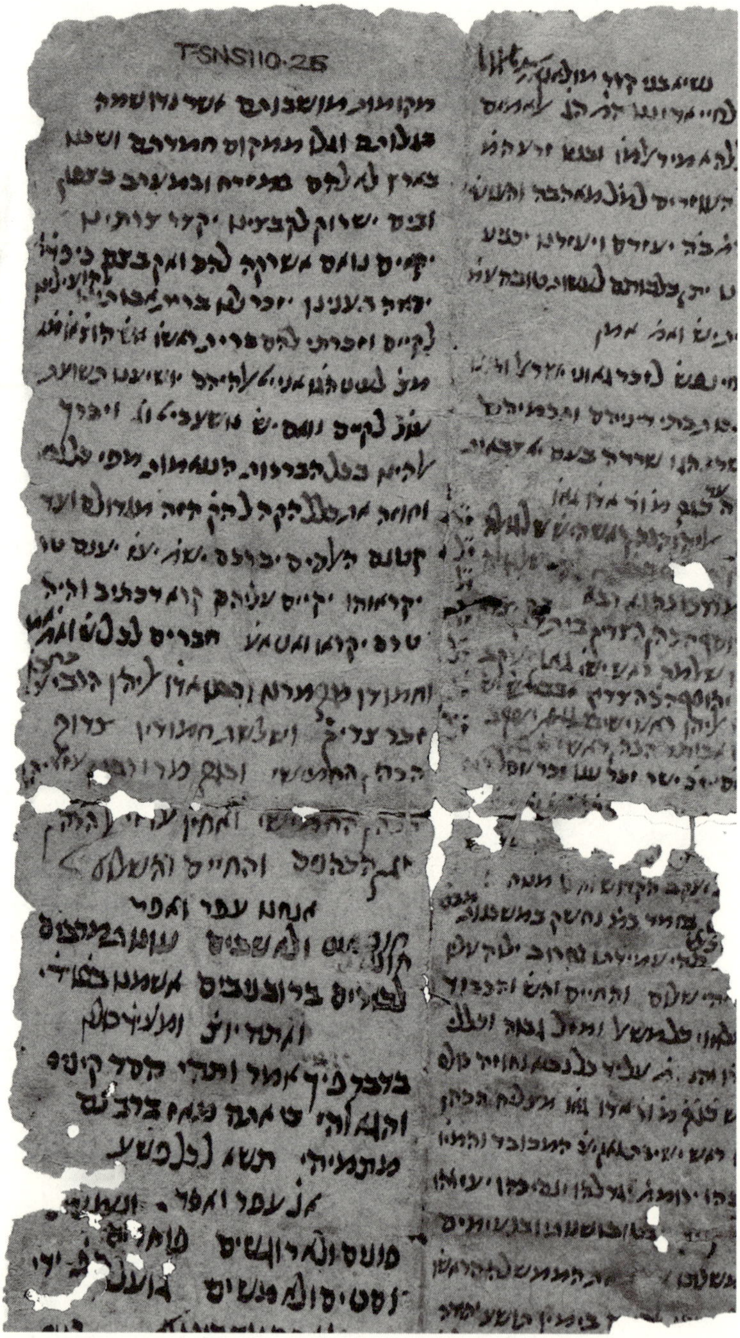

Figure 4. Petition for al-Āmir bi-Aḥkām Allah (Hebrew, Arabic, Judeo-Arabic). TS NS 110.26r. Reproduced by kind permission of the Syndics of Cambridge University Library.

to the office of *av bet din,* he used the root *lqb* to describe the process of bestowing a title: "Our elevating his station (*tarfī' manzilatihi*) and our giving him the title (*talqībuna*) *av bet din of the yeshivah.*"[70] In a panegyric, Sahlān Ben Avraham (d. 1050) was praised for the very fact that he held "seven titles" (*kinuyyin*).[71] In TS 8 J 16.18r, a certain Ovadiah is addressed as the "lofty lord (*al-sayyid al-ajall*), confidant of the state (*amīn al-dawla*), security of kingship (*thiqqat al-mulk*)." TS NS 246.22 is an early twelfth-century list, possibly a convenient reference for a scribe, of forty-three men along with their Hebrew titles. Each entry follows the same structure: "The sobriquets (*alqāb*) of So-and-So."[72]

Bestowers of titles stress that they did not dole them out lightly or haphazardly, and titles seem to have been fairly specific to their holders; when Avraham ha-Kohen, who already possessed two Hebrew titles, was given a third, *hod ha-zeqenim* (glory of the elders), he was told that the name had been given "many years before to the [now deceased] elder Abū 'Alī Ben Faḍlān at Baghdad" and "from then until now no one has been named this." The author, whom Mann suggests was Daniel Ben 'Azariah, specified his hope that the title would "elevate [Avraham's] honor, magnify his name, and extend his authority."[73]

State-oriented titles abound among addressees in the thirteenth-century *dīwān* of El'azar Ben Ya'aqov ha-Bavli. Here we encounter *shams al-dawla* (sun of the state), *sharf al-dawla* (nobility of the state), *'izz al-dawla* (might of the state), *najm al-dawla* (star of the state), and *amīn al-dawla* (confidant of the state).[74] In some cases, titles are hinted at within Hebrew panegyrics for these figures, as when *amīn al-dawla* Ben Manṣūr Ben al-Mashā'irī is called *pe'er misrah ve-ne'eman ha-melukhah* (wonder of dominion and confidant of sovereignty). Occasionally, Arabic *laqab*s are simply inserted into Hebrew poems.[75] The letters of Shemuel Ben 'Eli also provide a wealth of information on titles and epithets, especially as they were bestowed upon lower ranks by the author. Terms such as *amīn al-dawla*, *amīn al-mulk*, *thiqqat al-mulk*, *al-thiqqa*, *al-amīn*, all of which signify that the figure is a trusted proxy of "sovereignty" or the "state," are widely attested.[76] It is particularly interesting that Ben 'Eli continued to use the style of titulature characteristic of Shi'ite dynasties after, as Kramers suggests, such titles had been denounced by Sunni critics as emphasizing worldly over religious aspects of Islam.[77]

In Ben 'Eli's collection, the same individuals are sometimes described within a single letter both in Hebrew and in Judeo-Arabic, which allows for a useful comparison of political discourse in the two languages. In some cases, the Hebrew titles are much more elaborate and richer in literary references pertaining to Jewish dimensions of legitimacy. Two brothers described in Judeo-Arabic rather generically as "the two exalted elders" (*al-shaikhaini al-jalīlaini*) are described in Hebrew as "two precious elders, the praised brothers, the pure, the natives who are like bdellium and raised beds of spices [Sg 5:13], honest men [Gn 42:11], the priests, sons of the steadfast."[78] The Hebrew, in addition to being more ornate, draws on their lineage, both to their immediate progenitors and to their descent from a long line of priests.

On the other hand, the Hebrew and Judeo-Arabic sometimes mirror each other such that the Hebrew renders phrases whose origin is clearly Arabic. A certain Mevorakh is introduced in Judeo-Arabic as the "lofty minister, proxy of the nation, trusted one of sovereignty, beauty of the ministers"; in Hebrew, he is described as "our minister and noble one, the minister, the leader, the respected, our lord and master Mevorakh, minister of the nation, trusted one of sovereignty, splendor of the ministers, crown of the Levites, treasure of the yeshivah." Again, the Hebrew adds specifically Jewish dimensions and introduces a first-person plural voice ("our lord and master"). But most of the Hebrew formulations are translations of Arabic epithets (*amīn al-mulk = ne'eman ha-malkhut; jamāl al-ru'asā = hod ha-sarim*).[79] Thus, much innovation occurred within the Hebrew language to accommodate the feel of Arabic praise writing and to capture a new mode of political discourse.

An extraordinary amount of literary care went into the selection of terms of address, whether in Hebrew or in Judeo-Arabic. A fascinating example is ENA NS 18.30, a twelfth-century Geniza fragment that preserves three drafts of a single letter composed by Ḥalfon Ben Natanel for Maṣliaḥ Ben Shelomoh ha-Kohen, head of the Jerusalem academy, which at the time was in Fustat. The letter was written to initiate contact between the scholar-merchant, who already enjoyed significant fame, and the gaon, whom Ben Natanel hoped would maintain contact and promote his reputation. The existence of multiple drafts in Judeo-Arabic for the same purpose clearly attests to the deliberateness that Ben Natanel invested in getting the tone just right. Comparing the versions is revealing:

> 1. My lord, my master, the most high, my support, my refuge, the most revered, my help, my stay, the most excellent, crown of the Exile, lamp of the religious community, perfection of exaltedness, fit for the domains of religion and the material world, his virtue and beneficence are widespread.
> 2. My lord, the most high, my master, the unique, the most excellent, the most beautiful crown, and the most perfect splendor,

> banner of banners, the source of perfection, the beauty of thought, ornament of the age.
> 3. My lord, my master, august as is proper for him, the sublime, foremost in priority, his exalted and sublime Presence.

From the first version to the third, the terms of praise actually become fewer in number. On the other hand, the author moved away from one-word descriptions (the most high, my support, my refuge), which are fairly generic, to more complex constructions, though these are not absent even in the first example. Already in the first example, the author has drawn upon terms of praise common within Islamic political discourse and Arabic panegyric, most importantly "fit for the domains of Religion and the World" (*al-dīn wa'l-dunyā*), a theme that had a long life span in Jewish discourse. In the second and third examples, the author has dropped terms referring to the Jewish community specifically (the Exile, the religious community) and offered a more universal depiction. Most importantly, the text moves toward vocabulary that is much more rare, abstract, and particular to royalty ("banner," "Presence").

Official letters were sometimes enacted dramatically through the oral presentation of their contents. A long letter sent on behalf of the congregations of Alexandria by Yeshuʿa Kohen Ben Yosef to Ephraim Ben Shemariah, head of the Jerusalem congregation in Fustat, requests contributions for the freeing of captives; even in such an urgent matter, the author did not fail to include six lines of complicated rhymed prose in the introduction (praise in honor of the community) and thirty in the body of the letter. In thanking Ben Shemariah for a previous letter, the author writes, "the whole community (of Alexandria) enjoyed your letter . . ., the greatness of your wisdom and the beauty of your rhymes." Ben Yosef also requests that his letter be read to the community in Fustat.[80] Shemuel Ben ʿEli specifies that a letter should be read "in public and sweetly" (*meteq lashon*) and a joint letter from Sherirah and Hai Gaon to the Palestinian academy commands that the letter be read in public, "which was done there for our forefathers many times."[81] A letter of Maimonides to Yosef Ibn ʿAqnīn describes a highly ritualized public reading of a letter from an exilarch such that the community members rose while the reader stood with the elders of the community to his right and left.[82] The fact that epistles were frequently performed orally helps close the functional gap between epistles and oral panegyrics. And because epistles contained so much praise, their wide distribution demonstrates how public images of legitimacy could be disseminated and consumed.

Poetic Epistles, Epistolary Poems

As noted, many letters were written with a great deal of literary flair and made use of the same poetic techniques characteristic of "literature" proper. Similarly, many poems can be shown to have held an epistolary function. To be sure, letters and poems were distinguished in the medieval period and were theorized, respectively, in works on epistolography and poetics. At the same time, however, the Geniza preserves two book lists in which a *dīwān al-mukātabāt* (collection of correspondence) appears adjacent to a *dīwān al-shiʿr* (collection of poetry), which points to differentiation but also to the proximity of the two forms.[83] Further, no neat dichotomy can be maintained between texts that were "poems" and those that were "epistles." At the very least, both utilized praise as a dominant mode of address, which points to their common rhetorical goals. The shared function of praise is corroborated by similar organizational strategies in works of epistolography and poetics, in that both tend to be structured around hierarchy. We have already seen that al-Ḥumaydī and al-Qalqashandī organize blessings of address according to rank; similarly, the panegyric section of *Kitāb al-ʿumda*, a major work on Arabic poetics by Ibn Rashīq, is organized according to rank by specifying what qualities should be praised for occupants of different offices.[84]

One of our earliest Hebrew panegyrics, fragmentary though it is, is written in honor of Saʿadia Gaon. It consists of strings of words, between two and five words each, that maintain a common end rhyme from between four and ten strings. After praising the *mamdūḥ*, the author asks a particular question pertaining to a matter of exegesis and expresses hope for a response. Do we have here a poem or a piece of correspondence? The answer is both. The verso contains the beginning of the gaon's response, replete with the kind of wordplay that Saʿadia describes in his commentary on the Book of Creation (*Sefer yeṣirah*) as belonging to letter openings, thus reinforcing the reading of the poem as a letter.[85]

The same is also the case with the lengthy panegyric that opened this chapter; it is certainly a poem but also meets standard epistolary expectations (greetings, congratulations, thanks, updates, closings), not to mention that it was written in response to a letter proper. Another poetic panegyric by Hai Gaon is introduced in the manuscript with a revealing superscription, undoubtedly inserted by a scribe of the academy, "the correspondence (Ar., *mukātaba*) of our master Hai Gaon with master Avraham Ben ʿAṭa, Nagid of Qairawan."[86] In an important article on the Andalusian native Menaḥem

Ben Saruq, Ezra Fleischer stressed epistolary dimensions of Menaḥem's poetry and argued for the continuity, based on formalistic grounds, between the poet's writing and Eastern precedents. I am wholly in agreement with this aspect of Fleischer's article, which helps us situate Andalusian Jewish culture within the broader context of the Islamic Mediterranean.[87]

In the following section, I take the argument for the link in Jewish literary culture between the Islamic East and the Islamic West a step further by arguing for the basic continuity of panegyric performance as a hybrid oral-epistolary system. Although there are obvious structural differences between, for example, a gaon's thanking a donor and a poet's initiation of a relationship with a potential benefactor, the hybrid performance practice points to some level of shared function and interpersonal dynamic. This fact presses us to rethink the nature of Jewish culture in the Islamic West, particularly in al-Andalus, with respect to what has been termed its "courtly" quality. The section on the performance of Jewish panegyric in the Islamic West begins with a historiographic excursus on what I will call the "courtly hypothesis," which, I argue, has had a distorting effect on our perception of panegyric's function.

Jewish Panegyric Performance in the Islamic West

Andalusian Jewish culture has often been imagined as a kind of novum that broke forth ex nihilo, owed to the high degree of Arabization of Andalusian Jewry. If there is one word that is usually used to distinguish Andalusian Jewish culture from other Jewish cultures in the Islamic Mediterranean, it is "courtly," though scholars are seldom precise about what this term means. Seventy years have passed since Joseph Weiss delivered his paper "Tarbuṭ ḥaṣranit ve-shirah ḥaṣranit" (Courtly culture and courtly poetry) at the first World Congress of Jewish Studies in Jerusalem (1947).[88] By that time, research on the "court Jew" had gained momentum among researchers of different periods of Jewish history. Selma Stern had written her *Der Hofjude im Zeitalter des Absolutismus (1640–1740)*, in which she presented court Jews as "the forerunners of the emancipation," although debates raged over whether these Jews, who maintained contacts with and proved useful instruments of royalty, represented a people apart from their coreligionists or safeguarded their welfare (see, especially, the square critique of Stern by none other than Hannah Arendt).[89] Likely influenced by the tragedy of the Holocaust, Yitzhak Baer had portrayed the court Jews of Christian Iberia with a mixture of admiration and suspicion.[90]

Weiss aimed to elevate the study of Andalusian Hebrew poetry from philological-textual research and biographical description to create a "history of the spirit." His paper argued that the Hebrew poetry of al-Andalus reflected a Jewish "courtly" reality by drawing attention to the social manners idealized in the poetry as well as the lavish material surroundings described. Weiss wrote that "the Jews of the Arab courts who were close to royalty became the dedicated initiators of an independent Jewish court culture as a secular culture that was separate from Jewish society." He suggested that "Jews' experience in the Arab courts caused Jews to create their own similar culture and that the patron, in whose honor poets offered praise, stood at the center of this parallel culture." At the same time, Weiss opined, "courtly Jewish society could not be anything, of course, other than a spiritual semblance [of Muslim courtly society] (albeit one abounding in brightness and splendor), but was deprived of all real political power." Panegyric was marshaled as evidence in constructing this "court culture," and the presumed structure of the Jewish court, in turn, has determined how panegyric has been conceived and interpreted.

Weiss's paper became a classic in the field and remains cited widely, but its thesis has rarely been revisited.[91] Questions we might ask include: Where exactly was this Jewish court? Was the patron as central as Weiss had imagined? To what extent can we generalize about Jewish patronage structures across periods (Umayyad, Taifa, Almoravid)? Weiss's study had an impact on Schirmann, who, as discussed in the Introduction, saw the panegyric phenomenon as the paramount (and somewhat ugly) aspect of poetry as a "vocation." Weiss also had a deep impact on Eliahu Ashtor, who assented to the courtly image and saw the poet-patron relationship as key to understanding the great explosion of Jewish intellectual production during the "Golden Age" of al-Andalus. His influential *The Jews of Moslem Spain* portrays a performance scenario wherein Yiṣḥaq Ibn Khalfūn recites a Hebrew poem aloud before his Jewish patron and an audience, including competing poets, leading the patron to toss some coins into the poet's purse. Yet, as Ann Brener points out, there is really no evidence for this.[92] The image is undoubtedly constructed out of depictions of similar scenes in Arabic *adab* collections and what seem to be performative aspects of the poems themselves, such as first-person addresses, references to rival poets, and dedicatory sections. Because of the accepted view that Jews imitated the prevailing Muslim court culture on a smaller scale, not only textually but also materially, it would only be fitting that they practiced some version of public or semipublic adulation.[93]

Given that the courtly image is tightly bound up with the practice of panegyric—specifically, its oral recitation before a paying patron—it is worth revisiting the evidence for oral and written aspects of Andalusian Jewish poetic culture and panegyric practice in particular. It is clear that Hebrew poets sometimes met and exchanged poems and even competed to outdo one another within certain formal constraints, but we have exceedingly few anecdotes that recount panegyric performance or modes of remuneration. Some poems include specific requests for payment in the form of robes and the like, but one imagines that, had the direct payment of a poet for his panegyric before an audience been a norm, we would have at least a few anecdotes to that effect.[94] Despite some justification for the type of courtly performance that Weiss and others have imagined, I argue below that the preponderance of evidence points to a mixed oral-epistolary function similar to that described with respect to the Islamic East. Overall, the social structure of Andalusian Jewry represents more of a localized and less hierarchic (yet more elitist) version of its Eastern counterparts than a break with Jewish culture in the rest of the Islamic Mediterranean.

Insofar as at least some Hebrew panegyrics were performed orally in al-Andalus, the social setting is mostly reminiscent of the *majlis uns*, or, better still, the *mujālasa*, the more egalitarian salon of the middle strata. As Samer Ali has argued, the *mujālasa* was forged through bonds of mutual affection and "often prompted bacchic excess: banquet foods, wine, fruits, flowers, perfumes, singing, and of course, displays of sexuality and love."[95] This practice, too, may have had at least some precedent among Jews in the East prior to the year 1000, as suggested by one of the only wine poems to survive from that environment, "When I drink it I fill it for another, who gives it to his companion, and he, too, pours [lit., "mixes"] it. . . . All the lovers call out, 'drink in good health!'" (lit., "life"). The poem not only idealizes wine but also a host of social ideals of which wine is a metonym.[96] Still, it was only in al-Andalus that such social practices seem to have become the emblematic pastimes of a recognizable group.

At the heart of the matter is what is meant by the word "courtly" that is so often affixed to Andalusian Jewish culture. If it means tastes for wine drinking, garden settings, and an attraction to things worldly—then the Andalusians were more courtly than their counterparts in the Islamic East.[97] If it refers to Jews who held actual positions within Islamic courts, then this is a phenomenon that is well attested throughout the Islamic Mediterranean.[98] If it refers to a set of intellectual values that blends traditional Jewish learning with contemporary intellectual currents (whether termed "secular" or "Islamic"), then this, too, is something we find among Jews from Córdoba in the West to Baghdad in the East. But if it refers to the political practices associated with Islamic courts—a penchant for hierarchic structures, pronouncements of rank, and an imperial perspective—then Andalusian Jewish culture might be considered less courtly than its Eastern counterpart.

Oral and Written Elements of Panegyric Culture in al-Andalus

Generally speaking, the Hebrew poetic culture of al-Andalus had strong oral components.[99] Even Mosheh Ibn Ezra, who describes his own generation as a period of decline, testifies to the continued oral circulation of poetry through poetry transmitters (Ar., *ruwāʾ*; sing., *rāwī*). In fact, he characterizes oral transmission as superior to written recording, or at least that the latter is rendered unnecessary when the machinery of oral transmission is in place. Writing of the finest poets, he states: "I did not record any of the best poetry of this superlative group or an exalted word of their superior words, for they are well known and preserved in the mouths of the poetry transmitters (*al-ruwāʾ*). For the light of the morning obviates the need for lamps, and the sun obviates the need for candles!"[100]

A number of other pieces of evidence point to oral and even improvisational elements of this poetic culture in the generations prior to Ibn Ezra. Hebrew liturgical poems were certainly heard, and we imagine that many poems composed for weddings and funerals, which often contained praise, were recited aloud. In an epistle to his patron Ḥasdai Ibn Shaprut, Menaḥem Ben Saruq mentions, regarding laments that he had composed over the patron's father, that "all Israel lamented [them] each day of mourning" (one presumes orally).[101] As Schirmann notes, the Judeo-Arabic superscription preserved in a Geniza fragment to a well-known poem by Dunash Ben Labrat reads: "Another poem by Ben Labrat about the sound of the canals. . . . [here the scribe lists other subjects of the poem]. He described this at a gathering (*majlis*) of Ḥasdai the Andalusian."[102] Yehosef the son of Shemuel ha-Nagid relates, in a superscription to a poem, how his father improvised fifteen poems on the theme of an apple at a small social gathering (*maqom ḥevrato*).[103] Oral recitation at a small gathering is also suggested by a superscription in the *dīwān* of Yiṣḥaq Ibn Khalfūn: "And he wrote to him while drinking his medicine [i.e., wine] and his friends were with him at the gathering (*majlis*)."[104]

Again, such gatherings are reminiscent of the *majlis uns*, or the *mujālasa*, and, notably, there is no evidence for the presence of a patron paying professional poets.

Abū Walīd Marwān Ibn Janāḥ presents an anecdote that highlights a mixture of oral and written elements in Andalusian Hebrew poetic culture. While a young man, Ibn Janāḥ visited the poet Yiṣḥaq Ibn Mar Shaul and tried to impress his host by reciting one of Yiṣḥaq's poems. Ibn Janāḥ relates that he opened with the words *segor libi* (the enclosure of my heart) and then: "when I recited this poem before its author, he responded to me *qerav libi* (the innards of my heart)! I said to him, 'I have not seen it (like this) in any of the books but rather *segor libi*. If so, whence this change?' He said to me, 'When Ya'aqov and his sons recited this, he sent it from his city to Córdoba, and when it reached the transmitter (*rāwī*) Rav Yehudah Ben Hanija and with him Rav Yiṣḥaq Ibn Khalfūn, the poet had difficulty with the verse and changed it.'"[105]

Ibn Mar Shaul blames not the incompetent distortions of copyists but rather the intentional alterations made by the learned. Here we witness that a short poem was recited, then committed to writing, sent over a distance, and subsequently modified by a reciter whose version of the poem was copied in (apparently several) books and became the accepted standard. Transmission thus incorporated both oral and written aspects.

Ibn Janāḥ's anecdote calls attention to what I consider one of the most crucial aspects of Andalusian Jewish intellectual society. Only rarely do we find intellectuals gathered together; for the most part, they appear separated by distances and had meetings only occasionally.[106] This is the picture that emerges when reading the history of Hebrew poetry in al-Andalus as described by Mosheh Ibn Ezra. For the most part, Ibn Ezra describes an ever-shrinking constellation of intellectuals, often moving from place to place and spread out across al-Andalus. He does not describe a series of discrete Jewish courts, each with competing poets orbiting around a patron, but rather a coterie of scattered authors who exchange poems over distances. He mentions authors according to their generations, and then according to their cities, but hardly describes any organized court. The closest he comes pertains to the poets surrounding Ḥasdai Ibn Shaprut (further below), but any Jewish court culture must have been extremely short-lived; it seems to have been unique to the period of the Umayyad caliphate and was perhaps repeated, to some extent, in various Taifa states; but certainly by Ibn Ezra's generation, there barely seems to have been a trace of stable circles organized around patrons. This is how Ibn Ezra describes the generation of poets preceding his own:

> Among the poets of Toledo were Abū Harūn Ibn Abī al-'Aish, and after a period Abū Isḥāq Ibn al-Ḥarīzī. Among the poets of Seville were Abū Yūsuf Ibn Migash, originally of Granada and later of Seville, and Abū Zakariyya Ibn Mar Abun. And among the last of the generation in Granada was Abū Yūsuf b. al-Marah. Among the people of firm speech and clear poetry was my older brother Abū Ibrāhīm; he, may God have mercy on him, possessed gentle expression and sweet poetry due to his fluency in knowledge of Arabic expression (*'arabiyya*). He died in Lucena in 1120/21. And in the east of al-Andalus there was at this time Abū 'Umar Ibn al-Dayyan. . . . How deserted the earth is after them! How dark it is for their loss! Thus it is said, "The death of the pious is salvation for them but loss for the world. Our ancestors preceded in this with this saying, "*the death of the righteous is good for them but bad for the world*" (b. Sanhedrin 103b).[107]

Regarding his own generation, Ibn Ezra continues:

> Those of their generation who are at the end of their days, and those who come after them and follow in their paths, are an exalted small group[108] and a beautiful coterie that understands the goal of poetry. Although they were adherents of different schools (*madhāhib*) and [attained] distinct levels of speech, they came to [poetry's] gate and path, administered its purity and eloquence; they reached the extreme of beauty and splendor, nay they were mighty in likening and similitude. It has been said that men are like rungs of a ladder; there are the high rungs and the low and those in between. But all of them, in whatever cities they dwelled, were in the circle of beautifying, precision, and mastery.

He goes on to mention numerous figures by name, several of whom had migrated from one city to another, and concludes: "These skilled people (*naḥarīr*), I met all of them (except for a few) and selected their most famous and obscure [verses]. The poet [Abū Tammām] said concerning this, 'The coterie (*isāba*) whose values (*adābuhum*) are my values, though they are apart in the land, they are my neighbors.'"[109]

These intellectuals constituted a group largely by virtue of the literary and other intellectual ties maintained among them. If I might be permitted some anachronism, Andalusian Jewish courts were largely "virtual" and owed their existence to a web of connections and occasional moments of encounter. In Chapter 2, we will consider the role of panegyrics exchanged throughout such networks as "gifts." For now, we will continue to review the evidence for the oral and written elements of panegyric practice in al-Andalus.

A small subset of Andalusian panegyrics seems to be associated with installation to office or some other public acclamation of power. The most suggestive examples I have identified emanate from the *dīwān*s of Mosheh Ibn Ezra and Yehudah Halevi.[110] One of the poems by Ibn Ezra bears the superscription, "To a friend who was appointed to the position of judge (*tawallā al-qaḍā'*)" and includes verses that suggest a political ritual:[111]

All the masters of knowledge testify that your community adorned
and elevated itself through you.
[Your community] became your subject today, it inclined to be
ruled by your decree.
[Your community] raised up the wonder of dominion [before you]
for it is your possession and an inheritance from your fathers.
They said to you, "You are next in succession, come and redeem
your inheritance!
Arise and be our judge[112] for we have not found a leader[113] like you."
. . . .
Make a pledge with the sons of Wisdom for they, among all men,
share a pact with you . . .
Take delight in the might of the world but also beware lest it seduce
you. . . .
This is advice from a friend whose soul takes pride on the day of
your pride's exaltation.[114]

The immediacy of an occasion is suggested by such words as "today" and the second-person address to "arise and be our judge." The references to a "pledge" and "pact" likely allude to standard practices of Islamic installation rites, which center on the loyalty oath (*bai'a*) and making a bilateral compact (*'ahd*).[115] The poem was certainly written for the occasion of the friend's installation, though we do not know that it was recited as part of the ceremony; as is often the case, we are forced to rely upon the internal evidence of the poem, a method that can be only partly successful because poems that were not performed can contain performative elements.

A second example from Ibn Ezra's *dīwān* is a panegyric in strophic form, written, it seems, for the induction of another judge,[116]

How comely on the mountain are the footsteps of the herald announcing (Is 52:7)
that a shepherd has come to bring comfort to the flock wandering in the forest.
Behold, the sound of the people in its boisterousness (Ex 32:17) is heard calling him in song.

Our rejoicing before you is like the joy of a multitude on their holiday.
May you reign over us! You and your son and your son's son!

Gates of the House of God, lift up your heads and say, "Come, O blessed one of God!
The one who stands to serve by the name of God, to teach the law of God,
to teach the teachings of God that [they] may know the ways of God."

For these are a sign upon your right hand and a reminder between your eyes (cf. Ex 13:9).

Although the unprotected settlements[117] are no more, you restored their habitations!
Although prophecy and vision had grown rare, you spoke their wonders!
Although deprivation had wasted their souls, your wisdom revived them!

Your table satisfies them, your refreshing stream gives them drink.

From now on you will be minister over one thousand. May you be exalted and rule over Israel!
May your enemy pass away, may he be lost and not be redeemed;
God has unsheathed His sword against him, but you he has chosen like Ittiel [i.e., Solomon].

May a thousand fall at your left, ten thousand at your right! (Ps 91:7)

May your name be exalted and magnified in all the corners of the earth!
May you wipe out transgressive and iniquitous people and burden their yoke!
May you judge them by the laws of the Torah and teach [the laws'] general and specific principles!

May your tongue utter wisdom and God illumine your face!

Again, several elements suggest a ritual occasion: the boisterous singing, the blessing of welcome, and the words "from this day on." Again, we do not know that this poem was uttered within an initiation ceremony, but it seems likely that there was some sort of ceremony that involved the singing of songs. Unfortunately, we still know very little about the performance of public rituals among Andalusian Jews. It seems that there was at least some continuity with Jewish rituals of installation as known from the Islamic East, and in both locales we find parallels with contemporary Islamic rituals of power. However, the installation of a judge in al-Andalus was a less "imperial" occasion than the appointment of an exilarch in Baghdad. In any case, there is no reason to believe that this poem was commissioned by a paying patron.

As stated, the most likely testimonies for Jewish panegyric performance on a courtly model pertain to the brief period of Ḥasdai Ibn Shaprut. Mosheh Ibn Ezra writes concerning Menaḥem Ben Saruq and Dunash Ben Labrat that Ibn Shaprut "rejoiced at their wondrous poetry and their marvelous and eloquent addresses."[118] In all likelihood, at least some of these poems were the panegyrics for which these poets are known.[119] Yet many panegyrics were clearly not performed face-to-face by the poet before his *mamdūḥ*, such as one that Ben Saruq sent to Ibn Shaprut when the former was imprisoned by the latter.[120] Nonetheless, the poem presents elements of "performativity" we might expect from formal courtly performance such as first-person speech and a boast over poetic skill.[121] In the final verse of the poem, the poet captures the rhetorical function of the address, which is to assuage the anger of the *mamdūḥ* and to gain freedom, a purpose masterfully developed through the rhetoric of the appended letter. Was the poem recited by a *rāwī* subsequent to its reception before the *mamdūḥ* alone, in a small social gathering, or in a public assembly? Oral performance remains a possibility, but we have no evidence one way or the other. What is certain is the poem's function as part of an epistolary package.

The most extensive anecdote that we possess concerning the performance of a panegyric paints a picture quite different from that of a poet presenting a poem before a patron with the hope of remuneration. Yehudah Halevi, in a letter to Mosheh Ibn Ezra, recounts how he came from "Seir" (Christian Iberia) to "dwell in the light of the masters of great deeds, the great luminaries, the wise men in the west of Sepharad (al-Andalus),"[122] who ultimately befriended him. Recalling their generosity, he wrote: "Time took an oath not to make an end (of me) but in the house of my estrangement it sustained me, delighted me with songs of friendship, and satiated me with the wine of love after I had sworn to wander." The company was reciting a poem by "the prince of their host," Mosheh Ibn Ezra (who was not present), a panegyric in honor of Yosef Ibn Ṣadīq in *muwashshaḥ* form that concluded with an Arabic *kharja*, titled "Leil maḥshavot lev a'ira" (A night when I rouse the thoughts of my heart).[123] After the others attempted to imitate the poem but failed, Halevi invented a complete version (presumably orally), which he later memorialized in the letter.[124] In Halevi's version, it is now Ibn Ezra who is appointed the *mamdūḥ*.

What do we learn about the place of panegyric in Andalusian social culture through this anecdote? First, we learn that Ibn Ezra's panegyric to Ibn Ṣadīq circulated beyond the hands of its recipient; it was likely sent to Ibn Ṣadīq and then copied or circulated orally to others.[125] Halevi's letter might be alluding to some of the social practices associated with court culture (wine, music, poetry), particularly the *majlis uns*, and the reciprocity of the social relations recalls the *mujālasa* most directly. The oral recitation of poetry, including Ibn Ezra's panegyric for Ibn Ṣadīq and possibly other panegyrics (perhaps suggested by "songs of friendship") is clearly attested.[126] However, to the extent that Ibn Ezra was the "prince of their host," he was not actually present; there was no patron in the sense of one receiving praise and offering payment in exchange. Halevi also created a panegyric without the *mamdūḥ*'s being present, a poem that he subsequently sent within an epistle. What did Halevi want from Ibn Ezra in sending him the epistle embedded with the poem? The answer, quite simply, is recognition, association, protection, and possibly even financial support. However, he was not seeking quid pro quo cash remuneration but something much broader, the dynamics of which we explore further in Chapter 2.

While scholars often cite this anecdote in order to capture Halevi's remarkable skill and rise to fame, here I stress the social dynamics revealed. The poem, after all, was not any old *muwashshaḥ* but one dedicated to Ibn Ezra's honor. The events that Halevi describes might be viewed as a pretext for directing praise toward Ibn Ezra. The letter is essentially a "self-introduction" written in the hopes of formalizing a relationship. Praise is the expected rhetorical register for doing so and is highly attested both in the introduction to the letter and in the poem that it contains. It is possible that Halevi's poem was recited aloud after reception, but we do not know this with certainty. This turned out to have been the beginning of a beautiful friendship, as Ibn Ezra responded to Halevi's letter with a poem inviting the young poet to Granada. The poem praises the eloquence of Halevi's letter and the poem that it contained and reflects astonishment at the author's prowess despite his youth. On the other hand, Ibn Ezra's response did not praise Halevi himself; the poem is a type of panegyric sent from an older and more powerful "patron" to a younger and less powerful "client." The poem employs only circumscribed praises and thus defines the formality and vertical dynamic of the relationship during its formative stage.[127]

* * *

In discussing Jewish panegyric in the Islamic East above, I pointed out that many poems held a specifically epistolary function. The same is true of many poems from the Andalusian corpus. An important example is the poem "Afudat nezer," written by Menaḥem Ben Saruq as the introduction to an epistle on behalf of Ḥasdai Ibn Shaprut for Yosef, king of the Khazars. Adopting monorhyme (a standard feature of Arabic prosody), the poem opens with the kinds of blessings that one would expect in an epistle proper:

> May the priestly crown [be given] to the tribe that rules the far-off kingdom,
> May God's benefit be upon it and peace be upon all its governors and host,
> May salvation be a raiment upon its shrine, its holidays and sacred occasions.

In particular, the wishes for "God's benefit" and "peace"—*ne'imot* and *shelomot*—correspond precisely to Arabic epistolary standards and are actually cognates of the widely attested *ni'mat allah* and *salamāt*.[128] The epistolary style here is not surprising, given that the poem introduced an actual epistle, was used by Ibn Shaprut to introduce himself to the king, and was sent over a great distance.

Epistolary function is apparent even in many of the so-called courtly panegyrics exchanged among intellectuals *within* al-Andalus. Medieval scribes often indicate when a poem was written in response to another poem, and such sets of poems, generally written according to the same meter and rhyme, served as a type of correspondence. Previous scholars have assembled lists of such exchanges—between Abū Faḍl Ibn Ḥasdai and Shemuel ha-Nagid, Yiṣḥaq Ibn Khalfūn and ha-Nagid, Yehudah Halevi and Mosheh Ibn Ezra, Avraham Ibn Ezra and Yosef Ibn Ṣadīq, Todros Abulafia and Yosef al-Qarawi—and we need not rehearse them here; let it suffice to say that such exchanges demonstrate that the function of poems as correspondence was obvious and paramount.[129] Despite their performative aspects, these poems were clearly not performed by their authors before their *mamdūḥ*s, though it remains a possibility that they were recited orally subsequent to reception.

A significant number of poems originally accompanied letters. As Schirmann suggests, many of the freestanding poems that have reached us were likely affixed to letters and were severed through anthologizing processes and the vagaries of textual transmission. Shemuel ha-Nagid's famous war poem "Eloah 'oz" (God of might) bears a superscription: "He said this poem that commenced his letter."[130] Ha-Nagid also composed an Aramaic poem (a condolence sent to Ḥananel Ben Ḥushiel upon the death of his father) that is appended to a letter, also in Aramaic.[131] Mosheh Ibn Ezra's *dīwān* preserves two letters that were originally connected with poems, and Halevi's *dīwān* preserves several letters as well. The exterior of a letter bearing the address could bear a few verses of panegyric.[132] We also learn from a superscription that Mosheh Ibn Ezra had to resend a letter and include a new poem because the original had been lost at sea.[133] In modern (and some pre-modern) editions of Hebrew poetic oeuvres, poems appear segregated from the epistles for which they were composed, but we should remain attuned to the original function of the poems as an element of correspondence.[134]

Let us conclude by commenting on the epistolary function of one of the most famous Hebrew poems of al-Andalus, a panegyric by Abū Faḍl Ibn Ḥasdai for Shemuel ha-Nagid. The poem is nicknamed the *shirah yetomah*, the "orphan poem," taking on the sense of the Arabic cognate *yatīma*, meaning "orphan" but also "unique, one of a kind, unparalleled." The poem is a highly classicized panegyric that evokes pre-Islamic themes and lavishes praise upon the addressee's wisdom, writing, and generosity. It opens with the theme of the "night phantom" (Ar., *ṭaif lail*) who visits the poet during his sleep; just as the poet is imagining an erotic encounter with his beloved, an encounter marked foremost by arousing scents, he awakens to find that there is naught save the "scent that revives souls . . . like the name of Shemuel ha-Nagid," thus figuring the *mamdūḥ*'s broad reputation as his "scent."[135]

According to Mosheh Ibn Ezra, Ibn Ḥasdai sent this poem from the east of al-Andalus to the Nagid, then in Granada—and indeed, the content of the poem intimates separation and longing. For all its literary brilliance, the poem ultimately belongs to an established epistolary genre, *shafāʿa* (commending someone to someone else, a "letter of introduction"), whereby the author asks the Nagid to offer protection for two refugees.[136] Ibn Ḥasdai did not request monetary payment from the Nagid but rather the performance of a favor; the poem was Ibn Ḥasdai's "payment in advance" to the Nagid for fulfilling the request. The give-and-take of this relationship is captured succinctly toward the end of the poem:

> Take this poem most pleasing, a gift of love (*teshurat ahavah*) pure and of old,
> adorned in her jewels as a bride, wrapped in her ornaments as a maiden.
> You are her betrothed yet she will remain forever a virgin!
> She has a father but is still an orphan!
> In your hands I entrust, my lord (lit. gaon), two brothers, desolate exiles,
> whose inheritance is as though they were strangers, their land is (destroyed) like Admah (cf. Hos 11:8).
> Were it not for your shade, they would wander to the ends of the earth!

The dedication of the poem is immediately followed with the charge, as though constituting the poem as the Nagid's possession demanded his reciprocation.

By way of a nearly contemporary comparison, the Geniza manuscript TS 20.24r (Figure 5) is a *shafāʿa* sent to Fustat by three notables of Granada, described as "the city of our master Shemuel ha-Nagid and his son Yehosef." The document is written in large, clear letters in the style of some official Arabic correspondence. The opening lines, which consist of blessings for the recipients' welfare, are presented in rhyme. The letter describes (in very vague terms) the unfortunate circumstances under which the person being recommended

Figure 5. Shafāʿa (letter of introduction) sent from Granada. TS 20.24r. Reproduced by kind permission of the Syndics of Cambridge University Library.

fled "exiled before a whetted sword and a drawn bow" and commends him as "modest, demure (*baishan*), and subtle of speech ([*ba'al*] *devarim rakkim*)."[137] Just as Ibn Ḥasdai's poem offered "payment" through a panegyric in meter and rhyme, this letter also contained a poem (though not a panegyric) and was crafted as a beautiful material object for appreciation and possibly for display. Literary ornamentation and physical adornment were similar means of causing value to inhere within the material object of the letter or poem and thereby show esteem for the recipient and, quite possibly, obligate him to reciprocate.

Again, in the *shirah yetomah*, Ibn Ḥasdai did not request monetary payment but rather the performance of a favor. The Nagid's response poem, a panegyric composed according to the same meter and rhyme and playing on the same themes, assures Abū Faḍl that the requested protection has been granted.[138] These praise poems were not intended primarily as publicly performed panegyrics, and the authors were certainly not paid for their compositions. Yet it would be wrong to assume that the poems did not possess value, in some sense, a point that will be expanded upon in Chapter 2, on the function of panegyrics as "gifts." Further, the function of the poems as correspondence does not preclude their circulation or even their oral performance. The Nagid shared the poem with his son, at least, who included it in the *dīwān*, and the poem was cited with respect by later authors. Although assertions about the performance of the poem beyond these points is guesswork, it is evident that Ibn Ḥasdai's panegyric contributed to the construction of the Nagid's public image, probably in his lifetime and certainly for posterity.

In sum, the evidence that we have for panegyric practices among Andalusian authors points to a highly developed culture of textuality—with poems serving as or accompanying letters and circulating beyond the hands of their recipients—and also to an oral culture of sorts, but one only partly meeting the expectations of courtly performance in the sense of a poet appearing before a patron with the hope of remuneration. I have suggested that the dedication of panegyric pertained more often to the circumstance of separation between men rather than their unification. We have limited evidence for panegyric performance at public gatherings, possibly including political rituals, and slightly more for its recitation in small gatherings, but most of our record attests to panegyric being exchanged through writing. Again, the oral dimensions of panegyric practice might be underrepresented in the surviving corpus, and even those texts whose primary purpose was to be read might have been performed subsequently. In any case, panegyrics clearly enjoyed a broad circulation that confirms their essential role in constructing the images of their *mamdūḥ*s.

Throughout this chapter, I have highlighted what I see as some basic points of continuity in Jewish panegyric practice across the Islamic Mediterranean—a mixture of oral and written elements, the use of panegyric in exchange relationships, and its role in the promotion of public images and claims to legitimacy. I see the rise of Jewish panegyric writing in al-Andalus more as a continuation of the Eastern practice than a new courtly function. Still, I do not mean to minimize the differences between the world of the academies and the contours of social relations among intellectuals in al-Andalus. In subsequent chapters, we will investigate further the idealized representations of *mamdūḥ*s among the various regions and subcommunities of the Jewish Mediterranean. Al-Andalus was clearly not the world of the great academies of Baghdad, but what the gaons and the Andalusian intellectuals shared were elements of social exchange based on informal, and ultimately unenforceable, bonds.

CHAPTER 2

Poetic Gifts: Maussian Exchange and the Working of Medieval Jewish Culture

> The propositions that are known to be true and require no proof for their truthfulness are of four kinds: perceptions, as when we know that this is black, this is white, this is sweet, and this is hot; . . . conventions, as when we know that uncovering nudity is ugly and that recompensing a benefactor with something of greater honor is beautiful.[1]
>
> —Maimonides, *The Treatise on Logic*

The previous chapter discussed issues related to the performance of panegyrics, essentially the *Sitz im Leben* of the texts, while also making some broad observations about the nature of medieval Jewish culture in Islamic domains. This chapter will delve further into what function panegyrics actually held and why they were so pervasive across relations among poets and patrons, gaons and donors, and between friends. What was it about panegyric that was fitting to *all* these types of relationships? The answer, in part, can be found by analyzing panegyrics' metapoetic and self-referential discourse, how authors described them and how readers received them.

The most common terms for describing panegyric writing in medieval Hebrew discourse, apparent in the *shirah yetomah* that closed the previous chapter, belong to the semantic range of "gifts," most often in the mundane sense of gifts exchanged among humans and sometimes reaching over into the language of Temple sacrifice, offerings to God. The language of gift giving, and the constitution of panegyrics as gifts, permeates several levels of

Jewish social organization in the Islamic Mediterranean, from the relations between geonic academies and satellite communities, to those among poets and patrons in a given locale, to those among intellectuals across and within Mediterranean centers. What these sets of relations among individuals, institutions, and communities shared was a foundation on bonds of loyalty—elements that tied people to one another in relationships that were essentially voluntary, or at least not inviolable.

Referring to the well-known study by Roy Mottahedeh, *Loyalty and Leadership in Early Islamic Society*, which demonstrates the essentiality of loyalty-based relationships (more than formal legal relationships) for the functioning of Islamic court life, Marina Rustow has investigated patronage and clienthood in various Jewish contexts, including ties between rabbinic leaders and followers and bonds among more humble folk. Rustow shows that "parallels between courtly literature and everyday letters demonstrate how deeply the modes and manners that we ascribe to courtly etiquette permeated other realms of relationships whose stability rested on the binding power of loyalty."[2] In particular, she considers the dynamic of granting benefaction (*ni'ma*) and the gratitude (*shukr*) that such benefaction required, a dynamic that engendered the "continuity and coherence" of life, political and otherwise.

Jewish life in the Islamic Mediterranean may be said to have functioned according to what Marcel Mauss called (in French) a system of *prestations* and *contre-prestations*—usually rendered in English as a system of "total services" and "total counter-services"—in which the exchange of gifts provided an essential component of group coherence.[3] Mauss's classic book, *The Gift: Forms and Functions of Exchange in Archaic Societies*, demonstrates that, cross-culturally, the giving of a gift obligates the receiver to reciprocate not only in kind but rather with something of greater value than the original gift (a point also recognized by Rustow in her study). For Mauss, reciprocal relationships need not require exchange between equal parties; in fact, structural inequality is precisely what allows the cycle of benefaction to perpetuate. The ongoing and dynamic process of indebting and repayment is said to give societies their coherence and structure by tying individuals to one another within and beyond their kinship circles. Mauss's short book has enjoyed a remarkable afterlife, especially in anthropology and sociology but also in history and literary studies, and many elements of this seminal work have been developed, nuanced, or challenged.

I will not attempt here to describe all of the types of loyalty-based exchanges that made up the "continuity and coherence" of Jewish life in the medieval Mediterranean.[4] Rather, I wish to reflect upon the metapoetic trope by which medieval Jewish authors referred to their compositions, especially panegyrics, as "gifts," and upon the use of gift discourse more broadly. The rhetoric of gift giving pervades panegyric letters and poems throughout the region and reveals a great deal about the functions that their authors and readers ascribed them. I will argue that portraying panegyrics as gifts constituted them as material objects whose value either served as or demanded reciprocation, thus initiating or maintaining bonds of loyalty. Toward the end of the chapter, I consider the specific implications of describing such gifts through the language of the sacrificial cult of ancient Israel, as though these gifts were offered not so much for their human recipients as for the divine.

Fortunately, I am preceded in the application of Maussian theory to the study of panegyric by a number of scholars of Greek, Latin, and Arabic poetry.[5] For Arabic, Suzanne Pinckney Stetkevych discusses a panegyric by the pre-Islamic poet al-Nābighah intended to negotiate the poet's reentry into the Lakhmid court. With the *qaṣīda*, the "poet/negotiator virtually entraps his addressee by engaging him in a ritual exchange that obligates him to respond to the poet's proffered gift (of submission, allegiance, praise) with a counter-gift (in this case absolution and reinstatement), or else face opprobrium."[6] Beatrice Gruendler also draws Mauss (and Mottahedeh) into the exchange between patron and poet: "The poem is a token of the poet's ongoing allegiance just as the patron's gifts and benefits were tokens of his ongoing protection and benevolence. To this end, the poem performs a service and thereby repays the patron's gifts and relieves the poet of some of his liability. The relationship emerges as a mutual exchange. However, it is not one of discrete transactions of giving and thanking; rather, it represents an ongoing process."[7]

Before continuing, I wish to introduce two further concepts of gift exchange. First is the idea that gift exchange generally involves objects that are *incommensurate* and *inter-convertible*, at least one of which is more symbolic than material. Thus, I am not discussing the exchange of a stock for cash value or the trade of a quantity of flax for a quantity of silk but rather the exchange of praise for such things as elevation in rank, favors, luxury items, or even money itself. The disparate "goods" generally correspond to the social standings of the two men, each of whom has something to offer the other that he does not already possess. Because there is no exact "exchange rate" between goods, the relationship by which giver and receiver are bound does not dissolve once the transaction is complete but, as Gruendler suggests, remains dynamic. This leads to the second point, the distinction between what has been termed "disembedded" and "embedded" exchange. In the former, the exchange belongs to a sphere that has an independent and discrete economic reality (stock for cash) such that the transaction might be considered "complete"; the relationship dissolves once the transaction has been satisfied. In an embedded exchange, the transaction participates in and supports noneconomic institutions such as friendship, kinship, religious affiliation, and learned societies.[8]

This is not to say that money cannot be an element of embedded exchange. The matter is similar to what is sometimes said about marriage in our own day: it can involve money; it just can't be *about* money. Hence panegyric, even panegyric composed for money, is bound by an ethical structure wherein a strict quid pro quo was considered uncouth, blameworthy, and a violation of an unwritten social code (this will be discussed further in Chapter 5). Embedded exchange was always hailed as an ideal; disembedded exchange was sometimes suspected of being the reality. Jocelyn Sharlet writes that in "medieval Arabic and Persian discourse on patronage, there is widespread concern that the exchange of poetry for pay may have more to do with material wealth and individual ambition than ethical evaluation and communal relationships."[9]

Central to the issue is the nature of the institution of patronage (Ar., *walāʾ*; lit., "proximity") in the Islamic world, which has been the subject of a significant amount of scholarship in recent years.[10] Apart from the earliest usage of the term in the strict legal sense, referring to the arrangement by which non-Arabs could be grafted into the Muslim *umma* (nation), it had expanded by the tenth century to encompass a broad range of social relationships. The broad application of patronage is summarized nicely by Rustow, as:

> using one's influence, power, knowledge or financial means on behalf of someone else, with an eye toward benefiting both that person *and* oneself at the same time. Investments of this type could lead to the production of art, literature, architecture, science, philosophy, or works of public hydraulic engineering. Rulers and their courts used them to advance their claims as the bestowers of material and cultural benefits on their subjects, and thus to achieve legitimacy, and indeed, rulers were in a special position to accumulate (or better: extract) the material resources that allowed them to act as patrons. But others bestowed patronage too: village big-men, long-distance traders, elders of the community, or anyone with wealth or power to redistribute. Patronage also included the formation of narrowly or locally political alliances in which a person of higher rank protected or helped a protégé. To sound more

> sociological about it, patronage was *any investment of resources (material or not) for the purposes of giving benefit and receiving some social benefit in return.*[11]

Viewing the phenomenon of Jewish panegyric within this broad context allows us to link the vast range of bonds considered throughout this book and the use of writing, especially ornate writing, as a binding instrument.[12] The term *mawlā* itself is terribly ambiguous in that it can refer either to the more powerful or the less powerful person in the patronage relationship, the patron or the client. Yet the fluidity of this term, and hence the broadness of the institution, is key for understanding the dual role of a figure such as Hai Gaon, who was at once patron (in that he bestowed intellectual resources and prestige upon satellite communities and leaders) and client (in that he relied upon their largesse and recognition to maintain the academy and his own position). The inclusion of material exchange was permissible within patronage relationships but was not their defining characteristic, either. Failure to recognize this point has led to some of the misperceptions about professional poets and "courtliness" referred to in Chapter 1.

If we consider exchanges of praise for favors, recognition, honor, and protection, we see the dynamics of exchange—and the rhetoric of gift exchange, in particular—pervasively among Jews throughout the Islamic Mediterranean. Similar dynamics are operative in the discourse of the academies and in mercantile relationships, in friendships, in family bonds, and among communal members of equal or disparate social station. Any of these relationships could include exchanges of money, but monetary exchange need not have been part of any single exchange. We will see that the receiving of "gifts," one of which could be praise, essentially obligated the receiver to reciprocate in some way. Al-Andalus was no exception; although it is famed for the exchange of praise for objects of value, even here we need to conceive of a patronage system that encompassed, but was not limited to, remuneration through money, garments, wine, and the like; just as often, exchanges involved favors, honor, and praise itself.

Gifts in the Discourse of the Academies

The operation of the academies of Sura and Pumbedita, as well as the competing academy of Jerusalem, was dependent upon intellectual and monetary ties with communities throughout the Mediterranean. Satellite communities directed questions on legal and other topics to their gaon of choice, usually including a donation for the academy, and could expect a response in return. At the same time, the gaons had to pursue allegiances actively, especially since communities could turn to another academy if they chose. We therefore find geonim playing several roles simultaneously as respected leaders invested with authority but also as fund-raisers charged with maintaining relations with supporters.

Soon after he had assumed the office of gaon of Sura, Saʿadia Gaon sent a letter to Fustat in his homeland, Egypt.[13] The letter contained teaching about the nature of the Oral Law and promised that another letter containing "warnings and rebukes" (*hazharot ve-tokhaḥot*) would follow in order to lead the community toward the proper observance of God's law. Saʿadia also asks the recipients to "inform us every day of your well-being, for it is the welfare of our soul. Without an army, there is no king, and without students, there is no honor for sages." Saʿadia had an intuitive sense for the reciprocal and interdependent nature of even the most hierarchically structured power relationships.

In the second letter, which contains the promised "warnings and rebukes," Saʿadia begins by addressing the recipients with various honorific terms and offering greetings from ranks of the academy. In the present letter, Saʿadia describes the first as an *iggeret teshurah*, a "gift epistle." He probably meant that, whereas most epistles by gaons were sent *in response* to petitions from communities that contained contributions for the academy, this "gift epistle" was unsolicited and was sent *gratis*. The gaon thus used the "gift" to initiate a cycle of exchange and to promote bonds of loyalty. While calling the letter a "gift" may have suggested that no specific—or, at least, monetary—repayment was expected, Saʿadia knew that he could essentially impose a debt; following Mauss, we might say that there was no such thing as a "free gift."[14]

Gaons often refer to letters received from distant communities (especially those that were accompanied by contributions) as gifts.[15] What gaons offered their supporters in return was praise itself, which could take on various forms. Most ritually oriented was the mentioning of names during the recitation of the *qadish* prayer on the Sabbath (a practice that seems to relate to pronouncing the caliph's name during the Friday *khuṭba*). Natan ha-Bavli relates, in connection with the installation of the exilarch, that when the cantor recited the *qadish*, he included the exilarch's name and then offered separate blessings for the exilarch once again, the heads of the academies, the various cities that sent contributions to the academies, and individual philanthropists.[16] One version of a *qadish* containing praise for an exilarch and gaons

Figure 6. Qadish, including praise for an exilarch. ENA 4053.1r. Image provided by the Library of the Jewish Theological Seminary.

has come down to us (ENA 4053; Figure 6) and reveals that the practice involved more than simply citing names but also appending magnifying expressions of blessing and praise.[17]

Returning to the poem by Hai Gaon that opened Chapter 1, we see an obvious reciprocal exchange whereby the monetary gift was exchanged for praise; even if the composition of the panegyric may have been technically voluntary, it was in practice obligatory. Hai assures Yehudah that his monetary gift will gain him favor with God and that the money is being well spent. Yet, instead of offering simple gratitude, Hai composed for Yehudah the extensive and labor-intensive panegyric.[18] The exchange between Yehudah and Hai was not (or, at least, not primarily) about the wedding of Yehudah's son. The wedding served as a pretext for asserting the essential dynamics between the two men and the communities of Baghdad and Qairawan. Yehudah offered allegiance and financial support for the academy, and Hai offered Yehudah recognition and a panegyric that brought him fame among his contemporaries and, it would seem, for posterity. Without the panegyric, the cycle of exchange would have been incomplete, and the incommensurability of the "goods" ensured the cycle's continuation. Finally, Hai not only improved the reputation of his addressee but also bolstered his own image by presenting himself as the authority of the Exile who possessed the authority to declare a holiday for his students.

Similarly, in a poem addressed to Avraham ha-Kohen ha-Rofe (first half of the eleventh century) that laments the death of the recipient's father, the author opens: "My poem is set, metered, purified, and also ordered; in an eloquent tongue it is sent to the lord of my soul as a gift and offering (*minḥah u-teshurah*), to master Avraham ha-Kohen."[19] Although we cannot identify the author with certainty, it is likely that he was an associate of the Palestinian academy, perhaps even a gaon, since Jacob Mann identifies several other texts by prominent figures of this academy praising the recipient.[20] The poem was not, of course, a gift for the deceased father but rather for the son, whose own honor was enhanced through the memorialization of his father's merit and the brief praise included for the son.

Praising affiliates of the academy seems to have been one of the gaon's many functions. In the following letter, Sherirah Gaon of Pumbedita addresses an *aluf* in Fustat (possibly Avraham Ben Sahlān) who had praised Shemariah Ben Elḥanan and seemingly sought confirmation from the gaon. Sherirah holds that the praise is justified, reviews Shemariah's wisdom and rank within the academy, and adds a bit of hyperbole:

> We have dwelled upon what you mentioned, *aluf*, may God preserve you, concerning praise of the magnificent, our esteemed, strong and steadfast Rav Shemariah, head of the Nehardeah row in our academy, may the Holy One give him strength, might, aid, and encourage him, son of Rav Elḥanan, may his memory be for a blessing, for he is the Head of the Order. For it is truly so and we more than anyone know his praiseworthy qualities; for who like him do we have from the East to the West? He is a lion in its pride, a great one of the academy. We know of the wonder of his wisdom and the inner chambers of his knowledge . . . and his strength in Torah beyond others. Were this not the case, we would not have appointed him to be the *mashneh* and we would not have made him head of the most honored of the three rows of the academy. To praise him is our first priority (*shivḥo 'adeinu rav min ha-kol*).[21]

Praising affiliates was indeed a priority for the heads of the academies for at least two reasons: 1) in order to garner or reward loyalty among communal figures in satellite communities; and 2) to give communal figures something, an object of sorts, to signify their status as recognized by the gaon and before their communities. In the document above, we witness another dimension of the dynamic, which is the local *aluf*'s praise of Shemariah, which had to be corroborated by the gaon. Had the *aluf* praised someone whom the gaon did not deem worthy, it may have amounted to a kind of faux pas in the chain of command.

Not only individuals but also communities are told that they are praised far and wide (indeed, many "community panegyrics" have come down to us). In one letter by Shemuel Ben 'Eli to the community of al-Kirkānī, we read: "We—whether we are near or far—are with you [pl.] in prayers and good blessings and we praise you and extol your ethical qualities (*middot*) among the communities. The elder among you we consider like a father, the young we consider like a brother and son, and all of you are most dear to us."[22]

Offering and disseminating praise in exchange for loyalty was an expectation, and when the cycle of exchange was broken, it was noteworthy. In a Judeo-Arabic letter, Shemuel Ben 'Eli writes concerning a community that had "abandoned the paths of our love" (*hajaru subūl mawaddatina*) by ceasing to send letters and charitable contributions (*mabārrahum*). Still, Ben 'Eli writes, "we shall never cease invoking blessings unto God (*al-du'ā'*) on their behalf and extending them blessings (*muwāṣalatahum bi'l-berakhot*) wherever we can. We even follow our courteous practice of spreading their praise (*basṭ madḥihim*) and commending them (*batt shukrihim*)."[23] The fact that the head of the academy indicated that the praise would continue in the absence of the contribution demonstrates that praise was *expected* when a contribution was sent. Indeed, praise was a sufficient means of repayment, and Shemuel's confirmation of ongoing praise may have been enough to persuade (read: "guilt") the community to reestablish relations.

A letter sent on behalf of the "two congregations" (likely Rabbanite and Karaite) of Alexandria to Ephraim Ben Shemariah, head of the Palestinian academy in Fustat, opens with extensive literary praise for the academy and makes a transition to similarly elaborate praise of Ephraim. Dated 1029, the letter praises the gaon and the academy for assisting previously in a case of freeing captives and asks them to take up the cause again in a similar scenario. Yeshuʿa Kohen Ben Yosef, the author of the letter, describes praising the recipient as the very aim of writing: "The purpose of this letter of ours to your honor, our brother, the man of our redemption, is to complete your praise, to specify your laudation, and to offer glory for the beneficence of your deeds that you performed when you broadened your hearts, opened your hands, and acted with great generosity in order to free your captive brethren." The author assures the reader that a letter that Ephraim had previously sent had been contemplated "by all of the community" and that the people "praised you for the vastness of your wisdom and the beauty of your rhyme." Yeshuʿa also writes that his own letter should be read before the entire community of Fustat in order to exemplify proper behavior and to show them that they, too, are compelled to fulfill the commandment of freeing captives.[24] Again, we see a type of exchange of incommensurate objects (praise for money) embedded within a broad social relationship preceded by the current correspondence and in which author and recipient were allied by institutional context and common cause, even bound by the same religious obligation. They were part of a discrete group whose conventions of address centered on the offering of praise as an embedded exchange.

Gifts of Praise Among Individuals in the East

We have seen above that praise, especially when laboriously executed, could be constituted as a gift of material and even enduring value. Broadly speaking, poetry was recognized as a type of material object among Jews throughout the Islamic Mediterranean. As Miriam Frenkel points out, poetry was one of the key pursuits of the Alexandrian Jewish elite, all of them merchants, who maintained contact with one another through letters. This group created cohesion through informal yet ritualized bonds of friendship that focused on the profession of covenant and the exchange of favors and goods; the exchange of poems essentially filled the same role as the exchange of other goods and services. In one letter composed in Arabic script, the cantor Avraham Ben Sahlān places poetry (*qaṣīda wa-rahuṭ*) on the same level as other *ḥawā'ij*, "necessities," a term generally reserved for material goods. The author asks that the recipient send him a poem and includes a portion of a Hebrew poem with which "I praised Abū al-Faraj Hibba Ibn Naḥum," a respected figure in the Alexandrian community.[25] Poetic exchange was one factor among several that helped create the group's boundaries and exclusivity.

One panegyric by El'azar Ben Ya'aqov ha-Bavli specifies that the author sent it following a "settling of accounts" (Ar., *muḥāsaba*) between poet and *mamdūḥ*. This does not suggest that the poet was paid for the poem but rather that the poet and his *mamdūḥ* were already bound in some sort of financial relationship. The precise sum of money owed (three dinar and four *awqīn*) is given in the superscription, and the poem playfully casts the repayment in sacralized terms, "He sanctified himself in all matters so much that he made his payment the weight of the sanctuary weight" (cf. Ex 30:13). With the panegyric, Ben El'azar not only acknowledged receipt but also perpetuated the relationship.[26]

An early panegyric by the Eastern poet 'Alwan Ben Avraham includes a fictionalized dialogue in which he asks passersby about his *mamdūḥ*. They respond: "Why do you ask about your chief when he is very distant?" The poet replies that his heart has become a laughingstock because of the *mamdūḥ*'s absence. The dialogue continues, and in the conclusion the poet turns to the *mamdūḥ* and implores him to fulfill his pledge and respond. Failure to reciprocate in correspondence was tantamount to breaking a pledge.[27]

A very different dynamic is witnessed in a poem by 'Eli he-Ḥaver Ben 'Amram, who requested compensation for poems in more than one instance. In this case, the poet grumbles to Yehudah Ben Menasheh, a bridegroom whom the poet already knew, that he failed to invite 'Eli to his wedding. After praising Yehudah, 'Eli concluded the poem: "Read this that is given unto you; I inscribed it in order to testify to your name . . . and send me a 'freewill offering' (*nedavah*; cf. Ex 35:29) with a generous heart." Had the poet been invited to the wedding, one imagines, he may still have written a panegyric but not demanded compensation since the exchange of favors would have already been satisfied.[28]

In short, panegyric was used in the Islamic East as a mediating device within a host of relationships whose dynamics of exchange could be quite diverse. Most often, these involved institutional-communal connections or relations between individuals who already knew each other and were bound within a cycle of exchange.

In al-Andalus

The rhetoric of gift giving permeates the Andalusian panegyric corpus, apparent already in the *shirah yetomah* discussed in Chapter 1. Earlier than this, a fragmentary panegyric to Ḥasdai Ibn Shaprut by Dunash Ben Labrat recognizes the annual contributions that the *mamdūḥ* makes to the academies of the East and expresses gratitude for the material items that the poet received personally. Dunash uses the language of gifts throughout:

> [Ḥasdai] acquired a good name and built a wall of kindness. Every year he sends an offering (*minḥah*) to the judges [in Babylonia] . . .
> And to me he sent portions (*manot*), gave gifts (*matanot*), and filled vessels with thousands of measures,[29]
> onyx and gold, sealed-up purses, perfect and beautiful garments and wrappings.[30]

This is the last line of the poem to have reached us, though we know it continued at this point. One would expect, as Shulamit Elizur suggests, that after expressing thanks for the bounty that Dunash received from his patron, the poet would have offered in exchange a dedication in the remaining lines. I would further assume that the conclusion made reference to the poem's value and possibly described it as a gift (given in exchange for the gifts mentioned above). The ethical nature of the embedded exchange was not undermined by the fact that it included objects of value. The relationship was not predicated on a simple quid pro quo but rather on a deeper and more enduring bond whose cyclical nature would be expected to continue.[31]

The superscription to a panegyric by Yehudah Halevi to an anonymous recipient states that the poem was sent as "thanks (*todah*) to someone who had given him a gift."[32] Another addressed to Yosef Ibn Ṣadīq states that the *mamdūḥ* had sent Halevi "a gift of a poem and a gift" (*teshurat shir u-matanah*).[33] Thus poems could accompany, be given in exchange for, or quite simply be gifts. More elaborately, another poem by Halevi for the same figure was composed upon Halevi's departure from Córdoba; the poet adjures himself to glean all that he can from Ibn Ṣadīq's wisdom, which is described as provisions for a journey. The poem is an offering (*minḥah*) in exchange:

Take delicacies from [Ibn Ṣadīq's] mouth as a provision,
And his words, behold a cake baked on hot stones![34] Eat and go
  with the strength of the meal!
Gather for yourself manna today, for tomorrow you will seek it as
  one who seeks something lost.
In exchange give him (*hashev lo*) truth, a gift (*minḥah*) sent forth,
  pearls of poetry with every precious stone!
Perhaps it will delight him, and perhaps the gift of Yehudah
  (*minḥat Yehudah*) will be sweet.[35]

Here there is no monetary exchange, but there is an intellectual exchange that captures and reinforces the social bond between the two men. The place of panegyric in the mutuality of a relationship is sometimes stated expressly. After pleading with Abū al-Ḥasan Ibn Murīl to send him a letter, Halevi wrote: "Read my poem and forget not my covenant (*briti*)."[36] Failing to recognize the covenant between the two men could lead to the dissolution of the relationship.

A panegyric written during Mosheh Ibn Ezra's youth to a certain Abū al-Fatḥ Ben Azhar asks the *mamdūḥ* to intercede with another patron who had looked unfavorably upon the poet, requests a letter from the *mamdūḥ*, and offers him the poem, "Bind upon your throat a necklace made from the finest of our jacinth and beryl."[37] Here there is no request for money but rather for the performance of a favor.

The very first poem of Ibn Ezra's collection of homonymic epigrams, *Sefer ha-ʿanaq* (Book of the necklace), dedicated to Avraham Ibn al-Muhājir, refers to poetry as a gift and alludes to the name of the patron (father of many nations, i.e., Abraham; cf. Gn 17:4):

Listen to these [verses], O princes of poetry, singers of the age,
and raise up their preciousness as an offering and gift
to the father of many nations, a prince who holds power[38]
so much that he struggled with men and with God![39]

In all likelihood, Ibn Ezra received financial support from the known courtier though the patron-poet relationship likely extended beyond the dedication of a single book in exchange for pay. We might presume that the intellectual bond preceded the commissioning of the work and that the dedication functioned within a system of embedded exchange.

Gift language also permeates Ibn Ezra's poems sent to fellow intellectuals from the late stage of his life after he had left al-Andalus; one poem bears the superscription, "He wrote from Castile to the exalted Nasi, his brother, may God have mercy on him, before he met him." In the poem, Ibn Ezra refers to the "covenant of love" between himself and the *mamdūḥ* ("should I forget it, may my right hand wither"; cf. Ps 137:5) and concludes with a dedicatory section whereby the poet consecrates the poem to the *mamdūḥ* as a gift, "Here is a gift of poetry."[40] This subject brings us to the next section of this chapter.

Dedicating Poems

Beatrice Gruendler calls attention to the dedicatory section of Arabic panegyric as a "speech act," phrasing that combines "action and utterance," whereby the words of dedication have the effect of constituting the poem as the recipient's possession (even when delivered orally). Arabic panegyrics sometimes collapse the entire relationship between poet and patron, with the poem as a mediating device, into a single neat word, *manaḥtukahā*, "[Herewith] I dedicate it to you." Gruendler stresses the reciprocal nature of the patron-poet relationship, how the "benefits and duties of the patron mesh with the benefits and rights of the poet," engendered most poignantly in the dedication, "which ties a firm and far-reaching bond between the two."[41]

As Dan Pagis notes, Mosheh Ibn Ezra used dedications with great frequency both in poems and in letters, most often using phrases such as "take this poem" or "behold this poem."[42] In a poem appended to a letter for Shelomoh Ibn Ghiyat, itself a response to a poem, Yehudah Halevi includes a dedication that fills eight lines.[43] Prior to this, Shemuel ha-Nagid used dedications in the few panegyrics that he composed for others.[44] In one, the Nagid praises his *mamdūḥ*, "I love you, beloved of my soul, as I love my own soul" and stresses the *mamdūḥ*'s wisdom, knowledge in Talmud, and alacrity in religious observance before concluding: "Take from me words chosen from bdellium, rhymes on a scroll."[45] There is no reason to think that the Nagid was paid for these verses, especially given the intimacy of the language suggesting near social parity.

Again, dedicatory language appears in poems that participated in patronage relationships that included the bestowing of material objects. A poem by Ibn Gabirol begins with a dedication, "Take this poem and its hidden stores, its precision and poetic themes. . . . Lord of my soul, may his heart and ears be attentive to understand my eloquence, also my poem and its supplications." The poet thus gives the *mamdūḥ* the poem and hopes that his pleas will be heard in return. We do not know exactly what these requests entailed; they might have been for something tangible, such as money or a garment, or possibly something more abstract, but the exchange was portrayed as belonging to the world of embedded, rather than disembedded, exchange.[46]

Dedications seem to have been introduced into Hebrew panegyric in al-Andalus and to have spread from there to authors in the Islamic East. An anonymous panegyric sent to the Yemeni merchant and community leader Maḍmūn II refers both to the gifts given by the *mamdūḥ* to the community and to the poet's gift to the *mamdūḥ*. The poet praises the "*nagid* of the nation of God" for his valor and kindness and includes, "He succored the whole nation and supported its falling, young and old alike. His generosity is like the rain; those who seek his gifts are glad." In the lengthy dedication, the poet identifies himself as a Levite (i.e., a singer) and writes, "Hear this, *nagid* of the wise men of Torah,[47] lord of the rulers and glory of the gaons, take this gift that is here presented; I sent it to remove anguish."[48] The poet's gift was not presented in the hope of specific remuneration but was inscribed within a reciprocal bond between leader and community.

We close this part of the chapter with a translation and discussion of a fascinating epistolographic poem (TS 13 J 19.21; Figure 7) mentioned and transcribed by Goitein and later published by Yehudah Ratzhaby.[49] It was sent by the student (*talmid*) Yiṣḥaq Ibn Nissim Parsi to his peer Abū Zikri Yiḥye Ibn Mevorakh. The author had received a letter from the latter that contained verses based on a famous poem by Ibn Gabirol ("I am the poet and the poem is my slave!").[50] Parsi now responds with a letter of his own, opening with the Jewish version of the *basmallah* (*be-shem ha-raḥman*, "in the name of the Merciful") and two biblical verses, all typical of letter introductions. He then inscribes a poem in the same meter and rhyme as Ibn Gabirol's and undoubtedly of the poem he had received from Ibn Mevorakh. The metered poem begins in line four:

1. In the name of the Merciful,
2. The meek shall inherit the earth and shall delight (Ps 37:7).
3. Great peace unto them who love your Torah (Ps 119:165).

4. To you, O prince, beloved and friend of my soul! Peace unto you, my people's lord and confidant
5. whom mountains have raised up as a gift (*teshurah*)! I have sent you [this poem] to be a mantle.
6. If you please, let it be your mantle veil, wrap yourself and turn to its foundation
7. so that princes will consult you as an oracle (Jb 12:8) and poets will praise you for its splendor.
8. Verily, poetry is your eternal slave but the poems of others you enslave for your use!
9. May my poem be a friend of pure heart to you. Your heart hurt me by leaving;
10. it was connected to my heart all your days like a chain bound to a neck.
11. I delighted in your letter's arrival; in your kindness you gave me a choice gift.[51]
12. The poem came and I was in awe of its treasure, and on Shelomoh Ibn Gabirol it was based!
13. I was astounded by your words, my friend, "Write a letter and send it along!"
14. How can I write while my heart is with you? Woe, on the day you left it was taken captive.
15. By departing you seized my innards and so my heart mourns.
16. Behold I cry and do not know if it is for my heart or for you!
17. My heart's pain has grown with your separation and there is none to help.
18. [I am] tormented and have not found anyone pure of heart, intellect, or wisdom.
19. May God plant you in his garden as a pure seedling and reveal to us his beloved (the Messiah)!
20. May you delight in the knowledge of God and His splendor and enjoy the wisdom of His creation's[52] secret!
21. Then the poem will speak happiness for you, my prince, beloved and friend of my soul.

Following the poem, the letter continues with standard blessings, compliments for the recipient's writing, and requests for further correspondence; as

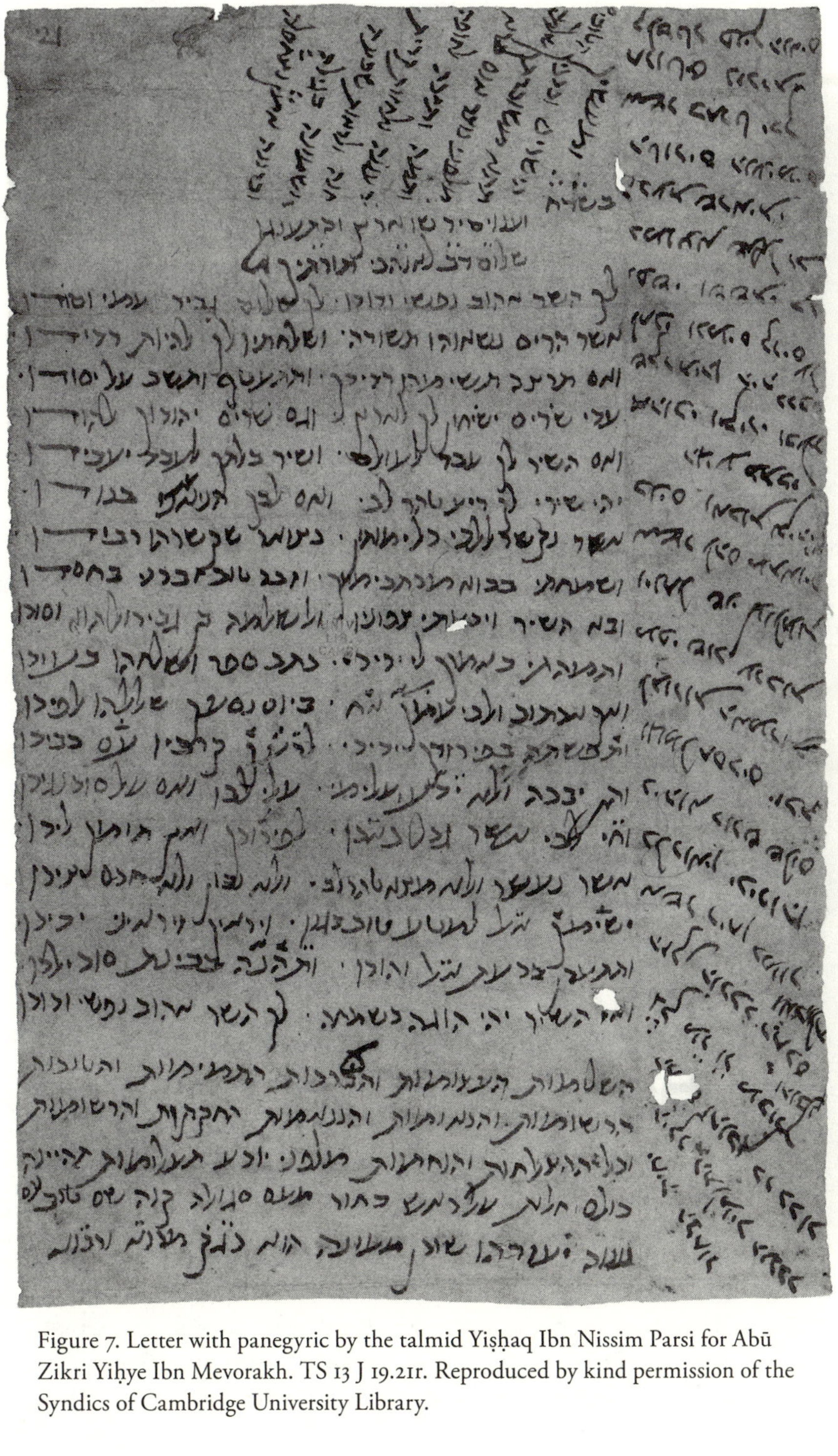

Figure 7. Letter with panegyric by the talmid Yiṣḥaq Ibn Nissim Parsi for Abū Zikri Yiḥye Ibn Mevorakh. TS 13 J 19.21r. Reproduced by kind permission of the Syndics of Cambridge University Library.

Goitein points out, the verso contains related content written in Judeo-Arabic.[53] The letter is fascinating on a number of levels. First, it attests to the widespread fame of Ibn Gabirol's poetry and the phenomenon of imitation (*muʿāraḍa,* contrafaction), even among students of a young age. Second, it was not composed by a known or professional poet but represents the attempt of an "amateur"; the poem exhibits numerous literary merits (opening and closing with the same phrase, clever plays on biblical verses) but also has its shortcomings (misuse of gender in pronouns and frequent deviations in meter). Third, it demonstrates the clear epistolographic purpose of the poem and is a response to another poem that itself made up part of a letter. Finally, the author refers to his friend as a "gift" (*teshurah*) offered by the mighty mountains (4). What gift can one offer a "gift"? The answer, of course, is a poem, a panegyric, described here as a "mantle." The friend's letter is likewise described as a gift (9); this reference is proximate to the author's dedication "May my poem be a friend of pure heart to you" (7); that is, the friend is a gift and the poem, the poet's gift, is a friend. The epistolographic poem thus draws extensively upon the metapoetic discourse of gift exchange, a discourse expressing—indeed, constituting—the mutual bond of the correspondents.

In short, Jewish culture in the Islamic Mediterranean functioned according to a shared discourse of gift exchange across a range of social relationships—among poetic correspondents, poets receiving material remuneration and their beneficiaries, heads of academies and their communal adherents, among merchants and students. Of course, these relationships were hardly uniform. Some involved financial aspects while others exhibit nonmaterial exchanges of different sorts, but all were premised on reciprocal bonds that were expected to be cyclical and enduring. Although praise was not the only aspect of these relationships, it constituted a "good" of great value, especially insofar as it could extend the *mamdūḥ*'s reputation before his peers.

The Rhetoric of Sacrifice

For the most part, the "gifts" referred to in the discussion above have been devoid of valences of sacrificial offering. In this concluding section, I consider the phenomenon of sacrificial language in the rhetoric of exchange relationships.[54] The central question is whether the introduction of God as a third party and the dynamics of atonement substantially alter the picture we have depicted about the mutuality of human exchange relationships, particularly in light of the Maussian framework.[55]

In the letter that opened Chapter 1, Hai Gaon describes the contribution from Rav Yehudah Rosh ha-Seder as a "gift [that] will be considered by God an offering and sacrifice (*minḥah ve-azkarah*). He made it ransom for him for pardoning and atonement." Play on the language of the sacrificial cult can also be far more extensive, as in the following letter by Shemuel Ben 'Eli, which deals primarily with the appointment of Zekhariah Ben Barkhael to the rank of *av bet din*.[56] Here the head of the Baghdad academy addresses the community to which Ben Barkhael was being dispatched: "That which arrived to us and him [Ben Barkhael] from you will be considered for you, our brethren, like a whole offering, like incense seasoned with salt, like a burnt offering, like a grain offering. . . . And when this letter arrives to you, read it in public with a sweet tongue . . . and a joyous voice."[57] "That which arrived" was, in all likelihood, a monetary contribution. What the community received in exchange, in addition to the presence of the sanctioned *av bet din*, was the letter itself, which was to be read aloud and intoned with beauty, thereby bringing glory upon the community and reinforcing its tie to the academy.

Did Ben 'Eli or the recipients of the letter *really* believe that the monetary donation had expiatory power for the givers? Does using sacrificial language rather than the language of human gift exchange truly alter the way in which the donation was considered? That is, did Ben 'Eli and the community both recognize that the donations were simply keeping the lights on (or the lamps lit, as it were) and read the language of sacrifice with ironic distance? Was the rhetoric a kind of inside joke among intellectuals, the kind of literary play for which the medieval Hebrew poets are famed (the language of sacrifice is, for example, exploited to describe the garden or the body of the beloved)?[58] Or should we view this as a kind of cultural practice that created or reinforced some core value of medieval Jewish society? The answers to these questions are, of course, difficult to glean from the sources, but I will try to evaluate the function of this discursive phenomenon.

There is little doubt that the representation of monetary contributions as sacrifices is on some level rhetorical, but this does not mean that the rhetoric is necessarily empty. It conveys to the reader that giving money to the academy is a type of divine service, and it is arguable that the sacrificial metaphor may have been important for claims of the academy's legitimacy. At the very least, the rhetoric allows the recipient of the letter to imagine something more complex than a two-party human exchange relationship but instead a three-party dynamic, whereby the academy head acts as a kind of mediator between the donor and God. Rather than participating in mutual back-scratching, both donor and recipient can act as though they are working together in a single cause, likely deepening the sense of embedded exchange. Thus we might ask whether the use of sacrificial language throws a proverbial wrench into the application of the Maussian framework in the study of medieval Jewish exchange practices.

Following a paradigm proposed for Late Antique Jewish culture by Seth Schwartz, Marina Rustow reflects upon medieval Jewish culture under Islam between the poles of "reciprocity" and "solidarity."[59] According to Schwartz's definitions, a reciprocity-based conception holds that "societies are bound together by densely overlapping networks of relationships of personal dependency constituted and sustained by reciprocal exchange." On the other hand, a solidarity-based model means that "societies are bound together not by personal relationships but by corporate solidarity based on shared ideals (piety, wisdom) or myths (for example, about common descent)."[60] In Schwartz's view, whereas Greco-Roman society was grounded in institutionalized reciprocal structures, biblical religion and rabbinic Judaism theoretically and largely eschewed such structures in favor of a solidarity-based system and, in this sense, did not constitute a "Mediterranean society." Adding a deeper dimension to Goitein's use of the phrase and noting the shift from the rabbinic to medieval periods, Rustow cleverly concludes that "the Jews of the tenth through twelfth centuries as reflected in the documents of the Cairo Geniza, then, unlike Schwartz's ancient Jews, *were* a 'Mediterranean' society."[61]

Geonic culture was clearly dependent upon reciprocal relationships, evidenced so richly by the exchanges of praise, loyalty, and material items detailed above. This culture of reciprocity was seen as fundamentally ethical in that the exchanges were of the "embedded" variety. Yet even this was sometimes not enough. Rather than portraying a gift to the academy as a mere contribution to a scholarship fund that brought its donor honor, it could be said to affect and delight the divine and to engender efficacious atonement. The rhetoric of sacrifice, whereby all donations are said to belong ultimately to God, intimates a system of solidarity.

Returning to the letters by Hai Gaon and Shemuel Ben 'Eli, do we have here a system of reciprocity merely masquerading as a system of solidarity? Should we doubt the gaons' sincerity? It would be cynical and exaggerated to view the leaders with the severity with which Martin Luther impugned the papacy for selling indulgences in order to raise funds for the erection of Saint

Peter's Basilica. The trajectories of reciprocity were portrayed, and quite possibly perceived, through a lens of solidarity. At least rhetorically, the language of ideological solidarity remained paramount.

Mauss, for his part, was hardly oblivious to reciprocal relationships that involved third parties such that exchange occurred between a donor and something otherworldly with the human recipient serving as a facilitator or intermediary. *The Gift* was preceded by some time with a work that Mauss had written (at the age of twenty-six) in collaboration with his fellow Durkheimian (also twenty-six, and a philo-Semite) Henri Hubert: *Sacrifice: Its Nature and Function*.[62] In classic Durkheimian fashion, the book characterizes sacrifice in social terms such that the phenomenon of sacrifice—far from being a self-abnegating act of total surrender—belonged to a system of reciprocity. Mauss later integrated this element within *The Gift*, where he titled the last part of the introduction, "Note: the present made to humans, and the present made to the gods," which itself includes a further "note on alms." Here, he argued that "destruction by sacrifice" is an "act of giving that is necessarily reciprocated."[63] Mauss sees here the beginnings of a theory of "contract sacrifice" wherein the "gods who give and return gifts are there to give a considerable thing in the place of a small one," a system characteristic within monotheistic religions as well. Rather than seeing a structural opposition between giving to the human and the nonhuman, Mauss focuses on giving to men who are manifestations of the nonhuman such that the realm of the nonhuman penetrates the realm of the human, "The exchange of presents between men, the 'namesakes'—the homonyms of the spirits, incite the spirits of the dead, the gods, things, animals, and nature to be 'generous toward them.'"[64]

Mauss was not dealing with the rhetoric of sacrifice so much as actual sacrifice, and it would be difficult to call the academies' leaders "manifestations" or "homonyms" of God rather than "mediators" or "representatives." The language of sacrifice simply deepened the claim of solidarity-based exchange. In any case, as Schwartz and Rustow stress, solidarity and reciprocity are not strict alternatives; they are paradigms, both opposing and complementary, through which we might meditate upon specific cultural practices, including rhetorical ones. In the case of exchanging donations to the academy for praise, reciprocity was plain to all; solidarity existed because it existed rhetorically.

The language of sacrifice is also apparent within correspondence that is relatively private or noninstitutional. TS 8 J 39.10, an unpublished epistolary formulary, preserves a copy of a letter addressed to "our lord and master Yeshayahu son of [. . .]ḥyah" that opens with extensive blessings. After acknowledging receipt of a gift "sent amid love and affection," the author goes on to express embarrassment for having needed the donation and adds "we asked the Creator of all to make it like the whole sacrifice upon the altar and like the regular meal offering in the morning and in the evening."[65] The author probably belonged the group that Mark Cohen has termed the "conjunctural poor," people of means who had fallen upon hard times. The financial assistance was given through a private, rather than an institutional, channel and was the cause of some "shame" for the recipient.[66] The rhetoric of the letter created the veneer—or, quite possibly, the true perception—of social solidarity involved with the donation.

Not all usage of sacrificial language was tied to monetary donation. An unpublished letter, TS 10 J 9.4v, contains a poem whose main purpose was to wish good health upon an addressee who had fallen ill. The anonymous poet, who laments that he could not offer a real "gift" (*teshurah*), calls his composition a type of sacrifice pleasing unto God:

> May the Lord of praises prepare healing balm and all types of remedies . . . and strengthen the respected, beneficent leader, the choice of His people, a turban upon all of the communities. To bring you a gift (*teshurah*) is not in my power, though I was determined and constituted it as prayer (*samtiha tefilot*) pleasing before the face of God as an offering (*qorban*); may it be considered like a sacrifice (*zevaḥ*) and burnt offering (*'olot*). It heals like spell-inducing water![67] We sing a song like the song over the splitting of the depths (i.e., the Song of the Sea, Exodus 15), and the daughters of my people go out with timbrels and drums and sing amid dance.[68]

The poet offered the "sacrifice" that will hopefully incite God to heal the sick recipient.[69] The letter certainly draws upon the grandeur of Israel's past and likens the delivery of the infirm addressee with the delivery of Israel from bondage. Solidarity is placed at the center of the relationship by stressing a shared historical and theological consciousness. What else the anonymous author wanted in return is unclear. I would presume that author and addressee were already involved in an unequal relationship involving the addressee's support of the poet and that the letter was intended to maintain that relationship.

Similar is the dynamic of a short letter, written in a beautiful hand, addressed to a certain Ḥiyya, "Pride of the God-Fearing." The letter requested wine, which had been prescribed by the author's doctor after bloodletting and had previously been promised to the author. The letter concludes with blessings of well-being in Hebrew rhymed prose and adds "may his offering (*minḥah*) bring prosperity quickly like a fragrant sacrifice (*qorban*), and peace."[70]

Is the function of sacrificial rhetoric different in private and institutional correspondence? Earlier in this chapter, I cited examples that I described as "playful," such as El'azar Ben Ya'aqov ha-Bavli's referring to a sum of money received as "the weight of the sanctuary weight"[71] or 'Eli he-Ḥaver Ben 'Amram's request from a *mamdūḥ* for a "freewill offering." How do we know when reference to a gift as a sacrifice is playful and when it is serious? The answer is that we cannot always know this with certainty, and our judgments are necessarily subjective. What is striking is how continuous the rhetoric of sacrifice was across the social and political strata of Jews in the Islamic Mediterranean. Both in the context of the geonic world and in Andalusian circles, the rhetoric of sacrifice played a role in group formation and cohesion, of building political and communal ties between center and periphery, on the one hand, and of boundary marking for a social elite, on the other. While I would assign greater import to the rhetoric of sacrifice in institutional contexts, it arguably presented some dimension of solidarity in personal contexts as well.

CHAPTER 3

"Humble Like the Humble One": The Language of Jewish Political Legitimacy

At various points, historians have tried to discern tidbits of biographical data, the "kernel of truth," from the broadly conventional representations of medieval Jewish panegyric. Regarding TS 16.68r, a panegyric by Shemuel ha-Shelishi Ben Hosh'anah for Shemariah Ben Elḥanan of Fustat, Jacob Mann wrote: "There is undoubtedly much flattery and exaggeration in all these praises of our Egyptian scholar, as was the fashion of the time in Muslim countries. Yet a genuine substratum remains which was certainly true to the Rabbi's great merits."[1] Menaḥem Ben Sasson makes a similar conclusion concerning a panegyric by Yiṣḥaq Ibn Khalfūn in honor of Avraham Ben 'Aṭa, specifically that the *mamdūḥ* was respected in his community, showed concern for students and the poor, and protected the community against enemies.[2] On rare occasions, praises refer to highly specific roles performed by the *mamdūḥ*; a letter from the Palestinian gaon Shelomoh Ben Yehudah (1025–51), likely to Ephraim Ben Shemariah of Fustat, includes: "[God] bestowed upon you patience and forbearance, a fearing heart to serve the people in all their needs, and to save those who were caught in the matter of taxes or in court. You seek the great ones in their homes and know how to make peace and a just settlement."[3] Such details as knowing trial procedures, assisting the tax-burdened (probably referring to those who owe the *jizya*), and working with specific officials are atypical in comparison with being patient and forbearing and likely refer to actual communal functions.[4] The same letter goes on to contrast the *mamdūḥ*'s qualities with the deficiencies of a rival, also given in detail: "[He is] impatient, does not know how to scrutinize in legal matters, and does not know how to work with the police, the ruler, the scribe,

Figure 8. Panegyric for 'Adaya Ben Menasheh Ibn al-Qazzāz / Peraḥiah. TS 32.4v. Reproduced by kind permission of the Syndics of Cambridge University Library

or the tax collector, though he does have other virtues that are esteemed and respected by the community. Not every man merits all the virtues of praise apart from him in whom they are all encompassed, none other than Moses our Master for he was 'exceedingly humble.'"[5] Such specific points suggest that authors did not use a one-size-fits-all model when representing *mamdūḥ*s.

The precision with which panegyrists modulated hyperbole is demonstrated richly by the fascinating Geniza document TS 32.4v (Figure 8), which actually presents two panegyrics: an original, beautifully calligraphed and vocalized poem in honor of 'Adaya Ben Menasheh Ibn al-Qazzāz, Karaite military governor of Palestine (a role he probably inherited from his father);[6] and a later poem, a rewriting of the first, written interlineally by 'Eli he-Haver Ben 'Amram, now dedicated to a certain Peraḥiah.[7] Many lines are left unchanged, but some are modified in minor yet interesting ways.[8] The opening of the poem for 'Adaya calls the *mamdūḥ* "mighty among ministers, son of a minister elevated above other ministers, captain of captains" (*rosh ha-rashim*).[9] In the later poem for Peraḥiah, the verse is altered, "mighty among *leaders*, minister elevated above other ministers, head of the *pure ones*" (*rosh ha-barim*); a verse in the original poem recalling 'Adaya's deceased father, Menasheh, "His banner is made precious with the majesty of sovereignty, an army captain like Yoav Ben Ṣeruya" becomes "He possesses a *reputation* and a *strong hand according to his measure* like Yoav Ben Ṣeruya." Yoav Ben Ṣeruya was King David's nephew set in charge of the army who attained the rank of captain (*rosh*) when he conquered Mount Zion from the Jebusites (2 Sm 8:16, 20:23; 1 Chr 11:4–6). The set of associations was ideally suited to Menasheh but was apt for Peraḥiah only insofar as it conveyed power in general. The poet certainly sensed that the hyperbole of the model poem was fitting for a military commander's function and status, whereas praise for Peraḥiah, who was of a lower but nonetheless significant rank, had to be modulated accordingly.[10]

Still, it does not seem, for the most part, that *mamdūḥ*s desired personalized, individualized portrayals of themselves; in fact, it was not uncommon for poets to praise several *mamdūḥ*s within a single poem without differentiating among them whatsoever (e.g., [Avun and Yosef are] "shepherds of faith, perfect in wisdom and kindness, forever a choice offering to God from among all His beings").[11] Instead, *mamdūḥ*s sought idealized depictions of social types that they were said to embody.

The problem of recovering realia from panegyric belongs to the general topic of discerning convention from reality, of finding details that might be considered reliable within a sea of undifferentiated representations. Dan Pagis argued in the case of medieval Hebrew love poetry that one might first establish convention and consider what diverges from it to be reality.[12] This seems a reasonable but not foolproof method in the case of panegyric. However, the purpose of this chapter is not to sift through panegyric in search of morsels of truth but rather to use convention itself as a historical source that yields not biographical data but the broader values of medieval Jews. The chapter thus steers a course away from the "convention versus reality" issue to explore a different set of questions pertaining to the construction of political legitimacy. What resonances were evoked when a panegyrist called a *mamdūḥ* the epitome of humility or a shepherd to his flock? What was the value of portraying a *mamdūḥ*'s wisdom, generosity, and eloquence when these very characteristics were predicated of so many *mamdūḥ*s before him? What can we learn about Mediterranean Jewish society that such characteristics were repeated so frequently in connection with political figures? How did references to archetypal figures and offices relate to claims of power in the present?

* * *

This chapter reviews some of the more dominant and ubiquitous elements of the language of Jewish political legitimacy that emerges from the panegyric corpus. The chapter is thus primarily interested in constructions of legitimacy for figures who held some position of authority, from gaons and exilarchs to their appointees, local leaders, judges, scribes, and even literary patrons, when they also held a political function.[13] Most of the discussion deals with particular traits (e.g., wisdom, generosity, discretion), metaphors of political office (shepherd), and the evocation of biblical ranks (kings, priests) and sacred objects (Ark of the Covenant, Tablets of the Law). There is also a brief discussion of portrayals of Jewish *mamdūḥ*s in their roles vis-à-vis non-Jews. Throughout, the chapter explores resonances of images of legitimacy within Islamic and Jewish literatures and demonstrates that Jewish political discourse combines traditional Jewish and contemporary Islamic idioms of power. Using insights from anthropology, especially the work of Victor Turner and Judith Butler, the conclusion of the chapter considers the significance of conventional, repetitive representation not only for the *mamdūḥ* and the author but also for the audience. In medieval Jewish panegyrics, *mamdūḥ*s are largely presented as instantiations of certain ideals of leadership that become more ingrained for the community each time a given man is praised for possessing them.

Dominant Images

Scholarship on the articulation of political legitimacy in Islamic contexts has demonstrated that images of power revolve around a number of dominant qualities—wisdom, generosity, eloquence, military prowess, and so on.[14] It has also been noted, at least in the context of al-Andalus, that Hebrew panegyrics focus on certain traits in imitation of the style of Arabic panegyric and in accordance with contemporary social values.[15] What has not been articulated sufficiently is how deeply Jewish political culture was shaped by Islamic political culture and that Jews' very conception of rightful dominion was a complex amalgam of traditional Jewish and contemporary Islamic images of legitimacy. Qualities such as modesty and wisdom are mediated through archetypal figures of Israel's ancient past and are combined with images of eloquence, generosity, ascension over enemies, and the suppression of heretics that are at the center of Islamic political discourse.[16] A seemingly universal characteristic such as "humility" can be shown to reverberate against highly specific diachronic and synchronic images of legitimacy. Further, Jewish panegyric evokes ancient offices as well as metonymic emblems of Israel's sanctity to create the sense that the legitimate structures of the past persisted into the present. This was important not only for the recipients of panegyric but for their authors and broader audiences as well.

Works on Arabic poetics, which often include sections on panegyric, abound in ideal character traits appropriate for praise in verse. The *I'yār al-shi'r*, by Ibn Ṭabāṭabā (d. 934) offers a long list of virtues (*faḍā'il*) for which the Arabs praised men: "generosity, courage, forbearance, resoluteness, determination, loyalty, virtue, reverence, intelligence, trustworthiness, temperance, sense of honor, truthfulness, patience, piety, gratitude, affability, forgiveness, justice, beneficence, ties of kinship, concealing secrets, bestowing provisions, clarity of judgment, scorn, shrewdness, aspiration, humility, eloquence, joy, [judgment of] refutation and confirmation."[17]

Similar sets of characteristics surface repeatedly in the Hebrew panegyric corpus for political figures and others. The following pages systematically present ideal character traits and related tropes predicated of Jewish *mamdūḥ*s: humility, generosity, eloquence, wisdom, discretion, the leader as shepherd, victor over enemies, and embodiment of ancient offices and sacred objects. All these would fit within Weber's categories of "traditional" and "charismatic" legitimacy claims.[18] The aim of this chapter is not merely to list these subjects but to explore, in a political context, their semantic depth against the backgrounds of Hebrew, Arabic, and Judeo-Arabic writings from the period. The selections focus on figures ascribed "sovereignty" or "dominion" and bring together strains of representation between the Islamic East and the Islamic West.

Humility

Humility enjoys a privileged place in Jewish and Islamic political discourse. It is the noted character trait of Israel's archetypal leader, Moses (Ex 12:3), and several passages in Proverbs extol this virtue (e.g., 22:4). It is also an ideal characteristic of several rabbis from the Talmud and persists in representations of sages in Ashkenaz.[19] The trait is highlighted in Judeo-Arabic ethical treatises, has a chapter dedicated to it in Ibn Gabirol's *Mivḥar peninim* (Choice of pearls), and occupies a prominent place in the political writings of Maimonides, who stresses humility among the requisite qualities of Israelite kings.[20] In the *Mishneh Torah*, he wrote: "[The king] should always behave with excessive humility. In this there is none greater than Moses our master. Behold he said, 'What are we?' (Ex 16:7). He withstood [the Israelites] trouble and burden, their complaint and wrath 'as the nurse bears an infant.' . . . [The king] should not treat Israel with haughtiness. He should conduct himself with great humility. He should bear the nation's burdens and complaints as a nursemaid cares for an infant."

Here Maimonides brings together God's command to establish a king who is not haughty (Dt 17:20) with archetypal images of Moses, both as exceedingly humble and as a nursemaid for the people (Nm 11:12).[21] Further, in the *Guide of the Perplexed*, Maimonides maintains that specific rituals, such as those surrounding the king's admission into the Temple precincts, were established to instill the feeling of humility in the monarch.[22]

Similarly, humility is a trait strongly associated with Muḥammad and the early caliphs and is frequently emphasized in Islamic political writing as a requisite quality of the ruler.[23] The great literary anthology known as *Al-'iqd al-farīd* (The unique necklace), by the Andalusian Ibn 'Abd Rabbih (860–940), for example, opens with a book on the ruler that contains a chapter on humility (*al-tawāḍ'u*) that includes sayings on the theme by the Prophet, caliphs, and various poets. Typical are the statements of 'Abd al-Malik b. Marwān, "The greatest of men is he who has humility concerning high rank, who swears off of dominion, and who apportions power," and the verses by Ibn al-'Atāhiyya:

> If you wish to see the most honored among men, look at a king in
> the garb of a beggar.
> This is the one for whom God magnified His favor; this is the one
> fitting for the world and religion.[24]

The sovereign's being fit for the twin domains of religion and the world, *al-dīn wa'l-dunyā*, is a constant motif throughout Arabic panegyric and has strong echoes in Jewish writing. Humility was also commonly attributed to those whom Marshall Hodgson called the "hadith folk" (those who study and repeat the *ḥadīth*), particularly in biographical presentations of scholars such as Aḥmad Ibn Ḥanbal.[25] In some cases, this presentation was paired with specific practices of asceticism meant to represent or induce the characteristic.

A Hebrew formulary preserved in the Geniza presents a suggested introduction for addressing a gaon that hinges on a balance of grandeur and humility:

> To the lord of Israel, their leader and prince, their pride (*geonam*), diadem and crown, their judge, light, and flame. To whom can I liken and compare his copious [knowledge of] Torah, his dear wisdom, his sought-out intelligence, his well-known humility, his recognized modesty, his known honesty, his faith, his righteousness, his alacrity, his radiance . . . , his reprimand and rebuke, the fruit of his mouth,[26] his asceticism (*perishut*) in eating and drinking, his ways and paths, and his sitting and departing. He surpassed those who came before him in his ability and his [deserving] praise. Although his status is high, his humility rises even higher. Even when the affairs of the masses overwhelm him, he does not neglect affairs of Torah.[27]

Interestingly, although the formulary that preserves this introduction includes praises for many types of figures (*ḥazan*s, a *ḥaver*, a clerk of merchants), only the gaon is attributed with humility;[28] at least within this document, humility is associated with only the highest rank. Most atypical is the attribution of asceticism (*perishut*).

Given that one sign of the true ascetic was that he shunned honor and praise, it is hardly surprising that panegyrics for ascetics are relatively rare.[29] Still, a number of panegyrics praise figures for giving up material objects toward higher goals within a rubric of humility such as Shemuel ha-Shelishi Ben Hosh'anah's praise for Shemariah Ben Elḥanan, "a man who encompasses all, a table filled with every good thing, who disregards the material world," or El'azar Ben Ya'aqov's praise for the "Nagid of the people of God" Shemuel Ben Karatha, "a lord who sold his desires to his intellect."[30] In Baghdad in the thirteenth century, Shemuel Ben 'Eli wrote a letter regarding the appointee Yiṣḥaq Ben Sasson: "He resembles an angel of God but he is simple (*tam*), a dweller in tents. . . . Humility, kindness, and preciousness are tassels on the hem of his robe"; with a "dweller in tents," 'Ben 'Eli evokes the biblical Jacob (Gn 25:27) and possibly the nomadic Rekhabites, who at least refrained from drinking wine (cf. Jer 35:10).[31] In the Islamic West, Mosheh Ibn Ezra praised Yehudah Ibn Abū al-Ḥajjāj:

> He chose toil of his body for his soul, but his soul does not toil for his body. . . .
> By his intellect he instructs [Wisdom] and exercises judgment with her constantly:
> "Little sleep, my child, little slumber, little laziness, and little food and drink."[32]

The first phrases of the final verse are derived from Prv 6:10, but the verse as a whole recalls the famous rhyming Sufi saying, "Little food, little sleep, and little speech" (*qillat al-ṭaʿām qillat al-manām wa qillat al-kalām*).[33] Similarly, in Judeo-Arabic, Yehudah al-Ḥarīzī praised the elder (*al-sheikh*) ʿAmram al-Hītī of Karkh, who "secluded himself for God in worshiping Him. . . . Throughout the day he continuously fasts and the night he spends in contemplation and wakefulness."[34]

Yiṣḥaq Ibn Khalfūn praised Avraham Ibn ʿAta of Qairawan as wise, courageous, generous, and humble: "He is superior like the palm, but humble like the hyssop."[35] Mosheh Ibn Ezra praised one figure: "He is pure, his Torah grows by the day but so does his humility! How he fled from dominion but it pursued him";[36] and another: "[He has] the countenance of a lion yet his humility is like *his* humility."[37] The paradigmatic force of Moses' humility was so strong that it could be alluded to only by the pronoun "his."[38] It is clear, then, that humility, more than a general character trait that should be cultivated among all people, was linked specifically with legitimizing leadership. Conversely, a lack of humility was enough to declare a person an illegitimate leader and disqualify him from office. Ephraim Ben Shemariah, a representative of the Jerusalem academy in Fustat, was sometimes accused of being haughty and, perhaps as (over)compensation, referred to himself as "the meek and lowly."[39] A Rabbanite heresiography recounts that ʿAnan Ben David, the figure associated with the founding of Karaism, was not selected for the exilarchate, despite his impressive learning and Davidic lineage, because of his "lawlessness and lack of piety"; instead, his younger brother Ḥananiah was chosen because of his "great modesty."[40] A letter sent on behalf of the community of Alexandria to Yehudah Halevi, then residing in Fustat, complains of a leader "who loves dominance and strife" (*taḥarut*); as Miriam Frenkel points out, love of rule is often cited as a trait that renders one wicked; humility is the ideal.[41] In the late twelfth century, Avraham Ibn Daud identified humility as the one character trait that Yehosef, son of Shemuel ha-Nagid, did not inherit from his father, a deficiency that precipitated his downfall and the massacre of the Jews of Granada in 1066.[42] We will probably never know exactly which leaders of the medieval Jewish world were truly modest and which were haughty; what is clear is that humility was a central aspect of representing political legitimacy that resonated with Jewish and contemporary Islamic discourses of power.

Generosity

Generosity, from pre-Islamic times onward, whether toward one's tribe, client, friend, pious foundation, religious community, or poet, was widely recognized as a quintessential virtue within Arab culture. A caliph's or governor's generosity, quite often figured simply as his "hand," symbolized the continuation of a pre-Islamic value system as well as a prime function of the state. One of God's beautiful names is *al-karīm* (the Generous), and the ruler's generosity might be viewed as an imitative act. Further, as Suzanne Stetkevych argues, the generosity of the more powerful agent in a reciprocal relationship was seen as a precondition for his nobility.[43]

Generosity is extolled as a virtue in Aristotle's *Nicomachean Ethics* and in Judeo-Arabic ethical writings, including a dedicated chapter in Ibn Gabirol's *Iṣlāḥ al-akhlāq* (Improvement of the moral qualities), where it is associated with the biblical Abraham and is said to secure honor for the one who exercises it; in fact, Ibn Gabirol writes, giving generously is likened to "lending unto God."[44] As Miriam Frenkel demonstrates, the value of *nedavah* (generosity, benevolence)—toward the poor, institutions, and students—recurs in the representation of Alexandrian Jewish leadership.[45] It is quite common for Hebrew authors to cast a *mamdūḥ*'s liberality through biblical allusion, either by association with Abraham or through language inflected with rituals of sacrifice.[46] The emphasis on generosity in the Jewish corpus derives from the contemporary focus in Arabic writing; by comparison, rabbinic laments focus on "humility, piety; scholarship, good lineage, and personal sanctity," but generosity does not play a significant role.[47]

The dedication of a panegyric by the Baghdadi poet Avraham ha-Kohen (c. 1000) for a certain Avraham Ben N[——][48] illustrates the centrality of generosity (and wisdom): "I have made your poem well like the Psalms,[49] sweet to the soul and restoring to the body, for your name is manifest upon us in might, our lord and master, strength of the tottering. Of you I speak when I wake and sleep for your love is better than old wine and the incense of your kindness is like a column of smoke, a burnt offering pleasing to the heavens."[50]

Generosity is a quality attributed to figures across a wide spectrum, including gaons, scribes, patrons of scholarship, and merchants. Most often, the exact nature of the *mamdūḥ*'s generosity is left unstated, though numerous examples are specific: a supporter of scholars, a feeder of the hungry, one who provides ransom for captives.[51] The commonality is that these figures set communal, intellectual, and supra-mundane values over worldly pleasure and material consumption.

The presentation of generosity was perhaps most complicated when the *mamdūḥ* enjoyed a luxurious lifestyle. Did his accumulation of wealth not signify a preoccupation with things worldly? How could a man be exceedingly generous when he preserved great wealth for himself? The tensions around these questions are implicit in such poems as Ibn Khalfūn's panegyric for Yehudah Rosh ha-Seder of Qairawan: "Whose merchandise is for giving, not taking, and on whose account the goods weep, for no sooner are they amassed and collected before he scatters them to all who ask."[52] In the same poem, Ibn Khalfūn compares the *mamdūḥ*'s many virtues with those of biblical archetypes. Abraham and Sarah(!) stand for generosity, "Both in word and in deed, his heart, wisdom, humility, and hand / are like the heart of David, the wisdom of Solomon,[53] the humility of Moses,[54] and the hand of Abraham and Sarah."

When Hai Gaon praised the same figure, he also noted his material wealth, offered blessings for prosperity in agricultural and mercantile endeavors,[55] and presented the *mamdūḥ*'s distribution of wealth as an act reminiscent of sacrificial offering: "His kindness is upon all like vapor rising and incense. All his oils are scented like spiced early rain, aloe, myrrh, and cinnamon, every powder burning."[56] Hai's poem also stresses Yehudah's generosity through attributed, fictionalized speech wherein words are set in the *mamdūḥ*'s mouth,

> I offer you aid, I make increase for you and grant you wealth!
> Ask, and I shall give, open your mouth and separate [your lips]!
> I shall fulfill all you request; I will neither diminish nor substitute.
> In my region and community, through writing and epistles,
> unto the ends of the earth, I am your emissary.
> Your wise men are like my children. I give them support.
> In a time of need I am like grapes in the desert.[57]

More than mere flattery, with this "scene" and through filial metaphors, Hai models Yehudah's place in the world of the academy both geographically and hierarchically.

As for the Andalusian corpus, a few examples by Yehudah Halevi will suffice to show how the trait could be related with others and function in disparate contexts. Halevi praised one *mamdūḥ*:

> A generous man (*nadiv*) whose soul gathered wisdom while his
> hand dispersed precious things. . . .
> Since you do not seek greatness, God has prepared you to uproot
> and to build,
> like Saul who found kingship when he went to seek she-asses.[58]

The generous man is not consumed with accumulating wealth, which speaks to his humility, which, in turn, destines him for greatness and even power. Thus, generosity is tied to rightful dominion in a specific way.

A panegyric by Halevi for Yosef Ibn Ṣadīq, a judge, scholar, and poet in Córdoba, sets generosity within the context of friendship, though the poem also stresses the *mamdūḥ*'s learning and power,

> Those who hold dominion and Torah as an inheritance are your
> younger brothers whereas you are the firstborn.
> For me you have mixed love with generosity and my soul is drunk
> with their wine.[59]

Dominion and Torah (*misrah ve-torah*) perfectly mirror the pair *al-dīn wa'l-dunyā* so often evoked in Islamic representations of legitimacy;[60] here they are mixed with generosity and the more intimate language of "love." Another poem by Halevi for a *nasi* in the East is similarly hyperbolic: "Were it not for his generosity, rhymes of praise would never have been created,"[61] as is his poem for the Andalusian Yosef Ibn Ezra: "His generosity is as though from the hand of God. . . . He is like a tree that bears new fruit daily and does not deny dainties to those who seek them."[62] In this last poem, liberality stands out as one trait among several (wisdom, eloquence, majesty), which combine to form a portrait of the Andalusian Jewish leader.

In the Islamic East through the thirteenth century, generosity remains a similarly central virtue predicated of Jewish leadership. TS 12.416 / ENA 1810.1 is an anonymous twelfth-century panegyric for Maḍmūn II of Yemen:

He helps the whole nation—young and old—and supports their
falling.
His generosity is like rain; those who seek his gifts are glad.
The living God established him for his community like a wall
around houses and gardens.[63]

Here the generosity focuses on communal leadership. A poem by El'azar Ben Ya'aqov for a Karaite known by the sobriquet *sharf al-dawla* (nobility of the state) opens with a prelude describing a beloved (rare in Ben El'azar's corpus), extols the *mamdūḥ*'s wisdom, celebrates how ministers and princes prostrate themselves before him, and includes an extended image of generosity in accordance with the Arabic style yet replete with biblical imagery,

He is like the sea that gives pearls to those near and sends rains to
those far off, and like the sun that dwells in the heavens whose
light illumines the ends of the earth.
His two hands are like the Mediterranean[64] and the Sea of Reeds,
his fingers are rivers.
He waters the earth with his kindness when the vapors of the sky
are stopped up. . . .
One who likens his generosity to the water of the sea is like one
who likens the smooth-skinned to the hairy.[65]

After comparing the *mamdūḥ* to the sea in several ways, the poet pronounces that even this comparison is tragically deficient and seemingly reprimands himself for having made the comparison. The preoccupation with generosity in the Hebrew panegyric corpus derives directly from Arabic panegyric and social values more than earlier Jewish literature; yet, insofar as generosity was a value intertwined with legitimacy, it was not only literary imagery that became Arabized but also politics more fully.

Speech, Writing, Eloquence

Words can do many things. They can cause comfort or distress, offer insult or praise, convey honesty or deceit, or bring about actions. In Jewish panegyric throughout the Islamic Mediterranean, speech and writing are associated with all these diverse functions and, in one form or another, constitute a pervasive motif. The power to affect action through word, whether in speech or in writing, is a fairly universal aspect of Near Eastern ruler representation. The regent, standing at the pinnacle of a political structure, implements his will in distant places with little more than a gesture or wish. Est 8:8 asserts that King Ahashverosh's writing, sealed with his signet ring, is so powerful that its decree cannot be reversed (see also Joseph's signet ring in Gn 41:42). The bureaucratic systems of the medieval Islamic world at least ideally provided rulers with an efficient system of enacting decrees, and so the image of the potentate surrounded by his scribes (*kuttāb,* sing. *kātib*) or wielding his pen were poignant representations of his power. The signet ring remained a prominent symbol of power; the famous Pamplona casket of al-Andalus, for example, represents an enthroned ruler (possibly Hishām II, 976–1009) wearing a signet, and the motif is exploited in a panegyric by Halevi for Yiṣḥaq Ibn Ezra, "a letter was inscribed by his mouth and signet; Majesty and Dominion are the sons of his pen and his speech."[66]

The ability to express oneself in classical Arabic with eloquence (*faṣāḥa*), grammatical precision, and learned expressions drawn from religious and other literature is a highly esteemed value in Arabic writing. A panegyric by al-Mutanabbī for a *wazīr* extols eloquence in writing and speech: "You pluck words when they are in bloom . . . and their beauty is multiplied when they are repeated. When you are silent, the most eloquent preacher is a pen which has taken your fingers as a pulpit."[67] Jews fully imbibed the value of eloquence with respect to the Hebrew language, particularly in its pure biblical form, and employed the Hebrew word *ṣaḥot* ("purity"; Is 32:4) with the full force of the Arabic *faṣāḥa*. They also extolled those Jews who demonstrated impressive control over Arabic;[68] in one panegyric, Mosheh Ibn Ezra praised a *mamdūḥ* who "eclipses all the light of the Arabs' eloquence" (*ṣaḥot*).[69] Naturally, mellifluous speech and writing were associated with figures that did not hold political office (e.g., poets) but held a special place within political discourse.

While some biblical rulers are said to have composed artful writings (David, Solomon), in Jewish tradition, eloquence is not an attribute whose absence might undermine legitimacy; Moses famously lacked this quality (Ex 4:10). Thus, when mediating images of eloquence through biblical archetypes, Hebrew panegyrists evoke the two monarchs but more often the later prophets and scribes. For example, Ibn Khalfūn praised Yehudah Rosh ha-Seder: "He speaks like Haggai, Zekhariah, and Malakhi, and behold, he writes like Ezra! He utters the Psalms of David."[70]

Several representations of Ḥasdai Ibn Shaprut focus on the *mamdūḥ*'s speech in various respects as powerful, eloquent, and even cunning. Menaḥem Ben Saruq set Ḥasdai within a *majlis* (using the Hebrew calque *moshav*):[71] "When he explains eloquent words (*meliṣot*) and makes wondrous a gathering (*moshav*) of nobles (*negidim*)." In the same poem, Ben Saruq sets Ibn Shaprut amid a circle of scribes striving, yet failing, to capture his lofty thoughts: "If every scribe were to inscribe the thoughts of his heart they would not attain but a hundredth. Were they to press with all their might, even with the expanse of their eloquence, could they show the degree of his greatness?"[72] Representing the *mamdūḥ* speaking within a *majlis* or reporting that his praise was uttered in governmental circles would not only flatter the addressee but also contribute to his legitimacy.[73]

Soon after Ibn Shaprut had persuaded the dethroned King Sancho I and Queen Toda of Leon to come to Córdoba to conclude an alliance with 'Abd al-Raḥman III, Ben Saruq's rival poet Dunash Ben Labrat extolled the Jewish diplomat: "He brought a mighty king like a prisoner . . . and drew [the king's] rebellious hag Toda, who wore kingship like a man, with the power of his intelligence, the strength of his cunning, his many designs, and his smooth speech." Later in the poem, Ibn Shaprut is praised for his words of judgment.[74] Menaḥem Ben Saruq's students likewise wrote a panegyric for Ibn Shaprut that includes extensive praise for his speech:

> Whose praise ascends on high, for whom powerful men wait as for dew and rain.
> They open their mouths wide for spring rain and for his word they thirst.[75]
> Before him the words of every minister are stopped up.
> They hide their thoughts and their mouths go dumb;
> before his wisdom they all grope about like the blind.
> They stream to him and the goodness of his deeds[76]
> and fawns lick the bottoms of his feet.[77]
> He is as swift in his eloquence as he is in his running,
> Asking him for advice is like consulting an oracle.[78]

Thus speech, while predictably included in panegyric, can bear very different valences, even when describing one and the same person.

Truthfulness of speech is also at the center of a panegyric by Shelomoh Ibn Gabirol for Yequtiel Ibn Ḥasan, "leader of ministers and rulers":

He is the light of the world, its foundation's base upon which the pillars of the heavens are set.
All rulers await him and all deputies hope for his word. . . .
His mouth brings good tidings for all men, his generosity is more precious than pearls. In his spirit is grace and in his heart kindness; his lips are always truthful.[79]

As in the verses by al-Mutanabbī quoted above, Yehudah Halevi praised Abū Yosef Yaʿaqov Ibn al-Muʿallim for both speech and writing and placed "Dominion and Torah," essentially *al-dīn wa'l-dunyā* (religion and the world), at the center of the portrait:

Dominion and Torah are two camps that war over him and compete jealously.[80]
One set a chain about his neck[81] and the other put wondrous deeds in his mouth—
words like the [gems] set on Aaron's heart;[82] when I query them they prophesy!
His pens have reeds of the heart, not reeds of wood; they draw from heart-troughs and never grow thirsty.[83]

As seen, skillful and powerful writing, often presented metonymically through the pen, was frequently predicated of caliphs and the scribes and *wazīrs* of their courts.[84] The best-known example of praise for writing in the Hebrew corpus is from the *shirah yetomah* in honor of Shemuel ha-Nagid of al-Andalus, famed to have risen through the ranks of power as an Arabic scribe for Muslim potentates and also as a Hebrew poet (the poem does not specify skill in one language or the other):

You possess the pen that is honored and graceful though it is lowly with neither beauty nor stature,
made from a reed yet it acquires Majesty and Dominion, the brother of the worm yet it is full of guile and deceit.[85]
It is proud, a man of valor when it rides though at rest it is nothing.
Its two teeth are whetted arrows; its spit can bring either kindness or revenge.
It scatters sapphires upon books inlaid with embroidery and silk.[86]

The poem draws a link between writing and dominion and reflects upon the pen's power to bring honor or shame.

Another poem that pairs writing with dominion is Halevi's lengthy panegyric for the Andalusian Yosef Ibn Ezra, which also dwells on the *mamdūḥ*'s wisdom and generosity:

To what man do the host of heaven bow, before whom do its
myriads prostrate?
They answered me, "Before a light that flashed from Sepharad who
rules over our day and night!
His name is Yosef, minister of grace and majesty. . . . "
His pen outruns the lightning; the wise thoughts it lays out are his
sisters.
With it he shames the lance of Taḥkemoni[87] and musters rebuke
against his enemies.
With it he rules so much that none can reverse what he writes with
his hand or seals with his signet.[88]

The final reference to King Ahashverosh demonstrates the long continuity of a Near Eastern theme, here mediated through the contemporary representation of Muslim potentates.

Powerful and eloquent speech and writing are similarly central in constructions of Jewish leadership in the Islamic East. Already from an early letter for Saʿadia Gaon, the panegyrist includes: "He pronounced wisdom and knowledge similar to Kalkol and Darda.[89] The fire of his speech is known, for it was redeemed from descending to the Pit."[90] A striking representation of powerful (if not necessarily eloquent) speech is found in a Hebrew letter by Abū Sulaiman David Ben Shekhaniah (d. 1024), a cantor and court scribe in the Palestinian community in Fustat, addressed to the Karaite David Ben Yiṣḥaq, who made appearances before the Fatimid caliph, "the respected minister who stands in the breach and advocates on Israel's behalf before the king and his ministers, the mistress[91] and her eunuchs. He is beautiful in his assembly (*moshav*, i.e., *majlis*), his scribes (*soferim*) surrounding him and hearkening to the sound of his speech. He abides in his place (cf. Ps 9:8), his hand raised against his enemies [as in the days of Passover],[92] his hand raised against the Casluhim and his dread over the Nephtohim,[93] like Joseph before Pharaoh and Mordechai before Ahashverosh."[94]

Here Ben Shekhaniah casts the *mamdūḥ* through the archetypes of the Jewish courtier but also as one who holds his own *majlis* and thwarts enemies in Egypt and Palestine (Casluhim and Nephtohim). Central to the depiction is the speech to which the scribes listen attentively—speech that becomes action through a calibrated political structure. Such a representation served not only as flattery but also as a kind of portrait that promoted a legitimate image of power beyond both author and addressee.

A letter of appointment by Shemuel Ben 'Eli for Yiṣḥaq Ben Sasson likewise includes: "His words are honeycomb flowing like rivers; they all serve him and are balanced in his intellect."[95] In a lengthy dirge (five manuscript pages!) included within a letter to the community of Mazdiya, Ben 'Eli laments a *rosh yeshivah* who died around the age of twenty, with emphasis on punctilious expertise in sacred texts and general eloquence:

> He was precise when chanting the Bible and recited with a sweet
> voice that woke the sleepers.
> The Mishnah was his younger sister and he deciphered the
> mysteries of *Talmud*,
> Tosefta, Sifra and Sifrei, as well as aggadot transmitted and passed
> on to him.
> He had a pleasing palette, a tongue eloquent (*ṣaḥ*) and long, his
> words like sharpened arrows.[96]

Here the values of eloquence are given specific roles appropriate to an academy head. The conclusion of the letter shifts to Judeo-Arabic and also recalls the deceased's qualities, including his "skillful tongue and eloquence" (*barā'at lisānihi wa-faṣāḥatihi*).[97]

Finally, El'azar Ben Ya'aqov ha-Bavli praised several figures for the power of their pens, including "the lofty sun of the state (*shams al-dawla*) Ben Karatha al-Nāẓir" and "the elder (*al-sheikh*) Abū al-Riḍā al-Ghaḍā'irī."[98] In a particularly striking lament over the *rosh yeshivah* Yiṣḥaq Ben al-Shuwaikh, a writer's case wails over the deceased, along with the dignitaries of the academy and ritual objects:

> A lord whose throne God established in Bavel though his
> reputation reached from the Gozan river unto No.[99]
> The scribes of the court bemoan his death, and so every judge and
> jurist after their kind.

Legal decision and reasoning,[100] the Torah of God, His judgment and Law, all weep for him,
and so weep those who heard the words of his teachings that were smoother than butter and oil.[101]
And so every community bewails him and weeps, every congregation, from the lowly to the great.
Legislators lament him and cry, every judge in his dwelling-place.
The writer's case[102] keens and says, "Woe for a lord whose tongue is his pitchfork."
His phylacteries and the fringes of his garment bewail him and weep.[103]

The lament not only bemoans the loss of the gaon but also presents the makeup of the world of the academy peopled with scribes, judges, and jurists, as well as personified ritual objects. Much of the rhetoric belonging to "secular" political discourse is found here, from the gaon's "throne" to the rhymed expression of eloquence, "his tongue is his pitchfork" (*leshono qilshono*), coined by Shelomoh Ibn Gabirol and used by subsequent Andalusian authors.[104] The lament honored the memory of the leader; but more than this, it impressed upon the community a structure with attending values that went beyond the deceased.

In sum, the focus on various aspects of speech and writing at once reveals the continuation of the Near Eastern theme in the Islamicate environment even as it testifies to the immediate and thorough Arabization of Jewish notions of legitimacy. Jewish figures were made to resemble contemporary Muslim rulers, and, in this way, their portraiture was tantamount to a kind of power production.

Wisdom

Wisdom is already predicated of many of the *mamdūḥ*s in the previous sections, often paired with humility, eloquence, or generosity, and sometimes with respect to specific areas of knowledge such as grammar or exegesis. That a ruler and his advisers should be wise is obvious, and this is only compounded when a figure also inhabits a scholarly position. Aphorisms sometimes bind wisdom and sovereignty closely, as in one preserved in Ibn Gabirol's *Choice of Pearls*: "Who is fit to rule? The wise man who attains sovereignty or the king who seeks wisdom."[105]

A rich and early representation of a *mamdūḥ*'s wisdom is the opening of Dunash Ben Labrat's panegyric for Shemariah Ben Elḥanan. Wisdom is figured as an ocean by an extended metaphor:[106]

> For the master who possesses a sea of knowledge, wisdom, cleverness, thoughts and ideas, and who makes them available to all;
> with their essence he brings water to those who desire Wisdom. In his seas sweet and delicious waters heap up.
> From him rain and dew arise, saturated [clouds][107] sent forth by winds of thought.
> All rivers with springs originate with him, all waters drawn with buckets and skins.
> Compared with his sea mine is like Rabbi Shammai. He makes my enemies and the Ibn Qaprons[108] into fools.
> In his sea neither sailors nor helmsman float; they launch neither boats nor vessels.
> There are no sea monsters or fish of any kind. But for the wise there are crystal ornaments,
> gems appointed for princes and ministers, brought to the House of God as gifts and offerings.
> Never haughty in wisdom, always fearing God, he ponders over rulings and for them people wait.[109]

The *mamdūḥ* had studied in Pumbedita under Sherirah Gaon and was given the rank "head of the Nehardeah row." Here, the wisdom is highly generalized, though the poem makes some reference to his rulings. In some cases, *mamdūḥ*s are praised for specific knowledge in matters of Jewish law or even for memorizing particular tracts of the Talmud. A tenth-century poem in a *payyetanic* style for a scholar includes:

> The lowly and the great step out to meet you,
> to take from your casuistry (*pilpul*) in matters [of law].
> The wise and intelligent rush to your door.
> You melt the reasoning of the two academies,
> the Talmud and interpretations with ninety-eight senses.[110]

TS 16.68r is a letter from Shemuel ha-Shelishi Ben Hosh'anah of Jerusalem to Shemariah Ben Elḥanan in Fustat that describes the *mamdūḥ* as "a man who encompasses all, a table filled with every good thing, who disregards the material world,[111] the right hand pillar, the strong hammer, who utters six [orders of Mishnah], who teaches four [tractates of Talmud], and who intones nine [blessings].[112] Happy is he and happy those who sit to hear the sweetness of his teachings, his lessons, and his interpretations."[113]

In a panegyric by Ibn Gabirol for Shemuel ha-Nagid, the *mamdūḥ* is described as one who "sought out Wisdom, made sense of its innermost secrets, gathered the scattered and stray; he plundered its spoils and concealed them among his treasures and secured their precious silver and gold."[114] In another, Ibn Gabirol likens the Nagid's Teaching to God's that "restores every soul" (cf. Ps 19:8):

> Your Wisdom, in truth, is broader than the sea, your Teaching
>   restores every soul.
> Your appearance is like the appearance of God's angels. Your form,
>   in truth, is stolen from them.
> The words you speak are noble, hewn from the ten [commandments].
> I am astounded that God created you in this generation even
>   though its men do not repent daily.[115]
> Your fathers begat you alone[116] but for them you are like thousands
>   of tens of thousands!
> With your wisdom you have built foundations and filled the face of
>   the earth with fruit.[117]
> Behold, if the students of Rav only knew you, they would call you
>   Shemuel head of the academy.[118]

The Egyptian poet 'Eli he-Ḥaver Ben 'Amram dedicated a panegyric to Yehosef and Eliassaf, the two sons of Shemuel ha-Nagid of al-Andalus, first praising them together for their generosity, modesty, and uprightness, and then praising them each in turn, beginning with Yehosef:[119]

> Glory of majesty, the respected minister and leader of the generation,
> head of all the wise, glory of knowledge, wisdom, and intellect,
>   chosen one of the community, foremost of all called [by the
>   name Yehosef].
> Yehosef is like Joseph in Egypt and is called Decipherer of Mysteries.[120]
> God gave him wisdom as an inheritance along with a spirit of pity
>   and compassion.

God gave him a wise heart regarding His Torah, exegesis, and laws,
interpretations more precious than gold and rulings that bring joy
to distress.
And Eliassaf, his wisdom emanates forth, his Teaching like a
flowing river.
His intelligence is known and established, set out like dainties of Eden.

The poem concludes with blessings that God increase sovereignty (*melukhah*) for the *mamdūḥs*' (future) children and cause them to reign unto the ends of the earth, as well as blessings for ingathering exiles to the Promised Land and vanquishing enemies. Wisdom is set within the rubrics of Torah, exegesis, and law; yet the *mamdūḥs*' influence is figured as a type of sovereignty.

The "sea of wisdom" motif is taken to another level by Mosheh Ibn Ezra in honor of the *wazīr* Abū Ayyūb Ibn al-Muʿallim, whose Hebrew name, Shelomoh, provided obvious association with King Solomon:

One who seeks [King Solomon's] wisdom, let him turn to a sea of
wisdom, expansive and broad;
[Ibn al-Muʿallim] made its shore ruby and its waters toss up spices;
its taste is honeycomb to the palate. . . . [121]
He is Wisdom's foundation and birthplace, just as [the number] one
is the foundation of thousands.[122]

Yehudah Halevi called Yosef Ibn Migash the "light of the West" and praised his deeds and wisdom extensively, again with obvious plays on the name of the *mamdūḥ*'s namesake:

Whereas men prostrated in a dream before [the biblical] Joseph,
awake they bow at [Yosef Ibn Migash's] feet,
for in him goodness and wisdom are more abundant! [Ibn Migash]
inherited [the biblical Joseph's] deeds and even his name!
O, you who seek Teaching, behold his heart is [Teaching's] ark! Go
and get its keys from his tongue!
Leave off Heman and Kalkol, abandon Darda,[123] and seek [Ibn
Migash's] pronouncements instead![124]

Turning to the Islamic East in the thirteenth century, Elʿazar Ben Yaʿaqov ha-Bavli praised a certain Saʿadia as "crowned with four crowns, a lord who understands all Wisdom and Knowledge (*ḥokhmah u-mad'a*) while others are like donkeys carrying books."[125] The theme of "four crowns" (Torah, priesthood, kingship, and a good reputation) derives from m. Avot 4:13, while the image of "donkeys carrying books" is qur'ānic (62:5, where it is predicated of Jews who rejected the Torah).[126] Interestingly, the "four crowns" motif is used by the same poet in praising a Karaite whose sobriquet was *sharf al-dawla* (nobility of the state). The rabbinic reference is fitting, the poet argues, for the *mamdūḥ* possesses not only general wisdom and precise knowledge of Hebrew grammar[127] but also expertise in matters civil and criminal (*dam va-din*) that impresses even the Rabbanites.[128] This type of rhetoric is paralleled when poets praise Rabbanites for possessing knowledge of Bible that bewilders even the Karaites.[129]

Gives Advice, Keeps Secrets

The intimate company of men, whether in a political or social setting, was a core value of medieval Near Eastern society. Essential were the keeping of secrets and the offering of valued advice. Adjacent sections of Ibn 'Abd Rabbih's chapter on the ruler within the *'iqd al-farīd* are dedicated to "consultation" and "keeping secrets."[130] Discretion was a requisite quality of both the *wazīr* and the friend. Ibn Ṭabāṭabā listed "keeping secrets" as a virtue extolled in Arabic panegyric, and the word *amīn*, "trusted one, confidant," frequently appears within Islamic political titulature in construct with "of the state" or "of sovereignty."[131]

In the Bible, both God and Moses are referred to as *ne'eman*, trusted (Dt 7:9, Nm 12:7), and this term figures frequently within medieval Jewish titulature and throughout the Hebrew panegyric corpus. One Jewish figure in thirteenth-century Iraq was known by the Arabic sobriquet *amīn al-dawla* (confidant of the state) and was praised in Hebrew as *pe'er misrah* and *ne'eman melukha* (wonder of dominion and confidant of sovereignty).[132] Praise for the trustworthy also centers on the Hebrew word *sod*, which can mean either "secret" or "counsel" (and thus can either be something that one keeps or gives), and refers at the most basic level to a small intimate circle.[133]

In the context of the academies and their ties to satellite communities, Sherirah Gaon praises Ya'aqov Ben Nissim of Qairawan, "treasure of our delight and our confidant (*ish sodeinu*), holder of our compact (*ba'al briteinu*), and delight of our heart."[134] A dynamic of concealing secrets but revealing wisdom is predicated of a certain Ḥananel, praised by Mosheh Ibn Ezra as generous, a protector of the God-fearing, and as one who "covers secrets but uncovers the secret of Teaching."[135] When wandering in Castile and hoping for reunification with Yosef "the exalted *nasi*," Ibn Ezra wrote: "We will take sweet counsel together (*namtiq beyaḥad sod*) and the oil of his mouth's speech will be spread upon the boils of my heart."[136]

In turn, Mosheh Ibn Ezra was praised frequently as "trusted" by Yehudah Halevi, sometimes playing directly on the *mamdūḥ*'s name in association with the biblical Moses—for example, "Mosheh is trusted (*ne'eman*) throughout my household (cf. Nm 12:7)."[137] In a remarkable *muwashshaḥ*, Halevi praised Ibn Ezra (a shift in the concluding *kharja* from Hebrew to Arabic, called the "language of men(!)," is in italics):

> When company met and princes counseled together,
> Dominion desired that he would be the leader of their intimate circle,
> And also the Torah spoke in the language of men,
> *O chiefs of knowledge, augustness and nobility,*
> *back away for Moses is in your midst!*[138]

Halevi also exploits the motif of the confidant when praising men of the East, as when he wrote hyperbolically of Shemuel ha-Nagid of Egypt:

> A just man who rules over men, who rules with the fear of God (cf. 2 Sm 22:3),
> He was determined to encounter God and so he was taken on high.
> Holy ones made him their confidant and so he stood in the counsel (*sod*) of the angels.[139]

Imagining the celestial realm as a court and setting the *mamdūḥ* within it as a trusted intimate surely enhanced the legitimacy of this figure's "reign" on earth. Setting the *mamdūḥ* among the angels or figuring him as an angel are treated further below.

Shepherd

A dominant image that echoes both against biblical precedent and a prevalent idealization of the ruler throughout the Near East is that of the leader as a shepherd tending his flock.[140] King David is referred to as a shepherd over his people (Ps 78:71), and the metaphor is used to describe divine guidance (e.g., Is 40:10–11; Jer 31:10; Mi 7:14). Because the biblical Moses shepherded the literal flock of his father-in-law (Ex 3:1), the midrash elaborated: "God saw his fitness to be the shepherd of His people . . . and gave him dominion over men" (Shemot Rabbah 2:2).

The political imagery of the shepherd was hardly unique to Jewish discourse. An early Arabic epistle attributed to al-Ḥasan al-Baṣrī and addressed to ʿUmar Ibn ʿAbd al-ʿAzīz (d. 720) describes the just ruler: "The just ruler, O commander of the Faithful, is like a shepherd who is tender toward his camels and kind to them; he takes them to the best pastures, prevents them from going to dangerous places, defends them against wild beasts, and protects them from the harms of the heat and cold." The text goes on to compare the just ruler to a father, a mother, a guardian of orphans, the heart among the organs, and calls him an intercessor between God and human beings.[141]

Maimonides recognized the shepherd as a key political metaphor in the *Mishneh Torah*; he notes that the Bible charges the king to follow the model of Moses and "pasture" his people like a shepherd. He also links the theme with the image of God as shepherd in Isaiah and hence presents pasturing as a kind of *imitatio dei* (*Laws of Kings and Their Wars*, 2:11).[142]

A *muwashshaḥ* in Mosheh Ibn Ezra's *dīwān*, probably deriving from a rite of induction into office, opens: "How comely on the mountains are the footsteps of a herald as he announces / that a shepherd has come to bring ease to the flock that wanders in forests."[143] Yehudah Halevi frequently refers to leaders as shepherds, such as Shemuel ha-Nagid of Egypt, "mightiest of all shepherds," whose sons are "anointed to be shepherds"; or Abū Isḥāq Avraham Ben Bassah, "father of a multitude who shepherds the remnant of his tribe with his staff" (cf. Mi 7:14).[144] The motif reflects the persistence of a longstanding trope of Near Eastern leadership inflected through Jewish texts and the immediate Islamic environment. Its centrality draws upon and reinforces a basic conception of leadership while promoting each *mamdūḥ* as a contemporary instantiation of the ideal.

Enemies

Historians have generally tried to identify enemies mentioned in panegyric—enemies whom the *mamdūḥ* has the power to thwart or whom the poet wishes God would eradicate—with specific figures or groups, whether these were doctrinal opponents such as Karaites, political competitors within the Rabbanite community, or religious Others.[145] Such references sometimes do allude to real and identifiable adversaries. Yet on a literary level, the inclusion of wishes against enemies is a fixed topos, one of the standard themes of praise that the addressee could expect to encounter. The topos is common throughout Near Eastern literatures and certainly has precedents in the Hebrew Bible (e.g., Numbers 22–24) and the Arabic panegyric corpus; in some Arabic panegyric, a rival Muslim dynasty can be portrayed as the enemy of Islam.[146] Also, as Mark Cohen points out, Hebrew Geniza letters frequently exploit Mi 5:8: "May all of your enemies be cut down" (*ve-khol oyvekha yikaretu*), likely in imitation of the convention in Arabic letter writing, *kabata allahu aʿdāhu* ("May God crush his enemies").[147]

A few, sometimes colorful, examples from the Hebrew corpus will illustrate the theme. Already in the late tenth century, a series of poems dedicated to Avraham ha-Baghdadi provide a rich sketch of idealized traits and contain several references to enemies, including non-Jewish ones.[148] The poems praise the *mamdūḥ*'s wisdom, generosity, and eloquence, as well as the beauty with which he recites prayer and poetry.[149] He is portrayed as loving his followers, as one who disperses Torah, and as a disseminator of wisdom.[150] In one poem, the poet asks that Avraham's enemies, identified as "Bavel and Edom," "be seized and enveloped by shame" and that God give the *mamdūḥ* the power to "unsheathe his sword from its scabbard and annihilate those who commit evil."[151] Moreover, it is Avraham's love of Torah that empowers him to fight these enemies: "His desire and passion is for the Torah of God; his banner is for it and toward its study does he skip; therefore, he smashes his enemy like a hammer that smashes rock."[152]

Enemies are identified broadly as non-Jews also in a panegyric by Yehudah Halevi for Shemuel ha-Nagid of Egypt:

> He does not desire wealth but desires the honor of God,
> to be an intimate of the world and a foundation for the altar.
> Like Joseph, he went out over all the land of Egypt
> to gather the Jerusalem exiles and to hew to pieces the enemies of
> Ephraim.[153]

Defeating the "enemies of Ephraim" was thus part of the Nagid's mission.[154] The identifications of non-Jewish groups in the corpus remain largely generic; even the most specific are coded through identification with biblical groups such as the "Casluhim and Nephtohim" (quoted above); "sons of Masa" (Gn 25:14), in a poem by Yehudah Halevi; and "Sons of Qedar" and "Togarmim," in panegyrics by 'Eli he-Ḥaver Ben 'Amram.[155]

Praise for subduing apostates such as Karaites presents a Jewish version of a theme found throughout Arabic praise traditions. One of the foremost activities of Muslim leaders was the eradication of apostasy (e.g., Sunni caliphs against Shi'ites and other sects), and the theme was exploited frequently within panegyric.[156] In the case of Rabbanite Judaism, the analogue was limiting and combating the influence of Karaism, even if it did not mean excluding Karaites on a social level. The formulary TS J 3.3 includes an address to a scribe: "[To] our elder, the esteemed, the beloved, the noble our master and teacher So-and-So, the scribe, the eloquent speaker. Every heretic and apostate (*poqer ve-kofer*) will be made his ransom (*kofer*). Those who revolt against him will be ashamed."[157] Although Karaism may have been a real concern for medieval Rabbanites, the prominence of the topos—here in an address to a hypothetical figure—reveals its importance as part of a construction of leadership. The topos also persists in Hebrew writing at least through the late twelfth century, when Avraham Ibn Dā'ūd depicted Yehudah ha-Nasi Ben Ezra as a great subduer of Karaism.[158] The point here is not that heresy was not a true concern in Castile but rather that Ibn Dā'ūd gave the suppression of heresy a privileged place in his selective representation of the new Jewish leader.

In many other cases, references to enemies, to the extent that they were real, pertain to other Jewish Rabbanites, some of whom were political competitors or detractors. In the Islamic West, verses preserved in the *dīwān* of Mosheh Ibn Ezra for a newly appointed judge likely take aim at other contenders for the office:

> May your enemy utterly pass away, become naught and never be redeemed!
> God has unsheathed His sword against him and has chosen you like Ittiel.
> May a thousand fall at your left and ten thousand at your right![159]

Similarly, when Yosef Ibn Migash replaced Yiṣḥaq Alfasi as head of the academy in Lucena, Halevi composed a strophic panegyric in which he described the academy as the "camp of God" and the *mamdūḥ* as "Mount Sinai before the Lord"; in the concluding stanza, the poet wrote: "Those who hate you shall wear shame and the tent of the wicked shall be naught."[160] In another poem, possibly for the same *mamdūḥ*, Halevi wrote: "By his hand, God gives his people strength, but beneath his hand, He subdues his enemies."[161] In general, however, the enemies topos is more a feature of Jewish panegyric in the Islamic East than in the Islamic West; in Halevi's corpus, it is utilized more often in praising figures in Egypt than in al-Andalus.

The enemies topos persists in the East strongly through the thirteenth century. El'azar Ben Ya'aqov ha-Bavli addresses the leader (*al-ra'īs*) Yosef Ben al-Barqūlī of Waṣīṭ: "His hand is against his enemies and his feet kick his foes" and concludes with the blessing "May God silence his enemies."[162] A panegyric for a certain Sa'adia by the same poet concludes: "May his name be magnified and may he be blessed by the mouth of God but may his enemies be cursed."[163]

In short, great men had enemies; without enemies, one was not a great man. Evoking a *mamdūḥ*'s enemies actually enhanced the image of his power (and, one might say, his "street cred"). TS 8 J 3.3 also presents blessings for "So-and-So, head of the yeshivah," "[May God] cut down his enemies like a small part of the finest wheat, subordinate them at the lowest level, make their end desolation and ruin (cf. Is 24:12), and execute the doom decreed against them (cf. Ps 149:9). . . . [God] is the star that shines upon So-and-So, head of the yeshiva. May He who is preeminent over ten thousand (God; cf. Sg 5:10) protect him from every opponent and harmer."[164] Presenting the enemies topos irrespective of any particulars demonstrates that the motivation for its inclusion was at least partly literary. Distinguishing between a literary topos and reality remains a difficult endeavor. While Jewish society in the medieval Mediterranean was certainly not devoid of intrigue, and tensions between Rabbanites and Karaites or Jews and non-Jews could be quite real, the recognition of the topos is an important starting point for the historian. Having enemies was simply a benefit when it came to representing legitimacy; lacking them could make one appear unimportant.

Between Jews, Muslims, and Christians

Numerous Hebrew panegyrics composed in Muslim territories portray *mamdūḥs*' positions vis-à-vis religious others. These representations range widely, from the *mamdūḥ*'s enjoying the respect of non-Jews, to his occupying advisory positions under Muslim rulers, to his saving Israel from the plight of subjugation under Muslims and, as seen, standing against Muslim or Christian enemies. 'Eli he-Ḥaver Ben 'Amram of Egypt praised Mosheh Bar Yeḥezqael:

"Bound with love, Jews together with Muslims (*yehudim ʿim yishmaʿelim*) praise you in assemblies (*maqhalot*)," thus creating an image of widespread respect across religious boundaries.[165] Similarly, Yehudah Halevi wrote of Shemuel ha-Nagid of Egypt: "Therefore nations (*le'umim*) praise him unto the desert and the sea islands for he stands as a banner for all nations and as a leader."[166] Hai Gaon's representation of Yehudah Rosh ha-Seder goes a step further, to focus on the benefit that the Jewish figure brings to his neighbors: "Through him nations in Togarmah and Qedar are blessed."[167] Elʿazar Ben Yaʿaqov praised the *ra'īs* Yosef Ben al-Barqūlī of Waṣīṭ as a political adviser of Muslims whose status brings honor to the Jews, "Through him the people of God wore honor and put on glory. . . . Nations are led by the light of his face."[168]

Other panegyrics focus on the role of the *mamdūḥ* as an intercessor on behalf of the Jews. Of Abū Isḥāq Avraham Ben Bassah, Yehudah Halevi wrote: "He softens the hearts of sons of Qedar with his words."[169] Halevi praised Abū Rabīʿa Shelomoh Ibn Qerishpin: "He raised the banner of freedom over the Exile and removed the yoke of forced labor of the sons of Masa," quite possibly referring to an actual event.[170] Above, we saw the representation of the Karaite David Ben Yiṣḥaq as an intercessor and courtier who vanquished enemies.[171]

In Menaḥem Ben Saruq's disciples' praise for Ḥasdai Ibn Shaprut, enemies are specified as Christian:

> From his bosom he cast out the people whom God cursed; he drew
> his sword and put an end to the oppressors
> who slumber away, sprawling out, lying dumb like dogs.[172]
> He hewed down those contaminated by abomination and the
> pig-eaters.[173]

The references to Christians as "contaminated by abomination and pig-eaters" mirrors what one might find in contemporary Arabic panegyric or war poetry, in which Christians are presented as heretical sinners marked by their consumption of pig. The martial imagery within the passage is discussed further below.

Praising Jewish figures for thwarting Muslim enemies is relatively rare. Menasheh Ibn al-Qazzāz was praised for his military expeditions against Bedouin tribes in Syria: "He subdued the sons of Kedar and Nebaioth and brought them low; the sons of Adbeel, Mibsam, and also Mishma were forced to flee and were decisively repelled."[174] All the figures named are sons of Ishmael

(Gn 25:13–14), and thus the poem might, at first glance, seem to present a conflict between Jews and Muslims. From the poem, one could hardly guess that these battles were waged on behalf of the Fatimid dynasty against other Muslims. The same is true of the war poems of Shemuel ha-Nagid of al-Andalus, which portray battles between Taifa states as assaults against the Jews.

There is thus no single mode of representing interreligious relations in the context of Jewish panegyric. Each portrayal relates the *mamdūḥ*'s role as a diplomat or an army commander in the entourage of a Muslim ruler or as a leader within the Jewish community, perhaps as a spokesman before Muslim power. This diversity points to the multifaceted and sometimes paradoxical aspects of Jewish life in the medieval Muslim world.

Martial Imagery

The Andalusian poet Shemuel ha-Nagid is generally credited with introducing the war poem genre into medieval Hebrew poetry.[175] Insofar as he set himself within battle scenes and boasted over his prowess while simultaneously praising God for granting his success, this is undoubtedly true. However, the Nagid was not the first to employ martial imagery, either in the literal or the figurative sense, in medieval Hebrew verse. Given the focus on enemies, it is hardly surprising that the corpus is rich with such imagery.

The disciples of Menaḥem Ben Saruq, to give an early and figurative example, praised Ḥasdai Ibn Shaprut as a "general (*aluf*) in Judah" and continued (this passage was partially quoted above):

> With words he conquered[176] cities and regions, not with arrows and swords.
> From his bosom he cast out the people whom God cursed; he drew his sword and put an end to the oppressors
> who slumber away, sprawling out, lying dumb like dogs.[177]
> He hewed down those contaminated by abomination and the pig-eaters.
> From every direction he abused the oppressor with his wit.
> Shield bearers are incinerated before him.
> Those who carry spears, who bear arms, who are girded with weapons of war all bow down before him.

Riders of horses also flee, melted and dissolved, scattered and
dispersed.[178]

The motif of "battles of words" or "battles of wits" dominated the representation of scholars, poets, and holders of political office and it is largely in this form that martial imagery and manly prowess appear within the medieval Hebrew literary tradition. However, also before the Nagid, martial language was utilized in a highly literal sense in Menaḥem Ben Saruq's poetic introduction to the famous epistle sent on behalf of Ḥasdai Ibn Shaprut to King Yosef of Khazaria. The poem does not praise the king for typical attributes such as wisdom, generosity, or eloquence but focuses instead on the one idea that most captured the minds of the Jews of al-Andalus, that somewhere in the world there was a Jew who wielded military might:

May the priestly crown [be given] to the tribe that rules the far-off
kingdom;
May God's benefit be upon it and peace be upon all its governors
and host.
May salvation be raiment upon its shrine, its holidays and sacred
occasions.
May its trained army and its warriors' shields be made mighty by
the wondrous hand.
May its chariots' horses and riders not retreat in a despondent mood.
May the standards of its marshals and the drawn bows of its
soldiers be clothed in triumph.
May its marksmen's arrows and the lightning of its spears come in a
thick column of smoke and split the heart of my lord's, the
king's, enemy to multiply their troubles.
In the necks of his chariots reside might, tumult, and terror.
Its horsemen win victory and return in tranquility from a terrible
land.
For this my soul pours out, "Happy is the eye that sees the king
coming out on a day of battle like the risen and wondrous sun!"
His soldiers run like lightning, one against a hundred and two
against ten thousand.
They press down their enemies as the full cart presses down.
Consider, O pillars of the earth, who has heard or seen such a
thing?[179]

> The remnant [of Israel] dominates mighty men who flee; they deliver up the city and its inhabitants.[180]

The poem begins, in classic epistolary form, with blessings that offer the king God's benefit and peace.[181] Menaḥem then offers blessings of victory, including wishes for the thwarting of the enemy, with an uncommon degree of martial imagery and expatiates on the power of the king's army. The words "Happy is the eye that sees the king" clearly echo the language of the Yom Kippur *'avodah* liturgy in praise of the high priest, "Happy is the eye that sees" (the pageantry of the high priest's ritual).[182] In fact, the poem goes on to mimic the style of the *piyyut* by likening the king's appearance to the sun. Further, the striking phrase that opens the poem, *afudat nezer* (translated here as the "priestly crown"), evokes the high priesthood by creating a construct out of the two ceremonial objects most associated with the office, the *ephod* and the crown (more properly, the "headplate" that was worn over the miter; Exodus 28).[183] Although Yosef is called a "king" within the poem, the association between Yosef and the high priest is unmistakable.

Why has the poet associated the Khazar king with the representation of a priest when he was not of priestly or even Israelite descent? Especially given the martial context, why not dwell more on images of kingship or offer a blessing that Yosef be given the crown of the monarchy? Avoiding monarchic imagery may have deflected any hint that Yosef was an illegitimate usurper of the Davidic line, which was seen as persisting in the office of the exilarch. The term *kohen* is applied in the Bible to non-Israelites (Gn 14:18) and for non-Aaronids, but priestly imagery may have been favored here since priests were not only ritual but also political officers who played a particular role in battle: "And it shall be, when you draw nigh unto battle, that the priest shall approach and speak unto the people" (Dt 20:1–2). In fact, the conditions of battle described in Deuteronomy—horses, chariots, a multitudinous opponent—are all present in the poem as well. The suggestion of the poem is not that Yosef became a priest but rather that, in his political and military capacities, he deserved the emblems of priesthood.

Kings, Priests, Levites, and Sages

Panegyric provided an opportunity for presenting the makeup and order of the Jewish community through offices of the distant past. Most generally, Israel as a whole is figured as a grouping of the monarchy, the priesthood, and the Levitic office (Temple singers). A poem for Avraham ha-Baghdadi extols the *mamdūḥ*'s power over his enemies and adds: "Be ashamed, O daughter of Edom, who lays waste to villages, O enemy of Moses, David, and Merayot!" (who represented the Levitic office, monarchy, and priesthood, respectively).[184] Yehudah Halevi praised Yosef Ibn Migash for descent through Moses and Aaron and adds that the emblems of their offices have not vanished but rather persist through the *mamdūḥ*: "The tablets were not broken, the ark and the cherub were not buried. . . . Torah and power (*gedulah*) were conjoined and then discussed by men of repute."[185] Again, thoroughly Jewish imagery was placed in the service of casting the *mamdūḥ* in the mold of the Muslim ruler in whom the domains of religion and the world (here, Torah and power) are conjoined.

The relative ranking of biblical offices was theorized frequently in rabbinic and medieval Jewish literature, and the ideal configuration of power among the offices has been treated extensively in scholarship on the Jewish political tradition.[186] A locus classicus is Maimonides' *Laws of Kings and Their Wars*, 2:5, where rank is indicated through bodily postures such as standing or prostrating before one deserving of respect: "Even a prophet prostrates himself before the king. . . . However, a high priest does not need to appear before the king when called. Rather the king stands before the high priest, 'And he shall stand before El'azar the priest' (Nm 27:21). Still, it is a commandment for the high priest to honor the king by having him seated and standing in his presence when he visits him. The king should only stand before the high priest when he consults *Urim* and *Tumim*. . . . It is a commandment for the king to honor students of Torah. He should stand before the Sanhedrin and Sages of Israel and seat them at his side. . . . However, in public, the king should not stand before anyone."[187]

Models of political structure are similarly worked into documentary sources, such as epistles by Shemuel Ben 'Eli in which the author combined praise for recipients with claims of legitimacy for himself, the yeshivah, and scholars more generally. In a letter to the community of al-Kirkānī, he wrote: "The rank of the Torah is more esteemed than that of the high priest and more exalted than kingship because four crowns descended from heaven, the foremost of which was the crown of Torah (Aramaic, *kelila de-oraita*). The sages, may their memory be for a blessing, said, 'There are three garlands: The garland of the ark, the garland of the altar of incense, and the garland of the table.' The ark corresponds to the sages of Israel, for in it were the tablets of the covenant and the book of the Torah, the altar of incense corresponded to the priests, and the table corresponded to the kings of Israel, and it is known that the ark is exalted above them all" (cf. b. Yoma 2b).[188] Even more elaborately, in a Judeo-Arabic epistle to Zekhariah, an *av bet din* in Aleppo, Ben 'Eli lavishes praise upon several communities in Syria and extols the status of the yeshivah (Hebrew in italics):

> The place[189] of the yeshiva is the *throne of the Torah*, which is the proxy (*al-nā'ib*) for Moses our Master in every age. . . . It is the place designated for teaching Torah and Talmud and transmitting law (*al-halakha*) from generation to generation extending back to Moses our master. . . . Anyone who disputes with it disputes with the lord of the Torah because [the yeshivah] is the [Torah's] place; he also disputes with Moses our master, may peace be upon him, for [the yeshivah] is [the Torah's] throne. . . . As for the king, [the Israelites] chose him because of their need for someone to lead them in battles and wars. But in the days of Exile (*al-galut*) they have no king, no war, nor anything else that would require a king; rather, they need someone to guide them (*yurshiduhum*), instruct them, and teach them the requirements of their faith, to render judgments, and to issue for them legal opinions (*yuftihum*). We know that King David, may peace be upon him, the prophet-king who combined the qualities of fear and wisdom, used to rely upon his sages for judgment and issued decrees only by their word.[190]

Israel thus had no need for a king in Exile; moreover, when there were kings, the wise and righteous king relied upon and deferred to his scholars. Despite the many references in Islamic writing to the caliph as possessing the domains of religion and the world, at least in the Sunni context a certain separation of powers emerged such that the ideal ruler was one who relied upon the opinion of the *'ulamā*, the scholars. As Goitein points out, "the best ruler is he who keeps the company of scholars"; this was a common aphorism in medieval Jewish and Islamic political thought, and this argument helped shore up claims of the yeshivah's legitimacy.[191]

In the panegyric corpus, authors seldom rank offices but rather extol whatever lineage a *mamdūḥ* claimed. Of the various offices, the monarchic received the greatest attention in Hebrew panegyric, especially in Eastern territories where exilarchs and *nasi*s claimed legitimacy as Davidic scions. TS 10 J 22.3v, an unpublished and beautifully calligraphed panegyric (dated 1146), praises Abū Saʿīd al-Dāʾūdi, whose relational name (*nisba*) clearly attests to a Davidic claim, as "of the people and crown of the *nasis* . . . associated by lineage (*meyuḥas*) to the father of the house of kingship. . . . He is anointed in the oils of wisdom like the Messiah."[192] Most often, individuals—especially those who claimed particular lines of descent—were cast through these ancient offices.

Panegyrists built representations of *mamdūḥ*s through the imagery of their forebears and their offices. More than serving as a quaint nod to tradition, the references lent an air of legitimacy to those empowered and allowed a system of undisputed authority to appear firmly established and current. The subject of lineage, especially in connection with the Davidic line, will be treated further in Chapter 4, on Mediterranean regionalism.

Sacrality

In an excellent article, Esperanza Alfonso touches on sacral metaphors of the *mamdūḥ* in Andalusian Hebrew poetry, especially insofar as they connect with the body. The "heart of the benefactor [becomes] the *locus par excellence* of the sacred" and is figured by such objects as the Tablets of the Law, the Ark of the Covenant, the Temple or its inner sanctuary; in funerary elegies, the grave is sometimes called the place where the "Tablets and the Ark are buried."[193] As she notes, literary criticism during the 1980s, especially following the book by George Lakoff and Mark Johnson titled *Metaphors We Live By*, reconceived metaphor beyond mere adornment to become a device that performs essential cognitive work by providing frameworks for articulating and interpreting the world. As Alfonso puts it, the cognitivists "conceive of metaphor as the mapping of relations, properties, and knowledge from the *source* domain into a *target* domain";[194] that is, metaphor allows us to interpret one concept through the categories of another, to think of something in terms of something else. Metaphors, although figurative, have an actual effect upon how members of a cultural group think and even live.[195]

The Andalusian examples brought by Alfonso represent only one segment of related instances of sacred hyperbole employed throughout the Mediterranean. Sacralizing metaphors are already presented in rabbinic literature, as in a lament wherein the deceased is figured as the Ark (b. Ketubot 104a).[196] Around the year 1000, one author praised Avraham ha-Baghdadi: "[God] has made with Avraham a covenant to pass on a flawless dominion of might and to make it an inheritance. . . . Here is the vessel that God has made precious! Here is the Temple (*heikhal*) that will not be uprooted! Here is the spring where kindness flows!" The imagery continues toward the end of the composition and creates an interesting tension in its political conclusion: "May God who is all powerful set his eyes upon the 'Temple' and nullify the counsel of the enemy who has slandered [Avraham] and maligned him to destroy him. . . . May He build for our 'Temple' a fortified Temple on a hill in order to magnify his might greatly. May He raise up in [Avraham's] lifetime the downtrodden Temple, erect in his day the fallen booth. May He illuminate for David the darkened flame; may He bring the seventh and hasten the eighth (Elijah and the Messiah; cf. b. Sukkah 52b)."[197]

In the first passage, the author affirms the role of the *mamdūḥ* as God's agent on earth. Avraham is the Temple—which, unlike the Jerusalem Temple, is indestructible—and also its vessels. His is a dominion of might that will persist into future generations. Thus, any need for political restoration or divine intervention would seem to be obviated. Yet the second passage calls upon God for just such an intervention, to restore the Temple (*heikhal*) in Jerusalem and to suppress Israel's enemies. The poet links the two passages with great irony by asking God to build for "our 'Temple'" (i.e., Avraham) a "Temple on a hill." This is more than a clever wordplay. On a discursive level, the poet poignantly explores the tension between the worldly power of Avraham and the ultimate disempowerment of the Jews. By figuring the *mamdūḥ* as the sacred Temple, the poet couples the current legitimacy of the *mamdūḥ* within the Jewish sphere with the political illegitimacy of the broader world.

Yet sacralization of *mamdūḥ*s is seldom connected so directly with politics. Most often, it simply involves the inter-projection of sacred objects and human beings. A particularly dense example from the Andalusian corpus is Mosheh Ibn Ezra's panegyric for Abū al-Fatḥ Ben Azhar: "If we desire to ascend to the Temple, behold you are our cherub and Sanctuary. / Or if we recall the Tablets of the Law, our holy Ark is concealed in the Ark of your heart."[198] The device is clearly hyperbolic; but again, such metaphors are more than ornamental and should be considered cognitive structures. Beyond flattery, the device enhanced legitimacy by associating *mamdūḥ*s with objects suggestive of divine election and assured listeners of a sacred presence in the world. The device persisted for centuries, as in El'azar Bar Ya'aqov's lament over Maimonides: "Woe, for the Ark of Faith was taken with the cherubs . . . the Tablets which are God's work."[199] Many other texts from al-Andalus and the East could be cited.[200]

A related trope is figuring the *mamdūḥ* as an angel—a being of the divine realm, or setting him among the host of heaven. Here, there is precedent in the Bible (2 Sm 14:20), and the examples in the medieval corpus are plentiful. Shelomoh Ibn Gabirol praised Shemuel ha-Nagid of al-Andalus: "Your appearance is like that of the angels; your form, in truth, is stolen from them."[201] Similarly, Ibn Khalfūn wrote for Abū al-Faraj Yehoshuʿa Ben al-Qumūdī: "They likened him to an angel of God and were all astonished upon seeing him. / Behold, they said, 'What has happened to this angel that he dwells among men on earth?'"[202] Shemuel Ben ʿEli praised Yiṣḥaq Ben Sasson: "He resembles an angel of God though he is a dweller in tents."[203] A bilingual poem by Elʿazar Bar Yaʿaqov for *najm al-dawla* (star of the state) Abū al-Barakāt al-Ṣulḥ is a poignant final example (Hebrew in plain font; Judeo-Arabic in italics):

> *When they saw you they said, "There is no God but God!" and "God is Great!"*[204] They were greatly astonished and so they said,
> "This is an angel of God, or a prophet, or *this is the Messiah who outshines the luminaries.*"[205]

What is the effect of figuring the *mamdūḥ* as an angel? It is, of course, a manner of hyperbolically praising a given trait, usually beauty or wisdom. Yet, just as figuring the beloved as an otherworldly being in love poetry may speak to the ontological status of beauty, so figuring the *mamdūḥ* as an angel suggests the divine origin of legitimate rule, of which the *mamdūḥ* is an instantiation.[206] This does not require that the listener considered the trope literally, that a *mamdūḥ* was truly sacred. It only requires that the listener imagined the *mamdūḥ* to be wise or beautiful in a way that set him within a divine order. Chapter 7 is dedicated to a related type of sacred hyperbole wherein the *mamdūḥ* is associated not only with divine objects or angels but with God Himself.

Conclusion

What was the effect of representing a *mamdūḥ* as a wise and generous shepherd, an eloquent speaker, and an angel on earth, when the same representation was made of countless *mamdūḥ*s before him? To the modern reader, such conventional, predictable representation might seem hackneyed, tired, and even absurd. Yet such repetitive portrayals served purposes in medieval Jewish society that went beyond the *mamdūḥ*, his panegyrist, and the relationship between them. The repetition of tropes of praise and pronouncements of legitimacy carried significance also for the third party in the performative complex: the audience. Few people would have read works of political philosophy, but more people (perhaps still not "many") would have political principles impressed upon them through panegyric. Yet we can also go beyond Weber's "ruler-centric" model of legitimacy wherein the power-subject volunteers his obedience to the power-holder due to effective persuasion from the top down.[207] Without romanticizing the status non-leaders, we can say that panegyric practice and the offering of loyalty also served to enhance the rank of the power-subject who gained greater proximity to leadership and was afforded at least some sense of place within a political, even an ontological and theological, structure. This may have been particularly important for a religious minority, for it granted legitimacy not only to the leader but also to the group.

Insights from anthropology might help explain what strikes us as a puzzling social practice. Panegyric may be seen as a type of social performance, which, as Victor Turner argued, involves acts that are repeated, or, as Judith Butler explained Turner, a "reenactment and re-experiencing of a set of meanings already socially established."[208] Butler puts the idea to use, for example, to explain gender identity—that the frequent repetition of "corporeal acts" contributes to an individual's sense of "gender" (that the repetition of an act such as putting on a skirt, already socially inscribed as a sign of femininity, establishes and affirms one's gender as female).

On the level of the group, the repetition of verbal pronouncements of legitimacy allowed for the creation of a particular political sensibility; calling countless *mamdūḥ*s wise and generous shepherds not only enhanced the legitimacy of those individuals but also gave the community a sense that these qualities resided within the group. Hyperbolic praise was not only about flattery but also about the constant reinscribing of core values of leadership without which the *group* could not claim legitimacy. A useful comparison might be the reiteration of marital values within wedding ceremonies; such pronouncements have relatively little to do with the couple undergoing the ritual, but the occasion of the wedding allows the witnessing group to affirm some of its primary commitments.

With the dedication of panegyric, Mediterranean Jews not only professed their admiration for given figures but also reified the core values of institutions of leadership. Panegyric bolstered images of power that combined contemporary Islamic and traditional Jewish idioms of power that both drew upon and deepened notions of group identity and legitimacy. Insofar as these values were mediated through figures, offices, and sacred objects of Israel's past, political panegyrics offered audiences a means of interpreting the structure of the world that both evoked preexisting meanings and allowed the past to exist in the present.

CHAPTER 4

"Sefarad Boasts over Shinar": Mediterranean Regionalism in Jewish Panegyric

> When making a speech of praise, we must also take into account the nature of our particular audience; for, as Socrates used to say, "it is not difficult to praise the Athenians to an Athenian audience." If the audience esteems a given quality, we must say that our hero has that quality, no matter whether we are addressing Scythians or Spartans or philosophers.
>
> —Aristotle, *The Rhetoric*

Despite their highly conventional character and relatively stable mode of representation, variations in panegyrics shed light on the subject of Jewish regionalism within the Islamic Mediterranean and beyond. First, we can see that panegyrics composed for *mamdūḥ*s in distinct locales sometimes focus on different attributes, not only because panegyrists were praising unique individuals but also because they were tapping into distinctive sensibilities of leadership in each place. Second, panegyrics often elucidate the dynamics between center and periphery, or between one center and another, by creating ordered or hierarchic representations of geography. In that panegyrics contribute to our knowledge concerning the interplay between local and central Jewish authority, between hierarchic and horizontal structure, they constitute an important source for charting what Marina Rustow has recently called the "jagged shape" of the Jewish community.[1] Taken together, the corpus reveals something of the pan-Mediterranean networks of Arabic-speaking Jews and justifies the

"Mediterranean" as a unit of study even as it presents multiple ways of conceptualizing the interrelation among regions.

Panegyrics, as historical testimonies, can modify received narratives of Jewish history. Al-Andalus, for example, has often been viewed as the prime example of a local Jewish leadership that broke away from Iraqi moorings. *Sefer ha-Qabbalah* (The book of tradition), by Avraham Ibn Dā'ūd, the proud Andalusian chronicler who wrote from Castile after the fall of Andalusian Jewry during the Almohad revolution, portrays the decline of the great academies of Baghdad in the tenth century and the divinely-ordained rise of an independent Andalusian academy just prior to that. As he relates it, "the King [the Umayyad caliph 'Abd al-Raḥman III] . . . was delighted by the fact that the Jews of his domain no longer had need of the people of Babylonia."[2] Although Ibn Dā'ūd's representation has held powerful sway over the reconstruction of events, his narrative of Baghdad's decline and the severance of Andalusian Jewry from Eastern authority by the mid-tenth century is far too neat.[3]

Ongoing relations between East and West, and the fidelity of the latter toward the former, are apparent in numerous panegyrics produced within al-Andalus. Writing in the tenth century, Menaḥem Ben Saruq praises Ḥasdai Ibn Shaprut as a *rosh kallah* (head of the assembly), a title that would have been bestowed upon him by a Baghdadi gaon, which testifies to the Andalusian Jewish courtier's fealty to the center in Iraq during the reign of 'Abd al-Raḥman III. Dunash Ben Labrat likewise praised Ibn Shaprut, "Every year he sends an offering to the judges [in Babylonia]."[4] Famed for his panegyrics for Ibn Shaprut, Ben Labrat is less well known for one that he wrote for Shemariah Ben Elḥanan, a leader of the Babylonian community in Fustat.[5] Shemuel ha-Nagid also viewed himself as part of a broader Mediterranean network; he authored a panegyric in honor of Sahlān Ben Avraham of Fustat, another for the Palestinian gaon Daniel Ben 'Azariah, and a lament upon the death of Hai Gaon of Baghdad.[6] A generation later, Shelomoh Ibn Gabirol composed a panegyric for two emissaries of the Sura academy who had arrived in al-Andalus.[7] Al-Andalus thus appears at least through the first half of the eleventh century as a satellite community like any other that exhibited strong local networks and ties to distant centers simultaneously.

Spatial representation is common in the panegyric corpus and conveys something about how authors and audiences conceptualized geography. Hai Gaon of Baghdad commands that his panegyric for Yehudah Rosh ha-Seder of Qairawan be recited "in all of Bavel . . . unto Ashur and Suriya . . . unto Elam and Paras" (i.e., Iraq, Syria, and Persia); by doing so, the gaon was essentially claiming his jurisdiction over these regions. A funerary elegy by Mosheh Ibn Ezra for a certain Barukh in al-Andalus maintains that lamentation shall not cease in "Bat Bavel, Admat Edom, Miṣrayim, and Em Sefarad" (Iraq, Christian Iberia, Egypt, and Córdoba; lit., the "mother of Sefarad").[8] Hai Gaon's imagined geography maps well onto the political boundaries of the Islamic Mediterranean, whereas Ibn Ezra's goes somewhat beyond.[9]

Another way in which panegyric allows us to approach the subject of regionalism is to consider fluctuations in representations of leadership over space. Returning once again to Hai Gaon's panegyric for Yehudah Rosh ha-Seder on the occasion of the *mamdūḥ*'s son's wedding, the gaon included an extensive section wherein he imagined the luxurious material setting of the wedding celebration and how he would "dwell there for the days of the feast (*mishteh*) among friends." An earlier section of the poem describes the patron's material possessions extensively. Hai was familiar with the cultural style of Jewish leadership in the Islamic West and undoubtedly accommodated his portrayal of Yehudah accordingly.[10]

The best way to observe shifts in representation as a function of geography is to consider how an individual panegyrist tailors representations when praising figures in or from different regions. The remainder of this chapter studies modes of portrayal and representations of geography in the panegyrics of Yehudah Halevi[11] and Yehudah al-Ḥarīzī, both of whom praised figures from the Islamic West to the Islamic East as well as in territories along the Christian Mediterranean.

Yehudah Halevi

Yehudah Halevi was a consummate "Mediterranean" figure in that he moved between Muslim and Christian territories in Iberia and then journeyed to the Islamic East (Egypt and probably Palestine). A number of his poems in the strophic *muwashshaḥ* form are dedicated to figures attributed with "dominion" (*misrah*) and make allusions to rituals of power acclamation. One such poem, "Clear a road and pay honor before our king!," is dedicated to Abū al-Ḥasan Meir Ibn Qamniel, a *wazīr* whom Halevi encountered during his early career in Seville. It is one of several poems for the same figure that, taken together, reveal a good deal about the development and vicissitudes of a poet-patron relationship. One was written when the *mamdūḥ* had journeyed to the

Islamic East, and the poet now stresses that "Separation" had "set a burning fire in my body," leading the poet to apostrophize the four winds:

O North Wind, rouse for me a scent that captures souls!
O South Wind, return to me the one who has fled on wings of dreams!
O East Wind, bring him greetings until the moon will be no more!

O West Wind that wafts and fans the flame [of my heart],
blow and answer me, is there any distress like mine? . . .

We shall ascend and cross the sea from Sefarad for a cherub,
Meir, who is flowing myrrh, unique in dominion.[12]

Although Halevi never names a specific place apart from Sefarad (i.e., al-Andalus), physical distance from the *mamdūḥ* inspires the poet's geographic imagination to think beyond the boundaries of his locale. In many ways, the device in this poem prefigures the wind imagery in Halevi's famous poetry for Zion.[13]

"Clear a road and pay honor before our king!" is the most political of Halevi's poems for Ibn Qamniel and may have been written for the day the latter ascended to office.[14] The poem includes a play on Ibn Qamniel's name Meir, meaning "he who illumines," and concludes with a *kharja* in Hispano-Romance, one of the vernacular languages of Jews in the Peninsula:

1. Clear a road[15] and pay honor before our king!

2. The heralding voice runs upon the earth like the running of lightning.
3. The hearts of those who wait for the repairer of the breach[16] rejoice as though they were drinking a goblet [of wine].
4. When his form emits a scent,[17] it is healing for all the maimed.

5. His memory is honeycomb to our mouths; he is our hopes' very desire.

6. His parents called him Meir and ever since then they could not conceal him,

7. for they found him to be a luminary of Truth; his name is like his essence.
8. They raised him at their bosom yet hewed his habitation[18] above the heavenly abode!

9. He peered from behind a lattice and illumined our darkness.

10. At your heels, Israel's straight path is revealed,
11. for your thoughts are [only of] wisdom, generosity, and fear of God.
12. Strengthen the cords and draw the hearts of those who say, "Be willing!"[19]
13. And speak to those that draw after you; speak in order to bless us!

14. The men of our age see your myriads, the host of heaven,
15. each calling before you and your chariots, "I kneel!,"[20]
16. saying in your ears, "Deck yourself with majesty[21] for so were your fathers.

17. They were our princes! You are the *nasi* of God in our midst."

18. O you raised in the bosom of Dominion, drink and delight in her love,
19. Since the day he was created, her necklace was fitting for his neck.
20. She plays a lovely song and so brings relief to her friends:
21. *"Son of foreign lands, you have drunk, now sleep upon my breast!"*[22]

It is likely that "Clear a road" mentions no place name and offers no representation of geography because Ibn Qamniel held claim to local authority only and because poet and addressee were then of the same place. This point is striking in comparison with Halevi's poem to Ibn Qamniel written during their separation, in which a geographic expanse came into view. The specificity of an Andalusian style and an intended local audience are apparent in the Hispano-Romance *kharja*, which would not have been intelligible in the rest of the Arabic-speaking Mediterranean. The language was quite possibly selected over Arabic in this case because the speaker, Dominion, *misrah*, is gendered feminine; in love poems in *muwashshaḥ* form, words placed in the mouths of female beloveds are often rendered in the Romance vernacular, quite possibly pointing to the gendered nature of language distribution in al-Andalus.[23]

In several respects, the political rituals suggested by the poem elicit comparison with the Islamic ceremony of swearing loyalty (*bai'a*): the heralding voice, the acclamations of allegiance, perhaps also Ibn Qamniel's peering from "behind a lattice," for men of power were often shut off from public view. The incipit, "Clear a road" is based on Is 57:14, famously evoked in the New Testament as John the Baptist's herald for Christ (Mt 3:3); here, the verse is directed toward a far more mundane "ruler." Yet allegiance is professed also in the celestial realm, for the hosts of heaven call out "*Avrekh!*" (translated here as "I kneel!"), the word that the Egyptians exclaim before Joseph at the moment of his ascension to power (Gn 41:43). As stated, the occasion of the poem may well have been Ibn Qamniel's ascension to office, though we do not know whether such a poem would have been recited as part of such a ceremony or simply for the occasion more generally. Professions of allegiance and boisterous singing repeat in other poems suggestive of similar occasions.[24]

Ibn Qamniel is portrayed in "Clear a road" as Israel's salvation and healing; the incipit phrase from Isaiah evokes the image of deliverer. His merits include wisdom, generosity, and fear of God. These traits are often at the center of Arabic panegyric poetry as well. The other focal point is Ibn Qamniel's lineage; the poem mentions his parents, "who raised him at their bosom," and his forebears, "our princes" (*nesikheinu*).

Ibn Qamniel is called a *nasi*, a term often reserved for one who traces his descent from King David.[25] In a recent book, Arnold Franklin demonstrates that Jews in the Islamic East were preoccupied with claims of Davidic descent, which emerged or intensified as a form of political capital that paralleled Muslim claims of descent from Muḥammad's noble family, the *ahl al-bayt*.[26] While there was certainly no guarantee that a *nasi* would rise to power, members of this family line held a claim that others did not. Franklin also calls attention to regional variation in the usage or emphasis of the term *nasi*. In Christian Europe, "the functional aspect of the title, signifying succession to a recognized office of authority, was brought to the foreground and transferred to new types of communal leadership, while the implied genealogical ties to David, which became so important in the East, tended to recede into the background."[27] Franklin also points out that Abraham Ibn Dā'ūd gives a "muted role to the scions of the royal line" when recounting the Andalusian myth of origins.[28]

What can we say about the term *nasi* in al-Andalus during the late eleventh and early twelfth century and Halevi's usage of it in this poem? First, it is possible that Halevi did not intend any association with the Davidic family. In the Bible, *nasi* can refer to a leader in the general sense prior to the rise of David (Nm 3:32, 16:2). Before Halevi, Shelomoh Ibn Gabirol praised Yequtiel Ibn Ḥasan with the terms *nasi* and *nagid* interchangeably; he was "the one who arose in the place of the three shepherds" (Moses, Aaron, and Miriam) but not as a replacement, let alone a descendant, of King David.[29] Mosheh Ibn Ezra used *nesi 'arav* to refer to a Muslim leader.[30] Further, among Jews in Christian Iberia, *nasi* seems to be the Hebrew appellation given to the rank titled *wazīr* in Arabic (irrespective of Davidic claims); this practice may have been carried over from al-Andalus.[31]

Avraham Ibn Ezra, writing in the twelfth century, identifies the "House of David" as a "great and powerful family in Baghdad"; hence David's descendants do not seem particularly prominent in the Islamic West.[32] However, Franklin and others have pointed out that members of the Davidic family had moved westward, even unto al-Andalus, by the tenth century.[33] Ibn Dā'ūd describes Ḥiyya Ben al-Dā'ūdī, who died in Castile in 1154, as "the last renowned person of the House of David" in Sefarad.[34] Yehudah Halevi concluded his praise for an unidentified leader from the East who had come to reside in al-Andalus: "Sefarad [al-Andalus] boasts over Shinar [Iraq] because of you, and through your name *nasi*s are blessed."[35] Halevi was probably careful about how he used the word *nasi* when addressing a migrant from the East and hence we might assume that this addressee claimed Davidic descent. But even still, in such a case Davidic ancestry is not emphasized as the foremost aspect of legitimacy.

To know with certainty when *nasi* is used in the general sense of "leader" and when in the specific sense of "Davidic dynast" is admittedly difficult.[36] The ambiguity of the term obtains in the case of Ibn Qamniel. Lineage is certainly a recurring motif in Halevi's panegyrics for him; regarding those who are astounded at Ibn Qamniel's wisdom despite his youth, Halevi wrote: "Had they known his fathers, they would say that [wisdom] is a quality that passes from father to son. / The honor of his fathers is a fitting crown for him just as the headdress was fitting for the head of Aaron."[37] But the type of lineage that is emphasized here is rather general and does not stress a progenitor from a distant past. By way of contrast, an unpublished, beautifully calligraphed, panegyric preserved in the Geniza and dated 1146 (a few years after

Figure 9. Panegyric for Abū Saʿīd al-Dāʾūdī. TS 10 J 22.3v. Reproduced by kind permission of the Syndics of Cambridge University Library.

Halevi's death) praises Abū Sa'īd al-Dā'ūdī, whose relational name (*nisba*) clearly attests to a Davidic claim (TS 10 J 22.3v; Figure 9):

> [He is] of the nation and crown of the *nasis*, majesty of all the fearing,
> associated by lineage to the father of the house of kingship
> and the dynasty of those selected as *nagids*.
> He is distinguished among the most eminent, for he is a lion while they are wild beasts. He is beautiful among the children of Adam and Eve and one who fears the Creator of created things,
> anointed in the oils of wisdom like the Messiah whom the prophets anointed.[38]

Further, insofar as Halevi may have included Davidic descent as a quality worth praising, this does not require that the poet viewed such status as a unique or ultimate claim to authority. That this was not the case is suggested by a panegyric for the well-known rabbinic scholar Yosef Ibn Migash; Halevi stresses the *mamdūḥ*'s lineage as the "seed of Moses and Aaron" and concludes: "Through him *nasis* are blessed and seek the status of lineage by associating (*yityaḥasu*) with his family."[39] The poem thus gives weight to lineage of noble stock yet gives no particular precedence for descent through David.

The movement of *nasis* from the Islamic East to the Islamic West may well have challenged existing power structures in al-Andalus, where those who claimed authority usually bore names such as Hakohen (the priest) or Halevi (the Levite).[40] This is not to say that Andalusians did not respect lineage, including lineage from David, or that they valued individual merit over bloodlines. It seems that the status of a *nasi* was given weight, but no greater weight than other claims of legitimacy. Panegyrists generally worked with the material they had; if an addressee claimed status as a Davidic dynast, the poet would praise him as such, just as he might praise the Levitic descent of one who bore the family name Halevi. The "muted role given to scions of the royal line" that becomes apparent in Christian Europe in the late twelfth century may already be present earlier in the Islamic West. Arguably, the multivalent usage of the term *nasi* in al-Andalus is indicative of this neutralized status.

Sometime after 1090, Halevi migrated to Christian Iberia, to the kingdom of Castile, and there he praised Jewish figures associated with the court of Toledo, among them Alfonso VI's doctor Yosef Ibn Feruzziel.[41] Apparently, the Jewish courtier had appeared in *Wādī al-ḥijāra* (Guadalajara), at the time under Christian control, for the place name is mentioned explicitly in the Hispano-Romance conclusion to one poem. Place comes into view because neither the poet nor the *mamdūḥ* was from the city. The poem associates the *mamdūḥ* with several biblical political figures: his namesake Joseph, Moses, and David. Brilliantly, the poet ties the place name *Wādī al-ḥijāra*, literally the "Wadi of Stones," with David, for it was at a riverbed that David picked up "five smooth stones" to fight Goliath (1 Sm 17:40). The poem opens with a ceremonial setting: "When the people's chiefs assemble, kings in their counsel, they all praise Yosef for he is the source of their honor." Yosef is called the man "full of God's glory, who stands among the myrtles . . . [whose] roar terrifies princes." The poem builds to pronouncements of acclamation and concludes with a *kharja* in Hispano-Romance:

21. Rivers of oil flood the wadi of stones[42]
22. when the lord who nurses God's people[43] with delights is heralded:
23. "May the prince live! And say, Amen!" And they broke out in song:

24. *"Whence does my master come? Such glad tidings!*
25. *It is as if a ray of sunlight appears in Wādī al-ḥijāra."*[44]

Verse 21 cleverly brings together two stages of David's life: the brave boy who slew Israel's enemy; and the mature anointed king. As stated, David is but one of several political figures evoked, and the poem makes no claims of the *mamdūḥ*'s descent from the king. More obscure is the reference to his being the man "who stands among the myrtles," which alludes to the angelic being that appears to the prophet Zechariah (Zec 1:8). Yet the word "myrtles" here is likely code for the Andalusian-style elite dwelling in Christian Iberia. Once a fixture of the Andalusian garden, the myrtle had become in Christian Iberia a metonym that symbolized Andalusian culture itself. Similarly, Mosheh Ibn Ezra referred to his circle of estranged friends ("men of culture," or *ahl al-adab*) among the less sophisticated Jews of the Christian north: "among them we are like myrtles among the trees of the forest, our leaves withering."[45] With this reference, along with the insertion of the Hispano-Romance dialect, Halevi marks this poem as highly particular to the context of Christian Iberia.

Famously, Halevi departed the Iberian Peninsula in 1140 to make pilgrimage to Palestine, en route disembarking at Alexandria and residing in

Cairo for a period. He wrote panegyrics for several Egyptian dignitaries, the most illustrious of whom was Shemuel Ben Ḥananiah, who held the title of *nagid*.[46] Among Halevi's four surviving panegyrics dedicated to this figure is the following *muwashshaḥ*:[47]

1. [Shouts of] "Grace, grace!" unto him who tends his vineyard, who fences in its vine at the time of planting.[48]
2. His name is Shemuel, for God appointed him to bear the shield of His salvation.[49]
3. They sounded[50] loud cymbals for his name, his reputation was heard in all the earth.
4. A *nagid* who seeks his people's welfare and pronounces peace for all his seed.[51]

5. A righteous man who rules over men, who rules with the fear of God.[52]
6. He came to strengthen himself through God and so he was taken aloft;
7. the holy [angels] brought him into their inner circle, and so he stood in the counsel of the shining ones.
8. Then his enemies were weakened and prophets and seers counseled together.

9. The Lord his God is with him; He is his fortress and rock.[53]

10. The day he arose as the prince of princes, people from afar set their faces [on him].[54]
11. They did not believe what was said until they beheld with their own eyes.
12. They reaped a hundredfold[55] because of what their ears heard.
13. They all appointed him prince[56] to rule over them and their children.

14. May God prolong dominion upon his shoulder[57] and choose rulers from among his seed.

15. Canaan envies Miṣrayim because it is illumined by the light of his face;

16. Shinar studies his ways and beseeches Majestic Full of Light
17. to behold the king who stands above the waters of the Nile.
18. Sefarad joins them to measure the extent [of his greatness].[58]

19. Perhaps [Sefarad] will be a treading ground for his footsteps, a treading ground for Pharaoh's chariots.

20. Ariel proclaimed, "This is my king whom I have awaited like dew!
21. I have accepted him as chieftain and prince to teach justice to Israel![59]
22. He called his name Shemuel because I asked the Lord for him.[60]
23. He has not withheld from me a redeemer so that my enemy cannot say, 'I have overcome him.'"

24. May He make peace above and grant kindness to David and his seed.

Halevi was likely still in Iberia when he wrote this, since verse 19 seems to invite the *mamdūḥ* to visit. The imagined geography presented in lines 15–18 is both expansive and ordered; Iraq (Shinar), Palestine (Canaan), and al-Andalus (Sefarad) all focus their gaze upon Egypt (Miṣrayim) because of the "king who stands above the waters of the Nile." By comparison, "When the people's chiefs assemble" mentions only Guadalajara, and "Clear a road" makes no reference to place name at all. The geographic representation in "Grace, grace" is likely a function of the magnitude of its addressee and the fact that it was composed by an Andalusian for an Egyptian. The expanse includes the Islamic East (*al-mashriq*) and the Islamic West (*al-maghrib*) and betrays a spatial ordering that is largely the opposite of what had traditionally been the intellectual and legal hierarchy of the Jewish world. Iraq and Palestine were generally seen as the main "centers" upon which those in Egypt and al-Andalus gazed. The relatively minor status of al-Andalus is preserved in that it "joins" the great centers of Iraq and Palestine and is mentioned only after them, while the status of Egypt is greatly augmented. However, this does not signify a reversal in power relations in the twelfth century so much as a hyperbolic representation of the Nagid's status.[61]

As with the previous poem, "Grace, grace" evokes rituals of acclamation, and it is conceivable that it was written for Ben Ḥananiah's initiation to the office of Nagid (probably around 1140).[62] The poem refers to the "day he arose as prince," when "they all appointed him prince to rule over them." Line 10 also refers to a gesture of loyalty; cf. 1 Kgs 2:15, "all Israel set their faces on me, that I should reign."[63] The ritual is further dramatized with a personified Israel (and specifically, Ariel, i.e., Jerusalem; cf. Is 29:1) taking an oath of allegiance: "I have accepted him as chieftain and prince." As with the other poems, these elements are highly reminiscent of the *bai'a* ceremony of caliphal acclamation.

Although Ben Ḥananiah is not called a *nasi* explicitly in this poem (he is called *sar ha-sarim* and, of course, *nagid*), Brody and Mann rightly pointed out that the emphasis on David's seed in the concluding verse suggests that Ben Ḥananiah emanated from a Davidic family. Here, the poet not only looks backward toward Davidic origins but forward toward future leaders from the same line and possibly even the Davidic Messiah. Lineage recurs as a central motif throughout Halevi's panegyrics for Ben Ḥananiah, sometimes centering on the expression *noḥel u-manḥil*, "one who inherits and passes on an inheritance."[64] The phrase itself derives from rabbinic literature (e.g., b. Baba Batra 142a), where it applies to the inheritance of property, but is employed in panegyric writing to describe the rightful transfer of power from father to son.[65] Although the interest in lineage is not exclusive for Davidic scions, it seems to amplify the claims of rightful "rule" in the case of Ben Ḥananiah.

Unsurprisingly, the poem draws heavily upon Davidic imagery, especially in describing Ben Ḥananiah as a "righteous man who rules over men, who rules with the fear of God" (2 Sm 23:3). Although David is only one political figure of Israel's past to be evoked, alongside Samuel, Mordechai, and Moses (lines 4, 21, 22), David occupies a place in this poem that the other figures do not; he is evoked further in lines 2 and 9, and, in line 14, the poet entwines the Davidic imagery with messianic expectation through a well-known reference to Is 9:5. Halevi hopes that God will "choose rulers from among his seed" and concludes with blessings for "David and his seed." Further, although David serves as an archetypal ruler in a number of Halevi's panegyrics, this poem stresses Davidic descent as a matter of political capital in the present. Messianism, with specific reference to the Davidic line, is evoked explicitly in other panegyrics by Halevi for Ben Ḥananiah. In the conclusion to one, Halevi addresses Israel: "Shemuel has arisen and David comes[66] after him! You will be tranquil as you were in days of old." By "David," Halevi likely intended a Messiah of Davidic stock.[67]

By comparison, there is a general absence of the messianic motif in Halevi's panegyrics for Iberian figures despite the fact that many of his liturgical poems dwell on messianic themes. Should the motif's inclusion in panegyrics for an Eastern figure be viewed as a function of the poet's age, that redemption became more pressing for the poet as his life progressed? Was messianic expectation emphasized in the panegyrics for Ben Ḥananiah because of the Davidic claims of the addressee? Or does the distinction reflect different conventions among Andalusian and Egyptian audiences? In general, the inclusion of messianic expectation within panegyric seems more a fixture of Hebrew writing from the Islamic East than from the Islamic West.[68] Although Halevi was probably unaware of Aristotle's prescription in the *Rhetoric*, it seems that he accommodated his praise to fit the expectations of *mamdūḥ*s and audiences within the several regions of the Mediterranean.

Yehudah al-Ḥarīzī

More than half a century after the death of Halevi, the same basic regional dynamics remain apparent in the works of Yehudah al-Ḥarīzī, who was born in Toledo (then under Christian control), was identifiable as a *maghribī*, and traveled widely in the Islamic East and some territories along the Christian Mediterranean. He went as far as Baghdad and ultimately settled in Aleppo, where he died. His writings survive in Hebrew, Judeo-Arabic, and Arabic.[69] Virtually all of al-Ḥarīzī's works, irrespective of language, contain large amounts of panegyric, in dedications, integrated into narratives, or as freestanding works. He praised an extraordinary number of individuals of different social varieties and often peppered depictions with the specific: the physical beauty of a young man; a musician who "rouses the strings of the oud (*kinor*) to sing like Levi when serving in the Levitic office"; for a doctor from Aleppo who is called "the tree of wisdom whose fruit is food yet its leaves are for healing," al-Ḥarīzī added: "And Pinḥas arose and executed judgment and so the plague came to an end" (cf. Ps 106:30). In praising Avraham the son of Mosheh Maimonides in a bilingual poem, al-Ḥarīzī drew upon key Arabic philosophical vocabulary (Judeo-Arabic in italics): "The ideas of the intelligent are like the precious spheres / *but his Active Intellect (ʿaqluhu al-faʿāl) encompasses them.*"[70]

Al-Ḥarīzī also praised the same figures in different works such that depictions modulate both as a function of time and of language.[71] In Hebrew, Menaḥem Ben Yiṣḥaq of Fustat is praised in al-Ḥarīzī's earliest dedication as rather generically generous. A later Hebrew dedication is rhetorically more elaborate: "My tongue is too short to praise him; if it spanned from sea to sea its praise would remain at the Nile; he is the benefactor of his generation, merciful to every petitioner; he gives from the blood of his heart and the heart rejoices. . . . Beholding his face is like seeing the face of God (cf. Gn 33:10)."[72]

But in Arabic, Menaḥem's generosity and lineage are mediated through pre-Islamic imagery and figures: "When he undertook generosity and kindness, one would forget the memory of Ḥātim!," referring to Ḥātim Ibn al-Ṭā'ī, proverbial for generosity. Menaḥem's fathers are like "a lion roaring in al-Sharā," a desert pass in Arabia known for the fierceness of its lions, a place neither author nor *mamdūḥ* would ever visit.[73]

Al-Ḥarīzī occasionally integrated praise through the narrative strategy of setting it within the mouth of a fictional character.[74] In "Iggeret leshon ha-zahav" (Epistle of the golden tongue, i.e., Hebrew), the wondrous mistress whom the narrator encounters reveals herself to be, "the Golden Tongue, whom God loves eternally, by way of [whom] ministers rule. . . . Of all the patrons of the world and all the ministers of the earth, I choose the elect of God, the respected minister master Shemuel. . . . I am his handmaiden and he is my king. He is the right-hand pillar who dwells in the tribe of Taḥkemoni, . . . the flame of the pure *menorah*, his face the *menorah*'s cups."[75] The portrayal revolves around wisdom and generosity and exploits the *menorah* as a symbol of sovereignty.

The same technique of narrative insertion is used in one version of al-Ḥarīzī's famous *Book of Taḥkemoni*, a work that the author rededicated to numerous patrons throughout his career and within which he praised tens of individuals from Toledo to Baghdad. In the first chapter, the author decries the sad state of patronage in his day. Another man (who ultimately turns out to be the collection's protagonist Ḥever ha-Qeni) encourages al-Ḥarīzī to undertake composition and not to "uproot a succulent garden on account of thorns like briars." He continues:

> and if you seek a lord with whose praise you might esteem your book . . . behold I saw a son of Yishai [Jesse] to whom kings bring a gift, upon him is the glory of sovereignty for an eternal covenant is preserved and set for him. On the day he was born, God heralded from His height before His people, "Behold, a son is born to the House of David, Yoshiahu is his name, and dominion shall be upon his shoulder! . . . The key of the House of David is upon his shoulder."
>
> Rule (*nesi'ut*) was created as a helpmate for him;
> the image of preciousness was created in his image.
> He set his spirit in the corpses of praise
> so much that one bone joined another.[76]

Already, it is clear that this *mamdūḥ*, whom we know to be Yoshiahu Ben Yishai of Damascus, is a great *nasi* who claimed descent from the House of David. The portrayal includes wisdom, generosity, and other qualities, but the preoccupation of this massive dedication (fifty-eight lines) is entirely on Davidic lineage. The poetry and prose go on to evoke several other biblical verses associated with David and the expected Messiah (Is 9:6; Mi 5:1) and also include a genealogy of fifteen named progenitors linking this *nasi* "directly" with the biblical king. The author cites praise of this *mamdūḥ* as the very purpose of composing the book, which is quite different from the protonationalist claims that al-Ḥarīzī makes elsewhere.[77]

Al-Ḥarīzī was fully attuned to the proper means of praising a Davidic *nasi* and refrained from applying the title to non-Davidic leaders in writing for patrons in the East. In fact, he dedicates the very same verses predicated of Ben Yishai ("Rule [*nesi'ut*] was created . . . one bone to another") to Mosheh Bar Ṣedaqa, a doctor and non-Davidic communal leader in Damascus, simply by replacing the word "rule" (*nesi'ut*) with "dominion" (*u-misrah*).[78] Al-Ḥarīzī undoubtedly sensed that the word *nesi'ut* could be misleading when writing for patrons in Damascus. Conversely, when praising figures in Iberia and Provence, he uses the title *nasi* with greater versatility. In praising the "nasi Rav Makhir," he wrote (with a double wordplay on *nasi*), "he eclipses the (Davidic) *nasi*s with his virtues and shames the clouds (*nesi'im*; lit., "vapors") with his generosity," which suggests that this *nasi* was not of Davidic descent.[79]

In praising figures from Provence, generally patrons of his works, the author focused almost exclusively on moral virtues and learning, particularly of Bible and rabbinic works. For the patrons of his translation of Maimonides' commentary on the first order of the Mishnah (*Zera'im*, Seeds), he wrote:

> Through Torah they turn darkness into light; if [Torah] were a *menorah*, they would be its cups.
> Herewith I present to the lofty ones, the shining lights, the priests of God, this gift of Seeds.

Al-Ḥarīzī frequently played on *mamdūḥs*' geographical associations. To David, Nagid of Yemen, he included, "Awaken, North wind, and come O South (*Teiman*)! Bring greetings to our lord, the Nagid, from a slave of his slaves who . . . came from the highlands of Sefarad and dwells in the land of Nod exiled and alone."[80] In Judeo-Arabic, he praised Daniel al-Baghdadi, who was "among the people of knowledge and virtue and the masters of faith and intelligence," then in Damascus, "His virtues are beautiful without my praise in the way a tender girl is more beautiful without ornament. / One who is glorified with Eastern majesty has no need of Western praise."[81]

In Jerusalem, al-Ḥarīzī recognized three distinct communities: the "Ashkelonim," by which he meant natives from the Levant (*al-shām*); the "Ṣarefatim," the French; and the "Ma'aravim," the *maghribīs*. The individuals selected from the first two groups are praised generally for religious wisdom. Interestingly, he lamented two "French" brothers in Judeo-Arabic, a language that the deceased may well not have understood; for one, the poet wishes that God will "water his tomb because of his augustness," a ubiquitous phrase in Arabic elegy, and waxes rhetorically: "Morning and night the Revelation (*al-shar'*, i.e., the Torah) weeps for him."[82] But still, the depictions focus exclusively on moral uprightness and religious learning. In contrast, he describes Eliahu ha-Ma'aravi, a *maghribī* he met in Palestine, as one "who possessed knowledge and culture (*'ilm wa adab*), partly inherited (*mawrūth*) and partly acquired (*muktasab*)."[83]

For al-Ḥarīzī, possessing *adab* was the highest cultural ideal, one that signified continuity with the Andalusian past. Throughout his travels, he sought but seldom found Eastern Jews who cultivated this quality, and the author took particular delight when it surfaced among the Jews of Fustat ("possessing characteristics of *adab*") and Cairo ("possessing individuals with *adab*").[84] Although *adab* was a quality that al-Ḥarīzī associated primarily with the West, finding and nurturing this ideal in the East was a key part of his intellectual and cultural vision.

CHAPTER 5

"A Word Aptly Spoken": The Ethics of Praise

Although it is obvious that praise was far more acceptable during the medieval period than it is in our own day, in which it is generally limited to funerals and a few other occasions—and even then, with little hyperbolic embellishment—this does not mean that uttering praise was without its ethical baggage or detractors.[1] Already in Aristotle's *Nicomachean Ethics*, praise is the subject of some reflection; the praiseworthy man should not speak about himself or others, "since he cares not to be praised nor for others to be blamed."[2] Among Muslim authors, al-Ghazzālī includes praise (*al-madḥ*) as one of the more dangerous categories of harmful speech in the *Iḥyā' 'ulūm al-dīn* (Revival of the religious sciences) and systematically divides potential harms into those that might befall the panegyrist (*al-mādiḥ*) or the *mamdūḥ*. The panegyrist might exaggerate to the point of lying, become a hypocrite by presenting love when feeling scorn, make statements that he cannot verify, or bring delight to a tyrannical or iniquitous *mamdūḥ*; the *mamdūḥ* might succumb to haughtiness or moral laxity.[3]

There is no systematic treatment by a medieval Jewish author that explores the ethics of praise in all its aspects, yet a good deal can be gleaned from comments in a variety of genres. The ethical misgivings surrounding the culture of praise were several, from the worldly desires of fame-seeking *mamdūḥ*s, to the sincerity of the person rendering the praise (especially when money was involved), the potential falsehood of poetic statements themselves, and the problem of praising men when, theologically speaking, all praise was properly due to God. This chapter considers some of the qualms about panegyric composition in Jewish writing and the ways in which authors tried to navigate or overcome the ethical concerns. The figures treated include Sa'adia Gaon, Baḥya Ibn Paquda, Yehudah Halevi, Mosheh Ibn Ezra, and Maimonides. The discussion falls into six main sections: (1) the general permissibility of praise; (2) the critique that praise, as a vehicle of worldly prestige, should not be sought; (3) the theological difficulty of rendering praise to men instead of to God; (4) the gross offenses of poetic plagiarism and the recycling of praise; (5) the problems surrounding poetry for pay; and (6) authorial sincerity and lying in poetry. Some of these questions are bound up intimately with the poetics of panegyric, especially its hyperbolic and intertextual elements, topics that will be touched on briefly here and will be developed further in following chapters.

The Permissibility of Praise

Occasionally, modern scholars have inaccurately ascribed opposition to the practice of panegyric among medieval Jewish figures. One text that Schirmann adduced in this regard is a curriculum of study written by Yosef Ibn 'Aqnīn (c. 1160–1226) from the Judeo-Arabic treatise *Ṭibb al-nufūs* (Healing for souls). Using standard genre divisions of Arabic poetry, Ibn 'Aqnīn prescribes that children between the ages of ten and fifteen should study Hebrew poetry, recommending poems of asceticism (*zuhdiyyāt*), in particular, but proscribes genres that might inculcate negative traits such as invective (*ahājī*) and the "praise of ignoble values" (*madḥ akhlāq radhīla*). Whereas Schirmann reads this as a broad ban on panegyric, I would suggest that it might prohibit praise for intoxication or sexual passion but not the generosity, wisdom, and eloquence of a *mamdūḥ*.[4]

For most medieval Jewish authors, the practice of praising men, at least within certain constraints, was seen as permissible or even meritorious. To begin, no writer doubts that recounting the deeds of great men of the past is desirable, though this is obviously not identical with the direct praise of contemporaries. In the introduction to his Judeo-Arabic Bible commentary, for example, Sa'adia Gaon writes that one of the reasons for which the Torah recounts the stories of Israel's forebears is to exemplify behavior so that one might be "diffident like Adam, beneficent like Abraham, forgiving like Isaac, compassionate like Jacob, one who repays wickedness with kindness like Joseph, zealous[5] for God like Pinḥas, patient like Aaron, humble like Moses, inspiring like Joshua, and all other practices that possess praiseworthy virtues (*akhlāq maḥmūda*). [The Torah] only recounted them for the sake of man's edification (*li-ta'adīb al-insān*)."[6]

Sa'adia extends this logic to the direct praise of contemporaries in his commentary on Prv 27:2: "Let another man praise you, not with your own mouth; a stranger, not with your own lips." Sa'adia glosses: "It is prohibited for a man to praise himself, but despite this it is not required that he prevent men from praising him. Rather, [Solomon] made it an intermediate state (*ḥāl mutawaṣiṭa*) so that no one will think that prohibiting praise altogether is more sound (*aṣlaḥ*) or that [prohibiting praise] is a component of humility (*al-khushū'*), for a friend's or another's saying [praise] is proper because it rouses in others a desire for pious behavior."[7] One imagines that there was a link in Sa'adia's mind between recounting the deeds of noble ancestors and the practice of praising contemporary men.

A different concern is expressed by Mosheh Ibn Ezra, who commented at length about the ideal moral posture of the poet. Ross Brann has called attention to Ibn Ezra's remorse over his "ignoble use of language" and "thematic indiscretions," what Ibn Ezra himself identifies as youthful flights of "amorous verse, some diversions, or *muwashaḥāt*. . . . I ask God's forgiveness for them."[8] In another autobiographical passage, Ibn Ezra expresses regret for having used poetry for self-aggrandizement, "In the days of my youth and times of my early life, I considered poetry something to boast over (*min al-mafākhir*) and considered it among the instruments of glorification (*min jumlat adawāt al-ma'āthir*); then I rejected it and desisted from it the way a gazelle flees its shadow and aspired to spend the rest of my life [doing] worthier things."[9]

Thus, a poet should not exploit his ability to gain worldly recognition, and the fact that composition brought Ibn Ezra so much glory led him to refrain from it entirely, at least for a time. However, his autobiographical musings continue: "I did not desist entirely from reciting poetry when the need arose. . . . Of my poems, men possess upward of six thousand verses pertaining to different subjects and various poetic themes. Among them are numerous words concerning the praise (*taqrīẓ*) of my brethren and confidants, eulogies over my close ones and dear ones."[10]

Notably, Ibn Ezra never identifies panegyric specifically as an offending or morally compromising genre. He continued to celebrate poetry precisely because it allowed the "great acts of the noble to become immortal" like an "engraving on stone."[11] Elsewhere, Ibn Ezra admits that he "exceeded bounds" (*afraṭtu*) in praise and invective, but this is a critique of a poetic technique, not a blanket rejection of the panegyric genre (further, see Chapter 6).[12] To be sure, for Ibn Ezra there were ethical guidelines involved in any sort of poetic composition; in addition to not exploiting poetry for self-glorification, there were further concerns surrounding the problems of poetry for pay, truth and falsity, and, as stated, the limits of hyperbole. But when executed within proper parameters, panegyric remained customary, necessary, and essentially ethical. Ibn Ezra may have abandoned some things in exchange for "worthier things," but at least some of the latter were still of this world.

In Maimonides' writing, the praise of contemporary men holds a somewhat ambivalent place but finds general approval. In his Judeo-Arabic commentary on m. Avot, Maimonides favors the praise of virtuous men because it can inspire others to emulate them. In the introductory overview, he writes that people should speak only on topics conducive to the welfare of the body and soul, whether his words concern "praise of virtue or of a virtuous man, or with blame of vice or an ignoble person." The Bible's censure of the Sodomites and other ignoble persons and "praise and magnification of those possessing virtue" (*madḥ al-akhyār wa taʿaẓīmuhum*) exist so that people will "follow the path of [the righteous] and avoid the path [of the wicked]."[13] Similarly, Maimonides expands the adage "Nothing is better than silence" (Avot 1:16) into a full-blown discussion of five categories of speech, which he arranges from the obligatory to the prohibited (according to the fivefold categorization of Islamic jurisprudence).[14] In the category of meritorious speech, he includes speech in praise of the intellectual and ethical virtues, which he extends to the praise of virtuous men: "[Meritorious speech] is discourse that moves the soul toward these virtues by speech and poetry and restrains it from vices the same way. It is to praise virtuous persons and to extol their virtues, so that their conduct will appear good to people, so that they will follow their way."[15] There is no indication that this praise should only be applied to men of the biblical past. Thus, for Maimonides, there is really nothing wrong with praise, which should have the benefit of goading others toward ethical behavior, as long as one does not grow accustomed to offering flatteries for personal gain.[16]

Maimonides recognizes, however, that praise can sometimes have unintended, deleterious effects. In a discussion of "gossip" (*lashon ha-raʿ*) in his commentary on Avot, he cites an anecdote that suggests that speech intended as praise can constitute inadvertent blame: "One of the wise praised the handwriting of a scribe (*kātib*) who had presented [his writing] in a large assembly (*majlis kabīr*). The master (*ustādh*) [of the assembly] censured him for praising the handwriting of this scribe and said to him, 'This is all gossip (*lashon ha-raʿ*). By praising him in public you are bringing blame upon him, for there are among [the assembled] those who love him but others who loathe him. When those who loathe him [hear the praise], they must mention his deficiencies [as well].'"[17]

Maimonides' source for the anecdote was probably b. Baba Batra 164b; what is interesting is the way in which he transforms the setting into a contemporary *majlis kabīr* with a *kātib* and an *ustādh*; Maimonides' version sounds like an Arabic literary anecdote.[18] Maimonides further recounts an anecdote that he encountered in *The Book of Moral Qualities* (*Kitāb al-akhlāq*) concerning a man who almost never spoke; when asked about his practice, the man explained that speech divides into four categories: that which has no benefit, that which brings benefit but also harm, that which neither benefits nor harms, and that which brings true benefit only. The second category is illustrated by "praise of a man (*madḥ insān*) in order to seek benefit from him," for it brings the one praised pleasure but rouses his enemies to harm him. Ideally, the speaker should abandon praise for the sake of avoiding harm.[19]

Maimonides' strongest reservations toward praise are limited to his well-known discussion of pedagogy in the commentary on m. Ḥeleq, though even here he notes that the pursuit of praise might motivate one to study. Recognizing that students at most stages of development will not pursue knowledge for its own sake, he recommends that the teacher encourage him with more tangible things. The child may be urged to read with incentives of "nuts," later "clothes," and then "money." When these are no longer enough, the mediating substitute can be the pursuit of worldly glory: "Although it is reprehensible (*madhmūm*), a teacher, if necessary to get someone to study, can say, 'Read so that you may become a master (*rav*) and judge and so that your name will become great during your lifetime and after your death such as So-and-So (*fulān wa fulān*),' so that [the student] reads and strives to be rewarded with this rank, his goal being people's magnification, aggrandizement, and praise (*ta'ẓīm, ijlāl, thanā'*)."[20]

Here Maimonides cites the famous adage that one should "not make [words of Torah] a crown by which to magnify oneself (*'atarah le-hitgaddel bahem*) nor a spade to dig with" (m. Avot 4:5). The practice is thus "reprehensible" for it enables the student to misuse Torah study as a tool for self-aggrandizement. Still, there is no blanket condemnation of magnifying or praising, per se, just as there is no condemnation of nuts or clothing; these simply should not be the goal of Torah study. The practice under scrutiny is permitted, for it is preferable to the alternative, the neglect of study. At the very least, the pursuit and attainment of glory and the act of praising seem perfectly normative. We know that Maimonides was the recipient of a good deal of panegyric himself and that he seems to have accepted it graciously.

A Pietist's Reservations

The association of praise with worldly prestige and the pursuit of renown naturally opened up the practice to broad criticism. As a semi-ascetic pietist with Sufi leanings, Baḥya Ibn Paquda was concerned with resisting the entrapments of the world. In his *Hidāya ilā farā'iḍ al-qulūb* (Direction to the duties of the heart), he divided these entrapments into two categories: (1) pleasures pertaining to the body, such as eating, drinking, and sexual intercourse; and (2) love of rule, nobility, pride, eminence, arrogance, and haughtiness. For Ibn Paquda, praise was an enabling device for the attainment of the second category. As pointed out by Bezalel Safran, Baḥya went so far as to call a person whose kind actions are motivated only by a desire to acquire "praise from men and their respect in this world" (*al-thanā' min al-nās wa-karāmatahum fī al-duny*ā) guilty of "secret polytheism" (*al-shirk al-khafī*). What Baḥya seems to mean is that such men mistakenly view themselves as bestowers of benefit and fail to recognize that all benefit derives from God; hence they see themselves as sharing or "partnering" in God's work, which is the very definition of polytheism in Islam (*shirk*; lit., "partnership"). The ideal man who "relies upon God" does not take pleasure in the "praise of men." Further, Baḥya excoriates "the groups of men . . . who love prestige (*al-karāma*) from among people and seek the spread of their renown (*nashr al-dhikr*) among the people" and warns the reader against pursuing the same. Undoubtedly, he had contemporary figures among Andalusian Jews in mind. Praise is implicated as a vehicle for the promotion of worldly prestige, itself seen as the antithesis of piety, and thus has a degenerative social effect.[21]

Further, in the fifth part of *Duties of the Heart*, Ibn Paquda rehearses a set of stratagems that the "evil inclination" uses to entice the souls of the pious and how the pious should respond. One of "his" enticements preys upon man's "love of praise and eulogy in this world" (*ḥubb al-madḥ wa'l-thanā' fi'l-dunyā*). The evil inclination argues by way of biblical prooftexts that God rewards the righteous with a good name and, moreover, that other men will learn through his deeds, the latter being the dominant justification for praise we have encountered. To this, the pietist should reply that this praise will bring no benefit when one realizes his shortcomings in religious matters.[22]

Also, when enumerating the qualities by which a truly humble person can be recognized, Ibn Paquda includes the man "who, when one offering praise praises him (*mādiḥ madaḥahu*) for some good he has performed, cuts off the one offering praise." This is proper because the humble man fears that whatever he has accomplished is insufficient in comparison with what God wants from him. Moreover, the humble man should say to one praising him, "Enough, brother! This [good deed] in comparison with my sins is like an ember of fire in the ocean!" And when one is praised falsely, all the more so he should press the one offering praise to desist.[23] While Baḥya may not have judged praise prohibited in the strictly legal sense, he clearly disagreed with Sa'adia, for whom the Book of Proverbs posited that praise was a permitted "intermediate state" that did not negate the cultivation of humility. The two thinkers were participating in the same discussion about the place of praise in Jewish society within the Islamic milieu.

Stealing from God

It is well known that Yehudah Halevi expressed various concerns dealing with the composition of Hebrew poetry according to the meters of Arabic poetry. He renounces the practice, or at least deems it inferior, in two works: one in his own voice in the *Treatise on Hebrew Meters*; and one through the voice of a fictitious Jewish scholar in the *Kuzari*. In both works, the crux of the issue is a prosodic one—namely, the use of Arabized quantitative meter over the nonquantitative meter of indigenous Hebrew verse. In the *Treatise on Hebrew Meters*, the concern is largely aesthetic. As Ross Brann points out, Halevi functions here both as "teacher and critic" in that he disparages Arabized Hebrew poetry as inferior to poetry composed in Hebrew's natural meter but still provides examples of Arabized Hebrew verses as his patron, Ḥalfon Ben Natanel ha-Levi, had requested. As Brann writes, "despite the general suggested ban, he carefully outlines which [meters] are more preferable to others." There is no hint here that panegyric is ethically compromising as a genre; in fact, each of the original epigrams composed to exemplify the twelve quantitative meters contains a wordplay on the root of the patron's name *ḥlf*—a device that serves as a type of dedication—and several of the examples are panegyrics. Thus, even as the work criticizes the prosody of Arabized Hebrew verse, it participates in the cultural practices of Arabized Jews, including the composition of panegyric in honor of a *mamdūḥ*.[24]

Halevi's later work, the *Kuzari*, includes, as Brann has shown, a far more extensive and ethically oriented discussion of Arabized Hebrew verse.[25] Here, the beauty of meter should be sacrificed for a "higher and more beneficial virtue"—namely, the accurate transmission of ideas. In Halevi's view, the cantillation marks of biblical Hebrew succeed in conveying all aspects of language beyond its mere words (gestures, pauses and continuation, intonations of interrogation or astonishment). Metered poetry, in contrast, "can only be recited one way" and is hence an inferior means of conveying meaning. In the Jewish scholar's and in the Khazar king's estimation, it is unfortunate that Jews have caused their language to take on the meters of other nations and "corrupted the composition of our language" (*nufsidu waḍaʿ lughatinā*). But again, the reservations (insofar as they can be identified as Halevi's own) are limited to the subject of meter, not genre, and certainly contain no disapprobation of panegyric. When Halevi did identify a specific poetic genre as corrosive, he cited "humorous erotic poems" (*al-ashʿār al-hazaliyya al-ghazaliyya*). For Halevi, this, along with coarse food, overabundant eating and drinking, the company of women, and the friendship of jokers could harm one who sought to "purify his thought for the demonstrative sciences or his soul for prayer and supplication."[26]

A dominant theme of Halevi's thought is the problem of being engaged in the social world while pursuing the true worship of God, two poles that Halevi designates the "service of men" and the "service of God" (using, in both cases, the Arabic word *ʿubūdiyya*, which carries a range from "enslavement" to "service" to "worship"). In the famous conclusion of the *Kuzari*, the Jewish scholar says: "I seek freedom from the service of the men whose favor I seek, though I would never attain it even if I strived for it all my life. And if I were to attain it, still it would not benefit me, I mean the service of men and seeking their favor. Instead, I will seek the favor of the One whose favor can be attained with even the slightest trouble (*mu'na*), [favor] which brings benefit both in this world and the next, and this is the favor of God, exalted. His service is freedom and humility (*al-tadhallul*) is the [only] true honor (*ʿizz*)."[27]

The idea is echoed perfectly, and with the same play on the Hebrew cognate term *ʿavodah* (service) in Halevi's poetry, in which the poet asks himself rhetorically, "Do you flee the service of God (*ʿavodat elohim*) and yearn for the service of men (*ʿavodat anashim*)?"[28] Panegyric was undoubtedly one element of what Halevi considered the "service of men," and composing it, if only out of social grace, might have been a frustration. Still, Halevi's point is not so much that engaging in worldly affairs is unethical but rather that it is pointless for it fails to bring true benefit; there is neither freedom nor true honor in courting or even attaining the favor of men.

Halevi is famed for having left al-Andalus to make a pilgrim's journey to Palestine, to flee the "service of men" to worship God alone, a choice that has often been presented as a conversion of sorts. The degree of sincerity and the completeness of this transformation have been discussed by many scholars, generally concentrating on the nine-month period that Halevi spent in Egypt on his way to Palestine. Whether his journey was interrupted for logistical reasons or otherwise, it is clear that in Egypt the pilgrim integrated into Egyptian Jewish society, accepted some dinner invitations while refusing others, received gifts, and wrote Hebrew poetry, including that in the Arabic style he had denounced in the *Kuzari*. Despite any enhanced commitment to serve God alone, Halevi composed a significant number of panegyrics for Jewish dignitaries and merchants during his sojourn, whether out of genuine desire or social obligation. The seeming hypocrisy of the pilgrim enmeshed with worldly matters was not missed by onlookers in Egypt who questioned Halevi's ongoing composition of several types of poetry, including panegyric, "Can a pilgrim (*ṭālib ḥajj*) speak such ravings?"[29] How could the unworldly pilgrim supposedly focused on serving God in the Holy Land have room for such base concerns? Could one serve both God and men?

The ethical tension of writing panegyric is captured in one of Halevi's poems written in Egypt. Importantly, the poem is itself a panegyric couched within a letter written in honor of Natan Ben Shemuel, scribe of the Nagid of Egypt, who had sent Halevi a letter. The poem opens with a description of the pleasures of "Eden along the Nile" and then makes a transition to praise of the *mamdūḥ* (the section also expounds a bit on the pilgrimage itself). I cite the verses in the poetic translation of Raymond Scheindlin:

> By singing [this poem], I steal a bit from God,
> to Whom alone my songs are promised.
> I have devoted, dedicated, put aside
> my songs to Him alone, the only God.
> But I permit myself this one exception:
> to honor and to thank His sons and scholars.
> I trust His clemency—it suits Him to forgive—
> and give Him thanks, as due to Him from me.[30]

Stealing from God was an ethical infraction of no small measure. But, of course, it is striking that even this seeming assault on panegyric, as Scheindlin states, "turns out to be merely a strategy of panegyric."[31] Still, the ethical problem of dividing praise between God and men was a very real one for Halevi and other medieval poets, both Arabic and Hebrew; this problem will be treated comprehensively in Chapter 7.

Plagiarism and Recycling

On a less theological note, panegyrists were sometimes charged with mundane ethical infractions, chief among them plagiarism and recycling, topics treated extensively in Arabic works on poetics and in scholarship on Arabic literature. The ethical nature of panegyric practice was dependent upon honest relations between poet and *mamdūḥ*, with the poem serving as a mediating device. Each poetic utterance had to be original and composed by a poet for a specific *mamdūḥ*, even if themes were static. Because of the highly conventional quality of panegyrics, it was all too easy for this tacit rule to be violated through some sort of depersonalization. Insofar as panegyric was seen as a material object, there was fear that a poet could simply pass along "bad goods."

The most notorious issue was plagiarism, which the medievals called "stealing" (Ar., *sariqa*) (this generally pertained to specific turns of phrase and sometimes images more than poetic themes).[32] Plagiarizing panegyric was wrong not only because it harmed the original poet, who exercised a kind of "copyright" over his verse, but also because it harmed the *mamdūḥ*, for the latter was duped into thinking that he had received a gift particular to the relationship. We have already seen how the exilarch Mar ʿUqba, according to Natan ha-Bavli, was discovered uttering Arabic praises for a caliph with poems he had stolen from a scribe's notebook. The offense (insofar as the events are true) was probably not only theft but also the inflicting of harm upon the caliph.[33] When a plagiarized poem was given to a different *mamdūḥ*, the offense became all the more severe; this would be the case even if the plagiarist truly believed that the words of praise were appropriate for his addressee.

An intimately related issue was recycling, the rededication of a poem of a poet's own composition to a different *mamdūḥ*.[34] Like plagiarism, presenting two men with the same poem undermined the requisite personal structure of the poet-poem-*mamdūḥ* complex. Again, there is an infraction of duping the *mamdūḥ*—not only the second one, who received the recycled gift, but also the first one, who, in a sense, lost his gift by its being dedicated to someone else. In the entire corpus of praise writing by Jewish authors, there are very few cases in which a single author dedicated nearly identical poems to two different *mamdūḥ*s. ʿEli he-Ḥaver Ben ʿAmram praised Yosef al-Tustari of Egypt and then Yehosef, son of Shemuel ha-Nagid, about twenty years later; despite some adjustments and expansions, the similarity is overwhelming, down to a name play on the biblical Joseph. It seems likely that when the need arose to praise the Andalusian Yehosef, the poet realized that he had a poem for a *mamdūḥ* of the same name "ready to go" and probably thought that no one would notice (as far as we know, no one did until the twentieth century).[35] In Chapter 4, we saw that Yehudah al-Ḥarīzī dedicated the same short Hebrew poem to two *mamdūḥ*s (with a change of a single word), and it seems that the same author also dedicated different versions of an Arabic poem to two *mamdūḥ*s, one Jewish and the other Muslim. The former version, which has come down to us in Judeo-Arabic, inscribes the *mamdūḥ*'s name within the poem, while the latter, preserved in an Arabic biographical dictionary, amplifies the political rhetoric.[36]

Money, Money, Money

In Chapter 2, a distinction was made between "embedded" and "disembedded" exchange. In the former, poet and *mamdūḥ* are aligned in an ongoing relationship toward some cause of a social, intellectual, or religious nature; the ethical quality of this relationship is not necessarily undermined by the presence of money as an object of exchange. In the latter, poet and *mamdūḥ* are not directed toward a mutual goal; there is essentially a quid pro quo exchange of praise for material goods. It is for this reason that Arabic literature abounds in anecdotes that humorously portray the situation whereby false praise is practically sold.[37] Such anecdotes provided a kind of "escape valve" that allowed for a social critique without truly undermining the system itself; much like modern political cartoons or mock news programs, they serve as much to perpetuate a structure as to challenge it.

It seems that Mosheh Ibn Ezra distinguished among poet-patron relationships according to the embedded/disembedded division. In his assessment of the career of Yiṣḥaq Ibn Khalfūn, Ibn Ezra wrote: "There was none among the Jewish poets who took up poetry as a trade (*ṣināʿa*) and who made use of verse as a commodity (*bidāʿa*) other than him (*ghairuhu*) and requested gifts for it (*wa-istamnaḥa bihi*)."[38] Ibn Ezra's use of the words *ṣināʿa* (as a trade) and *bidāʿa* (as a commodity) is not accidental. Ibn Rashīq, a towering Arabic literary critic whom Ibn Ezra mentions by name, used the same words when distinguishing between the poetry penned by caliphs and scribes, on one hand, and the poetry of professional poets, on the other. Caliphs and scribes write for leisure, without fear; the poetry of poets "whose trade (*ṣināʿa*) is poetry and whose commodity (*bidāʿa*) is panegyric" is subject to greater strictures and scrutiny.[39] Ibn Ezra's comment might therefore be seen as at least slightly derisive.

But how could Ibn Ezra call Ibn Khalfūn the *only* poet to make poetry a trade and a commodity? Surely, he knew that Dunash Ben Labrat and Menaḥem Ben Saruq sought and received the support of Ḥasdai Ibn Shaprut and that Shelomoh Ibn Gabirol was greatly reliant upon Yequtiel Ibn Ḥasan; Ibn Ezra probably received at least some remuneration himself. Some translators of this passage have rendered the word *ghairuhu*, "other than him," as "like him," as though others also made poetry a trade and commodity but only to a lesser degree. The distortion, I believe, stems from the erroneous assumption that the only motivation for writing panegyric was a need for funds; as argued in Chapter 2, a patronage relationship could encompass financial support without being solely about money.[40]

In recalling the days when Ibn Shaprut supported Menaḥem and Dunash, Ibn Ezra wrote that Ḥasdai rejoiced at their "wondrous poetry and their marvelous eloquent orations. Therefore their ranks (*manāzil*) were elevated with him and he awarded them the utmost of their requests and the extremity of their desires."[41] Fulfilling the poets' requests and desires, one imagines, involved some sort of monetary support. Equally important and far less tangible is the elevation in rank, a more abstract form of remuneration. Ibn Shaprut did not compensate poets for their poems on a quid pro quo basis or in purely monetary terms. The patron-poet relationship went well beyond the tossing of a little coin in exchange for flattering words; it was based on a deeper, enduring relationship between two men, one of whom had the power to elevate the social status of the other and to fulfill his requests, monetary or otherwise. Further, the relationship might be called "embedded" because the *mamdūḥ* and his poets were allied in a "higher cause"—namely, enhancing the intellectual culture and prestige of Andalusian Jewry through the production of works relating to the Hebrew language and biblical exegesis. There was clearly some gifting involved, but it was set within the higher purpose of elevating scholarship.

Ibn Khalfūn, in contrast, wrote simultaneously for many patrons in many places, some of whom he may not have known previously through personal ties. He often requested specific forms of remuneration (money, clothing, wine, firewood) and may not, in Ibn Ezra's view, have been allied with his *mamdūḥ*s in any mutual cause; seeking remuneration may have been the only purpose of writing.[42] Dunash and Menaḥem participated in embedded exchange, and Ibn Khalfūn in disembedded exchange. The formers' patronage relationships involved money, and the latter's were *about* money; in this sense, Ibn Khalfūn was alone among the Hebrew poets of al-Andalus. While I would not describe Ibn Ezra's remarks about Ibn Khalfūn as a severe indictment, it seems that the literary critic was making an ethical comparison.

Broadly speaking, Ibn Ezra is not critical of the existence of economic bonds between poet and *mamdūḥ*. He is hardly naïve about the link between a poet's ability to create a healthy economic environment. He recounts several aphorisms about how poetry flourishes when there is money, including: "It is fitting for the wise person (*al-ʿāqil*) to choose men for his panegyric (*madīḥ*) just as he chooses pure ground for his planting."[43] Further, he laments poetry's decline with a number of economic metaphors: "But the market (*sūq*) of this poetic art sold badly (*aksada*)[44] after its brisk trade (*nafāqiha*), and the faces of its people[45] darkened just after having shined; the flame of the excellent ones burned out and the water of the most noble dried up, and these were the ones who brought rain to the people. The people abandoned making prestige (*dhikr*) eternal and making pride (*al-fakhr*) everlasting."[46]

Immortalizing prestige through poetry is, ethically speaking, a good. At one point, Ibn Ezra discusses the comparative qualities of poetry and prose, generally arguing for the superiority of the former, but notes a decline of poetry in his own day: "Ever since men have made [poetry] a means of acquiring gain (*al-takassub*) and a ladder for requesting gifts (*al-istimnāḥ*), the garment of beauty has become shabby and the water of its comeliness has dried up and [prose] addresses (*al-khuṭab*) have become more esteemed."[47] The negative effect of composing poetry only in search of gifts (as Ibn Khalfūn did) is an aesthetic one. This does not render the composition of panegyric itself unethical.

Sincerity, Truth, and Falsehood

As stated, a poet's sincerity was most suspect in cases in which he received payment and remained a concern when any type of gain might be derived. But even beyond this, a poem by a well-intentioned and ethically upright panegyrist could be ethically troubling because all poetry relied upon "deception" as its very mode of discourse. Below, I consider two concerns: (1) that a poet would lie intentionally; and (2) that even when he meant to tell the truth, he lied.

There is a famous story wherein ʿAlī Ibn Abī Ṭālib is praised excessively by a poet and quips: "I am inferior to what you say but superior to what is in your soul."[48] Here the concern seems to be that the poet would intentionally deceive the *mamdūḥ*, a particularly grievous offense, given that the *mamdūḥ* in this case was ʿAlī.[49] Some Arabic literary critics assert that a verse might be evaluated based upon the speaker's reputation as a teller of truth; praise by a known liar should even be read as invective. Critics cited with approval verses that combined praise and blame in a single verse and even celebrated the literary feat of disguising blame as praise. Yet, ethically speaking, readers also feared that what seemed like praise could actually conceal blame.[50]

The Hebrew poets clearly absorbed this concern over insincerity. Mosheh Ibn Ezra sent a poem to a younger addressee (in response to a poem that he had received) that concludes with words of advice: "Do not be beguiled by words of one offering praise, even if he sacrifices to you an offering of well-being (Lv 22:21)! Every man speaks smoothly but sealed within [his speech] is falsehood."[51] In order to allay suspicions, poets stressed their sincerity as a constant refrain. We have already seen that Hai Gaon's address to Rav Yehudah Rosh ha-Seder assures the *mamdūḥ* that those who hear it will "not find all this praise strange or foreign" but rather "a word aptly spoken (Prv 25:11)." In Ben Saruq's poem to Ibn Shaprut from prison, the poet writes in order to assuage his *mamdūḥ*'s anger: "I begin with his praise though I cannot hope for his kindness for he has nullified hope. / This indicates that there is neither falsehood nor guile in my words."[52] As Schirmann notes, the verses mean that the words of praise can be trusted since they bring the hapless poet no benefit (though we might see this more a part of a complex rhetorical strategy to get the poet out of jail). Yehudah Halevi wrote in a panegyric for Shemuel Ben Ḥananiah of Egypt: "O lines of verse!—you spoke so eagerly when I lied, but now that I have truth to speak, are mute! . . . Come, gather round and let me make a diadem of you. Then see how splendid you can be!"[53] Halevi thus insists upon the sincerity of this praise, all the while calling attention to the practice of poets (including himself!) to lie in their poems. Writing in Judeo-Arabic, Yehudah al-Ḥarīzī introduced the praise of one figure "who possesses refined culture (*adab*) and who *used to* possess generosity"; he added, "were I to say that he possessed generosity, I would not be speaking truthfully."[54]

Similarly, in the concluding verses of a fifty-eight-line panegyric, Mosheh Ibn Ezra extols Abū ʿUmar [Yosef] Ibn Qamniel: "Poets who praised lords (*sarim*) other than Yosef, behold they lied and spoke vapor and emptiness with fervor. / But when [those who praised Yosef] made decrees of praise and spoke wondrously, even then they spoke the truth."[55] With the idea of "speaking wondrously," our discussion can move beyond the question of the author's sincerity and motivation toward the deeper question of whether his words—as poetic utterances—can ever be considered "true." The background necessary for understanding Ibn Ezra's verse is that poetic speech consists of statements that are metaphoric and hyperbolic—statements that, logically speaking, are not true. For this reason, poetry was sometimes denounced as deceit or at least not subject to evaluation through the categories of truth and falsehood. Either way, poetry hardly seemed the ideal medium for enumerating the virtues of a *mamdūḥ* that were meant to be taken as true. Here, Ibn Ezra turns the topos to rhetorical advantage by claiming that no praise directed toward a *mamdūḥ* other than Yosef could ever be true because of the unworthiness of its subject. However, even when poets "spoke wondrously"—hyperbolically and with exaggeration, essentially lying—about Yosef, they were being truthful. Chapter 6 delves more deeply into the theory and practice of "wondrous speech" with respect to panegyric, its sanctioned usages, and boundaries, as well as other elements of the poetics of praise.

CHAPTER 6

"A Cedar Whose Stature in the Garden of Wisdom . . . ": Hyperbole, the Imaginary, and the Art of Magnification

In the Introduction to this book, I cited, in the context of the social function of praise, a passage from the Hebrew introduction of the *Epistle to Yemen* in which Maimonides responds to a report that Jews in Yemen "praise, aggrandize, and extol me" (*mehalelim, marbim, umeshananim*) and that Rabbi Solomon "indulges in hyperboles in praise of me and speaks extravagantly in extolling me, exaggerates wildly according to his desire, and waxes enthusiastic out of his love and kindness."[1] There I used an idiomatic translation, but here I wish to call attention to a point that a more literal rendering yields: "He broadens his mouth in extolling us (*marḥiv pihu be-mahalaleinu*), lengthens his tongue in our praise (*ma'arikh leshono be-shivḥenu*), speaks in hyperbolic language (*lashon havai*) according to his desire, and magnifies to tell (*higdil le-sapper*) out of his love and kindness."[2] The commonality in most of these expressions is the act of enlarging, expanding, increasing.[3] It is thus not surprising that the Arabic and Hebrew words meaning "magnification" (Ar., *ta'ẓīm*; Heb., *giddul*) are synonymous with "praise" and that theoretical literature on medieval Arabic and Hebrew poetics is largely concerned with the different means of enhancing and intensifying praise (or blame).

The other key Hebrew term that appears in the passage by Maimonides is *havai*, usually translated as "hyperbole," a word of rabbinic origin. It appears in b. Tamid 29a, for example, paired as a synonym with *guzma* (exaggeration); there, several textual examples are given, including "cities great and fortified up to heaven" (Dt 1:28); and "the people played pipes . . . so that the earth rent with their sound" (1 Kgs 1:40).[4] By Maimonides' time, Mosheh Ibn Ezra had identified *havai*, with reference to this talmudic passage, as the equivalent of the Arabic literary device known as *al-ghulū* or *al-ighrāq* (hyperbole), one of the more extensively treated subjects among literary critics.[5] This subject will be treated in detail below, but here I will note only how the basic elements of Arabic literary thought had penetrated medieval Jewish writing on praise, not only for a proper critic such as Ibn Ezra but also for Maimonides, who did not discuss literary theory to any significant degree.[6]

The contemporary reader has a great deal of difficulty appreciating praise in a highly rhetorical or hyperbolic mode. Interestingly, we do retain a taste for this in satire and insult, even (or especially) of the extremely base variety. To re-create the medieval experience of panegyric, one must apply that same level of appreciation for hyperbole and rhetoric but in the opposite direction toward praise. Neither in blame nor in praise was the rhetoric considered true; it was simply considered deserved, and the more deserving a subject, the greater the degree of rhetorical invention and hyperbolic magnification.

A relatively basic level of rhetorical embellishment is observed in an epithalamium composed by Mosheh Ibn Ezra for Shelomoh, son of Abū al-Ḥasan Ibn Māṭir:

> He walks on paths of intelligence; his feet tread and march upon refined culture.
> Since youth his thoughts have been turned toward the heavens, his ideas borne above the Great Bear.
> His station above the people of his age is like the rank of human beings above beasts and creeping things.
> His deeds are more precious than theirs even as pearls are more precious than potsherds.
> They race to catch the dust of his feet, but how can an [ordinary] bird be the pursuer of eagles?[7]

As is typical, the praise centers on intelligence, refined culture (*musar*, i.e., *adab*), and deeds. The verses are, of course, not devoid of rhetorical figures, but these mostly center on the distinction between the *mamdūḥ* and other men as an analogue of conventional hierarchies (e.g., pearls over potsherds). Here, Ibn Ezra praises an individual belonging to a respected family, but the *mamdūḥ* is young and not one who has yet attained esteemed rank.

In contrast, when Ibn Ezra praised a figure described in a superscription as "one of the eminent (*kibbār*) among his friends," we find a richer rhetorical display:

12. He rose on the night of my distress like dawn and shined the light of friendship upon the gloom of my wandering.
13. My footsteps had slipped, but when I beheld the place of his habitation, I stood firm upon a rock and fortress.
14. I came with an anguished heart but, with the honey of his speech, his soul made me secure at the breast of tranquility.
15. Honeycomb to the mouth of the taster, sunlight to the eye of the seer, and flowing myrrh giving scent to the nose,
16. A pedestal to all kindness, a pillar to esteem, a beam and covering for the Tabernacle of Truth.[8]
17. Before he learned to call "Father, mother,"[9] his Maker made him feel fear of Him alone.
18. The designs of his mind bring pain to adversaries but gladden the souls of friends.
19. With the breath of his mouth he gives wisdom to the fool and his pen's spittle cleanses blood from the stupidity of the age.
20. A cedar whose stature in the garden of Wisdom is so great that its shoots offer shrubs before it;
21. before the wind, they fly away like straw, but it continues to flourish upon raging waters.[10]
22. His hand built Dominion with a hewn stone while other rulers merely daubed it with whitewash.[11]

Even the untrained reader can intuitively sense that there is something different about this poem. Ibn Ezra has pulled out all the stops. It is generally denser with devices of the Arabic poetic style known as *al-badīʿ* (the novel, original)—a self-conscious intensification of poetic figures that was cultivated among the so-called *muḥdath* ("modern") poets of the ʿAbbasid period; these devices include figures of wording (antithesis, parenthesis) and figures of thought (metaphor, hyperbole).[12] Moreover, there are differences in metaphorical and imaginative depth: the first poem's "Since youth his thoughts have been turned toward the heavens, his ideas borne above the Great Bear," while hyperbolic, is simply not as rich or complex as the second poem's "A cedar whose stature in the garden of Wisdom is so great that its shoots offer shrubs before it; before the wind, they fly away like straw, but it continues to flourish upon raging waters." The latter verses take the reader deeper into a fictional world and require more thought to interpret.

Ibn Ezra, who was steeped in works of Arabic literary criticism by Muslim authors, championed the composition of Hebrew poetry according to the poetics of the *badīʿ*. As Raymond Scheindlin has argued, *Kitāb al-muḥāḍara wa'l-mudhākara* as a whole can be viewed as a legitimization of Hebrew poetry composed according to Arabic poetics, and to this I will only add that the defense was not only of Arabized meter and rhyme but more specifically of the manneristic style of the *badīʿ* for which Ibn al-Muʿtazz, one of Ibn Ezra's sources, had also mounted a defense within Arabic literary criticism.[13] Sensitization to the elements of this poetics is an important tool not only for the scholar of medieval poetry but also for the historian who wishes to ascertain the prestige of a *mamdūḥ* based on the style of a poem.[14]

In a separate publication, I review the poetics of the *badīʿ* according to Mosheh Ibn Ezra, using as a heuristic device a verse-by-verse analysis of the panegyric that the author composed to illustrate the *maḥāsin al-shiʿr* (beautiful elements of poetry) as an appendix to his exposition on *al-badīʿ* within his *Kitāb al-muḥāḍara wa'l-mudhākara*.[15] Here, I will focus only on one of the figures of thought that Ibn Ezra discusses, *al-ghulū*, against the background of works on Arabic poetics. This will lead to a discussion of the related subject of the "imaginary" (*takhyīl*) and the "imagination" (*takhayyul*) in Ibn Ezra's poetics, including a translation and an analysis of an extended section of the *Kitāb al-muḥāḍara*. These topics are of great importance for the interpretation of panegyric and intersect with subjects of medieval thought as diverse as exegesis, logic, philosophy of language, and psychology.

Literary Theory in the Medieval Arab World

The independent genre of literary criticism was a relative latecomer among the disciplinary writings of Muslim scholars. Julie Scott Meisami writes: "As most medieval critics were associated with formalized 'sciences' such as philology, grammar, exegesis or logic, each of which had, by the fourth/tenth century, established both its own set of 'questions' (*masā'il*) for examination and its own methodology, the critics' treatment of matters bearing on aesthetics and stylistics varies with respect to the disciplinary contexts in which they occur."[16]

An exegete of the Qur'ān had to be versed in rhetorical and aesthetic effects (metaphor, hyperbole, assonance) in addition to the corpus of pre-Islamic poetry; the grammarian would turn to poetry for textual citations; and the logician had to understand the poetic as a mode of speech alongside the demonstrative, dialectic, rhetorical, and so on. Only in the tenth century, with the work known as *Naqd al-shiʿr* (The criticism of poetry), by Qudāma Ibn Jaʿfar (d. 948), did literary theory emerge as an independent genre. Literary theory continued to develop throughout the Middle Ages along multiple tracks, as an ancillary topic within other disciplinary genres and as a self-contained and self-referential corpus of texts.

In addition to building upon early Arabic evaluations of good and bad poetry, something of the Arabic discourse on poetics can be traced to the peripatetic tradition. Bonebakker shows that Qudāma Ibn Jaʿfar draws on Aristotle and Galen explicitly and seems familiar with Plato's notorious condemnation of the mendacity of poets in the *Republic*.[17] Further, to understand the impact of Aristotle on Arabic poetic thought, not only in works of literary criticism but also within philosophical writing, one must recall that Aristotle's *Poetics* and *Rhetoric* originally made up the seventh and eighth parts of the Organon, the suite of works dedicated to the art of logic. The modern severing of these works from the Organon has created the false impression that poetry and logic are diametric opposites. But for major Muslim philosophers (al-Fārābī, Ibn Sīnā, Ibn Rushd), poetics was a natural subject of inquiry *within* logic.[18] Al-Fārābī, we will see, was a central source for Mosheh Ibn Ezra, and, as is well-known, Maimonides followed al-Fārābī in arraying syllogisms along a spectrum with the demonstrative at one end and the poetic at the other, depending upon the types of statements that serve as the premises of the syllogism: true, conventional, false, or mimetic.[19] Of all of Aristotle's ideas on poetics, it is his definition of the poetic statement as mimetic—one that imitates reality much as a sculpture imitates its subject—that had the greatest impact on classical Arabic literary criticism.[20]

It is in the *Rhetoric*, more than in the *Poetics*, that Aristotle systematically discusses praise as one of the varieties of epideictic, or demonstrative, speech (the other main variety being blame).[21] There he stresses such rhetorical strategies as *auxesis* (translated variously as magnification, amplification, heightening the effect), a word that, like panegyric itself, suffered significant devaluation in the modern period.[22] *Auxesis* could take on numerous forms, such as claiming the superiority of the one praised over famous or ordinary men, asserting that the one praised was the only one or the first to accomplish a particular thing; one might censure in invective for the opposite reasons.[23]

This discussion belongs to the *Rhetoric* rather than the *Poetics*, since such constructions, strictly speaking, are not poetic; that is, they need not depend upon mimetic, or imitative, speech. The Arabic version of the *Poetics* substituted excerpts of Greek poetry with Arabic ones and set praise and blame (of people, of virtues) as the central categories of poetic speech in place of tragedy and comedy.[24] Thus, the substantive treatment of eulogy found in the *Rhetoric* became the centerpiece of the Arabic life of the *Poetics*. Praise and blame remained the central topics of inquiry in Arabic commentaries on the *Poetics* and in original works of Arabic literary criticism where the subjects were studied systematically, both according to rhetorical strategies (such as auxesis) and poetic figures (metaphor, hyperbole, antithesis).

By the late eleventh century, when Ibn Ezra composed the *Kitāb al-muḥāḍara*, the *naqd al-sh'ir* genre had grown to be quite expansive, and, as occurred within the Western tradition of rhetoric and poetics, the number of identifiable literary devices had multiplied exponentially. Ibn al-Mu'tazz (d. 908) listed 12 "beautiful elements of poetry" whereas al-'Askarī (d. 1005) counted 39, and al-Ḥillī (d. 1348) 151.[25] Also, as in Western criticism, the genre exhibits tremendous variety regarding both the definition of literary terms and the taxonomy of their interrelation (further below).

Although Mosheh Ibn Ezra cites Aristotle and al-Fārābī (as well as Plato, Socrates, Isokrates, and Galen) as authorities in *Kitāb al-muḥāḍara*, it is with the authors of the *naqd al-shi'r* genre that he most explicitly aligns himself: "Concerning most of the chapters of this work, the Banners of Eloquence from within Islam (i.e., Muslim scholars of rhetoric)—and they are the most worthy regarding speech in prose and poetry—laid out numerous books, such as the book of Qudāma (d. 948) concerning criticism (*al-Naqd*), *al-Badī'* (The novel style), by Ibn al-Mu'tazz (d. 908); *Ḥilyat al-muḥāḍara* (The ornament of lecturing), by al-Ḥātimī (d. 998); *al-Ḥāli wa'l-'ātil* (The ornamenting and the denuding), by him;[26] *al-'Umda* (The pillar), by Ibn Rashīq (d. 1063 or 1071); *al-Shi'r wa'l-shu'arā* (Poetry and poets), by Ibn Qutaiba (d. 889); and others."

Of these, *Ḥilyat al-muḥāḍara* and *al-'Umda* seem to have been of the greatest direct influence, though the former, as Yosef Tobi stresses, has received very little treatment despite the fact that the word *muḥāḍara* appears in the title and the paired terms of Ibn Ezra's title (*al-muḥāḍara* and *al-mudhākara*) appear in near-succession within the work.[27]

Just as works of exegesis could contain substantive discussions of poetics, so works of poetics often subsumed discussions of exegesis, not only reflecting but also producing in the process a kind of exegesis focused on aesthetics (in the Islamic case, this held particular import for the doctrine of the Qur'ān's inimitability). Before writing *Kitāb al-muḥāḍara*, Ibn Ezra wrote a work on exegesis, *Kitāb al-ḥadīqa fī ma'anā al-majāz wa'l-ḥaqīqa* (Book of the garden concerning figurative and literal speech), and many sections of *Kitāb al-muḥāḍara* continue this line of inquiry.[28] That is, in introducing biblical examples into his discussion of the "beautiful elements of poetry," the critic was effectively inventing a new approach to biblical criticism that Mordechai Cohen describes as an "aesthetic exegesis" according to the standards of Arabic literary criticism.[29]

Throughout his *Kitāb al-muḥāḍara*, Ibn Ezra systematically gives examples of praise and invective (as well as other genres) that depend upon many of the *maḥāsin al-shi'r*; the final section of the book is a catalog of these devices. Ibn Ezra generally illustrates figures with verses from the Qur'ān or Arabic poetry, the Hebrew Bible, and Andalusian Hebrew verse, quite often his own. For the most part, Arabic verses are taken from citations given in the aforementioned Arabic books on poetics rather than Ibn Ezra's independent survey of Arabic poetry (but see some likely counterexamples below).[30] Ibn Ezra's definitions of poetic figures are sometimes more clumsy and opaque than the definitions presented in the Arabic sources from which he drew.

Alongside *al-isti'āra* ("loan metaphor, borrowing"),[31] the most important figure of thought that Ibn Ezra treats is *al-ghulū*, which can roughly be translated as "hyperbole" (from the Greek, "throwing beyond"), one of the richer and more ambiguous areas of the philosophy of language and Western literary criticism. In Western criticism, one thorny problem is to understand "hyperbole's" relationship with "exaggeration" (from the Latin, "to heap up"). Are the two synonymous? Is one a subspecies of the other? Is hyperbole strictly a "figure of thought" defined by the impossibility of content, or can it encompass a device such as "amplification" as a "figure of wording"?[32] The problem is equally complicated in Arabic criticism. First, different authors use terminology differently. The word *mubālagha* is sometimes understood as the umbrella category "hyperbole" with several subvarieties but can also be defined specifically as "exaggeration," similar to but not identical with hyperbole. Hence the fourteenth century al-Qazwīnī divides *mubālagha maqbūla* (acceptable hyperbole) into three categories: (1) what is exaggerated within what is customarily possible (*tablīgh*); (2) within what is theoretically possible (*ighrāq*); (3) and what pertains to the strictly impossible (*ghulū*).[33] But in the tenth and eleventh centuries, critics such as al-'Askarī distinguished between *al-mubālagha* as what "reaches the outer limit and furthest end in meaning" and *al-ghulū* as what "passes over the limit (*ḥadd*) of meaning and rises above it."[34] Ibn Rashīq, a key source for Ibn Ezra, similarly sees *al-mubālagha* as "following something to an end (*al-taqaṣṣi*), the poet's reaching (*bulūgh*) the extreme (*aqṣa*) of what is possible in describing a thing"[35] but *al-ghulū* as "impossibility because of its divergence from reality, its departure from the existing (*al-wājib*) and the generally accepted."[36]

Already at the beginning of this chapter, I noted that Ibn Ezra identified the Hebrew term *havai* with the Arabic device known as *al-ghulū* or *al-ighrāq*.[37] In his *Kitāb al-ḥadīqa*, Ibn Ezra seems to differentiate between *al-mubālagha* as "exaggeration, reaching the limit" (illustrating with the biblical verse "Joseph stored up huge quantities of grain, like the sand of the sea" [Gn 41:49]), and *al-ghulū* as "hyperbole, going beyond the limit" (illustrating with Prv 25:15, "A gentle tongue can break a bone").[38] The example in Gn 41:49 brings description of quantity to its limit, but it is nonetheless a description of quantity. The content of the proverb is more strictly impossible and contrafactual. In this way, Ibn Ezra seems to follow the definitions of Ibn Rashīq.

In his section on *al-ghulū* within the presentation of the *maḥāsin al-shi'r*, Ibn Ezra uses a number of terms of art more or less interchangeably as hyperbole (*ghulū*, *ighrāq*, *ighāl*, *taghmīq*, *ta'ammuq*). The commonality in this terminology, over against *mubālagha*, is that hyperbole, in Ibn Ezra's words, "departs from the class of the possible and enters the class of the impossible." The subtleties in Ibn Ezra's terminology become clearer with a close reading of his exegetic interventions in the *Kitāb al-muḥāḍara*. He cites numerous biblical verses that make use of *al-ghulū*, including: "great cities and fortresses up to the sky" (Dt 9:1, also quoted in b. Tamid 29b); and "their land shall be drunk with blood, their dust saturated with fat" (Is 34:4).

Ibn Ezra's comments on Nm 13:33, "And we were in our eyes like grasshoppers, and so we were in their eyes," are also illustrative of his categories. The first phrase, he opines, is "exaggeration, reaching a limit" (*taghyī*),[39] but the second he calls "utter falsehood" (*kidhb maḥḍ*), "since no one knows the hidden except for God, exalted" (i.e., the inhabitants of the land did not actually *see* the spies); this type of falsehood is distinct from both *al-mubālagha* and *al-ghulū*. Both exaggeration and hyperbole ultimately express truth, though with different relationships to possibility, whereas "utter falsehood" does not correspond to truth in any way. A rich sequence of verses is found in Is 34:3–4, which deals with God's fury against the nations and their ensuing destruction,

3. their slain shall be cast out, the stench of their carcasses shall rise,
4. the mountains shall be melted with their blood, and all the host
   of heaven shall be dissolved.

While verse 3 does not even constitute exaggeration, the two images in verse 4 exemplify hyperbole, especially since the angels are viewed as inviolable. The destruction of the angels, writes Ibn Ezra, refers to "the overturning (*taqallub*) of the nations, and [Isaiah] coined a similitude (*mathal*) with the transformation (*taḥawwul*) of the angels." "The mountains shall be melted with their blood" and "the host of heaven shall be dissolved" are both examples of *ghulū*.[40] Distinguishing between figurative and literal expressions has obvious implications for the interpretation of eschatological passages of the Bible, for the exegete must consider whether the Bible intends seemingly impossible statements that do not correspond with human experience as true. For example, Ibn Ezra views seemingly false expressions concerning the "awaited polity" (i.e., the Messianic era) and the miracles as nonfigurative.

After the lengthy excursus on biblical interpretation, Ibn Ezra quotes verses of Andalusian Hebrew poetry that make use of hyperbolic devices, including a panegyric by Ibn Khalfūn that seems to liken a *mamdūḥ* to God[41] and another by the poet "who uses hyperbole the most in his poetry," by which Ibn Ezra meant himself: "I am astonished that his pens did not bloom from the rivers of his hands, which flow." The verse combines two praiseworthy attributes: the *mamdūḥ*'s generosity (the rivers of his hands) and his skill in writing (his pens), which are linked because the poet is amazed that the *mamdūḥ*'s wondrous writing is not a product of his generosity.

Earlier in *Kitāb al-muḥāḍara*, prior to the systematic classification of the "beautiful elements of poetry," Ibn Ezra defends his own use of hyperbole, partly by way of appealing to precedent, but also on poetic grounds. Here I translate the entire lengthy passage to illustrate how rich the topic was for Ibn Ezra and eleventh-century critics generally and also to illustrate some of the subtleties of his thinking on the subject. The pertinence of the subject to panegyric is manifest throughout.

> If I exceeded bounds (*afraṭtu*)[42] when lauding (*taqrīẓ*) a man or blaming contemporaries, or when I praised (*madaḥtu*) by way of poetry or sought protection by way of vainglorious poetry, I only followed the path of our predecessors and adhered to the opinion of members of both religious communities [i.e., Muslim and Jewish] who speak with hyperbole (*al-mutakallimīn fī al-ghulū*) and immoderation (*iṭnāb*), embellishment of speech (*zukhruf al-qawl*) and expatiation (*ishāb*), for exceeding the usual bounds (*al-taʿammuq*)[43] in the composition of poetry is the goal among those

learned in this matter. There were some who found fault with verses of hyperbole (*al-ighrāq*) and those who approved of them, though [the latter] are the majority. They made this quality mandatory for [poetry's] creators and said, "What is intended by hyperbole (*al-ighrāq*) is exaggeration (*al-mubālagha*)."[44] They added that the poet, when he speaks hyperbolically (*awghala*) and goes beyond what exists (*yakhruj 'an al-mawjūd*) and enters the category of the non-existent (*bab al-ma'adūm*), only intends by this similitude (*al-mathal*) and reaching the limit (*bulūgh al-ghāya*) of description.

However, if it were said, "One part of a definitive proof is conveying something that intellects (readily) accept," and if it were said, "The best of speech is the most true," this would be a correct statement. However, it does not apply to poetry, for it is said, "the best of poetry is the most false." A question was asked concerning poets and the answer was, "Let it suffice you to know that no people approve of falsehood apart from them." It was said, "Sincerity (*al-ṣidq*) and deceit (*al-kidhb*) pertain to utterances, correctness and error pertain to opinions,[45] good and bad pertain to acts, truth (*al-ḥaqq*) and falsehood (*al-bāṭil*) pertain to legal judgments, and benefit and harm pertain to things that can be perceived by the senses." [It is written] in the Qur'ān of the Arabs, "As for poets, the erring follow them. Do you not see that they stray in every valley and that they say what they do not do?" (Qur'ān 26:224–26). If poetry were stripped of deceit, even if it remained unclear after contemplation, it would cease to be poetry. One of the earlier poets said:

He is the sea from whatever direction you approach! Its expanse is beneficence and generosity is its shore.

He was so accustomed to extending his hand that, were he to renounce grasping, his fingertips would not even respond.

If you came to him rejoicing [in praise], he would appear[46] as though you gave him that which you were seeking.[47]

Even if there were nothing in his palm but his soul, he would give of it generously; therefore one who entreats him should fear God.[48]

All of these are deceitful similes (*tashbīhāt*) and that which is intended by them is that he is generous.

The one who engages[49] the art of logic does not permit [a statement] unless he takes its premises as true, whether through reason, things perceived through the senses, conventions, or trustworthy reports that contain no doubt, such as that Baghdad is in the world. Conventions are of higher rank according to the distinction of the speaker. [Another source of truth is] reports that [the speaker] shares with those other than the speaker; [yet another source of truth is] reliable experience—that is, that [the plant] scammony reduces bile.[50] One who deems true that which the intellect does not, apart from what [God] set in the path of the miracles in order to establish revelation and confirm the prophets, makes light of God's greatest gifts.[51]

Aristotle categorized speech and said, "Regarding speech, there is that which is true, that which is false, and that which is intermediate between truth and falsehood. The true is proof and everything that follows from proof, while the false is the speech of the poets according to the manner of their speech but not its essence. As for that which is intermediate between truth and falsehood, there is that whose truth is greater than its falsehood, such as the speech of dialecticians (*mujādilīn*), and that whose falsehood is greater than its truth, such as the speech of sophists, and that whose truth and falsehood are equivalent, such as the speech of rhetoricians and orators."[52] When the poet praises, he says that the face of the *mamdūḥ* is more luminous than the sun, that his hand waters more than copious rain, that he is more courageous than a lion, that his chest is broader than the sea, and what is similar to this. All of it is falsehood from the perspective of truth, though the requirements of speech compel it.

Abū Naṣr al-Fārābī said in his book on the *Enumeration of Sciences*:[53] Poetic statements are those that are composed of things whose concern is imagining the matter (*al-takhayyul fī al-amr*) that is being addressed, whether with respect to ugliness and beauty, or with respect to loftiness and baseness. Through their utterance, a likeness (*shabah*) comes to our[54] minds through the imagination (*al-takhayyul*) just like that which comes to our minds when we look at a thing to which we have an aversion such that it frightens us and we avoid it, even though we have verified that it is not so; similarly, this happens to us with poetic statements. Frequently do men follow their imaginings (*takhayyulāt*) more than their opinions, as we said happens when one looks at depictions that imitate a

> thing or things that resemble the matter. For this reason, a man should not precede his seeing [something] hastily with his imagination, lest [the imagination] will overwhelm him before seeing what results from the matter. One of the wise summarized this statement and captured its essence when he said, "The poet is like one who makes a sculpture, perfect and wondrous to the eye, though it contains nothing real." This is utterly convincing.[55]

The passage begins, in an autobiographical mode, with particular poetic devices and concludes with a discussion of the "imagination" (*al-takhayyul*), a term that al-Fārābī had advanced as the operative site of producing and processing visual images, poetic speech, divination, and prophecy.[56] Between the two ends of the passage, Ibn Ezra explores the well-known dialectic between truth and falsehood and whether the best statements are the most true or the most false, clearly siding with Qudāma and others that the "best of poetry is the most false."[57] The admixture of rhetorical and emotive aspects of poetry with the logical valuation of statements is explained, as stated toward the beginning of this chapter, by the fact that poetics and rhetoric were both considered branches of logic in the classical and medieval worlds. At another point in the *Kitāb al-muḥāḍara*, Ibn Ezra briefly summarizes the content of Aristotle's *Poetics* and identifies it as the eighth part of the Organon.[58] It is Ibn Ezra's location of poetry *within* logic that allows us to make sense of the argument's rather convoluted structure. Throughout the discussion, Ibn Ezra reveals his full immersion in the literature on poetics as known in his day, drawing upon passages by Aristotle[59] and al-Fārābī, as well as the Qur'ān and the poetry of Abū Tammām.

In the first paragraph, Ibn Ezra defends hyperbole by arguing that it is essentially a form of exaggeration and that going beyond "what exists" (*al-mawjūd*) and entering the nonexistent (*al-ma'adūm*) is still "reaching the limit." Using almost identical language, Ibn Ezra's source Qudāma notes a dispute among critics and stresses the defense of hyperbole among the "Greek philosophers."[60] Ibn Ezra presents leaving what exists (*al-mawjūd*) and entering the nonexistent (*al-ma'adūm*) as the distinguishing characteristic of *al-ghulū*. Later, in the review of the *maḥāsin al-shi'r*, Ibn Ezra shifts his language slightly to speak of hyperbole as what "leaves the class of the possible (*'unṣur al-mumkin*) and enters the class of the impossible (*'unṣur al-mamnū'*)." Although, for some later critics, these are different points (i.e., something might "not exist" but still be "possible"), Ibn Ezra seems to use the terminology interchangeably.[61]

In general, Ibn Ezra subscribes to the well-known "content/form" dichotomy of poetic speech, distinguished in the passage with the "manner" (*tarīqa*) of speech and its "essence" (*nafs*). A statement (e.g., "his hand is the sea"), even when its "manner" relies upon falsehood (a hand is not a sea), is considered true as long as its "essence" corresponds with reality (it is predicated of a generous person and not of a miser).[62] The famous qur'ānic verse of "the poets" is cited here as supporting evidence that poetic speech is built upon falsehood and not to argue (as was sometimes done) that one should shun poets and poetry altogether.[63] At another point in the *Kitāb al-muḥāḍara*, Ibn Ezra argues that a poetic statement must also correspond with the poet's opinion about his subject. He cites a famous *ḥadīth* (attributed to "one of the jurists"):[64] "Deeds are [judged] according to intentions, and every man has his intention" and continues with a story about 'Alī Ibn Abī Ṭālib (again, without specific reference to the Muslim figure): "A man praised one of the great and was excessive in his praise and overstepped bounds (*zāda fī madīḥihi wa afraṭa*). However, [the poet's] opinion was not like the outer expression of his speech (*ẓāhir qawlihi*), and so the soul of the *mamdūḥ* did not accept his words and [the *mamdūḥ*] responded to him saying, 'I am inferior to what you say but superior to what is in your soul.'"[65]

This anecdote is usually cited in Arabic writings as a critique of the praise enterprise as a whole, similar to Muḥammad's urging people to throw dirt in the faces of panegyrists, cutting out poets' tongues, or paying for praise in honor of God but not in honor of himself.[66] For Ibn Ezra, the story is not a blanket indictment of *madīḥ* but rather a prescription that a poem's content should correspond with the poet's opinion. That is sufficient as a standard of truth.

An essential element of Ibn Ezra's passage is the appeal to al-Fārābī's concept of the "imagination" (*al-takhayyul*). In several works, al-Fārābī details the workings of the "imaginative faculty" (*al-quwwa al-mutakhayyila*) as the site of retaining and combining images in the absence of perceptible objects. Central to the reception of prophecy, the imaginative faculty is also the site of producing and interpreting poetic imagery in the mode of *al-takhyīl* (translated by such terms as the "phantastic, imaginary, or make-believe").[67] In the *Iḥsā al-'ulūm* (Enumeration of sciences), al-Fārābī was clearly concerned with the psychological effects of poetic statements, the emotive qualities produced in the listener as though he were encountering a physical object.[68] In the work titled the *Risāla fī al-shi'r* (Treatise on poetry), al-Fārābī takes his discussion of the imagination one step further to argue that the quality of a poetic statement corresponds to its degree of remove from reality;

the more it relies upon layers of imitation and the work of the imaginative faculty, the better: "[Statements of imitation] may be constructed of things that imitate the matter itself, or of what imitate the things that imitate the matter itself, or of what imitate those things. Thus, statements of imitation create a distance of many degrees from the matter. In a similar vein, the imagining (*takhayyul*) of the thing by those statements [of imitation] leads to the same distance. . . . Many people find that the imitation of a thing by that which is farthest from it is better and more complete than imitating it by that which is nearest."[69]

We do not know that Ibn Ezra read al-Fārābī's Treatise on Poetry; *Kitāb al-muḥāḍara wa'l-mudhākara* does not present a similar statement. Still, Ibn Ezra certainly pursues such imaginative effects in his poetry. Dan Pagis seemed to understand this when he noted that, in Ibn Ezra's poetry, "the specifics of the depiction, or the various depictions, develop one inside the other, and each one adds further to the distancing of the subject from its appearance or quality in reality."[70] In the second panegyric that introduced this chapter, Ibn Ezra referred to the *mamdūḥ* as a "cedar in the Garden of Wisdom" before which shoots present offerings of shrubs and adds that the "shoots are blown away with the wind" while the cedar, representing the *mamdūḥ*, endures. The reader is taken deep into the world of the imagination. Although, in medieval Hebrew poetry, imaginative devices are not unique to panegyric, they play a particularly important role in conveying the esteem of the *mamdūḥ*.

A couplet from *Sefer ha-ʿanaq* presents layers of representation in the service of presenting a man's power, specifically over Time (i.e., Fate):

> He brandished swords over the head of Time and made [Time's]
> daughters into sheaths;
> he enslaved [the daughters] as though they were his handmaidens
> who were shamed like whores who pay their lovers![71]

Disturbing images of rape and sexual humiliation aside, the verse is rich in imaginative depth. The "daughters of Time," themselves merely an extension of Time, are subdued as enslaved (and seemingly penetrated) handmaidens, who, in turn, are likened to whores, not only whores who receive payment but whores who offer payment to their lovers (an image of utter disgrace in Ez 16:33). From the last image, one must retrace several steps to reach the *mamdūḥ*. The couplet includes degrees of falsehood and certainly evokes the emotive qualities that al-Fārābī saw as the hallmark of poetic speech.

The *takhalluṣ* (transitional verse of the formal ode) is a particularly ripe poetic node for the display of imaginative devices, since by definition it seeks to relate things that do not have an obvious association. Among the "beautiful elements of poetry," Ibn Ezra illustrates *ḥusn al-takhalluṣ* (beauty of the transitional verse) with a highly imaginary example by Ibn Gabirol:

> Knowledge is the first among the paths of God, from the might of the Lord God stored it up
> and established it as a king over everything and wrote Yequtiel's name upon its standard.

The might of the Lord establishes Knowledge (foremost of God's paths) as a king who holds a standard, which bears Yequtiel's name. Yequtiel is made into the epitome or telos of Knowledge through several degrees of imaginary remove.

Again, Ibn Ezra did not discuss the imagination in any depth. Still, he clearly focused on the hyperbolic devices (*al-ghulū* and *al-ighrāq*) that were at the core of the imaginative process, devices that, as Beatrice Gruendler remarked, "shocked, or thrilled, audiences and critics with their imaginary potential" even before al-Fārābī pondered their emotive power. Gruendler also highlights the social power of imaginative tropes and their particular connection to panegyric. Through the study of works on ʿAbbasid poetics as well as reports (*akhbār*) that detail audience reactions, she concludes:

> The *muḥdath* ["modern"] poets produced complex tropes with arresting fantastic features that purported to be true. They all shared the blurring of the borderline between reality and image and the interpenetration of these two planes with an illogical or fantastic effect, construed with logical tricks[72] and figures of speech. There was something new and strange, even absurd, about this, which fascinated audiences. The accounts about poets, patrons, and critics overwhelmingly demonstrate the success of verses that contained such elements of the imaginary. It was enjoyed by contemporary listeners, and it was most prized by those who benefited from poetry's aesthetic appeal, namely the political elite praised with it and their bureaucrats and entertainers.[73]

As with Arabic poetics, the imaginative devices pondered and employed by Mosheh Ibn Ezra and his contemporaries cannot be dissociated from the social circumstances in which poetry circulated; these devices were undoubtedly of great import to the recipients of Hebrew panegyric and for the construction of their public images.

CHAPTER 7

In Praise of God, in Praise of Man: Issues in Political Theology

On November 6, 1995, Noa Ben-Artzi Filosof, granddaughter of the assassinated Prime Minister Yitzhak Rabin, eulogized her grandfather (in Hebrew): "You were the pillar of fire before the camp and now we are left only the camp, alone, in the dark." No one could miss the stirring power of the image from Ex 13:21, where God makes Himself manifest in order to lead the Israelites in a pillar of cloud by day and a pillar of fire by night. The image was effective, even apt, on many levels: the prime minister as a unitary leader before his people; his power akin to raging fire (better the fire than the cloud); the nation as the "camp"; the political situation as desert and darkness. One might argue that the secular Zionist context allowed the biblical image to be stripped of any specific association with the divine and that the "pillar of fire" was nothing more than an image of leadership. Yet I would argue that the image was particularly effective due to the rhetorical, even theological, tension produced. Rabin was not Moses, who followed God's direction; Rabin was God.

One might assume that a literary device of this sort, which associated man so closely with the divine, perhaps even allowing the human to displace the divine, would not have occurred in the devout context of Jewish society in the Middle Ages. However, such images are not altogether uncommon among the many panegyrics that survive from the pens of medieval Jewish authors. We have already witnessed occasional examples in earlier chapters of this book.

Dunash Ben Labrat's "Know, my heart, wisdom," for example, opens with self-exhortation wherein the poet urges his heart to praise God and then his patron Ḥasdai Ibn Shaprut:

Thank the Former of hearts, the Protector of souls, who reins in
mighty winds,
with innovative, metered and distinguished poems, with
expressions that are measured, refined and well-conceived,
and set a song of praise for the prince, the *rosh kallah* who utterly
ruined foreign troops.[1]

In almost a single breath, the poet implores his heart to give thanks to God through poetry and to eulogize his patron in panegyric. In fact, one might say that God is simply exploited as a pivotal device for making the transition between the self-exhortation and the panegyric. The fact that God's qualities are restricted to two lines while the patron's occupy nineteen might be significant in itself. Most striking is the parallelism set up between Ibn Shaprut and God with the poet describing the *mamdūḥ* through divine imagery no fewer than five times:

He put on wonder and glory (Ps 104:1) and wore God's victory. He
conquered ten fortifications of the insolent. . . .
Nations hurry in alarm and peoples quake; those who thought
themselves mighty grew weak for fear of him (Ps 99:1, 104:7), . . .
He is friend to many, forgiving their transgressions (Mi 7:18), yet he
lowers his arm [in judgment] (Is 30:30) while sitting at the gate.[2]

The poet conveys essential values of political legitimacy—military prowess, clemency, and judgment—all of which are typically predicated of a sovereign. Yet the poet takes the portrayal a step further by basing his depiction on phrases predicated of God in the Bible. This intertextual technique raises several issues, starting with the most basic question of whether it carries significance in a theological sense at all, and, if so, what it articulates about the culture of the Jews in the Islamic Mediterranean. Does the sharing of epithets and other phrases suggest a kind of "power sharing" between God and the *mamdūḥ*, the quasi-deification of the *mamdūḥ*, a partial displacement of the divine, an analogy between divine and human sovereignty?

The first question I will address, essentially a poetic one, is whether the praises for God in the Bible were treated by medieval Hebrew poets as desacralized "raw material" that could be recast in a manner entirely dissociated from original context. In favor of this position is a statement wherein Mosheh Ibn Ezra lamented the limited capaciousness of the Hebrew language that resulted from the condition of exile; nothing of the language had been preserved apart from what is found in the "twenty-four books" (of the Bible), and from these "the community intertextually borrowed (*iqtabasat*)[3] everything, whether with respect to prayers, invocations, renunciation of worldly things, panegyric (*al-madḥ*), poetry (*al-taqrīḍ*),[4] lament, elegy, and all other types of speech and oration."[5] Thus the Hebrew poet, who sought to compose in a register of pure biblical Hebrew, was bound to draw on the reservoir of phrases that the Bible directed toward God; to avoid this entirely might have taken significant effort. Although Hebrew poetry is famously context-driven such that lacing a text with a biblical allusion can evoke an archetypal figure or scenario with resounding depth, it need not be the case that every quotation is meant to conjure up its original context.[6] A second argument in favor of this position is that the Bible's praises for God are drawn from mundane metaphors in the first place and need not be seen as "belonging to God" in any real sense. This might have been the reaction of a reader such as Maimonides, who subscribed to a radical apophatic theory of God's attributes; the Bible spoke "in the language of men" and described God through metaphors, often rather crude ones, so the redirection of such metaphors back to men would be neither surprising nor offensive.[7]

In contrast with the position that the redirection of "God references" to men was not tension-producing or meaningful, one might argue that the practice intimated an essential point about politics whereby legitimacy involved resonance with tropes of divine rule. In the discussion below, I largely take this latter position, though I remain cognizant of the critique suggested by the first. My reasons for this are several, foremost among them being that contemporary Arabic panegyric makes similar use of divine tropes, including those borrowed intertextually from the Qur'ān, and that the poetic technique was suggestive enough that it evoked condemnation on the part of literary critics. Further, Muslim and Jewish theologians addressed the subject of names and epithets shared between the human and the divine, sometimes with explicit connection to panegyric composition. The technique was one element of the broader phenomenon of sacralizing the *mamdūḥ*.

We will see that, in adopting the practice of praising men through divine imagery, poets were pressing against and, in the minds of some, overstepping a boundary between the human and the divine. The question of what exactly was being suggested, on a political level, through resonance with divine tropes is complicated. Was the "ruler" himself in some sense divine, such that we might speak of a "divine-human" complex wherein both power and names were shared? Was the "ruler" one whose legitimacy derived from God's direct manifestation, divine selection, imitating God's ways, or a mere analogy of divine and mundane powers?

The main purpose of this chapter is to look systematically at the phenomenon of praising Jewish *mamdūḥs* with divine tropes from poetic and theological perspectives. I will examine panegyrics that quote the Bible directly as well as those that allude to divine qualities more generally. My ultimate argument is that divine references provided a type of cognitive metaphor through which political culture was conceptualized, thus affording the "ruler" a place in the "polity" analogous to that of God in the universe. However, before presenting further examples from Hebrew panegyric, the chapter will range widely through bordering territories. It begins with a general discussion of issues in "political theology" that are provoked when divine imagery is put to work in the service of representing men. Following this, I will review texts and scholarship on the idea of political theology in biblical, rabbinic, and medieval Jewish sources. I then turn to Islamic sources and sites in Islamic writing that treat what I am calling "theological poetics," wherein the tensions of praising men with divine imagery are contemplated. From here, I present further examples from the Arabic panegyric corpus to create a taxonomy of models of divine-human relation as suggested by the texts. The chapter will then return to Jewish sources on theological poetics and further examples from the Hebrew panegyric corpus and conclude by evaluating the implications of this study for understanding the political culture of Jews in the Islamic Mediterranean. The chapter thus takes a rather circuitous path from medieval Hebrew poetry and back again, and it is my hope in doing so that the discussion will provide areas of resonance and differentiation for scholars in related areas of literature and political philosophy.

Political Theology

The premodern world—and, some would argue, the modern world—was predominated by theories of sovereignty that associated the ruler intimately with divinity. This was the case both in Christendom, where agnatic kingship was seen as deriving from a divine source, and in the Islamic world, where the construct *khalīfat allah*, "God's caliph," was taken in a range of meanings, from a caliph loyal to God, to a caliph selected by God to be His deputy, to God's manifestation on earth.[8] As a reflection and element of politics, the representation of the sovereign drew upon a wellspring of divine imagery, mostly from sacred books and liturgical traditions.

Political theology is an area of political philosophy made famous in the 1920s by the German legal theorist Carl Schmitt, who posited that political culture, even in ostensibly modern, secularized forms, is not devoid of theological elements, as when eternality is ascribed to the body politic, or when a ruler is afforded a place in the state that parallels that of God in the universe. For Schmitt, the matter was not only one of vestigial motifs but rather of a deeper theological structure that undergirds all politics, even unto modernity.[9]

The roots of this structure have been studied in premodern periods, particularly in theories of sovereignty and modes of power acclamation in Christian contexts. Thus, the great medievalist Ernst Kantorowicz evoked the subject in the subtitle of his book of 1957, *The King's Two Bodies: A Study in Medieval Political Theology*.[10] A decade before this, Kantorowicz studied the interpenetration of divine and human images of sovereignty in his *Laudes Regiae: A Study in Liturgical Acclamations and Mediaeval Ruler Worship*.[11] Here he argued that royal panegyrics integrated into the medieval Latin liturgy (beginning in Frankish-Gaul in the eighth century) articulated a kind of sacral kingship such that the potentate shared imagery and power with Christ as conqueror, emperor, and king.[12] In *The King's Two Bodies*, Kantorowicz deepened his discussion of what he called the "God-man," the sovereign portrayed as both human and divine or, to use a phrase of the medieval period, "human by nature and divine by grace."[13] The book explains the sovereign's "immortality" as an embodiment of the body politic as well as divine aspects of his present sovereignty. Moreover, the book studies the legal constructs by which the king possessed a body like other men but also a transcendent body that made his sovereignty an instantiation of divine rule. In a recent retrospective marking fifty years since the book's publication, Stephen Greenblatt wrote that *The King's Two Bodies* remains "a remarkably vital, generous, and generative work" that treats an "astonishing range of devices invented by theologians and lawyers for defeating [the] death [of the sovereign] by extending bodily existence far beyond carnal boundaries."[14]

Kantorowicz's idea of the transcendent sovereign is probably captured most poignantly by the famous image of Emperor Otto II enthroned in the Aix-la-Chapelle Gospels—Christ-like in appearance, an orb in one hand, hands extended in crucifixion form, supported from beneath by a representation of the earth, and surrounded by the four beasts of Ezekiel's vision and a nimbus while the hand of Christ sets a crown upon his head. The emperor is the "God-man," his sovereignty bestowed by Christ even as he imitates and embodies Christ; he is simultaneously of the mundane and the celestial worlds, distinct domains that can be traversed by the person of the sovereign. For Kantorowicz, this suggested a cult of medieval "ruler worship," a subject for which he had a strong concern (perhaps even an obsession) after witnessing the atrocities of fascism. The image and its interpretation are memorable; yet, as Greenblatt puts it, "the gift of *The King's Two Bodies*" is that it presents its central argument not only "in physical grotesqueries like the effigy but in abstract, abstruse theological and legal doctrines."[15]

The thesis of *The King's Two Bodies* can be felt in an extraordinary range of studies that treat sovereignty and models of kingship in the ancient Near East, Byzantium, the Sassanian Empire, rabbinic Judaism, and the Islamic world.[16] Given the power that Kantorowicz ascribes theological aspects of political philosophy in Christian realms, we might ask the degree to which his theory is applicable or transferable to non-Christian contexts. Does divine embodiment of the sovereign require a theology whereby God becomes flesh? For the emperor to be "divine by grace," is a theology of divine grace not prerequisite? Other particularities of the formulation of divine kingship—such as the king's healing touch, or his transcending death—are arguably resonant only as Christomimetic tropes. Extending Kantorowicz's approach to the study of Islam, with its principle of succession through "consultation" (*shūrā*),[17] or postexilic Judaism, for which sovereignty was more a fantasy than a reality, is complicated. Below I offer a limited treatment of the topic in biblical, rabbinic, and medieval Jewish and Islamic sources.

Biblical Models

The Hebrew Bible presents competing models of kingship in different books. The literature on this subject is too vast to consider here, and for convenience I point to a recent treatment by Yair Lorberbaum that offers a tripartite taxonomy of biblical notions of kingship (which the author uses to introduce his discussion of political theory in rabbinic literature).[18] Lorberbaum calls the first notion "Direct Theocracy" (exemplified in Judges), whereby God Himself serves as king, thus obviating any need for monarchy and even negating its validity. The second is "Royal Theology," the dominant biblical view (exemplified in Psalms and other texts), whereby the Israelite king serves as an extension of God upon earth. The third is "Limited Monarchy" (exemplified in Deuteronomy 17, the "chapter of the king"), which places strict limits on monarchs such that true power resides with God only. The most relevant of these for our purposes is, of course, the second, though the Bible provides little detail about the precise nature of divine "extension" or the metaphysical conditions that it presumes.

Some biblical passages are particularly suggestive, or at least provide a locus classicus for seeing how later interpreters considered the issue of "Royal Theology." The most important in this regard is 1 Chr 29:23, "Solomon sat on the throne of Yahweh as king in place of his father David." The Bible, unfortunately, in no way clarifies whether this means that the king sat upon a celestial throne or an earthly throne that was created by Yahweh, or whether the "throne" was merely a symbol for reign. A related but even more ambiguous verse is Ps 45:7, clearly a part of a panegyric for a king. The Hebrew reads *ki-sakha elohim ʿolam va-ʿed*, most literally but oddly rendered, "Your throne God is everlasting." Should this be read as "Your throne is God everlasting," "Your throne, O God is everlasting," or "Your throne is [the throne of] God everlasting"? Even if it were taken in the final sense, we would still be left with the same questions that we had in the case of Solomon's throne. In any event, the divine inflection of Solomon's reign—and, in some cases, also David's—became a point of departure for thinking on divine kingship in the Jewish, Christian, and Islamic traditions.

Rabbinic and Medieval Jewish Sources

If we may return to Lorberbaum's thesis, models of biblical kingship enjoyed extended trajectories within rabbinic literature, often revolving around the reading and redirection of particular biblical passages. The model of "Limited Monarchy"—whereby a very mundane king stands subservient to God—dominates tannaitic literature, likely as a counterpoint to Roman conceptions of imperial omnipotence. However, traces of the "Royal Theology" model can also be observed, especially in later rabbinic writings.[19]

In a persuasive essay, Raʿanan Boustan argues that Lorberbaum's division of kingship models maps well onto changes in traditions pertaining to "Solomon's throne": "The earlier rabbinic sources that elaborate on this biblical image use descriptions of the throne's design and operation to highlight the severe limitations that should be placed on royal power. By contrast, midrashic and targumic sources from the sixth and seventh centuries increasingly downplay this 'disciplinary-pedagogical' function of the throne in favor of an emphasis on the throne's heavenly resonances; this cosmic or sacral dimension of the throne imbues its royal occupant with quasi-divine powers."[20]

An opinion is attributed already to the third-century amora Resh Laqish that Solomon first sat on the throne in the upper world and then sat on the throne in the lower world.[21] Another striking reading is a passage in Exodus Rabbah that expounds upon why God is called *melekh ha-kavod*, king of honor: "because He distributes (*ḥoleq*) his honor to those that fear him." By way of associated biblical verses, the midrash claims that God seated Solomon upon His throne, Elijah upon His horse, gave Moses His scepter, His garment of might to Israel, and reserves His crown for the Messiah. Such passages (which Kantorowicz would have loved) do not maintain an impenetrable barrier between the mundane and the divine realms but allows some, His "fearers," access to the metonymic symbols of divine power.[22]

Among medieval Jewish exegetes, there is a tendency to retain a fairly firm boundary between the human and the divine while still allowing for a type of "Royal Theology" by way of selection or analogy. Sa'adia Gaon translates the aforementioned Ps 45:7 as "Your [David's] throne, God erected it (*naṣabahu*) forever and for eternity."[23] Although this is not as dramatic as seating the king upon God's actual throne, it still maintains a theory of divine selection and affirmation. Avraham Ibn Ezra and David Kimḥi reject Sa'adia's reading but explain it instead as an implied construct, "Your throne is the throne of God," and defend the reading with 1 Chr 29:23, which might suggest close association with divinity.[24] However, accepting the verse as an implied construct does not exclude a metaphoric interpretation. While neither exegete explains Ps 45:7, Kimḥi discusses 1 Chr 29:23 in his commentary on Psalm 72, which he reads as David's deathbed testament. David says to God: "Just as You judge and render sentences without witnesses, so may my son judge and render sentences without witnesses." God responds: "By your life so I shall do, as it is said, 'And Solomon sat upon the throne of God.'" Kimḥi continues (following some early midrash): "Can a man of flesh and blood sit upon His throne? Behold it is written, 'His throne was tongues of flame' (Dn 7:9). Rather, the 'throne of God' means that he rendered sentences like his Maker without witnesses."[25] That is, the claim of Solomonic "divinity" is delimited to the sphere of judgment and is purely one of analogy. Solomon and David do not *really* sit upon God's throne. Interestingly, the views of the medieval exegetes seem more aligned with earlier tannaitic literature than with amoraic or early medieval aggadic literature.

Maimonides' political philosophy strongly associates the just sovereign with living in imitation of God. In the *Mishneh Torah*, he explains that all people, and especially the sovereign, are commanded to "walk in His ways" (cf. Dt 2:9) and to be "gracious and merciful" (*ḥonnen u-meraḥem*) with reference to a well-known rabbinic dictum, "Even as God is called gracious, so you be gracious; even as He is called merciful, so you be merciful; even as He is called holy, so be you holy." The prophets also described other attributes "to teach us that these qualities are good and right and that a human being should cultivate them, and thus imitate God, as far as he can."[26] In *The Guide of the Perplexed*, Maimonides is even more specific about what it means for the sovereign to imitate God with respect to mercy and grace: "[The governor] should be merciful and gracious, not out of mere compassion and pity but in accordance with what is fitting." That is, just as God need not *feel* pity in order to perform actions that suggest mercy, so the sovereign should perform similar actions, not because he is moved by pity but rather because these actions are just. Similarly, "with regard to some people, he should be *keeping anger and jealous and avenging* in accordance with their desserts, not out of mere anger."[27] In any case, Maimonides' perspective is one of divine imitation, certainly not divine manifestation.

Despite the significance of Jewish thinking on "Royal Theology," it seems that medieval Jewish thinkers, hence those closest in time to the panegyrics under discussion, delimited the divine associations of biblical figures by circumscribing their God-like qualities within specific spheres (such as judgment) and by presenting the God-human relationship as one of imitation and analogy.

Association with Divinity in Classical Islam

There is no question that the caliph in the Umayyad, 'Abbasid, and Fatimid dynasties was presented as elevated over other men. His power was enunciated through well-choreographed ceremonies, appearances with emblematic objects of power (such as the mantle, staff, and ring of the Prophet), and verbal articulations. He held unique regnal titles, dressed in splendid colors, and, beginning with the 'Abbasids, was literally hidden from public view.[28]

But do such power-enhancing practices intimate an element of divinity? Only in rare circumstances did Muslim thinkers, especially Shi'ites, create a theory of politics that allowed for the sovereign to be imbued ontologically with divinity in a literal sense.[29] For the most part, Islamic political dogma inscribed the caliphal role as a very human one. Aziz al-Azmeh, who has offered the broadest treatment of "Muslim Kingship," wrote: "It was [the caliph's] duty to imitate God, so that his subjects could imitate him. . . . He was living law in the sense of embodying and exemplifying the law, not in the sense of overruling it. On the contrary, he had to be ruled by God's law in order to rule legitimately himself."[30]

At the same time, however, al-Azmeh stresses that political rhetoric created images of the absolute ruler as the "best of all mankind" or even as sacred: "In all, the rhetorical and visual assimilation of the caliph to prophecy, to divinity, to a charismatic line, and his conception in terms of inviolability, incommensurability, ineffability, and sheer potency, produced a critical mass creative of a sublime and holy authoritarianism, one which flows in the social and imaginary-conceptual capillaries of Muslim political traditions."[31]

The phrase *khalīfat allah*, "God's caliph," offers a key entry point into questions of divine association in Islamic culture. In the view of Patricia Crone and Martin Hinds, the designation was used in the first Islamic centuries in a literal sense: that the caliph was God's deputy on earth with power over the mundane and the religious and that the title was only subsequently desacralized through an appellation of later coinage, "The caliph of God's Messenger" (*khalīfat rasūl allah*)—the successor of Muḥammad—thus neutralizing divine association and even religious authority.[32] Already in Qur'ān 38:26, King David is called God's "representative (*khalīfa*) upon the earth," and the usage of the term *khalīfa* during the Umayyad period arguably carried something of this sense and had little to do with the "succession" of a human ruler.[33] Throughout Umayyad panegyric, Crone and Hinds point out, the caliph is presented as God's representative on earth: "God's rope," "dispeller of darkness," "a refuge," one who "makes the blind see" and "stands between God and His servants."[34]

Crone and Hinds's book was received with significant criticism, from technical points to broad denunciations of a supposed "Orientalist" stance, and it is not my intention to engage these arguments here.[35] Instead, I wish to make two interrelated methodological observations. First, if Crone and Hinds are correct that "God's caliph" was meant in a literal sense that intimated divine association, the phrase still does not delineate the exact nature of God's relationship to the Muslim ruler. Did it convey that the caliph (or David, for that matter) was a direct manifestation of God, a divinely selected ruler, or a leader who lived in imitation of God? Did he represent God by extension or by analogy? Second, because much of Crone and Hinds's argument is based upon panegyric, we must evaluate the utility of this genre for reading political philosophy. On the one hand, poetic texts can be valuable testimonies to political culture in practice and may better reflect the period in which they were recited than later historical accounts. On the other hand, given their hyperbolic and performative qualities, our ability to interpret them is checked by our knowledge of political philosophy as presented in nonpoetic texts.[36] What is clear is that divine associations in some panegyrics were provocative enough to rouse the ire of literary critics who sometimes saw them as tantamount to polytheistic blasphemy.

In the following section, I will discuss aspects of what I am calling "theological poetics" in Islamic literature, including works belonging to poetic or theological genres that treat problems in divine/human "name sharing" and "power sharing" and the inter-projection of divine and mundane imagery. From the perspective of Islamic theology, "power sharing" between God and men carries the risk of ascribing partners to God (Ar., *shirk*), the very definition of polytheism.[37] Islamic writings exhibit concern for maintaining a recognizable boundary between human and divine epithets, with important implications for panegyric writing in particular. Following this, I will review examples from the Arabic corpus and then return to the study of Jewish texts and Hebrew panegyric.

Theological Poetics in Arabic-Islamic Sources

The tensions implicit in directing divine predicates toward men surfaces most clearly in Islamic theological writing within the expansive rubric of divine attributes and the "beautiful names" (*al-asmāʾ al-ḥusna*, sometimes called the "ninety-nine names of God").[38] Like the Bible, the Qurʾān often describes God in terms borrowed from the realm of human experience—essentially projections of the mundane onto the divine—yet tension and dissonance can occur when those very terms are projected back into the realm of the human. The root of the problem is at least partly one of language, such that "name sharing" and "power sharing" are intimately connected. Qurʾān commentators and theologians categorized the beautiful names according to different strategies, from simple alphabetical listings to sophisticated theological taxonomies. Among the several systems of classification indicated in the Qurʾān commentary of the Muʿatazilite Abū Manṣūr al-Baghdādī (d. 1037), for example, is a division according to names that can be applied to God alone (e.g., *khāliq*, Creator; *muḥyī*, Giver of Life; *mumīt,* Bringer of Death) and those that can also be applied to beings other than God (e.g., *ḥayy*, living; *ʿālim*, knowing; *mālik*, possessor), even if the terms do not mean exactly the same thing when speaking about God and other creatures.

Unsurprisingly, there is wide consensus that the name Allah can be applied to God alone. At least some theologians (e.g., al-Ghazzālī) hold the same to be true of *al-raḥmān* (the Merciful), even if it is similar in meaning to *al-raḥīm* (the Compassionate), a divine name that can also be predicated of human beings. A name in an intensive form such as *ʿalīm* (Knowing) is associated with omniscience and is generally applied to God alone, whereas a human being might be called *ʿālim*.[39] Some names (e.g., *mutakabbir*, "haughty"), as Haggai Ben Shammai has put it, "can have a laudatory connotation when referred to God or a derogatory, pejorative one when referred to humans."[40] For our purposes, the essence of this subject is the question of what names of God can also be predicated of men and hence be uttered in their praise.

In Arabic poetics, the problem of directing qur'ānic "God references" toward men, whether involving the beautiful names or not, is treated under the subject of *al-iqtibās* (lit., "taking a firebrand from a fire")—the intertextual technique of quoting from the Qur'ān verbatim, with slight modification, or by allusion. Broadly speaking, the phenomenon of *al-iqtibās* is recognized in both poetry and prose. Scholars generally approve of the practice in prose and point to *ḥadīth* wherein the Prophet quotes from the Qur'ān verbatim (similarly, the companions and early caliphs). With respect to poetry, most scholars cite the practice with approval, although a minority reject it because it seems to transform the Qur'ān into poetry, potentially undermining the central tenet that the Qur'ān is not poetry but a distinct and inimitable mode of speech.[41]

Yet, even those who approve of *al-iqtibās* prohibit or look unfavorably upon certain applications. The jurisprudent Mālik, whose school was predominant in al-Andalus, is reported to have disapproved of *al-iqtibās al-qabīḥ* (shameful or ugly *iqtibās*), including cases in which a poet transfers to the addressee "what God attributes to Himself."[42] Similarly, in the *Kitāb al-ʿumda*, Ibn Rashīq critiques a verse in which al-Mutanabbī boasts, "As if I flattened the earth (cf. Qur'ān 79:30) from my knowledge." The critic censured, "He likened himself to the Creator—God is far more sublime than whatever the transgressors say!"[43] These criticisms of what we might call "divine *iqtibās*" go beyond the appropriation of the beautiful names only. In his book *al-Iqtibās min al-qur'ān al-karīm*, which is largely a catalog of approved instances of *iqtibās*, Abū Manṣūr al-Thaʿālibī (961/62–1037/38) includes a short chapter on *al-iqtibās al-makrūh* (contemptible *iqtibās*). Here we find disapproval for exploiting the Qur'ān for the purpose of folly and for "mentioning a created thing with attributes possessed by God alone" (*fī dhikr al-khalq mimā ista'athara allah bihi min al-ṣifāt*). Al-Tha'ālibī illustrates the latter with a couplet from a panegyric by al-Ṣūlī in honor of the military commander Abū Aḥmad al-Muwāfaq (842–91) upon the occasion of his wresting Baghdad from the two sons of 'Abd Allah b. Ṭāhir:

> O sons of Ṭāhir! The soldiers of God have come to you! Between
> the two of them [the two sons of Ṭāhir] even death is given over
> to perdition.
> Amidst the armies of their leader, Abū Aḥmad is the most excellent
> protector and the most excellent helper.[44]

The final verse includes a verbatim quotation from Qur'ān 8:40: "Know that God is your protector, the most excellent protector and the most excellent helper," hence the approbation.[45] Similar is the blame that Ṣafī al-Dīn al-Ḥillī (d. 1350) assigns a ruler who once signed a proclamation: "They shall come before Us and We shall call them to account" (Qur'ān 88:26).[46]

Irrespective of the proscriptions of legal scholars and literary critics, their preservation of examples of contemptible *iqtibās* provides sufficient evidence that poets associated their *mamdūḥ*s with God, sometimes drawing upon imagery that was unmistakably qur'ānic. Reservations toward certain practices in poetry in no way describe what the poetic effects of those practices were. Poetic criticism is one thing; poetry is another. In fact, literary criticism might be most useful in reconstructing poetic culture insofar as it reveals where the fault lines lay, the boundaries of sanctioned expression against which the poet could bristle.[47] Poets found exploiting the language of the Qur'ān a productive means of creating hyperbolic effects, whether or not these were intended to constitute a particular political philosophy. In some cases, play on divine references was clearly not political at all, as when al-Mutanabbī boasted over his poetic prowess. But in others, divine association may have suggested something about the nature of politics.

What can we actually learn about the political meaning of calling a *mamdūḥ*, for example, the "most excellent protector and the most excellent helper"? Did the poet intend actual divinization? Did the *mamdūḥ* displace God or occupy a place in mundane affairs analogous to but distinct from God's place in the universe? Was the *mamdūḥ* a conduit for the performance of God's work? Was the qur'ānic phrasing only a hyperbolic way of emphasizing his role as protector? The precise mechanics of a divine-human complex are difficult to discern from an isolated verse and will remain elusive because of the hyperbolic nature of poetic texts. Below I present a limited survey of examples of divine *iqtibās* in the Arabic panegyric corpus toward creating a taxonomy of divine references within political contexts.

Divine *Iqtibās* in Arabic Panegyric

My purpose in this section is to review select examples of divine *iqtibās*, as a type of sacred hyperbole, from the Arabic literary corpus and to analyze what types of divine-human interaction they seem to imply. Again, divine *iqtibās* need not convey a single understanding of a divine-human complex that holds for all of Islamicate civilization, diverse as it was with respect to region, period, and sectarian and ontological underpinnings. In all the examples, poets flirt with divine association, some tending toward a model of direct manifestation and others toward relatively light literary play. The predominant model, however, is based in analogy such that the ruler occupies a place in the world or the state that is parallel to God's place in the universe.

In numerous instances, the Andalusian Shiʿite poet Ibn Hānī offered praise for the Fatimid caliph al-Muʿizz li-Dīn Allah (932–75)[48] drawing directly on the beautiful names, such as, "That which you desire is none other than what divine decree (*al-aqdār*) desires! Go and judge, for you are the One, the Subduer (*al-wāḥid al-qahār*)!"[49] The verse bestows two of the beautiful names upon the caliph and presents him as one who follows the divine will; in fact, the poem insists that his very desires are identical with God's. While the caliph may not be God, he is deserving of God's titles. The divine associations are further intensified because these beautiful names occur in this precise order in Qur'ān 40:16, which also pertains to sovereignty, "To whom belongs sovereignty this day? To God the One, the Subduer." Has the *mamdūḥ* displaced God? Is God made manifest through the caliph? Is he one who lives in imitation of God? Again, it is difficult to discern the precise mechanics of a divine-human complex.

In another poem, Ibn Hānī praises al-Muʿizz:

> I consider the praise of him like the praise of God: obedience and glorification by which sin is diminished.
>
> He is the Inheritor of the world (*al-wārith al-dunyā*),[50] the one for whom men were created, until the time when the two poles of the earth will meet.

From the cradle [his father] al-Manṣūr was not ignorant of his
nobility; banners and flags gleamed with bedazzlement.
[Al-Manṣūr] saw that he would be elevated to be Possessor (*mālik*)
of all the earth, and when he saw him he said, "This one is the
Everlasting, the Unequaled" (*al-ṣamad al-watr*).[51]

On the one hand, al-Mu'izz is a part of God's creation—its goal, its telos, but a created being nonetheless. On the other, the *mamdūḥ* is sacralized in several ways, specifically by attributing expiatory power to praising him and by naming him with no fewer than four of the beautiful names. "Obedience and glorification" (*qunūt wa tasbīḥ*) are likewise associated with serving God specifically. Two of the divine names are circumscribed by the mundane; al-Mu'izz is Inheritor and Possessor of the world, *al-dunyā*, whereas God holds these names with respect to everything, especially the afterworld—*al-ākhira*. This technique is common, and I am labeling it "delimitation." The political significance of the device here seems to define al-Mu'izz's role as analogic and mimetic. At the same time, the use of the "Everlasting" and the "Unequaled" veer more toward terms specific to God and perhaps even suggest God's manifestation through the person of the caliph. The tension between delimitation and manifestation makes this panegyric particularly rich, even as it reminds us of the limited utility of panegyric as a source for political philosophy. Whether Ibn Hānī overstepped a boundary or simply brushed against it, the conceit of these verses suggests that some limit between the mundane and the divine was presumed and could be exploited by the poet.

The high degree of divine association in Ibn Hānī's panegyric for al-Mu'izz likely relates to Shi'ite, particularly Isma'ili, theories of the imamate, which set the imam cum caliph within a particular cosmology and deemed him infallible.[52] Yet sacralized portrayals of sovereigns are not reserved for Shi'ite potentates only. The poet Ibn al-Ta'awīdhī (d. 1188) praised the 'Abbasid caliph al-Mustaḍī' Bi'amr Allah: "After God, yours are the prohibition, the creation and the command; in your outstretched hand are benefit and harm."[53] The bringer of harm and the bringer of benefit (*al-ḍār, al-nāf'i*) are among the beautiful names, and the verse exploits Qur'ān 7:54: "Surely His is the creation and the command." Again, the caliph is distinguished from God but possesses what God possesses, at least secondarily so. There is a kind of "delimitation" as well as a technical eschewal of *shirk* (polytheism), even as the verse intimates a kind of power sharing. The caliph is like God and is sacralized by being praised with

God's praises. The attribution of divine qualities does not demonstrate that panegyric simply "secularized" or "desacralized" divine language; rather, the association with God, however hyperbolic, remained a meaningful and essential aspect of ruler representation. In this case, the association seems to be mimetic and analogical.

To take an Andalusian non-Shiʿite example, the poet Ibn ʿAbd Rabbih praised the Umayyad emir ʿAbdallah Ibn Muḥammad (844–912) upon his accession to power:

> The reign (*khilāfa*) of ʿAbd Allah is a pilgrimage for all mankind; in
> its time there is neither lewdness nor abuse!
> He is the Imam of Guidance (*imām al-hudā*) who brought to life
> for us the very lifeblood[54] of Guidance; [the lifeblood] was
> gasping for breath while it was dying.
> He is true with what his hands presented of augustness, and that
> which was presented to us from [his hands] through him is true!
> He conducts the kingdom of the two sunsets! Lo, he is fit for the
> kingdom of the two sunrises![55]

In Qur'ān 55:17, God is called "Lord of the two sunrises and Lord of the two sunsets." Here, the verse is used playfully in reference to the Islamic West, where ʿAbd Allah held power (however exaggerated here), and to the Islamic East, where his power was purely aspirational. But despite the specificity of the play, the emir is given a divine epithet, which would undoubtedly have troubled certain critics. I do not consider the divine association here to be as strong as in Ibn Hānī's praise for al-Muʿizz. But still, a kind of sacralization is put to effect, enhanced by portraying ʿAbd Allah's reign as a sacred time similar to *ḥajj*, when "lewdness and abuse" (*rafath wa fusūq*) are banned (cf. Qur'ān 2:197).[56]

As Suzanne Pinckney Stetkevych has shown, the boundaries of divine association are pressed even in the *burda* tradition in praise of the Prophet Muḥammad. Al-Buṣīrī (1211–94) suggestively employs diction that is commonly associated with God but with a certain delimitation; Muḥammad is called "free of any partner" with respect to "inner and outer beauty," a verse that Stetkevych describes as "uncomfortably close to the Islamic deific formula for Allah 'who has no partner.'"[57] At the same time, the poet is careful to distance this statement from "what the Christian's claim," that is, the deification of a prophet. Another verse from al-Buṣīrī's *burda* reads:

For indeed both this world and the next come from your generosity,
And our knowledge of the Pen and Tablet comes from your knowledge.[58]

Again, the association with God is close, dangerously close, to being transgressive. The first hemistich exploits Qur'ān 92:13, "To Us [God] belong this world and the next"; the "Pen and Tablet" of the second hemistich refer to the archetypes set by God, and the verse may thus imply that the Prophet possesses "knowledge of the unseen" (*al-ghayb*), which only God possesses (Qur'ān 27:65; 6:59). Further, the word translated here as "from" (*min*) might defensibly be understood in the sense of "through"; thus the Prophet would be a conduit associated more closely with God than the rest of humanity, but a human nonetheless. On the other hand, it might be that "this world and the next" and "knowledge of the Pen and Tablet" literally come *from* the Prophet, that these things are, in a sense, his. Such associations have bothered readers of the poem down to the present.[59] Perhaps the verse falls within the bounds of proper expression, or perhaps it trespasses into the territory of *shirk*, but it is certain that the verse's power stems from its provocation of this boundary.

A final related Arabic example, by the Andalusian poet Ibn Muqāna al-Ushbūnī, is composed for the Fatimid caliph Idrīs Ibn 'Alī Ibn Ḥamūd (who had traveled to Málaga). The poem involved a dramatic performance practice wherein the poet recited with a veil separating himself from the caliph and, when the poet reached the verse "See that when we are lit by your light, it is from the light of the Lord of the Worlds," Ibn Ḥamūd would order the veil to be lifted.[60] Although not involving a technical *iqtibās*, the poem intimates a two-part association of the caliph with God: that the caliph speaks to other men as God speaks to all humanity, "through a veil" (Qur'ān 42:51), and that the caliph's light is God's light, following the famous verse (Qur'ān 24:35) "God is the light of the heavens and the earth." An analogical relationship is posited such that God stands in relation to His creation as the caliph does to his subjects. Still, there is a delicious ambiguity in the verse. On the one hand, it might be that the divine light that reached the poet from the caliph was a *reflection* of God's light such that the caliph was a conduit of God's sovereignty. On the other, the poet might be saying that the caliph's light *is* divine light.[61] Ultimately, poetry remains a difficult source for discerning political theory, but there is certainly sufficient evidence that Arabic poets productively exploited qur'ānic language in provoking the boundary between the human and the divine.

Reverberations of Theological Poetics in Jewish Sources

Some of the concerns of Islamic theological literature surface, albeit with less philosophical rigor, in premedieval rabbinic writings. The problem of "name sharing" between humans and God is implicit in abstruse legal areas such as oath taking (which names of God are considered valid or binding when sworn upon) and the copying of Torah manuscripts (which names can and cannot be erased by a scribe). In m. Shevuʿot 4:13, an opinion attributed to Rabbi Meir states that one is liable for an oath taken by proper names of God (such as the tetragrammaton or *Elohim*) and epithets such as *ḥannun ve-raḥum* (Gracious and Merciful), *erekh apayim* (Slow to Anger), *rav ḥesed* (Abounding in Kindness), and "all other nicknames" (*kinuyyim*). However, the majority opinion is that one is exempt from liability if the oath is taken over one of the nicknames, since these are also predicable of humans. B. Shevuʿot 35a goes on to ask whether *ḥannun* and *raḥum* should be considered divine names sufficient and binding for the purposes of an oath and turns to the related case of names that can and cannot be erased when a scribe writes a Torah scroll. The judgment there is clear that names borrowed from the realm of the human are not fully divine, even when they belong to the "thirteen attributes of God" named in Ex 34:6.[62] Names including *ha-gadol* (the Great), *ha-gibbur* (the Valiant), *ha-nora* (the Terrible), *he-ḥazaq* (the Strong), *ha-ʿazzuz* (the Mighty), *ḥannun ve-raḥum* (Gracious and Merciful), *erekh apayyim* (Slow to Anger), and *rav ḥesed* (Abounding in Kindness) can all be erased and are thus not binding in the case of an oath.

At the heart of the discussion is whether the names that the Bible uses to describe God are essentially and exclusively divine. They are considered nonbinding for oath taking and can be erased because they are, in effect, human names; their application to God is derivative and metaphoric. Even according to the minority opinion of Rabbi Meir, whereby all the "nicknames" are fully valid for oaths, there is no denial that these same nicknames can also be attributed to human beings. The question itself only makes sense when one assumes that such names carry ambiguity.

Moving now to the geonic, and hence the Islamic, period, the *Halakhot gedolot*, a legal compendium by Shimʿon Qayyara (late tenth century), rules against the majority opinion in the Talmud that an oath taken by one of the nicknames is binding despite the fact that such names can be erased, "for who is intended . . . other than the Holy One, blessed be He, He who is Gracious, He who is Merciful."[63] It seems likely that the departure from the Gemarah's opinion relates to the weight of the "beautiful names" in contemporary Islamic discourse. Still, Qayyara's position does not resolve whether such names as *raḥum* and *ḥannun* are permissible appellations for human beings.[64] In eleventh-century al-Andalus, Ibn Janāḥ viewed the term *raḥum* as particular to God. Under the root *rḥm* in his *Kitāb al-usūl* (Book of roots), he wrote that "the attribute that is particular to God (*al-ṣiffa al-khāṣṣa li'llah*), sublime and exalted, is *raḥum ve-ḥannun* because of the *ḥah* of intensification, likewise the *nun* of *ḥannun*. The general attribute of the light construction is *raḥman*."[65]

The impact of medieval Islamic, especially Mu'atazilite, thinking on Jewish writing on "name sharing" is felt most strongly in an obscure Judeo-Arabic work attributed to Shemuel Ben Ḥofni Gaon, the original title of which was probably *Kitāb al-asmā' wa'l-ṣifāt* (The book of names and attributes).[66] The purpose of the book was to explore what names and attributes are appropriate for praising both God and men, and which are reserved for God alone: "[We] will mention the names of God, may He be exalted, and the attributes of His essence and His actions, and what of the attributes of the Creator, may He be exalted, is permitted to be attributed to the created (*al-makhlūq*) since this does not require making them alike or similar, and what is not permitted of this."[67]

Importantly for our purposes, the entire work is framed by a desire to praise a certain Abū Isḥāq Mar Rav Avraham Ben Mar Rav 'Aṭa al-Ṭabīb, who is credited with expertise in natural science and matters of law (*sharī'a*) and as a supporter of the Sura academy. At the beginning of the treatise, the author writes that the work was written as an introduction to the terms with which "we shall designate the virtuous lord, the most exalted leader Abū Isḥāq. . . . —may God prolong his exaltedness—concerning the titles of leadership and praise that convey his merit and virtues and require esteeming, exalting, magnifying, and revering him as he justly deserves."

The treatise itself is divided into five main subsections: (1) names by which God alone is called; (2) names by which humans can be called but not in specific formulations whereby they can only be applied to God—for example, "I am the first and I am the last" (Is 44:6); (3) names of action applicable to God, some of which cannot be predicated of men; (4) names of God's essence; and (5) actions that can be predicated of Him and those that cannot. The end of the treatise includes subsections on actions that can be performed by God alone, things that can never be predicated of God, twenty names that can be applied either to God or men, and ten names for humans that cannot be attributed to God (all from Psalm 15).

In general, the author takes a rather liberal view of what names can be applied to both God and humans. In most cases, one must bear in mind that the names do not imply equivalence or similarity between the two, especially of terms that refer to God's essence but human actions. God and man may both be called *yode'a*, "Knowing," but in the case of God, it refers to his essence (that he knows all things at all times), whereas a person might know a specific thing at a particular point in time; God can be called *qadosh*, "Holy," as can a human, but a human is only called such because he refrains from prohibited things (*muḥarramāt*).[68] Interestingly, Ben Ḥofni sees all "thirteen attributes" as predicable of humans. The author opines that God and humans may be called "removing guilt" and "passing over transgression" and even writes that "we have found that men are called *raḥum*." Although *raḥum* and *ḥannun* are understood as "the utmost of mercy and graciousness," they are not reserved for God alone.[69]

Toward the conclusion of the treatise, the author returns to praise the *mamdūḥ*: "We did all of this because we were glad that there was in this land one like [Abū Isḥāq]." The author concludes by stating that he found ten terms with which to praise the *mamdūḥ*; these divide into two categories, the first of which is appropriate for the "people of knowledge" (*ahl al-'ilm,* i.e. scholars). We see the first two terms—wise (*ḥakham*) and clever (*navon*)—and here the manuscript unfortunately ends. One may presume that the second category pertains either to generous patrons or to those specifically trained in matters of law.

There is no discussion in a work of poetics by a medieval Jewish author that explicitly considers the problem of directing phrases predicated of God toward human beings. Still, it is clear that the general theory and practice of *al-iqtibās* was embraced and largely celebrated by Jewish authors in al-Andalus. Mosheh Ibn Ezra was clearly versed in *al-iqtibās* and referred to the device by name.[70] We have already seen how he noted that Hebrew authors "intertextually borrowed" (*iqtabasat*) from the Hebrew Bible for all poetic genres; elsewhere, he extolled the practice of Arabic poets who "took verses from their Qur'ān" (*min qur'ānihim*) and Jewish poets who beautified their poetry through the analogous technique.[71] Undoubtedly, Ibn Ezra considered the fact that biblical praises for God were being used in panegyric whether as a matter of necessity or as a productive means for creating desired effects.

Some sense of a limit to setting men in God's place may be indicated by Ibn Ezra's critique of a particular verse by Ibn Khalfūn. The verse reads: "Were it not for you, there would be no created beings, their fathers and grandfathers would not have been created."[72] Ibn Ezra thought that this was going too far in the poetic device *al-ghulū*, hyperbole.[73] Arguably, the offense, in Ibn Ezra's view, was that Ibn Khalfūn, even without employing *al-iqtibās*, placed the *mamdūḥ* in God's place as Creator.[74]

Yehudah Halevi likely expressed reservations toward divine *iqtibās* in a Hebrew panegyric dedicated to Natan Ben Shemuel. Written during Halevi's pilgrimage, the poet concludes with a metapoetic reflection on panegyric:

> I have committed a trespass with the song of God's holiness,
> to whose name my praises are appointed;
> I have dedicated them, distinguished them, and made them
> unique utterances to God the Unique,
> but I have permitted them at a time such as this to His
> sons and students as praise and thanks.[75]

The word *em'al* with the preposition *bet* in the first line, "to commit a trespass with [something]," appears in the Bible in the sense of "misappropriation, using something sacred for the wrong purpose," as in Jo 7:1, "the children of Israel committed a trespass with the devoted thing [*ḥerem*], the thing set apart for Yahweh." (This usage also produced the common rabbinic term *me'ilah*, the misappropriation of sacred objects or funds.) Whether Halevi refers here specifically to misappropriating his own liturgical poetry or biblical laudations for God is not clear, but certainly he identifies the problem of redirecting God's praises toward men and the misuse of words that properly belong to God. Importantly, he does not maintain that God's praises could simply be decontextualized or desacralized; God's praises remain God's, and redirecting them toward men is permitted in rare circumstances for *mamdūḥ*s who are worthy of them.

Divine *Iqtibās* in Hebrew Panegyric

Clearly, there is a rich background of Islamo-Arabic thought and literature against which we might read Hebrew sources that weave descriptions of God into panegyrics for men. While I do not hold that poets intended an intimate association between a *mamdūḥ* and divinity each time a divine epithet or a biblical verse was quoted, I also do not believe that we can simply discount all such examples as radically decontextualized or as desacralized metaphors. The

Hebrew corpus reveals countless characterizations of men through divine imagery, whether by assigning them names associated with God (including the "thirteen attributes"), by directing biblical praises for God toward them, or by associating them with divinity in other ways. In most cases, these are found in texts dedicated to Jewish leaders of significant rank—gaons, exilarchs, *nagid*s, scribes, courtiers, and other men of status. There are, of course, differences in allusion type and the application of intertextual references ranges from the "serious" extolling of virtues to "light" literary plays. Below, I discuss several examples, beginning with the "light," followed by some that might be called "personal" and concluding with some that are truly political.

In some cases, reference to God can be entirely humorous or ironic. Yehudah Halevi praised Meir Ben Qamniel, whose name "Meir" means "giver of light," as "Meir who illuminates the Torah." However, the poet also fears that the *mamdūḥ* has disfavored him: "He gives light like dawn to all of his friends but to me he brings on evening" (*ma'ariv 'aravim*). In the liturgy, God is called *ma'ariv 'aravim*, "bringer of evening." Obviously, Halevi was not associating the *mamdūḥ* with any positive quality of God but was only making a play on this sobriquet. Still, the verse works not because *ma'ariv 'aravim* was deemed neutral but precisely because of its resonant association with God.[76]

In numerous cases, a poet uses divine association in a personal key as a way of capturing the degree to which he longs for or respects the *mamdūḥ*. Shelomoh Ibn Gabirol praised Nissim Ben Ya'aqov Ibn Shahīn of Qairawan, who had been the poet's teacher in al-Andalus: "I meditate upon you always; you are like One and I am the one who elongates [its pronunciation]." "I meditate upon you always" recalls Ps 63:7; "one who elongates" is a learned reference to the punctilious requirement of elongating the pronunciation of the word "One" (*eḥad*) when reciting Dt 6:4 in the *Shema'* prayer.[77] Similarly, Avraham Ibn Ezra praised Barukh Ibn Jau: "He is more precious to me than pearls. . . . He is One without a second; he is without measure or form."[78] In such cases, the poet sets the *mamdūḥ* in the place that the worshiper places God; the references may have been humorous on some level; but analogically, they evoke the difference in status between poet and *mamdūḥ*.

Addressing Mosheh Ibn Ezra, Yehudah Halevi wrote (speaking of himself in the third person): "His lips fall short of recounting your goodness. Can your praise be counted or told? He fails for he does not know the number [of your praises]" (Ps 71:15); Halevi thus set the older *mamdūḥ*, who served as a protector and patron, in the place where the psalmist placed God.[79] Another panegyric by Ibn Khalfūn to an unknown recipient opens:

> Toward the goodness of your name I fly like an eagle, toward your
> reputation I skip like a fawn,
> and toward your image I hurry like a swift cloud, as though by
> these [your name, reputation, and image] I took vows unto
> God.[80]

The incipit may well have been the opening words of a devotional poem.[81] The differentiation between the addressee and God does not emerge until the second hemistich of line 2, and even here the name, reputation, and image all retain a sacral valence. One might compare the final verse with the Arabic panegyric by Ibn Hānī above, "I consider the praise of him like the praise of God." Again, the divine association relates to the personal connection between the two men rather than between a leader and his community. Perhaps a more general or communal function is suggested later in the poem: "With your words and choice teachings you revive and quicken those who sleep in graves." The reference to reviving the dead, generally viewed as predicable of God alone, is used here hyperbolically and should not be mistaken for divinization. Yet divine association is brilliantly created through the ambiguity of the addressee in the opening verse and the continued use of divine imagery throughout.[82]

Turning now to the most political examples, divine association was an important device for depicting men of power. While association with God was probably not intended every time a divine epithet was directed toward a man, the richer, denser, and more explicit examples may convey a political philosophy wherein association with the divine carried meaning.[83] After considering several Hebrew panegyrics for men of power from the Islamic East and from al-Andalus, the discussion will return to the phenomenon's significance within the rubric of political theology.

An early panegyric for Sa'adia Gaon contains several examples of divine *iqtibās*: "You who purify seven times in the furnace (Ps 12:7), who derives the precious from the vile . . . who gathers lambs and leads the mother sheep (Is 40:11). . . . The fire of his speech is known for it was redeemed from descending into the Pit (Jb 33:24)."[84] The focus of the portrayal is on Sa'adia's eloquent speech, exegetic prowess, and communal leadership. It is difficult to see in these rather general associations any sort of deification. Yet, like God, and through the Bible's precise wording, the *mamdūḥ* purifies his speech and protects his flock. A particularly dense grouping of divine *iqtibās* references is found in a panegyric for a hypothetical gaon (from the epistolary formulary

TS J 3.3): "Our lord and master So-and-So, head of the academy of the pride of Jacob, the honored and precious, who has taught Torah all his life and sought teaching with his all. He leads the holy nation on the paved path and leads them along the straight road. He removes stones from rough places (Is 42:16) and straightens ridges (Is 40:4). He strengthens the weak (Ez 34:16); heals the sick and bandages the wounded [liturgical]. He looks for the lost [sheep] and brings back the strayed (Is 49:10). He holds dominion in tranquility and tends with repose. He guides them to springs of water (Is 49:10); He causes them lie down along watercourses."[85]

The gaon is shepherd, healer, guide, and restorer. He performs many of God's vital functions, however metaphorically. The shepherd, of course, is one of the more universally recognized metaphors of legitimate rule, though the quotation here is predicated of God. Even the verses that do not use divine *iqtibās* recall God's roles. I do not see the divine allusions as casual or incidental but rather, especially given their density, an essential element of constructing the gaon's image of legitimacy. This document is of particular importance because it addresses a hypothetical figure; the imitation of God is thus a requisite quality of the idealized leader.

Numerous God references are preserved within the correspondence of Shemuel Ben 'Eli. In praise of Avraham, head of the Palestinian academy, he wrote: "He redeems her who stumbles [i.e., Israel] from descending into a pit."[86] In a letter to a *melammed* (teacher), Shealtiel, we read: "He curbs the spirit of princes, inspires awe in kings" (Ps 76:13).[87] To Natanel, a *rosh yeshivah*, he wrote: "His rod and staff comfort the community" (Ps 23:4).[88] To an *av bet din*, he wrote: "His foundation is on holy mountains" (Ps 87:1). Again, these examples do not suggest divine manifestation so much as the *mamdūḥs*' imitation of the divine. Interestingly, they were not composed by one of lower rank for *mamdūḥs* of higher rank but rather the opposite; these panegyrics were not intended to flatter their recipients but rather to establish the *mamdūḥs*' legitimacy before their communities and ultimately to uphold the legitimacy of the gaon himself.

The prevalence of God references in political poems from al-Andalus is already suggested by the panegyric of Ben Labrat for Ibn Shaprut at the beginning of this chapter, which employs such images with striking density. With rich intertextual associations, Ibn Shaprut wears God's glory and victory, forgives transgressions, lowers his arm in judgment, and inspires dread in the nations of the world.[89] The poet does not go so far as to suggest the patron's superiority over God; one verse explicitly denies this by referring to the *mamdūḥ*'s "delight in the Law of God and his fear of Him" (line 37). Still, the poet has presented his patron through divine *iqtibās* several times, suggesting a double-sided analogy: the patron lives in imitation of God's work and, like God, is deserving of praise.

Yosef Ibn Ḥasdai praised Shemuel ha-Nagid, highlighting his role as a *wazīr* of Granadan kings: "Kings walk by the light of his face (Ps 89:16)."[90] Another political function, that of protector, is highlighted in a panegyric epigram in Mosheh Ibn Ezra's *Sefer ha-'anaq*, a work dedicated to the courtier Abū Yiṣḥaq Avraham Ibn Muhājir:

The prince is a fortification of fire surrounding his people (Zec 2:9)
in a time of oppression; he is a wall (*shur*).
He dwells in Sefarad though the shade of his kindness extends to
Shinar and Shur.[91]

Several examples of divine *iqtibās* are contained in a poem by Yehudah Halevi to Abū Isḥāq Avraham Ben Bassah: "he dressed in a garment of justice like a coat of mail (Is 59:17); he is a "tower of might" (cf. Ps 61:4, Prv 18:10) and "shepherds the remnant of his tribe with his staff (cf. Mi 7:14)."[92] Of Yosef Ibn Ezra, Halevi wrote: "His generosity is as though from the hand of God, without sorrow he makes many gifts (Prv 10:22); [he] rides on clouds (Is 19:1)."[93] Halevi also wrote a series of poems and letters to Shemuel Ben Ḥananiah, Nagid of Egypt, whom the poet once designated as *negid adonai*, "God's Nagid," a construct that echoes the Arabic *khalīfat allah*.[94] In his poems to this dignitary, Halevi wrote: "All nations praise him (Ps 117:1)"; "[he is] praised with loud cymbals (Ps 150:5)"; and "your shade is a canopy over all of their glory" (Is 4:5).[95] Again, Halevi has permitted the misappropriation of God's praises for His "sons and students."[96] God's praises are sanctioned here not in the sense that they are universally permitted or because the words ultimately derive from mundane analogies; rather, they are appropriate for these specific men because the men, like the words, are associated with the divine.

A final example from Halevi's corpus is the following, translated in its entirety, to an unidentified recipient. It begins with a description of a flower, which is a stand-in for the *mamdūḥ*, and then turns to more direct praise:

1. Rose of kindness and lily of beauty,
praised with good favor,
a bud of preciousness that flourished on a root of glory,

the splendor of its honor is never diminished,
whose stature is that of God's [lofty] cherub,
which He established for greatness, praise, and sovereignty.
A wise man—opposite him the polish of the
sun's surface is like a potsherd.
God took him from the skies to the earth
in order make her [the earth] his gorgeous raiment.
Through him she put on delight to such an extent that
Comeliness [itself] praised [her].
Through him she wrapped herself in joy and
dressed in might; through him she found hope and faith.
God installed him over her hosts
and gave him grace and power.
He is a gazelle but attacks like a lion cub.
How his hand pierces the dragon! (Is 51:9)
Though there is delight in the garden of his face,
the sword in his eyes can leave one bereft.
His favor is a dew cloud; the moisture of his dew
drips and flows upon the hearts of men.
But, in a time of anger, his haughtiness will
take men captive and plunder them.
O, captain of gazelles! When separated from you
the heart burns hot like coal
out of much longing and desire.
My soul cries for you like a hind (Ps 42:2)!
Abandon anger and bring it to an end!
May the right hand of your kindness
receive the downtrodden and misfortunate.
I have no other guide (Is 51:18);
may your soul guide me along waters of repose (Ps 23:2).[97]

Both in the "floral" introduction and in the direct praise, the *mamdūḥ* is associated with the celestial and is selected by God to rule. The portrayal moves toward divine association through intertextual allusions, such as the *mamdūḥ*'s "piercing the dragon" (line 17), culminating in the highly personal conclusion wherein the poet longs for the *mamdūḥ* as the psalmist longs for God and where the *mamdūḥ*, rather than God, is the poet's only guide. The *mamdūḥ* is selected and empowered by God and is therefore deserving of praises, even the praises of

God. The divine references within the poem thus have two functions, magnifying the image of the *mamdūḥ* with respect to power and sovereignty and capturing the intimacy and intensity of the relationship between the poet and his *mamdūḥ*. There is a brilliant play between line 15, in which God appoints the *mamdūḥ* over the earth's hosts (*ṣevaeha*), and line 25, in which he is called *sar ṣevaim*, "captain of gazelles," likely referring to the social group of the poet and patron; however, there may be a deeper resonance with Joshua 5, where an angelic being identifies himself as *sar ṣeva Yahweh*, "the captain of the host of the Lord," adding further dimensions of power and sacrality.

Divine *iqtibās* is not utilized frequently by the Baghdadi poet El'azar Ben Ya'aqov ha-Bavli. However, the device appears effectively in one poem written on the occasion when "R. Zekhariah, son of 'Eli Head of the Yeshivah (*ra's al-mativah*) married the daughter of the leader (*al-ra'īs*) Abū al-Ṭayb Ben Faḍlān." The poem contains praise for several members of the groom's family, beginning with his father:

> Pride of the House of Jacob, awesome to praise (Ex 15:11), since
> eternity by him all actions have been measured (1 Sm 2:3) . . .
> Whose throne is suspended above the earth; his paths are in the
> ancient highest heavens (Ps 68:34) . . .
> Who possesses signs like [Isaiah] Ben Amoṣ when he spread figs
> upon the rash of my sin (cf. Is 38:21–22).
> [He is] the sacred Ark of the Covenant, the Oral and Written Law
> are truly great with him.[98]

The brief portrait contains several images of sacralization and presents the *mamdūḥ* through some of the most famous of God's praises from the Song of the Sea and Hannah's prayer; the image from Isaiah is also a reference to divine healing and restoration. The density of the images paired with the general absence of such imagery in Ben El'azar's oeuvre suggests that the device here was very much intentional and was reserved for the most august political figures.

If we look beyond the technical employment of *al-iqtibās*, many more panegyrics set the *mamdūḥ* as analogous to God. The correspondence is captured richly in TS 12.416 / ENA 1810.1, an anonymous panegyric dedicated to Maḍmūn II, Nagid of Yemen and a leading figure in the India trade:

> I thank You, Lord of lords, for your established goodness and
> kindness,

that You look upon the humiliation of Your community, which is
dispersed among the multitudes,
and that You sent her a man of valor and might to save her from
bonds of misery,
the lord Maḍmūn, Nagid of the nation of God and their glory,
whose praise rises above the clouds,
because of his great kindness and goodness, both new and old.[99]

God and His Nagid are both characterized, within a few lines of each other, by "kindness and goodness." The Nagid's legitimacy derives from divine appointment, and his position before the community is analogous to the divine's. His praise rises "above the clouds."

The same basic analogy obtains in other documents from the Geniza, including letters from people of status and petitions from the poor. Daniel Ben ʿAzariah thanks an unidentified person (possibly a Karaite Nasi) for financial support: "After God, I rely upon you and put my full trust (*attakkul*) in you with all my matters; in you I put my faith and in you I seek refuge."[100] The word *attakkul*, "to put full trust in something" (the verbal noun is *tawakkul*), is usually used in association with God only, and its usage here is revealing.[101] In petitions from the poor, the sentiment is captured in the constant refrain "I throw myself before God and you."[102] The expression might strike the modern ear as odd or as overblown and ingratiatory rhetoric. I would argue, however, that the formula conveys a vital analogy between God's place and the benefactor's that was very real; the latter's bestowing of favor is parallel to—and, in some ways, an extension of—God's beneficence.[103]

Likening appearance before the *mamdūḥ* to appearance before God or approaching holy ground is a more rhetorically elaborate way of capturing the same idea.[104] Among Andalusian authors, Ḥasdai Ibn Shaprut is praised by the students of Menaḥem Ben Saruq: "[The enemies of Ḥasdai] hide, frightened and afraid, and come before him in the cleft of a rock" (Ex 33:22).[105] Thus, Ḥasdai's enemies stand before him as Moses stood before God, hidden in fear yet shielded from His awesome power. Yehudah Halevi wrote of Abū Rabīʿa Shelomoh Ben Qerishpin that "seeing the glory of his face is like seeing the face of God" (cf. Gn 33:10).[106] Halevi likened journeying to visit Yehudah Ibn Ghiyat to going on pilgrimage, "to seek early the face of master Yehudah I ascend like one going on pilgrimage" (*ʿoleh la-regalim*).[107] To Shemuel Ben Ḥananiah ha-Nagid of Egypt, he wrote: "I stand in his house as though in the house of God."[108] In a panegyric to the scribe Natan bar Shemuel, Halevi wrote that chaffs of wheat swaying in the wind appear like "[people] bowing before God and thanking him, just as the cultured man bows before the prince, master Natan."[109] All these examples are, in a sense, hyperbolic and rhetorical; no one *really* thought that appearing before a Jewish dignitary was tantamount to coming into God's sacred presence. At the same time, the category of the sacred provided a vital metaphor for the conceptualization of political culture. This argument is not undermined by the fact that Jewish leaders did not possess true sovereignty; one need not subscribe to a Romantic notion of Jewish nationalism to see that Jews in medieval Islamic empires imagined themselves as belonging to a kind of polity with distinctive structures and ultimate sources of authority. What strikes us in the present context is the extent to which these structures were ingrained within and informed by contemporary Islamic political culture.

Conclusion: Metaphor and the Working of Politics

To review my argument thus far, I have demonstrated that divine praises were woven into the fabric of Hebrew and Arabic panegyrics over a wide domain of the Islamic Mediterranean and over several centuries. I have also demonstrated that Jewish and Muslim readers alike recognized the tensions involved in predicating such praises of men. However, these tensions did not cause poets to avoid association with the divine but rather allowed them a productive space for creating hyperbolic effects. This is not to say that such references were intended literally. It is a unique quality of poetic speech that it can produce statements that are meaningful, irrespective of any claim to truth.

In an earlier section of this chapter, I introduced the concept of political theology as articulated in the writings of Carl Schmitt and Ernst Kantorowicz. In particular, I highlighted Kantorowicz's concept of the medieval Christian ruler as a "God-man" whose transcendent qualities demanded his worship, as well as Schmitt's argument that all politics, even the ostensibly modern and secular, preserves an essentially theological structure. I also introduced certain strains within Jewish and Islamic thought that related to these concepts, noting both impulses toward intimate association between the ruler and the divine but also limits on that impulse.

Ultimately, I believe that the vast majority of panegyrics discussed here use association of the *mamdūḥ* with the divine as a type of metaphor or analogy, what might best be described as a "cognitive metaphor." In Chapter 3, I noted that Esperanza Alfonso introduced this idea into the study of Hebrew panegyric with respect to the polis as a body; it has a head (or heart) and limbs; it can be healthy or infected.[110] Further, she argues that Hebrew panegyrics display sacralizing elements; the "heart of the benefactor [becomes] the *locus par excellence* of the sacred" such as the Ark of the Covenant or Jerusalem. The ruler as God is another such metaphor, albeit one that is more theologically fraught.

Although Schmitt did not think in such literary terms, he essentially had it right that politics operated according to a theological structure, and this, more than a cult of ruler worship, seems to characterize the medieval Islamicate world, including the Jewish sub-polity that it contained. The place of the ruler in the state (whether a real or an imagined one) was like that of God in the universe; he related to his subjects as God relates to His creation or people and, like God, was deserving of praise. Importantly, the use of this cognitive metaphor did not entail the source domain's desacralization or secularization; on the contrary, it allowed for the *mamdūḥ* to be conceptualized through the category of the sacred.

Again, I have not argued in this chapter that medieval Muslims or Jews worshiped their leaders as divine beings. What intrigues me about Kantorowicz for the present study is that he contemplated some sort of divine-human complex that hovers around the perceived boundary between the human and the divine. In medieval Jewish and Islamic thought, there *was* a boundary between the human and the divine that was meant to be respected. But this is precisely the boundary that panegyrists pressed against and, in the minds of some critics, transgressed.

In Hebrew panegyric, we are likely encountering images of divine analogy more than divine manifestation, whether the *mamdūḥ* is depicted as lowering his arm in judgment, putting on wonder and glory, forgiving transgression, comforting with his rod and staff, or providing shade over humanity. As was the case with the representation of Muslim sovereigns, Jewish authors maintained that their leaders were God's humble and fearing servants even as they portrayed them as a little bit divine. To be sure, such representations were hyperbolic and rhetorical. But more than hyperbole should be considered verbal pyrotechnics or, even worse, gratuitous flattery, it should be viewed as the cognitive framework through which a cultural group interpreted the world. Associating *mamdūḥ*s with divinity in panegyric did not make addressees divine so much as it presented a theological structure within politics.

CHAPTER 8

"May His Book Be Burnt Even Though It Contains Your Praise!": Jewish Panegyric in the Christian Mediterranean

The Hebrew literary culture of the Christian Mediterranean during the later Middle Ages maintained an intimate bond with the Andalusian tradition. It took on different forms throughout the region, with significant variations in Christian Iberia, southern France, Norman Sicily, and on the Italian Peninsula. Because areas now separated by political boundaries were often not differentiated and were linguistically continuous, it is reasonable to treat the region as a whole within a single chapter. Arguably, one should not draw a firm dividing line even between Islamic and Christian territories within the Mediterranean; people, books, and ideas flowed fairly freely across religious borders, and cities like Toledo and Palermo, though ruled by Christian kings, remained very much Arabo-Islamic in character. A figure such as Anatoli Ben Yosef (late twelfth–early thirteenth century) was active in Marseilles and Lunel but also in Alexandria and Sicily. Hence the positing of a "Christian Mediterranean" as a rubric for studying Jewish panegyric is somewhat artificial. Still, it is useful for charting the movement of an Arabized Hebrew style after the fall of Andalusian Jewry, the accommodation of existing forms to new literary trends and cultural values, and the ultimate development of novel traditions through the fifteenth century.

The state of research in the field of late medieval Hebrew literature is heavily indebted to the extraordinary life's work of Jefim Schirmann, in whose many writings we follow the engaging narrative of Hebrew literature's efflorescence under Muslim aegis and its ultimate decline on Christian soil. Despite the presence of a significant number of talented poets in Christian Iberia and southern

Figure 10. King David as depicted in Kennicott 1, f. 185r (c. 1476). Courtesy of the Bodleian Library, University of Oxford.

France and notable creativity in the area of rhymed prose composition, Hebrew writers seemed, in Schirmann's view, to have succumbed to a kind of epigonism—alternately for failing to attain the standards of the Andalusian school and for pursuing a manneristic style that signified decadence. Of the genres that Schirmann valued most—love poetry, metaphysical reflection, and liturgical verse—the contributions of Jewish poets in Christian lands (with certain exceptions) seemed both paltry and pale in comparison with the Andalusian classics. The expulsion of the Jews from France in 1306 seemed to thwart a budding literary culture. By the middle of the fifteenth century, amid the many conversions of Iberian Jews to Christianity and mounting tension over the converso problem, Hebrew poetry seemed moribund, collapsing under the weight of its own failures and the hysteria that brought Jews to the threshold of expulsion. On the

Italian peninsula, where some literary activity had predated the influx of Andalusian material, the seeds were planted for an ongoing literary engagement that would last through the Renaissance and the Baroque.

In fact, the Hebrew literature of the Christian Mediterranean lacks the same depth of metaphysical reflection paired with the zestful celebration of life's delights that had characterized the Andalusian tradition. On the other hand, we find literature produced by social types across a broader spectrum, a wider range of themes and forms, more examples of the proverbial and moralizing genres, special penchants for social satire and textual parody, and a great deal more to laugh about. And when it came to panegyric, the authors of Hebrew poetry in Christendom wrote reams of it, truly extraordinary quantities, a fact that could only corroborate Schirmann's dim view. In the present chapter, I will suspend questions about "quality" vis-à-vis the Andalusian tradition but will attempt, rather, to understand the Hebrew panegyric of the region on its own grounds. The chapter will pick up on many themes that have been treated throughout this book, such as social bonds, poetics, and leadership representation and also introduce new intellectual elements that left an imprint on the panegyric corpus such as the kabbalah, Jewish-Christian polemics, and Romance vernacular literature.

On the one hand, we can speak of an "international" or "Mediterranean" Hebrew literary culture wherein authors traversed political borders, which resulted in the transmission and cross-pollination of styles. In addition to the aforementioned Anatoli Ben Yosef, figures such as Yehudah al-Ḥarīzī and Qalonymos Ben Qalonymos (1286–d. after 1328) traveled widely.[1] On the other hand, the Christian Mediterranean can be characterized by Hebrew literary "micro-cultures." Virtually all authors operated within fairly localized networks, which could center on patrons or webs of relationships maintained among social equals (or near equals). Small pockets of poets praising one another appear in numerous areas—Norman Sicily, Castile, Catalonia, southern France—and it is through their panegyrics that we readily glimpse the nature of their social relationships and cultural values. Most literary pursuit occurred in urban centers, but some activity is also recorded in the countryside.[2] In some cases, this activity gave rise to what we recognize as distinctive "schools" (groups of authors who adhered to identifiable styles), though the medievals would not have used this term, and, in fewer cases, actual "circles" of poets, which the medievals recognized themselves.

The arrival on Christian soil of great Andalusian poets such as Mosheh Ibn Ezra or Avraham Ibn Ezra did not spawn the immediate creation of new literary centers. Still, there is a notable interest in things Andalusian. The Andalusian style of *piyyut* enjoyed absorption among some authors in Ashkenaz already before the Crusades and continued to gain influence over the coming centuries.[3] However, there does not seem to have been any significant practice of panegyric among Jews in Christendom prior to the twelfth century.[4] Avraham Ibn Ezra, who left the Islamic West to seek patronage in Christian cities on the European continent, imbued his panegyrics for figures in Christian centers with values markedly different from his panegyrics for Andalusian and Maghrebi figures.[5] One short poem is dedicated to a French exegete, possibly Shemuel Ben Meir (Rashbam):

> Peace upon his coming,
> he and his host.
> Are you from Sinai
> or from [the wilderness of] Ṣin?
> Or from [the stock of] Ittiel and Yequtiel?
> He came like Samuel
> from Ramah. . .
> He made a wondrous commentary
> for the Torah.
> Therefore he is called
> Parshandata.[6]
> His book is a redeemer
> for all who ask. . . .
> Rule is established for him,
> also kingship
> is fitting for him.[7]

The depiction is tailored to fit a biblical commentator. Terms of sovereignty are used metaphorically to refer to intellectual rank.

A number of Ibn Ezra's panegyrics for figures in the Christian Mediterranean derive from book dedications, either for students or patrons. A good example is the dedication to the patron Mosheh Ben Me'ir that prefaced the Torah commentary. The poem begins with praise for God, autobiographical statements about Ibn Ezra's old age and sickness, and how

> Mosheh Ben Meir supported him and made
> his body[8] fresh like a palm frond.

Mosheh, for whom all wisdom is but a portion,
like tossing a bit of water into the Gihon river
or setting a candle before the sun or moon.
God concealed him so that he might be a light in darkness.
His hand is like the generosity of a cloud. . . . The Law of Moses by the hand of Mosheh shall I explicate;
it is the trustworthy testimony of God.[9]

A playful correspondence between Ibn Ezra and the Tosafist Yaʿaqov Ben Meir (Rabbenu Tam) demonstrates the portability and popularity of the Andalusian literary style. We do not know how the correspondence began; the earliest poem we have is Ibn Ezra's response to one that he had received from Rabbenu Tam, which was likely written according to the meter and rhyme of Arabized Hebrew poetry. Ibn Ezra jokes about the Tosafist's "foreignness" in the "holy place" of poetry:

Who has brought the Frenchman (*ha-Ṣarfati*) to the Temple of poetry?
A foreigner has passed and trampled through a holy place.

Rabbenu Tam responded: "To Avraham I am a slave gained by purchase. I bow down and prostrate before his face." Ibn Ezra ultimately responded in kind and with requisite humility: "Forefend that an angel of God would bow and prostrate before Bilʿam!"[10]

Another of Ibn Ezra's panegyrics for Rabbenu Tam is presented, quite originally, in the shape of a tree yet nonetheless adheres to the quantitative meter of Andalusian verse.[11] In sum, the correspondence demonstrates that Arabic prosodic features in Hebrew poetry could be appreciated and mastered by the non-Arabophone.[12]

Ibn Ezra's panegyrics for figures in Christendom carefully avoid certain themes. There are no gazelles to lust after, no water channels irrigating flower beds, no wine burning like fire within hailstones. However, Ibn Ezra does transport to Christendom the rhetorical strategies of the *qaṣīda* (formal ode). Among the more famous of his panegyrics is one that he wrote for Rabbi Menaḥem and his son Mosheh of Rome. It begins with praise of God ("Every morning, the works of God are new), specifically for endowing humans with eyes, ears, mouth, and limbs. Then the poet recounts:

I was asleep though my heart was awake when my organs stood
firm to argue like enemies.
The eye said, "By the moment I see, behold, and seek that which is
in the inner chamber
and in the heavens and the earth without taking a single step."

The eye's boast continues until the ear interjects:

"Be silent! What power do you have when you require light?
If you cannot see unassisted, then what authority do you possess?
My domain is over all six directions!"

The debate develops further with the tongue and the hand getting into the act, until the poet awakes to the intrusion of a heavenly voice:

I awoke and within me were battles, one camp armed against
another.
And the heavens spoke, "Why do you fight? Go and seek the proper
judgment!
Go unto Rabbi Menaḥem, who shows compassion for souls so
much that they return to their bodies!"[13]
Happy is the eye that sees his glory, and the ear that hears words
from his mouth.
Though every tongue speaks his praise, even books fail to
encompass it.
His eye has seen the wonders of God and his ears have heard the
heavenly voice of ancestors.
My tongue speaks a word of Teaching, but in his mouth the six
orders (of the Mishnah) are ordered.
He cast his eye upon the wealthy and the poor like a shepherd
tending flocks.
His ear is blocked from hearing vanity; his mouth and speech are
the life of flesh.
If there is a gate for everyone who understands wisdom, before him
a hundred gates are open.
His hands pour generous rains so much that he sets rivers in
deserts.

The poem concludes with blessings for the *mamdūḥ* and his son. The rhetorical development of the poem is highly reminiscent of Ibn Gabirol's panegyric in which the flowers, statues, and birds of a palace garden engage in a boasting match, until the poet silences them and urges them to praise the *mamdūḥ*; but here, body organs replace garden furnishings, and a heavenly voice replaces the poet's. Ibn Ezra joins the prelude and the praise intimately by repeating the organs and other themes (six directions/orders of Mishnah) in each section. In the prelude, the organs are God's creations and rival factions within the poet's body; in the *madīḥ*, they are instruments with which people praise the *mamdūḥ* and his own agents of virtue. Hence God is praised for creating organs whose purpose is to praise the *mamdūḥ*. A contrast is set up between the poet, for whom the organs battle inwardly, and the *mamdūḥ*, whose organs perform righteous acts.[14] The portrayal of the *mamdūḥ* focuses on his knowledge of the Mishnah, his generosity toward the poor, his righteousness, and his role as a "shepherd," all themes that are familiar by now. However, there are no gazelles or goblets, and the *mamdūḥ* is not a cast as a literary patron, a thwarter of enemies, a cultivator of Greek wisdom, or an eloquent speaker (apart from his knowledge of Mishnah). But even if the representation of the *mamdūḥ* only partly overlaps with earlier tradition, the persistence of the *qaṣīda* form, a form that would be utilized among Jews in Christendom for centuries, attests to a basic continuity with the Arabized Hebrew tradition.

Norman Sicily in the Twelfth Century: Anatoli Ben Yosef

The *dīwān* of Anatoli Ben Yosef (b. c. 1150–d. a. 1212), known best as a *dayyan* (judge) of Alexandria and a correspondent of Maimonides', presents a large number of panegyrics that the poet wrote and received during his sojourn in Norman Sicily. S. M. Stern estimates that this stint fell roughly between 1170 and 1180, not long after the death of Roger II (1095–1154), who actively cultivated an Arabic-Islamic style political culture by adopting the regnal title al-Mu'tazz Bi'llah and patronizing Muslim panegyrists who praised him in Arabic.[15] Even during the reigns of Roger's relatively weak successors before Frederick II, Palermo was probably still very much an Arabized city.[16] One of Anatoli Ben Yosef's friends in Sicily wrote a poem upon the scholar's arrival from "Edom," Christian territory, suggesting, as Stern writes, the degree to which "the Jews of Sicily still regarded themselves as a part of Islamic civilization";[17] Sicilian Jews also favored the Muslims during the years of the Norman conquest.[18]

As a native of Marseilles who had not yet set foot in Alexandria, Ben Yosef's exposure to Arabic poetics was probably indirect and mediated through Arabized Hebrew poetry.[19] Although Stern is probably right in characterizing the Sicilian Hebrew poets as "*dilettanti* . . . simple imitators of the great Spanish pathfinders," it is more productive to consider them for what they were than for what they were not: a circle of men who established and maintained social bonds through the practice of panegyric on the Andalusian model.[20] Hence the writings of this group attest that al-Andalus had become a template not only for the literary production of Mediterranean Jews but also for their ways of socializing and their *habitus* more generally.[21]

Anatoli's *dīwān* often illuminates the circumstances of panegyric composition: a poetic exchange after Anatoli had visited a certain Eliakim when ill; the departure of friends from Palermo; an extended epistolary exchange with Shemuel Ben Menaḥem al-Nafūsī, from initial meeting to separation; a friendship with a cantor in Messina. One poem suggests that a certain Peraḥiah Ibn al-Khayr al-Ḥalabī had heard Anatoli recite a poem and now requests verses in writing. The exchange of poetry clearly played a seminal role in establishing Anatoli's status in Sicily. One poem (a circle poem, beginning and ending with the same phrase)[22] illuminates the continued role of poetry as an aspect of gift culture:

> It is your hands' duty to repay the lord (*gevir*) just as it is your heart's duty to guard your words,
> so much that poetry will fall like rain or song drip like dew.
> Great is your virtue to recount; I only cease because I lack the strength and power to finish! . . .
> Your scent wafts over me and I snatch the fragrance of a bundle of myrrh.
> I give you this [poem] as a gift (*teshurah*) because it is your hands' duty to repay the lord.[23]

There is no evidence that this exchange involved money, however. Stern argues that the context of friendship separates the poems in Anatoli's corpus from the contexts of "patronage" and "court" characteristic of al-Andalus, but the social practice, as argued in Chapter 2, is actually continuous with one major strain of poetry's function in al-Andalus.[24]

On the level of poetics, the verse of this group reveals a selective absorption of Arabized Andalusian motifs: weeping over ruins, dream visions, the insomnia of the poet yearning for a friend, *mamdūḥ*s whose faces illumine goblets. One of Anatoli's poems is a *mu'āraḍa* (contrafaction) of a poem by Yehudah Halevi. Yet the corpus preserves no poems on erotic motifs (whereas Arabic poetry from Sicily does). *Mamdūḥ*s are praised for wisdom and eloquence, for mastery of the Holy Tongue, for performing commandments and upholding God's Law. Although Anatoli expresses gratitude for kindness, no *mamdūḥ* is likened to the rain; no one is a keeper of secrets who dwells in the counsel of the angels. There are no shepherds, no enemies to thwart. "Dominion" appears very seldom and with little pomp or substance; what might be the only occurrence of the word in the *dīwān* appears in the following verses, which, generally speaking, are typical of Anatoli's style:

> Those who draw water from their springs do not thirst, and those
> who eat of their bread do not hunger.
> The stems of plantings of love that had aged after drying out
> quickly stood on their feet and became succulent.
> Their lips drip honeycomb and their words are honey that heals
> every bone and is sweet to every heart. . . .
> They revive the dying Law of God with their intellects and restore
> spirit to the bodies of Teaching.
> The shoulder of Dominion was set upon their shoulders as a sign
> that they alone were fit [. . .] were defiant.
> They spread out beds of friendship for loved ones and trimmed
> them with the fine linen of their love.
> They guided me gently along waters of repose, a place of streams
> and broad rivers.[25]

Neither political dominion nor its ethical twin, humility, appears in Anatoli's portraits. Although Anatoli wrote a number of poems for Peraḥiah Ibn al-Khayr al-Ḥalabī, it is only in a dirge over this figure that the poet even bestows upon him the (rather ambiguous) title *sar*.[26] In addition to the fact that Jews seem to have played a diminished role in Sicilian government in comparison with the Toledan courts (further below), the lack of grandeur presented in Anatoli's corpus also likely relates to the author's Provençal origins; his panegyric is already one step removed from the Andalusian tradition.

Toledo in the Thirteenth Century: Todros Halevi Abulafia

Whereas Avraham Ibn Ezra's movement to Christian territories involved a significant change in his poetic style, the Hebrew poetry of Todros Halevi Abulafia (1247–d. a. 1298), who spent his entire life in the city of Toledo under Christian rule, adhered closely to the Arabized style of Hebrew verse characteristic of al-Andalus. Todros's poetry maintains the dynamic integration of Arabic motifs and style so faithfully that it is often analyzed by scholars together with the poetry of the major Andalusian poets. Once an Islamic center (through 1085), Toledo remained a highly Arabized city well into the thirteenth century, especially since its sovereign, Alfonso X "the Wise" of Castile, promoted Arabic knowledge within his court. Todros himself had become a courtier in Alfonso's multireligious court and dedicated Hebrew panegyrics to the learned king (on these poems, see Chapter 9).[27]

Despite the change in Toledo from Muslim to Christian rule, relatively little changed with respect to the poetic tastes of its Jewish population. It is obvious that Abulafia earned money by composing poetry, yet he wrote in the Hebrew introduction to his anthology on the topic of panegyric: "If I wrapped one of the elite[28] in a mantle of praise [Is 61:3], it was not in the hope of earning wealth from poetry or a gift of ruby and topaz from speech but rather to perfect the art of poetry according to its measure or because of great love burning like the fire of steel [Na 2:4], like the prophecy of Deborah."[29] In his youth, Todros dedicated two collections of poems to Jewish patrons with Judeo-Arabic introductions, one for Shelomoh Ben Ṣadoq and another for Todros Ben Yosef Halevi Abulafia (who, confusingly enough, shared a nearly identical name with the poet). In numerous respects, these collections are reminiscent of Mosheh Ibn Ezra's *Sefer ha-'anaq*. The collection for Abulafia is divided into ten chapters organized according to poetic themes, deals with *al-badī'* (the novel style), and is introduced with a Judeo-Arabic preface. Lamenting the fate dealt him by the vicissitudes of Time, Todros quotes a verse by al-Mutanabbī about offering poetry as a gift[30] and continues in praise of his patron:

> Because of the kindness presented to me, it was incumbent upon me to thank the just, renowned, and perfect master Abū al-Ḥasan Todros Ibn al-Lawi (Halevi), may God guard his augustness, and, in order to give thanks to the one of magnanimous disposition—may

> God increase his station and not deplete his generosity—I ennobled this book in his name and marked it with his marking. I divided it into ten chapters, each consisting of fifty verses according to the novel elements of poetry (*badā'i al-shi'r*) in the most beautiful garb including elegant arts of culture (*adab*) and rare and graceful verses of love and praise (*al-ghazl wa al-madḥ*). At the beginning and end of each chapter I composed verses of his praise and laudation that will outlast the passage of time.[31]

Indeed, the first chapter is dedicated to "describing some of his virtues and the generosity of his good qualities," and the other chapters open and close by weaving panegyric together with other themes.

A similar work, even more like *Sefer ha-'anaq* in that all its poems are homonymic (*tajnīs*), also presents panegyric as the theme of its first chapter. The Judeo-Arabic preface identifies the patron as Abū al-Rabī' Shelomoh Bar Ṣadoq, on whose epithets the author expounds, "possessor of hearts of men, gatherer of praiseworthy qualities in perfection and completeness, he who possesses virtue, majesty, intelligence, and perfection, the one who possesses the two ministries, the lofty, the magnanimous, the unique, the radiant, the most respected, scion of the generous and the life-giver of generosity, an ocean of kindness, poison to enemies, Creation's generosity and the most generous of created beings (*al-makhluq*), Abū al-Rabī' Ibn Ṣadoq."[32]

Especially by preserving such epithets *dhū al-wizāratain* "the one who possesses the two ministries" (i.e., *al-dīn wa al-duny*ā, religion and the world), this work attests richly to the powerful sway that the Arabic language and panegyric tradition held over the representation of Jewish leadership even once removed from direct Islamic political aegis. The Hebrew panegyrics within the work praise Ibn Ṣadoq's generosity, righteousness, power over enemies, the "dominion on his shoulder," his humility, courage, and his eloquence and occasionally fold in divine hyperbole: "The writing of his hands is like the writing of God, His speech like the speech of the Lord of Hosts."[33]

Over the course of his career, Todros wrote a great many panegyrics to many addressees, some of whom were his direct patrons while others were poetic correspondents. The two most important patrons were those mentioned above, but many other names appear in the *dīwān* and constitute what might be seen as a circle of Toledan poets in the orbit of the court of Alfonso X.[34] Given the sheer number of poems, we can reconstruct a great deal about the nature of patronage and friendship in this circle, including some rather delicate moments. In general, even the patrons who did not compose poetry themselves were learned connoisseurs who offered "feedback," sometimes substantive criticism, on Todros's verse.

One striking argument over poetics alluded to in a poem for Yiṣḥaq Bar Ṣadoq pertained to sacred hyperbole. It seems that in an earlier panegyric (not preserved), Todros had followed the theme of Ibn Gabirol and praised his *mamdūḥ* with the words "you are like One," which readers took as comparing him to God. Bar Ṣadoq had apparently responded: "You are also like One," and now Todros writes: "You wrote, 'You are also like One,' as though my soul were whoring [after other gods]. Many people mocked me and scoffed when you sent your white scroll."[35] It seems that Bar Ṣadoq thought that Todros had overstepped the bounds of hyperbole with "you are like One"; by redirecting the verse back to the poet, Bar Ṣadoq simultaneously reprimands Todros for an irreverent comparison and neutralizes the simile because, if one person can be "like One" in the sense of being unique, then anyone can, and the compliment loses all meaning.

Todros included in the *dīwān* not only the poems that he had addressed to others but also a good number of poems that he had received from them. The *dīwān* preserves many poetic correspondences, often including secondary poems that were set on the exterior of envelopes. Several of these relationships were not based solely in friendship and praise but also reveal a good deal of invective, either primarily or secondarily. Thus, within Todros's otherwise friendly correspondence with Ibn Sasson, we learn that the latter called Todros's horse a mule, to which the poet responded: "Whenever I see you, I behold a judge of Gomorrah."[36] More famous is Todros's extensive invective exchange with a poet named Pinḥas, which began after the two had exchanged poems of friendship and complaint over separation. Angel Sáenz-Badillos described this invective exchange, apart from formal elements, as "closer to the Romance type of invective than to the Arabic one."[37]

Additionally, Pinḥas wrote a long panegyric in honor of Don Çag (Yiṣḥaq) Ben Ṣadoq, son of the aforementioned Shelomoh Ben Ṣadoq and a courtier in the service of Alfonso X (whom the king ultimately executed), in which the poet included insulting words toward Todros. The poem to the courtier was subsequently shared with Todros, who wrote an extensive response in which he mixed panegyric for Ben Ṣadoq with invective for his rival poet. After answering Pinḥas's charges, Todros pleaded with the patron: "Let us return to our friendship of old . . . like sun after rain, like days of youth after old age" and named him by eight virtues in a single verse: justice, truth, uprightness, humility, generosity, preciousness, wisdom, and intelligence.[38]

Truth be told and despite Todros's greater renown, Pinḥas's poem seems the superior in terms of overall conception and execution of language. "The hidden praises of Time have I seen" is a circle poem in which the speaker conveys a "prophetic" vision, a gathering in which poets come from all directions to boast over their specific locales. After the representatives of the East, North, and South speak, they call for the prince of the West, but no one answers until Pinḥas steps forth and boasts its qualities:

> [In the West] there is a gazelle who is figured (*nimshal*) as the Garden of Eden; moreover, in truth, I have likened his fruit to the Tree of Knowledge.[39]
> His hands are like a Tree of Life that revives all who fall to the ground, and in them I live.
> I speak truthfully about him; may I be found right and free from guilt before you. Do you understand in what I erred?
> [I erred in] how many of the gazelle's virtues I recall but do not tell, and also those I forgot!

The other participants "whisper to one another about the one for whom kingship is fitting," and then the poet turns to the direction of the gazelle[40] and says in a tone of quasi-messianic expectation: "Would that the good I have awaited would come!" The voice that answers is Time itself:

> Why do you worry, O mortal, for I have done as you wished.
> What have I to do with North, East, and South? The West have I acquired.
> Behold, my seal and its cord[41] are yours; the mark of Dominion I have set on your beloved's forehead.
> His throne shall endure beside me forever; him have I chosen to execute my covenant in the world.

Further, Time vows to lay the gazelle's enemies low and ultimately continues: "Every year they shall have a celebration and feast for the day I appointed Yiṣḥaq as minister!" The poem now reverts to the poet's voice and ultimately to a second-person address toward the *mamdūḥ*:

Then Time made Yiṣḥaq king in the council (*ba-maʿamad*)
and gave you an honorific even as I have given you an honorific. . . .
The day that word of your kingship reached me, how my face
rejoiced and how I was beautified.

At this point, the poet directs an invective excursus against Todros, including the verse, "May his book be burnt even though it contains your praise!" Finally, Pinḥas concludes with a blessing and returns to the theme of his prophetic vision—indeed, to the opening words of the poem:

In your welfare will I have welfare, a vision of peace have I beheld
for you.
The year of your redemption has already come, for the hidden
praises of Time have I seen.[42]

Many motifs of dominion encountered throughout this book are present: election, objects symbolic of sovereignty, rituals of enthronement. Given the internal references to rites of initiation, the poem may have been composed for the period around such a ritual if not an initiation itself.[43] Perhaps importantly, and despite the poem's overtones of prophecy and messianism, God is absent; it is Time that selects the *mamdūḥ* as deputy on earth and identifies him as the "expected good." In most respects, the poem would be entirely at home in Islamic al-Andalus. One exception might be the amount of space dedicated to the rivalry with Todros; although invective was not uncommon in al-Andalus, its setting within panegyric and its reference to a specific correspondence set it apart.

Returning to Todros's panegyric, much of its originality is found within verbal and orthographic plays. In addition to the *tajnīs* poems, Todros composed according to numerous constraints that served as conceits: a poem in which every word contains the letter *mem*; a (shorter) poem dedicated to a man named Mosheh in which every word, like the name, contains the letters *mem* and *shin*; poems in the shape of a tree (following Avraham Ibn Ezra); two collections of twenty-two poems, arranged alphabetically, wherein each poem takes a given letter of the alphabet as the first letter in each verse; an alphabetic acrostic where the first word of each line uses the name of the letter in a different meaning (hence *beit*, in the sense of "house"; *qof*, in the sense of "monkey"). Actually, this last poem presents every letter except for *gimmel* and *ṭet*, which Todros also transforms into a further conceit with a follow-up poem whose premise is that "the daughter of your love married the son of my poem":

> The tongue of the Talmud offers her a blessing for I gave her the
> Hebrew tongue.
> *Gimmel* and *ṭet* are missing for I shall never issue her a writ of
> divorce (*geṭ*).[44]

Todros's corpus attests to the trend toward mannerism that earned late medieval Hebrew poetry blame in the eyes of many modern scholars. More sympathetically, we might see the development as the next logical step in the cultivation of *al-badīʿ* and the emergence of a poetics that took the exploration of language's possibilities as its subject. Clearly, the consumers of such verse saw in it not decline but rather novelty, ingenuity, and delight.

Related to this development is what might be called Todros's metapoetic turn, wherein not only language but also the art of poetic composition became the substance of exploration, play, and abuse. In a fascinating pair of panegyrics for Yosef and Todros Abulafia, son and father, the poet draws on the "dissembling poet" motif with multiple inversions.[45] The presumption is that Todros had written the father a poem (not preserved) in which he called the *mamdūḥ* a "generous cloud" and his generosity the "rain of Mount Hermon" but the *mamdūḥ* failed to offer compensation. Now, within a poem dedicated to the son, the poet invents a speaker who blames the poet for abusing speech, for lying in his poems despite the renown he enjoys:

> "Why do you lie in your poems, making your poetry and your
> words loathsome.
> Your poetry is already known in the East and West of Time . . .
> Why do you call the valiant weak and the miser of the age its
> patron?
> You called Rav Todros 'generous of heart' though his heart never
> possessed this.
> You have gave the name 'sea of kindness' to a rock, 'spring of water'
> to a desert.
> If your desire were to praise him and your heart loved him deeply,
> his wisdom, culture, and intellect, along with his other virtues,
> would have sufficed for the length and breadth of Time!

But what has he to do with generosity? What has Gilboa to do with Ḥermon or its rain?"[46]
I responded, "Don't judge according to the first thing [you hear] in an argument!
I sinned by mistake, not out of malice, when I called him a cloud and mist of kindness.
Forefend that my poem would lie maliciously, whether to give him praise or pleasure.
I thought him generous, though he is not, only because the lord Yosef is his relative!"

The poem goes on to praise the son's generosity at length. The circumstance was probably not entirely fictitious; it is probable that the poet had written Todros the patron a poem that went uncompensated and that the present poem is a "claim [for payment]" (*iqtiḍā'*).[47] While it was sent to another member of the family rather than Todros himself, the poem was probably intended to be shared with the father (and it was; further below). As is typical of an *iqtiḍā'*, the poet combines blame with praise—in this case, praise of the father's other virtues together with the son's generosity, undoubtedly in the hope of receiving delayed or even greater remuneration. Cleverly, Todros uses the father's neglect as a pretense for praising the son, effectively transforming the "error" of praising Todros's generosity into a poetic prelude leading to a *takhalluṣ*. The insult that the poet directed toward the father was not expected to sever the relationship but rather fell within the bounds of invective play that could be tolerated within a patronage relationship.

Still, what Todros may have intended as a light jab seems to have elicited a stronger response. In the superscription to a second poem, the poet describes Todros the patron's anger "when he heard that I called the sea of his kindness a desert and so I sought atonement from him with poems more precious than gold."[48] In this poem, Todros disavows any claims of the father's miserliness by declaring them poetic inventions, the types of lies for which poets are known. As Ross Brann has argued, the introductory prelude of this poem is a "meta-qaṣīda, a poem on how to compose, or more precisely, how *not* to compose a poem."[49] Using the topos of the dissembling poet as a defense, Todros begins and ends his poem with the words, "A poet speaks nothing but deceptions (*hatulim*)." The entire prelude is a meditation on this theme: "What is a poem apart from lying words. . . . Sometimes [a poet] calls a miser a generous man and sometimes a generous man a scoundrel. . . . [or a poet claims that] the sky is dark when the sun is at high noon." Again, Todros has created an entirely novel prelude, though it leads, as always, to a *mamdūḥ* and his praise:

> This is the rule: Poetry has no beauty without lying and false words.
> Therefore, when I made a praise poem for the minister Yosef, God's leader (*nesi el*) and most valiant of the troops,
> I mixed it with falsehood and cursed the lord Todros, father of praises.
> Among all lies and worthless words there is no falsehood like the lie of cursing him.
> These are his well-known names: generous of heart, Taḥkemoni, mighty of deeds, light of the generation who has no gloom, a sea of preciousness that has no boundary. . . .
> His heart's only desire is to make the poor wealthy, to revive the spirit of the downtrodden. . . .
> Every poet who praises you, his words are without falsehood, pure like gold without dross,
> but if he writes poems for another, "a poet speaks nothing but deceptions."

Importantly, Todros here disrupts the standard "content/form" dichotomy of poetic speech, which Mosheh Ibn Ezra described as poetry's "manner" (*ṭarīqa*) and "essence" (*nafs*). To revisit Chapter 6, a statement (e.g., "his hand is the sea"), even when its "manner" relies upon falsehood (a hand is not a sea), is considered true as long as its "essence" corresponds with reality (it is predicated of a generous person and not a miser).[50] In these remarkable poems, Todros invents a speaker who calls him a liar for transgressing what is permitted according to the manner/essence dichotomy; that is, the poet figured a miser as a "sea of kindness"; the verse would have been fine had it been predicated of a generous man. Todros's defense in the first poem is not that his lie was merely hyperbolic but rather that his error was not malicious. But in the second poem, the poet defends having called the patron Todros a miser but not as a matter of hyperbole or neglect; the defense now is that poetic statements need not correspond to reality *either* in "manner" *or* in "essence."

Of course, the argument in a sense collapses in the final verse, where the poet states, appealing to a rather hackneyed convention, that praises for the *mamdūḥ* are true but that praises for others are deceptions. Would not a poet who praised another enjoy the same defense that Todros affords himself, that a lie of "essence" is permitted within poetic speech? Or perhaps Todros would argue that his fabrication was exceptional since it was not gratuitous but rather created for the ultimate purpose of praising Yosef? Was the second poem really intended to convince the patron that the insult was merely a minor infraction? Or did Todros assume that the learned patron would see through the feebleness of the defense, essentially reifying rather than overturning the manner/essence dichotomy? It might be that the aim from the outset of the first poem was to disrupt but ultimately affirm a standard poetics and to create delight through layers of metapoetic inversion and unexpected twists in the most predictable of all genres. Such a position would help explain the rather surprising superscription with which Todros introduced the *first* poem: "To the leader and master Yosef Halevi I composed this poem and set my mouth in the sky of the generosity of master Todros."[51]

Southern France in the Late Thirteenth and Early Fourteenth Centuries

The anonymous scribe who compiled the poetry of Avraham Bedersi authored superscriptions that delineate circumstances of composition.[52] One rhymed prose Hebrew text by Bedersi is dedicated to praise of the courtier Todros Ben Yosef Halevi Abulafia, the very man praised by the poet Todros Abulafia above, and the Castilian king Alfonso X, who had come to Perpignan in 1275 en route to meet the pope in Beaucaire. The text is introduced: "The great king, the king of Castile, spent many years in our territory and pitched the tent of his honor in this city for a period of days. Amid the camp came the great minister, the leader (*nasi*), leader of the leaders of the Levites, our lord and master Todros (may his soul be in Eden), who was a powerful and honorable man before the lady, the queen of Castile, who accompanied the king."

The rhyming prose that follows illuminates ritualized aspects of the Jews' receiving the king in Perpignan and possibly alludes to the appointment of the Jewish courtier with the dubbing of a sword. Although many of the appellations clearly address Abulafia because of their distinctly Jewish character, the merciless use of pronouns and constant subject shifting sometimes leave it ambiguous whether the *mamdūḥ* is the courtier or the king. Below, I attempt to delineate which praises are directed toward whom, though other possible interpretations are indicated in the notes:

> Happy are you, O land, whose king comes unto you! Behold it is the time of love, the rains have passed! Who has revealed to us this great sight? Who has given us this honor? We have seen honor we never imagined! We have worn glory we never considered! O generation! See the virtue you merited the day you beheld your king [Alfonso][53] in his glory! This is a day you never expected; a time you did not await has arrived. Upon the wings of wonder you flew! And though [Alfonso's] height is above the heavens, you did not [need to] ascend to heaven to behold the one whom your soul loves! A man of God [Alfonso] has passed before us and a star that rose from Jacob [Abulafia] rises within our borders.[54] How beautiful were your bells in going out to meet [Alfonso]. You did not have to go armed over the sea to behold his glory. No man [even] had to leave the door of his house and you saw his honor and the precious majesty of his power. [Alfonso][55] scoffs at [other] kings and his sheaf stands upright. How honored is this day that our lord, king of Israel [Abulafia], was revealed before our eyes like the revealing of the king at his table.[56] [Abulafia is][57] the great eagle, the one who pierces the dragon and hews Rahab. The one [Alfonso] who seeks power and honor by his bow, who appoints with his sword, selected him [Abulafia] and extended his golden scepter and established [Abulafia's] place above his courtiers.[58] [Abulafia] is the great master, *nasi* of the *nasi*s of the Levites, a chief among his people, our lord and master Todros Halevi, whose name is greater than *rabban*.[59]

Bedersi inscribes Abulafia both within Christian court culture and within Jewish political structures. He is an appointee of the king and also a king in Israel. He (or possibly Alfonso) is the great eagle (further on this term, see Chapter 9) and, borrowing some language predicated of God, the slayer of primordial sea monsters (Is 51:9). More might be said about some of the appellations (e.g., "man of God"), but the ambiguity of referents leaves too many questions unanswerable.

This is only one of the many praises that Bedersi penned in honor of Abulafia; Bedersi immortalized him as the "father of Dominion, father of Wisdom, and father of Song" toward the end of his long list of literary figures—including most of the major Iberian Hebrew authors of poetry and rhymed prose, the Arabic authors al-Ḥarīrī and Ibn Quzmān, and the troubadours

Cardénal and Folquet—within his lengthy *Ḥerev mithapakhat* (Ever-turning sword).[60] But the most telling record of panegyric in this context consists of the correspondence between the two men. The scribe recounts how, at one gathering, Abulafia recited a Hebrew epigram that imitated an Arabic panegyric on the pen and the sword that praised a king as the only man who possessed both. Bedersi also "prophesied," that is, invented, a similar poem and, some time after the event, sent his version to Abulafia, now concluding with a third verse identifying the courtier as a man of power and as a poet, a possessor of the sword and the pen.[61]

Much of the correspondence adheres perfectly to the style and values of the Andalusian poets, including homonymic poems praising eloquence with rather hackneyed hyperbole; others trend toward the manneristic innovations promoted by the poet Todros Abulafia of Castile, likely with influence from al-Ḥarīzī as well. One exchange arose after the authors debated the etymology of the word *kidod* ("spark") but came to agree after they consulted the lexicons of David Kimḥi and Yonah Ibn Janāḥ.[62] More will be said about their correspondence below.

The fact that the most extensive Hebrew panegyric exchange preserved from southern France in this period involved a Castilian may make it appear as though the phenomenon was largely an extension of the practice in Castile. Yet other evidence suggests a more robust literary culture in this locale, beginning before the generation of Bedersi.[63] Bedersi wrote panegyrics for a number of other local figures and also received one from Yiṣḥaq ha-Gorni before the relationship between the two poets devolved into a bitter and extensive invective exchange. Schirmann characterized ha-Gorni as a "Jewish troubadour," whereas Susan Einbinder has called this a myth, seeing the poet instead as a "temperamental but mainstream member of an intellectual elite."[64] The superscription to ha-Gorni's panegyric for Bedersi reads: "God was good to Gorni when he went . . . to Perpignan, and there he met the poet Rabbi Avraham Prof[iat] Bedersi, who found favor in his eyes and so he wrote verses for him." In the poem, a voice calls to the poet:

> "Lift your eyes and behold the land of Sefarad![65] There Bedersi is
> the most precious of my great ones,
> father of all players who play the lute with elegance, greatest of
> those who pluck the lyre."

Ha-Gorni had already known Bedersi by reputation but adds:

Who could describe his form to me when it is inscribed on the wall
[of my heart] in vermilion?
I desired not only to see him but also to hear him; I sought him
though I did not know the way.
Your hands' deeds, Avram, are victorious even though the day is
short and the workers are lazy (cf. m. Avot 2:20).
I set them as frontlets between my eyes, as fringes upon my
garment (Dt 6:8).
And may your heart not become haughty when I call, "Please, lord"
and "If only [my lord]."
My son, if my hand were to grow strong like yours, it would be
[only] to play songs on my instruments like David![66]

In short, the poem is a familiar type of panegyric whereby one poet introduces himself to another in the hope of forming a bond and extending his reputation. Bedersi's response seems to have been critical, which led ultimately to the devolution of their relationship into hostility. Ha-Gorni did not always receive such poems warmly, either, as when he took offense that a young poet had praised him as a "minister of teaching" (*sar te'udah*), whereas he considered himself a "king."[67]

Although ha-Gorni states that he composed hundreds of poems, only twenty-six survive, and most of these are invectives. Still, the invectives are not necessarily emblematic of the poet's original corpus, which, one imagines, contained more panegyric. A poem that he wrote in praise of his birthplace, Aire-sur-l'Adour (which, "if the Messiah knew of it, would choose to be born there rather than in Bethlehem"), also praises four individuals as masters of Talmud and helpers of the poor.[68] Occasional snippets of praise are also included in the invectives that ha-Gorni launched against nearby cities such as Carpentras, which he portrayed as Sodom lacking even ten righteous men, a city that he will destroy with his poetry, sparing only the "sons of Yiṣḥaq" and the "sons of David."[69]

Returning to Bedersi's correspondence with Abulafia, the most memorable and innovative turn in panegyric is a text written after the style of the Passover Haggadah in a way that wittily transforms the symbolic foods, textual themes, and *piyyutim* that praise God into praise for the *mamdūḥ*. Some excerpts will surely delight (or perhaps puzzle) the reader familiar with the Passover seder, beginning with the three foods that Rabban Gamliel maintains that the seder participant is obliged to mention: the paschal lamb, the unleavened bread, and the bitter herb. "The paschal lamb (*pesaḥ*), because [Abulafia] passed over (*pasaḥ*) the souls of those who rebelled against him and poured out a spirit of generosity upon them and saved their children. Unleavened bread (*maṣah*), because he does not 'allow his dough to sour' day and night. . . ."[70]

A section follows this on the "four sons," corresponding to the Torah's four statements "concerning [Abulafia's] righteousness" and, continuing with the order of the seder, a song in imitation of the hymn "Dayyenu" ("It would have been enough!"),

> How much dignity and glory you possess, O minister, and how many virtues have [you set] upon our lives (*ḥayyenu*)[71]:
>
> If your palace extended only to this point but did not reach great heights and elevations, it would have been enough (*dayyenu*)!
> If our lord reached great elevations but did not cause a [comforting] wind to pass over us, it would have been enough (*dayyenu*)!
> If your trade and marble were Faith (*dat*) but you did not seek the honor of kings, it would have been enough (*dayyenu*)!

Through this very novel approach, Bedersi covers many of the standard motifs of panegyric: teaching faith, poetic composition, possessing a king's beauty, eloquence, dominion, humility, love, generosity toward the lowly and the wanderer. The experiment seems to have delighted Abulafia, who responded in kind "after the manner of *hallel*" (sections of the Psalms recited at the seder and on other occasions), to which Bedersi responded with more panegyrics that imitate other Passover *piyyutim*, as well as one modeled after the afternoon service (Musaf).

Israel Davidson called the exchange the "first important attempt at [Hebrew] parody in France," in that the texts were imitative of a ritual and "turn the religious hymns into compliments" though they contained "nothing of the humorous or satiric."[72] It is difficult to say exactly what the medieval reader considered humorous, though making light of canonical and reverent texts seems to belong to the trend of what the Russian formalist Mikhail Bakhtin called the *parodia sacra* of the late Middle Ages, including parodies of liturgies, Gospel readings and sayings, litanies, hymns, and psalms. These texts, which Bakhtin saw as echoing "carnival laughter" as a form of folk humor, could be heard in marketplaces, universities, and even religious institutions; Bakhtin expounds especially upon the *risus paschalis* ("paschal laughter"), wherein preachers encouraged laughter among congregants as a "joyous regeneration" following "lenten sadness."[73] That Bedersi's imitation of the Haggadah fell during the same season as Easter may not be a mere coincidence.

Meshullam DaPierra and the Gerona School

Geographically more proximate to Toledo than Perpignan but culturally and intellectually more distant was the city of Gerona in Catalonia, and the panegyric composed there was fairly distinct, as exemplified by the corpus of Meshullam DaPierra (born in southern France). Despite certain surface similarities to the Andalusian style regarding meter and rhyme, his panegyric, as well as his poetry more broadly, is unique in the corpus. Ross Brann has elegantly noted: "The reader familiar with Andalusian courtly poetry presumes to be at home in da Piera's verse but nothing in his work is ever what it appears to be at first reading. Andalusian genres, motifs, and rhetoric seem to resurface but in fact these elements are usually recast by an acute socio-religious sensibility which is altogether a product of the cultural climate of thirteenth-century Jewish Catalonia."[74] Brann illustrates this nicely with a reading of the one panegyric by DaPierra that opens with a prelude on erotic themes, dedicated to none other than Naḥmanides, the ranking rabbinic authority of the day. Brann argues that the prelude, despite the appearance of stock characters and motifs, hails from a new environment. Bernard Septimus has described the Gerona intellectuals as "'new men,' merchants, talmudists, and mystics, striving for spirituality and full of fresh energy."[75]

It seems that a search for patronage motivated the poet's initial relocation from Provence to Catalonia, where he became ensconced in what Ezra Fleischer reasonably named the "Gerona school," both because of the close social connections among its authors and shared elements of literary style.[76] It has been suggested that DaPierra was appointed head of the Catalonian *aljama*, the political body representing the Jewish community, though this view is based only on two verses appearing in a single poem:

> For they elevated me as head of the circle (*mesibah*); I shined upon
> those who know office (*yod'ei ba-ma'amad*), men of rank[77]. . . .
> However much Time may remove me from being a lord (*gevir*), I
> shall never abandon dominion (*misrah*) even if I perish.[78]

Without doubt, the poet associated with communal leaders who were also men of letters. The "circle" (*mesibah*) could conceivably refer to a political council, though the word is not generally used in this way; literally meaning a "place of sitting around (in a circle)," the word was used in earlier centuries, like *moshav*, as a calque of the Arabic *majlis*, a "gathering, session of learning."[79] Dominion (*misrah*) here could refer to actual political status, though we might expect corroborating evidence that DaPierra attained the highest office over others—for example, Naḥmanides—who were in Gerona at the time. Since all other references to this group within the poem emphasize social intimacy (they are called "associates," "sons of society," "loved ones," "friends," "men of the compact"),[80] it seems more likely that DaPierra's "dominion" here refers to his rank as a man of letters within the group rather than a leader of Catalonian Jewish political culture. What is perhaps most interesting about the Gerona poets is the degree to which the lines among the political, the social, and the literary blur.

The first thing that the reader of DaPierra's poetry notices is just how difficult it is. Schirmann argued that the poet was cultivating the troubadour style known as the *Trobar clus*, whose raison d'être was to be opaque, one of several links that Schirmann made between DaPierra's poetry and the troubadour lyric. Another thing that the reader notices is how little panegyric there is in the corpus, despite the fact that many of the poems are dedicated to individuals or small groups of men who held positions of authority. Apart from mentioning the names of addressees, extremely little is said about them. One is far more likely to find long sections of boasting or invective against enemies, perhaps with some dedicatory praise tacked on, which is a thematic progression typical of the *sirventes* of the troubadours. For example, Peire Cardénal (first half of thirteenth century) wrote: "I have always despised fraud and treachery and lived according to truth and justice; and if this makes my fortunes vary, I don't complain, for life seems fine and good to me. . . . Great barons feel as much pity for others as did Cain for Abel; they steal more readily than wolves and lie more easily than whores. . . . Faidit, go and sing this *sirventes* to En Guigon at Tournoël, for in worthiness he has no equal in the world, except milord En Eble of Clermont."[81]

By the early thirteenth century, the troubadour lyric had come to be studied systematically in works of poetics that, as John Dagenais has noted, read the lyric through the lens of Aristotelian epideictic categories with "praise and blame" as the basis of analysis; genre classification included the types of subjects—love, lords, and ladies—that could be praised or blamed.[82] Still, among the genres assigned (either by medieval or modern critics)—*canso*, *sirventes*, *alba*—none approximated panegyric; hence readers did not see the praise of a patron as the rhetorical aim of any troubadour genre despite the fact that direct praise is contained within several. Panegyric dedications were largely devoid of elaboration, and even the most extensive examples tend to list qualities rather than expand upon them hyperbolically.[83]

Returning to the panegyric of DaPierra, one of the richest ones is addressed to "ha-Seniri," possibly Yiṣḥaq Ben Yehudah Ben Natanel. It opens with a vision of the friend who "appears in flame from the Burning Bush, the embers of the Bush also burn me," turns to blame against those who have attained dominion (*misrah*) in the poet's homeland of Provence, and then to the generosity of the people of Gerona—in particular, the *mamdūḥ*:

> I write for his honor; when I praise him in song, Intellect's lips sing its words.[84]
> I utter verses that contain honor but upon those deserving of death I am merciful.

Following this, DaPierra viciously attacks those whom he calls "scoundrels" for seven lines (apparently his idea of being "merciful") and ultimately returns to the *mamdūḥ*:

> Unto you, watchman over men of the age, before whom thoughts become straight,
> establish and prepare yourself and beneath your feet the ideas of your mind will subdue the earth!
> Your glory is honored because of the breadth of your intellect even when those men of the age oppress you. . . .
> Friends love you and you love them; they make your heart drunk with love.
> They make your mention honeycomb and manna in their mouths; they speak your name like the finest of spices.
> May the writing of my hand go forth like a fawn sent forth, my letters fly like a hawk.
> Dominion in the house of Ḥasdai has been passed on from their ancestors since eternity; through their forefathers' honor they are crowned.
> How great is the dominion of your fathers that they can sell some to others but not deplete it![85]

The only qualities mentioned are the *mamdūḥ*'s intelligence and his dominion as a matter of inheritance, a far cry from the *mamdūḥs* composed of intellectual prowess, generosity, eloquence, humility, courage, and power over enemies in nearby Toledo.

This is not to say that such qualities are not present in DaPierra's poetry; the poet frequently predicates them of *himself* even as he insists upon his humility. One poem contains the verse "I possess humility and do not praise myself; I do not show my tassel to any man" (did he fail to see the irony?) before briefly praising four kabbalists in Gerona who also functioned within the poet's social and poetic circle:,

> My friends' sounding praises for me is like bells upon the hem of
> my garment.
> I am known only to one or two, or truthfully there are only four in
> my world!
> I am known to Yiṣḥaq Ben Shemuel, and to Avram, my portion
> and rope,
> and my leader Ben Ḥasdai who is light to my eyes and the bud and
> crown and the healing.
> My whole salvation is in Ben Naḥman; my nard and aloe give forth
> scent in his name.[86]

The poem cleverly plays on the poetics of esotericism associated with the kabbalah, such that the poet, like esoteric knowledge itself, is "known only to one or two." The praise of kabbalists is an aspect of DaPierra's poetry that makes it unique in the tradition. In general, one might delve further into studying kabbalistic imagery within DaPierra's panegyric and lines of continuity between medieval Hebrew panegyric and the ways in which holy men, such as Shim'on Bar Yoḥay, are addressed in the *Zohar*.[87]

The poem in DaPierra's corpus that can most reasonably be called "political panegyric" was composed for a friend who had been granted a courtier position by King James I of Aragon. This poem, too, is extremely reticent about the characteristics of the *mamdūḥ*. The introduction describing a spring garden is reminiscent of the Andalusian style and may be intended to hark back to the prototype of poetry associated with the Jew in royal service. The exaltation of the *mamdūḥ* is announced by a heralding musician within the garden scene:

Amid reed and cinnamon the tongue of a musician sings, birds of
every feather after their kind.
My beloved hastened upon the hills of spices, the Garden of Eden,
to gather his cinnamon.
Know that the myrtle has yielded new fruit; its smoke rose from a
bundle of myrrh!
He is consecrated among his brethren,[88] the one who sat upon a
throne; [the king] prepared for him a throne of sovereignty in the
palace.
A mighty king obtained for him grace and honor and appointed
him as adviser of the advisers.
They selected him[89] like a dragon in a river and a lion whelp leaping
forth from Bashan.[90]
Ornament of pride, my soul's friend and grandeur, [the king] set
upon your neck his crescent-ornament.
His bracelets are fitting for your wrists, his necklace from his neck.
Who else would honor you, my love, when the honor of your
dignity comes from the glory of his status?
Would you take a gift from a scoundrel, or milk from a wrathful
spider?[91]

Most of the poem's remaining forty-five verses advise the *mamdūḥ* to avoid involvement with a particular enemy, variably called a "scoundrel" or "pig." DaPierra positions his *mamdūḥ* within general, non-Jewish political culture; the poem suggests rituals of empowerment, and "adviser of advisers" (*yo'eṣ yo'aṣim*) seems more of a title than a general description.[92] The *mamdūḥ* is known by his relation to the king, who is the ultimate source of sovereignty (notably, it is not God who is given this position). But again, the panegyric says little about the *mamdūḥ* except that the honors bestowed upon him are fitting. The near absence of "dominion" in DaPierra's corpus, let alone its characterization through hyperbole, sacred or otherwise, certainly speaks to a subdued assertion of Jewish political claims in Gerona at the time.

The Saragossa Circle

Perhaps the most fascinating of Iberian Hebrew literary circles, which explicitly identified itself as such, is the one that sprouted up around Saragossa in the late fourteenth and early fifteenth centuries. It involved such poets as Shelomoh DaPierra (a relative of Meshullam's), Vidal Ben Lavi, Don Vidal Benveniste, and Shelomoh Bonafed. DaPierra was the founder of the group and enjoyed the patronage of three generations of the prominent Ben Lavi family. Others in the group, such as Benveniste, do not seem to have had or needed patronage. The group identified itself by various names—*kat meshorerim* ("group of poets"), *ḥevrat nognim* ("society of singers"), *'adat nognim* ("assembly of singers")—all of which point to a self-conscious group identity.[93] The mass conversions of Iberian Jewry, beginning in 1391 and continuing after the Tortosa disputation (1413–14), included some seventeen members of the Ben Lavi family and members and affiliates of the *ḥevrat nognim*. Yet, as historians readily recognize, the ties between conversos and Jews remained strong and, as Frank Talmage put it, "it was poetry, Hebrew poetry, that continued to bind together many of the figures in this drama—conversos and professing Jews—for years to come."[94]

Panegyric, together with invective, makes up the great majority of this group's literary output, much of which survives in the form of correspondence; the medieval manuscripts tend to present the lengthy poems along with other short accompanying ones (some copied from the "backs of sheets") in the chronological order of the literary exchange, often with paratextual comments by the poet-anthologizers that explain the circumstances of composition. Hence this poetic culture was largely one of reading and writing, which was also a feature of at least some vernacular literary culture at the time (but see below about occasional oral performances and competitions).[95]

The earliest stratum of the circle was active even before the mass conversions of 1391, with continued activity afterward and beyond the Tortosa disputations. Works from the earlier periods display a political sensibility largely continuous with patterns witnessed throughout this book. Ram Ben-Shalom has demonstrated that letters and panegyrics by Yom Tov Ben Ḥannah (late fourteenth–early fifteenth century) to Aragonese Jewish courtiers appeal to the language of dominion and kingship as an expression of sustained religious political identity in exile.[96] In the most striking example, a wedding poem, likely for Yehudah Lavi, the poet expounds upon the theme of kingship; the poem begins with the heavens, which were "created before a king ever reigned," and then recounts generations of Israelite kings (Saul, David) until the poet finally reaches blessings for the bridegroom: "Have you seen the one whom God has chosen as a son, for nothing like him soars in the heavens of Dominion! How much sweeter than honey and how much mightier than a lion!"[97] The poem evokes God's choosing a "son" in Is 9:5–6; although certainly not the first political poem to refer to this passage, its use is particularly poignant, given the contemporary Christological reading (the poem also draws on Gn 49:10, another contested verse).

After the Tortosa disputation, Shelomoh DaPierra wrote a lament for Don Benveniste Ben Lavi de la Cavalleria, a poet and translator who was active in the disputation and seems to have enjoyed further status at court, at least prior to the disputation.[98] The deceased, whose connections with royalty are well documented,[99] is recalled as a "mighty shepherd through whom the stumbling were strengthened," a "cherub with wings spread out by whom the ministers of the age increased in valor" and because of whose "departure deputies quaked and said. . . . How can kings continue to exercise sovereignty when by his advice they wore pride as a necklace? . . . The laws of his mind's counsel were inscribed for the kings of the age instead of religious laws." The lament goes on to praise his wisdom, eloquence, virtues, generosity toward the poor, and faith, as well as the translations that he made from various languages into Hebrew.[100] But apart from this lament, the representation of Jews in DaPierra's *dīwān* is strikingly apolitical or, at least, not in the concrete sense of courtly status. This corresponds, it seems, to the change of Jewry policies that followed the death of King Martin I, who died without heir, and the ascent to the throne of Fernando I of Aragon in 1412.[101] More generally, the role of the Jewish courtier was significantly diminished with the progression of the fifteenth century; Jews appear mostly as tax farmers rather than in their former roles as diplomats, astronomers, and advisers.[102] Notably, the only living person in DaPierra's *dīwān* to be praised in a manner typical for a powerful man—as an amalgam of wisdom, strength, humility, virtue, and mighty in deed—is the Christian Don Juan de Ixar, in a poem that DaPierra wrote when he came to the "city of his governance" to "find favor in his eyes."[103]

Praise in DaPierra's corpus is centered almost solely on poetic skill, and the language of "dominion" becomes transferred to the realm of the poetic. Typical is the praise found throughout DaPierra's correspondence with Don Vidal Benveniste:

> You are a lord of Wisdom, a mighty one of song for whose ascent
> song has awaited.
> The mark of song was written and sealed upon the wall of your
> mind's heart, friend, and my soul is in your speech.

Time has removed the dominion of preciousness from the shoulder
of musicians and set it upon your shoulder.
[Time] has dried the sea of players; all streams of song now flow to
your rivers and lakes.

The poem continues to mix praises for poetic skill with other virtues but comes back to poetry:

Those who dwell at the furthest extremes love your name; they give
your name glory, majesty, and honor.
The hosts of Sheba and Sava bow before your house and hall, even
before mention of your name!
The hearts of giants fall in fear of you, ogres[104] are terrified of
you. . . .
Your name spreads like the scent of flowing myrrh amid a bundle of
spices, so who can hide you?
The dream-words of your speech are visions of prophets[105] and so
song's prophets[106] are your diviners.

Although a focus on literary ability is not a new theme and is obviously quite appropriate for correspondence, the nearly singular obsession with the topic marks a new cultural moment. The poem concludes with the language of dominion:

May [God] magnify your power and raise your loftiness above the
height of your leaders and above your exalted ones.
And with much pride, dominion, and majesty may he elongate your
days, with much tranquility and delight.[107]

All this language of power and majesty refers most likely to Don Vidal's station among poets or his esteemed lineage; the rest of the correspondence does not indicate political power. It was after Don Vidal's conversion to Christianity that he came to occupy governmental positions.

Shelomoh Bonafed corresponded with members of the *kat meshorerim* and was the last great Hebrew poet in Iberia. Even as he feared that with his death, "Yedutun and Heman will die" (i.e., Hebrew poetry will come to an end),[108] he was also aware that his literary moment was already one of revival. In one poem, presented as consolation to a friend, Bonafed names a number of poets of the thirteenth century (Meshullam DaPierra, Avraham Bedersi, Yedaia ha-Penini) and of Islamic al-Andalus (the "sons of" Ezra, Ibn Gabirol, Halevi) and adds: "With their deaths poetry died . . . until [Don Vidal] Ben Benvenist arose and was established as the father of poetry."[109]

Of the poets of his age, Bonafed wrote: "In the streets they glean new poetry and old."[110] In fact, the poetry of the Saragossa circle reflects an admixture of a classical style with new developments, both on the levels of prosody and theme: series of homonym poems (*tajnīs*); beginning a verse with the last word of the previous line; numeric mnemonics; responding to a poem received with another not only in the same meter and rhyme but also reusing a word from each line.[111] But still, there is evidence for a simultaneous reining in of poetic devices, as when Bonafed urged younger poets with whom he corresponded, "don't come in the hollow way of rhymes or the yoke of *tajnīs* lest its yield will spoil."[112]

As for thematic shifts, Raymond Scheindlin studies a panegyric *qaṣīda* by Don Vidal Benveniste, which imitates an earlier one by Yehudah Halevi, wherein a beautiful maiden in a garden directs her attention not to the *mamdūḥ* but rather to the poet, who, in turn, spurns her in favor of the only true beauty, thereby adding a layer of complication to the *takhalluṣ*: "My soul yearns to dwell alone with wisdom . . . so I went up to the presence of the noble Shneur." Scheindlin concludes: "Although Vidal's imitation of Halevi is a clever adaptation of an earlier form to a new situation, it is also an example of the continued use of a form that is no longer relevant to the situation."[113] Also, reusing and secularizing a motif from Ibn Gabirol's *Keter malkhut* (with ultimate origins in a *ḥadīth*), Bonafed concluded one panegyric, "Take, lord, a gift of poetry and soldiers of song which *fled in fear of you but unto you they fled*."[114] This poetic universe was both old and new.

Most of the Hebrew prose introductions with which poets preface their praise poems reveal social circumstances that are extraordinarily banal and not unlike those encountered earlier in this book: a wedding; a condolence following a death; a man who lost his wealth; the donation of an ornamental Torah "crown"; a man who traveled to the "land of Yishmael" (which, by the way, is represented as far preferable to "Edom"); praise for a homily given in the synagogue; a poet joining the "group of poets"; recovery after illness; even an exchange when Shelomoh DaPierra had a toothache.[115] In sum, they remind us that very ordinary life continued for Iberian Jews even following the tumultuous events of 1391 and the Tortosa disputation. A particularly fascinating scenario, unique to the period, arose when (prior to his conversion) Astruc Ramokh sent a poem in the vernacular to Shelomoh DaPierra and hoped for a response in the same; although DaPierra "praised" the poem received ("he made a mouth for a mute tongue, made a goat like a lion"), he also pleaded the case of Hebrew over the vernacular: "One should compose in the Hebrew tongue; what have I to do with the language of Kasdim or the murmurings of Ashkenazim?"[116]

But by far the most interesting social dynamics in this circle are those that arose out of the circumstances of conversion, especially following the Tortosa disputation. First, the stressful months of the disputation also occasioned a kind of poetic convention insofar as Jewish intellectuals from many locales were summoned to Tortosa. Bonafed recounts his arrival in Tortosa: "the wind was the wind of poetry flowing like water since many of the great poets in the kingdom were there along with most of the scholars." Bonastruc Demaistre presented a poem in honor of Yosef Ben Lavi (Vidal de la Cavalleria); Ben Lavi apparently replied in kind, which led Bonafed to compose an original poem in the same meter and rhyme ("speaking the language of his poem") and lamenting the conversions ("shrieking bitterly over the bitter waters and raising a voice of complaint in the camp of the Hebrews"). The poem begins: "A precious sun that set in our West, why will it not rise on the circuit of our circle?" Mixed with the voice of lament is praise for Ben Lavi:

> [Time] instilled fear and summoned the whole community of those who know Law and Faith (*dat ve-din*), among them a lord who restores our souls,
> a flame in the dark place of hidden wisdom, light in the gloom of thought's hidden place. Behold his shining around us!
> We were sons of giants on the necklace of his honor, but we became grasshoppers because of the transgressions of our loved ones.
> But what more can the Sons of Days do [to us] when the springs of his intellect extinguish our flames?[117]
> How can the gloom of their darkness endanger us when his light rises over the deep darkness that surrounds us?
> The tablet of his song is a shield against sorrow,[118] his hand's pen a spear to hurl at the camp of our enemies.
> We sing his song not for pride but to terrify Time's many soldiers lest it make us grieve.
> The embroidery of his writing is a wonder to man's eye, how can we imagine likening our writing to its beauty?
> Arise, silent pipe, mute lyre, and be brave! Drive out our misery and distress!

Arise and awaken the army of singers whom the army of Time has
taken, for whom the vicissitudes of the Sons of Days lie in wait.
Release the fetters of their hearts' distress with cords of song; lift up
your voice and the wings of our cherubs will be lifted.
O Tent of Testimony, Assembly of Dominion, Epitome of Majesty!
May there be peace in their troops and power to battle those who
wage war against us.
May there be peace in their troops; quickly may they and we go in
the light of a precious sun that set in our West.[119]

In this circle poem, the "precious sun that set in our West" first signals the opening passage of lament but, in the final verse, refers to the luminous *mamdūḥ*. The portrayal of Ben Lavi centers on his skill as a poet, now inflected with the urgency of the moment as a weapon fighting the tide of conversion. Despite the poem's references to "dominion" and "majesty," the representation is not that of a political man.

Despite the "distress" and "deep darkness" brought on by the conversions, the bifurcation of the community into Jews and conversos did not amount to the total severing of social or literary ties across the boundary. Shelomoh DaPierra converted to Christianity around the age of seventy and continued to exchange Hebrew poems with Don Vidal Benveniste.[120] Shelomoh Bonafed wrote Hebrew poems to converts and corresponded with Francesc de Santa Jordi (formerly Astruc Ramokh the Jew) in Hebrew, even offering a rhymed prose critique of central Christian doctrines.[121] In the absence of bonds of faith, the bonds of literary culture persevered.

As Avraham Gross points out, some of the panegyrics between Jews and converts call attention to the circumstance of religious difference whereas others make little mention of it. Of the latter variety is Bonafed's poem for "the exalted Maestro Iṣaaq Aderet [Ben Lavi] after he changed his honor" (*hemir kevodo*), which makes only the most oblique reference to conversion through the standard language of "departure":

Wind of friendship, bring my greetings to the son of Lavi for whose
departure my soul was exiled,
the lord who protected the heights of my verse and upon whose tel
of love the city of my speech was built.[122]

In another poem, Bonafed praised Aderet's wisdom as more essential to his being than his religious affiliation, which is presented as an outer garment (the poem makes several plays on the *mamdūḥ*'s name):

> If the way of your faith has become hidden, your power and wisdom are revealed!
> If your sun is darkened for our eyes, behold it has risen on the circuit of your wisdom!
> If Time, in truth, has stripped off your cloak (*aderet*), it did not plunder your honor and glory (*aderet*). . . .
> He who has beheld a dream-vision of an angel of God will be satisfied in beholding your image while awake.[123]

Bonafed and Aderet make light and sometimes ironic play of their state of religious difference. Aderet, after converting to Christianity, boasted over his own verse and diminished Bonafed's:

> Who is it that seeks to spoil the glory of my anointed? Who can compare with Ben Yiṣḥaq in poetry?
> Be glad and rejoice when you see that the daughter of your song has become a concubine and maidservant in his household.[124]

Calling his poetry "my anointed" (*meshiḥi*, "my Messiah") draws attention to religious difference, for it would seem that Iṣaaq is also blaming (lightly, I think) Bonafed for despising Christ.[125] In his response, Bonafed ultimately seeks reconciliation: "Ben Lavi is as valued in poetry as I; the two of us rule over proverbs" (*moshlim be-moshlim*) and adds deferentially, while playing on the original verse: "If your king is a garden of grace, then I am a river, and if your anointed (*meshiḥakha*) is the sea, then I am dry land."[126] All this is not a Jewish-Christian polemic but rather a playful repartee that exploits motifs of interreligious disputation. Simultaneously, it creates a world, bracketed off from the "real world," wherein the Messiah is neither Christ nor an expected savior but rather Hebrew poetry.

Polemical valences carry a deeper significance in Bonafed's correspondence with Francesc de Santa Jordi. In one poem, Bonafed mixes praise for de Santa Jordi with rebuke:

Answer, O pure and ruddy who comes from Edom, for whom the
heights of the city are a footstool,
exalted in the faith of his religion, his mind is his folly; because of it
his eye became blind.
In his high station, he forgot the plight of his people as though the
dominion on his shoulder sounded [only] the glory of his name.
His anger was kindled because he did not believe that the fugitive[127]
would survive.
The staff of the righteous became a serpent, a bright and pure light
became a sore.

These few verses are dense in allusions to Christianity and contested biblical verses within Jewish-Christian polemic. De Santa Jordi is "from Edom"; designating neither familial lineage nor geographic territory, Bonafed uses Edom here to denote religious community. It is perhaps half-facetiously that Bonafed calls him "pure and ruddy," evoking Sg 5:10, a verse sometimes taken by Jewish and Christian commentators as alluding to the Messiah.[128] The phrase "dominion on his shoulder" (cf. Is 9:6, which begins "For unto us a child is born, unto us a son is given") is a touchstone of the Jewish-Christian debate; Bonafed uses it with some frequency to refer to Christianity, stripping it of association with Christ and reducing it to worldly rule. The staff becoming a serpent reminds us first of Moses' and Aaron's miracles before Pharaoh's magicians (Exodus 7), but perhaps also to Moses' erecting a serpent on a bronze pole in the wilderness (Nm 21:8–9), taken already in Jn 3:14–15 as prefiguring the crucifixion. Hence poems within the polemical exchange between Bonafed and de Santa Jordi exploit key verses of Jewish-Christian debate in a calculating manner.

We do not have direct evidence that other leading members of the *kat meshorerim*, notably Don Vidal Ben Lavi and Shelomoh DaPierra, continued to correspond with Bonafed after conversion, despite numerous attempts over many years by the latter. In a poem that he wrote to the two of them, Bonafed seems to hope for their return, presumably to Judaism:

My eye beheld your return to early days (*qadmut*); nay, it didn't see
it but dreamed it in a dream.
It beheld you upon a chariot of Truth bridled with the hand of Faith,
shepherds in the garden of Knowledge in the shade of the Living
God; He is not dead for Truth lives within your souls.

When Bonafed referred to the conversions of DaPierra and Ben Lavi, however, he wrote that they "contravened the law of language and broke the covenant of eloquence" and that their "love passed" when they stopped writing Hebrew.[129] That is, he speaks much more about poetry than about religion, per se. The question is whether Hebrew poetry is simply a synecdoche for Judaism or whether Bonafed would have been satisfied with his former coreligionists' return to Hebrew poetic exchange. In the case of Aderet, such an arrangement seemed quite tolerable. Don Vidal, now Gonsalo de la Cavalleria, came to occupy governmental positions closed to Jews, which made his return unlikely, not to mention that religious recidivism was a punishable offense. In another poem, though Don Vidal was clearly a Christian at the time, Bonafed praised him: "the honor of your wisdom is like a consuming fire at the top of the mountains of Israel." He does not suggest, through lineage or belief, that the *mamdūḥ* was a Jew but rather that his wisdom (still?) benefited Israel. Thus through Hebrew poetry, Bonafed attempted to create an interreligious or supra-religious intellectual circle, perhaps as an attempt to create normalcy within a radically transformed religio-social environment.

Angel Sáenz-Badillos already noted that "one gets the impression that [Bonafed] alludes to poetry in almost every poem. Hebrew poetry is the leitmotif of his whole life."[130] More than a pastime or one of several intellectual pursuits, Hebrew poetry for Bonafed seemed a source of stability in a world turned upside-down. We have already seen that a focus on poetry was emblematic of DaPierra's praise writing, and with Bonafed this tendency took on a deeper dimension bound up with social and political reconfiguration. In the fifteenth century, Hebrew poetry became the fixation of its own discourse, thereby producing a self-referential, hermetic, and inward-gazing universe that existed beyond the social and political organization of the time. Dominion became almost exclusively an aspect of this world apart, and all the poetic tropes traditionally applied to the political, including sacred hyperbole, were marshaled in the service of poetry itself.

In his correspondence with Shelomoh DaPierra, Mosheh 'Abbas apparently boasted over his poetry by calling it "Lord, God of eternity" (*Adonai el 'olam*). In his lengthy prose response, DaPierra upbraided him: "['Abbas] went far beyond the fence of associative metaphors so much that he called his poem 'Lord, God of eternity.' We have been greatly admonished against this from the paths of eloquence and poetry and one should not to diverge from it. However, I sent to his honor poetry and eloquent prose in which I alluded to this by way of respect."

In the epistle, DaPierra set three poems that take the sacred hyperbole to a further extreme and prefaced them: "I shall set profane words in the Holy of Holies." Among the poems is a five-verse homonymic (*tajnīs*) poem wherein each line concludes with the equivocal word *elohim* (which can mean God, angels, or rulers of cities); it closes:

> Therefore I rise to thank you with all [my] might, for your name is
> greater than every ruler (*elohim*),
> True! Your pen is the Lord of Lords (*adonei ha-adonim*) and your
> poetry is the God of Gods (*elohei ha-elohim*).[131]

Of course, DaPierra's "rebuke" seems only half-hearted, since he clearly took pleasure in continuing this irreverent game. Indeed, this sort of play continued among the poets of Saragossa, for when En Bonaguda [Yehudah] Yaḥseel ha-Kaslari praised Shelomoh Ben Reuven Bonafed as "God in song," Bonafed responded: "If in song Ben Reuven is God (*elohim*), then Yehudah is God of Gods" (*elohei elohim*).[132]

* * *

In 1946, María Rosa Lida proposed that the *hyperbole sagrada* characteristic of Spanish poetry in the fifteenth century resulted from the influx of converso poets into the courtly literary scene. Indeed, panegyrics by converso poets sometimes pressed the boundaries of blasphemy, such as a poem by Antón de Montoro for Queen Isabel (the monarch who expelled the Jews) that claimed that, had Isabel been alive, God would have selected her as Christ's mother instead of Mary (note the structural similarity to ha-Gorni's boast over his birthplace, "If the Messiah knew of it, he would choose to be born there rather than in Bethlehem").[133] As Roger Boase points out, a poem by Pedro de Cartagena, also addressed to the queen, can be taken as an apt commentary: "You should silence the eulogies addressed to you . . . because in making you known the people commit idolatry."[134] It should now be clear that, in the fifteenth century, we are not witnessing a blasphemous invention of the conversos but rather the continuation of a distinct Arabic-Hebrew poetics that can be traced over centuries.

CHAPTER 9

The Other "Great Eagle": Interreligious Panegyrics and the Limits of Interpretation

The synagogue built in 1357 by Shemuel Halevi Abulafia in Toledo, best known as the Tránsito, is constructed in a *mudejar* style, replete with geometric lattice windows, vegetal and arabesque stucco reliefs, and inscriptions along the ceiling in Arabic script.[1] Calligraphic Hebrew inscriptions cover the walls, many of them evoking figures of Israel's past, including kings (especially Solomon), the archetypal courtier Mordechai, and the prophet Samuel, whose name the patron bore. Past glory is similarly evoked through numerous comparisons between the new synagogue and Solomon's Temple. At the same time, the synagogue famously displays the Castilian coat of arms, whose emblems were the castle and lion. An inscription just to the right of the Torah niche presents a lengthy poetic dedication in Hebrew for the patron, chief treasurer (*tesorero mayor*) of King Pedro I of Castile (r. 1350–69), who is also praised in Hebrew. The letters of the words "Don Pedro" are about double the size of those in the rest of the inscription and are underscored with decorative designs.

The dedicatory panegyric begins with praise for God who has "established judges and ministers to save us from the hand of enemies and oppressors. And though there is no king in Israel, He has not deprived us of a Redeemer who is the bulwark of the tower; since the Exile of Ariel none has arisen like him in Israel." Below, parts of the dedication to Shemuel and the entire dedication for Pedro are translated:

> [Shemuel] is the ruler of the land, the great tamarisk, citadel of strength and greatness. He attained the rank of dominion (*misrah*)

> in accordance with his praise, and great and holy shall he be called.[2] [He is] the right-hand pillar upon which the House of the Levite and the House of Israel are fixed. Who can count his praises? Who can recount his virtues and his deeds? And who can recount and complete his praise? [He is a] turban of Dominion and the most precious of Majesty. He stands at the head of the order, chief leader of the Levites of God, Shemuel Halevi, the man raised on high. May God be with him and cause him to ascend. He found grace and favor in the eyes of the great eagle with great wings, the man of war and the champion[3] whose dread has fallen upon all peoples. Great is his name among the nations, our lord and protector,[4] King Don Pedro. May God aid him and increase his glory and majesty and guard him as the shepherd of his flock. The king has made [Shemuel] great and has exalted him and elevated his throne above all the ministers. . . .[5] Without him no man lifts his hand or foot. Nobles prostrate themselves before him so that his nobility may become known throughout the land and be heard among the people. And it shall be pronounced among all the kingdoms, "Hear! There is unto Israel a Savior!"[6]

The praise for Pedro is framed by the much longer praise for Abulafia, who, as a courtier, functions as Israel's "Redeemer" and "Savior." Shemuel possesses virtues and dominion; the author emphasizes his Levitic descent. Why is he called the "great tamarisk"? This tree is used already in rabbinic literature as a metaphor for a great man, especially a scholar,[7] though the association here is as specific as a tradition that the "tamarisk in Ramah" beneath which Saul sits in 1 Sm 22:6 alludes to the biblical Samuel (from Ramah);[8] but in this case, Samuel would be the patron rather than his biblical namesake.

Pedro's elevation of Abulafia, along with Pedro López de Ayala's (1332–1407) portrayal of Pedro I as lavishing favor upon Jews, has led to the modern perception of a judeophilic king. Clara Estow argues, however, that Ayala's representation is a vilifying caricature of a Jew-loving king created to undermine Pedro's authority and champion the counterclaims of his archrival Enrique de Trastámara (it was also Ayala who bestowed upon Pedro his enduring sobriquet "the Cruel"). Considering all the available evidence, Estow concludes that, although Pedro's Jewry policies were "essentially benign," there is no "unique or especially pro-Jewish royal bias."[9] In fact, Pedro famously imprisoned Shemuel Halevi, exacted enormous taxes from the Jews after 1366, and did not hesitate, when a need for funds arose in 1368, to allow three hundred Jews to be sold into slavery in Jaén (though, of course, none of these events had occurred at the time of the synagogue's construction).[10]

As a whole, the dedication points to many tensions surrounding the political condition of Jews in the Middle Ages—the absence of Jewish sovereignty paired with God's appointment of Jewish "judges and ministers" for the Jews' protection and the rule of a Gentile king in whose eyes a particular Jewish minister found favor; Jewish power is paradoxically attained through the graces of their "subjugators." The praises for Pedro, "our lord and protector," focus on temporal aspects of rule, especially military power that inspires fear in "all nations." The blessings include his preservation as a "shepherd to his flock," which begs the question of whether the author considered Jews to be a part of this flock or not, whether the flock was a religious or a political body (compare "[God] established judges and ministers to save *us*"). Also, of Pedro we read "great is his name"; but of Abulafia "great and holy shall he be called."

Pedro is the "great eagle," a title that had only been predicated previously of Maimonides and a few other figures.[11] The appellation derives from a parable in Ezekiel 17, where the "great eagle with great wings" crops the top of a cedar of Lebanon and plants its seeds in a distant city, where they grow into a vine that brings forth shoots and branches. This eagle is explicitly identified with the Babylonian king who took Jerusalem's "seed of royalty" to Babylon. In exile, the leadership swears an oath of loyalty to the king, an act that humiliates Israel yet allows it to survive. A second "great eagle with great wings" appears, toward which the vine bends its root to be watered. This eagle is identified with God, who swears to defeat the Babylonian king and plant the vine "upon a high mountain of Israel" so that "every bird of every feather" might dwell in its shade.[12]

At the very least, the dedication presents a Gentile king whose authority, however worthy, is bracketed by its temporality; the dedication thus does not abandon an entrenched view of Jewish sacred history wherein a redemption is awaited. After all, it is Shemuel, and not the king, who is called "Savior" and "Redeemer." The allusion to the "great eagle" raises a further important question: Did the author of the dedication intend only positive associations with the appellation, or might he have embedded a barb to suggest that Pedro is the first "great eagle" who enjoys the loyalty of Israel humiliated in exile but who will ultimately be vanquished by God, the other "great eagle"?

In an important article, Amnon Linder studies carefully scripted encounters between popes and Jews that, in some cases, included Jews' offering hyperbolic *laudes*. Although these late-medieval and early-modern rituals devised by Christian authorities were intended as performances of Jewish loyalty, Jewish sincerity was sometimes considered suspect by Christian onlookers. According to Linder, these suspicions were not without cause. With reference to a book by Gerd Baumann, Linder refers to Jews' "'dual discursive competence,' which is typical of dominated subgroups which can switch between their own discourse and that of the dominating community."[13] Baumann's idea can involve speech matters as simple as contextual pronunciation or shifting grammatical patterns but can also rise to the level of subversive double meaning. Linder opines that Jews' pronouncements of praise could be viewed as "expressing complete compliance and subjection, but covertly transmitting to its members a subversive, counteracting message"; he finds "reversals of meaning" in many *laudes* from the early modern period. Thus, in Linder's view, popes were praised for traits that a learned Jewish audience might recognize as belonging to biblical villains, an "instantly recognizable rogues' gallery."[14] Although I am not convinced by all of Linder's arguments, the question he asks is essentially a good one.[15]

Should the dedication of the Tránsito be read according to a poetics of resistance, whereby the subjugated Jewish minority appears to esteem temporal authority outwardly while harboring a fantasy of subversion beneath the surface? Related questions are explored in a classic book by the anthropologist James Scott (1990) that argues that many dominated subgroups present themselves to power with deference—a "public transcript" beneficial to all parties involved—but simultaneously engage in subversive "backstage discourse"; moreover, "hidden transcripts" are often presented in plain sight through "a politics of disguise and anonymity that takes place in public view but is designed to have a double meaning or to shield the identity of the actors."[16] Of course, such messaging would have to be executed covertly and with plausible deniability, which makes identifying reliable instances rather difficult. Reading a submerged poetics of resistance can, at best, be a circular process, since "hidden transcripts" can be found only if one presumes that they might be present; judgments must remain necessarily subjective, and there is always the risk that scholars are creating what they claim to be revealing. In this regard, we must be mindful of historiographic trends that extol the Jew as a loyal servant of political authority (useful, for example, among Jewish emancipationists in nineteenth-century Europe to combat anti-Semitic claims) *and* of the more recent countervailing trend that emphasizes Jewish agency and resistance, whether executed through violence, ritual, art, or words (flexibly exploited in Zionist but also in postcolonial discourse).[17]

The purpose of this chapter is to explore aspects of "dual discursive competence" among Jews as manifest in their panegyrics for non-Jewish figures. In addition to the question of subversion, the chapter looks more generally at how Jews negotiated—through language, form, imagery, and allusion—political status and religious difference when presenting panegyrics for non-Jewish figures. Panegyric dedication might be viewed as a kind of "pressure point" that demanded the articulation of an interreligious relationship that could otherwise remain undefined, amorphous, and noncommittal. Jewish panegyrics for non-Jewish figures offer careful constructions of non-Jewish legitimacy, and close readings of these texts—both what they say and what they do not—yield important data on interreligious dynamics in Mediterranean contexts. Some panegyrics actively inscribe Jewish presence within a political structure while others efface religious difference altogether.

The range of texts includes panegyrics in Hebrew, Arabic, Judeo-Arabic, and Castilian from al-Andalus, Egypt, Syria, Castile, and Aragon. Panegyrics were sometimes written in the *mamdūḥ*'s mother tongue, which, of course, was also the mother tongue of the Jewish author, while others were dedicated in languages of intellectual or political significance that the *mamdūḥ* may not have understood. Apart from this initial section on the Tránsito inscription, the texts will be presented almost entirely chronologically, beginning with Ḥasdai Ibn Shaprut's/Menaḥem Ben Saruq's Hebrew praise for the Byzantine emperor Constantine VII and circling back to Pedro I, with the Castilian panegyric that concludes Santob de Carrión's *Proverbios morales*.[18] Questions considered include: To what extent do Jewish authors, whether through choice of language or internal reference, inscribe themselves as Jews within their panegyrics? That is, is religious difference an aspect of performance, and how does this inform the texts' constructions of authority? When writing in Arabic or Castilian, are panegyrics by Jewish authors distinguishable from those of non-Jews? To what extent do Jewish authors echo contemporary non-Jewish panegyric conventions, including religiously specific formulations of power? Do Jewish panegyrists meet *mamdūḥs*' expectations without abandoning a Jewish worldview that insists on the ultimate illegitimacy of non-Jewish authority? Finally, the chapter will attempt to ascertain the extent to which a "poetics of resistance" can be detected in these interreligious panegyrics. Whether offering truly subversive ideologies or not, it seems that authors did imagine dual Jewish/non-Jewish audiences, discursive communities that could interpret the texts in different ways. Still, the number of texts that suggest true subversion are very few in number, and again, in these cases, subversion might seem present only because we are looking for it.

Ḥasdai Ibn Shaprut's/Menaḥem Ben Saruq's Hebrew Missive to Emperor Constantine VII of Byzantium

An early medieval Hebrew address to a non-Jewish figure is contained in a missive, one of two that Ḥasdai Ibn Shaprut sent to rulers in Byzantium.[19] The opening bears resemblance to Ibn Shaprut's address to King Yosef of Khazaria and is likely also penned by Menaḥem Ben Saruq. Probably intended for Emperor Constantine VII Porphyrogennetos (912–59), known as a learned king who revived sciences and sponsored the *Book of Ceremonies*, the letter opens with much pomp and in rhyme:

> To the crown of the great king who is set on high (*'elyon*), to whom nothing in the imagination (*dimyon*) can compare: Of all creatures on earth . . . existing things (*hevyon*), who understands enigmas with preparations of thought (*ra'ayon*). No secret (*ḥevyon*) matters[20] are obscure for him. He is wondrous[21] going forth in battle in garments of combat[22] and raiment of armor (*siryon*) to tread upon his many enemies like grapes and to leave them bereft, utterly destroyed (*khilayon*). May it be the will of his Rock who sets streams in the desert[23] (*ṣayon*) to spread his compassion and kindness over him like a palanquin (*apiryon*) so that the work of his hand shall not grow weak (*rifyon*). May He rouse him . . . and strengthen him in all that he asks with speech (*higayon*). So may God Most High (*el 'elyon*) do and so may He increase his wellbeing. I inform my esteemed lord, the king. . . .[24]

The letter goes on to inform the emperor that an epistle that he had sent to 'Abd al-Raḥman III had arrived and pleased the caliph. Why was the missive composed in Hebrew rather than in Greek or Arabic? While it is not clear that either Ibn Shaprut or Ben Saruq could have composed a Greek letter (despite the former's role in translating Galen from Greek), it would not have been more difficult to commission a Greek scribe in al-Andalus than a Hebrew translator in Byzantium. The letter might have been interpreted with the aid of Jewish courtiers in Byzantium, but this is speculative.[25] Since correspondence between the

Figure 11. Seal of Constantine VII (Catologue of Byzantine Seals at Dumbarton Oaks and in the Fogg Museum of Art, no. 63.2.). © Dumbarton Oaks, Byzantine Collection, Washington, D.C.

emperor and the caliph was well under way, Arabic might have been the easiest solution, though Ibn Shaprut might be emphasizing the role of Jews as intermediaries between Muslims and Christians. Given that a second letter from Ibn Shaprut to Byzantium pleaded for the improvement of Jewish status, the author's calling attention to his Jewishness may have been part of a rhetorical strategy.

The portrayal of Constantine VII creates the image of a learned man of war that is similarly conveyed in Byzantine historical writing; were it not for the emerging alliance between the Andalusian Umayyads and the Byzantines, the author would probably not have emphasized military power. Eliyahu Ashtor suggests that the opening formula corresponds with Byzantine conventions of addressing the emperor as the "great and exalted king" (*basileus*).[26] It is true that Byzantine emperors had been known by the title "king" (as opposed to "emperor") since Herakleios (629). Further, a seal of Constantine VII (Figure 11) bears a more specific inscription, quite possibly an official title: Con[stan(tinos)] aut(ocrator) basi[l(eus) R(o)]maion (Constantine, sole ruler and king of the Romans).[27] Although the panegyric seems largely attuned with audience expectations, it does not echo "autocrator," since this would undermine the legitimacy of the Umayyad caliph whom Ibn Shaprut served, not to mention any Jewish political sensibility.[28] It is possible that the rare rhyming syllable (*yon*) maintained throughout the Hebrew passage was selected to match the last word of the title (*Romaion*). If the letter were recited to the emperor in Hebrew (and presumably translated), this assonantal allusion to his Greek title could still be appreciated. Although not composed in the dominant language of the target audience, the panegyric exhibits a "dual discursive competence" both in content and in form.

The first rhyming word (*ha-husam ʿelyon*, "set on high, exalted") is identical with the last (*el ʿelyon*, "God Most High"), and the entire passage is likely structured as a buildup to this final phrase. Importantly, "God Most High" is the name by which Melkhizedeq, the righteous non-Israelite king of Salem, knew the God of Abraham (Gn 14:18). Hence, the God who is to bestow favor upon the emperor is the biblical God in His most universal formulation. This provided the panegyrist a space for offering God's favor to one who was not a blood descendant of Abraham in a way that was compatible with both Jewish and Christian worldviews. The only phrase that might present a hidden transcript is "No secret matters are obscure for him," possibly an allusion to the mock panegyric for the prince of Tyre in Ez 28:3, but this phrase was sometimes plucked from context to praise Jewish figures as well (e.g., Saʿadia Gaon).[29] What the text does do is negotiate praise for a Christian ruler by a Jew who served a Muslim caliph by delimiting legitimacy to the temporal realm and evading comparison with contemporary Muslim rule or allusion to Jewish disempowerment.

Shelomoh ha-Kohen's Hebrew Panegyric for al-Mustanṣir Bi'llah and Badr al-Jamālī

Following the Fatimid repulsion of Seljuk troops that had invaded Cairo in 1077, Shelomoh Ben Yosef ha-Kohen composed a Hebrew poem that included extensive praise for the imam al-Mustanṣir Bi'llah and his military commander

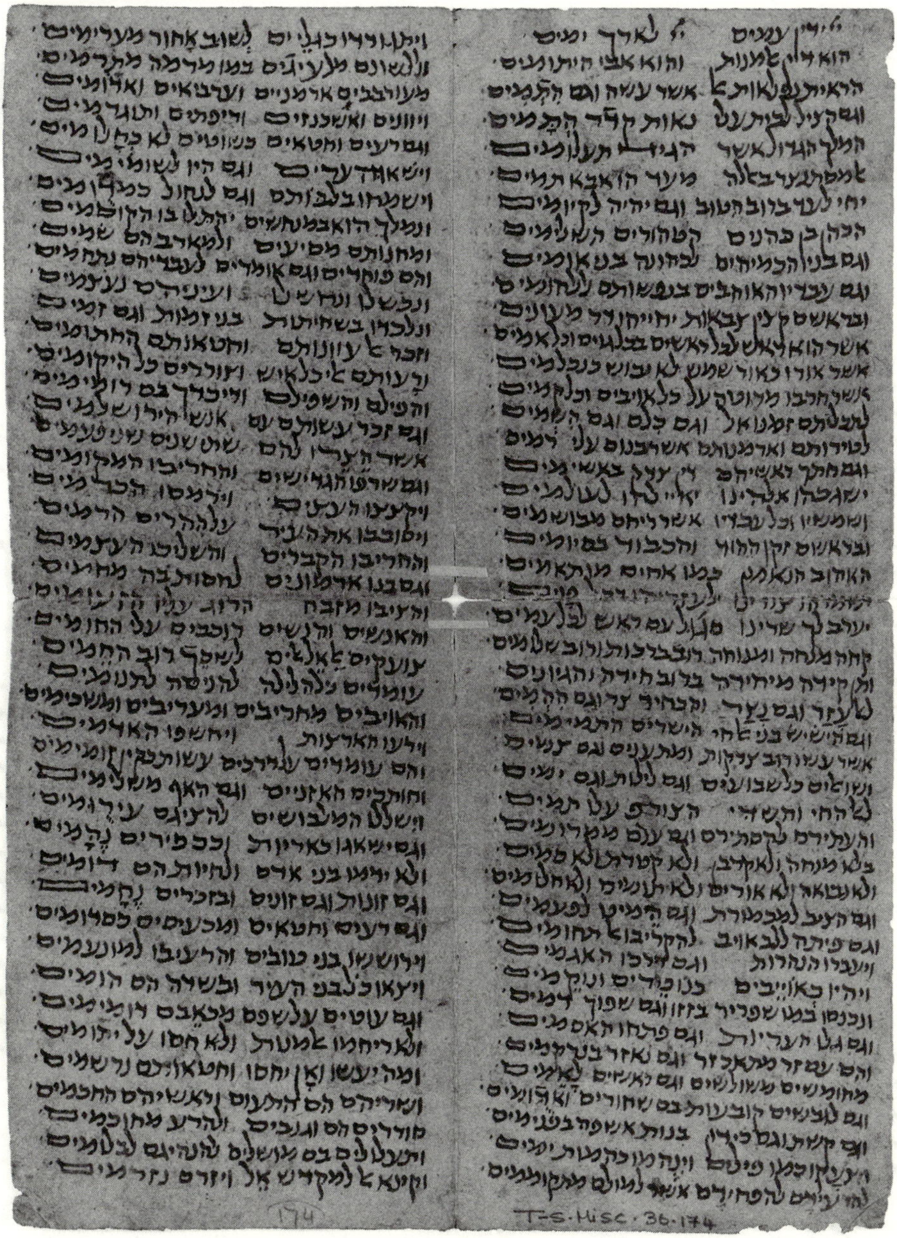

Figure 12. Panegyric by Shelomoh Ben Yosef ha-Kohen, including praise for al-Mustanṣir Bi'llah and Badr al-Jamālī. TS Misc 36.174r. Reproduced by kind permission of the Syndics of Cambridge University Library.

Badr al-Jamālī. The poem was originally published from TS Misc 36.174 (Figure 12) with English translation over a century ago, by Julius Greenstone, and was the subject of a recent article by Johannes den Heijer and Joachim Yeshaya that offers a vocalized Hebrew text, a new English translation, and discussion.[30] Den Heijer and Yeshaya concentrate on the poem as an example of the Hebrew war poetry genre that is most often associated with Shemuel ha-Nagid. The poet recounts the destruction that the Seljuk army had brought to Jerusalem and Damascus and the enemy's ultimate defeat (including vivid descriptions of rotting corpses and the like) at Cairo, all thanks to God's vengeance and Badr al-Jamālī's able command.

Al-Mustanṣir Bi'llah Ma'ad Abū Tamīm was the eighth Fatimid imam-caliph. As Irene Bierman has put it, the "Fatimid Ismāʿīlī ruler functioned in a dual role: both as caliph to all those within his empire (all Muslims, Jews, and Christians) and as Living Imām to Believers (Ismāʿīlīs)." The imam claimed authority by descent from Muḥammad through his daughter Fāṭima and her husband, ʿAlī, and was considered by Isma'ilis to be a "divinely guided and infallible Imām, vested with ultimate authority to interpret the Qur'ān in his lifetime," an authority that "rested on his knowledge of the true reality found in the esoteric dimensions (*bāṭin*) behind the literal or obvious (*ẓāhir*) words of the Qur'ān."[31] Further, he was head of the *da'wa*, the group of religious dignitaries who were privy to his esoteric teachings and acted as missionaries or propagandists (*dā'ī*, *du'āt*) throughout the empire. In comparison with that of his predecessors, al-Mustanṣir's reign was characterized by the imam's retreat from worldly politics, administration, and warfare, spheres that were turned over to appointees.

Badr al-Jamālī, a Fatimid military commander (*amīr al-juyūsh*) of Armenian extraction in Acre, was appointed by al-Mustanṣir as governor of Cairo in 1073. He rapidly transformed the urban landscape by expanding its footprint, building its fortifications, and constructing numerous urban monuments, many of which bear his names and titles. The inscriptions (twenty-one have been identified) generally emphasize al-Jamālī even over the imam, whose name is also included but with little elaboration; as Bierman writes, the inscriptions left little doubt as to who was "the person with real power."[32] Al-Jamālī's militarized transformation of the Fatimid capital, formerly an Isma'ili royal enclosure, was accompanied by a reorganization of the city's ethnic makeup. The Fatimid armed forces were organized according to ethnically defined regiments (North African, African, Armenian, Arab), and the capital was divided according to neighborhoods that housed the respective troops.[33] It was also during al-Jamālī's reign that Jewish and Christian elites moved from the suburbs into Cairo proper. The year 1077, that of ha-Kohen's poem, also marked an important year in the career of al-Jamālī in that he gained the title *Hādī du'āt al-mu'minīn*, "Guide for the missionaries of the believers," which is remarkable, given that he was not known as a man of letters.

It was only with al-Mu'ayyad, court poet of al-Mustanṣir, that specifically Shi'ite conceptions of the imamate came to be celebrated in poetry. As Tahera Qutbuddin demonstrates, al-Mu'ayyad eschewed characterizations of military prowess and earthly power in favor of religious imagery to create a sharp distinction between the imam and the 'Abbasid caliphs, whom the Fatimids portrayed as strictly mundane and hence illegitimate kings. Praise of the imam centered on a number of motifs, some of which are listed here to highlight what is (and is not) reflected in the Hebrew poem: descent from Muḥammad through 'Alī and Fāṭima; attributes and functions (e.g., pillar of hereafter, succor for the sinner, treasure in both worlds, sanctuary, shield from hellfire, salvation of mankind, protector of the Ka'aba, leader of rites); similarity to prophets (especially Jesus); titles of appointment (imam, imam of the age, elect, commander of the faithful, progeny of the cloak), as well as titles of genealogy (pure progeny, family of Muḥammad, People of the House); victor over enemies who are portrayed as errant idol worshipers.[34]

Insofar as ha-Kohen's poem captures many of these elements, the Jewish poet was imitating or participating in a court practice that was au courant. Yet the poem cannot simply be considered a Hebrew version of an Arabic panegyric for the imam in that it inscribes and negotiates Jewish presence within the empire. Despite the relative simplicity of its language, the poem is complicated on many levels. It recognizes the imam not only as a mundane temporal leader but also within a specifically Isma'ili theological framework. It casts one Muslim dynasty as the safeguard of religion but another as wayward idolatry. It expresses hopes simultaneously for the continued power of the imam but also for Jewish political restoration and the rebuilding of the Jerusalem Temple specifically.

The performance context is not very clear. Did ha-Kohen present it to the Muslim figures directly? If not, would the Fatimid imam or his commander know of its composition? Was praise in Hebrew valued within Fatimid court culture as a type of tribute on behalf of the Jewish author, Jewish courtiers, or the Jews more generally?[35] Could the poem have circulated among Jews only, and, if so, what was the value of praising the Muslim figures? We will return to these issues below. Given the poem's length (149 lines), only the opening section is translated here, though other verses will be included in the discussion. Lines 20 and 21 are translated with intentional ambiguity to reflect the Hebrew and a consequent interpretive difficulty.

1. Lord who judges nations, judge for the length of days,
2. He is the protector of widows, the father of orphans.
3. Have you beheld the wonders of God, who made, perfected
4. and preserved the pastures of Qedar for the flawless house of ʿAlī,
5. the great king who explicates the hidden,
6. al-Mustanṣir Bi'llah Maʿad Abū Tamīm—
7. May he live forever in an abundance of good and for all time,
8. the priest, son of the pure and unblemished[36] priests,
9. and also his sons who long for the priesthood, sons of nations,
10. and also his servants who desire to wage battle at the risk of their lives.
11. And at their head is the commander of armies, may He who resides in the heavenly abode grant him life.
12. He is captain to all the captains of all peoples and all nations,
13. whose light is like the light of the sun, who is never ashamed like the disgraced,
14. whose sword is whetted against all enemies and adversaries.
15. God appointed him to annihilate them; he destroyed them, and laid waste to
16. their palaces and citadels, which they had built to lofty heights.
17. He decapitated them—a just sentence for the guilty!
18. May God exalt and empower him forever!
19. And his servitors and servants whose scent is spiced.
20. At their head is the elder of utmost glory and honor,
21. the beloved, the trusted, like twin brothers—
22. May our Rock protect and preserve him come what may!
23. May it please you, our prince, treasure of the people, head of all nations,
24. Take a gift and repose, abundant blessings and [wishes of] peace!
25. And from your soul, offer prostration[37] full of expressions and utterances
26. to God who succored and protected, who terrified and destroyed the oppressor.

The imam is named by his adopted regnal title (al-Mustanṣir Bi'llah; lit., "he who seeks victory through God"), his given name (Ma'ad), and his patronymic (Abū Tamīm); the poem, in fact, makes several interlingual plays on the name by calling God "He who succored and protected" (*naṣar*, line 26), and multiple rhymes on the Hebrew words *tamim/temimim* ("unblemished, perfect, blameless") with respect to the House of 'Alī, Jews, and God (lines 4, 27, and 30, respectively).

In accordance with the Shi'ite conception of the imamate, al-Mustanṣir is of the "House of 'Alī" and the explicator of esoteric knowledge (4, 5). Where one would expect an Arabic text to praise him as the "imam son of imams," the Hebrew has "priest (*kohen*) son of . . . priests" (8). Den Heijer and Yeshaya are right that the word choice demonstrates a "fascinating process of adaptation of an Islamic concept to a Jewish cultural frame of reference."[38] In fact, Sa'adia Gaon had already established the Arabic word *imām* as the standard translation of *kohen* in his *Tafsīr*, likely because it combined religious function with hereditary office. The poem's employment of *kohen* may have been facilitated further by the biblical application of the term to non-Israelites (Gn 14:8, 41:45, which Sa'adia also translates as *imām*), and to non-Aaronids, "and the sons of David were *kohanim*" (2 Sm 8:18).[39] Still, in calling the imams "the pure, unblemished" (lit., "perfect," 8), the poet emphasized legitimacy as a matter of heredity more than morality, though he certainly could have implied both.

The house of 'Alī, already introduced in the opening, surfaces again in verse 121: "And the faction of 'Alī (*'adat 'Alī*, probably a translation of *shi'at 'Alī*), aided by the descendants of Zamzumim, vanquished them." Although it is true that in the Bible, "Zamzumim" refers to a particular people (Dt 2:20), its usage here might evoke the well of Zamzam near the Ka'aba in Mecca where, according to tradition, God revealed water to Hagar to save the thirsting Ishmael; thus the "descendants of Zamzumim" might be the family of Ishmael through the Prophet, the *ahl al-bayt*, which also constitutes a significant motif in Isma'ili panegyric. In general, relations with Mecca were a priority for Badr al-Jamālī. One of his greatest accomplishments was the successful petitioning of the *sharīf* of Mecca to remove the names of the 'Abbasid caliph and the Seljuk sultan at Zamzam and also to replace the black covering of the Ka'aba that displayed the 'Abbasid caliph's name with a white one bearing al-Mustanṣir's.[40] The reading of Zamzumim as Meccans is further supported by the verses that follow: "And the sons of the merciful Abraham and Ishmael cried unto Him who strikes down great kings and kills mighty sovereigns." God hears not only the prayers of Jews but of Muslims as well. This poem speaks volumes to Jews' "dual discursive competence."[41]

The imam's sons are called "sons of nations" (9), which may well refer to the ethnic diversity of al-Mustanṣir's family and the maternal lineage of the imams more generally. As Delia Cortese and Simonetta Calderini put it, not only did the "family pedigree of the imām-caliphs' mothers play no role in arguments aiming at authenticating their lineage," but also "male members of the ruling elites often . . . chose wives and concubines with as diverse a background as one can possibly imagine." One of al-Mustanṣir's wives was Byzantine (*rūmiyya*); his mother was the slave girl Rasad (bought from the Karaite Abū Saʿd al-Tustari), whose origin is said to have been Sudanese, Abyssinian, or Nubian; one of the wives of al-Mustanṣir's great-grandfather al-ʿAzīz was a Melchite Copt; and so forth.[42] The recognition of non-Arabs within the Fatimid Empire, even within the royal family, may well have been seen as a cause for celebration and an ingredient of legitimacy, including in the minds of Jews who sought to carve out their own place within the empire.

Another point in the poem consistent with al-Mustanṣir's reign, again in contradistinction with ʿAbbasid panegyrics for caliphs, is the partitioning of religious and worldly affairs.[43] Al-Mustanṣir is not praised for his valor or his sword; preeminence in these spheres is reserved for Badr al-Jamālī, "commander of the armies" (reflecting the title *amīr al-juyūsh*), "captain of all captains" (lit., "head of all heads"), whose sword is whetted against enemies and who executes God's justice (11–17). Equally important in the poem is the representation of the enemies, again consistent with Arabic panegyrics for al-Mustanṣir, who are cast not as a competing Muslim faction but as sinners, madmen, "builders of an altar for accursed things" and "worshipers at high places" (lines 68, 124), whores, fornicators, and those who "inflame themselves with males" (line 79; cf. Is 57:5, which also has a tinge of idolatry). As Qutbuddin notes, representing intra-religious struggles as interreligious, even monotheist-pagan, is a standard trope in panegyrics for al-Mustanṣir.[44]

What has puzzled scholars most about this poem concerns the identity of the figure(s) in verses 19–22; the question has important implications for how we ultimately understand the function of the poem. The history of scholarship has been reviewed by Den Heijer and Yeshaya and need not be repeated here in detail. The main questions have been: (1) whether verse 19 refers to the servants of Badr al-Jamālī or is a recapitulation of verse 10, hence referring to other servants of al-Mustanṣir; (2) contingent on the first question, whether verse 20 continues praise of Badr al-Jamālī (now called "elder of utmost glory and honor") or introduces a new subject of praise; and (3) if the latter, whether it refers to one person or two and who this might be.

At stake is essentially whether there is a Jewish *mamdūḥ* in the poem. Den Heijer and Yeshaya follow Greenstone in viewing verse 20 as continuing praise for al-Jamālī, whereas Yosef Yahalom follows Jacob Mann in seeing a new and Jewish subject of praise. But whereas Mann identified two figures ("twin brothers") as Yehudah and Mevorakh Ben Sa'adia, Yahalom sees only one whom he identifies with Avraham ha-Kohen Ben Yiṣḥaq Ibn Furāṭ, who held the title "the glorious elder."[45] I generally agree that verse 20 does not refer to Badr al-Jamālī, since there is no Arabic analogue for "the glorious elder" among the commander's known titles; this title is simply not sufficiently grand.[46] I also believe that the poet has now turned to a Jewish *mamdūḥ* and see further support for Yahalom's identification, since, when Daniel Ben 'Azariah granted Ibn Furāṭ the title, the gaon emphasized that it had not been bestowed upon anyone for many years since the death of its previous holder.[47] A Jewish audience is suggested by a concluding second-person plural address that hopes that the "stone that the builders rejected shall become the cornerstone" and that the Temple will be rebuilt (lines 140–42). It might also be that verses 10 and 19 refer to two different classes of "servants": soldiers ("who desire to wage battle"); and a nonmilitary group ("whose scent is spiced"). Conceivably, the poet could intend by the latter Jewish courtiers in particular, based on Sg 4:10, which reads, "the scent of your ointments is better than spices"; the female beloved here is allegorically understood to be Israel.

A secondary Muslim audience, at least for part of the poem, is possibly suggested by material aspects of the manuscript; the verso of the poem is written over a few words in large (upside-down) Arabic script, seemingly the conclusion of an official decree;[48] although this certainly does not prove that the poem was brought back to court, it does indicate the general permeability of borders between religious communities. What would be the utility of a Hebrew poem in the Fatimid court? We do know that knowledge of Hebrew Bible, including in its original language, had been actively cultivated in the *da'wa* for nearly a century prior to the composition of the poem;[49] hence the poem was composed in a recognized language of learning, though one doubts that the *mamdūḥ*s would have understood it themselves.[50] Hebrew panegyric so aligned with a Fatimid political vision may have held value for a Muslim ruler who could appreciate it in translation or paraphrase, especially given the new multiethnic configuration of Cairo. However, one imagines that the Fatimids would have little use for the poem's hope of rebuilding the Temple or even find it subversive.

But if we imagine a solely Jewish audience, how do we understand the Isma'ili formulations of legitimacy, especially those that refer to the ontological distinctiveness of the imam? Ultimately, many questions remain with respect to the *Sitz im Leben* of the poem, and the way in which we read verses 20–26 affects, or perhaps rests on, how we imagine the place of Jews within the Fatimid state. The most likely performance scenario in my view is that ha-Kohen's panegyric had an immediate Jewish recipient, a courtier in the ranks of al-Mustanṣir, who may have shared with a Muslim audience at least part of the poem, presumably in translation, or the mere fact that the celebratory poem had been composed. That the poem was in Hebrew rather than Arabic may have only added to its significance as a tribute emanating from one of the capital's numerous ethnic and religious sectors.

Religious difference and Jewish particularism are also manifest in several parts of the poem. In addition to the concluding address discussed above, God brings joy to the "sons of the living God" and answers their prayers, though they came "without offering, sacrifice, incense, or spices" (30–32). God remembers the sins of the enemy, "what they did to the people of Jerusalem" (though the inhabitants could include non-Jews) and that they "erected an altar to sacrifice accursed things" (61). In turn, God "took vengeance for the sake of the sanctuary of God" (89). Though the poem also mentions destruction in Damascus and Fustat, the author's concentration on Jerusalem gives the poem a decidedly Jewish feel.

Terms for "nations" (*'amim, 'amamim, le'umim, goyim*) repeat as rhyming words throughout the poem and constitute a major theme. The enemy comes in haste to the "royal city . . . known as Qāhira to all peoples and nations" (117–18). At the same time, the enemy is called a "strange and wicked nation" and their leaders "heads of nations" (40–41). We have already mentioned that al-Mustanṣir's sons are called "sons of nations" and that Badr al-Jamālī and also the addressee of the poem are called "head of all nations." The poem thus constructs a multiethnic world, a Fatimid state consisting of many nations fighting an enemy that is similarly variegated, though only the Fatimids seem to count Jews among the nations under their rule. The inscription of Jews within a multiethnic state is most fitting for the period of Badr al-Jamālī's urban reforms and reflects Jews' attempt to negotiate, whether before Muslim officials or only for themselves, their place within the empire.

In sum, ha-Kohen's poem combines praise for Fatimid rulers according to Shi'ite ideology with eschatological hopes for Jewish restoration, all within a world that is divided between monotheism and "idolatry" yet within an empire that is multiethnic and religiously diverse. Can all these ideological strands be harmonized? It would be more typical in Jewish writing to represent the current situation as the best of political circumstances but one that should ultimately be supplanted, that even a sovereign who is "good to the Jews" should be overthrown in favor of Israel's political restoration. Yet the praise for the imam goes beyond this and seems to assent to his place not only in the present but also within Isma'ili ontology and sacred history. If the wish that the imam would "live forever" were fulfilled, the possibility of Jewish restoration would be forever deferred.

Is there any reason to suspect a hidden transcript that only a Jewish reader could detect? Apart from the general tension discussed above, there is only one verse that evokes a biblical passage associated with anti-Muslim polemic with any frequency. In describing how the Seljuk enemy was defeated, ha-Kohen includes "the mouth that spoke great things became silent stones" (line 135); hence, the boastful Seljuk enemy was silenced. The first words (in Aramaic, *u-fum memalil ravrevanim*) derive from Daniel's famous vision of four beasts, the last of which possesses a small horn "speaking great things" before which the other horns fall; the small horn represents a king who will conquer previous kings, "speak words against the Most High," and "change the seasons and the Law" until a time when dominion shall be given to the "nation of the holy of the Most High" (Daniel 7). Jewish exegetes take the passage as a blueprint for the evolution of world politics and understand the fourth beast as the last kingdom and the small horn as a political figure who fells preceding kings. In the Islamic world, the "mouth speaking great things" was associated with Muḥammad, either because of a supposed haughtiness or the Qur'ān's eloquence; that Muḥammad changed seasons (i.e., holidays) and the Law seemed obvious enough.[51] In encountering the verse of the poem, was the Jewish reader expected to evoke the entire exegetical tradition such that the "mouth speaking great things" would refer not only to the Seljuks but rather to Muslims, including the Isma'ili Fatimids, more generally? Or is it unfair to read the verse through the exegetic tradition at all? While a covert subversive reading cannot be ruled out, it seems unlikely or at least not supported by corroborating evidence.

Yehudah al-Ḥarīzī's Arabic Panegyrics for the Ayyubids

As Joseph Sadan revealed, Yehudah al-Ḥarīzī spent the end of his career in Aleppo and Irbil, composing Arabic panegyrics and other genres for Ayyubid patrons.[52] One of these panegyrics was recited by al-Ḥarīzī directly to Abū al-Fatḥ Muḥammad al-Tabrīzī, an otherwise unknown figure. Although it is not certain that al-Tabrīzī was the *mamdūḥ* of the poem, it was clearly composed for someone of authority and for the occasion of a festival, possibly *ʿeid al-aḍḥā*.[53] The poem opens with an exquisite and lengthy introduction about a "land whose springs[54] irrigated its fields and whose branches flourished on its hills." With reference to the famous qur'ānic houris of paradise (56:22–23 and elsewhere), the poet speaks in the first person: "Its houri-eyed and graceful-necked stole my heart; its girls and supple maidens assailed me." The poem goes on to describe the flowers that "became drunk at [the land's] wine cup," constellations, more beautiful maidens who fell the mighty, again tree branches, and ultimately birds, which leads to the *takhalluṣ*:

13. Its birds clamor and respond to one another, they exchange and trade their melodies
14. for [the land's] ruler, the one who illumines it, its protector, the one who lends it beauty that beholding it reveals,
15. its wisest, most perfect and most generous, the leader upon whom its garland was bound.
16. [He is] the great tree of fortune, sweet of the harvest, high of radiance, and clouds of abundance that quench its thirsty.
17. Its days are renewed with his splendor; its pillars are made firm by his loftiness.[55]
18. His hand bestows the rain of his generosity upon all souls; it shall never vanish until lack [itself] has vanished.
19. [He is a] lion of *al-Sharā*, abundant rain of mankind, a star of night-travel, a blaze of hospitality to which guests are guided in the dark.[56]
20. His beauty is his deeds and beneficence; [as for] his wealth, those who petition him are its guardians.
21. He is a noble who has become the path of Right Guidance; when he kindled the flame of generosity, he made the enemy a sacrifice.
22. Thanks to his Honor, Right Guidance hoisted its banners whose fluttering resembled the enemies' [quaking] hearts.
23. He is the firmness of the Creator's heaven,[57] one who pierces with [sword] tip; whatever sword [is against him], its blades do not become bloodied.

24. O perfect one, O noble one, O you who accomplishes what many of the eminent have failed!
25. Enjoy the festival and be exceedingly joyous on account of authority whose boughs are flourishing![58]
26. By your glorious deeds, you possess power, sole authority, and territory[59] over whose expanse riders take victory.[60]

The introductory prelude (*nasīb*) and the *madīḥ* are tightly bound together; the land never disappears in the second part of the poem, and specific motifs repeat across the *takhalluṣ* (flourishing branches, garlands, praise). It turns out that the utopian land of the prelude is the very territory over which the *mamdūḥ* presides, and the *madīḥ* answers the question of *why* the land is flourishing; the paradisial setting derives from the rightful dominion of the *mamdūḥ*.

The *mamdūḥ* is characterized according to standard traits: generosity, courage, hospitality, military prowess, power over enemies, and political dominion. Al-Ḥarīzī employs a register of Arabic typical of the age's poetry. He is sure to include archaizing terms, such as the proverbial "lion of *al-Sharā*" (line 19) for "courageous."[61] In the same verse, "hospitality" renders *al-qirā*, literally the "guest meal," which is similarly a central term in pre-Islamic Arabia and fully signals the literary tradition in which al-Ḥarīzī was inscribing his *mamdūḥ*.

Most interesting are the two references (lines 21, 22) to "Right Guidance," which the *mamdūḥ* both embodies and promotes. In classical Arabic, "Right Guidance" (*al-hudā*) is most often a way of referring to "True Religion" and hence Islam itself. Is al-Ḥarīzī writing as though he were an adherent of Islam, essentially removing religious difference from the performance of the poem? Or is he, as a Jew, stating that the *mamdūḥ* safeguards Islam while refraining from commenting on whether Islam is a good? Sadan argues that although al-Ḥarīzī certainly draws on particular Islamic vocabulary in his Arabic verse (e.g., in wishing the *mamdūḥ* a joyous *'eid*), the poet would not go so far as to contradict or betray his Jewishness.[62] Sadan thus translates *al-hudā* in the first instance as "giving"[63] and in the second as "truth," though he also recognizes that, to the Muslim ear, the verses would sound like a typical celebration of Islam's success owed to the *mamdūḥ*'s qualities.

Another possibility is that al-Ḥarīzī is using *al-hudā* in a more generic sense as a just political order grounded in revelation or a profession of monotheism; at the very least, al-Ḥarīzī might have appreciated that the *mamdūḥ* kept polytheism at bay. Jewish assimilation of the term is evident in a Judeo-Arabic poem wherein al-Ḥarīzī praises the biblical Moses: "God sent Moses the prophet to negate darkness and to spread Right Guidance" (*al-hudā*);[64] similar is his lament for Maimonides: "the sons of the age went about in the dark until one day he revealed the path of Right Guidance (*jalla al-hudā*) and was a guide."[65]

An astonishing fact that has gone virtually unnoticed is that the panegyric for al-Tabrīzī appears in a nearly identical form in al-Ḥarīzī's Judeo-Arabic *Kitāb al-durar* (Book of pearls) dedicated to the Damascene Jewish doctor 'Imrān Mosheh Bar Ṣedaqa (the teacher of Ibn Abī 'Usaibiyya).[66] Al-Ḥarīzī tailored the panegyrics for their respective addressees; the poem for Bar Ṣedaqa alludes to the *mamdūḥ*'s Arabic name, does not call him a "leader" or "ruler," and omits references to swords and wishes for a joyous *'eid*. However, Bar Ṣedaqa *is* presented as a protector of "Right Guidance."[67] In short, al-Ḥarīzī's Ayyubid *mamdūḥ* probably registered *al-hudā* as Islam, but the word did not refer to Islam exclusively in al-Ḥarīzī's lexicon; al-Ḥarīzī was quite adept in his dual discursive competence. Still, there is nothing here that one might consider subversive.

Many questions remain regarding the poem's performance. Was it recited by the Jewish poet before an otherwise Muslim audience during the very feast of *'eid*? Was it recited beforehand or afterward to the *mamdūḥ* alone or before an audience that was either strictly Muslim or religiously mixed? In any case, the poet in no way announced his Jewishness within the poem and imagined it functioning within a Muslim space; the poem could have been written by a Muslim author.

A shorter Arabic panegyric by al-Ḥarīzī does call attention to Jewish–Muslim difference. The poem is written for Muẓaffar al-Dīn Mūsā Ibn Abī Bakr Ayyūb (d. 1237), who ruled over Damascus and territory in Mesopotamia along the Armenian border. The poem is not associated with any particular occasion. I have translated verse 8 literally and hence ambiguously in order to call attention to a difference between Sadan's understanding and my own:

1. Judgment attacks with the swords of your resolve and the sharpness of your might is a spearhead[68] in [your resolve's] hands.
2. To the refined workmanship of your sword belong luster from your splendor; from [the luster and splendor] the water of majesty flows round.
3. You have acquired your splendor with generosity; the two of them will forever possess whetted swords and torrents.

4. You have bound the lion,[69] so now it is your prey; you have forsaken abundant rain, so now it is a miser.
5. When you are mentioned to the enemy on a day of battle,[70] the souls of the valiant stream forth from your mention.
6. Why should I explain your attributes when they are like the dawn, which requires no proof?
7. Describing you dumbfounds people of intellect; the wise and the boor in this are alike.
8. The enemy said: "What is with the Jews and generosity?" I answered them: "Your learning has failed you!
9. Moses split the sea of generosity before mankind only so that Israel might pass through!"[71]

The portrayal revolves around powers of judgment, generosity, and military prowess and is quite conventional. Sadan sees the concluding verses as a counter to the common stereotype of Jewish miserliness.[72] According to Sadan, the "Moses" in the poem stands for the Jews, who display generosity before mankind. However, it is more likely that the Moses of the poem refers to the *mamdūḥ* whose name, after all, was *Mūsā* Ibn Abī Bakr; he is likened to the biblical Moses in that he offers patronage (splits the sea of generosity) before the general public (mankind) for the benefit of Jews (Israel), including the poet.[73] The verses thus call attention to an inherent strain in the Muslim-Jewish patronage relationship. The poem is not a retort to a stereotype but rather a defense of the poet's place in the *mamdūḥ*'s entourage and possibly the latter's supporting Jewish favorites more generally. Still, the poem does not call attention to doctrinal difference or to broader politics by presenting a challenge to Muslim hegemony or by enhancing the *mamdūḥ*'s legitimacy as protector of a multireligious polity. The poem thus presents interreligious relations within a very limited scope and eschews further tensions of Muslim–Jewish relations that are explored in al-Ḥarīzī's Hebrew *Book of Taḥkemoni*.[74] Such themes would obviously have no place in a panegyric for a Muslim patron; the differences point to al-Ḥarīzī's skill at navigating numerous religio-cultural spaces.

Interestingly, it is to a Jewish audience that al-Ḥarīzī praises the Ayyubids most explicitly and in theological terms. In the *Kitāb al-durar*, when praising the judge Menaḥem Ben Yiṣḥaq, who had aided the Jewish community during years of a crusader siege on Cairo, al-Ḥarīzī expatiated on the "Muslim kings" (*mulūk al-Islām*), "who are granted victory with the never-ending victory of the Mighty

One. Through them He unsheathed a sharp-bladed sword. . . . Through their hands God gave victory to all worshipers and with their prosperity He brought ease to the land. . . . Praise God for this sublime grace! It is not a slight thing but rather is among the great miracles; for our people it is a sister to the splitting of the Sea, for in their time too they despaired of living and were on the verge of death, but just then God relieved their troubles. . . . All this was with the help of the Ayyubid kings (*mulūk banī Ayyūb*) who rose as suns of fortune in the highest heavens. Through them God protected religion and the world" (*al-dīn wa'l-dunyā*).[75]

The theological motif of God working through non-Israelite kings for Israel's benefit (or harm) extends back to the Hebrew Bible, but here God's favor brings succor to "all worshipers," apparently encompassing Muslims and Jews (possibly Copts as well, but certainly not crusaders). At the same time, al-Ḥarīzī poignantly notes specific resonances for Jews, that the siege produced suffering like that of the Israelite slaves under the Egyptians and that its end was "for our people . . . a sister to the splitting of the Sea [of Reeds]." Most striking is the reference to God's protecting through the Ayyubid kings "religion and the world" (*al-dīn wa'l-dunyā*), which we have seen is a central theme within claims of Islamic political legitimacy that was also mimicked within Jewish political discourse; what is unique here is that al-Ḥarīzī presents the Muslim kings to the Jewish audience as the agents through whom God works to promote *religious* authority and justice. As with the word *al-hudā*, al-Ḥarīzī has "de-Islamicized" a key term of Islamic political discourse to encompass the interests and perspectives of non-Muslim subjects. There is no indication that this praise was intended for Ayyubid ears; the formulation does not perform Jewish loyalty before Muslim power so much as it structures the meaning of political events for a Jewish audience. There does not seem to be any "hidden transcript."

Ibrāhīm Ibn al-Fakhkhār's Arabic Panegyric for Alfonso VIII of Castile

Arabic continued to be heard in the streets and courts of Toledo for at least two centuries after the Castilian conquest of the city (1085).[76] Men with expertise in Arabic language and culture offered particular utility in the administration of the city and in newly conquered territories. Jonathan Ray has demonstrated that Jewish courtiers played key functions in establishing Castilian settlements along the Christian-Muslim frontier, and Yosef Kaplan writes: "The conquering kings found the Jews necessary and useful in consolidating their regimes, in establishing administrative infrastructure, for colonization following the expansion of their borders, and for the development of commerce in newly conquered urban centers."[77] Of particular import were the Arabic language and its accompanying political discourses and practices.

Abū Isḥāq Ibrāhīm (Avraham) Ibn al-Fakhkhār was active as a diplomat largely during the long reign of Alfonso VIII of Castile (r. 1158–1214). The early years of Alfonso's rule were characterized by weakness and disorder and the expansion of neighboring Christian and Muslim kingdoms into his territory. Alfonso remained king through the reigns of the most potent Almohad caliphs and famously defeated Muḥammad al-Nāṣir in 1212 at Las Navas de Tolosa, arguably the tipping point in the struggle for power between Castile and the Maghrib. Al-Fakhkhār appeared at the court of Marrakech in 1203 and again in 1214 and also worked as a tax collector under Alfonso; additionally, he functioned as a communal leader and patron among Jews. As a figure who moved easily among the settings of the Jewish community and Christian and Muslim courts, al-Fakhkhār was able to speak several languages and assume various modes of cultural discourse.

Arabic poems by al-Fakhkhār are preserved in a number of anthologies compiled by Muslim anthologists. Ibn Sa'īd al-Maghribī (1213–86) relates that he met al-Fakhkhār personally and describes the Jew as a "doctor" who "was prevalent in Toledo and became an emissary on behalf of its Christian king Alfonso (Adhfunsh) to the nation of the Banū 'Abd al-Ma'amūn at the court of Marrakech. My father described him as a master of poetry, learning in ancient sciences, and logic." Al-Maghribī also relates that, while he and al-Fakhkhār were both in Seville, the latter recited a couplet he had composed in honor of Alfonso VIII:

> The court of Alfonso is a wife still in her succulent days;
> Take off your shoes in honor of its soil for it is holy.

First, we might ask whether the verses were recited before Alfonso or were disseminated among Arabic speakers only; Ibn Sa'īd reports only that he heard the verses in Seville, not that they were recited before the king. Still, the verses must have been composed long before the encounter between Ibn Sa'īd and al-Fakhkhār, since Alfonso died just after Ibn Sa'īd was born and the content of the poem suggests that the court was fully functional. The emphasis on the court is suggestive of the original performance setting, and it is possible that the verses originally stood as part of a longer panegyric.[78]

If the verses were recited directly to Alfonso, we must ask whether the king understood the Arabic or whether they were translated for him; in either case, the king could certainly appreciate that he was being acclaimed in a manner characteristic of Muslim sovereigns.[79] Being praised in Arabic presented Alfonso VIII as a king with all the pomp characteristic of his Almohad foes, thus promoting an essential image of royalty within the culture of Christian expansionism. If al-Fakhkhār's verses, alone or as part of a longer panegyric, were recited before Alfonso VIII himself, they would speak further to an Arabized court culture in Christian Toledo, though it remains possible that the sole purpose of the verses was to spread the monarchal image among Castile's Arabic-speaking subjects and abroad.

The second line of al-Fakhkhār's couplet—*fa-akhla' al-na'alaini takrimatan fī tharāha innahā qudus*, "Take off your shoes in honor of its ground for it is holy"—is a clear play on Moses' appearance before the Burning Bush recounted both in the Qur'ān (20:11–12) and in the Hebrew Bible (Ex 3:5). The Arabic phrasing closely mimics the Qur'ān, *fa-akhla' na'alaika innaka bi'l-wādī al-muqaddasi Tuwan*: "Take off your shoes for you are in the holy valley of Tuwa!" and thus constitutes a clear example of the intertextual technique known as *al-iqtibās*. Further, the verse evokes a point of overlap between two (really three) scriptural traditions and resonates within multiple religious, literary, and cultural worlds.[80]

The dynamics of a Jewish poet evoking the Qur'ān in an Arabic panegyric in honor of a Christian king are intriguing, to say the least. The *iqtibās* here not only beautifies the verse but also likens appearing in Alfonso's court with encountering the sacred. Does calling the soil of Alfonso's court "holy" in any way compromise a Jewish worldview on the part of al-Fakhkhār? Does the representation not cast the Christian sovereign, as it was phrased in Chapter 7, as "a little bit divine"? In any case, al-Fakhkhār's verses do not address broad political questions such as whether Christian sovereignty is preferred over Muslim or how this current political structure relates to Jewish subjugation or eschatological schema. Such issues are bracketed or submerged beneath the more mundane and immediate contexts of empire, diplomatic mission, and al-Fakhkhār's establishing his place at court. There is certainly no hint of subversion, but the sample is exceedingly short.

Did al-Fakhkhār perform this poem specifically "as a Jew" or more as an Arabized subject of a Christian king? Was the text perceived as a Jewish composition? Would it have made a difference to the Christian king or to Muslims in al-Andalus and the Maghrib if the poet were Muslim or Christian? One imagines that Alfonso VIII, to the extent that he was aware of the verses, would have been equally or more pleased had the author been a Muslim. What could confer greater legitimacy upon a Christian king than to have Muslim subjects aggrandize him within their own mode of political discourse (as was the case with Roger II of Sicily)? For the Muslim listener in Almohad territory, Jewish performance would not be as poignant as Muslim performance, though it was also likely significant that the author was not a Christian. The Jewish courtier loyal to a Muslim ruler was certainly a familiar type to Muslims in al-Andalus and the Maghrib, and the redirection of Jewish fidelity toward a Christian sovereign was probably noteworthy. The Muslim listener may have been struck that a Jew as thoroughly Arabized as al-Fakhkhār would pay homage to a king who was Christian and not Muslim.

Todros Halevi Abulafia's Hebrew Panegyrics for Alfonso X of Castile

In the second half of the thirteenth century, Todros Halevi Abulafia composed at least two Hebrew panegyrics for Alfonso X (the Wise, r. 1252–84) of Castile.[81] Alfonso, whom Robert Burns described as an "Emperor of Culture," is renowned for constructing a multireligious court and for sponsoring (and, to some extent, authoring) intellectual projects such as translations, histories, treatises on games, and astronomical works—in some cases, with the collaboration of Jewish scholars.[82] Abulafia worked in Alfonso's court as a tax collector and, at one point, for reasons that are not altogether clear, was imprisoned by the king. While serving Alfonso, Abulafia was not cordoned off in his clerical capacity but, like other courtiers, was an active participant in the habitus of the court, including the poetic performances that were a part of its script. As Aviva Doron has argued, Abulafia was greatly influenced by the Andalusian school of Hebrew poetry, but "one must assume that his encounter with poets of his time and place made its contribution."[83] The numerous poems in Romance languages preserved in honor of Alfonso X cover a wide range of traits, such as Izan Marques's poem that praises him as "generous, noble, genuine, humble, and discrete."[84] Unsurprisingly, there is nothing comparable in Todros's poems to Guirat Riquier's praise for Alfonso's "spiritual life."[85]

In comparison with Arabic, Hebrew was esteemed in Christian contexts not only as a general language of learning but also as a scriptural tongue of which Jews had special knowledge. Although Alfonso may not have understood Todros's Hebrew poems without translation, they were likely of value to him as tokens in an esteemed language and as gifts offered by a Jewish subject signifying the fealty of the Jew (or maybe even the Jews). The selection of language surely calls attention to religious difference. The earlier of Todros's panegyrics was inscribed on a chalice presented to the king when the courtier first entered royal service. In Todros's *dīwān*, the poem is introduced with a superscription that offers a rare glimpse into the material presentation of a poem:

> When I went to the king to enter his service, I gave him a chalice—
> embroidered work and designer's craft—and on its forehead I
> placed a mark,
>
> Faith saw that vengeance was naught ever since the day Don
> Alfonso arose as king.
> I came to serve you and brought a chalice for your splendor, upon it
> a poem embroidered.
> As God commanded, "On every pilgrimage festival, none shall
> appear empty handed."[86]

Service itself is celebrated as a theme of the poem. The superscription evokes Ez 9:4–6, where a mark is placed on the forehead to spare one from God's judgment and destruction. The superscription creates an analogy between God and the king as judge; the chalice, in addition to functioning as a gift, stands for the poet who seeks the king's favor and protection. The final verse (cf. Ex 23:15) sets appearing before the king on par with religious pilgrimage and thus utilizes a technique similar to that in al-Fakhkhār's Arabic verses where the court is likened to sacred ground. Further, as is common in Arabic panegyric, the poem presents the period of the king's reign as one free of conflict (when "vengeance was not") and recalls such verses as Ibn 'Abd Rabbih's praise for an Umayyad emir: "The reign of 'Abdallah is a pilgrimage for all mankind; in its time there is neither lewdness nor abuse!" (cf. Qur'ān 2:197, regarding *ḥajj*).[87]

The second panegyric is a longer, strophic poem that adheres not to any existing Arabic or Hebrew form but seemingly follows the troubadour form known as *coblas unisonans* (all of the stanzas of the poem have the same rhymes in corresponding lines).[88] Alfonso X, who was praised by troubadours and, indeed, titled himself the "Troubadour of the Virgin Mary," could have appreciated the meter and rhyme in an unmediated fashion even if he did not understand the actual meaning of the words; "dual discursive competence" can pertain not only to content but also to form:

> How good it is to obey the orders of the king, Don Alfonso, who annihilates all bitterness! His desire is fulfilled the moment he decrees it!
>
> . . . .
>
> In him is nothing evil and there is no good that he lacks.
> There is no one who can finish praising him,
> for no song can encompass his praiseworthiness.[89]
> Who can recount[90] every good that the Creator placed in him? The work is great but the day is short![91]
> Were all creation to gather together to speak [his praises], they would fail.
> He has no equal among the living and he has no like. His only sin is that he brought poverty to an end.
> His kindness turns every poor man into a magistrate.
> Valiant, yet justice is a sash for his loins.
> On a day of battle, he dashes on his horse so that [the phrase] "a horse brings victory" shall not be deemed a lie.[92]
> He has no desire for wealth except to distribute it.
> "There is none" is not a part of his vocabulary, neither for lords nor the lowly. His desire is always to answer "yes" after "yes."
> His kindness rises like the sun and morning light.
> His rank ascended among other ranks like light.
> His reputation flew off in every direction for his kindness gave it wings to fly.
> Kings are stars, yet he is a luminary—
> [A moon] that never wanes and which no cloud obscures, [a sun] with no night and from whose scorching heat none can hide.[93]
> He brings light and is like a cloud that gives rain to every passerby.[94]

The poet begins by inscribing himself as the king's loyal servant, again celebrating service itself. The representation of the king focuses on generosity and military prowess with further reference to broad reputation and stern justice. Although the recipients of the king's generosity likely include the poet, there is no reason to think that the poem is only about Todros's desire for remuneration. The two rabbinic references—"there is no one who can finish praising him" and "the work is great but the day is short" (b. Ta'anit 28b, m. Avot 2:20)—both derive from contexts about serving or praising God and suggest that composing Hebrew panegyric is a kind of service. The poet draws on further tropes often associated with God—Alfonso surpasses all praise, and his word causes things to be—though Todros also underscores that the king's qualities are gifts bestowed by the Creator. These elements, far from being subversive, would only be enhanced for the Jewish audience that would readily catch the references.

The poem is decidedly universalistic in that it neither praises the king as preeminent among Christians only nor specifically as a sovereign over a multireligious population; he is praised by "all creation" and is generous to "every passerby." God, too, is named most universally as the "Creator." The poem thus eschews religious difference even as its very language calls attention to it. Alfonso's court comprised a specific habitus wherein courtiers of different religions played their parts as individuals, representatives of their religious communities, and as symbols within a Castilian political project.

Shelomoh DaPierra's Praise for Don Juan de Ixar

By the late fourteenth century, an increased knowledge of Hebrew among Christians, not only clergy but laymen as well, allowed for a greater opportunity for Jews to praise them in the language that had been a more exclusive inheritance of the Jewish people. Shelomoh DaPierra dedicated Hebrew poems to two Christian *mamdūḥ*s in his *dīwān*, which offers information about the circumstances of each poem. Of an event while traveling in Aragon, he introduced a poem:

> I sent this to the lord, the minister, the exalted Don Juan de Ixar when I came to the aforementioned city of his governance for they told me that he was expert in proverbs and poems. I lifted up my parable to find favor in his eyes.

The panegyric itself is unique in DaPierra's corpus in its focus on character traits associated with power throughout this book (whereas the poet's Jewish *mamdūḥ*s do not possess these to the same degree): he performs great deeds, possesses noble lineage, wisdom, a powerful arm that strengthens the weary, and even humility. The poem offers much of the standard rhetoric—"your name is the praise of praises. . . . In your hand are the keys of all praises; in the hands of others they are borrowed," and continues with a seemingly strong endorsement of Don Juan's political dominion:

> In you, O lord, Time has set sovereignty and established you as
> head over all the nobles.
> Dominion chooses you and says, "Adorn yourself in pride, take
> power and rule over the rulers!"
> One who prefers another is like the eaters of manna who preferred
> onions![95]

The final verse quoted here refers to Nm 11:5, where Israelites complain to Moses about the lack of meat in the desert and yearn for the foods of Egypt, including onions. The analogy of Don Juan and other rulers with manna and onions is clear and fits the mood of the poem. The poem limits power to the mundane; sovereignty is bestowed not by God but by Time. Hence there is a clear bracketing of authority that does not negate Jewish political claims; a more legitimate sovereign, one appointed by God, remains possible.

Santob de Carrión's Castilian Praise for Pedro I

Probably not long before Shemuel Halevi Abulafia constructed the Tránsito synagogue with its inscription bearing the name of Pedro I, Santob de Carrión (a.k.a. Shem Tov Ibn Ardutiel) dedicated his Castilian *Proverbios morales* (Moral proverbs) to the very same monarch and included a panegyric for the king at the end. Santob was also a learned author of Hebrew works, including a penitential poem for Yom Kippur, other liturgical pieces, and the rhymed prose narrative in the *maqāma* style titled *Ma'aseh ha-rav* (Story of the rabbi), more commonly known as the "Debate Between the Pen and the Scissors" (completed 1345).

The *Proverbios* is a meditation on the vicissitudes of the world, the nature of evil (especially human malice), and what modern scholars have called the author's "relativism"—recognition that what brings benefit to one can bring harm to another and therefore no subject is wholly worthy of praise or blame.[96] In the prologue, Santob famously announces himself as a Jew and assumes a self-deprecating posture to justify the value of his composition before the king: "For being born on the thorn bush, the rose is certainly not worth less, nor is good wine if taken from the lesser branches of the vine . . . nor are good proverbs [of less value] if spoken by a Jew."[97] The prologue thus calls attention to religious difference and constitutes what was perhaps a requisite performance of minority identity.

The *Proverbios* concludes with three, or possibly four, logically linked sections. The first (stanzas 670–707) deals with the nature of evil and human sin wherein animals appear blameless by comparison; whereas animals kill to eat but are then contented, men remain greedy and malicious no matter what they possess and will rob and kill to acquire more. Therefore, the virtuous man requires armor and protection, a point that leads naturally to the second section (708–22), on the role of the just king, including praise for Pedro as the embodiment thereof; this section might be further subdivided between direct praise for Pedro (708–15) and a series of apothegms on an idealized king (716–22). This then leads to a concluding dedication to Pedro I (723–25), which also contains praise.[98] The panegyric, apothegms, and concluding dedication are translated here:

> Never have I seen a better piece of woven embroidery,
> nor a taut striped fabric, nor a better blend, (708)
>
> nor a bundle of white teeth between ruddy lips,
> than keeping the strong and the feeble, the old and the young (709)
>
> together in balance, in honor, and in peace.
> The deeds of the king who can do this are perfect! (710)
>
> With the good he sports but the wicked he shoves away.
> He protects the ewe and the lame goat from the wolf and the wild ass. Why expatiate further? (711–12a)
>
> In the noble King Don Pedro we see these [deeds];
> All of these are complete in him. His deeds are stars, and he is the sphere (712b–13)
>
> of heaven that sustains the earth in just balance.[99]
> He supports the good but subdues the wicked. (714)

If he alone were the right hand of the world,
a thousand kings could not make up its left.[100] (715)

Power without restraint[101] is half-hideous.
May God never allow such a robe to be long! (716)

For if it were very long, it would cut many short,
and he who wore it would strip many. (717)

Power with restraint is a very handsome thing
like a white face mixed with red; (718)

restraint, which raises up humility and good sense, and
power, which smashes pride and folly. (719)

Two things sustain the world: one is the Law,
which gives order,[102] and the other is the king, (720)

whom God set as guard so that none would contravene
what God orders—lest he be sentenced—(721)

and to prevent people from devising evil,
and to keep the strong from consuming the feeble. (722)

May God grant life to the king, our support,
who sustains the law and is a defender! (723)

May He bring all the people of his land into his service
and remove from [the land] all war and revolt! (724)

And may [the king] fulfill the favor, which was promised by his
noble father[103]
and to which he is duty-bound, for Santob the Jew! (725)

The concluding sections vacillate between praising Pedro directly and describing a just king more generically. One question is whether the apothegms on the just king (716–22) are descriptive of Pedro, edificatory for him, or present some other interpretation. In 708–15, Pedro is equated with the one whose deeds preserve equilibrium between the strong and the weak and who is wholly righteous. This corresponds with the dedication in which he is called "our support" and "defender" and one who "sustains the law" (723). In general, the portrait comports well with Pedro's image in the Tránsito synagogue as "protector" and "shepherd," though in the Tránsito, Pedro is also a "man of war" and a "champion."[104] Twice, Santob refers to *las gentes*, which can justifiably be translated either as "people" or "peoples" (722, 724). Hence, the poet might express hope that the king will prevent all people qua individuals from performing evil and that they will come into his service. Alternatively, these verses might be read that all *peoples* qua religious communities should serve the king and that the monarchic imperative is to prevent one group from harming another—perhaps most specifically, Christians harming Jews.

In what is probably the climactic verse of the panegyric (713–14), marked by an enjambment, Pedro is called the "sphere of heaven," which is certainly hyperbolic but might also reflect, most positively, a specific conception of the ideal sovereign. Earlier in the *Proverbios*, in reflecting upon men's tendency to blame the world for their misfortunes, Santob concludes that the "celestial sphere has neither love nor desire for any thing" and is thus blameless.[105] A king should emulate what does not act out of emotion but rather through justice, an idea reminiscent of Maimonides' sovereign, who, in emulating God, is wholly dispassionate and only appears to possess the emotions that drive the actions of others.[106] But if we carry this metaphor to its logical conclusion, it must also be the case that the king, like the celestial sphere, brings benefit to some but harm to others.

In the panegyric section, "a bundle of white teeth between ruddy lips" (709) signifies the social harmony that Pedro maintains. A second reference to "a white face mixed with red" (718) appears as a metaphor for "power with restraint," a reading that harks back to a Jewish interpretation of Sg 5:10, "my lover is white and ruddy," where the lover is identified with God, whiteness with His Mercy, and redness with His Justice.[107] Hence the ideal king emulates God by exercising justice and mercy in equipoise.[108]

A number of distinctions emerge if we compare the panegyric and dedication, on the one hand, and the apothegms on the ideal sovereign, on the other. First, the direct praise for Pedro emphasizes his role as protector, but he is not necessarily, or at least not yet, a king who exercises "power with restraint." Second, in the dedication, Pedro is called one who "sustains the law" (723), and in the apothegms we read: "Two things sustain the world: one is the Law, which gives order, and the other is the king whom God set as guard"

(720). Thus, the law does not derive from the king but rather both the law and the king flow from God.[109] Are we to believe that Santob would call the temporal law that Pedro enforces divine? Did Santob see Pedro as a divinely appointed king? Santob may well be playing here with two senses of the word *ley* (law) that could signal, at least to a learned Jewish audience, a qualified but not wholly subversive endorsement of Pedro. Like the Arabic *sharīʿa* and *torah* in medieval Hebrew, *ley* can bear a double meaning either as *nomos*—mundane law formulated by a temporal ruler—or as divine Law.[110] The ideal king's law might be divine but the law that Pedro maintains is a law that is a *nomos*. Thus, *ley* might be (human) "law" in stanza 723 but (divine) "Law" in stanza 720 (I have translated it this way). In such a reading, the law of Pedro would fulfill the king's essential function of protecting weaker communities and might be exercised with dispassion, but it is still not God's Law.

The passage may well have been interpreted differently by Christian and Jewish audiences and conveyed a "hidden transcript"; what a Christian might have read as an edificatory prescription for a young king, a Jew might have read as a bifurcation between temporal and divinely elected sovereigns. This point might be underscored by the reliance on Jewish sources for stanzas 720 and 722. Already in 1845, Leopold Stein located the source of 720 in a Hebrew aphorism by Ibn Gabirol.[111] Sanford Shepard suggests that "and to keep the strong from consuming [lit., "eating"] the feeble" in 724 echoes a teaching in m. Avot 3:2, "Pray for the welfare of the kingdom; were it not for fear of it, men would swallow one another alive."[112] That is, amid praising the king through a Jewish proverb, Santob is justifying to the Jewish audience *why* he is praising the king, because he performs the mundane function of protecting the weak but not because his order is divine. Such intertextual references may have signaled to the Jewish reader that the ideal king selected by God to sustain divine Law was not identical with Pedro but rather with a past Israelite king or a future Davidic Messiah ("ruddiness" is especially associated with King David, "a boy, ruddy and handsome" (1 Sm 17:42), from whose seed the Messiah is expected).[113] Still, even according to such a "hidden transcript," Santob has not wholly subverted the king nor lampooned him but rather circumscribed his role to that of beneficent mundane ruler.[114] Finally, we might surmise that Santob regarded the king as he regarded all objects of praise, with a sense of relativism: "I can neither praise nor denounce a thing [entirely], nor call it beautiful or ugly. According to the circumstances and the nature of a thing, fast can be called slow and heads can be called tails."[115] Like the celestial sphere, the king could bring benefit to some but harm to others.

Conclusion

As inhabitants and players in non-Jewish political structures, Jews participated in the rituals of power that made up political life, the practice of panegyric among them. With panegyric, Jews not only performed the expected "public transcript" but also negotiated their political position within local and imperial structures, before the eyes of rulers and also for themselves. Recognizing the temporal authority of non-Jewish potentates while maintaining traditional Jewish stances on sacred history could certainly be fraught. Interreligious panegyrics reveal various strategies of accommodating these claims, most often through the careful construction of images of sovereigns and political structure. Such representations appear to be consistently laudatory and inoffensive; some evade or bracket issues so as not to betray Jewish claims, while others opt for universalist representations of sovereigns or even adopt theological claims to authority as expressed within the hegemonic group. Authors were mindful of dual Jewish/non-Jewish audiences and seem to have written texts that could be interpreted on multiple levels; while there is relatively little evidence for an outright mocking of temporal power, the very bracketing of authority set Jews apart as subjects of Mediterranean rulers.

AFTERWORD

The twenty-first century is a tough time to be a panegyrist. In 2013, when the Dutch-British composer John Ewbank composed "Het Koningslied" (The king's song) to be performed at the inauguration of Prince Willem-Alexander as king of the Netherlands, the song was met with fierce opposition that culminated in an online petition with some 40,000 signatories who threatened renunciation of Dutch citizenry. Beleaguered by the controversy, Ewbank ultimately posted on Facebook "Dear compatriots, after having to block yet another insult on my Twitter account, I am now totally done," and withdrew his song from the inaugural ceremonies.

What was it that so enraged the Dutch citizenry (not exactly known for their fury)? In the *Financial Times*, their complaints were cited as the "song's poor grammar, eclectic mix of styles [including rap] and lack of a memorable refrain." Of equal significance were the "imbecilic" lyrics with their patriotic kitsch, "One flag! Two lions! . . . It doesn't matter we're small! Our actions speak loud!"; hackneyed promises of protection set in Willem's voice, "I will be your beacon in the night. . . . I will fight like a lion for you"; and the quintessentially Dutch "I'll build a dyke with my bare hands and keep the water away from you!" (This theme, recalling the greatest engineering achievement of earlier Dutch rulers, is reiterated in the rap section).[1] One signatory of the petition complained to the Huffington Post: "The song makes it sound like Willem-Alexander is some kind of god and we're his underlings to whom he gives his life. . . . Away with it!"[2] All this, even though the lyricist had carefully avoided second-person laudation (e.g., "you fight like a lion") but opted instead for the voice of royal commitment ("I will fight like a lion"). The vow form was probably intended to reshape the prince's reputation as a youthful drinker and spendthrift by showing that he was now ready to rule (or to be a responsible figurehead, at least). Had Ewbank followed the more traditional panegyric form of praising attributes presently "held" by the ruler, he would undoubtedly have been accused of sycophancy, if not outright lying.

* * *

Dominion Built of Praise has, I hope, brought the reader into contact with a lost world of praise culture in which social habits, rhetorical practices, politics, and even cognitive perceptions were very different from our own. Taking empathy with the medieval subject as a guiding principle, the book has sought to explicate the inner logic of this culture of praise, not only its practicalities but also its seriousness, ambiguities, complications, boundaries, and pitfalls. Without this empathy, we would entirely misperceive what the panegyric enterprise was about. While I doubt that the book will usher in a new age of panegyric writing—a "golden age of poetry and power," as Robert Frost put it—I hope that the reader has developed at least an appreciation for this genre of writing that is rich, brilliant, and, in a certain sense, beautiful. As seen, panegyric writing intersected with virtually every aspect of medieval Jewish life, from its formal and informal bonds of loyalty, to its political rituals and rivalries, regional identities, interreligious relations, and intellectual concerns ranging from ethics, biblical exegesis, the philosophy of language, poetics, psychology, and the nature of the human-divine relationship.

This book has followed medieval Jewish praise writing like a river wending its way through the massive slab of earth that was the medieval Mediterranean. It is my hope in doing so that I have revealed not only the river but also something of the canyon.

NOTES

INTRODUCTION

1. These two poems are translated and discussed in Scheindlin, "The Hebrew Qasida in Spain." See also idem, "Poet and Patron."

2. Schirmann, "The Function of the Poet in Medieval Spain," 236.

3. Schirmann, *Toledot ha-shirah ha-ʿivrit bi-Sefarad ha-muslemit*, 56.

4. Cited in Rowland, *Faint Praise and Civil Leer*, 15.

5. Burrow, *The Poetry of Praise*, 3.

6. J. Stetkevych, "Arabic Poetry and Assorted Poetics." I first encountered this citation in Ali, "Praise for Murder?." Interestingly, Ali notes that in twentieth-century Egypt, attraction toward nationalist socialism under Nasr also led to a condemnation of panegyric; see 7n2.

7. Ginzberg, *Geonica*, 2:277 (my italics).

8. Goitein, *A Mediterranean Society*, 5:35.

9. I will address reservations toward specific aspects in Chap. 5 on the ethics of praise.

10. Braunn, "Arabic Verses in *Kitāb al-muḥāḍara wa'l-mudhākara*," 134–35.

11. Mann, *Texts and Studies in Jewish History and Literature*, 1:107–8, 367–68.

12. On portraiture, see, e.g., Rosenthal et al., *Citizens and Kings*.

13. On the idea of facades, see Hackett, "Dreams or Designs, Cults or Constructions?"

14. Weber, *The Theory of Social and Economic Organization*, 328; idem, "Social Psychology of the World Religions." Naturally, sociology, religion, and political science have all had a great deal to say about Weber's formulation, including different classifications and taxonomies of legitimacy. See, e.g., Matheson, "Weber and the Classification of Forms of Legitimacy."

15. See also Merquoir, *Rousseau and Weber*, 32.

16. Lakoff and Johnson, *Metaphors We Live By*; to see where this field has gone, see Dirven, *Metaphor and Metonymy in Comparison and Contrast*. Alfonso, "The Body, Its Organs, and Senses." I extend and elaborate upon her argument in subsequent chapters.

17. Ibn Ezra, *Shirei ha-ḥol*, 300 (dedicatory poem to *Sefer ha-ʿanaq*), line 15. "Whitewash and plaster," cf. Ez 13:10, with reference to a false prophet. The dominion of others is

thus illegitimate but also constructed. See also *avnei shevaḥot* in line 12 of the same poem (in this book, all citations to "Ibn Ezra, *Shirei ha-ḥol*" refer to Mosheh Ibn Ezra; other citations will refer to Avraham or Yiṣḥaq Ibn Ezra explicitly).

18. E.g., Biale, *Power and Powerlessness in Jewish History*; Penslar, *Jews and the Military*.

19. The number of communal titles can be bewildering, and it is not my aim in this study to delineate exactly how each title was assigned or what responsibilities each entailed. Certain aspects, however, will be discussed at various points.

20. On the Cairo Geniza in general, see Goitein, *A Mediterranean Society*, 1:1–28. For a good read on the history of its discovery and portraits of the scholars involved, see Cole and Hoffman, *Sacred Trash*.

21. A fine introduction is Whitby, *The Propaganda of Power*. Many other studies of panegyric in various languages and periods, but especially classical Arabic, will be cited at specific points throughout this book. See also Marin, *Portrait of the King*.

22. The field of classics has a highly specific vocabulary for differentiating genres and forms of praise: panegyric (poetry for a festival), epideictic (which includes praise and blame), encomium (generally praise in prose address). Further, see Russell, "The Panegyrists and Their Teachers." In this book, I am not adhering to this strict terminology but use terms for praise writing fairly interchangeably whether presented orally or in writing, in an assembly or in private, in poetry or in prose.

23. In addition to Whitby, *The Propaganda of Power*, see Rees, *Layers of Loyalty in Latin Panegyric*; Roche, *Pliny's Praise*; Hägg, Rousseau, and Høgel, *Greek Biography and Panegyric in Late Antiquity*.

24. See also Hackett, "Dreams or Designs, Cults or Constructions?."

25. See the introduction to Whitby, *The Propaganda of Power*, esp. essays by Braund and Rapp.

26. See Dennis, "Imperial Panegyric," 135.

27. It is called the *burda* tradition because Muḥammad bestowed his mantle upon the poet Ka'b Ibn Zuhayr when the latter recited a poem in his honor. See S. Stetkevych, *The Mantle Odes*.

28. See S. Stetkevych, *The Poetics of Islamic Legitimacy*, esp. 185–87, 241–82; Sharlet, *Patronage and Poetry in the Islamic World*, 47; Gruendler, *Medieval Arabic Praise Poetry*; Ali, *Arabic Literary Salons in the Islamic Middle Ages*.

29. On panegyric performance in association with public processions in the Fatimid Empire, see Sanders, *Ritual, Politics, and the City in Fatimid Cairo*. On the various types of *majālis* (pl. of *majlis*) and the associated social behaviors, see the excellent overview of Newman, "Madjlis," in *The Encyclopaedia of Islam*, 2nd ed. See also Robinson, *In Praise of Song*, 67–74.

30. Ali, *Arabic Literary Salons in the Islamic Middle Ages*, 48.

31. Ibid., 17.

32. On Ibn Qillīs, see Mark Cohen and Somekh, "In the Court of Ya'qub Ibn Killis." On Ibn al-Munajjā, see Ashtor, "Abū Al-Munajjā Solomon ben Shaya." On the Jewish poets cited by al-Jāḥiẓ, see Ratzhaby, "Shirah 'aravit be-fi yehudim be-Andalusiya."

33. For an English translation of this responsum, see Scheindlin, *Wine, Women, and Death*, 32.

34. See Chap. 9 in this vol.

35. The context here was not a *majlis ʿām*, and *duʿā* is not identical with *madīḥ*, but the anecdote allows for the plausible scenario of a Jew standing before a caliph to recite his praise. See also the entertaining anecdote from the *Ansāb al-ashrāf* cited by Goitein, wherein a Jew recited one of his father's vainglorious poems before the Caliph Muʿāwiyya and the poet was upbraided, since "such glory belonged only to the ruler"; see Goitein, *A Mediterranean Society*, 4:227.

36. The full text reads: "O God, perfume his tomb with exaltation and. . . ./ And forgive us our sins and transgressions! / [Ask God to pray] for the one who brought us our clear religion in truth, / And [who] put an end to stinking gloom [i.e., polytheism], for through him the universe is adorned. / [Ask God to] pray for him and grant him peace! (cf. Qur'ān 33:56) / In the hereafter you will surely be honored, / In its delight you will take pleasure as a gift from [our Lord]." What the text was doing in the possession of a Jew and how it made its way into the Geniza is a matter of speculation. The text may have been valued primarily for the contents of the recto, the "flip side," which is an excerpt from some version of a biography of the Prophet, presumably based on Ibn Hishām.

37. Further, see Chap. 2 in this vol.

38. On Ibn Naghrīla, see Brann, *Power in the Portrayal*, including the discussion of Ibn Khayra's panegyric in chap. 3.

39. On the caliphal image of ʿAbd al-Raḥman III, see J. Safran, "The Command of the Faithful in al-Andalus"; idem, *The Second Umayyad Caliphate.*

40. Ibn Bassām, *Al-dhakhīra fī maḥāsin ahl al-jazīra*, 233–35.

41. Ibn Janāḥ, *Kitāb al-uṣūl*, 729. See also the commentaries of Gersonides as well as Avraham Ben Shemuel to 1 Sm 18:6–8.

42. Ibn Paquda, *Torat ḥovot ha-levavot*, 341–42. See also B. Safran, "Bahya Ibn Paquda's Attitude Toward the Courtier Class," 159. On Baḥya's reservations toward panegyric, see Chap. 5 in this vol.

43. A. Ben Maimon, *Sefer ha-maspiq le-ʿovdei ha-shem*, 2:2, 81.

44. Most of these types will be treated throughout the book. For the examples, see Mosheh Ibn Ezra, *Shirei ha-ḥol*, 170–71 [172]; Halevi, *Diwan des Abu-l-Hasan Jehuda ha-Levi* (hereafter Halevi, *Dīwān*), 40 [33]; Van Bekkum, *The Secular Poetry of Elʿazar Ben Yaʿaqov ha-Bavli*, Hebrew sec., 85–87.

45. Bourdieu, *The Logic of Practice*, esp. chap. 3.

46. Halkin, *Moses Maimonides' Epistle to Yemen*, 2–3 (my trans. from the Hebrew). There is also a translation of the entire epistle in idem and Hartman, *Epistles of Maimonides*; for this passage (similar to my trans.), see 95. See also my discussion of this passage in Chap. 6 in this vol.

47. Such a group might reasonably be called a "community of practice," a term that emerged first in the study of education and then in sociolinguistics to refer to an aggregate of voluntary adherents aligned in a common cause who mark their "membership"

through verbal or other practices; the idea is more specific than a "speech group," which is not predicated on voluntarism or alignment. A good entry point is Holmes and Meyerhoff, "The Community of Practice."

48. On royal hymns in the ancient Near East, see, e.g., Klein, *The Royal Hymns of Shulgi King of Ur.* I wish to thank Tzvi Abusch for this reference.

49. Mack, *Wisdom and the Hebrew Epic.*

50. C. Roth, "Ecclesiasticus in the Synagogue Service." On the liturgical genre, see Swartz and Yahalom, *Avodah*; Münz-Manor, "As the Apple Among Fruits, So the Priest When He Emerges."

51. In the *'avodah* liturgy, these poems are usually followed with two other poems, the second of which begins with the words *ashrei 'ayin ra'ata*, "Happy is the eye that sees," and follow with a visual description of the high priest's pageantry.

52. *Maḥzor qatan ke-minhag qoṣantina*, 83. It is possible that the attribution to Yosi Ben Yosi is incorrect. On the helmet as a Hellenistic and Roman symbol (particularly of Caesar in the time of Herod), see Ariel, "The Coins of Herod the Great in the Context of the Augustan Empire."

53. Mosheh Ibn Ezra, *Shirei ha-qodesh*, 307–9; lines 26–27, 32–33. For Ibn Ghiyat, see Ha-Kohen, *Siftei rananot kolel seliḥot ve-baqashot*, 235. On the significance of surveying territory and other aspects of caliphal pageantry in al-Andalus, see Barceló, "The Manifest Caliph."

54. Although marble is listed among the materials used in the construction of the Temple, a pavement of marble is associated in the Bible only with a palace (Est 1:6).

55. The presentation of the same requirement in the *pesuqei de-zimrah* of the morning liturgy, however, is not predicated on exchange.

56. D. Stern, *Parables in Midrash*, 19–21.

57. For "great man," see b. Eruvin 80a; b. Avodah Zarah 76b; and elsewhere. For "he is not a mortal," b. Eruvin 24a. Interestingly, the Gemarah cites a disagreement concerning what Rav Ḥiziqiyah said, the alternative being "One like him is a great person," a discrepancy that suggests that there might have been discomfort with the hyperbole of "he is not a mortal." For Ben Zakkai, m. Avot 2:8.

58. Schwartz, *Were the Jews a Mediterranean Society?*. See also Weitzmann, "Mediterranean Exchanges," 495; Rajak, *The Jewish Dialogue with Greece and Rome,* 373–92. See also below on recent work by Rustow.

59. Sysling, "Laments at the Departure of a Sage."

60. Titulature is discussed extensively in Chap. 1 of this vol.

61. See also the comments by Rustow in Chap. 2, n. 61, below. Whether the political use of panegyric in Islamic empires should be seen as an outgrowth of an Arab practice or as an extension of a Late Antique Roman and Byzantine one is beyond the scope of this project.

62. R. Brody, *The Geonim of Babylonia and the Shaping of Medieval Jewish Culture*, xix.

63. See also Herman, *A Prince Without a Kingdom.* At least some "imperial" practices were associated with the exilarchate prior to the geonic period.

64. See Mark Cohen, *Jewish Self-Government in Medieval Egypt*. Further, merchants wielded significant influence as representatives or agents of Jewish authorities, both local and distant, and could also play the role of "kingmaker" through their professions of allegiance and financial backing. See Rustow, "The Genizah and Jewish Communal History."

65. Again, these maps are overlapping; many intellectuals were also merchants.

66. E.g., we know that trade between Egypt and al-Andalus suffered a decline in the second half of the eleventh century, but the movement of books from the latter to the former (including luxury editions of the *dīwān*s of Mosheh Ibn Ezra and Yehudah Halevi) seems to have continued unimpeded.

67. Ha-Nagid, *Dīwān Shemuel ha-Nagid*, 164–69 [51]; 231–36 [85] for the lament on Hai Gaon.

68. On the debate over whether the turn to biblical purity represented Jewish accommodation or competition with the Islamic value of *'arabiyya*, see Brann, *The Compunctious Poet*, chap. 1.

69. Halevi, *Dīwān*, 1:53–57 [40], lines 23–47.

70. See, e.g., Ibn Janāḥ, *Kutub wa rasā'il*, 247–48. Also, Andalusian poets often refer to one another as "brothers in *adab*," occasionally within hierarchic contexts. E.g., Halevi compares how the "brother in *adab*" (*aḥi musar*) bows before a particular *mamdūḥ* just as men bow before God; see Halevi, *Dīwān*, 1:112 [78], lines 19–21. See also references to al-Ḥarīzī in Chap. 4 of this volume. I interrogate the term "courtier rabbi" in Chap. 1 and am preparing a separate article, "The Jewish *Ahl al-Adab* of al-Andalus."

71. I.e., to measure his greatness. *Dīwān*, 76–77 [57]. On Shemuel Ben Ḥananiah, see Mann, *The Jews in Egypt and in Palestine*, 1:229–30; this poem will be discussed further in Chap. 4.

72. On Pirenne and Braudel and the development of Mediterranean scholarship, see Horden and Purcell, *The Corrupting Sea*, 31–39. The latter book is an important example of the renewed interest in Mediterranean studies.

73. See, e.g., the recent synthetic project by Catlos, *Infidel Kings and Unholy Warriors*; Horden and Kinoshita, *A Companion to Mediterranean History*.

74. Horden and Purcell, *The Corrupting Sea*, 2.

75. See Herzfeld, "Practical Mediterraneanism."

76. Stroumsa, *Maimonides in His World*, 4.

77. Although Yemen appears occasionally within the pages of *A Mediterranean Society*, it belonged, in Goitein's view, more properly to the route of the India trade. See Goitein and Friedman, *India Traders of the Middle Ages*.

78. Mark Cohen, *Jewish Self-Government in Medieval Egypt*; Frenkel, *The Compassionate and Benevolent*; Bareket, *Fustat on the Nile*; Gil, *A History of Palestine 634–1099*; Rustow, *Heresy and the Politics of Community*; Goldberg, *Trade and Institutions in the Medieval Mediterranean*.

79. Astren, "Goitein, Medieval Jews, and the 'New Mediterranean Studies,'" 524.

80. See also Horden and Purcell, *The Corrupting Sea*, 405.

81. On Anatoli Ben Yosef, see Schirmann, *Ha-shirah . . . Ṣarfat*, 440–52; the discussion there is by Fleischer.

82. On the in/of distinction, see Horden and Purcell, *The Corrupting Sea*, 2. For another grand history of the Mediterranean (that focuses on the individual), see D. Abulafia, *The Great Sea*.

83. A fascinating question is the degree to which the panegyric traditions of Christian states changed under the impact of Arabic practices. This question is largely beyond the scope of the present project; but see some comments in Chap. 9.

84. See also Gutwirth, "Models of Patronage in Medieval Spain."

CHAPTER I

Note to epigraph: Fleischer, "Shiro shel rav Hai Gaon," 1325–26, lines 176–80, 191–92. A smaller portion of the poem, along with the surrounding letter, was published by Mann, *Texts and Studies*, 1:129–34.

1. Including praise for a living woman, even when associated with her husband or another man, is quite rare; the most extensive I am aware of is for the wife or daughter of a *rosh yeshivah*, possibly Shemuel Ben ʿEli. See Assaf, "Qoveṣ shel iggerot rav Shemuel Ben ʿEli," 3:26 (the article was published in three parts; references are cited by part and page number).

2. Fleischer, "Shiro shel rav Hai Gaon," 1325, lines 158–68 = Mann, *Texts and Studies*, 1:130. I have laid out the poem in prose form, here and below. Similarly, Hai refers to a letter received from a certain *aluf* as a "sweet offering and a satisfying gift" (*minḥah ʿarevah ve-eshkar raṣon*). See TS 20.100, lines 23–24; Mann, *Texts and Studies*, 1:119–22.

3. Fleischer, "Shiro shel rav Hai Gaon," 1322–23, lines 106–14. "Lifting spirits and exchanging gifts," following Fleischer's interpretation.

4. On his scholarly activity, see Meacham-Yoreh, ed., and Frenkel, trans., *The Book of Maturity by Rav Shemuel Ben Ḥofni Gaon and the Book of Years by Rav Yehudah Ha-Kohen Rosh Ha-Seder.*

5. Mann, *Texts and Studies*, 132. See also partial transcription and discussion (and part of the poem with vocalization) by Ben Sasson, "Rashei ha-ṣibbur be-ṣafon Afriqa," 142–46.

6. As Fleischer points out, because Hai was sending his poem to a *mamdūḥ* in the Islamic West, he was likely trying to appeal to the donor's literary tastes and expectations. For the poem by Dunash Ben Labrat, see Schirmann, *Ha-shirah ha-ʿivrit*, 1:35–40, esp. lines 37–38. See also TS 13 J 19.18 in Chap. 2 of this vol.

7. In addition to other examples below, Shemuel ha-Nagid's "Eloah ʿoz" concludes with similar instructions. See ha-Nagid, *Dīwān Shemuel ha-Nagid*, 14, lines 146–49.

8. See p. 10.

9. One fascinating case that captures oral performance at a funeral derives from the *dīwān* of the thirteenth-century Baghdadi poet Elʿazar Ben Yaʿaqov ha-Bavli. An exceptionally detailed superscription for a funerary elegy reads: "And by him, a lament, when a son of the *rosh yeshivah* Daniel Ben Abī Rabīʿa died; he included in its introduction a diatribe

(*murāshaqa*; lit., "pelting one another") concerning the community (*fī al-jamāʿa*) against the people at the mourning ceremony from among the exalted great ones who were reciting poetry because all that they recited was stolen. He himself stood to present [the lament] before the community." One can hardly imagine a stranger time to appeal to standards of plagiarism, but the description certainly captures the public and oral nature of lament poetry. See Van Bekkum, *The Secular Poetry of El'azar Ben Ya'aqov ha-Bavli*, 45–46 (my trans. of the Judeo-Arabic, based on Van Bekkum's).

10. The section is published in Neubauer, *Medieval Jewish Chronicles*, 2:83–85. The most comprehensive treatment of Natan's report is Ben Sasson, "The Structure, Goal, and Content of the Story of Nathan Ha-Babli." Surviving portions of the Judeo-Arabic original of Natan's text are published here. See also my article on the installation, "The Hidden Exilarch."

11. On this term, see the Introduction, p. 10. In the same text, the story about how Mar 'Uqba addressed the caliph uses the term *duʿā*, which is translated at that point with *berakhot*.

12. Ben Sasson suggests that the al-Bardani family, a dynasty of synagogue precentors in Baghdad, may have fulfilled this role. See his review of Beeri, *The Great Cantor of Baghdad*: Ben Sasson, "Review: Geniza Research at the Turn of the Millenium," 259–60. As Beeri points out, it is possible but not certain that a lament by al-Bardani was written for an exilarch (see *The Great Cantor of Baghdad*, 13, 157). The opening of one poem that was definitely dedicated to an exilarch can be found in Ḥ. Brody, "Piyyutim ve-shirei tehillah me-rav Hayya Gaon," 57 [13].

13. Sanders, *Ritual, Politics, and the City in Fatimid Cairo*, 126.

14. Decter, "The Hidden Exilarch," 188, with reference to Geertz, *Negara*, 120. Since this publication, I have rethought, to a certain extent, the idea of the "theater state," largely following the hesitations of Bertelli, *The King's Body*, 67. To think of political ritual merely as a performance can cynically reduce its contents to a means of social control wherein elites create a dramatic experience for the masses without necessarily subscribing to the religious and cosmological messaging presented. While the ceremony was certainly very dramatic, I have little doubt that even the elites performed the ritual not as actors but as full participants. This is why I prefer now to speak of "political rituals."

15. On Ben 'Azariah in general, see Mann, *The Jews in Egypt and in Palestine*. For Shemuel ha-Nagid, see Jarden, 139–42 [40].

16. Published in Fleischer, "Qavim ḥadashim li-demuto shel rav Daniel Ben 'Azariah, nasi ve-gaon." Fleischer gives the date 13 Nisan 1052; Gil suggests the year 1057, *History of Palestine*, 660n125. I wish to thank Arnold Franklin for helping me clarify this.

17. An *'avodah* would make a transition here to a description of the rituals of the high priest in the Temple on Yom Kippur, which is also a kind of political culmination.

18. Franklin, "Cultivating Roots," 98, and, more recently, in his *This Noble House*, 89–90, 116–18. I will discuss the issue of lineage at greater length in Chap. 4. An interesting comparison, which likewise begins with God and Creation but lacks any pedigree, is one of several panegyrics for Shelomoh Abū al-Munajjā Ibn Shaiʿa, a renowned Jewish courtier in

Egypt: "The Lord of all for Whom all are His worshipers, Who possesses all and upon all is His kindness, Who suspended the circuit of the earth upon nothing . . . and set for His witnesses the pride of His might and the majesty of His wonders (i.e., Ibn al-Munajjā) before the eyes of all the created." See Mann, *The Jews in Egypt and in Palestine*, 2:268–69 (text), 1:215–17 (description). The opening verse echoes a verse by Ibn Gabirol, *Shirei ha-ḥol* [74], "the secret of all is because of the All who has all in His hands" (all citations in this book to Ibn Gabirol, *Shirei ha-ḥol*, refer to the ed. by Jarden, unless otherwise noted).

19. The epistles were anthologized already in the medieval period, likely by a scribe of the yeshivah. The anthology was published by Assaf, "Qoveṣ shel iggerot rav Shemuel Ben 'Eli."

20. Ibid., 1:106–7.

21. As Assaf points out, this practice is known with respect to the gaon centuries earlier from the *Epistle of Sherirah Gaon*. See Assaf, "Qoveṣ shel iggerot rav Shemuel Ben 'Eli," 1:111.

22. Assaf, "Qoveṣ shel iggerot rav Shemuel Ben 'Eli," 2:61–62.

23. The laying of hands was incorporated into the rabbinic ordination ceremony *semikha*, "laying (of hands)." This is distinct from the "extending of hands" that Natan ha-Bavli describes in the case of swearing loyalty to a new exilarch, which seems more resonant with the Islamic *bai'a* ceremony. See Decter, "The Hidden Exilarch," 189n8. The difference between the two hand gestures is also confirmed by the letters of Ben 'Eli. Cf. this passage with Assaf, "Qoveṣ shel iggerot rav Shemuel Ben 'Eli," 3:69, which details the appointment of Natanel Ben Mosheh Halevi, "that [those of lower rank] will extend their hands to him in truth" (*yitnu lo yad be-emet*), a sign of loyalty. On signet rings, see, e.g., Marsham, *Rituals of Islamic Monarchy*, 141, and "seal ring" in the index. Also see Yefet Ben 'Eli on Dn 7:14.

24. I changed the verbal noun "our appointment of him" to the perfect tense.

25. Assaf, "Qoveṣ shel iggerot rav Shemuel Ben 'Eli," 2:69.

26. The one epistolary genre that has been shown to lack praise for the most part (and even keeps salutary blessings to a minimum) is what Jessica Goldberg terms "commercial letters." These do not include letters from merchants that are devoid of commercial content. A counterexample, she notes, is ULC Or 1080 J248. See chap. 3 of her *Trade and Institutions in the Medieval Mediterranean*.

27. Mann, *Texts and Studies* 1:107–8. Further on Mann's use of "verbiage," see p. 3.

28. A useful collection of merchant letters from the Geniza is Udah, *Ha-mikhtavim ha-'araviyim shel ha-soḥarim ha-yehudim bi-genizat Qahir*; see also Motzkin, "The Arabic Correspondence of Judge Elijah and His Family."

29. Assaf, "Qoveṣ shel iggerot rav Shemuel Ben 'Eli," 1:114–15. See also Assaf's valuable comparison of Jewish epistolary forms in the Islamic East and the Islamic West.

30. Gafni, "Epistles of the Patriarchs in Talmudic Literature."

31. On the timing of the significance of the movement to Baghdad, see R. Brody, *The Geonim of Babylonia*, 36–37.

32. Sources of this mail system have been sought in Sassanian, Byzantine, and now Arabian precedents. For an overview, see Silverstein, *Postal Systems in the Pre-Modern*

Islamic World. See also Bosworth, "Abū 'Abdallāh al-Khwārazmī on the Technical Terms of the Secretary's Art," esp. 141–43.

33. On all these systems, see Silverstein, "Jews and the News"; also Goldberg, *Trade and Institutions in the Medieval Mediterranean*, 189–93.

34. The discussion of Arabic epistolography is drawn from secondary articles and my own review of many of the primary sources. In general, see Arazi, "Risāla"; Latham, "The Beginnings of Arabic Prose Literature"; Lecomte, "L'introduction du Kitāb adab al-kātib"; Arazi, "Une épître d'Ibrāhīm b. Hilāl al-Ṣābī sur les genres littéraires."

35. An English trans. of 'Abd al-Ḥamīd's epistle can be found in Ibn Khaldūn, *The Muqaddimah*, 2:29–35; Ibn Qutaiba, *Adab al-kātib*; al-Ṣulī, *Adab al-kuttāb*; al-Ḥumaydī, *Tashīl al-sabīl ilā ta'allum al-tarsīl*; al-Qalqashandī, *Ṣubḥ al-a'ashā' fī ṣinā'at al-inshā'*.

36. Arazi, "Risāla."

37. Bosworth, "Abū 'Abdallāh al-Khwārazmī on the Technical Terms," esp. 158–64.

38. On this definition of *sulṭāniyya*, see Mark Cohen, "Correspondence and Social Control in the Jewish Communities of the Islamic World," 40. In other works, the foremost division is between *ikhwāniyya*, "personal," and *dīwāniyya*, "bureau, chancery," correspondence, apparent in sections of the *Ṣubḥ al-a'ashā'*.

39. For the chap. that provides greeting differentiated by rank, see al-Ḥumaydī, *Tashīl al-sabīl ilā ta'allum al-tarsīl*, 62–89. Although wishing a merchant "profit" is prescribed in this manual, I have hardly found any similar formulas in Geniza merchant letters.

40. Father to son, *Ṣubḥ al-a'ashā'*, 8:131; inferior to superior, 8:128–30.

41. See Guo, *Commerce, Culture, and Community in a Red Sea Port in the Thirteenth Century*.

42. Partially transcribed and translated by Gottheil, "Fragments of an Arabic Common-Place Book." Goitein believes that the scribe was Ḥalfon Ben Natanel; see *A Mediterranean Society* 2:572n16; *Sidrei ḥinukh*, 44n23. The twenty-one chapter titles are given on 2a. Cf. al-Qalqashandī, *Ṣubḥ al-a'ashā'*, 8:126, which has many of the same terms.

43. For a qur'ānic quotation and reference to the Prophet, see fol. 6a. Also, among the numerous qualities for which Shemuel ha-Nagid was praised by Muslim authors was his ability to write epistles in Arabic with control over Islamic formulas; see Brann, *Power in the Portrayal*, 37.

44. TS K 20.9 / TS Misc 36.147, line 56, published in Allony, *The Jewish Library in the Middle Ages*, 11–27 [4] (not doc. 5, as in the index; also the Hebrew letters are reversed in the note ad locum).

45. Ben Shammai wrote the section on Judeo-Arabic in the aforementioned Arazi, "Risāla." See also Goldberg's discussion of Goitein's scattered treatment of epistolography, "On Reading Goitein's *A Mediterranean Society*." Some additional sections of *A Mediterranean Society* on epistolary practices include 1:11–12; 3:22, 115, 224, 239, 244; 5:46–47, 230–32, 422–24.

46. This is in his commentary on *Sefer yeṣirah* (Book of Creation), titled *Kitāb al-mabādī* in Arabic. See Sa'adia Ben Yosef, *Sefer yeṣirah (kitāb al-mabādi)*, 49–50.

47. Schechter, *Saadyana*, 58; Mann, *Texts and Studies*, 1:72–73.

48. See Beeri, "Seridei igronim qadumim min ha-geniza." For a *gaon*: 32; a *baḥur*: 8; a *ḥazan*: 31, 34, 36; a *ḥaver*: 35; a mercantile clerk: 37.

49. Beeri, "Seridei igronim." In this doc., most of the introductions are addressed to "So-and-So" (*ploni*), though some preserve actual names. Other formularies preserve names of original addressees, such as TS 8 J 39.10 (I discuss this document in Chap. 2). Beeri lists other unpublished manuscripts of this type on 54nn45–47. See also Oxford Heb e.74.71b–72a, mentioned by Mann, *The Jews in Egypt and in Palestine*, 2:192; Mann also describes Or 5544.1b as a "formulae of letters to a Gaon, the academy, and other communal leaders." See Mann, *The Jews in Egypt and in Palestine*, 2:191. See also TS NS 108.40, published by Allony, "A Twelfth-Century List of Personalities and Their Titles."

50. Mark Cohen, "On the Interplay of Arabic and Hebrew in the Cairo Geniza Letters." On some of the standard formulations in personal and business Arabic letter writing, see Guo, *Commerce, Culture, and Community in a Red Sea Port in the Thirteenth Century*; also Diem, *Arabische Geschäftsbriefe des 10. bis 14. Jahrhunderts*; idem, *Arabische Privatbriefe des 9. bis 15. Jahrhunderts.*

51. E.g., ULC Or 1080 J25 is a rather mundane family letter by Avraham Abū Ḥasan from the city of Kutz (in upper Egypt) that contains a number of verses of poetry, quite likely composed by Avraham himself. See Goitein, *Sidrei ḥinukh*, 46. See also the rhymed prose introduction in Judeo-Arabic to Oxford Heb d.74.41 in praise of Ḥalfon Ben Natanel by Yiṣḥaq Ben Barukh; pub. in Gil and Fleischer, *Yehudah Halevi u-venei ḥugo*, 379–83, also trans. in Goitein, *Letters of Medieval Jewish Traders*, 259–63.

52. See also the Introduction, pp. 22–23.

53. Further, it is not always easy to tell whether a title was bestowed within Jewish institutional contexts or within a Muslim court. See, e.g., Mann on Abū al-Munajjā, *The Jews in Egypt and in Palestine*, 1:215, where the title "exalted of the state" seems to refer to the Ayyubid state.

54. Al-Qalqashandī notes that epistolary practices are sometimes imitations of ritual practices; regarding the phrase "the slave kisses the ground" (before the caliph), which became standard in the petition sometime during the Fatimid period, he notes that "they transferred it from action to expression" (*naqalūhu min al-fi'l ilā al-lafẓ*). See Khan, "The Historical Development of the Structure of Medieval Arabic Petitions," 25.

55. Bosworth, "Laḳab."

56. See Dietrich, "Zu den mit ad-dīn zusammengesetzten islamischen Personnamen."

57. Kramers, "Les noms musulmans composés avec Dîn."

58. S. M. Stern, "Three Petitions of the Fāṭimid Period"; Khan, "The Historical Development of the Structure of Medieval Arabic Petitions."

59. It may seem surprising that someone other than the caliph could be called "king," but this might be the precise point. The caliph was *not* a (mundane) king but rather God's deputy. This concept will be discussed further in Chap. 7.

60. S. M. Stern, "Three Petitions of the Fāṭimid Period," 182–84.

61. Goitein also notes a petition wherein a caliph is called "The Pure Majesty" (lit., "presence") (*al-ḥaḍra al-ṭāhira*). See Goitein, "Petitions to Fatimid Caliphs from the

Cairo Geniza," 30. As the letters become increasingly standardized in later periods, the forms of address actually become less ornate (see Khan below). See examples in S. M. Stern, "Petitions from the Ayyūbid Period"; idem, "Petitions from the Mamlūk Period." For a diachronic study of structural changes, see Khan, "The Historical Development of the Structure of Medieval Arabic Petitions."

62. See also Goldziher, "Zu Saadyana XLI," 73–75, who notes the use of adjectives such as "holy, Alawide, Imāmī, prophetic, pure" (*al-muqaddasa al-ʿalawiyya al-imāmiyya al-nabawiyya al-zakiyya*) to describe the station of the Fatimid caliph.

63. Goitein, "Prayers from the Geniza for Fatimid Caliphs, the Head of the Jerusalem Yeshiva, the Jewish Community and the Local Congregation," 52. The same caliph is addressed (entirely in Arabic) similarly in a petition from a Jewish merchant with the addition of the phrase "Imam of Our Time and Age" (S. M. Stern, "Three Petitions," 179).

64. *Al-mawāqif*, an honorific that indicates place or station (*laqab makānī*), similar to *al-ḥaḍra*, "the Presence."

65. Assaf, "Qoveṣ shel iggerot rav Shemuel Ben ʿEli," 3:72. The document is TS 8 J 2.

66. See also Chap. 9 for a Hebrew poem that includes praise for the caliph al-Mustanṣir Bi'llah and his military commander Badr al-Jamālī that describes the caliph through several phrases that held particular resonance within the Ismaʿili conception of the imamate.

67. Mann already appreciated that Jews "followed the train" of Islamic practice; he also notes that such titles became "commonplace and soon lost all real significance"; *The Jews in Egypt and in Palestine*, 1:277–80. See also Bareket, *Fustat on the Nile*, 82.

68. Bareket, *Fustat on the Nile*, 119–22. Goitein also kept a card file of titles.

69. However, Bareket also points out that honorifics were sometimes given to those who did not play specific roles; *Fustat on the Nile*, 99–100.

70. Assaf, "Qoveṣ shel iggerot rav Shemuel Ben ʿEli," 2:69.

71. Similarly, a letter from Shelomoh Ben Yehudah to Sahlān Ben Avraham addresses the latter, "who is given four honorifics" (*kinuyei shel kavod*). TS Misc 35.14, published in Gil, *Ereṣ Yisraʾel*, 2:261–63 [146].

72. Published by Allony, "A Twelfth-Century List of Personalities and Their Titles."

73. Or 5544.8r, published in Mann, *The Jews in Egypt and in in Palestine*, 2:86. See also Mann, 1:86.

74. See the superscriptions in Van Bekkum, *The Secular Poetry of Elʿazar Ben Yaʿaqov ha-Bavli*, Hebrew sec., 11, 19, 21, 55, 112, 158. Two of these are also referred to by Mann, *Texts and Studies*, 1:172–73. Note that the figure called *sharf al-dawla* on 19 was a Karaite. See also Fischel, "The Divan of Eleazar the Babylonian as a Source for the Social History of the Jews of Baghdad in the XIII Century," 233–36, where some of these figures and families are identified within Arabic chronicles (along with their titles).

75. Van Bekkum, *The Secular Poetry of Elʿazar Ben Yaʿaqov ha-Bavli*, 21–22.

76. E.g., Assaf, "Qoveṣ shel iggerot rav Shemuel Ben ʿEli," 2:43, 45, 47–48; 3:42, 44, 51, 53.

77. Kramers, "Les noms musulmans composés avec Dîn."

78. Assaf, "Qoveṣ shel iggerot rav Shemuel Ben 'Eli," 3:49–50. See also the *paqid* Rabbi Yefet 2:43–44; here, *paqid* seems to render *wakīl.*

79. Similarly, Shemuel al-Barqūli is praised "Sun of the Ministers" (*shemesh ha-sarim = shams al-ru'asā*). Assaf, "Qoveṣ shel iggerot rav Shemuel Ben 'Eli," 3:41–42.

80. Ox Heb a.3.28. Pub. by Cowley, "Bodleian Geniza Fragments," 250–56. In addition to the praise for the community, there is an extensive panegyric for Ephraim. Also referenced in Goitein, *A Mediterranean Society*, 5:423.

81. In addition to the poetic epistle that opened this chap., Hai Gaon refers to two of his letters as "open letters to all of the West" (i.e., the Maghrib) (*iggerot petuḥot el kol ha-ma'arav*) and asks that they be copied and shared, though not necessarily orally. Note the similarity with the term *petiḥei* used above by Shemuel ha-Nagid when writing in Aramaic.

82. Some of this information is collected in Assaf, "Qoveṣ shel iggerot rav Shemuel Ben 'Eli," 1:115, esp. n. 4. In addition, see Or 5544.8r, pub. in Mann, *The Jews in Egypt and in Palestine*, 2:86, *wa waqafa 'alaihi wa qara'hu ilā al-j[amā'a].* The oral presentation of letters is also attested in Sicily. A rabbinic term for an open letter is *peshiṭ*. Also, according to Arazi, "Risāla," "[Arabic] letters were intended to be read by more than one person." Especially eloquent passages were admired. On the reception of one letter, "the meeting held to hear it resembled a veritable *majlis*, complete with drinks and selected delicacies."

83. TS K 3.44 and ENA 2687.36, pub., respectively, in Allony, *The Jewish Library in the Middle Ages*, 379–81 [101], 396–99 [104].

84. Ibn Rashīq, *Kitāb al-'umda fī maḥāsin al-shi'r wa adābihi.*

85. See n. 47 above.

86. For the superscription, Ḥ. Brody, "Piyyutim ve-shirei tehillah me-Rav Hayya Gaon," 27.

87. Fleischer, "On the Beginning of Hebrew Poetry in Spain"; despite the value of this article, I am in disagreement concerning Fleischer's essentializing argument for the "purely Jewish" nature of Menaḥem's writing. Further, I do not know that "competition" for patrons necessarily separated the Andalusians from their Eastern counterparts; even Hai Gaon had to deal with the competition of other academies, which might further explain his adopting poetic discourse as the proper means of addressing his donors.

88. Subsequently published in 1952, Weiss, "Tarbuṭ ḥaṣranit ve-shirah ḥaṣranit."

89. Arendt, "*The Court Jew.*" Arendt associated court Jews with Jews who collaborated with the Nazis.

90. In fact, Baer was almost certainly present when Weiss delivered his paper, since both scholars are included as speakers on the history panel at the World Congress. See Decter, "Before Caliphs and Kings"; Horowitz, "The Court Jews and the Jewish Question."

91. The only critiques I am aware of are N. Roth, *Jews, Visigoths, and Muslims in Medieval Spain*, 6; Roth writes that the poetry was "not intended for any 'aristocracy' but precisely for the 'masses.'" Unfortunately, though Roth's intuition to move away from the

courtly model is well placed, he does not develop or justify his argument for the position stated here. He simply moves from one extreme to the other without nuance or measured reflection upon the sources. Better is the reading by Tobi, *Between Hebrew and Arabic Poetry*, 23, who concludes that the poets were largely not paid for their compositions, including panegyrics, but rather that they wrote them "out of true esteem for the extolled persons" (23). I do not see the same dichotomy between payment and sincerity (see Chap. 2 of this vol.).

92. Brener, *Isaac Ibn Khalfun*, 49.

93. Perhaps the best evidence we have for the existence of a distinct group of men we might call "courtly" is the critique of a group with a particular set of educational and social values leveled by the eleventh-century Andalusian pietist Baḥya Ibn Paquda, though "courtly" certainly is not Baḥya's term. See B. Safran, "Bahya Ibn Paquda's Attitude Toward the Courtier Class." Baḥya identifies a group consumed with wealth, the pursuit of prestige, and pride to the point of haughtiness, which seems to map well onto the tastes represented in Andalusian Jewish poetry. His critique is directed toward intellectual tastes as well as certain social practices such as drinking excessively in company (*isrāf*). See Ibn Paquda, *Torat ḥovot ha-levavot*, 400.

94. Ibn Ezra's remarks concerning Ibn Khalfūn, "who made poetry a commodity and trade" will be treated in Chap. 5.

95. Ali, *Arabic Literary Salons in the Islamic Middle Ages*, 18. See also my discussion in the Introduction, p. 10.

96. See Pagis, "Shirei yayyin me-lifnei tequfat Sefarad," 25–26.

97. Although Gerson Cohen's construction of the "courtier rabbi" pertains to figures who actually served in office, the portrayal of this idealized type extends beyond such figures as well. See his "The Typology of the Rabbinate," in Ibn Dā'ūd, *Sefer ha-Qabbalah*, 263–303.

98. Before Ibn Shaprut rose to power in Umayyad al-Andalus, Yosef Ben Pinḥas and Aharon Ben 'Amram were powerful bankers in 'Abbasid Baghdad; Fischel, *Jews in the Economic and Political Life of Mediaeval Islam.* Contemporary with Ibn Shaprut was Ya'aqūb Ibn Qillīs, who held powerful positions at Fatimid outposts and ultimately converted to Islam. Mark Cohen and Somekh, "In the Court of Ya'qub Ibn Killis." Abū al-Munajjā Ibn Shai'a became a minister of agriculture in Egypt in the twelfth century. Ashtor, "Abū al-Munajjā Solomon ben Shaya."

99. Some of the following information is also assembled in Schirmann, *Toledot . . . muslemit*, 70–77. I discuss some additional sources and generally draw different conclusions.

100. Ibn Ezra, *Kitāb al-muḥāḍara wa'l-mudhākara*, 47a (Halkin, 86). "Sun," lit., "suns" (*shumūs*). See also Schirmann, *Toledot . . . muslemit*, 77n299. In addition, Ibn Ezra recounts anecdotes pertaining to the performance and aural aspects of Arabic poetry, though these seem to be drawn from works of Arabic literary criticism and do not necessarily correspond to the performance practices of Hebrew poetry in al-Andalus. See *Kitāb al-muḥāḍara*, 190.

101. Schirmann, *Ha-shirah ha-'ivrit*, 1:23–24, lines 281–92.

102. TS 8 K 15.8. See the transcription in Schirmann, "Ha-meshorerim benei doram shel Mosheh Ibn Ezra vi-Yehudah ha-Levi," 127n30. Another version of the poem has surfaced that demonstrates that the poem also, and perhaps originally, circulated as part of a panegyric in honor of Ibn Shaprut (it also lacks the much discussed conclusion of TS 8 K 15.8). See Geneva 29, pub. in Elizur, "Shirat ha-ḥol ha-'ivrit bi-Sefarad." It is debatable whether Dunash originally wrote the poem with the panegyric such that the prelude subsequently circulated independently or whether Dunash wrote the short version as a freestanding poem and later appended a panegyric to it. I would guess the former scenario, but the evidence is judiciously reviewed by Elizur.

103. The full story is that at a social gathering (*meqom ḥevrato*), Yehosef served apples, which led one of the participants to share a verse of an Arabic poem. Another guest translated the verse into Hebrew and then the Nagid improvised fifteen short poems on the theme. See Ha-Nagid, *Dīwān Shemuel ha-Nagid*, 274–78, discussed also in Schirmann, *Toledot . . . muslemit*, 223.

104. Brener, *Isaac Ibn Khalfun*, 174–75; Ibn Khalfūn, *Shirei Yiṣḥaq Ibn Khalfūn*, 39. The translation is Brener's, though I changed the word "party" to "gathering." Although the text uses the word *majlis*, rather than *mujālasa*, as Samer Ali points out, the two terms lose formal distinction. See Ali, *Arabic Literary Salons in the Islamic Middle Ages*, 16.

105. The anecdote can be found in the Hebrew version (trans. Ibn Tibbon), *Sefer ha-riqmah*, 226–27.

106. A letter from Yiṣḥaq Ibn Ezra also reflects how intellectuals would flock together around the holidays for intellectual enjoyment. He writes that a certain poet had recently arrived at his house joining a company of friends. The letter was sent with Yiṣḥaq's friend Mar Yosef, who was traveling to Granada for the holiday. Yiṣḥaq included some "foolish poetry" of his own, selected by Mar Yosef, presumably to be read at the gathering. See Goitein, *A Mediterranean Society*, 5:16.

107. Ibn Ezra, *Kitāb al-muḥāḍara*, 76–78.

108. "Small group," *'itra*; lit., "nearer portion of a tribe."

109. Ibn Ezra, *Kitāb al-muḥāḍara*, 78–80.

110. The poems by Halevi are discussed in Chap. 4. Yet another similar poem of unknown authorship is preserved in the Geniza. TS H 11.3 is identified in the manuscript as "Andalusian," probably referring to its form if not its origin. Ratzhaby, "Shnei shirim sefardiyyim me-oṣar ha-geniza." The contents are described by Schirmann, *Shirim ḥadashim*, 178.

111. Avraham Ibn Dā'ūd specifies that certain people (Yosef Ibn Sahl, Yosef Ibn Ṣadīq) were appointed judges (*nismakh ba-dayyanut*), it seems by a laying on of hands, in particular years. Ibn Dā'ūd, *Sefer ha-Qabbalah*, 61 (Hebrew sec.), lines 236, 239.

112. *Qaṣin*, usually trans. as "chief" or "ruler," but here it seems to be used in the sense of the Arabic *qḍ'*, which occurs in the superscription.

113. *Ḥovesh*, lit., "binder," as in one who dresses a wound, e.g., Is 3:7, where it is also used in parallel with *qaṣin*.

114. Ibn Ezra, *Shirei ha-ḥol*, 249–51 [240], lines 23–25, 32, 37, 42.

115. See Marsham, *Rituals of Islamic Monarchy*, 40–58; Mottahedeh, *Loyalty and Leadership*, 50–54; Tayan, "Bay'a," 1:1113.

116. The poem is in Ibn Ezra, *Shirei ha-ḥol*, 272–73 [257]. Pagis notes that it is "a song of blessing to one of the rabbis (*rabbanim*) upon his entry to power" and suggests, based on stylistic features, that the author was not Ibn Ezra. The poem is followed in two manuscripts by poems of Mosheh Ibn Gikitilla, so there may have been some confusion among anthologists. In any case, precise authorship is not as important for our purposes as the Andalusian origin.

117. *Perazon*, a hapax legomenon in Jgs 5:7, *ḥadlu perazon be-yisra'el*, something that ceased to exist until Deborah arose. Although the translation of the Jewish Publication Society as "deliverance" would be fitting, the medieval commentaries all refer to unfortified and unprotected settlements.

118. "Addresses," *khuṭab*; usually, but not always, orations. Elsewhere, Ibn Ezra simply uses it to describe prose writing, as opposed to metered verse.

119. Also, in the introduction to Shemuel ha-Nagid's *dīwān*, his son Yehosef wrote that he included in "this *dīwān* his metered utterances (*min aqwālihi al-mawzūna*) and poems in various meters (*al-qita'āt 'alā a'āriḍ shatta*) that were sung in his presence (*kānat tughanna bi-ḥaḍratihi*)" (Jarden, 1). The passage is usually understood to mean that the Nagid had his own poems recited before him by *rāwīs*. On the other hand, the final phrase, *kānat tughanna bi-ḥaḍratihi*, might refer to poems by other poets that were composed in the Nagid's honor, especially since such poems were included in the *dīwān*. Conceivably, the phrase might even be translated as "extolling his Excellency" (*taghanna* with the preposition *bi* can mean "to praise, extol," and the word *ḥaḍra* is frequently used as an honorific, "Presence," in the sense of "Highness" or "Excellency"). By the way, although the word *qiṭa'* is usually understood as a short poem, it is used in the *dīwān* to refer to long poems as well, as in the superscription to "Eloah 'oz," which is 149 lines long. Ha-Nagid, *Dīwān Shemuel ha-Nagid*, 4 [1].

120. The exact circumstances of the imprisonment are murky.

121. Schirmann, *Ha-shirah ha-'ivrit*, 1:8–10.

122. Alternatively, this could mean "the West, Sepharad." We do not know exactly where this gathering took place—probably somewhere around the frontier between Christian and Islamic Iberia or possibly in the environs of the kingdom of Granada.

123. Ibn Ezra, *Shirei ḥol*, 274 [258]. The *kharja* is not preserved in Ibn Ezra's poem but is presumably the same one that concludes Halevi's. Schirmann agrees that the poem is by Ibn Ezra for Ibn Ṣadīq whereas Fleischer claims that the poem is by Ibn Ṣadīq himself and that the "Yosef" mentioned in the poem is some Yosef apart from Ibn Ṣadīq. See Schirmann, *Toledot ha-shirah . . . muslemit*, 431 and n. 51 by Fleischer and also 489n41. Fleischer's reconstruction seems possible but not necessary. This point does not affect my discussion significantly.

124. Abramson, "A Letter of Rabbi Judah ha-Levi to Rabbi Moses Ibn Ezra."

125. If one accepts Fleischer's reconstruction, then Ibn Ṣadīq shared his own composition (for a *mamdūḥ* also named Yosef), which Halevi then tried to imitate. Although Ibn

Ezra was in Granada and Ibn Ṣadīq in Córdoba, it seems likely that the two met. One poem by Ibn Ṣadīq and addressed to "Mosheh," quite possibly Ibn Ezra, expresses longing following the departure of the addressee after a visit. The poem is found in David, ed., *Shirei Yosef Ibn Ṣadīq*, 27.

126. Maimonides also provides evidence for the performance of *muwashshaḥ*s in Hebrew and Arabic, *Commentary on the Mishnah, Neziqin*, Maimonides, *Mishneh 'im perush rabeinu Mosheh Ben Maimon*, 419. Further, Schirmann cites some evidence for actual poetic competitions, such as a passage by al-Ḥarīzī that quotes an Egyptian poet (Yiṣḥaq Ben Barukh) in Damascus wherein the poet calls upon a *mamdūḥ* to pay attention to his poetry but to disregard all others (Schirmann, *Toledot . . . muslemit*, 71–72). However, I see no clear evidence here of oral presentation or an actual competition. We have clearer evidence for Hebrew poetry competitions from Christian settings (see Chap. 8 in this vol.). For the passage on Ben Barukh, see Yehudah al-Ḥarīzī, *Taḥkemoni*, 398–417. We also have evidence from al-Ḥarīzī of another type of performance, the plagiarizing of verses by Ibn Gabirol in taverns; see *Taḥkemoni*, 225, line 340.

127. Ibn Ezra, *Shirei ha-ḥol*, 1:22–23. It is interesting that Ibn Ezra did not respond with yet another *muwashshaḥ* concluding with the same *kharja* but rather he wrote a more formal poem in monorhyme; I believe that this was selected because Ibn Ezra, despite his warm reception of Halevi, was also keeping the relationship from seeming too "chummy." Another poem by the elder Ibn Ezra for a younger recipient, Abū al-Ḥasan 'Ezra b. El'azar, similarly contains extensive praise for a poem received but not for its author; Ibn Ezra, *Shirei ha-ḥol*, 131–33 [137]. See also Halevi, *Dīwān*, 74 [56], which is similar.

128. See also Mark Cohen, "Correspondence and Social Control," on epistolographic conventions, and Rustow's treatment of *ni'ma* discussed in Chap. 2 in this vol.

129. See the list compiled by, e.g., Abramson, "A Letter of Rabbi Judah ha-Levi to Rabbi Moses Ibn Ezra," 400–402; T. Abulafia, *Gan ha-meshallim ve-ha-ḥiddot*, 2:1–11 [439–55].

130. Ha-Nagid, *Dīwān Shemuel ha-Nagid*, 4.

131. Ibid., 256–60 [107]. The letter also contains significant praise for Ḥananel in Aramaic, "Happy is Rabbi Ḥushiel who passed on and left as a remembrance a wise son, perfect in Torah, captain of Talmud, like Samuel, Sinai and the one who uproots the mountains of this generation, like the first prophet (Moses) whose weight is like that of 60,000." See Jarden's notes for rabbinic references.

132. This is indicated, e.g., in the superscription to a poem by Mosheh Ibn Ezra for a certain Elḥanan; see Ibn Ezra, *Shirei ha-ḥol*, 155.

133. Ibn Ezra, *Shirei ha-ḥol*, 180 [181]; 191 [192]. Halevi, *Dīwān*, 2:329 [118] (letter), 1:137 [94] (poem); 1:207 (letter), 1:99–102 [70] (poem); 1:211 (letter preserves a short poem within). Also, internal evidence from poems indicates that writings were sent by carrier pigeon, such as Halevi's reference to a letter being "fixed in the pinions of a far-flown dove"; Halevi, *Dīwān*, 1:137–41 [94], line 52.

134. In addition, some letters follow the structural and thematic development expected of poems. A letter in rhymed prose by Yiṣḥaq Ibn Ezra follows the thematic organization of

a classical *qaṣīda*, a multipartite poem beginning with an amatory prelude and making a transition to panegyric; it is executed with all the literary imagination of a poem but without adhering to the formal requirements of meter and monorhyme. Yiṣḥaq Ibn Ezra, *Yiṣḥaq Ben Avraham Ibn 'Ezra*, 3–8.

135. Schirmann, *Ha-shirah ha-'ivrit*, 172–75, lines 11–12. The motif of reputation as scent is already known from the Sg 1:3, "Your name is oil poured forth."

136. On the Jewish internalization of *shafā'a* as a genre, see also Mark Cohen, "Correspondence and Social Control," 47n5; Goitein, *A Mediterranean Society*, 1:347, and also 1:489n5.

137. The event was likely the massacre of Granadan Jewry in 1066. If this is correct, the authors still refer to the city as the "city of Shemuel ha-Nagid," even though the Nagid was already dead. Importantly, the authors do not refrain from referring positively to Yehosef, even though later writers (both Jewish and Muslim) would identify Yehosef's arrogance as the spark that caused the massacre. The document was first published by Schechter, "Genizah Specimens," 112–13, and later with modifications and a Spanish translation by Ashtor, "Documentos españoles de la Genizah," 60–63. Another good example is TS 16.68r, a letter sent from Shemuel "the third" Ben Hosh'anah to Shemariah Ben Elḥanan in Fustat, which praises the addressee extensively and asks that he "keep an eye on and teach the proper path" to the youth Natan Ben Avraham, who was traveling to Egypt to claim his inheritance following his father's death. Natan is described as a "pure and innocent boy" (*yeled zakh tamim*) and learned in Torah. Published in Gil, *Ereṣ Yisra'el* 2:24–25 [18]. For a Judeo-Arabic example, see TS 13 J 16.13 in Ashtor, "Documentos españoles," 68–71.

138. Schirmann, *Ha-shirah ha-'ivrit*, 1:172, lines 65–69.

CHAPTER 2

1. My translation largely follows that of Efros, "Maimonides' Treatise on Logic," English sec., 47. However, for "something of greater honor," I follow Ibn Tibbon's translation, *be-yoter nikhbad*, which seems to read the Arabic as *majāzāt al-muḥsin bi'l-afḍal*. Efros reads *ifḍāl*, "bestowing kindness," which might be preferable. See 17, 40 (Hebrew sec.).

2. Rustow, "Formal and Informal Patronage Among Jews in the Islamic East," 343. This entire vol., edited by Alfonso, is dedicated to the topic of patronage; it contains a very valuable introduction and a number of useful contributions.

3. Mauss, *The Gift*. We need not consider here whether the premodern or nonindustrial models that Mauss discussed paralleled or provided a counterpoint to the impersonal systems of exchange that he witnessed unfolding in his own day. See the discussion in the introduction to the 1990 ed. by Mary Douglas.

4. The more concrete type of gift dynamic that Mauss describes is apparent in everyday letters, such as TS 10 J 7.18, from Shelomoh Ben Elijah (a wine merchant, among other things) to an addressee simply called *al-sheikh al-rashīd* ("the noble elder"). The letter accompanied a gift (*hadiyya*, l. 16) of wine and states no fewer than five times that

the recipient should not "shame" the author by "returning the gift." The social gap between writer and addressee is apparent, as is the norm of reciprocation. The document is described by Motzkin, "A Thirteenth-Century Jewish Trader in Cairo," 54–55.

5. Kurke, *The Traffic in Praise.* Other citations below.

6. S. Stetkevych, *The Poetics of Islamic Legitimacy,* 18. See also "Mauss" in the index.

7. Gruendler, *Medieval Arabic Praise Poetry,* 233, with a reference to Mauss in n. 8. See also Latham, "The Beginnings of Arabic Prose Literature," esp. 173, on the exchange of writing for material gifts.

8. The distinction between "embedded" and "disembedded" is made by Karl Polanyi, cited in Sharlet, *Patronage and Poetry in the Islamic World,* 7.

9. Ibid. Such dynamics surrounding the composition and reception of panegyrics are apparent in Jewish praise writing and in characterizations of patron-client relationships. In Chap. 5, I will discuss the nuances between sanctioned and suspect patronage relationships; concern over "disembedded" exchange is apparent.

10. Bernads and Nawas, *Patronate and Patronage in Early and Classical Islam.*

11. Rustow, "Patronage in the Context of Solidarity and Reciprocity," 25. Italics in the original.

12. Classical Jewish sources also reveal some tradition of patronage, at least in the sense of a "division of labor" between full-time scholars and those who provided for their material needs. The dynamic is illustrated richly by a midrash concerning Joseph's brothers Issachar and Zebulun; the former was said to engage in commerce and support the intellectual endeavors of the latter. See Gutwirth, "Models of Patronage in Medieval Spain." Still, the particular dynamics of *walāʾ* seem to define better the relationships under discussion in the present chapter.

13. Most recently published by Gil, *Be-malkhut Yishmaʿel,* 2:29–30 [8].

14. Revel, "Iggeret rav Saʿadia Gaon," 181–88; addendum by Y. N. Epstein, 189–90. Revel thought that this letter was sent to Spain, but this was doubted by Epstein, who linked the two letters as part of the same correspondence. Because the letter *resh* was smudged, Revel thought that this might be *iggeret teshuvah,* "repentance epistle" (Epstein was also unsure), but Abramson agrees with the reading as *teshurah.* Abramson, *Ba-merkazim u-va-tefuṣot bi-tequfat ha-geonim,* 129n39. Abramson believes that *teshurah* here essentially means "addressing" or "turning to" (as though from the root *shwr*; see n. 55 below on this etymology), since he doubts that Saʿadia would "praise his own letter" by calling it a gift. I agree that the usage has to do with initiating a relationship but would stress its relevance for a cycle of "gifting."

15. In Islamic contexts, we also find letters referred to as gifts. An anecdote from *al-ʿiqd al-farīd*: "Nuʿaym Ibn Ḥammād said: 'The king of India sent a letter to ʿUmar Ibn ʿAbd al-ʿAzīz, which contained. . . .' I have sent you a gift. However, it is not a gift but a greeting. . . .By 'gift' he meant the letter." Ibn ʿAbd Rabbih, *Al-ʿiqd al-farīd,* 2:72.

16. Natan's account is published in *Seder ʿolam zuta* in Neubauer, *Medieval Jewish Chronicles,* 2:83–85. There is a full English translation of the investiture ceremony by Stillman, *The Jews of Arab Lands,* 171–75.

17. B. Levin, "Qadish ʿatiq miyemei ha-geonim." The text lavishes blessings and praise upon the exilarch ("May He make great his welfare and the welfare of his generation like the water of the Euphrates. . . . May he be as a tree planted along water, sending forth its shoots by a stream; it does not sense the coming of heat, its leaves are ever fresh; it has no care in a year of drought, it does not cease to yield fruit" (Jer 17:8)). See also Y. Epstein, *Studies in Talmudic Literature and Linguistics*, 938–39; Mann, *The Jews in Egypt and in Palestine*, 1:226 (corresponding text, 2:277–79), where an addressee is told that his "name is given a prominent place in the benedictions on every Sabbath and Festival in the presence of the gaon."

18. Hebrew poets often emphasize the amount of labor that went into composing a poem, as though to remind the reader of the poem's value. Several poems call attention to being composed according to strict meter (by Dunash Ben Labrat, Hai Gaon, and the author of TS 13 J 19.18). In a poem "to one of the great of the East," Halevi instructed his *mamdūḥ*: "Read, my lord, the fallen fruit that I gathered as a shepherd gathers lambs / By the glory of your name, I tamed them; I haltered them after they had been wild." Halevi, *Dīwān*, 1:65–67 [49], lines 41–48.

19. TS 13 J 19.18; published by Mann, *The Jews in Egypt and in Palestine*, 2:86. The verso of the poem introduces the opening words of the poem with *shirati ʿarukha*, which, I assume, had to do with some sort of filing system.

20. Mann, *The Jews in Egypt and in Palestine*, 1:84–86.

21. Gil, *Be-malkhut Yishmaʿel*, 2:100–101 [doc. 30], p. 9, line 4–p. 10, line 2 of Gil's reconstruction, Heb e.44.80–81. My translation (there is a somewhat different translation in Bareket, *Fustat on the Nile*, 196, though "is our first priority" is also there).

22. Assaf, "Qoveṣ shel iggerot rav Shemuel Ben ʿEli," 3:21.

23. Ibid., 1:39.

24. Heb. a.3.28, published by Cowley, "Bodleian Geniza Fragments," also mentioned in Chap. 1, p. 49.

25. Frenkel, *The Compassionate and Benevolent*, 220–21, with ref. to doc. 95, pp. 624–25 (ULC TS 16.6). The panegyric included is highly atypical in structure. See also doc. 77 on pp. 557–61 (TS 13 J 24.14), in which an Alexandrian cantor, part of a circle that included cantors, *parnasim*, and doctors, writes that he copies down and sends the recipient whatever "special word or elegant poem" that he hears.

26. Van Bekkum, *The Secular Poetry of Elʿazar Ben Yaʿaqov ha-Bavli*, 79.

27. Davidson, "Poetic Fragments from the Genizah III," 235–36.

28. Beeri, "ʿEli he-Ḥaver Ben ʿAmram," 298–300, lines 18–20. The poet also asks for compensation in the poem on p. 308, line 22, "Pay attention to my words [. . .] your praise and reward them."

29. This may, as Elizur suggests, refer to wine. Conceivably, it could also refer to filling vessels with money, which is attested in Arabic anecdotes about panegyric exchange, though the suggestion of wine seems more convincing.

30. Elizur, "Shirat ha-ḥol ha-ʿivrit bi-Sefarad," 204, lines 21, 23–24.

31. Further, see Chap. 5 in this vol.

32. Halevi, *Dīwān*, 1:52 [39].

33. Ibid., 1:118 [83].

34. Cf. 1Kgs 19:6, which an angel gives Elijah to sustain him on a journey.

35. Halevi, *Dīwān*, 1:12 [10], lines 10–18. The "gift of Judah" harks back to Mal 3:4, "Then the offerings of Judah and Jerusalem shall be pleasing to the Lord"; the phrase is picked up again in the thirteenth century by Yehudah Ibn Shabbetai, who titled a work *Minḥat Yehudah sone ha-nashim* (The gift of Judah the misogynist).

36. Halevi, *Dīwān*, 1:201–4 [138], line 63.

37. Ibn Ezra, *Shirei ha-ḥol*, 229–31 [225].

38. "Power," lit., "who holds in his hand"; cf. Gn 31:29.

39. Ibn Ezra, *Shirei ha-ḥol*, 302 [1]. The final verses refer to Jacob, Gn 32:39.

40. Ibn Ezra, *Shirei ha-ḥol*, 62–63 [64].

41. Gruendler, *Medieval Arabic Praise Poetry*, chap. 5; quotations, 66, 71.

42. See Pagis, *Shirat ha-ḥol ve-torat ha-shir*, 193–96; also I. Levin, *Me'il tashbeṣ*, 235.

43. Halevi, *Dīwān*, 1:137 [94], lines 72–88.

44. Also earlier, Dunash Ben Labrat wrote a panegyric for Ḥasdai Ibn Shaprut that likely concluded with a dedication.

45. Ha-Nagid, *Dīwān Shemuel ha-Nagid*, 213–14. Similar is the dedication of a poem by the Nagid addressed to "one of the heads of yeshivah in the East": "Take words from your friend, cast in molds of heaven, forged in the plain of Orion," 215–16.

46. Ibn Gabirol, *Shirei ha-ḥol*, 142–43 [71], lines 1, 6–7.

47. Lit., "testimony."

48. TS 12.416 / ENA 1810.1, Goitein and Friedman, *India Book II*, 464–67 [B69a]. The content is also summarized in idem, *India Traders of the Middle Ages*, 523.

49. I first encountered the poem prior to its publication while writing a seminar paper under Mark Cohen. I included a translation of the poem based on the manuscript and Goitein's transcription. Subsequently, the poem was published by Ratzhaby, "Shnei shirim sefardiyyim me-oṣar ha-geniza," 11. The text is also discussed by Goitein, *A Mediterranean Society*, 5:286–87.

50. Schirmann, *Ha-shirah ha-'ivrit*, 1:192. The references to the poem are in lines 7, 10. Ibn Gabirol wrote the poem at the age of sixteen, which likely hints at the young age of the correspondents. Although *talmid* is a title that is sometimes held by older men, it seems likely to me (and to Goitein) that the correspondents were young, in this case.

51. Lit., "dowry"; cf. Gn 30:20.

52. Lit., "child's."

53. Goitein presumes that this was to be read aloud to family members who did not know Hebrew.

54. See also Hasan-Rokem, "Gifts for God, Gifts for Rabbis," 221–44.

55. The Bible has many terms for the word "gift," some of which pertain to exchange among humans, some only to God, and some whose semantic range bleeds over from one category to the other. A *minḥah* is given most often among humans (Gn 25:6, 32:14; Ez 46:16–17; Ps 68:19; Prv 15:27; Eccl 7:7; Est 9:22; 2 Chr 21:3) but sometimes indicates an offering of grain or animal to God (Gn 4:3; Nm 16:15, 18:6–7, 29; 1 Sm 2:29; Jer 14:12; Ex 28:38) or

even an idol (Ez 20:31, 39). This is the most common term for "gift" in the medieval Hebrew corpus, quite possibly under the influence of the Arabic *mnḥ* (see above). A *maset* is generally for humans (usually translated as "portion, gift, contribution, tax," Gn 43:34; Est 2:18; 2 Chr 24:6, 9) and, in one instance, is a contribution specified for God (Ez 20:40). An *eshkar* is mentioned only in connection to humans (Ps 72:10; Ez 27:15). The word *teshurah* occurs only once in the Bible (1 Sm 9:7); although its exact meaning is uncertain, it is clearly some sort of a gift for a man. Menaḥem Ben Saruq defines it as "an offering (*tiqrovet*) for 'seeing the face' of the king or an important man." (Menaḥem derives it from the root *shwr* and relates it to the verse *umigeva'ot ashurenu* "and from the hills I shall *see* him [Jacob]" (Nm 23:9). Menaḥem's opinion is also cited by Rashi; and see n. 14 above). Beyond this, many types of offerings are rendered unto God alone, from the general to the specific, attested in many places in the Bible: *zevaḥ* (sacrifice); *qorban* (offering); *'olah* (burnt offering); *asham* (guilt offering); *ḥaṭṭat* (sin offering); *todah* (thanks offering); *shelamim* (offerings of well-being), *nedavah* (freewill offering). In addition, there is a wide variety of meal offerings and spice offerings that we need not enumerate here.

56. On this circumstance, see Chap. 1, pp. 36–38.

57. Assaf, "Qoveṣ shel iggerot rav Shemuel Ben 'Eli," 2:83. See Lv 6:15, Ex 30:35.

58. E.g., Ibn Gabirol, "[The cloud] sprinkled its drops with a skillful hand like the hand of Aaron at the altar"; see Decter, *Iberian Jewish Literature*, 85; Mosheh Ibn Ezra, "Take [of the beloved] what is rightly yours, the breast and thigh"; see Scheindlin, *Wine, Women, and Death*, 90–91.

59. Rustow, "Patronage in the Context of Solidarity and Reciprocity."

60. Schwartz, *Were the Jews a Mediterranean Society?*, 14–16.

61. Rustow, "Patronage in the Context of Solidarity and Reciprocity," 32.

62. Hubert and Mauss, *Sacrifice*. For a recent treatment of the genesis, politics, and aftereffects of this book, arguing for a basic anti-Christian thrust to the book's argument, see Strenki, *Theology and the First Theory of Sacrifice.*

63. Here he considers not only gifts to gods but also to the dead and to nature and touches on implications for the history of monotheism (generally subscribing to an evolutionist view of religion, whereby "higher" forms of religion develop from but do not eradicate the core elements of more "primitive" forms). The implication, as Strenki suggests, is that the idea of Christ's sacrifice in Christianity did not involve a new or enlightened theology.

64. All passages from *The Gift* are from 14–18. In his discussion of "alms," Mauss also points out that the biblical concept of *ṣedaqa*, "justice," is quite different from the sense of "alms" or "charity" that it later takes on.

65. TS 8 J 39.10r, lines 15–22 (unpublished). It seems most likely that this formulary was utilized within an institutional setting, though it is conceivable that it refers to a more personal relationship (examples below). The recto preserves only this one letter; the verso includes the introductory blessings of three different letters.

66. On conjunctural poverty and the "shame" associated with it, see Mark Cohen, *Poverty and Charity in the Jewish Community of Medieval Egypt*, 36–51.

67. Spell-inducing water. Lit., "bitter water"; cf. Nm 5:24 and elsewhere. Although these waters usually bring a negative effect (e.g., causing the suffering of the adulterous woman), the image is evoked here because of its magical power.

68. TS 10 J 9.4v. The recto preserves a twelfth-century response to an endorsement on a petition (in Arabic script); see Khan, *Arabic Legal and Administrative Documents in the Cambridge Genizah Collections*, 418–19 [107].

69. Perhaps related is a poem by Mosheh Ibn Ezra written when Abū al-Walīd b. Faraj recovered from an illness. After praising the *mamdūḥ*'s kindness and intelligence, Ibn Ezra wrote, "His fat and blood are gifts to God; he sacrificed them willingly, not because of rebellion." That is, the fat and blood lost due to illness constitute a volitional offering rather than a sin offering; in exchange, the poem continues, "God had mercy upon him like a father upon a son and did not recall his sin or rebellion." *Shirei ha-ḥol*, 86–87 [86].

70. The document is mentioned by Goitein, *A Mediterranean Society*, 4:255 (though he does not mention the sacrificial reference).

71. Though not exactly sacrificial, it is still related to Temple ritual.

CHAPTER 3

1. Mann, *The Jews in Egypt and in Palestine*, 1:28, text transcribed in 2:23–24, Gil, *Ereṣ Yisra'el*, 2:24–25 [18]; partial trans. in Bareket, *Fustat on the Nile*, 202–3. See a similar statement in Mann, *The Jews in Egypt and in Palestine*, 1:20.

2. Ben Sasson, "Rashei ha-ṣibbur be-ṣafon Afriqa," 149–51. The argument is based on parallels in "historical sources," by which Ben Sasson means letters.

3. TS 10 J 12.17, lines 12–17; Gil, *Ereṣ Yisra'el*, 2:180–81 [95]; Bareket, *Fustat on the Nile*, 133. See a similar set of skills in Judeo-Arabic in TS 13 J 7.25, lines 19–23 in Gil, *Ereṣ Yisra'el*, 2:592–94 [324].

4. See Goitein, "Evidence on the Muslim Poll Tax from Non-Muslim Sources," 6:278–95.

5. TS 10 J 12.17, lines 17–21; above, n. 3.

6. This figure surfaces numerous times in Rustow, *Heresy and the Politics of Community*, 127–28 and elsewhere (see index).

7. Cf. the poems in Beeri, "'Eli he-Ḥaver," 315, lines 2, 4; Mann, *The Jews in Egypt and in Palestine*, 2:11–13, lines 2–4. There is mention in Geniza documents of a Peraḥiah Ben 'Adaya, but I doubt that there is any connection; for this name, see Rustow, *Heresy and the Politics of Community*, 128n42.

8. This document will be discussed again in Chap. 5, in the context of ethics.

9. "Head of heads," a rendering of the Arabic *ra'īs al-ru'asā*, probably in the sense here of military captain (see below). Also Rustow, *Heresy and the Politics of Community*, 125–28.

10. See also a poem Yehudah al-Ḥarīzī dedicated to a *nasi* and to a non-*nasi* in Chap. 4, pp. 142–43.

11. Ibn Ezra, *Shirei ha-ḥol*, 137–39 [134], line 11; see also 75–76 [74]; 99–101 [99]; 111–12 [110]. See also Fleischer, "On the Beginning of Hebrew Poetry in Spain," 1:25–26. Other panegyrics praise several people separately and focus on a different quality of each, e.g., Ibn Ezra, *Shirei ha-ḥol*, 191 [192]; Halevi, *Dīwān*, 1:178 [119]. The practice of praising several *mamdūḥs* individually within a single poem was far more common among Eastern poets, such as Mosheh Dar'i and El'azar Ben Ya'aqov.

12. Pagis, *Hebrew Poetry of the Middle Ages and the Renaissance*, 45–79.

13. Of course, not all Jewish panegyrics were directed toward political figures as such, and even other social types (poets, Talmudists, doctors) were represented according to fairly stable sets of characteristics. Gaons and poets could both brandish pens like swords, though the former's enemies might be religious dissenters while the latter's might be rival poets; a "head of the Jews" (*ra'īs al-yahūd*) might extend a generous hand toward the poor but a literary patron toward his poets and scribes.

14. See my comments in Introduction, pp. 9–10.

15. I. Levin, *Me'il tashbeṣ*, 80. See also Ratzhaby, *Moṭivim she'ulim be-sifrut Yisra'el*, 459–80 (on kingship and rule).

16. One might compare the dominant images with those presented in Ashkenazi responsa. There one finds, to be sure, images of wisdom as well as associations with kings and priests, but several of the traits, such as eloquence and ascension over enemies, are absent. See the survey by Goldin, "'Companies of Disciples' and 'Companies of Colleagues.'"

17. Ibn Ṭabāṭabā, *I'yār al-sh'ir*, 17.

18. See Introduction, p. 5.

19. See Feldman, "The Rabbinic Lament"; Goldin, "'Companies of Disciples' and 'Companies of Colleagues,'" 134–38.

20. E.g., Ibn Gabirol, *The Improvement of the Moral Qualities*, 63–65; idem, *A Choice of Pearls*, 65 (chap. 31).

21. *Laws of Kings and Their Wars* (2:6, 11). The "nursemaid" is not an uncommon image in Hebrew panegyric. See, e.g., Halevi, *Dīwān*, 157 [102], line 22. Arabic writings sometimes liken the ruler to a "mother" who nurses and weans and is saddened at her infant's pain. See Ibn 'Abd Rabbih, *Al-'iqd al-farīd*, 1:33–35.

22. *Guide of the Perplexed*, 3:45, Pines trans., 580; 3:47, Pines trans., 594.

23. See also Afsaruddin, *Excellence and Precedence*.

24. Ibn 'Abd Rabbih, *Al-'iqd al-farīd*, 1:35–36; see also 2:201.

25. See Melchert, "The Piety of the Hadith Folk," 425–39 (with reference to Hodgson's term); Cooperson, *Classical Arabic Biography*, 107–53.

26. I.e., his speech.

27. Beeri, "Seridei igronim," 76–77 [32]; see also Davidson, "Poetic Fragments from the Genizah III," 232, line 3.

28. Interestingly, humility also receives relatively little play in the *dīwān* of El'azar Ben Ya'aqov ha-Bavli.

29. See pp. 9–10.

30. Van Bekkum, *The Secular Poetry of El'azar Ben Ya'aqov ha-Bavli*, 11 [11], line 10. The text is quoted more fully below.

31. Assaf, "Qoveṣ shel iggerot rav Shemuel Ben 'Eli," 2:71. See also Ben 'Eli's claims of his own humility, 3:19.

32. Ibn Ezra, *Shirei ha-ḥol*, 104–6 [105], line 15. Of course, Ibn Gabirol is famous for representing his own asceticism; see Schirmann, *Toledot . . . muslemit*, 303–6; see also chap. 44, on asceticism, in *A Choice of Pearls*, 98–113.

33. Schimmel, *Mystical Dimensions of Islam*, 114. Still, there is no evidence that the figure in Ibn Ezra's poem held any political function.

34. Al-Ḥarīzī, *Kitāb al-durar*, 210–12.

35. See Brener, *Isaac Ibn Khalfun*, 116–17; see, similarly, Ibn Ezra, *Shirei ha-ḥol*, 170–71 [172], line 24.

36. Ibn Ezra, *Shirei ha-ḥol*, 191 [192], lines 3–4; cf. b. Eruvin 13b.

37. Ibn Ezra, *Shirei ha-ḥol*, 315 [*Sefer ha-'anaq*, 1:71].

38. Similarly, Ibn Khalfūn wrote: "He is humble like the humble one" (*'anav kemo 'anav*); Brener, *Isaac Ibn Khalfun*, 154–55.

39. Bareket, *Fustat on the Nile*, 133.

40. Nemoy, *Karaite Anthology*, 4.

41. Frenkel, *The Compassionate and Benevolent*, 200. See also the invective by Ibn Ezra, *Shirei ha-ḥol*, 221–22 [218], lines 14–15, "You have been prideful! . . . With your deeds you have acted haughtily (*ta'oz*) like a ruler (*moshel*) such that you have become a byword (*mashal*) [of cruelty] in the mouth of every man and woman!" See also Ben Shammai, "The Judaeo-Arabic Vocabulary of Sa'adya's Bible Translation as a Vehicle for Eschatological Messages," 191–225.

42. Ibn Dā'ūd, *Sefer ha-Qabbalah* (Book of tradition), 75–76 (English sec.).

43. S. Stetkevych, *The Poetics of Islamic Legitimacy*, 200.

44. Ibn Gabirol, *The Improvement of the Moral Qualities*, 5:1 (Arabic, 31–32; English, 93–95). On the place of generosity in ethical discourse, see references in Decter, "Concerning the Terminology of al-Harīzī's Virtues Debate," 159–73.

45. Evident in the quotation that serves as the title phrase of Frenkel's book *The Compassionate and Benevolent* (*ha-ohavim ve-ha-nedivim*); see, esp., 186–87.

46. In linking various biblical characters with different virtues, Sa'adia Gaon associates Abraham with beneficence. Sa'adia Ben Yosef, *Perushei rav Sa'adia Gaon li-vereshit*, 10.

47. Feldman, "The Rabbinic Lament," 63.

48. The precise identity of this *mamdūḥ* has been the matter of some speculation. Scheiber simply calls him Avraham ha-Baghdadi. Gil believes that he is Avraham Ben 'Ata of Qairawan: "The Babylonian Yeshivot and the Maghrib in the Early Middle Ages," 112–14. Other poems in honor of this Ben 'Ata likewise highlight generosity and the giving of alms, but these are broadly conventional.

49. Lit., "the poems of Oṣem's brother" (David; cf. 1 Chr 2:15); thus the poet states that his poems are like the Psalms.

50. A. Scheiber, "Two Additional Poems of Praise in Honour of Abraham of Baghdad," 26, lines 29–36.

51. For the ransoming of captives, see Beeri, "'Eli he-Ḥaver Ben 'Amram," 315–16, [11], line 12.

52. Brener, *Isaac Ibn Khalfun*, 164–65; Ibn Khalfūn, *Shirei Yiṣḥaq Ibn Khalfūn* [6], lines 9–12. The poem is also discussed by Brener, 67–70; Ben Sasson, "Rashei ha-ṣibbur," 144–46. See also Avraham Ibn Dā'ūd's presentation of Yehudah the Nasi of Calatrava: "Since he had no regard for silver, nor did he delight in gold, he did not keep for himself any of his share of the King's pay. All of his deeds were patterned after the son of Agrippa, who said: 'Whereas my father stored up his treasures below, I shall store up my treasures above.' Nonetheless, he conducted a huge business." Ibn Dā'ūd, *Sefer ha-Qabbalah*, 98–99 (English sec.).

53. Lit., "his [David's] son."

54. Lit., Yequtiel, a nickname for Moses in b. Megillah 13a.

55. On the blessings for mercantile, agricultural (including vineyard cultivation), and related activities, see lines 25–53, esp. line 53.

56. Fleischer, "Shiro shel rav Hai Gaon," 1325, lines 159–62.

57. Ibid., 1317, lines 1–7.

58. Halevi, *Dīwān*, 193 [132], lines 1–4, 17–20; for the concluding story about Saul, see 1 Kings 9–10.

59. Halevi, *Dīwān*, 1:118 [83], lines 11–14. See also Halevi's panegyric for Shemuel ha-Nagid of Egypt; Halevi, *Dīwān*, 144 [97].

60. See above, pp. 95–96. Also common is the rhyme, *Torah 'im gedulah* (Torah with power).

61. Halevi, *Dīwān*, 65 [49], lines 19–20.

62. Ibid., 123 [87], lines 49–60.

63. Published in Goitein and Friedman, *India Book II*, 464–67 [B69a], lines 6–8.

64. *Yam ma'arav*; lit., "western sea."

65. Van Bekkum, *The Secular Poetry of El'azar Ben Ya'aqov ha-Bavli*, 19 [17], lines 10–14, 17. See Van Bekkum's notes for biblical references. Lines 15–16 are tattered but clearly make reference to his "gifts" and his being so great that other ministers of the age seem like strangers.

66. On signet rings in Islamic government, see Chap. 1, p. 37. For the Pamplona casket, see Dodds, *Al-Andalus*, 198–99 (catalog sec., text by Renata Holod). For Halevi, see *Dīwān*, 178 [119], line 16. Also, a letter by Shemuel Ben 'Eli (c. 1190) regarding the appointment of Ben Barkhael references a signet ring: "He also possesses a signet ring to sign documents, rulings and epistles that are appropriate for him to sign." Assaf, "Qoveṣ shel iggerot rav Shemuel Ben 'Eli," 2:61.

67. Trans. Arberry, *Poems of al-Mutanabbī*, 132, lines 28–31.

68. See also Brann, *The Compunctious Poet*, 23–58, esp. 26–27.

69. Ibn Ezra, *Shirei ha-ḥol*, 29–30, line 23. Whether Ibn Ezra refers here to eloquence in Hebrew or Arabic is unclear; it stands to reason that the latter is intended.

70. Brener, *Isaac Ibn Khalfun*, 164–65, lines 16–17.

71. Both *majlis* and *moshav* are derived from roots that mean "to sit."

72. Schirmann, *Ha-shirah ha-'ivrit*, 1:8–10, lines 5–6, 19–22. The wordplay of the first line is extraordinary: *ilu khol meḥoqeq ḥiqeqei ḥeiqo yeḥoqeq*. "Eloquence," *ṣiḥṣuḥam*, lit., "their dazzling," but the root is linked with the Arabic *faṣāḥa* (see above). "Degree of his greatness," lit., "strength of his superiority."

73. In another panegyric, also possibly for Ibn Shaprut, Ben Saruq expounds upon eloquence and again sets the *mamdūḥ* within a *majlis*: "When he speaks lofty words and speaks eloquently, his listeners are astounded and together are greatly surprised. . . .He is established in a gathering (*moshav*) of youths who understand conversation just as apertures are set upon jacinth." Fleischer, "On the Beginning of Hebrew Poetry in Spain," 31. See also Beeri, "'Eli he-Ḥaver Ben 'Amram," 310–12 [9], line 9, a panegyric for Elḥanan Ben Shemariahu: "He is good in session (*yeshivah*) and comely in a gathering (*mesibah*)."

74. Schirmann, *Ha-shirah ha-'ivrit*, 1:35–40 [5], lines 47–50, 64. Speech is also a theme of Ben Labrat's panegyric for Shemariah Ben Elḥanan of Fustat; see Mann, *The Jews in Egypt and in Palestine*, 2:21–22, lines 10–11; Dunash Ben Labrat, *Shirim*, 88.

75. *Niḥaru*; lit., "are parched."

76. Cf. Jer 31:12.

77. Perhaps this alludes to a throne with gazelles at its base, though I do not know of a corresponding image (lions, on the other hand, are quite common). Perhaps there is some reference to gazelles in relief work, or perhaps the allusion is to beloveds or simply youths acting obsequiously.

78. Oracle; lit., *urim* (cf. Ex 28:30 and elsewhere). The panegyric is published in Robles and Sáenz-Badillos, *Tĕšubot de los discípulos de Mĕnaḥem contra Dunaš Ben Labraṭ*, 1–4, lines 33–37. This is the introductory panegyric to their response to Dunash's critique of Menaḥem; interestingly, and perhaps ironically, they adopt the system of quantitative meter that Dunash introduced and that Menaḥem rejected.

79. Ibn Gabirol, *Shirei ha-ḥol*, 27–29 [13], lines 7–8, 10–11.

80. See Brody's notes on the midrashic references to the biblical Jacob (i.e., the *mamdūḥ*'s namesake).

81. As Pharaoh did when elevating Joseph's rank (along with giving him his signet ring). Cf. Gn 41:42.

82. Cf. Ex 28:29–30; these are especially linked with judgment.

83. Halevi, *Dīwān*, 1:4–5 [5], lines 9–16.

84. See also I. Levin, *Me'il tashbeṣ*, 119.

85. "Guile and deceit," probably in the sense that poetic writing is based upon falsehoods, not that the Nagid literally used the pen to trick people.

86. Schirmann, *Ha-shirah ha-'ivrit*, 1:172–75, lines 29–33.

87. One of King David's warriors in 2 Sm 23:8; the root of the word means "wise."

88. Halevi, *Dīwān*, 123 [87], lines 29–35, 61–66. The last line is based on Est 8:8. See also *Dīwān*, 178 [119], lines 16–17.

89. Wise men in 1 Kgs 5:11.

90. "Redeemed . . . Pit"; cf. Jb 33:24. Schechter, *Saadyana*, 58, lines 10–11.

91. There is some debate in the literature over the meaning of the term *gevirah* here. It can mean "female ruler," perhaps the wife or mother of the caliph, or (male) "regent." I have chosen "queen" because of the analogous parallelism of king: ministers; queen: eunuchs. Eunuchs had a particular role at court, most importantly as attendants for women. On royal Fatimid women being addressed as *malika*, see Cortese and Calderini, *Women and the Fatimids in the World of Islam*, 109. On eunuchs in Islamic contexts, see the entry "Khāṣī" in *Encyclopaedia of Islam*.

92. The bracketed text is difficult both to read and interpret but perhaps evokes the ruin visited upon the Egyptians at the time of the ten plagues.

93. Casluhim, Gn 10:4, one of the sons of Miṣrayim. Nephtohim, one of the groups in Palestine; cf. Jo 15:9. The author thus refers to inhabitants of Egypt and Palestine seen by the Israelite spies.

94. Halper 401r, lines 14–19. Gil, *History of Palestine*, 585–86. Gil associates the *mamdūḥ* with a certain "David the Jew" who is mentioned in a chronology as an employee in the bureau of tax revenues; for bibliography and discussion, see Rustow, *Heresy and the Politics of Community*, 178. Rustow, 180, also partially translates the text and notes how the poet "paints him in his *majlis* . . . with a team of *kuttāb*."

95. Assaf, "Qoveṣ shel iggerot rav Shemuel Ben 'Eli," 2:71.

96. Ibid., 2:74, lines 6–12.

97. Ibid., 2:78.

98. Van Bekkum, *The Secular Poetry of El'azar Ben Ya'aqov ha-Bavli*, 55–56 [39], line 19; 5 [4], line 14.

99. 2 Kgs 17:6; Ez 30:15; i.e., from Iraq to Egypt.

100. *Gemara* and *savra*.

101. I follow Van Bekkum's emendation of *maḥma'ot* in the note. However, I read *ḥalqu* instead of *ḥelqo*.

102. *Qeset*, occurring only in Ez 9:2–3, 11, Ibn Janāḥ translates *dawā*, which probably is a writer's case, usually containing ink and writing instruments, that can be bound to a belt, though the word can also denote the inkhorn only (see Lane, *Arabic-English Lexicon*, 940). Ibn Janāḥ notes that others understand it to be the writing tablet.

103. Van Bekkum, *The Secular Poetry of El'azar Ben Ya'aqov ha-Bavli*, 7–9 [9], lines 18–25.

104. Ibn Gabirol used it as a boast; Ibn Gabirol, *Shirei ha-ḥol*, ed. Jarden, 230 [111], line 28. For a concise history of the expression, see the wonderful note by Brody in Halevi, *Dīwān*, 1:89 (nn. to lines 51–54).

105. Ibn Gabirol, *A Choice of Pearls*, 2. On the other hand, in the same book, "Kings are the judges of the world but the wise are judges of kings," 6.

106. Mann, *The Jews in Egypt and in Palestine*, 2:21–23; Ben Labrat, *Shirim*, 89–92. Their readings differ in some places.

107. The poetic device of including the modifying adjective but omitting the modified noun is called *al-tatbī'* (following). See Decter, "Panegyric as Pedagogy."

108. *Ḥakhmei ha-gediyyim*; lit., "wise men of the goat kids," which is probably a reference to the Ibn Qapron (*cabrón*, goat) family. Ibn Qapron was a student of Dunash's rival Menaḥem Ben Saruq. Allony, however, following Abramson, here reads *ḥakhmei hagriyyim*, "Muslim wise men," which seems less likely but also fits the meter.

109. Allony vocalizes differently, meaning "people imitate him with them." The continuation of the same poem is translated above in the discussion of speech.

110. Schirmann, *Shirim ḥadashim*, 25. "Two academies," Sura and Pumbedita; "ninety-eight faces," as Schirmann explains. Cf. Song of Songs Rabbah, 2:4: the interpreted Torah has forty-nine pure senses (lit., "faces") and forty-nine impure ones. The poet is Nisī al-Nahrawānī, who died in the early tenth century.

111. Following Mann. See also the references to asceticism above.

112. Four tractates of the Talmud, nine blessings; see notes by Mann.

113. On TS 16.68r, see Gil, *Ereṣ Yisra'el*, 2:24–25 [18]; partial translation in Bareket, *Fustat on the Nile*, 202–3. Also transcribed in Mann, *The Jews in Egypt and in Palestine*, 2:23–24 and discussed there in 1:27–28.

114. Ibn Gabirol, *Shirei ha-ḥol*, 15–17 [4], lines 14–15. It is common in Arabic to refer to rare bits of knowledge as "scattered" and to praise men for "gathering the scattered."

115. I.e., an unrepentant generation would not merit so great a gift as the *mamdūḥ*.

116. "Alone." The manuscript has a lacuna here. In the Brody and Schirmann edition, the editors supply the word "alone" (*levad*), a logical contrast with "thousands of tens of thousands," but then use this to question whether the poem was dedicated to Shemuel ha-Nagid, since he was not an only child. Jarden leaves the lacuna and includes the superscription that the poem was written for Shemuel ha-Nagid specifically. If *levad* is the correct word, its sense might simply be "unique."

117. Cf. Is 27:6, i.e., knowledge.

118. Ibn Gabirol, *Shirei ha-ḥol*, ed. Jarden, 19–20 [8], lines 1–7 = Brody and Schirmann, 7 [4]. "Students," lit., "sons."

119. Beeri, "'Eli he-Ḥaver Ben 'Amram," 293–94 [2], lines 11–18.

120. *Ṣofnat pa'aneaḥ*; cf. Gn 41:45, trans. according to the rabbinic interpretation.

121. Palate; lit., "jaws."

122. Halevi, *Dīwān*, 96–98 [95], lines 19–20, 25.

123. Wise men whom Solomon surpasses in 1 Kgs 5:11.

124. Halevi, *Dīwān*, 191–92 [130].

125. Van Bekkum, *The Secular Poetry of El'azar Ben Ya'aqov ha-Bavli*, 24–25 [21], lines 5–6.

126. The donkey image had already been used in a similar way by Baḥya Ibn Paquda, *Torat ḥovot ha-levavot*, 148. The poet uses qur'ānic language elsewhere as in a bilingual poem, "Because of your paths which are straight when the success and victory of God come" (*idh jā' fatḥ allah wa'l-naṣr*); cf. Qur'ān 110:1. See Van Bekkum, *The Secular Poetry of El'azar Ben Ya'aqov ha-Bavli*, 111 [138], line 1.

127. Lit., "the difference between plene and defective spellings."

128. Van Bekkum, *The Secular Poetry of El'azar Ben Ya'aqov ha-Bavli*, 19–20 [17].

129. E.g., above, Ibn Khalfūn for Yehudah Rosh ha-Seder.

130. *Al-'iqd al-farīd*, 57–63. Ibn Gabirol's *Choice of Pearls* has a short chap. on keeping secrets, 63 (chap. 29) and also one on the need to ask for advice (but not on giving it), p. 53 (chap. 21).

131. See Chap. 1, pp. 43–48.

132. Van Bekkum, *The Secular Poetry of El'azar Ben Ya'aqov ha-Bavli*, 158–59 [181]. Nearly the same appellations are found, both in Judeo-Arabic and in Hebrew, in a letter by Shemuel Ben 'Eli (*amīn al-mulk ne'eman ha-melukha*). Assaf, "Qoveṣ shel iggerot rav Shemuel Ben 'Eli," 3:51.

133. A related term *'eṣah* (advice, counsel) is similarly esteemed and harks back to social values already in the Bible; even God is presented as one who possesses and offers counsel (Ps 16:7, Jb 12:13). See, e.g., praise for Avraham ha-Baghdadi for giving advice to kings; A. Scheiber, "Panegyrics in Honor of a Baghdad Dignitary," 112 [1], line 25). *'Eṣah* is also used in medieval Hebrew to mean "intelligence."

134. TS Misc 36.203.2; Mann, *Texts and Studies*, 1:107–8.

135. Ibn Ezra, *Shirei ha-ḥol*, 180–81 [181], line 11. On drawing water, see Is 30:14.

136. Ibn Ezra, *Shirei ha-ḥol*, 62–63 [64], line 22. Also, Ibn Ezra wrote about himself, "he brought his friend's secret to the chamber of his heart and bolted the doors of his tongue," 68–70 [69], line 15.

137. Halevi, *Dīwān*, 135 [93], line 20; see also 69–70 [52], line 29.

138. Ibid., 122 [86], lines 18–22. The phrase "The Torah speaks in the language of men," deriving from b. Berakhot 31b, was quite famous in the medieval period, largely in connection with explicating the allegorical form of the Bible (particularly, but not exclusively, in the thought of Maimonides). See, e.g., Klein-Braslavy, "Bible Commentary," esp. 249. I believe that the use of the expression here to refer to Arabic (i.e., the vernacular) is unique.

139. Halevi, *Dīwān*, 1:76 [57], lines 5–7. "Made him their confidant," lit., "brought him into their intimate circle (*hevi'uhu be-sodam*)"; "angels," lit., "shining ones."

140. Within Christian representations of Christ, the shepherd is also dominant (though it partly gives way to a more imperial image).

141. Ibn 'Abd Rabbih, *Al-'iqd al-farīd*, 1:33–35.

142. See also Chap. 7, n. 7.

143. Ibn Ezra, *Shirei ha-ḥol*, 272–73 [257], lines 1–2. "How comely . . ."; cf. Is 52:7.

144. Halevi, *Dīwān*, 110–11 [76], lines 4, 10. Also for the same figure *Dīwān*, 144 [97], 5–8. For Ben Bassah, *Dīwān*, 34–36 [25], lines 28, 35–36; cf. Gn 17:4–5. See also *Dīwān*, 87–88 [62], lines 17–18; 171 [113], lines 8–10. Other examples of shepherd imagery include Ibn Ezra, *Shirei ha-ḥol*, 11 [9], line 30; 182–85 [183], line 34 (of a *wazīr*); El'azar Bar Ya'aqov, in Van Bekkum, *The Secular Poetry of El'azar Ben Ya'aqov ha-Bavli*, 7 [9], line 26; and many others.

145. See n. 2 above, concerning Menaḥem Ben Sasson on Yehudah Rosh ha-Seder.

146. See S. Stetkevych, *The Poetics of Islamic Legitimacy*, 270. On enemies more generally, see 89, 174, 251. For more ancient Near Eastern sources (including incantations to

utter against one's enemies), see, e.g., Collins, "The First Soldier's Oath," 164–67. I wish to thank David Wright for this reference.

147. Mark Cohen, "On the Interplay of Arabic and Hebrew," 28.

148. S. Scheiber, "Two Additional Poems of Praise in Honour of Abraham of Baghdad," 123–27; Schechter, *Saadyana*, 63–74.

149. Giving to poor, etc.: Schechter, *Saadyana*, 66, lines 4–5; 70, lines 25–28; 72, line 10; 73, lines 14–25. Giving to/founding the academy: Schechter, *Saadyana*, 66, lines 8–9; 68, lines 2–4; 71, lines 17–18; 72, lines 2–3, 6–7. Some of the poems include praise for Avraham's generosity, both for general charitable acts (feeding the hungry, clothing the poor, aiding the orphan) and for giving money to the academy specifically.

150. Schechter, *Saadyana*, 72, lines 7–8; S. Scheiber, "Two Additional Poems," 124, line 4; 125, line 18.

151. Schechter, *Saadyana*, 68, line 22; 70, line 11; see also S. Scheiber, "Two Additional Poems," 124, line 15; Schechter, *Saadyana*, 70, line 12.

152. Schechter, *Saadyana* 72, lines 8–9.

153. Halevi, *Dīwān*, 81 [59], lines 6–7, 11–15; see also *Dīwān*, 76 [57], lines 7–8.

154. See also, for Aharon Ibn al-ʿAmāni: Halevi, *Dīwān*, 93 [67], lines 8–9, 21–22.

155. See p. 105. For "Togarmim" and "Sons of Qedar," see Beeri, "ʿEli he-Ḥaver Ben ʿAmram," 309 [8], line 23; 316 [11], line 18. See below also on the enemies of Menasheh Ibn al-Qazzāz. On the phenomenon of coding Muslim foes in Hebrew poetry in al-Andalus, see also Brann, *Power in the Portrayal*, 119–39.

156. See, e.g., J. Safran, "The Command of the Faithful in al-Andalus."

157. Beeri, "Seridei igronim," 170 [15].

158. See Ibn Dāʾūd, *Sefer ha-Qabbalah*, 97.

159. Ibn Ezra, *Shirei ha-ḥol*, 272–73 [257]. Ittiel probably refers to Solomon. "A thousand fall"; cf. Ps 91:7. On the poem's authorship, see above in Chap. 1, n. 116. See also Ibn Ezra, *Shirei ha-ḥol*, 29 [24].

160. Ibn Ezra, *Shirei ha-ḥol*, 141 [95]. The poem has also been attributed to Levi Ibn al-Tabban.

161. Ibn Ezra, *Shirei ha-ḥol*, 87 [62], lines 15–16.

162. Van Bekkum, *The Secular Poetry of Elʿazar Ben Yaʿaqov ha-Bavli*, 3–4 [3], lines 19, 31. (There seems to be some confusion because the superscription has the *mamdūḥ* as Yosef Ben al-Barqūlī, but the poem, line 2, clearly names "Shemuel" as the *mamdūḥ*). Also, to the elder (*sheikh*) [Mishael] Abū Riḍā Ben al-Ghaḍāʾirī and his two sons Ezekiel and Ezra: "For how long will the disputers [attack] the lord upon whom the wine of love flows? How can you believe his enemies when they spoke falsehood against me?" We do not know who these enemies were, exactly; but apparently, they had spread calumny against the poet as well. Van Bekkum, *The Secular Poetry of Elʿazar Ben Yaʿaqov ha-Bavli*, 5–6 [4].

163. Van Bekkum, *The Secular Poetry of Elʿazar Ben Yaʿaqov ha-Bavli*, 24–25 [21], line 13.

164. Beeri, "Seridei igronim," 76–77 [32].

165. Ibid., 306–7 [7], line 11.

166. Halevi, *Dīwān*, 1:110 [76], lines 14–15.

167. Mann, *Texts and Studies*, 1:130, line 8.

168. Van Bekkum, *The Secular Poetry of El'azar Ben Ya'aqov ha-Bavli*, 3–4 [3], lines 24, 28. See, similarly, Hai Gaon for Yehudah Rosh ha-Seder, "Kings walk by the light of his face." Fleischer, "Shiro shel rav Hai Gaon," 1325, line 158,

169. Halevi, *Dīwān*, 1:34 [25], line 31.

170. Ibid., 1:27 [20], lines 17–18.

171. See pp. 105–6.

172. Is 56:10.

173. Robles and Sáenz-Badillos, *Tĕšuḇot de los discípulos de Mĕnaḥem contra Dunaš Ben Labraṭ*, 1–4, lines 26–31 (Hebrew sec.).

174. TS 32.4, lines 19–20; trans. Rustow, *Heresy and the Politics of Community*, 128.

175. Schirmann, "Samuel Hanaggid."

176. Lit., "opened," probably absorbing some of the sense of the Arabic *ftḥ*, which means both "opened" and "conquered."

177. Is 56:10.

178. Robles and Sáenz-Badillos, *Tĕšuḇot de los discípulos de Mĕnaḥem contra Dunaš Ben Labraṭ*, 1–4, lines 26–31 (Hebrew sec.).

179. Is 66:8, a song of redemption.

180. Schirmann, *Ha-shirah ha-'ivrit*, 1:6–8, lines 1–16.

181. Epistolographic aspects of the poem are discussed in Chap. 1, pp. 61–62.

182. See Introduction, n. 51.

183. Fleischer sees the phrase as a construct of two synonymous terms meaning "crown"; in any case, what is essential here is the priestly association. See Fleischer, "On the Beginning of Hebrew Poetry in Spain," 12.

184. Schechter, *Saadyana*, 72, line 22. There are actually three biblical references to the name Merayot. In addition to the priest in Neh 12:15, there is also a "chief officer of the House of God" (Neh 11:11, 1 Chr 9:11), and a Levite (Ezr 7:3, 1 Chr 5:32).

185. Halevi, *Dīwān*, 1:173 [114], lines 13, 15. Here Moses might be associated more with prophethood than the Levitic office.

186. E.g., S. Cohen, *The Three Crowns*; Goodblatt, *The Monarchic Principle*.

187. See also m. Avot 6:5.

188. Assaf, "Qoveṣ shel iggerot rav Shemuel Ben 'Eli," 2:51.

189. *Manṣib*, the place where something is planted, set up, or erected. It also means office, dignity, rank, position.

190. Assaf, "Qoveṣ shel iggerot rav Shemuel Ben 'Eli," 2:64–66.

191. See Goitein, *Studies in Islamic History and Institutions*, 205–7.

192. Gil, *A History of Palestine*, 595n81, believes that it is in the handwriting of Sahlān Ben Avraham. Mentioned also in Franklin, *This Noble House*, appendix B, 7. More of the poem is trans. in Chap. 4 of this vol.

193. Alfonso, "The Body, Its Organs, and Senses," 7–8.

194. Ibid., 2; Lakoff and Johnson, *Metaphors We Live By*. See also Dirven, *Metaphor and Metonymy in Comparison and Contrast*.

195. The concept is illustrated well by different operative metaphors for thinking about life. "Life is a journey," it is often said; it has stations, forks in the road, can be straight or winding, begins in one place and heads toward another. Alternatively, another prevalent metaphor for life is the "carnival"; it is celebratory, dramatic, and subject to reversals but is not teleologically oriented. Of course, life is neither a journey nor a carnival. They are both cognitive metaphors, and, it turns out, the adopted metaphor has a great deal to do with how one actually thinks about and even lives life.

196. See Feldman, "The Rabbinic Lament," 53. See also y. Berakhot 9:4, 32b.

197. Schechter, *Saadyana*, 70–71.

198. Ibn Ezra, *Shirei ha-ḥol*, 229–31 [225], lines 8–9.

199. Van Bekkum, *The Secular Poetry of El'azar Ben Ya'aqov ha-Bavli*, 52–54 [38], lines 1–2.

200. Some examples: Cherub—Mosheh Ibn Ezra: 117–20 [117], line 56; 229–31 [225], line 8. Yehudah Halevi: 120 [84], lines 1, 5–6; 173 [114], line 14; 182 [123], line 14; 186 [126], line 16. El'azar Ben Ya'aqov: 10 [10], line 2; 11 [11], line 4; 52–54 [38], lines 1–2. Sanctuary—Mosheh Ibn Ezra: 229–31 [225], line 8. Halevi: 195 [133], line 14. Ark, Tablets—Mosheh Ibn Ezra: 93–95 [93], line 32; 208–12 [207], lines 62–63. Halevi, 38 [28], lines 1–2; 173 [114], line 14; 184 [124], line 14; 191 [130], line 15. El'azar Bar Ya'aqov: 11 [11], line 4; 33–34 [27], line 9.

201. Ibn Gabirol, *Shirei ha-ḥol*, ed. Jarden, 19–20 [8], line 2.

202. Brener, *Isaac Ibn Khalfun*, 110 (my trans.). See also Halevi, *Dīwān*, 144 [97], line 15.

203. Assaf, "Qoveṣ shel iggerot rav Shemuel Ben 'Eli," 2:71; see also 3:30, 3:69.

204. Lit., *tashahhadu* ("they bore witness," but referring to the first part of the *shahāda*, "There is no God but God") and *kabbaru* (magnified, i.e., said *Allahu akbar*, "God is Great"). On the political use of the *shahāda* in a Judeo-Arabic historical source, see also Franklin, *This Noble House*, xi–xiii.

205. Van Bekkum, *The Secular Poetry of El'azar Ben Ya'aqov ha-Bavli*, 112 [139], lines 5–6. Messiah, *al-masīḥ*, which is interesting, since in Arabic the term usually refers to Jesus.

206. On beauty in medieval Hebrew love poetry, see Scheindlin, *Wine, Women, and Death*, 93–94.

207. See p. 5.

208. Turner, *Dramas, Fields, and Metaphors*, 44; Butler, "Performative Acts and Gender Constitution," 526.

CHAPTER 4

1. Rustow, "The Genizah and Jewish Communal History." Rustow's model seeks to go beyond geonic or Mediterranean models to integrate mercantile, religious, and political authority and the multiple allegiances that they involve.

2. Ibn Dā'ūd, *Sefer ha-Qabbalah*, 66 (English sec.).

3. See, e.g., Ashtor, *The Jews of Moslem Spain*, 1:230–41.

4. See Elizur, "Shirat ha-ḥol ha-ʿivrit bi-Sefarad," 204.

5. Mann, *The Jews in Egypt and in Palestine*, 1:27.

6. For Sahlān, see Jarden, *Dīwān Shemuel ha-Nagid*, 200 [62]; 139 [40]; 231–36 [85]. Also within the western Mediterranean, the Nagid sent a letter of condolence and a lament (both in Aramaic) to Ḥananel Ben Ḥushiel upon the death of his father in Qairawan, 256–60 [107].

7. Ibn Gabirol, *Shirei ha-ḥol*, ed. Jarden, 76–78 [42].

8. *Shirei ha-ḥol*, 92–94 [93], lines 19–20. It is conceivable that by *admat Edom*, the poet intends the Levant, i.e., where the biblical Esau actually settled, rather than the territory of the Christian Roman Empire that was ultimately associated with Edom.

9. See also my discussion of imagined geography in Decter, *Iberian Jewish Literature*, 188–206; Goldberg, *Trade and Institutions in the Medieval Mediterranean*.

10. Fleischer, "Shiro shel rav Hai Gaon," 3:1323, lines 128–33. Fleischer also believes that Hai adjusted his poem to the addressee's tastes. However, Fleischer goes so far as to suggest that Hai may not have introduced his letter with a panegyric at all had it not been for Yehudah's "Sefardi" predilections. The gaon also wrote other panegyrics; see Ḥ. Brody. "Piyyutim ve-shirei tehillah me-rav Hayya Ga'on." One is dedicated to an exilarch, 57 [13] (though Brody is uncertain about the attribution to the gaon). Also, there is at least one early Eastern panegyric for Avraham ha-Baghdadi that includes an elaborate description of the *mamdūḥ*'s palace, so the theme is not strictly Western. See S. Scheiber, "Panegyrics in Honour of a Baghdad Dignitary," 112–14 [2].

11. I offer a more extensive treatment of Halevi in Decter, "Mediterranean Regionalism and the Hebrew Panegyric Tradition."

12. Halevi, *Dīwān*, 186–87 [126].

13. See Scheindlin, *The Song of the Distant Dove*, 226–29.

14. Halevi, *Dīwān*, 176–77 [118].

15. Is 57:14.

16. Is 58:12.

17. Lit., "is spat from his form."

18. Lit., "nest."

19. I.e., be willing to accept this office.

20. *Avrekh*; cf. Gn 41:43. Commentators differ significantly on this word. My translation follows Avraham Ibn Ezra. Ibn Janāḥ takes it as an imperative of the same root, "Kneel!" Saʿadia Gaon translates it as the sobriquet by which people refer to Joseph, *al-ẓarīf*, "The Elegant."

21. Cf. Jb 40:10.

22. This is the translation of Benabu, "Rivers of Oil Inundated the Valley of Stones," 25. Cf. S. M. Stern, *Hispano-Arabic Strophic Poetry*, 138; Sola-Solé, *Corpus de Poesía Mozárabe*, 243.

23. López-Morillas, "Language," 45–50.

24. See my discussion in Chap. 1 for rituals of investiture and examples by other authors, pp. 36–37.

25. See also the discussion of a panegyric for Daniel Ben ʻAzaria in Chap. 1, pp. 35–36. The specific formulation "*nasi* of God," which appears also in the poem below for Shemuel Ben Ḥananiah of Egypt, appears in the Bible with respect to Abraham (Gn 22:6); still, it seems redolent here with the Islamic formulation *khalīfat allah*, "caliph of God." On the controversial meaning of the latter, see Crone and Hinds, *God's Caliph*, and critiques thereof.

26. Franklin, *This Noble House*.

27. Franklin also points out that for Ibn Dā'ūd, "*nasi* signified above all else someone who was entrusted with communal authority." See ibid., 45–47. See also further below.

28. Ibid., 226n69; see also his comments on 45 concerning Ibn Jau.

29. See Schirmann, *Toledot . . . muslemit*, 274–75, nn. 105, 106, and 109.

30. "The Christian general, the Muslim leader (*nesi ʻarav*), and the Greek sage are all silenced from speaking before him." *Shirei ha-ḥol*, 195–98 [195], line 33.

31. Fleischer believes that *wazīr* was a title bestowed upon those who already held the title *nasi* among Jews. See his comment in Schirmann, *Toledot . . . Ṣarfat*, 287–88n38. It seems more likely that the case was the opposite: that *nasi* was a title bestowed upon a *wazīr*.

32. See his commentary to Zec 12:7; also Franklin, *This Noble House*, 52.

33. Franklin, *This Noble House*, 53–55.

34. Ibn Dā'ūd, *Sefer ha-Qabbalah*, 45 (Hebrew sec.); *ve-aḥarav lo nishar be-ereṣ Sefarad adam mefursam shehu mi-beit David*. Ibn Dā'ūd does not describe him as a *nasi*, which suggests that his usage of *nasi* elsewhere may have been in the broader sense. However, Ibn Dā'ūd also describes Yehudah the *nasi*, who was appointed ruler of Calatrava under Alfonso VI, and some of his relatives as "of royal seed from the nobility" (cf., Dn 1:3, where the "royal seed" is Davidic); English, 98; Hebrew, 71.

35. Ibn Ezra, *Shirei ha-ḥol*, 62 [64]; 113–14 [112]; 182–85 [183]. Halevi, *Dīwān*, 65–67 [49], lines 52–53. See my extended treatment in Decter, "Mediterranean Regionalism."

36. E.g., Halevi calls Abū Saʻīd Ḥalfon Halevi of Damietta 23 [17], *nasi levi*, a "Levite *nasi*"; perhaps he simply meant a Levite leader or perhaps one who claimed descent from David and also belonged to a Levite family.

37. Halevi, *Dīwān*, 127 [88], lines 38–40.

38. TS 10 J 22.3v. Partly trans. in Chap. 3. Gil, *A History of Palestine*, 595n81, believes that it is written in the handwriting of Sahlān Ben Avraham. Mentioned also in Franklin, *This Noble House*, appendix B, 7. Goitein left a transcription, which is available through the Princeton Geniza Project; line 1 should read *al-ra'īs al-jalīl* (not *al-ḥalīl*).

39. Halevi, *Dīwān*, 173 [114].

40. This is apparent simply by perusing names in Gerson Cohen's index to Ibn Dā'ūd, *Sefer ha-Qabbalah*.

41. On this figure, see Baer, *A History of the Jews in Christian Spain*, 1:50–51; the present poem is mentioned on 1:68–69, and Schirmann, *Toledot . . . muslemit*, 437.

42. *Naḥal*, "river"; but this can be in the sense of a dry riverbed, i.e., a wadi.

43. Like Moses; cf. Nm 20:11.

44. The Hispano-Romance *kharja* integrates the Arabic word *bishāra* (tidings) and the Arabic city name. Like other *kharjas*, it has been the subject of significant philological research. This is the version in Benabu and Yahalom, "The Importance of the Genizah Manuscripts for the Hispano-Romance *Kharjas*," 153.

45. On the association of the addressee of panegyric with sacrality, see Chap. 3, pp. 123–25. On referring to "cultured" men of al-Andalus as "myrtles," see Decter, *Iberian Jewish Literature*, 37.

46. Mann believes that he is identifiable with the Jewish court physician Abū Manṣūr, who served the caliph al-Ḥāfiẓ. See *The Jews in Egypt and in Palestine*, 1:229–30.

47. Halevi, *Dīwān*, 76–77 [57].

48. References to Zec 4:7; Sg 1:16; Is 17:11.

49. Cf. 2 Sm 22:36, of David.

50. Lit., "set, established."

51. Est 10:3, of Mordechai.

52. Again, 2 Sm 23:3, of David (David's final words).

53. Cf. 2 Sm 22:2.

54. Cf. 1 Kgs 2:15.

55. I.e., they prospered; cf. Gn 26:12.

56. *Ma'amirim*; cf. Dt 26:17–18. As Brody points out, Sa'adia Gaon reads the word as though derived from the Arabic *amīr*, prince.

57. Cf. Is 9:5.

58. Halevi, *Dīwān*, 76–77 [57]. "To measure out his boundary," i.e., to measure his greatness. "Majestic Full of Light," i.e., God.

59. Ex 2:14, of Moses.

60. Cf. 1 Sm 1:20; "[Hannah] named him Samuel, meaning, 'I asked the Lord for him.'"

61. Similar are the verses of Shelomoh Ibn Gabirol, *Shirei ha-ḥol*, 14, lines 52–55.

62. According to Mark Cohen, the earliest reference to Ben Ḥananiah as Nagid is from 1140, hence just before Halevi's departure from al-Andalus; *Jewish Self-Government in Medieval Egypt*, 35.

63. The words are Adonijah's. However, I do not think that the verse is meant to elicit Adonijah specifically, since he was the "illegitimate" contender with Solomon for the throne after David.

64. Halevi, *Dīwān*, 110 [76], lines 6, 8 ("For whom does majesty await? Only for one who inherits greatness and passes it on as an inheritance . . . from generation to generation their crown will stand"; see also 111 [77], line 7.

65. However, the phrase also appears in connection with the inheritance of authority among those lacking ties with archetypal figures such as David, e.g., Aharon Ibn al-'Amani. See Halevi, *Dīwān*, 93 [67], line 14, and Brody's comment, p. 159 of the notes. It occurs most often in connection with figures in the East, though Mosheh Ibn Ezra uses it in a poem of comfort for Abū 'Umar Ibn Qamniel; *Shirei ha-ḥol*, 37 [39], lines 21–22.

66. Lit., "came," possibly referring to David arising as king in the days of the biblical Samuel. However, I agree with Brody here, who interprets: "Samuel has already come and soon David [the Messiah son of David] will come after him."

67. Halevi, *Dīwān*, 144 [97], lines 91–92. See also *Dīwān*, 110–11 [76], lines 14–17; Franklin also sees a messianic overtone in one of Halevi's letters to Ben Ḥananiah; *This Noble House*, 133.

68. Some other examples of messianic conclusions in panegyrics for figures in the Islamic East: Mann, *The Jews in Egypt and in Palestine*, 2:21–23; Beeri, "'Eli he-Ḥaver Ben 'Amram," [11]; TS 8 J 1.3, lines 1–5, pub. in Schechter, *Saadyana*, 71; TS 10 J 22.3v (above). An early example is Davidson, "Poetic Fragments from the Genizah III," 231, line 6. Also, one might compare the conclusions to Dunash Ben Labrat's panegyrics for Shemariah Ben Elḥanan and Ḥasdai Ibn Shaprut (poems cited above; see nn. 4, 5).

69. For biography and corpus, see Decter, *Iberian Jewish Literature*, 126–30; Sadan, "Rabbi Judah al-Ḥarīzī as Cultural Crossroads." In the present discussion, I move rather freely among al-Ḥarīzī's works and their various versions to provide a holistic thematic discussion. The chronology of works is discussed in the various publications by Yahalom below.

70. These poems in order are al-Ḥarīzī, *Taḥkemoni*, 585 [148]; 593 [170]; *Wanderings of Judah Alḥarīzī*, 260 [8]; *Wanderings of Judah Alḥarīzī*, 247 [3].

71. See also Yahalom's comments about Yosef ha-Ma'aravi in *Wanderings of Judah Alḥarīzī*, 18.

72. Al-Ḥarīzī, *Wanderings of Judah Alḥarīzī*, 80.

73. Al-Ḥarīzī, *Kitāb al-durar*, 112–13. For *al-Sharā*, see Lane, *An Arabic-English Lexicon*, 155. I am writing a separate article on al-Ḥarīzī as a bilingual author.

74. In this regard, he follows Yehudah Ibn Shabbetai, who also set praise of his patron within the narrative of his "Gift of Judah the Misogynist." See the trans. by Scheindlin, "The Misogynist."

75. *Iggeret lashon ha-zahav* (published in al-Ḥarīzī, *Taḥkemoni*, 597–98); cf. Ex 25:31.

76. One bone joined another; cf. Ez 37:7.

77. The whole dedication is in al-Ḥarīzī, *Taḥkemoni*, 91–92.

78. Ibid., 453, 493. See also Yahalom, "Redacción y reelaboración"; idem, "Arabic and Hebrew as Poetic Languages Within Jewish and Muslim Society."

79. Al-Ḥarīzī, *Wanderings of Judah Alḥarīzī*, 52. One wonders whether the *nasi* Qalonymos, whom al-Ḥarīzī calls a "*nasi* of God in our midst" and to whom he dedicated his (unpublished) *Sefer ha-goralot* (Book of fates), was of Davidic descent. See al-Ḥarīzī, *Taḥkemoni*, 541.

80. Al-Ḥarīzī, *Taḥkemoni*, 61.

81. Al-Ḥarīzī, *Kitāb al-durar*, 142.

82. Ibid., 122.

83. In fact, al-Ḥarīzī mixes praise and blame in characterizing this figure. Al-Ḥarīzī, *Taḥkemoni*, 436–37; *Kitāb al-durar*, 124. Another *maghribī* whom al-Ḥarīzī encountered was Yosef ha-Ma'aravi, whom he extolled in Hebrew: "In your heart is a house that [God]

built for the holy tongue to dwell, and there an Arab pitched a tent. / In the West you were a lord and master, but in the East God anointed you a prophet! / Aleppo (*Aram Ṣova*) is like a sanctuary and in it you are like a Western lamp." *Wanderings of Judah Alḥarīzī*, 207, lines 179–81.

84. On Fustat and Cairo, see *Kitāb al-durar*, 44.

CHAPTER 5

1. Panegyric is absent, notably, even in poems delivered at American presidential inaugurations. The poet laureate usually addresses visions of the state or the age rather than the president's qualities as a leader. Actually, Robert Frost's "Dedication" (which he composed for, but ultimately did not read at, Kennedy's inauguration in 1961) comes somewhat close: "The glory of a next Augustan age/ Of a power leading from its strength and pride,/ Of young ambition eager to be tried. . . . A golden age of poetry and power." According to Frost, he was unable to read this poem because of excessive glare from the sun and recited "The Gift Outright" from memory instead. One hears more hyperbole at political conventions.

2. Aristotle, *Nicomachean Ethics*, 1775; see also 1740.

3. Al-Ghazzālī, *Iḥyā' 'ulūm al-dīn*, 3:138–41.

4. Schirmann, "The Function of the Poet in Medieval Spain," 237. The Judeo-Arabic is found in Güdemann, *Das jüdische Unterrichtswesend während der spanisch-arabischen Periode*, 10. I do not know how to account for Schirmann's mistake. It is translated correctly in the Hebrew translation by Epenshtein as *shivḥei middot ra'ot*; see Epenshtein, "Perek 27 me-sefer merapei ha-nefashot," 376.

5. Lit., "one who seeks protection for."

6. Sa'adia Ben Yosef, *Perushei rav Sa'adia Gaon li-vereshit*, 10. A similar point is made in Ibn Gabirol's *Iṣlāḥ al-akhlāq*. See Ibn Gabirol, *The Improvement of the Moral Qualities*, Arabic sec., 33; English sec., 98.

7. Sa'adia Ben Yosef, *Mishlei 'im targum u-feirush ha-gaon rabbeinu Sa'adia Ben Yosef Fayyumi*, 218. See also Aristotle, *Nicomachean Ethics*, 1740, "Praise is appropriate to excellence; for as a result of excellence men tend to do noble deeds." Also, al-Ghazzālī held that self-praise was abhorrent (*qabīḥ*); see al-Ghazzālī, *Iḥyā' 'ulūm al-dīn*, 139.

8. Ibn Ezra, *Kitāb al-muḥāḍara wa'l-mudhākara*, 106; Brann, *The Compunctious Poet*, 77.

9. Ibn Ezra, *Kitāb al-muḥāḍara wa'l-mudhākara*, 90. Also, in recounting the life of Ibn Ezra, Avraham Ibn Dā'ūd, perhaps based on this passage, writes that he "renounced this world and looked forward to the world to come"; Ibn Dā'ūd, *Sefer ha-Qabbalah*, 102–3 (English sec.).

10. Ibn Ezra, *Kitāb al-muḥāḍara wa'l-mudhākara*, 102.

11. Ibid., 26.

12. Ibid., 114.

13. Mosheh Ben Maimon, *Mishnah 'im perush rabbeinu Mosheh Ben Maimon*, 4:389.

14. See also Kraemer, "The Influence of Islamic Law on Maimonides: The Case of the Five Qualifications."

15. Mosheh Ben Maimon, *Mishnah 'im perush rabbeinu Mosheh Ben Maimon*, 4:417. See also 4:419, where songs in praise of "courage, honor, or wine" are included in the legal category of recommended speech (even when sung in Arabic).

16. Ibn Ḥazm goes even one step further to argue that praising a profligate (*fāsik*) for qualities that he does not possess can lead him to desist from his wicked ways; Ibn Ḥazm, *Kitāb al-akhlāq wa'l-siyyar*, 121. For Maimonides on the dangers of flattery, see Twersky, *A Maimonides Reader*, 56.

17. Mosheh Ben Maimon, *Mishnah 'im perush rabbeinu Mosheh Ben Maimon*, 4:420.

18. See also the general sentiment in b. 'Arakhin 16a.

19. Mosheh Ben Maimon, *Mishnah 'im perush rabbeinu Mosheh Ben Maimon*, 4:416–17. I am not sure what work he intends by *Kitāb al-akhlāq*, but the subject parallels al-Ghazzālī's discussion. The anecdote is not found in Ibn Ḥazm's work of that title, Miskawayh's *Tahdhīb al-akhlāq*, or in the standard commentaries on Aristotle's *Nicomachean Ethics*.

20. Edition in Blau, ed. *Judeo-Arabic Literature: Selected Texts*, 211. Cf. Twersky, *A Maimonides Reader*, 405.

21. Ibn Paquda, *Torat ḥovot ha-levavot*, 159, 155, 225, 216, 262; B. Safran, "Bahya Ibn Paquda's Attitude Toward the Courtier Class," 167.

22. Ibn Paquda, *Torat ḥovot ha-levavot*, 262.

23. Ibid., 294–95.

24. Brann, *The Compunctious Poet*, 101–6. For bibliographic information on the *Treatise on Hebrew Meters*, see Schirmann, *Toledot . . . muslemit*, 475n239.

25. Brann, *The Compunctious Poet*, 113.

26. Halevi, *Kitāb al-radd wa'l-dalīl fī al-dīn al-dhalīl*, 76 (2:60).

27. Ibid., 228–29 (5:25).

28. The key poem in this regard is "Ha-tirdof na'arut aḥar ḥamishim" (Do you chase youth after fifty?); Halevi, *Dīwān*, 2:160–63 [5]. See Scheindlin, *Song of the Distant Dove*, 185; Brann, *The Compunctious Poet*, 116. See also Halevi, *Dīwān*, 184–87 [23], "They congratulate him for being in the service of kings, which to him is like the service of idols."

29. TS 13 J 24.8, Gil and Fleischer, *Yehudah ha-Levi u-venei ḥugo*, 464.

30. Scheindlin, *The Song of the Distant Dove*, 125–26. In Chap. 7, I offer a more literal translation in order to make a specific point.

31. Scheindlin, *The Song of the Distant Dove*, 127.

32. Tellingly, the same term can also refer to "legitimate borrowing." The boundary between appropriate referencing and plagiarism was blurry and subjective. A recent article that also provides the relevant bibliography is Naaman, "*Sariqa* in Practice." One might also consider the anecdote regarding El'azar Ben Ya'aqov ha-Bavli in which the poet, in the context of a mourning ceremony, excoriated community members who uttered "stolen" verses in lamenting the deceased. See Chap. 1, n. 9.

33. See Introduction, p. 11.

34. See Sharlet, *Patronage and Poetry in the Islamic World*, 14–15.

35. See Beeri, "'Eli he-Ḥaver Ben 'Amram," 292–95; Mann, *The Jews in Egypt and in Palestine*, 2:75–76. Both poems contain praise for other people as well. Perhaps notably, the lines regarding knowledge of biblical commentary and law are redirected from Sa'adia al-Tustari to Yehosef the Andalusian, while the praise for Yosef al-Tustari's "wisdom" is far more general than Yehosef the Andalusian's. Also, the Andalusian's brother Eliassaf enjoys several more lines of praise than the secondary figures among the Tustaris. The same poet also once "reused" an earlier poem by another poet; see the discussion of TS 32.4 in Chap. 3, pp. 91–92.

36. I am treating the Arabic poems in a separate article, "The (Interreligious?) Rededication of an Arabic Panegyric by Judah al-Ḥarīzī." See also the articles by Yahalom mentioned in Chap. 4, n. 78.

37. See, e.g., S. Stetkevych, *The Poetics of Islamic Legitimacy*, 181–82. Many others can be found in Sharlet, *Patronage and Poetry in the Islamic World*.

38. Ibn Ezra, *Kitāb al-muḥāḍara wa'l-mudhākara*, 58.

39. See Gruendler, *Medieval Arabic Praise Poetry*, 8.

40. See pp. 69–71.

41. Ibn Ezra, *Kitāb al-muḥāḍara wa'l-mudhākara*, 56.

42. In several instances, he was not paid at all, a point that so incensed him that he composed many of what Brener has called "payment poems," in which he mixed praise for his addressee with rebuke for his miserliness. See Brener, *Isaac Ibn Khalfun*, 51–61. She notes there that this type of poetry is related to the classification of *al-iqtiḍā' wa'l-istinjāz*, "claims [for payment] and the fulfillment of promises."

43. Ibn Ezra, *Kitāb al-muḥāḍara wa'l-mudhākara*, 88–90.

44. *Aksada*, "became stagnant," a word particular to markets.

45. Either its creators or recipients.

46. Ibn Ezra, *Kitāb al-muḥāḍara wa'l-mudhākara*, 88–90.

47. Ibid., 26.

48. See, e.g., Sharlet, *Patronage and Poetry in the Islamic World*, 10.

49. The story is cited in an almost identical form by Mosheh Ibn Ezra, who obscures the attribution to 'Alī and uses it toward a slightly different purpose, which I will discuss in Chap. 6.

50. Sharlet, *Patronage and Poetry in the Islamic World*, 18. Al-Ḥarīzī's invention of an epistle (as well as verses) that, read forward, offered praise but, read in reverse word order, offered invective, should be considered in this light. See Al-Ḥarīzī, *Taḥkemoni*, 153–60. It is also possible that Maimonides' comment about Yosef Ibn Ṣadīq in a letter to Shemuel Ibn Tibbon, often taken as praise, was intended as blame. See Stroumsa, "A Note on Maimonides' Attitude to Joseph Ibn Ṣadīq."

51. Halevi, *Dīwān*, 1:131–33 [137], lines 36–37.

52. "Guile," lit., "blinding"; cf. Ex 23:8, which warns that "bribes blind the clear-sighted." "Secure," lit., "find." Schirmann, *Ha-shirah ha-'ivrit*, 1:8–10, lines 23–34. See also Ibn Ezra, *Shirei ha-ḥol*, 1:35 [33], lines 27–28.

53. Trans. Scheindlin, *Song of the Distant Dove*, 115–16.

54. Al-Ḥarīzī, *Kitāb al-durar*, 136.

55. Ibn Ezra, *Shirei ha-ḥol*, 1:201 [199].

CHAPTER 6

1. See pp. 14–15.

2. Trans. from the Hebrew in Halkin, *Moses Maimonides' Epistle to Yemen*, 2–3. See also Maimonides' use of *ta'aẓīm* in Chap. 5, p. 148.

3. The expressions *tarḥivu peh* and *ta'arikhu lashon* occur together in Is 57:4, there in parallel with *hit'angu*, "to make sport of, mocking" and thus in a decidedly negative sense. See also Ps 35:21. However, Maimonides clearly does not have mockery in mind. In earlier chapters, we have already seen tongues called "long" (Chap. 3, p. 96) and "short" (Chap. 4, p. 141) in reference to degrees of eloquence.

4. The passage notes that hyperbolic and exaggerative language is found in the Torah, the Prophets, and in the discourse of the rabbis. In some cases, *havai* is paired with *hevel*, "vapor, vanity," and can hence carry the meaning of "nonsense," which is also the sense in modern Hebrew.

5. Ibn Ezra, *Kitāb al-muḥāḍara*, 266. This subject will be discussed in detail below.

6. Maimonides does discuss poetic speech in the context of syllogistic reasoning in the *Treatise on Logic*, chap. 8, and some basic elements of al-Fārābī's poetics are apparent in his treatment of the imagination and prophecy in other works (further below). Maimonides was not the enemy of poetry that he has sometimes been characterized as having been. A verse from a Hebrew poem (a panegyric by Halevi) is cited as an aphorism within Maimonides' famous letter to Ibn Tibbon; see M. Ben Maimon, *Iggerot ha-Rambam*, 530. Although the letter is generally written in Judeo-Arabic, this section is preserved in Ibn Tibbon's Hebrew translation only; it is conceivable that Maimonides actually quoted an Arabic poem here and that Ibn Tibbon substituted it with an existing Hebrew verse.

7. Ibn Ezra, *Shirei ha-ḥol*, 159–61 [160], lines 16–20.

8. All these architectural elements are found in Ex 35:11.

9. Cf. Is 8:4.

10. This verse presents two full paronomasias (*ḥalof/yaḥlif*; *yifraḥ/yafriaḥ*).

11. Mosheh Ibn Ezra, *Shirei ha-ḥol*, 64–65 [66], lines 12–22.

12. E.g., the "breast of tranquility" (line 14) is an example of *al-isti'āra* (loan metaphor). Verses 15–16 (Honeycomb to the mouth . . . Tabernacle of Truth) both demonstrate *al-taqsīm* (classification), which Ibn Ezra defines: "The poet expounds upon (*yufassir*) what he opens with and does not leave out any class (*qism*) that the meaning requires but rather he presents it" (*Kitāb al-muḥāḍara*, 242–44). In these verses, the "classes" are sensory organs and architectural fixtures. In fact, in the theoretical discussion in Ibn Ezra, *Kitāb al-muḥāḍara wa'l-mudhākara*, he illustrates the device with these very verses.

13. Scheindlin, "Rabbi Moshe Ibn Ezra on the Legitimacy of Poetry."

14. Of course, several factors need to be accounted for in ascertaining this: the skill of the poet, the literacy of the *mamdūḥ*, even the occasion of the poem. But something can be learned from comparing poems by a single poet for different *mamdūḥ*s.

15. Decter, "Panegyric as Pedagogy." See there for a full bibliography on the subject.

16. Meisami, "Literary Criticism, Medieval," 472.

17. Bonebakker, *The* Kitāb Naqd al-Š'ir *of Qudāma b. Ǧa'far al-Kātib al-Baġdādī*, 36–44. However, Qudāma does not reference Aristotle's *Poetics* or *Rhetoric*, despite the fact that at least the first was available in Arabic by this time.

18. See Black, *Logic and Aristotle's Rhetoric and Poetics in Medieval Arabic Philosophy*; Kemal, *The Philosophical Poetics of Alfarabi, Avicenna, and Averroes.*

19. See Efros, "Maimonides' Treatise on Logic," 47–49.

20. Beginning with Aristotle, *Poetics*, 1447a and several subsequent paragraphs, pp. 2316–40. Importantly, a poetic statement (e.g., the metaphor "the man is a lion") can occur within forms of speech apart from poetry proper.

21. Praise is not a central topic in Aristotle's *Poetics* but, in recounting the history of poetry, he refers to the early existence of "those who praised gods and men." See Aristotle, *Poetics*, 1448b–1449a, p. 2318.

22. See Rowland, *Faint Praise and Civil Leer*, 13. In 1577, the term was defined as "when we use a greater word for a lesse, or thus, when the word is greater than the thing is in deede." By 1729, the word's valence had turned decisively negative: "*Auxesis*, a Figure, when any thing is magnified *too much*." But in premodernity, using a "greater word for a lesse" was not necessarily morally compromising, let alone aesthetically displeasing.

23. Aristotle, *Rhetoric*, 1.9, 1368a, p. 2177. Unlike the *Poetics*, which was cited by medieval Arabic-speaking Jewish authors with some frequency, Aristotle's *Rhetoric* seems to have received no attention, despite the fact that it had been translated into Arabic by Ibn al-Samḥ (d. 1027) and had received a commentary by Ibn Rushd in the thirteenth century; S. M. Stern, "Ibn al-Samḥ."

24. See, e.g., the works by Black and Kemal cited above in n. 18.

25. Heinrichs, "Badī'."

26. This work has not been discovered. See Bonebakker, *Materials for the History of Arabic Rhetoric*, 14–16.

27. Partly because much of it was incorporated into Ibn Rashīq's text but also because of the relatively poor state of the manuscript. See, however, the preliminary survey by Tobi, "Preliminary Study in Ḥilyat al-Muḥāḍara by Abū 'Alī Muḥammad al-Ḥātimī." By the way, al-Tha'ālibī composed a work titled *Al-tamāthul wa'l-muḥāḍara*, which also circulated under the title *Ḥilyat al-muḥāḍara.* See Orfali, "The Works of Abū Manṣūr al-Tha'ālibī," 292, work 25.

28. See Fenton, *Philosophie et exégèse dans le Jardin de la métaphor de Moïse Ibn 'Ezra.*

29. See also Mordechai Cohen, "The Aesthetic Exegesis of Moses Ibn Ezra."

30. The Arabic verses in *Kitāb al-muḥāḍara* are studied in comparison with *dīwān*s and works of literary criticism by Braunn, "Arabic Verses in *Kitāb al-muḥāḍara wa'l-mudhākara.*"

31. On Ibn Ezra's concept of metaphor, see Mordechai Cohen, "Moses Ibn Ezra vs. Maimonides."

32. See, e.g., the essays on "amplification" and "hyperbole" in *Princeton Encyclopedia of Poetry and Poetics*, 46, 647.

33. Heinrichs, "Rhetorical Figures," 658.

34. This is the wording of Abū Aḥmad al-ʿAskarī, *Kitāb al-ṣināʿatayn*, 327, 365. Similar is the definition of *mubālagha* with Bonebakker, *The* Kitāb Naqd al-Šʿir *of Qudāma b. Ǧaʿfar al-Kātib al-Baġdādī*, 7, though, like Ibn Ezra, he also defends the use of *al-ghulū* by equating it with *al-mubālagha* (see below). Al-Ḥātimī does not include a chap. on *al-mubālagha*.

35. And this can include figures of wording.

36. Ibn Ezra does not include a chap. on *al-mubālagha* in *Kitāb al-muḥāḍara*.

37. The etymology of the word *havai* is unclear. Ben Yehudah suggests the Arabic cognate *hby*, "dust that has risen into the air." Perhaps it is related to the Greek *hyper*?

38. Fenton, *Philosophie et exégèse dans le Jardin de la méthaphor de Moïse Ibn ʿEzra*, 334–35.

39. Derived from *ghāya* ("limit"), hence "reaching a limit."

40. The second phrase is actually called *ighāl*, since it reiterates the hyperbolic theme at the end of the verse. Hence it is a "figure of wording" as much as a "figure of thought." See also Fenton, *Philosophie et exégèse dans le Jardin de la méthaphor de Moïse Ibn ʿEzra*, 334–35. Interesting also is Ibn Ezra's comment on Job's image of his former glory: "And the rock poured me out rivers of oil" (Jb 29:4), as well as Job's image of how he had imagined his future happiness prior to his suffering: "My glory refreshed, my bough renewed in my hand" (Jb 29:20). Ibn Ezra adds that an Arab poet saw or heard about the latter image and invented a verse in imitation: "If you heard about a lucky man who held a branch in his hand and it flourished, it would be true."

41. Discussed in Chap. 7, pp. 195–96.

42. Ibn Rashīq sees *al-ifrāṭ* as a synonym of *al-ghulū*.

43. See Lane, *Arabic-English Lexicon*, 2157.

44. This and the following few lines are cited in nearly identical form by Ibn Rashīq, in the name of al-Ḥātimī.

45. Lit., "minds."

46. Lit., "you would see him."

47. I.e., he would be thankful as though he received money from you.

48. I.e., the petitioner would be asking another man to give up his life.

49. Lit., "speaks with."

50. The entire passage has similarities to Maimonides, *Treatise on Logic*, chap. 8.

51. This corresponds with Ibn Ezra's position on miracles within the *maḥāsin al-shiʿr* sec.; see p. 168 above.

52. Halkin identifies this with *De Anima*, 3, 6 (430, lines 25–31).

53. Al-Fārābī, *Iḥṣā al-ʿulūm*, 42. By the way, this work was translated into Hebrew in the fourteenth century by Qalonymos Ben Qalonymos; see Zonta, *La "Classificazione delle Scienze" di al-Fārābī nella Tradizione Ebraica*." This passage is on pp. 11, line 25–pp. 12, line

5. Numerous similar statements are in al-Fārābī's *Kitāb al-sh'ir*; see Mahdi, "Kitāb al-sh'ir"; Matar, "Alfārābī on Imagination."

54. The manuscripts have "their" here, though it is "our" in the Arabic editions and in the later translation by Qalonymos. "Our" simply makes more sense. Otherwise, "their [i.e., the listeners'] minds."

55. Ibn Ezra, *Kitāb al-muḥāḍara*, 114–18.

56. In fact, we might say that al-Fārābī's thinking on poetics is really an outgrowth of his conception of the imaginative faculty as the site where mimetic functions are processed. As it is known, this had profound implications for al-Fārābī's and ultimately Maimonides' political philosophy.

57. Ajami, *The Alchemy of Glory*.

58. Ibn Ezra, *Kitāb al-muḥāḍara*, 134.

59. The final line, likening the poetic craft to sculpture, is certainly Aristotle's. The attribution about statements that mix truth and falsehood belong more properly to al-Fārābī as well as others. On similar passages in al-Fārābī and Qudāma Ibn Ja'far (who was a source for Ibn Ezra), see Bonebakker, *The* Kitāb Naqd al-Š'ir *of Qudāma b. Ǧa'far al-Kātib al-Baġdādī*, 36–37. The classification of demonstration, dialectic, and so on is close to Maimonides' presentation in chap. 8 of the *Treatise on Logic* since both are based upon al-Fārābī; in Maimonides' discussion, the arrangement is a logical one and not an ethical one, i.e., poetic speech is listed after sophistry because it is constructed out of imitative premises rather than those that can be evaluated by the standards of truth and falsehood, not because poetry is less ethical than sophistry.

60. The last two sentences of this paragraph are nearly identical with Bonebakker, *The* Kitāb Naqd al-Š'ir *of Qudāma b. Ǧa'far al-Kātib al-Baġdādī*, 27, lines 1–4. See also 77, lines 7–10.

61. Ibn Ezra, *Kitāb al-muḥāḍara*, 266. See above regarding the classification of *mubālagha* by al-Qazwīnī. Maimonides critiques the *mutakallimūn* for considering anything that can be conceived by the mind as possible; *Guide*, 1:71. Ibn Rushd looks unfavorably upon employing the nonexistent (*al-ghair mawjūda*) and insists that "the imitative things" be "existing matters" (*umūr mawjūda*). Thus he disapproves of a verse in which Generosity is personified and seated at a fire alongside the *mamdūḥ* (there would be no difficulty in personifying Generosity as long as it stayed within its own fictional frame). See Ibn Rushd, *Talkhīṣ kitāb Arisṭūṭālīs fī al-sh'ir*, 90–91; Butterworth, *Averroes' Middle Commentary on Aristotle's Poetics*, 84–85. Some critics simply warn against descending into the realm of the impossible and the absurd (e.g., wishing the *mamdūḥ* eternal life).

62. Pagis distinguished between poetic lies that were "qualitative (formal-stylistic)," on the one hand, and "pragmatic (factual-content)," on the other.

63. The way in which Ibn Ezra uses the verse is common among Arabic literary critics, though a minority hold the more conservative opinion. See, e.g., the discussion by Bonebakker, *The* Kitāb Naqd al-Š'ir *of Qudāma b. Ǧa'far al-Kātib al-Baġdādī*, 37–38.

64. The dropping of attribution is common to many Jewish renderings of *ḥadīth*, qur'ānic citations, and teachings concerning Muslim figures.

65. Ibn Ezra, *Kitāb al-muḥāḍara*, 192. See Halkin's references for original sources.

66. See Sharlet, *Patronage and Poetry in the Islamic World*, 10.

67. See the recent volume on the subject by Van Gelder and Hammond, *Takhyīl.*

68. Cf. the passage with Black, *Logic and Aristotle's Poetics*, 232–33.

69. Matar, "Alfārābī on Imagination," 107–8. *The Treatise on Poetry* seems to have circulated as an appendix to *The Enumeration of Sciences*, though Ibn Ezra does not quote from it directly.

70. Pagis, *Shirat ha-ḥol ve-torat ha-shir*, 84. See also further examples there. One difficulty within Hebrew scholarship on the subject stems from the fact that the word *dimmui* is used both for "simile" and "imagination."

71. Lit., "whores who give gifts." In Ez 16:33, God calls Israel a whore worse than other whores, for all whores receive gifts, but she gives gifts to her lovers! The poem is Ibn Ezra, *Shirei ha-ḥol*, 219 [1:93 of *Sefer ha-ʿanaq*].

72. Note that I am not treating "logical tricks" in the same way; an example would be the verse discussed in n. 61 above.

73. Gruendler, "Fantastic Aesthetics and Practical Criticism in Ninth-Century Baghdad," 215.

CHAPTER 7

1. Schirmann, *Ha-shirah ha-ʿivrit*, 1:37, lines 17–20.

2. Lines 21, 26, 32.

3. This term will be discussed extensively below.

4. This word has several meanings, from "poetry" in general, to "praise" but also "dispraise." Although any of these might be possible, Ibn Ezra seems to use the word in the most general sense. See Lane, *Arabic-English Lexicon*, 2515.

5. *Kitāb al-muḥāḍara wa'l-mudhākara*, 52.

6. E.g., in the panegyric dedicated to Saʿadia Gaon, we read, "In no hidden matter can one eclipse him." The phrase derives from Ezekiel 28, in which God directs the prophet to stand before the prince of Tyre and offer a mock panegyric that betrays the prince's haughtiness. If we insisted upon an absolute association with context, the gaon would stand in for the haughty prince, which was surely not the author's intention.

7. Let us imagine how Maimonides might have reacted to the direction to a man of a "God reference" such as "He gathers lambs and leads the mother sheep" (Is 40:10–11). For Maimonides, God is called a shepherd only metaphorically, so there would be no difficulty in describing a flesh-and-blood leader as a shepherd as well. In fact, the Bible itself already uses this metaphor to describe human leadership. In the *Mishneh Torah* (*Laws of Kings and Their Wars*, 2:11), Maimonides reviews praiseworthy characteristics of ancient Israelite kings and notes that the Bible charges the king to follow the model of Moses and "pasture" his people like a shepherd. Recognizing that the passage does not explain what shepherding entails, he searches the Bible for the relevant characteristics of the shepherd

and lands upon the aforementioned verse from Isaiah where the shepherd is God. It is of no difficulty whatsoever that the shepherd is a man in one instance and God in the other. Arguably, theological tensions would have been more pronounced for readers who subscribed to a cataphatic theory of God's attributes (such as that embraced by many Muʿatazilite thinkers, both Muslim and Jewish), which would have entailed a more relational, though still metaphoric, association between man and God.

8. Further below.

9. Schmitt, *Political Theology.*

10. Kantorowicz, *The King's Two Bodies.*

11. Kantorowicz, *Laudes Regiae.*

12. Kantorowicz also recognizes that these images themselves are transferred from the acclamations and liturgy of imperial Rome.

13. Kantorowicz, *The King's Two Bodies*, 65.

14. Greenblatt, "Introduction: Fifty Years of *The King's Two Bodies*," 63.

15. Ibid., 65.

16. See, e.g., recent bibliography in Bertelli, *The King's Body*; and Brisch, *Religion and Power.* However, the Brisch volume does not cite Kantorowicz as the generative text so much as Frankfort, *Kingship and the Gods.* On Judaism and Islam, see the volumes by Lorberbaum, al-Azmeh, and Moin below.

17. This refers to the electoral method of succession followed in the early decades of (non-Shiʿite) Islam, though it soon gave way to succession within lineage under the Umayyads. On the erosion of *shūrā* and ongoing calls for its implementation, see Crone, *God's Rule*, 34–39.

18. Lorberbaum, *Disempowered King.*

19. Within this model, Lorberbaum offers a further and useful distinction between a harder version of "divine kingship" and a softer version of "sacral kingship"; in the latter, the king need not be divine himself but is nevertheless elevated to the realm of the sacred.

20. Boustan, "Israelite Kingship, Christian Rome, and the Jewish Imperial Imagination," 175. Boustan also notes that the throne of Solomon had continued place in the culture of sovereignty in Umayyad Islam; see n. 13 of his article.

21. B. Sanhedrin 20b.

22. *Midrash Rabbah*, ed. Mosheh Arieh Mirkin, 5:117–18 and parallels to Tanḥuma in n. 2. The motif is echoed in a panegyric for the courtier ʿAdaya Ben Menasheh, "those far off heard the rumor and thanked the Rock who pities the downtrodden, who in his kindness apportioned from his glory (*ḥalaq mi-kevodo*) to the minister, who is great like Ezra Ben Serayah." Mann, *The Jews in Egypt and in Palestine*, 2:12, lines 11–12.

23. Saʿadia essentially supplies a missing *mem* as though the verse read *kisakha* me-*elohim*, "Your throne is from God." Yefet Ben ʿEli translates into Arabic *kursika min ʿind allah li'l-abad wa li'l-dahr*, ("Your throne, which is from God, is forever and everlasting"). See Ben ʿEli, *Kitab al-zabur: Libri psalmorum, versio Arabica*, 89.

24. Ibn Ezra also rejects the vocative reading, "Your throne, O God!"

25. Rashi, on Ps 45:7, is similarly delimited: "Your throne is minister and judge forever; your verdicts are true and you deserve to rule." Kimḥi also expands the argument to negate a Christian reading that the throne belongs to both son and king, hence Christ.

26. Quoted in Maimonides, *A Maimonides Reader*, 53. See also Maimonides, *Mishneh Torah, Laws of Kings and Their Wars*, 2:10.

27. Maimonides, *Guide of the Perplexed*, 1:54; trans. Pines, 126.

28. See Abel, "Le Khalifeh, présence sacrée"; and al-Azmeh, *Muslim Kingship*, 131, 135–36. On hiding from view, see Barceló, "The Manifest Caliph," 427. See also Decter, "The Hidden Exilarch."

29. Al-Azmeh, *Muslim Kingship*, 189–219. On the Mughal Empire in the sixteenth century, see Moin, *The Millennial Sovereign*.

30. Al-Azmeh, *Muslim Kingship*, 40.

31. Ibid., 162.

32. Crone and Hinds, *God's Caliph*. The origins of the idea of God's having a deputy on earth remain opaque; see ibid., 114–15.

33. Also, Adam is referred to as a caliph in Qur'ān 2:30.

34. Crone and Hinds, *God's Caliph*, 39.

35. See reviews by Rippin; Calder; and also Afsaruddin's review of the more recent book by Crone, *God's Rule*.

36. Crone and Hinds address this, to some extent, on 56. Similar is al-Azmeh, *Muslim Kingship*, 162.

37. See also Chap. 5, p. 150, regarding Baḥya Ibn Paquda's description of panegyric as a type of *shirk*.

38. See discussion in Gimaret, *Les noms divins en Islam*; Gardet, "Al-asmā' al-ḥusna"; Böwering, "God and His Attributes." See also Gimaret, *Dieu à l'image de l'homme*.

39. Note that there is nothing about the *fa'īl* form itself that makes it intensive; meaning is determined by context.

40. Ben Shammai, "The Judaeo-Arabic Vocabulary of Saadya's Bible Translation as a Vehicle for Eschatological Messages," 213.

41. In general, see Van Gelder, "Forbidden Firebrands."

42. Al-'Askarī, *Al-iqtibās*, 63–64.

43. Ibn Rashīq, *Kitāb al-'umda fī maḥāsin al-shi'r*, 2:14–15.

44. See also al-Tha'ālibī, *al-iqtibās min al-qur'ān al-karīm*, 2:57–58. For the general sec. on *al-iqtibās* in panegyric, see 2:175–79. When I gave a talk on this subject at Ohio State University, Bilal Orfali kindly shared his (then forthcoming) articles with me: "In Defense of the Use of Qur'ān in Adab"; idem, with Pomerantz, "I See a Distant Fire."

45. The offending usage, in al-Tha'ālibī's view, may have been that the poet transferred a *superlative* description of God to a man (the *most* excellent protector and helper). See, similarly, Van Gelder, "Forbidden Firebrands," 11. Also noteworthy is a Persian manuscript that critiques Shi'ites who ascribe God's attributes to the imams; see Mahdjoub, "The Evolution of Popular Eulogy of the Imams Among the Shi'a," 56–57.

46. The anecdote is cited by Van Gelder, "Forbidden Firebrands," 8–10. This is at the end of a tripartite taxonomy that al-Ḥillī offers of *al-iqtibās*: (1) praised and acceptable; (2) permitted and lawful; and (3) prohibited and contemptible. The last includes directing statements that God attributes to Himself toward men.

47. I liken the poet, in this regard, to the contemporary comedian. A statement is often funny when it transgresses a boundary, and it is through the act of transgression that the boundary itself becomes visible.

48. The title "al-Mu'izz," the "One who raises honor," is one of *al-asmā' al-ḥusna*. It was not uncommon for caliphs to take such names, suggesting divine association but also avoiding it by appending such terms as *li-dīn allah*, hence "the One who raises honor for the sake of God's religion." On titulature in general, see my discussion in Chap. 1. Bosworth, "Laḳab," writes that Isma'ili "titulature reflected the role assigned in Ismā'īlī cosmogony to the *Imāms*, in the hierarchy of intelligences emanating from the godhead, and it actively associated the holders of these titles with God's direct working in the world."

49. Ibn Hānī al-Andalusī, *Dīwān Ibn Hānī*, 146, line 1. After this opening comparison with God, the poem continues to press the boundaries of expression, "As though you were the Prophet Muḥammad and your followers were the Followers" (*al-anṣār*).

50. "Inheritor" can apply in the Qur'ān either to God (e.g., 15:23, where it follows "Giver of life, Bringer of death"), or to human beings, e.g., the Israelites in 28:5. "Inheritor of the Earth" does not occur in the Qur'ān in this form.

51. Ibn Hānī al-Andalusī, *Dīwān*, 135, lines 1– 4. *Al-watr* is not included in all lists of the *asmā al-ḥusna.* It occurs in Qur'ān 89:3, *wa'l-shaf'i wa'l-watr*, often translated obliquely, "by the even and the odd." In some interpretations, this is taken to mean "by [the animals who are created in] pairs and by the Unequaled [i.e., God]." Hence Lane identifies *al-watr* among the names of God. Lane, *Arabic-English Lexicon*, 2918. *Ṣamad* is sometimes translated as "besought by all."

52. In general, see Daftary, *The Ismā'īlīs*, 2nd ed., esp. chaps. 3 and 4; S. M. Stern, *Studies in Early Ismā'īlism*; Bosworth, "Laḳab"; Madelung, "Das Imamat in der frühen ismailitischen Lehre." There is a brief discussion of the phenomenon in question in Smoor, "The Master of the Century," 146–50.

53. Ed. Margoliouth, *Dīwān shi'r Abī al-Fatḥ Muḥammad Ibn 'Ubayd Allāh*, 173, line 1.

54. *Muhja*, "core, heart, lifeblood."

55. Ibn 'Abd Rabbih, *Dīwān Ibn 'Abd Rabbih*, 114. Although the original sense of the qur'ānic verse does not concern us, it likely refers to the rising and setting of the two luminaries, the sun and the moon. Some Qur'ān commentators associate it with the different locations of the sun's rising and setting at the times of the two equinoxes.

56. Also, the same poet praised the Caliph al-Nāṣir li-Dīn Allah: "He is a just ruler through whose extended hand God gives sustenance." Ibn 'Abd Rabbih, *Dīwān Ibn 'Abd Rabbih*, 122.

57. S. Stetkevych, *The Mantle Odes*, 102.

58. Stetkevych's trans., ibid., 144, line 154.

59. On the Tablet and Pen, see Wensinck and Bosworth, "Lawḥ." For contemporary criticism of the verse, see http://www.alsiraj.net/poetry/html/page04.html.

60. The poem and the anecdote are recounted in Ibn Sa'īd al-Maghribī, *Al-mughrib fī ḥulā al-maghrib*, 1:413–14.

61. *Nafḥ al-ṭīb*, 1:434. Also discussed in Ashraf Maḥmūd Najā, *Qaṣīdat al-madīḥ fī'l-Andalus*, 99.

62. Just after God passes before Moses, the following exclamation is pronounced: "The Lord! The Lord! A God compassionate and gracious, slow to anger, abounding in kindness and faithfulness, extending kindness to the thousandth generation, forgiving iniquity, transgression, and sin." A grammatical ambiguity in the text allows that the speaker here could be Moses or God; rabbinic tradition and medieval Jewish readers ascribe the speech to God Himself, who pronounced for Moses some of His attributes, what came be known as the thirteen characteristics or qualities. These lent themselves nicely to the philosophical concern with attributes.

63. *Halakhot gedolot, hilkhot shevu'ah*, 572. On this work and its dating, see R. Brody, *The Geonim of Babylonia*, 223–30.

64. In his *Mishneh Torah* (*Yesodei ha-Torah*, 6:1–5), Maimonides discusses the "holy, pure names" (*ha-shemot ha-qedoshim ha-tehorim*) and identifies names that cannot be erased and explains that "the rest of the nicknames used to praise" God can be erased (he names several, including *ḥannun ve-raḥum* (Gracious and Merciful). Another work, which has also been attributed to Maimonides, goes through verses of the Torah pericope by pericope and declares "according to tradition and reason" whether given terms in context are "holy" (*qodesh*, i.e., cannot be erased) or "profane" (*ḥol*, i.e., can be erased). In the introduction to the work, the author explains that only the tetragrammaton is not amphibolous and refers only to God. Even *Adonai* is "derived from [human] lordship" (though it cannot be erased when written with a *qamaṣ gadol* under the *nun*). Also *Elohim*, which Maimonides famously saw as amphibolous (alternately meaning God, divine beings, and rulers of cities), can be erased when it does not refer to God. All the nicknames are considered derivative and descriptive and can be erased. Regarding parallels in Islamic and Jewish law concerning divine names valid for oaths, see Rosenblatt, "The Relations Between Jewish and Muslim Laws Concerning Oaths and Vows"; Johannes Pedersen, *Der Eid bei den Semitin*, 206.

65. Ibn Janāḥ, *Kitāb al-uṣūl*, 676. I.e., the *dagesh* in the first *nun* of *ḥannun* and the implied *dagesh* in the *ḥet* of *raḥum*.

66. Originally published by Goldziher, the work has been republished recently with a Hebrew translation by Schlossberg, "A Booklet on the Names of the Lord and His Attributes" (Hebrew).

67. Schlossberg, "A Booklet on the Names of the Lord and His Attributes," 8.

68. In other cases, the author writes, subscribing to an apophatic theory, that man shares names with God out of some type of similarity (*mushabbihan li'llah*), as when they are called "righteous" or "pious" (*ṣadiq*, *ḥasid*).

69. Schlossberg, "A Booklet on the Names of the Lord and His Attributes," 15. Only very rarely have I found *raḥum* predicated of a man, and, even then, its meaning can be

ambiguous. For example, Ibn Khalfūn praised Abū Ayyūb Sulaiman Ben Dā'ūd: "Prince of my people, beloved of its soul, its merciful one" (*reḥumo*); however, it is possible that *raḥum*, in this instance, is being used in the sense "beloved." See the note by Mirsky to the poem by Ibn Khalfūn, *Shirei Yiṣḥaq Ibn Khalfūn*, 137 [54], line 1, with reference to Ibn Janāḥ, who notes that *rḥm* is the root in Aramaic that translates *'hv*. Ibn Khalfūn may have intended the ambiguity. 'Eli ha-Kohen describes King David as *gannun ḥannun be-mif'aleihu*; see Fleischer, "Qavim ḥadashim li-demuto shel rav Daniel Ben 'Azariah, nasi ve-gaon," 69, line 133. Todros Halevi Abulafia also uses it in panegyric (see Chap. 8, n. 35). Some versions of *mi-pi el*, a Sabbath song, contain *ein qadosh kadonai ein raḥum ke-ven 'Amram* (none is holy like God and none is merciful like Ben 'Amram, i.e., Moses).

70. Although Ibn Ezra does not mention al-Tha'ālibī by name, Halkin notes parallels (see *Kitāb al-muḥāḍara*, 14–15n29; 96–97n48). Additionally, I note parallel interpretations of Qur'ān 4:66 in al-Tha'ālibī, *al-Iqtibās*, 2:225; and Ibn Ezra, *Kitāb al-muḥāḍara*, 2–4. However, it is possible that Ibn Ezra learned this interpretation from another source.

71. Ibn Ezra, *Kitāb al-muḥāḍara*, 296.

72. Ibid., 268.

73. See Chap. 6 in this vol.

74. This is how the verse is understood by Dana, *Torat ha-shir be-sefer ha-'iyyunim ve-ha-diyyunim*, 99. I can imagine an alternative interpretation whereby the *mamdūḥ* is the ultimate goal of all creation (corresponding with Ibn Hānī's praise of al-Mu'izz above, "the one for whom men were created"). See also the end of Chap. 8 in this vol.

75. Halevi, *Dīwān*, 1:112–15 [78], lines 61–66. These verses were discussed in Chap. 5 using the poetic translation of Scheindlin, *Song of the Distant Dove*, 125–27; they are translated more literally here to highlight a point.

76. Halevi, *Dīwān*, 1:57 [42], lines 9–10.

77. Ibn Gabirol, *Shirei ha-ḥol*, 103–4 [50]. One elongates the final *dalet* in *eḥad* so that it will not be confused with the word *aḥer*, "another." See also a similar verse by Todros Abulafia in Chap. 8, p. 217.

78. A. Ibn Ezra, *Qoveṣ ḥokhmat ha-Rav Avraham Ibn Ezra*, 55–56, lines 44–45.

79. Halevi, *Dīwān*, 77 [58], line 44.

80. Brener, *Isaac Ibn Khalfun*, 158–59; Ibn Khalfūn, *Shirei Yiṣḥaq Ibn Khalfūn*, 8. Brener discusses the poem from a different perspective, 51–55.

81. Cf. Yehudah Halevi, "Toward the source of life, of truth, I run," in Scheindlin, *The Gazelle*, 198–201; even the use of the word *demut*, "image," does not clarify that the poem is about a man (for God also has a *demut*, Gn 1:27).

82. Similar is Ibn Khalfūn to an unknown *mamdūḥ*. See Ibn Khalfūn, *Shirei Yiṣḥaq Ibn Khalfūn*, 36; Brener, *Isaac Ibn Khalfun*, 146–47. "I knew you, but not upon knowledge did I rely but upon reputation. / I heaped my hopes upon you as the Jews hope for salvation. / I relied upon you like one who relies and leans upon a tower of strength (Ps 61:4, Prv 18:10) and a protective wall of fire (Zec 2:9). / With your name I donned a mantle of honor and girded myself in salvation." Brener's translation, with slight modification. There are two divine references in succession (line 3), and the tone is quasi-devotional.

83. An interesting case is a verse in Hai Gaon's panegyric for Rav Yehudah Rosh ha-Seder, however unclear. With Fleischer's emendation, "[Scholars'] eyes look toward his hand expectantly as though toward dew" (Ps 145:15). See Fleischer, "Shiro shel rav Hai Gaon," 1321, line 80.

84. Schechter, *Saadyana*, 57 (lines 1, 3, 7).

85. Beeri, "Seridei igronim qadumim min ha-geniza," 76–77.

86. Assaf, "Qoveṣ shel iggerot rav Shemuel Ben 'Eli," 2:80, lines 20ff.

87. Ibid., 22. On *melammed* as a title of significant status, see Goitein, *A Mediterranean Society*, 2:190.

88. Assaf, "Qoveṣ shel iggerot rav Shemuel Ben 'Eli," 2:66.

89. See pp. 176–77.

90. Schirmann, *Ha-shirah ha-'ivrit*, 1:174.

91. Ibn Ezra, *Shirei ha-ḥol*, 308 [37].

92. Ibid., 34 [25], lines 22, 28, 36. Also, when Yosef Ibn Migash replaced Yiṣḥaq Alfasi as head of the academy of Lucena, Halevi gave him the epithet "mighty of deeds" (Jer 32:19) and wrote that he made "faith and wisdom wondrous" (cf. Is 28:29). *Shirei ha-ḥol*, 141 [95], lines 14–15.

93. *Shirei ha-ḥol*, 123 [87], line 52.

94. Halevi, *Dīwān*, 1:144 [97]. See also expressions such as "The prince created by God" (Brener, *Isaac Ibn Khalfun*, 164–65; Ibn Khalfūn, *Shirei Yiṣḥaq Ibn Khalfūn*, 6, line 4); also "God's prince, son of His anointed" (Brener, *Isaac Ibn Khalfun*, 168–69; Ibn Khalfūn, *Shirei Yiṣḥaq Ibn Khalfūn*, 19, line 4). See also El'azar Ben Ya'aqov ha-Bavli, regarding "Shemuel *shams al-dawla* (sun of the state), "God's Nagid" (*nagid ha-el*); Van Bekkum, *The Secular Poetry of El'azar Ben Ya'aqov ha-Bavli*, 55, line 2. Far more common are expressions such as "Nagid of the People of Israel," which creates remove in a manner similar to "caliph of the Messenger of God."

95. Halevi, *Dīwān*, 110 [76], line 14: the poem also uses a messianic image, "a banner over all nations" (Is 11:10); 75 [57], line 3; 85 [61], line 11.

96. The word "sons," in particular, has a political resonance, since Israelite kings are sometimes called "God's son" (e.g., Solomon).

97. Halevi, *Dīwān*, 1:133 [91].

98. Van Bekkum, *The Secular Poetry of El'azar Ben Ya'aqov ha-Bavli*, 33–34, lines 4–7 (Hebrew sec.). Other poems in the *dīwān* include suggestions of divine selection, e.g., 88 [86].

99. TS 12.416 / ENA 1810.1, Goitein and Friedman, *India Book II*, 464–67 [B69a]. See also the English summary in idem, *India Traders of the Middle Ages*, 523 [II, 69]. A similar panegyric to the same *mamdūḥ* is ENA 3363.1 in *India Book II*, 468 [B69b].

100. TS 13 J 23.4, pub. in Gil, *Ereṣ Yisra'el*, 626–27 [343], lines 11–13. I have changed third-person to second-person address.

101. On the concept of *tawakkul*, see Scheindlin, *Song of the Distant Dove*, *tawakkul* in index.

102. Mark Cohen, *Poverty and Charity in Medieval Egypt*, 186. There, Cohen also recognizes the counter-impulse to this common refrain, that one should rely upon God alone and not upon fellow created beings.

103. See also Rustow, "Formal and Informal Patronage Among Jews in the Islamic East," esp. 353–55, on *ni'ma*; and Mottahedeh, *Loyalty and Leadership*, inter alia.

104. In addition to examples below, we will see in Chap. 9 that the device is even used when Jewish poets praise non-Jewish *mamdūḥs*.

105. Robles and Sáenz-Badillos, *Tĕšuḇot de los discípulos de Mĕnaḥem contra Dunaš Ben Labraṭ*, 7, line 32 (Hebrew sec.).

106. Halevi, *Dīwān*, 1:27 [20], line 19, already in Gn 33:10, though commentators, including Avraham Ibn Ezra, often take the word *elohim* here to mean "angels." Describing the *mamdūḥ* as an angel is quite common (e.g., Brener, *Isaac Ibn Khalfun*, 110; Ibn Khalfūn, *Shirei Yiṣḥaq Ibn Khalfūn*, 10).

107. Halevi, *Dīwān*, 1:53 [40], line 22.

108. Ibid., 1:81 [59], line 6.

109. Ibid., 1:112 [78], lines 19–21. "Cultured man," lit., "brother of culture" (*aḥi musar*), taken like the Arabic *ṣāḥib al-adab*.

110. Another common metaphor (or metonymy) for the structure of the Jewish polity is the *menorah*, the candelabrum that stood outside the Temple: the academy, the gaon, or another leader as its base and emissaries or followers as its branches and cups. Jews of France praised Ḥasdai Ibn Shaprut: "[You are] Our support, shield and buckler, who joins together our dispersed ones. From us, the communities of France (*Faranṣa*) . . . the shaft and branches [of your Menorah, Ex 25:31], your nose rings and finery." Mann, *Texts and Studies*, 1:27–30. Ibn Gabirol praised two emissaries of the Babylonian academy who had reached al-Andalus as "two flanks of the *menorah*." Ibn Gabirol, *Shirei ha-ḥol*, 76–78 [42], line 5. See other examples by Yehudah al-Ḥarīzī in Chap. 4, pp. 150–51.

CHAPTER 8

1. S. M. Stern, "A Twelfth-Century Circle of Hebrew Poets."

2. In the fourteenth century, Shemuel Ibn Sasson was active in the relatively small town of Carrión and nearby Fromista. Ibn Sasson wrote a number of poems to renowned Jewish personalities of his day, probably in the hope of establishing formal and mutual connections, though his poems seem to have gone unrecognized. Importantly, Ibn Sasson did not operate in a vacuum; he, too, belonged to a kind of poetic circle replete with *mamdūḥs*, correspondents, and rivals. See Brann, Sáenz-Badillos, and Targarona Borrás, "The Poetic Universe of Samuel Ibn Sasson, Hebrew Poet of Fourteenth-Century Castile."

3. See the review of the evidence by Kanarfogel, *Intellectual History and Rabbinic Culture of Medieval Ashkenaz*, 382–87, 442–43.

4. One exception might be the letter of Jews of *Faranṣa* for Ḥasdai Ibn Shaprut, though, of course, this was sent to an Andalusian; see Mann, *Texts and Studies*, 1:27–30.

5. The state of Ibn Ezra's corpus of nonliturgical poetry is still in a surprisingly unscientific state. We still use the edition by Kahana, *Qoveṣ ḥokhmat ha-Rav Avraham Ibn Ezra*. See also Bernstein, "Poems from an Unknown Diwan of R. Abraham Ibn Ezra," esp. poems 4 and 5 for panegyrics. See also I. Levin, *Avraham Ibn Ezra*. Among the poems for Andalusians and Maghribis, see Kahana, 48–49 [25], 52–54 [31], 56–59 [33].

6. Parshandata; cf. Est 9:7, but used here for its meaning, "Interpreter of the Law."

7. Kahana, *Qoveṣ ḥokhmat ha-Rav Avraham Ibn Ezra*, 59–60. Although it is often cited that the poem is about Rashi (on the grounds that "Parshandata" became a nickname for him), I agree with Kahana that this is difficult to reconcile with the other content of the poem, which suggests that the *mamdūḥ* is alive. See his commentary, 226–27.

8. Lit., "back."

9. Kahana, *Qoveṣ ḥokhmat ha-Rav Avraham Ibn Ezra*, 69–70 [46].

10. Ibid., 80–81 [51–52].

11. Ibid., 168 [125]. See also Pagis, "Shirei temunah ʿivriyyim ve-ʿod ṣurot melakhutiyot."

12. Schirmann, *Toledot . . . Ṣarfat*, 29–30.

13. Avoiding the problem of the *mamdūḥ* (even metaphorically) resurrecting the dead, Weinberger translates, "who brings comfort to the soul and restores the body." This does not seem warranted. Also, it is possible that the quoted speech continues at this point.

14. Here I am employing the technique of structuralist analysis employed with respect to the Arabic *qaṣīda* by Sperl, "Islamic Kingship and Arabic Panegyric Poetry in the Early Ninth Century." I did not write about this method in earlier chapters of the book, but I have studied the phenomenon of semantic and thematic repetition in the Andalusian Hebrew *qaṣīda* and the method often reveals the types of parallels and contrasts that Sperl documents in the case of Arabic.

15. In general on Roger II, see Mallette, *The Kingdom of Sicily 1100–1250*, 17–46, and translations 139–45. On his practice of personally hearing the petitions of subjects as an imitation of a caliphal practice, see Rustow, "The Legal Status of Ḏimmīs in the Fatimid East," 328.

16. On the fascinating rise of courtly literature in Sicily under Frederick II, again see the study of Mallette, *The Kingdom of Sicily 1100–1250*.

17. See S. M. Stern, "A Twelfth-Century Circle of Hebrew Poets," 68–69, quotation n. 29.

18. See Simonsohn, *The Jews in Sicily*, 1:xxxv. Simonsohn seems to place the years of Anatoli's sojourn a bit later, during the Hohenstaufen period (after 1194). He also raises a few critiques of Stern, most saliently that, with certain exceptions, we do not know conclusively exactly which figures in the *dīwān* were in Sicily or native to Sicily. Still, I think that there is enough evidence to speak of a Sicilian circle.

19. S. M. Stern argues that the poetry of the Sicilian natives also bears "no traces of a direct influence of Arabic poetry"; "A Twelfth-Century Circle of Hebrew Poets," 62.

20. For Stern's quotation, see pt. 2 of the article, p. 112.

21. Unfortunately, neither the *dīwān* nor other sources reveal much about Jewish communal organization or leadership during this period. In general, see Simonsohn, *The Jews in Sicily*, 1:xxxv–l. The sources reveal more about trade, which remained robust, and some shifts in status from the Norman to the Hohenstaufen periods, most importantly that during the latter, Jews were designated *servi camerae nostri*.

22. Scheindlin writes about the device of the "return verse" in "Secular Hebrew Poetry in Fifteenth-Century Spain," 25–37 and nn. on 301–7. One might collect instances of circle poems over many centuries (beginning with Ibn Gabirol's *ṭerem heyoti ḥasdekha ba'ani*) and the unique poetics involved. A number of examples are treated below.

23. S. M. Stern, "A Twelfth-Century Circle of Hebrew Poets," 76, first poem, vv. 1–3, 5–6.

24. Ibid., 78.

25. Ibid., 67.

26. Ibid., 77.

27. Relevant for the court culture of Toledo before the period of Alfonso X was the activity of Avraham ha-Fakhar, who praised Alfonso VIII in Arabic and was praised in Hebrew rhymed prose by Yehudah Ibn Shabbetai; see Decter, "Ibrāhīm Ibn al-Fakhkhār al-Yahūdī."

28. *Qeru'ei ha-'edot*, lit., "those called among the communities."

29. Deborah, lit., "wife of Lapidot"; cf. Jgs 4–5. The entire passage is T. Abulafia, *Gan ha-meshallim ve-ha-ḥiddot*, vol. 1, part 1, p. 2 (1,1:2), lines 13–15.

30. "You possess no horses to offer as a gift, no wealth or riches; if the state of affairs (*al-ḥāl*) won't help you, speech will!"

31. T. Abulafia, *Gan ha-meshallim ve-ha-ḥiddot*, 1,1:26–27 (of the commentary section).

32. Ibid., 1,1:45–46 (commentary section).

33. Ibid., 1,1:72 [200].

34. In one of his articles, Sáenz-Badillos wrote that an article on this group was in press. However, I have not been able to locate this article and am not certain that it was ever published. The planned title was "Poetas menores de la Corte Alfonsi"; the citation can be found in Sáenz-Badillos, "Hebrew Invective Poetry," 68n7.

35. T. Abulafia, *Gan ha-meshallim ve-ha-ḥiddot*, 1,1:128–32 [398], lines 59–60. For Ibn Gabirol, see Chap. 7, p. 197. Todros praises *mamdūḥ*s with terms such as Merciful (*raḥum*) and "One who clothes the naked" (*malbish 'arumim*) with some frequency.

36. T. Abulafia, *Gan ha-meshallim ve-ha-ḥiddot*, 2,1:17–18 [465], line 4.

37. Sáenz-Badillos, "Hebrew Invective Poetry," 66–67.

38. T. Abulafia, *Gan ha-meshallim ve-ha-ḥiddot*, 1,1:128–32 [398], lines 18–19, 80–81.

39. The text here has "Tree of Life," but I have emended it to avoid a repetition of "Tree of Life" with the next verse. "Fruit" is also a more frequent metaphor for "knowledge," often specifically "speech." The emendation does not affect the meter.

40. *Le-'ever ha-ṣevi*. Yellin emended the text to say, "I turned in the direction of Time," since later it is Time that answers. Still, it makes sufficient sense to just turn westward hopefully and speak to the general audience.

41. Seal and its cord; cf. Gn 38:18.

42. T. Abulafia, *Gan ha-meshallim ve-ha-ḥiddot*, 1,1:126–28, lines 19–22, 26–29, 40, 43, 46, 52, 66–67

43. On rituals of initiation generally, see Chaps. 1, pp. 57–59, and 4., pp. 133–40.

44. These poems can be found, in order, 1,1:190–91 [434]; 1,1:70 [574]; 1,1:180 [430]; 1,2:79 [590]; 1,1: 7–29 [3–48]; 2,1: 42–43 [532–33].

45. In general, see Brann, *The Compunctious Poet*; these specific poems are discussed on 149–56.

46. A variation of the widespread image of generosity, "dew of Ḥermon," substituting "rain" because of the rhyme. Gilboa, on the other hand, had been cursed by King David: "Let there be no rain nor dew upon you" (2 Sm 1:21).

47. See p. 325, n. 42.

48. Hebrew superscription, 1,1:117 of commentary.

49. Brann, *The Compunctious Poet*, 154.

50. See p. 172.

51. The superscription is preserved in T. Abulafia, *Gan ha-meshallim ve-ha-ḥiddot*, 1,1:123.

52. On the scribe, see Kfir, "Center and Periphery in Medieval Hebrew Poetry," 280. This excellent dissertation also includes the most updated critical edition of many poems of these poets.

53. Kfir agrees that the referent is ambiguous.

54. I read the "man of God" and the "star that rose" as two distinct subjects. If only one, then Abulafia.

55. Here, Kfir sees the subject as Todros, which is also possible. If so, one may omit "[other]" later in the sentence. Regarding "his sheaf stands upright," see Gn 37:7, Joseph's dream, i.e., others bow before him.

56. Cf. Sg 1:12.

57. Conceivably, the following appellations, the most interesting in the group, could refer to Alfonso, which might present some interesting interpretive issues. See Chap. 9 in this vol.

58. "Courtiers," lit., "those who see the face [of the king]."

59. "Whose name is greater than *rabban*"; cf. Tosefta *'eduyot* 3:4, "He who has disciples and disciples of disciples do they call *rabbi*. [When] his disciples' disciples are praised, they call him *rabban*. When these and those have been praised, they call him by his name." Trans. Neusner, *The Tosefta*, 4:309. Text in Kfir, "Center and Periphery in Medieval Hebrew Poetry," 317–19.

60. See *Ḥerev mithapakhat*, ed. Steinschneider, in the appendix to Bedersi, *Sefer ḥotam tokhnit*, 13–21; the quotation is 21, line 204.

61. Kfir, "Center and Periphery in Medieval Hebrew Poetry," 8, 320 [32].

62. Ibid., 321 [35, 36]; 322–24 [38–42]; 324–25 [43–44]. Schirmann referred to these exchanges as *tensonot hafukhot* (inverted *tensons*), an inversion of the troubadour *tenson* exchanges that focused on invective. *Toledot . . . Ṣarfat*, 472.

63. E.g., a short panegyric by Zeraḥya Gerondi for two figures in Mezliś, *Shirat ha-Maor*, 163.

64. See Einbinder, *No Place of Rest*, 33.

65. He included southern France within his parameters of Sefarad; on Sefarad as an area defined by culture rather than geography, see Decter, *Iberian Jewish Literature*, 211.

66. Kfir, "Center and Periphery in Medieval Hebrew Poetry," 232–34, lines 26–27, 34, 38–41.

67. Ibid., 237 [12], line 8. In this case, the two worked out their differences in subsequent correspondence.

68. Ibid., 229–30.

69. Ibid., 224–25. Other cities attacked are Manosque and Aix.

70. "Does not allow his dough to sour," an expression for performing religious commandments without delay.

71. Cf. the standard opening in the Haggadah, "How much dignity and glory and how many virtues has God [lit., "the place"] set upon us."

72. Davidson, *Parody in Jewish Literature*, 16.

73. Bakhtin, *Rabelais and His World*, quotations from 11, 14, 78. Bakhtin's thesis is not without its problems, beginning with the fact that "parody" was not a term of medieval genre classification, and also because of the teleological employment of the evidence wherein a medieval anti-authoritarianism became the seed of a trend that blossomed in the early modern and modern periods. For an excellent review on the state of the question, see Burde, "The *Parodia Sacra* Problem and Medieval Comic Studies." Historiographically speaking, Davidson's study, now over a century old, also seems bound up with issues of modernization and Jewish modernity, in particular. The entire subject is worth revisiting.

74. Brann, *The Compunctious Poet*, 141.

75. Septimus, "Piety and Power in Thirteenth-Century Catalonia," 213.

76. Fleischer, "The 'Gerona School' of Hebrew Poetry." I am less convinced, however, of Fleischer's opinion that, due to DaPierra's "religiosity" (*datiyuto*), references in his verse to the "generosity" of *mamdūḥ*s indicate the giving of alms to the exclusion of literary patronage. See Fleischer's note in Schirmann, *Toledot . . . Ṣarfat*, 297n76.

77. "Men of rank," *yoshvim*; lit., "sitters."

78. All quotations from DaPierra's poetry are from the ed. by Ḥ. Brody, "Shirei Meshullam Ben Shelomoh DaPierra," here pp. 81–83 [36], lines 22, 40.

79. E.g., see Beeri, "Eli he-ḥaver Ben ʿAmram," 310–12 [9], line 9, a panegyric for Elḥanan Ben Shemariahu: "He is good in a session (*yeshivah*) and comely in a gathering (*mesibah*)."

80. *Meyudaʿim*, *benei ḥevrah*, *ohavai*, *yedidai*, *anshei ha-brit* (18–20, 26, 29).

81. Bonner, *Songs of the Troubadours*, 199–201. Faidit is the name of another troubadour. See another example by Bertran de Born (c. 1140–94), 146.

82. Dagenais, "Genre and Demonstrative Rhetoric."

83. One of the longer ones concludes a love poem (*canso*) by Aimeric de Péguilhan (early thirteenth century) for Frederick II, "Song, go now in my name and in Love's, to

the good, the fair, the valiant and the praiseworthy, to him whom Latins and Germans serve, to whom they bow down as to a good Emperor; above the most eminent he has such eminence, liberality, merit, honor, and courtliness, wisdom, and knowledge, judgment and discernment—great in that greatness by which great merit is won." Quoted in Press, *Anthology of Troubadour Lyric Poetry*, 226–29. See also dedications, 310–15.

84. Brody reads the verse somewhat differently and paraphrases, "when I praise my friend in song his soul speaks in my throat and my words sing the intelligence of his lips."

85. Ḥ. Brody, "Shirei Meshullam Ben Shelomoh DaPierra," 97–99 [43], lines 21–22, 30–32, 35–36, 40–41.

86. Ibid., 42–44 [17], lines 14–19.

87. DaPierra describes *mamdūḥ*s in this circle with imagery that, while not atypical for the medieval Hebrew corpus, might have carried specific resonances for the kabbalist audience; see, e.g., Ḥ. Brody, "Shirei Meshullam Ben Shelomoh DaPierra," 105–8 [45], esp. lines 14–22, 50, 54–55. DaPierra also describes them as date palms, incense lamps, and crowns.

88. Cf. Gn 49:26.

89. Cf. Gn 18:19.

90. "Dragon in a river"; cf. Ez 29:13, but there of the enemy Pharaoh; "lion whelp . . . Bashan," Dt 33:22, of Dan.

91. Ḥ. Brody, "Shirei Meshullam Ben Shelomoh DaPierra," 62–65 [28], lines 7–16. As noted by Brody, the odd final image is based on Ps 140:4.

92. In fact, DaPierra almost consistently praises *mamdūḥ*s as "advisers," where one would more readily expect "wise men" (*ḥakhamim*).

93. A significant amount of scholarship has been dedicated to these poets over the past couple of decades, though much of the corpus remains in manuscript. Vardi, "'Adat ha-nognim be-Saragosa"; Scheindlin, "Secular Hebrew Poetry in Fifteenth-Century Spain"; Huss, *Meliṣat 'Efer ve-Dinah le-Don Vidal Benveniste*. Further bibliography on specific poets is given below.

94. Talmage, "The Francesc de Sant Jordi-Solomon Bonafed Letters," 340.

95. Whereas most modern editions of the *dīwān*s of these poets tend to excerpt the poems of the individual author from the correspondence, recent attempts have been made to present both sides of correspondences as in the manuscripts, which is preferable. E.g., Targarona Borrás and Vardi, "Literary Correspondence Between Vidal Abenvenist and Solomon De Piera"; Targarona Borrás and Scheindlin, "Literary Correspondence Between Vidal Benvenist Ben Lavi and Solomon Ben Meshulam De Piera." On Romance literary competition and correspondence in the late fourteenth and early fifteenth centuries, see Targarona Borrás and Vardi, 410n21.

96. Ben Shalom, "The Courtier as the Scepter of Judah."

97. The poem is in ibid., 210–11, lines 9–10, 19–20.

98. The figure lamented was also the father of Vidal Benveniste, the great poet who converted to Christianity and took the name Gonsalo. This figure should not be confused with Don Benveniste de la Cavalleria, whom Baer called "the last Aragonese Jew to wield

political influence" in Spain and who died in 1411 (before the Tortosa disputation); see Baer, *A History of the Jews in Christian Spain*, 2:173.

99. See Targarona Borrás and Scheindlin, "Literary Correspondence Between Vidal Benvenist Ben Lavi and Solomon Ben Meshulam De Piera," 68n40.

100. DaPierra, *Divan*, 10–13 [2]; the verses quoted are between lines 10 and 34. See also Bernstein, "Shir tehillah shel Shelomoh de Pierra li-khevod rabbah shel Qastiliah Rav Me'ir Alguadex."

101. On these circumstances, see Targarona Borrás and Scheindlin, "Literary Correspondence Between Vidal Benvenist Ben Lavi and Solomon Ben Meshulam De Piera," 67–68.

102. For a brief summary of Jewish courtiers in Christian Iberia, see Decter, "Before Caliphs and Kings."

103. DaPierra, *Divan*, 80 [81]. On this poem, see Chap. 9, pp. 270–71.

104. Ogres, *emim*, Gn 14:4.

105. Taking *ṣofim* as a noun, figurative of prophets; cf. Hos 9:8 and elsewhere.

106. Lit., "a company of song's prophets."

107. Targarona Borrás and Vardi, "Literary Correspondence Between Vidal Abenvenist and Solomon De Piera," 462–66, lines 9–13, 61–62. On the truly dizzying data on identifying and distinguishing this and other figures with similar names, see the discussion in the introduction of this article.

108. Quoted in Schirmann, *Toledot . . . Ṣarfat*, 630. Heman and Yedutun are Levites (1 Chr 25:1 and elsewhere), hence singers.

109. The *dīwān* of Bonafed is published by Escanilla, "Shelomoh Bonafed," 1:228 [48], lines 30–31.

110. Ibid., 1:212–24 [41], line 7.

111. For *tajnīs*, see DaPierra, *Divan*, 62–66; for first word/last word, DaPierra, 18 [5]; for numeric mnemonics, Targarona Borrás and Scheindlin, "Literary Correspondence Between Vidal Benvenist Ben Lavi and Solomon Ben Meshulam De Piera," 112; the main poems treated in this article also exhibit the feature of reusing a word from each line of the model poem in the response poem.

112. Escanilla, "Shelomoh Bonafed," 1:278–83 [62], line 65.

113. Scheindlin, "Secular Hebrew Poetry in Fifteenth-Century Spain," 29–30.

114. Escanilla, "Shelomoh Bonafed," 198–200 [35], line 23. For an excellent study of the "from you, to you" motif, see I. Levin, *Keter malkhut le-rabi Shelomoh Ibn Gabirol*, 131–50.

115. For a wedding, see Vardi, "Wedding in Agramont"; loss of income, Escanilla, "Shelomoh Bonafed," 131 [8]; donation of "crown," Prats, "A Hebrew Poetry Contest in Early-Fifteenth-Century Zaragoza"; travel to Muslim territory, Escanilla, "Shelomoh Bonafed," 54 [49]; homily, DaPierra, *Divan*, 29 [14]; joining the *kat meshorerim*, Escanilla, "Shelomoh Bonafed," 61 [57]; recovery from illness, Escanilla, "Shelomoh Bonafed," 162 [21]; toothache, DaPierra, *Divan*, 46 [39].

116. DaPierra, 87–89 [91]. The poem is also discussed by Wacks, *Double Diaspora in Sephardic Literature*, 132–33. Bonafed is also reported to have written a letter in a Romance

vernacular, but this text does not survive. See Sáenz-Badillos, "Shelomoh Bonafed at the Crossroads of Hebrew and Romance Cultures," 353–54.

117. Lit., "flames of flames."

118. *Magen meginnah*, shield, covering (of heart—*meginnah* appears only once in the Bible in this form: Lam 3:65, *meginnat-lev*, "covering of heart"). See similar usage in another poem in Escanilla, "Shelomoh Bonafed," 112 [2], line 27.

119. Escanilla, "Shelomoh Bonafed," 105–7 [1], lines 13–25.

120. One poem bears the superscription "a poem sent, after becoming a Christian, by En Solomon de Pierra, when he was older than seventy years, to his friend Don Vidal." However, in other manuscripts, it would appear that the poem was sent *to* DaPierra after his conversion. See DaPierra, *Diwan*, 2. See also Schirmann, *Toledot . . . Ṣarfat*, 588–92, though the assumptions of DaPierra's crypto-Judaism are largely unfounded.

121. Talmage, "The Francesc de Sant Jordi-Solomon Bonafed Letters."

122. I have translated from the version in Gross, "Ha-meshorer Shelomoh Bonafed," 1:51, lines 16–17.

123. Ibid., 53, lines 1–7.

124. Ibid., 51, lines 1–2.

125. As Gross suggests, Aderet might be playing on a textual ambiguity in Am 4:13, which can be read, "God proclaims for man *his anointed*" (*meshiḥo*, which the Septuagint translated as *Christos*, which, in turn, lent itself naturally to a Christological reading); or it can be read, "God proclaims for man *his speech*" (*mah siḥo*) (which is how the Masoretes vocalize it). Hence Aderet's verse exploits the ambiguity and alludes to competing reading traditions.

126. These verses are in Gross, "Ha-meshorer Shelomoh Bonafed," 54, lines 1, 7.

127. I.e., Israel.

128. On the other hand, the *adom/edom* play is quite widespread.

129. Gross, "Ha-meshorer Shelomoh Bonafed," 54, superscription to poem 4.

130. Sáenz-Badillos, "The Literary World of Shelomoh Bonafed," 167.

131. Habermann, "Iggerot Shelomo DaPierra le-Mosheh 'Abbas," 174–77. See also Schirmann, *Toledot . . . Ṣarfat*, 595, including the helpful n. 58 by Fleischer. The poem is also printed in DaPierra, *Divan*, 37 [26].

132. Escanilla, "Shelomoh Bonafed," 142 [14], line 2. See also a further example in Patai, "Shirei ḥol shel Shelomoh Bonafed," 71.

133. Lida, "La hyperbole sagrada en la poesía castellana del siglo XV" (for the verse by ha-Gorni, see above, p. 226).

134. Boase, *The Troubadour Revival*, 116–17.

CHAPTER 9

1. The exact contents of the Arabic inscriptions, apart from a few words, and even whether sections are in a real or ersatz Arabic, have puzzled scholars for over a century. In general, see Gerber, "The World of Samuel Halevi."

2. Cf. Ps 99:3.

3. *Ish ha-beinayyim*; lit., "man in the middle," i.e., between two armies, e.g., 1 Sm 17:4. Cantera Burgos likewise translates "campeador."

4. "Protector"; lit., "man."

5. Inscription illegible at this point.

6. Hebrew text in Burgos and Vallicrosa, *Las Inscripciones Hebraicas de España*, 338 [fig. 221]. I also consulted his Spanish translation and the English translation by Gerber.

7. See Jastrow, *Dictionary of the Targumim, Talmud Babli and Yerushalmi, and Midrashic Literature*, 128.

8. See Rashi's commentary ad locum.

9. Estow, *Pedro the Cruel of Castile*, 166.

10. Ibid., 202.

11. A quick survey of the phrase *ha-nesher ha-gadol* in the Bar-Ilan Responsa project yields that the appellation was used by: Meir Abulafia (1170–1244) for Maimonides; Asher Ben Yeḥiel (1250–1327) for Rav Asher; Yiṣḥaq Ben Sheshet (1326–1408) for the Ashkenazi Meir ha-Levi; Shim'on Ben Ṣemaḥ Duran (1361–1441) for Maharam of Rothenburg; Joseph Karo (1488–1575) for Abravanel. Bedersi uses "the great eagle" for Todros Abulafia (or possibly Alfonso X; see Chap. 8, p. 224) as well as for the (otherwise unknown) poet Avraham Shaqil. See Steinschneider's appendix to Bedersi, *Sefer ḥotam tokhnit*, 21, line 161. Also, in the *Zohar*, Ilai of Neṣivin is called the Great Eagle (in Aramaic); see Matt, *Zohar*, 9:58. In short, the appellation does not become associated with Maimonides exclusively until the early modern period, likely because of the history of printing Maimonides' works as well as the fact that he became known as the Aquila Synogogae (the Eagle of the Synagogue) in Latin works; see S. Scheiber, "Introduction" to *Codex Maimuni*, 11. I would like to thank Raymond Scheindlin for suggesting this direction of research.

12. There are other possible biblical intertexts in play. On the positive side, God is likened to an eagle in Dt 32:11; but in Ob 1:4, the prophet issues a pronouncement for a haughty Edom: "Should you nest as high as the eagle . . . even from there I will pull you down." These verses are discussed in relation to a Hapsburg-era Jewish synagogue painting in M. Epstein, *Dreams of Subversion in Medieval Jewish Art and Literature*, 34–35.

13. Linder, "The Jews Too Were Not Absent . . . Carrying Moses's Law on Their Shoulders," 326.

14. Ibid., 391.

15. E.g., on 391, Linder argues that praises for popes that draw upon biblical epithets for God yield an absurdity that renders them subversive. However, we have seen that this technique was also used by Jews when praising coreligionists. Incidentally, although Linder does not identify any malintent, one Jewish laud of 1721 calls Pope Innocent XIII the "great eagle" (381). The association, in this case, is based on the pope's former name and title, the initials of which correspond with the initials of the final words of Ez 17:3 in its Latin translation, i.e., "Aquila altera grandis **m**agnis **a**lis **m**ultisque **p**lumis" = Michael Angelus Max Pont.

16. Scott, *Domination and the Arts of Resistance*, xii, 19.

17. Several excellent books in Jewish studies make use of Scott. Horowitz, *Reckless Rites*, 85, 196; Boyarin and Boyarin, *Powers of Diaspora*, esp. 54–55; Seidman, *Faithful Renderings*, 4–5. Scott's ideas also seem implicit in M. Epstein, *Dreams of Subversion in Medieval Jewish Art and Literature*, 6; Yuval, *Two Nations in Your Womb*. On countervailing trends that portray Jews as docile or wholly loyal, see historiographic discussions in Horowitz above.

18. The only place where I break chronology is in presenting Shelomoh DaPierra before Santob de Carrión so that I can treat the Castilian text separately and end again in the Castile of Pedro I. There are other medieval texts that I am not addressing here. In Latin, Qalonymos Ben Qalonymos described Robert of Anjou as "Solomon the Second" in the introduction to his translation of Ibn Rushd's *Taḥāfut al-taḥāfut* (Incoherence of the incoherence); Schirmann, *Toledot . . . Ṣarfat*, 520–21. One should also see the multilingual epitaphs for Ferdinand III of Castile (d. 1252); while all versions praise him for capturing Seville, only the Latin adds, "from the hands of the pagans." See Dodds, Menocal, and Balbale, *The Arts of Intimacy*, 199–201. See also Bedersi for Todros Abulafia and Alfonso X in Chap. 8, p. 224.

19. For a plausible reconstruction of events surrounding the letter, see Ashtor, *The Jews of Moslem Spain*, 1:188–91; Mann, *Texts and Studies*, 1:10–12. The other letter, partly preserved in the same document, is intended for Empress Helena; more of the substance of the letter is preserved, but there is no opening address.

20. Lit., "hidden places."

21. I accept Mann's emendation of *nehedar* and the association in his note with the Yom Kippur liturgy. The manuscript reads *ne'edar*, "dear," which is reasonable and what Fleischer prefers.

22. *Bigdei tofes*. I am following Mann over Fleischer here, since the manuscript clearly denotes a *t* and not a *ḥ*. Fleischer reads *bigdei ḥofesh*; cf. Ez 27:20, "precious clothing" (appropriate for riding), which is a reasonable emendation. Although Mann notes that he does not understand the phrase, I believe that *tofes* could be used here in the sense of "one who lays siege, capture" (e.g., Dt 20:19; 1 Sm 15:8) and may stand for the phrase *tofsei milḥamah* (Nm 31:27). Either way, it is clearly a martial image.

23. Cf. Is 43:19, substituting *ṣayon* for *yeshimon* because of the rhyme.

24. TS J 2.71.1v, transcribed in Mann, *Texts and Studies*, 1:22–23, and (with improvements) in Fleischer, "Le-toledot shirat ha-ḥol ha-'ivrit vi-Sefarad be-reishitah," 58. My translation is based on Fleischer and the original manuscript, with some preferences for Mann's readings. Golb and Pritsak hold that this text was actually addressed to Romanus Lecapenus, based on their conclusion that a second fragment belongs to the same letter, a connection that Mann had considered but rejected. See their *Khazarian Hebrew Documents of the Tenth Century*, 83–86. Most of my discussion is not affected if one accepts Golb and Pritsak.

25. Although Byzantine courts appear as multiethnic and multilingual (e.g., Persian, Armenian), I do not see any direct evidence for Jewish courtiers at this time. See Kazhdan and McCormick, "The Social World of the Byzantine Court."

26. Ashtor, *The Jews of Moslem Spain*, 190.

27. Nesbitt, *Catalogue of Byzantine Seals at Dumbarton Oaks and in the Fogg Museum of Art*, no. 63.2. See also the excellent online exhibit: http://www.doaks.org/resources/seals/gods-regents-on-earth-a-thousand-years-of-byzantine-imperial-seals/rulers-of-byzantium/constantine-vii-27-january20136-april-945.

28. Cf. the letter of the Armenian Katholikos Yovhannēs V Drasxanakertc'I to Constantine VII in Yovhannēs V, *History of Armenia,* trans. Krikor H. Maksoudian, 192, which does include "autocrator." I wish to thank Sergio La Porta for this reference.

29. See Schechter, *Saadyana,* 57, line 13.

30. Den Heijer and Yeshaya, "Solomon ben Joseph ha-Kohen on Fāṭimid Victory"; Greenstone, "The Turkoman Defeat at Cairo."

31. Bierman, *Writing Signs*, 60.

32. Ibid., 107.

33. See the useful review essay by Den Heijer, "Religion, Ethnicity, and Gender Under Fatimid Rule."

34. Qutbuddin, *Al-Mu'ayyad al-Shirāzī and Fatimid Da'wa Poetry*, esp. 143–72.

35. Also, in the twelfth century, Benjamin of Tudela described the Abbasid caliph in Baghdad as one "versed in Mosaic Law [who] reads and writes the Hebrew tongue." See Adler, *The Itinerary of Benjamin of Tudela*, 55 (Hebrew sec.).

36. *Shelemim*; lit., "perfect, complete."

37. This follows den Heijer and Yeshaya's interpretation ("and give thanks"), though *qidda* is more literally a "bow." Greenstone, although admitting that he does not understand the verse, translates "cassia" (an aromatic plant). This could also be made intelligible in consideration of Ex 20:24, where cassia is the main ingredient of sacred oil. Hence one might translate, "and from your soul, offer sacred oil with abundant expressions and utterances," which would not alter the meaning significantly.

38. Den Heijer and Yeshaya, "Solomon ben Joseph ha-Kohen on Fāṭimid Victory," 162.

39. In the latter instance, Ibn Janāḥ translates *wazīr, wuzarā* (vizier, viziers); similar is his explanation of 2 Kgs 10:11. Abravanel in 2 Sm 8:18 also explains *kohanim* as *nesi'im ve-sarim* (princes and ministers).

40. Bierman, *Writing Signs*, 103–4.

41. See also the specifically Isma'ili terminology in Judeo-Arabic petitions in Chap. 1, p. 45.

42. See Cortese and Calderini, *Family Ties*, chap. 2; quotation, p. 44. Recognizing the multiethnic nature of the empire in ha-Kohen's poem is striking, given that later in the poem, the enemy is characterized as a hodgepodge of Armenians, Arabs, Greeks, and other groups; lines 48–49. Togarmah is quite reasonably associated with Turkomans. Rifatayyim might be Berbers, as den Heijer and Yeshaya speculate.

43. However, an address (by a Muslim) for al-Mustanṣir preserved in the Geniza (the document concerns a synagogue) uses the typical language of his being fit for "religion and the world" (*al-dīn wa'l-dunyā*); see Gottheil, "An Eleventh-Century Document Concerning a Cairo Synagogue."

44. Qutbuddin, *Al-Mu'ayyad al-Shirāzī and Fatimid Da'wa Poetry*, 171–72.

45. Cf. translations in Greenstone, "The Turkoman Defeat at Cairo," 161; Mann, *The Jews in Egypt and in Palestine*, 1:208; Yahalom, "The Temple and the City in Liturgical Hebrew Poetry," 289. Yahalom does not try to explain the phrase "like twin brothers." Perhaps it simply refers back figuratively to the two qualities predicated earlier in the verse: "the beloved" and "the trusted" (or perhaps to "glory" and "honor" in the previous verse).

46. Cf. titles in den Heijer, "Le vizir fatimide Badr al-Ǧamālī," esp. 98–99; Brett, "Badr al-Ǧamālī and the Fatimid Renascence."

47. See Chap. 1, p. 47. This figure's other titles were *sar ha-'edah* (prince of the community) and *pe'er ha-kohanim* (wonder of the priests); the former might be reflected in v. 23.

48. The Arabic writing is so large that only twelve words (some partial) fit on the entire sheet; the original decree must have taken up many pages and been for public viewing. I wish to thank Marina Rustow and Naïm Vanthieghem for sharing with me their transcription of the Arabic (correspondence with Rustow).

49. Kraus, "Hebräische und syrische Zitate in ismāʿīlitischen Schriften"; S. M. Stern, "Heterodox Ismaʿilism at the Time of al-Muʿizz"; Hollenberg, "Disrobing Judges with Veiled Truths."

50. But see above, n. 35.

51. Yefet Ben 'Eli takes Daniel 7 as an extended allegory about Islam. See also Saʿadia Gaon's more veiled comments on Dn 7:24–25; David al-Fasī, *Kitāb jamīʿ al-alfāẓ* also alludes to Islam and Muḥammad. All this can be found in the article by Ben Shammai, "The Attitudes of Some Early Karaites Toward Islam." See also Yefet's critique of Ismaʿili interpretation of the Bible in S. M. Stern, "Heterodox Ismaʿilism at the Time of al-Muʿizz."

52. Sadan, "Rabbi Judah al-Ḥarīzī as Cultural Crossroads."

53. This is Sadan's suggestion, based on references to sacrifice within the poem.

54. *Aʿatān*, lit., "resting places for camels near water."

55. Both these phrases have a very biblical ring to them; cf. Lm 5:21, "Renew our days as of old," and Ps 75:4, "It is I who make the pillars of the earth firm." Such a verse reflects how the Jewish poet may have "thought in Hebrew" or drawn upon Hebrew poetics when writing Arabic, much as he drew upon Arabic when composing in Hebrew.

56. Lit., "the blaze of the guest meal (*al-qirā*), [the land's] guests go to it night-blind" (*taʿashū*).

57. Lit., "firmness of the height of the Creator's sky."

58. "Authority," lit., "hands," but this figurative sense is common. Sadan has "more [generous] hands whose boughs." I see the *min* in the sense of "on account of, because of" rather than in the comparative sense.

59. Lit., a "place of roaming."

60. Sadan, "Rabbi Judah al-Ḥarīzī as Cultural Crossroads," 58–61.

61. On the expression, see Chap. 4, p. 142.

62. Sadan, "Rabbi Judah al-Ḥarīzī as Cultural Crossroads," 50n71.

63. Although the root *hdy* can also relate to "giving" (e.g., *hidāya*, gift), I do not see this meaning associated with the lexeme *hudā*.

64. Al-Ḥarīzī, *Kitāb al-durar*, 104, lines 182–83.

65. Al-Ḥarīzī, *Wanderings of Judah Alharīzī*, 248.

66. Al-Ḥarīzī, *Kitāb al-durar*, 126–30, lines 27–82. The overlap is noted briefly in two articles by Yosef Yahalom, "Redacción y reelaboración," 179–80; idem, "Arabic and Hebrew as Poetic Languages Within Jewish and Muslim Society," 312–13.

67. For a complete comparison of the two poems, see Decter, "The (Interreligious?) Rededication of an Arabic Panegyric by Judah al-Ḥarīzī" (in progress).

68. Lit., "spearheads."

69. For *thny*, generally to "bend," as "binding an animal," see Lane, *Arabic-English Lexicon*, 356.

70. "Battle," lit., "tumult."

71. Sadan, "Rabbi Judah al-Ḥarīzī as Cultural Crossroads," 56–58.

72. Ibid., 36–37.

73. One of the poems preserved for Ibn Abī Bakr, actually an invective, likewise plays on the biblical Moses: "We hoped that after Jesus, Muḥammad would come to deliver us from intense suffering and affliction / But he set us down confused in the wilderness of Moses with none to guide and none to console." Al-'Asqalānī, *Shifā al-qulūb fī manāqib banī Ayyūb*, 259.

74. See Brann, *Power in the Portrayal*, 140–59.

75. Al-Ḥarīzī, *Kitāb al-durar*, 110.

76. The discussion below is based on Decter, "Ibrāhīm Ibn al-Fakhkhār al-Yahūdī." See fuller bibliographic information there.

77. Ray, *The Sephardic Frontier*, 15.

78. Praise of the court also appears as a theme in some poems in honor of Alfonso VIII by contemporary troubadours. See, e.g., verses by Ramón Vidal de Bresalú in Alvar, *La poesía trovadoresca en España y Portugal*, 87–88, 127. See also a poem on the court of Alfonso X in Alvar, 243, as well as the discussion of Todros Abulafia below.

79. At least in Sicily, we know that the Norman king Roger II, who was praised in Arabic by Muslim panegyrists, knew Arabic and was praised by Muslim authors for his knowledge of Arabic language and culture. See Mallette, *The Kingdom of Sicily 1100–1250*.

80. This technique is discussed at length in Chap. 7 in this vol.

81. Schirmann, *Toledot . . . Ṣarfat*, 376–77.

82. Burns, *Emperor of Culture*.

83. Doron, *Meshorer be-ḥaṣar ha-melekh*, 41. Doron compares elements of Todros's verse with the poetry of two contemporary troubadours who appeared in Alfonso's court: Guirat Riquier and Bonifaci Calvo. Although her point is right, the comparisons that she draws are overly generic (e.g., the king as a source of light). See also Einbinder, *No Place of Rest*, 21–22.

84. Alvar, *La poesía trovadoresca en España y Portugal*, 244.

85. Ibid., 220.

86. Schirmann, *Ha-shirah ha-'ivrit*, 2:441–42 [388].

87. See p. 191. See also the discussion of pilgrimage as a motif in Chap. 7, p. 203.

88. Schirmann, *Toledot . . . Ṣarfat*, 376n41 (the note is by Fleischer). Doron simply calls it a *canso*; *Meshorer be-ḥaṣar ha-melekh*, 151. Brody, who first edited the poem, already suggested that the form was taken from Castilian poetry. The general rhyme scheme (with slight variation) is abbacca. Unlike most of Todros's poetry, this poem does not follow Arabic quantitative verse.

89. Cf. with Guirat Riquier: "About King Alfonso, everyone should speak well when praising him. No one who magnifies his praise can lie. He is worth so much that not beginning praise is to lie." See Alvar, *La poesía trovadoresca en España y Portugal*, 216. It is not my aim to characterize the poetics of Castilian court panegyrics as specifically Hebrew or Arabic, though such an investigation, which would require a more systematic review of all contributing panegyric traditions, is a desideratum.

90. Lit., "complete."

91. M. Avot 2:20.

92. Cf. Hos 1:7.

93. More generously, Yellin interprets, "there is none who needs to hide from his wrath." However, the verse is probably describing the power of his wrath more than his mercy.

94. T. Abulafia, *Gan ha-meshallim ve-ha-ḥiddot* 3, 56 (of *shirei ezor*). See also Doron, *Meshorer be-ḥaṣar ha-melekh*, 151.

95. DaPierra, *Divan*, 80–82 [81]. The poem on 83 [82] is for the same *mamdūḥ*. Also on 82 are two poems [83, 84] for another Christian figure described as "expert in our language" (he is not named, though the content of one of the poems suggests that his name was Gabriel). The poems for the latter figure include a high degree of sacred hyperbole; the poet writes of the "indwelling (*shekhinah*) of his wisdom" for which "the stranger who approaches it is sanctified."

96. See Perry, *The Moral Proverbs of Santob de Carrión*, 116–20.

97. This is Perry's translation, ibid., 20, lines 185–89. See also Perry's notable discussion of the "rose among thorns" motif as an engagement with Jewish–Christian polemics, 65–73.

98. The translation is from de Carrión, *Proverbios morales*, stanzas 708–25. I wish to thank Luis Girón for reviewing my translation with me.

99. "In equilibrium," *a derecho*, which can also mean "according to law." Hence, Perry translates "through the rule of law," which is also possible or intended secondarily.

100. There have been other interpretations of this ambiguous verse.

101. *Mesura*, an idealized chivalric characteristic in French epic and related literature, such as the *Poem of the Cid*.

102. Perry has "which is ordained," which might lend itself further to the argument presented below, but does not seem justified.

103. Here Santob alludes, as at the beginning of the work, to money that was owed him by Pedro's father, King Alfonso IX, at the time of his death.

104. I believe that this points to a slightly later date for the synagogue than the *Proverbios*, wherein Santob only hopes that the king will "subdue revolt" (724), undoubtedly referring to the contestations over sovereignty that cast a shadow over the early part of his reign. Not known as a king particularly dedicated to artistic or intellectual endeavors, Pedro was ultimately remembered by historians as a "proud and warlike" king for whom "knightly vigor and uncompromising action" were paramount. See Estow, *Pedro the Cruel of Castile*, 130.

105. Perry, *The Moral Proverbs of Santob de Carrión*, v. 2489; De Carrión, *Proverbios morales*, ed. Díaz-Mas and Mota, stanza 657.

106. Maimonides, *Guide of the Perplexed*, 1:54, Pines trans., 126.

107. See Rashi, ad locum; Abravanel on Lv 3:1. Nicholas of Lyra, who read Rashi, also follows this allegory, though Christian commentators more often associate white and red with Christ's divinity and humanity. See Kiecker, *Postilla of Nicholas of Lyra on the Song of Songs*, 86–87.

108. Secondarily, "ruddiness" can be associated not with God but with the Messiah (further below).

109. Note also the statements "judgment is God's only, and the king's" and that the judge is "at the same time of God and the King" (Perry, *The Moral Proverbs of Santob de Carrión*, vv. 1413–17; Díaz-Mas and Mota, stanzas 370–71).

110. Maimonides, e.g., uses the Arabic *sharīʿa* for law, whether of human or divine provenance, evident in the distinction in *Guide* 2:40 between "divine Law" (*sharīʿa ilāhiyya*) and "law that is a *nomos*" (*sharīʿa nāmusiyya*); Shemuel Ibn Tibbon translates *sharīʿa* as *torah* in both instances: *torah elohit* and *torah nimusit*.

111. Stein, *Untersuchungen über die Proverbios morales von Santob de Carrión*, 108. See also the note in Ibn Gabirol, *A Choice of Pearls*, 163n364.

112. Shepard, *Shem Tov*, 40–42.

113. See also messianic poems by Ibn Gabirol in Scheindlin, *The Gazelle*, 90–103.

114. In a recent book, David Wacks argues for a highly subversive interpretation of Santob's oeuvre, based on a reading of the paratextual material in the Escorial manuscript of the *Proverbios* in conjunction with Santob's major Hebrew composition, the "Debate of the Pen and the Scissors," a text for which several allegorical interpretations have been suggested (pen and scissors as philosophy and tradition, Jewish and Christian doctrine, Jews and political adversaries). Introducing yet another attempt to decipher the allegory, Wacks suggests that the scissors and pen represent vernacular and Hebrew writing, respectively—the former used for utilitarian, pedestrian purposes and the latter for sacred and intellectual ones. Wacks concludes: "If we read the critique of the vernacular in the *Debate* as a key, available only to a Hebrew-reading audience, the scissors-writing episode in the *Proverbios* [the Escorial appendix] becomes a coded satire of the very man to whom Ardutiel dedicates the text. The *astroso* or wretch is Pedro I himself and the 'carta vacía' devoid of reason and substance . . . is nothing other than the much celebrated *Proverbios.*" Wacks's thesis of authorial subterfuge, while intriguing and in some ways attractive, seems farfetched because the paratextual material of the "Debate" identifies the

work, the *Hebrew* work, with the scissors, the precise opposite of Wacks's identification. While *maqāmas* are famous for their paradoxes and reversals, Wacks's claim, which relies upon a one-to-one correspondence (wherein pen=Hebrew/scissors=Castilian), collapses since the single piece of evidence that testifies to a Jewish reading tradition suggests the opposite correspondence. Also, we do not know that the Escorial appendix circulated among Jews. See Wacks, *Double Diaspora in Sephardic Literature*, chap. 4, quotation p. 124. See his notes for bibliography on the "Debate."

115. Perry's translation, *The Moral Proverbs of Santob de Carrión*, 22, lines 309–13.

AFTERWORD

1. See the story in the *Washington Post*, http://www.washingtonpost.com/blogs/worldviews/wp/2013/04/23/heres-the-song-so-bad-its-got-the-netherlands-in-an-uproar-and-is-ruining-the-kings-big-day/, accessed July 22, 2013.

2. See http://www.huffingtonpost.com/2013/04/21/kings-song-dutch-king-willem-alexander-imbecilic-scrapped_n_3127671.html, accessed July 22, 2013.

BIBLIOGRAPHY

ABBREVIATIONS

AJSR	*Association for Jewish Studies Review*
BSOAS	*Bulletin of the School of Oriental and African Studies*
HUCA	*Hebrew Union College Annual*
IJMES	*International Journal of Middle East Studies*
JAL	*Journal of Arabic Literature*
JJS	*Journal of Jewish Studies*
JQR	*Jewish Quarterly Review*
JSQ	*Jewish Studies Quarterly*
JSS	*Jewish Social Studies*
PAAJR	*Proceedings of the American Academy for Jewish Research*
WCJS	*World Congress of Jewish Studies*

* * *

Abel, Armand. "Le Khalife, présence sacrée." *Studia Islamica* 7 (1957): 29–45.

Abramson, Shraga. *Ba-merkazim u-va-tefuṣot bi-tequfat ha-geonim*. Jerusalem: Mosad ha-Rav Kook, 1965.

Abramson, Shraga. "A Letter of Rabbi Judah ha-Levi to Rabbi Moses Ibn Ezra" (Hebrew). In *Hayyim (Jefim) Schirmann Jubilee Volume*, ed. Shraga Abramson and Aaron Mirsky, 397–411. Jerusalem: Schocken, 1970.

Abulafia, David. *The Great Sea: A Human History of the Mediterranean*. Oxford: Oxford University Press, 2011.

Abulafia, Todros Ben Yehudah. *Gan ha-meshallim ve-ha-ḥiddot: Osef shirei Todros Ben Yehuda Abu al-ʿAfia*. Ed. David Yellin. 2 vols. Jerusalem: Weiss, 1932–34.

Adler, Marcus Nathan. *The Itinerary of Benjamin of Tudela*. London: Henry Frowde, 1907.

Afsaruddin, Asma. *Excellence and Precedence: Medieval Islamic Discourse on Legitimate Leadership*. Leiden: E. J. Brill, 2002.

Afsaruddin, Asma. "*God's Rule: Government and Islam* by Patricia Crone." *Speculum* 81, no. 4 (2006): 1176–78.

Ajami, Mansour. *The Alchemy of Glory: The Dialectic of Truthfulness and Untruthfulness in Medieval Arabic Literary Criticism*. Washington, D.C.: Three Continents Press, 1988.

Al-'Askarī, 'Abd al-Muḥsin Ibn 'Abd al-'Azīz. *Al-iqtibās: Anwā'uhu wa aḥkāmuhu: Dirāsah shi'riyyah balāghīyyah fī'l-iqtibās min al-qur'ān wa'l-ḥadīth*. Riyad: Maktabat Dār al-Minhāj li'l-Nashr wa'l-Tawzī' bi'l-Riyāḍ, 2004.

Al-'Askarī, Abū Hilāl al-Ḥasn Ibn 'Abd Allah. *Kitāb al-ṣinā'atayn*. Ed. Muḥammad 'Ali al-Bajadi and Muḥammad Abū al-Faḍl Ibrāhīm. Cairo: 'Isā al-Bābī al-Ḥalabī, 1952.

Al-'Asqalānī, Aḥmad Ibn Ibrāhīm. *Shifā' al-qulūb fī manāqib Banī Ayyūb*. Ed. Madīḥah Sharqāwī. Cairo: Maktabat al-Thaqāfah al-Dīniyyah, 1996.

Al-Azmeh, Aziz. *Muslim Kingship: Power and the Sacred in Muslim, Christian and Pagan Polities*. London: I. B. Tauris, 2001.

Al-Fārābī. *Iḥṣā' al-'ulūm*. Ed. 'Uthmān Amīn. Cairo: Maktabah al-Anglo al-Miṣrīyyah, 1968.

Al-Fārābī. *Kitāb al-shi'r*. Ed. Muhsin Mahdi. *Shi'r* 3, no. 12 (1959): 90–95.

Al-Ghazzālī, Abū Ḥāmid Muḥammad. *Iḥyā 'ulūm al-dīn*. 5 vols. Cairo: Maktabat wa-Maṭbu'ah Muḥammad 'Alī Ṣabīḥ, 1956.

Al-Ḥarīzī, Yehudah. *Kitāb al-durar: A Book in Praise of God and the Israelite Communities* (Hebrew and English). Ed. Joshua Blau, Paul Fenton, and Yosef Yahalom. Jerusalem: Ben-Zvi Institute, 2002.

Al-Ḥarīzī, Yehudah. *Taḥkemoni o maḥberot Heman ha-Ezraḥi*. Ed. Naoya Katsumata and Yosef Yahalom. Jerusalem: Ben-Zvi Institute, 2010.

Al-Ḥarīzī, Yehudah. *Wanderings of Judah Alharizi: Five Accounts of His Travels* (Hebrew). Ed. Yosef Yahalom. Jerusalem: Ben-Zvi Institute, 2002.

Al-Ḥumaydī, Muḥammad. *Tashīl al-sabīl ilā ta'allum al-tarsīl*. Frankfurt am Main: Frankfurt University, 1985.

Al-Qalqashandī, Aḥmad Ibn 'Alī. *Ṣubḥ al-a'ashā' fī ṣinā'at al-inshā'*. 14 vols. Cairo: Al-Mu'assasa al-Miṣriyya al-'āma, 1964.

Al-Ṣulī, Muḥammad. *Adab al-kuttāb*. Ed. Aḥmad Ḥasan Basaj. Beirut: Dār al-Kutub al-'ilmiyya, 1994.

Al-Tha'ālibī, 'Abd al-Malik Ibn Muḥammad. *Al-iqtibās min al-qur'ān al-karīm*. Ed. Ibtisām Marhūn Ṣaffār and Mujāhid Musṭafa al-Manṣūrah. Cairo: Dār al-Wafā', 1992.

Alfonso, Esperanza. "The Body, Its Organs, and Senses: A Study of Metaphor in Medieval Hebrew Poetry of Praise." *Middle Eastern Literatures* 9, no. 1 (2006): 1–22.

Ali, Samer M. *Arabic Literary Salons in the Islamic Middle Ages: Poetry, Public Performance, and the Presentation of the Past*. Notre Dame, Ind.: Notre Dame University Press, 2010.

Ali, Samer M. "Praise for Murder? Two Odes by al-Buhturi Surrounding an Abbasid Patricide." In *Writers and Rulers: Perspectives on Their Relationship from Abbasid to*

Safavid Times, ed. Beatrice Gruendler and Louise Marlow, 1–38. Wiesbaden: Reichert, 2004.

Ali, Samer M. "The Rise of the Abbasid Public Sphere: The Case of al-Mutanabbī and Three Middle-Ranking Patrons." *Al-Qantara* 29, no. 2 (2008): 467–94.

Allony, Neḥemiah. "A Collection of Hebrew Letters from Twelfth-Century Spain" (Hebrew). *Sefunot* 16 (1980): 63–82.

Allony, Neḥemiah. *The Jewish Library in the Middle Ages: Book Lists from the Cairo Genizah* (Hebrew). Ed. Miriam Frenkel and Haggai Ben-Shammai. Jerusalem: Ben-Zvi Institute, 2006.

Allony, Neḥemiah. "A Twelfth-Century List of Personalities and Their Titles" (Hebrew). *Sefunot* 8 (1964): 127–36.

Alvar, Carlos. *La poesía trovadoresca en España y Portugal.* Madrid: Cupsa, 1977.

Arazi, A. "Une épître d'Ibrāhīm b. Hilāl al-Ṣābī sur les genres littéraires." In *Studies in Islamic History and Civilization in Honour of Professor David Ayalon*, ed. Moshe Sharon, 473–505. Leiden: E. J. Brill, 1986.

Arazi, A. "Risāla." In *Encyclopaedia of Islam*, 2nd ed., ed. P. Bearman et al. Brill Online, 2014. http://referenceworks.brillonline.com/entries/encyclopaedia-of-islam-2/risa-la-COM_0926.

Arberry, A. J. *Poems of al-Mutanabbī: A Selection with Introduction, Translation and Notes.* Cambridge: Cambridge University Press, 1967.

Arendt, Hannah. "*The Court Jew: A Contribution to the History of the Period of Absolutism in Central Europe*, by Selma Stern." *Jewish Social Studies* 14, no. 2 (1952): 176–78.

Ariel, Donald T. "The Coins of Herod the Great in the Context of the Augustan Empire." In *Herod and Augustus: Papers Presented at the IJS Conference, 21st–23rd June 2005*, ed. David M. Jacobson and Nikos Kokkinos, 113–26. Leiden: E. J. Brill, 2009.

Aristotle. *Nicomachean Ethics.* In *The Complete Works of Aristotle*, vol. 2, trans. William D. Ross and James Urmson, ed. Jonathan Barnes, 1727–867. Princeton, N.J.: Princeton University Press, 1995.

Aristotle. *Poetics.* In *The Complete Works of Aristotle*, vol. 2, trans. I. Bywater, ed. Jonathan Barnes, 2316–40. Princeton, N.J.: Princeton University Press, 1995.

Aristotle. *Rhetoric.* In *The Complete Works of Aristotle*, vol. 2, trans. W. Rhys Roberts, ed. Jonathan Barnes, 2152–269. Princeton, N.J.: Princeton University Press, 1995.

Ashtor, Eliahu. "Abū al-Munajjā Solomon ben Shaya." In *Encyclopaedia Judaica*, vol. 1, 2nd ed., ed. Michael Berenbaum and Fred Skolnik, 335. Detroit: Macmillan Reference USA, 2007.

Ashtor, Eliahu. "Documentos españoles de la Genizah." *Sefarad* 24, no. 1 (1964): 41–80.

Ashtor, Eliahu. *The Jews of Moslem Spain.* Philadelphia: Jewish Publication Society, 1973.

Assaf, Simḥa. "Qoveṣ shel iggerot rav Shemuel Ben 'Eli u-venei doro." *Tarbiz* 1, no. 1 (1929): 102–30; no. 2 (1929): 43–84; no. 3 (1930): 15–80.

Astren, Fred. "Goitein, Medieval Jews, and the 'New Mediterranean Studies,'" *JQR* 102, no. 4 (2012): 513–31.

Baer, Yitzhak. *A History of the Jews in Christian Spain.* 2 vols. Trans. Louis Schoffman. Philadelphia: Jewish Publication Society, 1966.

Bakhtin, Mikhail. *Rabelais and His World.* Trans. Helene Iswolsky. Cambridge, Mass.: MIT Press, 1968.

Barceló, Miquel. "The Manifest Caliph: Umayyad Ceremony in Córdoba, or the Staging of Power." In *The Formation of al-Andalus, Part 1: History and Society*, ed. Manuela Marín, 425–55. Aldershot: Ashgate Variorum, 1998.

Bareket, Elinoar. *Fustat on the Nile: The Jewish Elite in Medieval Egypt.* Leiden: E. J. Brill, 1999.

Bedersi, Abraham Ben Isaac. *Sefer Ḥotam Tokhnit.* Ed. Samuel David Luzzatto. Amsterdam: Yisra'el Levisson, 1865.

Beeri, Tova. "'Eli he-Ḥaver Ben 'Amram: Hebrew Poet in Eleventh-Century Egypt" (Hebrew). *Sefunot* 23, no. 8 (2003): 279–344.

Beeri, Tova. *The Great Cantor of Baghdad: The Liturgical Poems of Joseph Ben Hayyim al-Bardani* (Hebrew). Jerusalem: Ben-Zvi Institute, 2002.

Beeri, Tova. "Seridei igronim qadumim min ha-geniza." *Qoveṣ 'al Yad* 18 (2004): 45–79.

Ben 'Eli, Japheth. *Kitab al-zabur: Libri psalmorum, versio Arabica.* Ed. J. J. L. Bargés. Paris: Lutetiae Parisorium, 1861.

Ben Labrat, Dunash. *Shirim.* Ed. Neḥemiah Allony. Jerusalem: Mosad ha-Rav Kook, 1947.

Benabu, Isaac. "'Rivers of Oil Inundated the Valley of Stones': Towards a Methodology for Reading the Hispano-Romance *Kharja*s in Hebrew Characters." In *Studies in the Muwashshah and the Kharja*, ed. Alan Jones and Richard Hitchcock, 16–28. Oxford: Ithaca Press for the Board of the Faculty of Oriental Studies, University of Oxford, 1991.

Benabu, Isaac, and Yosef Yahalom. "The Importance of the Genizah Manuscripts for the Hispano-Romance *Kharjas*." *Romance Philology* 40, no. 2 (1986): 139–58.

Ben Maimon, Avraham. *Sefer ha-maspiq le-'ovdei ha-shem.* Ed. Nissim Dana. Ramat Gan: Bar-Ilan University Press, 1989.

Ben Maimon, Mosheh. *The Guide of the Perplexed.* 2 vols. Trans. Shlomo Pines. Chicago: University of Chicago Press, 1963.

Ben Maimon, Mosheh. *Iggerot ha-Rambam.* 2 vols. Ed. Isaac Shailat. Ma'aleh Adumim: Ma'aliyot Press, 1987.

Ben Maimon, Mosheh. *A Maimonides Reader.* Ed. Isadore Twersky. Tel Aviv: Behrman House, 1972.

Ben Maimon, Mosheh. *Maimonides' Treatise on Logic: The Original Arabic and Three Hebrew Translations.* Ed. Israel Efros. New York: American Academy for Jewish Research, 1938.

Ben Maimon, Mosheh. *Mishnah 'im perush rabeinu Mosheh Ben Maimon.* 3 vols. Ed. Yosef Qafiḥ. Jerusalem: Mosad ha-Rav Kook, 1963.

Ben Sasson, Menaḥem. "Rashei ha-ṣibbur be-ṣafon Afriqa: Ha-demut ve-ha-tadmit." *Pe'amim* 26 (1986): 132–62.

Ben Sasson, Menaḥem. "*Review: Geniza Research at the Turn of the Millennium (I)—A Survey of Recent Publications*" (Hebrew). *Pe'amim* 101–2 (2005): 251–74.

Ben Sasson, Menaḥem. "The Structure, Goal, and Content of the Story of Nathan Ha-Babli" (Hebrew). In *Culture and Society in Medieval Jewry: Studies Dedicated to the*

Memory of Haim Hillel Ben-Sasson, ed. Menaḥem Ben-Sasson, Robert Bonfil, and Joseph R. Hacker, 137–96. Jerusalem: Zalman Shazar Center, 1989.

Ben Shalom, Ram. "The Courtier as the Scepter of Judah: The Letters and Panegyrics to Courtiers of Yomtov ben Hana, Scribe of the Jewish Community of Montalbán" (Hebrew). In *Ot le-Tova: Essays in Honor of Professor Tova Rosen*, ed. Eli Yassif et al., 196–224. Beersheva: Heqsherim Institute for Jewish and Israeli Literature, 2012.

Ben Shammai, Haggai. "The Attitudes of Some Early Karaites Toward Islam." In *Studies in Medieval Jewish History and Literature*, vol. 2, ed. Isadore Twersky, 2–40. Cambridge, Mass.: Harvard University Press, 1984.

Ben Shammai, Haggai. "The Judaeo-Arabic Vocabulary of Saadya's Bible Translations as a Vehicle for Eschatological Messages: The Case of Saadya's Usage of the 8th Form of Arabic QDR." In *Esoteric and Exoteric Aspects in Judeo-Arabic Culture*, ed. Benjamin H. Hary and Haggai Ben Shammai, 191–225. Leiden: E. J. Brill, 2006.

Ben Yosef, Sa'adia. *Book of Beliefs and Opinions*. Trans. Samuel Rosenblatt. New Haven, Conn.: Yale University Press, 1948.

Ben Yosef, Sa'adia. *Mishlei 'im targum u-feirush ha-gaon rabbeinu Sa'adia Ben Yosef Fayyumi*. Ed. Yosef Qafiḥ. *Jerusalem:* Ha-Va'ad le-Hoṣa'at Sifrei Rasag, 1975/76.

Ben Yosef, Sa'adia. *Perushei rav Sa'adia Gaon li-vereshit*. Ed. Moshe Zucker. New York: Jewish Theological Seminary, 1984.

Ben Yosef, Sa'adia. *Sefer yeṣirah (kitāb al-mabādi)*. Ed. Yosef Qafiḥ. Jerusalem: Va'ad le-Hoṣa'at Sifrei Rasag, 1972.

Bernads, Monique, and John Nawas, eds. *Patronate and Patronage in Early and Classical Islam*. Leiden: E. J. Brill, 2005.

Bernstein, Simon. "Poems from an Unknown Diwan of R. Abraham Ibn Ezra" (Hebrew). *Tarbiz* 5, no. 1 (1934): 61–74.

Bernstein, Simon. "Shir tehillah shel Shelomoh DaPierra li-khevod rabbah shel Qastiliah Rav Me'ir Alguadex." In *Sinai: Sefer yovel*, ed. Y. L. ha-Kohen Maimon, 205–19. Jerusalem: Mosad ha-Rav Kook, 1957.

Bertelli, Sergio. *The King's Body: Sacred Rituals of Power in Medieval and Early Modern Europe*. Trans. R. Burr Litchfield. University Park: Pennsylvania State University Press, 2001.

Biale, David. *Power and Powerlessness in Jewish History*. New York: Schocken, 1986.

Bierman, Irene. *Writing Signs: The Fatimid Public Text*. Berkeley: University of California Press, 1998.

Black, Deborah L. *Logic and Aristotle's Rhetoric and Poetics in Medieval Arabic Philosophy*. Leiden: E. J. Brill, 1990.

Blau, Joshua, ed. *Judeo-Arabic Literature: Selected Texts*. Jerusalem: Magnes, 1980.

Boase, Roger. *The Troubadour Revival: A Study of Social Change and Traditionalism in Late Medieval Spain*. London: Routledge and Kegan Paul, 1978.

Bonebakker, S. A. *The* Kitāb Naqd al-Š'ir *of Qudāma b. Ǧa'far al-Kātib al-Baġdādī*. Leiden: E. J. Brill, 1956.

Bonebakker, S. A. *Materials for the History of Arabic Rhetoric from the Ḥilyat al-Muḥāḍara of Ḥātimī*. Naples: Istituto Orientale di Napoli, 1975.

Bonner, Anthony. *Songs of the Troubadours.* New York: Schocken, 1972.

Borrás, Judit Targarona, and Raymond Scheindlin. "Literary Correspondence Between Vidal Benvenist Ben Lavi and Solomon Ben Meshulam De Piera." *Revue des Études Juives* 160, no. 1 (2001): 61–133.

Borrás, Judit Targarona, and Tirza Vardi. "Literary Correspondence Between Vidal Abenvenist and Solomon De Piera." *Revue des Études Juives* 167 (2008): 405–509.

Bosworth, C. E. "Abū 'Abdallāh al-Khwārazmī on the Technical Terms of the Secretary's Art: A Contribution to the Administrative History of Mediaeval Islam." *Journal of the Economic and Social History of the Orient* 12, no. 2 (1969): 113–64.

Bosworth, C. E. "Laḳab." In *Encyclopaedia of Islam,* 2nd ed., ed. P. Bearman et al. Brill Online, 2014. http://referenceworks.brillonline.com/entries/encyclopaedia-of-islam-2/lakab-COM_0563.

Bourdieu, Pierre. *The Logic of Practice.* Cambridge: Polity Press, 1990.

Boustan, Ra'anan. "Israelite Kingship, Christian Rome, and the Jewish Imperial Imagination: Midrashic Precursors to the Medieval 'Throne of Solomon.'" In *Jews, Christians, and the Roman Empire,* ed. Natalie B. Dohrmann and Annette Yoshiko Reed, 167–82. Philadelphia: University of Pennsylvania Press, 2013.

Böwering, Gerhard. "God and His Attributes." In *Encyclopaedia of the Qur'ān,* vol. 2, ed. Jane Dammen McAuliffe, 316–31. Leiden, E. J. Brill, 2002.

Boyarin, Daniel, and Jonathan Boyarin. *Powers of Diaspora: Two Essays on the Relevance of Jewish Culture.* Minneapolis: University of Minnesota Press, 2002.

Brann, Ross. "Competing Tropes of Eleventh-Century Andalusi Jewish Culture." In *Ot le-Tova: Essays in Honor of Professor Tova Rosen,* ed. Eli Yassif et al., 7–26. Beersheva: Heqsherim Institute for Jewish and Israeli Literature, 2012.

Brann, Ross. *The Compunctious Poet: Cultural Ambiguity and Hebrew Poetry in Muslim Spain.* Baltimore: Johns Hopkins University Press, 1991.

Brann, Ross. *Power in the Portrayal: Representations of Jews and Muslims in Eleventh- and Twelfth-Century Islamic Spain.* Princeton, N.J.: Princeton University Press, 2002.

Brann, Ross, Angel Sáenz-Badillos, and Judit Targarona. "The Poetic Universe of Samuel Ibn Sasson, Hebrew Poet of Fourteenth-Century Castile." *Prooftexts* 16, no. 1 (1996): 75–103.

Braunn, Noah. "Arabic Verses in *Kitāb al-muḥāḍarah wa'l-mudhākarah*" (Hebrew). *Tarbiz* 14, no. 214 ;39–126 :(1943) , nos. 3–4 (1943): 191–203.

Brener, Ann. *Isaac Ibn Khalfun: A Wandering Hebrew Poet of the Eleventh Century.* Leiden: E. J. Brill, 2003.

Brett, Michael. "Badr al-Ǧamālī and the Fatimid Renascence." In *Egypt and Syria in the Fatimid, Ayyubid and Mamluk Era IV,* ed. Urbain Vermeulen and Kristof D'hulster, 61–78. Leuven: Peeters, 2005.

Brisch, Nicole, ed. *Religion and Power: Divine Kingship in the Ancient World and Beyond.* Chicago: University of Chicago Press, 2008.

Brody, Ḥayyim. "Piyyutim ve-shirei tehillah me-rav Hayya Gaon." *Yedi'ot ha-makhon le-ḥeqer ha-shirah ha-'ivrit* 3 (1936): 5–63.

Brody, Ḥayyim. "Shirei Meshullam Ben Shelomoh DaPierra." *Yedi'ot ha-makhon le-ḥeqer ha-shirah ha-'ivrit* 4 (1938): 3–118.

Brody, Robert. *The Geonim of Babylonia and the Shaping of Medieval Jewish Culture.* New Haven, Conn.: Yale University Press, 1998.

Burde, Mark. "The *Parodia Sacra* Problem and Medieval Comic Studies." In *Laughter in the Middle Ages and Early Modern Times*, ed. Albrecht Classen, 215–42. Berlin: De Gruyter, 2010.

Burgos, Francisco Cantera, and José María Millás Vallicrosa. *Las Inscripciones Hebraicas de España.* Madrid: C. Bermejo, 1956.

Burns, Robert I., ed. *Emperor of Culture: Alfonso X the Learned of Castile and His Thirteenth-Century Renaissance.* Philadelphia: University of Pennsylvania Press, 1990.

Burrow, John Anthony. *The Poetry of Praise.* Cambridge: Cambridge University Press, 2008.

Butler, Judith. "Performative Acts and Gender Constitution: An Essay in Phenomenology and Feminist Theory." *Theater Journal* 40, no. 4 (1988): 519–31.

Butterworth, Charles E. *Averroes' Middle Commentary on Aristotle's Poetics.* Princeton, N.J.: Princeton University Press, 1986.

Calder, Norman. "Review of *God's Caliph: Religious Authority in the First Centuries of Islam* by P. Crone and M. Hinds." *Journal of Semitic Studies* 32, no. 2 (1987): 375–78.

Catlos, Brian. *Infidel Kings and Unholy Warriors: Faith, Power, and Violence in the Age of Crusade and Jihad.* New York: Farrar, Straus, and Giroux, 2014.

Cohen, Mark R. "Correspondence and Social Control in the Jewish Communities of the Islamic World: A Letter of the Nagid Joshua Maimonides." *Jewish History* 1, no. 2 (1986): 39–48.

Cohen, Mark R. *Jewish Self-Government in Medieval Egypt: The Origins of the Office of the Head of the Jews, ca. 1065–1126.* Princeton, N.J.: Princeton University Press, 1981.

Cohen, Mark R. "On the Interplay of Arabic and Hebrew in the Cairo Geniza Letters." In *Studies in Hebrew and Arabic Letters in Honour of Raymond P. Scheindlin*, ed. Jonathan Decter and Michael Rand, 17–35. Piscataway, N.J.: Gorgias Press, 2007.

Cohen, Mark R. *Poverty and Charity in the Jewish Community of Medieval Egypt.* Princeton, N.J.: Princeton University Press, 2009.

Cohen, Mark R., and Sasson Somekh. "In the Court of Ya'qub Ibn Killis: A Fragment from the Cairo Genizah." *JQR* 80, nos. 3–4 (1990): 283–314.

Cohen, Mordechai Z. "The Aesthetic Exegesis of Moses Ibn Ezra." In *Hebrew Bible / Old Testament: The History of Its Interpretation*, vol. 1: *From the Beginnings to the Middle Ages (Until 1300)*, part 2: *The Middle Ages*, ed. M. Sæbø, 282–301. Göttingen: Vandenhoeck & Ruprecht, 2000.

Cohen, Mordechai Z. "Moses Ibn Ezra Vs. Maimonides: Argument for a Poetic Definition of Metaphor (*Isti'āra*)." *Edebiyāt* 11 (2000): 1–28.

Cohen, Stuart A. *The Three Crowns: Structures of Communal Politics in Early Rabbinic Jewry.* Cambridge: Cambridge University Press, 1990.

Cole, Peter. *The Dream of the Poem: Hebrew Poetry from Muslim and Christian Spain 950–1492*. Princeton, N.J.: Princeton University Press, 2007.

Cole, Peter, and Adina Hoffman. *Sacred Trash: The Lost and Found World of the Cairo Geniza*. Jerusalem: Schocken, 2011.

Collins, Billie Jean. "The First Soldier's Oath." In *The Context of Scripture*, vol. 1: *Canonical Compositions from the Biblical World*, ed. William W. Hallo and K. Lawson Younger, 164–67. Leiden: E. J. Brill, 1997.

Cooperson, Michael. *Classical Arabic Biography*. Cambridge: Cambridge University Press, 2000.

Cortese, Delia, and Simonetta Calderini. *Women and the Fatimids in the World of Islam*. Edinburgh: Edinburgh University Press, 2006.

Cowley, Arthur. "Bodleian Geniza Fragments." *JQR* 19, no. 2 (1907): 250–56.

Crone, Patricia. *God's Rule: Six Centuries of Medieval Islamic Political Thought*. New York: Columbia University Press, 2004.

Crone, Patricia, and Martin Hinds. *God's Caliph: Religious Authority in the First Centuries of Islam*. Cambridge: Cambridge University Press, 1986.

Daftary, Farhad. *The Ismāʿīlīs: Their History and Doctrines*. Cambridge: Cambridge University Press, 2007.

Dana, Yosef. *Torat ha-shir be-sefer ha-ʿiyyunim ve-ha-diyyunim*. Tel Aviv: Tel Aviv University Press, 1977.

DaPierra, Shelomoh Ben Meshullam. *Divan*. Ed. S. Bernstein. New York: Alim, 1942.

Davidson, Israel. *Parody in Jewish Literature*. New York: Columbia University Press, 1907.

Davidson, Israel. "Poetic Fragments from the Genizah III: From a Divan of ʿAlvan ben Abraham." *JQR* 2, no. 2 (1911): 221–39.

Dagenais, John. "Genre and Demonstrative Rhetoric: Praise and Blame in the *Razos de trobar* and the *Doctrina de compondre dictats*." In *Medieval Lyric Genres in Historical Context*, ed. William D. Padden, 242–54. Urbana: University of Illinois Press, 2000.

De Carrión, Santob. *Proverbios morales*. Ed. Paloma Díaz-Más and Carlos Mota. Madrid: Cátedra, 1998.

Decter, Jonathan. "Before Caliphs and Kings: The Jewish Courtier in Medieval Iberia." In *The Jew in Medieval Iberia*, ed. Jonathan Ray, 1–31. Boston: Academic Studies Press, 2012.

Decter, Jonathan. "Concerning the Terminology of al-Harizi's Virtues Debate." In *Giving a Diamond: Essays in Honor of Joseph Yahalom on the Occasion of His Seventieth Birthday*, ed. Wout van Bekkum and Naoya Katsumata, 159–73. Leiden: E. J. Brill, 2011.

Decter, Jonathan. "The Hidden Exilarch: Power and Performance in a Medieval Jewish Ceremony." In *Visualizing Medieval Performance: Perspectives, Histories, Contexts*, ed. Elina Gertsman, 179–91. Aldershot: Ashgate, 2008.

Decter, Jonathan. *Iberian Jewish Literature: Between al-Andalus and Christian Europe*. Bloomington: Indiana University Press, 2007.

Decter, Jonathan. "Ibrāhīm Ibn al-Fakhkhār al-Yahūdī: An Arabic Poet and Diplomat in Castile and the Maghrib." In *Beyond Religious Borders: Interaction and Intellectual*

Exchange in the Medieval Islamic World, ed. David Freidenreich and Miriam Goldstein, 96–111. Philadelphia: University of Pennsylvania Press, 2012.

Decter, Jonathan. "The (Interreligious?) Rededication of an Arabic Panegyric by Judah al-Ḥarīzī." In progress.

Decter, Jonathan. "Mediterranean Regionalism in Hebrew Panegyric Poetry." In *Regional Identities and Cultures of Medieval Jews*, ed. Talya Fishman and Ephraim Kanarfogel. Liverpool: Littman Library of Jewish Civilization, forthcoming.

Decter, Jonathan. "Panegyric as Pedagogy: Moses Ibn Ezra's Didactic Poem on the 'Beautiful Elements of Poetry' (*maḥāsin al-shi'r*) in the Context of Classical Arabic Poetics." In *Studies in Near Eastern Languages and Cultures*, ed. Adam Bursi and Hamza M. Zafer. Leiden: E. J. Brill, forthcoming.

Den Heijer, Johannes. "Religion, Ethnicity, and Gender Under Fatimid Rule: Three Recent Publications and Their Wider Research Context." *Bibliotheca Orientalis* 65, nos. 1–2 (2008): 38–72.

Den Heijer, Johannes. "Le vizir fatimide Badr al-Ǧamālī (466/1074–487/1094) et la nouvelle muraille du Caire: Quelques remarques preliminaries." In *Egypt and Syria in the Fatimid, Ayyubid and Mamluk Era V*, ed. Urbain Vermeulen and Kristof D'hulster, 91–107. Leuven: Peeters, 2007.

Den Heijer, Johannes, and Joachim Yeshaya. "Solomon ben Joseph ha-Kohen on Fāṭimid Victory: A Hebrew Ode to al-Mustanṣir Billāh and Badr al-Jamālī Reconsidered." *Al-Masāq: Journal of the Medieval Mediterranean* 25, no. 2 (2013): 155–83.

Dennis, George T. "Imperial Panegyric: Rhetoric and Reality." In *Byzantine Court Culture from 829–1204*, ed. Henry Maguire, 131–40. Washington, D.C.: Dumbarton Oaks, 2004.

Diem, Werner. *Arabische Geschäftsbriefe des 10. bis 14. Jahrhunderts aus der Österreichischen Nationalbibliothek in Wien.* Wiesbaden: Otto Harrassowitz Verlag, 1995.

Diem, Werner. *Arabische Privatbriefe des 9. bis 15. Jahrhunderts aus der Österreichischen Nationalbibliothek in Wien.* Wiesbaden: Otto Harrassowitz Verlag, 1996.

Dietrich, Albert. "Zu den mit ad-dīn zusammengesetzten islamischen ersonennamen." *Zeitschrift der Deutschen Morgenländischen Gesellschaft* 110, no. 1 (1960): 43–54.

Dirven, René. *Metaphor and Metonymy in Comparison and Contrast.* Berlin: De Gruyter, 2002.

Dodds, Jerilynn D., ed. *Al-Andalus: The Art of Islamic Spain.* New York: Metropolitan Museum of Art, 1992.

Dodds, Jerilynn D., María Rosa Menocal, and Abigail Krasner Balbale. *The Arts of Intimacy: Christians, Jews, and Muslims in the Making of Castilian Culture.* New Haven, Conn.: Yale University Press, 2008.

Doron, Aviva. *Meshorer be-ḥaṣar ha-melekh, Todros Abulafia: Shirah 'ivrit bi-Sefarad ha-noṣrit.* Tel Aviv: Dvir, 1989.

Einbinder, Susan. *No Place of Rest: Jewish Literature, Expulsion, and the Memory of Medieval France.* Philadelphia: University of Pennsylvania Press, 2009.

Einbinder, Susan. "Pen and Scissors: A Medieval Debate." *HUCA* 65 (1994): 261–76.

Efros, Israel. "Maimonides' Treatise on Logic." *PAAJR* 8 (1937–38).

Elizur, Shulamit. "Shirat ha-ḥol ha-'ivrit bi-Sefarad: Le-nusaḥo u-le-sugo shel ha-shir 've-omer al-tishan' le-Dunash Ben Labrat." In *The Cairo Geniza Collection in Geneva: Catalogue and Studies*, ed. David Rosenthal, 200–207. Jerusalem: Magnes Press, 2010.

Epenshtein, Shimon. "Perek 27 me-sefer merapei ha-nefashot li-rabi Yosef Ibn 'Aqnin." In *Sefer ha-yovel li-khvod Naḥum Sokolov*, 371–88. Warsaw: Shuldberg, 1904.

Epstein, Marc. *Dreams of Subversion in Medieval Jewish Art and Literature.* University Park: Pennsylvania State University Press, 1997.

Epstein, Ya'aqov. *Studies in Talmudic Literature and Linguistics* (Hebrew). Vol. 3. Ed. Ezra Zion Melamed. Jerusalem: Magnes Press, 1988.

Escanilla, Ana María Bejarano. "Shelomoh Bonafed: Poeta y Polemista Hebreo S. XIV–XV." Ph.D. diss., University of Barcelona, 1989.

Estow, Clara. *Pedro the Cruel of Castile 1350–1369.* Leiden: E. J. Brill, 1995.

Feldman, Emanuel. "The Rabbinic Lament." *JQR* 63, no. 1 (1972): 51–75.

Fenech, Soledad Gilbert. "La escritura de tijera en unos versos de al-Rusafi." *Al-Andalus: Revista de las Escuelas de Estudios Árabes de Madrid y Granada* 33, no. 2 (1968): 471–73.

Fenech, Soledad Gilbert. "Sobre una extraña manera de escribir." *Al-Andalus: Revista de las Escuelas de Estudios Árabes de Madrid y Granada* 14, no. 1 (1949): 211–13.

Fenton, Paul. *Philosophie et exégèse dans le Jardin de la méthaphor de Moïse Ibn'Ezra, philosophe et poète andalou du XIIe siècle.* Leiden: E. J. Brill, 1997.

Fischel, Walter. "The Divan of Eleazar the Babylonian as a Source for the Social History of the Jews of Baghdad in the XIII Century" (Hebrew). *Tarbiz* 8 (1937): 233–36.

Fischel, Walter. *Jews in the Economic and Political Life of Mediaeval Islam.* London: Royal Asiatic Society, 1937.

Fisher, Max. "Here's the Song So Bad It's Got the Netherlands in an Uproar and Is Ruining the King's Big Day." April 23, 2013. http://www.washingtonpost.com/blogs/worldviews/wp/2013/04/23/heres-the-song-so-bad-its-got-the-netherlands-in-an-uproar-and-is-ruining-the-kings-big-day.

Fleischer, Ezra. "The 'Gerona School' of Hebrew Poetry." In *Rabbi Moses Naḥmanides (Ramban): Explorations in His Religious and Literary Virtuosity*, ed. Isadore Twersky, 35–49. Cambridge, Mass.: Harvard University Press, 1983.

Fleischer, Ezra. "'Iyyunim be-Shirato shel Rav Hayya Gaon." In *Shai le-Heman: Meḥqarim ba-sifrut ha-'ivrit shel yemei ha-beinayyim*, ed. Z. Malachi, 239–74. Tel Aviv: Tel Aviv University Press, 1977.

Fleischer, Ezra. "Le-toledot shirat ha-ḥol ha-'ivrit vi-Sefarad be-reishitah." In *Ha-shirah ha-'ivrit bi-Sefarad u-vi-sheluḥoṭeha*, vol. 1, ed. Shulamit Elizur and Tova Beeri, 47–77. Jerusalem: Ben-Zvi Institute, 2010.

Fleischer, Ezra. "On the Beginning of Hebrew Poetry in Spain: Poems and *Piyyutim* by R. Menahem ben Saruq" (Hebrew). *Asuphoth* 2 (1988): 227–69.

Fleischer, Ezra. "Qavim ḥadashim li-demuto shel rav Daniel Ben 'Azariah, nasi ve-gaon." *Shalem* 1 (1974): 53–74.

Fleischer, Ezra. "Shiro shel rav Hai Gaon el rav Yehudah Rosh ha-Seder me-Qairawan: Nesibotav u-sevivotav." In *Ha-shirah ha-'ivrit bi-Sefarad uvi-sheluḥoṭeha*, vol. 3, ed. Shulamit Elizur and Tova Beeri, 1295–1327. Jerusalem: Ben-Zvi Institute, 2010.

Frankfort, Henri. *Kingship and the Gods.* Chicago: University of Chicago Press, 1948.

Franklin, Arnold E. "Cultivating Roots: The Promotion of Exilarchal Ties to David in the Middle Ages." *AJSR* 29, no. 1 (2005): 91–110.

Franklin, Arnold E. *This Noble House: Jewish Descendants of King David in the Medieval Islamic East*. Philadelphia: University of Pennsylvania Press, 2012.

Frenkel, Miriam. *The Compassionate and Benevolent: The Leading Elite in the Jewish Community of Alexandria in the Middle Ages* (Hebrew). Jerusalem: Ben-Zvi Institute, 2006.

Gafni, Isaiah. "Epistles of the Patriarchs in Talmudic Literature" (Hebrew). In *"Follow the Wise": Studies in Jewish History and Culture in Honor of Lee I. Levine*, ed. Zeev Weiss et al., 3–10. Winona Lake, Ind.: Eisenbrauns, 2010.

Gardet, L. "Al-asmā' al-ḥusna." In *Encyclopaedia of Islam*, 2nd ed., ed. P. Bearman et al. Brill Online, 2014. http://referenceworks. brillonline.com /entries/encyclopaedia -of-islam-2/al-asma-al-husna-COM_0070.

Geertz, Clifford. *Negara: The Theatre State in Nineteenth-Century Bali.* Princeton, N.J.: Princeton University Press, 1980.

Gerber, Jane S. "The World of Samuel Halevi: Testimony from the El Tránsito Synagogue of Toledo." In *The Jew in Medieval Iberia*, ed. Jonathan Ray, 33–59. Boston: Academic Studies Press, 2012.

Gil, Moshe. "The Babylonian Yeshivot and the Maghrib in the Early Middle Ages." *PAAJR* 57 (1990–91): 85–120.

Gil, Moshe. *Be-malkhut Yishma'el bi-tequfat ha-geonim*. 4 vols. Tel Aviv: Tel Aviv University Press, 1997.

Gil, Moshe. *Ereṣ Yisra'el bi-tequfah ha-muslemit ha-rishona, 634–1099*. 3 vols. Tel Aviv: Tel Aviv University and the Ministry of Defense, 1983.

Gil, Moshe. *A History of Palestine 634–1099*. Trans. Ethel Broido. Cambridge: Cambridge University Press, 1992.

Gil, Moshe, and Ezra Fleischer. *Yehudah ha-Levi u-venei ḥugo*. Jerusalem: World Union of Jewish Studies, 2001.

Gimaret, Daniel. *Dieu à l'image de l'homme: Les anthropomorphismes de la sunna et leur interprétation par les théologiens.* Paris: Cerf, 1997.

Gimaret, Daniel. *Les noms divins en Islam.* Paris: Cerf, 1988.

Ginzberg, Louis. *Geonica*. 2 vols. New York: Jewish Theological Seminary, 1909.

Goitein, S. D. "Evidence on the Muslim Poll Tax from Non-Muslim Sources: A Geniza Study." *Journal of the Economic and Social History of the Orient* 6, no. 3 (1963): 278–95.

Goitein, S. D. *Letters of Medieval Jewish Traders.* Princeton, N.J.: Princeton University Press, 2015.

Goitein, S. D. *A Mediterranean Society: The Jewish Communities of the Arab World as Portrayed in the Documents of the Cairo Geniza*. 6 vols. Berkeley: University of California Press, 1967.

Goitein, S. D. "Petitions to Fatimid Caliphs from the Cairo Geniza." *JQR* 45, no. 1 (1954): 30–38.

Goitein, S. D. "Prayers from the Geniza for Fatimid Caliphs, the Head of the Jerusalem Yeshiva, the Jewish Community and the Local Congregation." In *Studies in Judaica,*

Karaitica, and Islamica Presented to Leon Nemoy on His Eightieth Birthday, ed. Sheldon R. Brunswick, 47–57. Tel Aviv: Bar-Ilan University Press, 1982.

Goitein, S. D. *Sidrei ha-ḥinukh bi-yemei ha-geonim uve-ʿeit ha-Rambam: Meqorot ḥadashim min ha-genizah*. Jerusalem: Ben-Zvi Institute, 1962.

Goitein, S. D. *Studies in Islamic History and Institutions*. Leiden: E. J. Brill, 1968.

Goitein, S. D., and Mordechai Akiva Friedman, eds. *India Book II: Madmun Nagid of Yemen and the India Trade* (Hebrew). Jerusalem: Ben-Zvi Institute and the Rabbi David and Amalia Rosen Foundation, 2010.

Goitein, S. D., and Mordechai Akiva Friedman. *India Traders of the Middle Ages: Documents from the Cairo Geniza ("India Book")*. Leiden: E. J. Brill, 2008.

Golb, Norman, and Omeljan Pritsak. *Khazarian Hebrew Documents of the Tenth Century*. Ithaca, N.Y.: Cornell University Press, 1982.

Goldberg, Jessica. "On Reading Goitein's *A Mediterranean Society*: A View from Economic History." *Mediterranean Historical Review* 26, no. 2 (2011): 171–86.

Goldberg, Jessica. *Trade and Institutions in the Medieval Mediterranean: The Geniza Merchants and Their Business World*. Cambridge: Cambridge University Press, 2013.

Goldin, Simha. "'Companies of Disciples' and 'Companies of Colleagues': Communication in Jewish Intellectual Circles." In *Communication in the Jewish Diaspora: The Pre-Modern World*, ed. Sophia Menache, 127–38. Leiden: E. J. Brill, 1996.

Goldziher, Ignaz. "Zu Saadyana XLI." *JQR* 15, no. 1 (1902): 73–75.

Goodblatt, David. *The Monarchic Principle: Studies in Jewish Self-Government in Antiquity*. Tübingen: J. C. B. Mohr (Paul Siebeck), 1994.

Gottheil, Richard J. H. "An Eleventh-Century Document Concerning a Cairo Synagogue." *JQR* 19, no. 3 (1907): 467–539.

Gottheil, Richard J. H. "Fragments of an Arabic Common-Place Book." *Bulletin de l'Institut Francais d'Archéologie Orientale* (Cairo) 34 (1933): 103–28.

Granat, Yehoshua. "Polémica, equívoco, o ambivalencia?: Nuevas consideraciones sobre el primer poema báquico hebreo andalusí." In *Poesía hebrea en al-Andalus*, ed. Judit Targarona Borrás and Ángel Sáenz-Badillos, 27–38. Granada: Universidad de Granada, 2003.

Greenblatt, Stephen. "Introduction: Fifty Years of *The King's Two Bodies*." *Representations* 106, no. 1 (2009): 63–66.

Greenstone, Julius H. "The Turkoman Defeat at Cairo by Joseph Ben Solomon ha-Kohen: Edited with Introduction and Notes." *American Journal of Semitic Languages and Literatures* 22 (1906): 144–75.

Gross, Avraham. "Ha-meshorer Shelomoh Bonafed u-me'ora'ot doro." In *The Frank Talmage Memorial Volume*, vol. 1, ed. Barry Walfish, 35–61. Haifa: Haifa University Press, 1993.

Gruendler, Beatrice. "Fantastic Aesthetics and Practical Criticism in Ninth-Century Baghdad." In *Takhyīl: Source Texts and Studies*, ed. Marle Hammond and Geert J. Van Gelder, 196–220. Cambridge, UK: Gibb Memorial Trust, 2008.

Gruendler, Beatrice. *Medieval Arabic Praise Poetry: Ibn al-Rūmī and the Patron's Redemption*. London: Routledge, 2003.

Güdemann, Moritz. *Das jüdische Unterrichtswesen während der spanisch-arabischen Periode*. Vienna: Verlag von Carl Gerold's Sohn, 1873.

Guo, Li. *Commerce, Culture, and Community in a Red Sea Port in the Thirteenth Century: The Arabic Documents from Quseir.* Leiden: E. J. Brill, 2004.

Gutwirth, Eli. "Models of Patronage in Medieval Spain." In *Patronage, Production and Transmission of Texts in Medieval and Early Modern Jewish Cultures*, ed. Esperanza Alfonso and Jonathan Decter, 45–76. Turnhout: Brepols, 2014.

Habermann, A. M. "Iggerot Shelomoh DaPierra le-Mosheh 'Abbas." In idem, *Mi-peri ha-'eṭ veha-'et: Qoveṣ ma'amarim u-reshimot bi-śedeh ha-sifrut veha-tarbuṭ*, 155–79. Jerusalem: R. Mas, 1981.

Hackett, Helen. "Dreams or Designs, Cults or Constructions? The Study of the Images of Monarchs." *Historical Journal* 44, no. 3 (2001): 811–23.

Hägg, Tomas, Philip Rousseau, and Christian Høgel, eds. *Greek Biography and Panegyric in Late Antiquity.* Berkeley: University of California Press, 2000.

Ha-Kohen, Sha'ul. *Siftei rananot kolel seliḥot ve-baqashot . . . ke-minhag Tripoli ve-Jerba.* Livorno, 1837.

Halevi, Yehudah. *Diwan des Abu-l-Hasan Jehuda ha-Levi.* 4 vols. Ed. Ḥayyim Brody. Berlin: Schriften des Vereins Mekize Nirdamim, 1894–1930.

Halevi, Yehudah. *Kitāb al-radd wa'l-dalīl fī al-dīn al-dhalīl (Kitāb al-Khazari).* Ed. David Hartwig Baneth and Haggai Ben Shammai. Jerusalem: Magnes, 1977.

Halkin, Abraham S. *Moses Maimonides' Epistle to Yemen.* New York: American Academy for Jewish Research, 1952.

Halkin, Abraham S., and David Hartman. *Epistles of Maimonides: Crisis and Leadership.* Philadelphia: Jewish Publication Society, 1985.

Halsall, A. W., and T. V. F. Brogan. "Amplification." In *Princeton Encyclopedia of Poetry and Poetics*, ed. Roland Greene, Stephen Cushman, and Clare Cavanagh, 45–46. Princeton, N.J.: Princeton University Press, 2012.

Ha-Nagid, Shemuel. *Dīwān Shemuel ha-Nagid: Ben tehilim.* Ed. Dov Jarden. Jerusalem: Hebrew Union College Press, 1966.

Hennop, Jan. "King's Song for New Dutch Ruler Willem-Alexander Called 'Imbecilic,' Scrapped by Organizers." April 21, 2013. http://www.huffingtonpost.com/2013/04/21/kings-song-dutch-king-willem-alexander-imbecilic-scrapped_n_3127671.html.

Hasan-Rokem, Galit. "Gifts for God, Gifts for Rabbis: From Sacrifice to Donation in Rabbinic Tales of Late Antiquity and Their Dialogue with Early Christian Texts." In *The Gift in Late Antiquity*, ed. Michael Satlow, 221–44. Malden, Mass.: John Wiley and Sons, 2013.

Heinrichs, Wolfhart. "Badī'." In *Encyclopedia of Arabic Literature*, ed. Julie Scott Meisami and Paul Starkey, 1:122–23. London: Routledge, 1998.

Heinrichs, Wolfhart. "Rhetorical Figures." In *Encyclopedia of Arabic Literature*, ed. Julie Scott Meisami and Paul Starkey, 2:656–62. London: Routledge, 1998.

Herman, Geoffrey. *A Prince Without a Kingdom: The Exilarch in the Sasanian Era.* Tübingen: Mohr Siebeck, 2012.

Herzfeld, Michael. "Practical Mediterraneanism: Excuses for Everything, from Epistemology to Eating." In *Rethinking the Mediterranean*, ed. W. V. Harris, 45–63. Oxford: Oxford University Press, 2005.

Hollenberg, David. "Disrobing Judges with Veiled Truths: An Early Ismāʿīlī Torah Interpretation in Service of the Fāṭimid Daʿwa." *Religion* 33, no. 2 (2003): 127–45.

Holmes, Janet, and Miriam Meyerhoff. "The Community of Practice: Theories and Methodologies in Language and Gender Research." *Language and Society* 28, no. 2 (1999): 173–83.

Horden, Peregrine, and Sharon Kinoshita, eds. *A Companion to Mediterranean History.* Oxford: Wiley-Blackwell, 2014.

Horden, Peregrine, and Nicholas Purcell. *The Corrupting Sea: A Study of Mediterranean History.* Oxford: Wiley-Blackwell, 2000.

Horowitz, Elliot. "The Court Jews and the Jewish Question." *Jewish History* 12, no. 2 (1998): 113–36.

Horowitz, Elliot. *Reckless Rites: Purim and the Legacy of Jewish Violence.* Princeton, N.J.: Princeton University Press, 2006.

Hubert, Henri, and Marcel Mauss. *Sacrifice: Its Nature and Function.* Trans. W. D. Halls. Chicago: University of Chicago Press, 1964.

Huss, Matti. *Meliṣat 'Efer ve-Dinah le-Don Vidal Benveniste: Pirqei ʿiyyun u-mahadurah biqortit.* Jerusalem: Magnes, 2003.

Ibn ʿAbd Rabbih, Aḥmad Ibn Muḥammad. *Dīwān Ibn ʿAbd Rabbih.* Ed. Muḥammad Riḍwān al-Dāyah. Beirut: Mu'assasat al-Risāla, 1978.

Ibn ʿAbd Rabbih, Aḥmad Ibn Muḥammad. *Al-ʿiqd al-farīd.* Ed. Mufīd Muḥammad Qumayḥa. Beirut: Dār al-Kutub al-ʿilmiyya, 2006.

Ibn Bassām, Abū al-Ḥasn ʿAlī. *Al-dhakhīra fī maḥāsin ahl al-jazīra.* Ed. Iḥsān ʿAbbās. Beirut: Dār al-Thaqāfa, 1979.

Ibn Dā'ūd, Avraham. *Sefer ha-Qabbalah: A Critical Edition with a Translation and Notes of the Book of Tradition.* Ed. Gerson D. Cohen. Philadelphia: Jewish Publication Society, 1967.

Ibn Ezra, Avraham Ben Meir. *Qoveṣ ḥokhmat ha-Rav Avraham Ibn Ezra: Shirav u-meliṣotav, ḥidotav u-mikhtamav.* Ed. David Kahana. Warsaw: Hoṣa'at Aḥi'asaf, 1922.

Ibn Ezra, Mosheh. *Kitāb al-muḥāḍara wa'l-mudhākara.* Ed. Abraham S. Halkin. Jerusalem: Mekize Nirdamim, 1975.

Ibn Ezra, Mosheh. *Shirei ha-ḥol.* Ed. Ḥayyim Brody. Jerusalem: Schocken, 1978.

Ibn Ezra, Mosheh. *Shirei ha-qodesh.* Ed. Yisrael Levin and Tova Rosen. Tel Aviv: Tel Aviv University Press, 2012.

Ibn Ezra, Yiṣḥaq Ben Avraham. *Yiṣḥaq Ben Avraham Ibn 'Ezra: Shirim.* Ed. Menahem H. Schmelzer. New York: Jewish Theological Seminary, 1980.

Ibn Gabirol, Shelomoh. *A Choice of Pearls.* Trans. B. H. Ascher. London: Trübner, 1859.

Ibn Gabirol, Shelomoh. *The Improvement of the Moral Qualities.* Trans. Stephen S. Wise. New York: Columbia University Press, 1901.

Ibn Gabirol, Shelomoh. *Shirei ha-ḥol.* Ed. Ḥayyim Brody and Ḥayyim Schirmann. Jerusalem: Schocken, 1974.

Ibn Gabirol, Shelomoh. *Shirei ha-ḥol.* Ed. Dov Jarden. Jerusalem: Dov Jarden, 1975.

Ibn Hānī al-Andalusī, Abū al-Qāsim Muḥammad al-Azdī. *Dīwān Ibn Hānī al-Andalusī.* Ed. Karam al-Bustānī. Beirut: Dār Ṣādir, 1980.

Ibn Ḥazm, Muḥammad. *Kitāb al-akhlāq wa'l-siyyar*. Ed. Evá Riyāḍ. Beirut: Dār Ibn Ḥazm, 2000.

Ibn Janāḥ, Yonah. *Kitāb al-uṣūl*. Ed. Adolf Neubauer. Oxford: Clarendon Press, 1875.

Ibn Janāḥ, Yonah. *Sefer ha-riqmah*. Ed. Michael Wilensky. 2 vols. Reprint. Jerusalem: Ha-Akademiah, 1964.

Ibn Janāḥ, Yonah. *Kutub wa rasā'il: Opusculers Et Traités D'abou'l-Walîd Merwân Ibn Djanâh (Rabbi Jonah) de Córdoba*. Ed. Joseph Derenbourg and Hartwig Derenbourg. Amsterdam: Philo Press, 1969.

Ibn Khaldūn. *The Muqaddimah*. Vol. 2. Trans. Franz Rosenthal. Princeton, N.J.: Princeton University Press, 1967.

Ibn Khalfūn, Yiṣḥaq. *Shirei Yiṣḥaq Ibn Khalfūn*. Ed. Aharon Mirsky. Jerusalem: Bialik Institute, 1961.

Ibn Paquda, Baḥya. *Torat ḥovot ha-levavot*. Ed. Yosef Qafiḥ. Jerusalem: Va'ad ha-Kelali li-Yehude Teman bi-Yerushalayim, 1973.

Ibn Qutaiba, 'Abd Allah Ibn Muslim. *Adab al-kātib*. Ed. Muḥammad Dālī. Beirut: Mu'assasat al-Risālah, 1986.

Ibn Rashīq. *Kitāb al-'umda fī maḥāsin al-shi'r wa-adābihi*. Ed. Muḥammad 'Abd al-Qādir Aḥmad 'Atā. Beirut: Dār al-Kutub al-'Ilmiyyah, 2001.

Ibn Rushd, Abu al-Walīd. *Talkhīṣ kitāb Arisṭūṭālīs fī al-shi'r*. Ed. Sālim Muḥammad Salīm. Cairo: 1971.

Ibn Sa'īd al-Maghribī. *Al-mughrib fī ḥulā al-maghrib*. Ed. Shawqi Dayf. Cairo: Dār al-Ma'ārif, 1964.

Ibn Ṣadīq, Yosef. *Shirei Yosef Ibn Ṣadīq*. Ed. Yonah David. New York: American Academy for Jewish Research, 1982.

Ibn Ṭabāṭabā, Muḥammad Ibn Aḥmad. *I'yār al-sh'ir*. Ed. 'Abd al-'Azīz ibn Nāṣir Māni'. Riyād: Dār al-'Ulūm, 1985.

Jastrow, Marcus. *A Dictionary of the Targumim, Talmud Babli and Yerushalmi, and the Midrashic Literature*. Reprint. New York: Judaica Press, 1996.

Kanarfogel, Ephraim. *Intellectual History and Rabbinic Culture of Medieval Ashkenaz*. Detroit: Wayne State University Press, 2012.

Kantorowicz, Ernst. *The King's Two Bodies: A Study in Medieval Political Theology*. Princeton, N.J.: Princeton University Press, 1957.

Kantorowicz, Ernst. *Laudes Regiae: A Study in Liturgical Acclamations and Mediaeval Ruler Worship*. Berkeley: University of California Press, 1946.

Kaplan, Yosef. "Court Jews Before the 'Hofjuden.'" In *From Court Jews to the Rothschilds: Art, Patronage, and Power, 1600–1800*, ed. Vivian B. Mann and Richard I. Cohen, 11–25. Munich: Prestel, 1996.

Kazhdan, Alexander P., and Michael McCormick. "The Social World of the Byzantine Court." In *Byzantine Court Culture from 829 to 1204*, ed. H. Maguire, 167–97. Washington, D.C.: Dumbarton Oaks Research Library and Collection, 1997.

Kiecker, James G., ed. and trans. *Postilla of Nicholas of Lyra on the Song of Songs*. Milwaukee: Marquette University Press, 1998.

Kemal, Salim. *The Philosophical Poetics of Alfarabi, Avicenna, and Averroes: The Aristotelian Reception.* London: Routledge, 2002.

Kfir, Uriah. "Center and Periphery in Medieval Hebrew Poetry: Secular Poetry from a Provincial and Provençal Perspective" (Hebrew). Ph.D. diss., Tel Aviv University, 2011.

Khan, Geoffrey. *Arabic Legal and Administrative Documents in the Cambridge Genizah Collections.* Cambridge: Cambridge University Press, 1993.

Khan, Geoffrey. "The Historical Development of the Structure of Medieval Arabic Petitions." *BSOAS* 53, no. 1 (1990): 8–30.

Klein, Jacob. *The Royal Hymns of Shulgi King of Ur: Man's Quest for Immortal Fame.* Transactions of the American Philosophical Society, vol. 71, pt. 7. Philadelphia: American Philosophical Society, 1981.

Klein-Braslavy, Sara. "Bible Commentary." In *The Cambridge Companion to Maimonides,* ed. Kenneth Seeskin, 245–72. Cambridge: Cambridge University Press, 2005.

Kraemer, Joel L. "The Influence of Islamic Law on Maimonides: The Case of the Five Qualifications" (Hebrew). *Te'udah* 10 (1996): 225–44.

Kramers, J. H. "Les noms musulmans composés avec Dîn." *Acta Orientalia* 5 (1927): 53–67.

Kraus, Paul. "Hebräische und syrische Zitate in ismāʿīlitischen Schriften." *Der Islam* 19, no. 4 (1930): 243–63.

Kurke, Leslie. *The Traffic in Praise: Pindar and the Poetics of Social Economy.* Ithaca, N.Y.: Cornell University Press, 1991.

Lakoff, George, and Mark Johnson. *Metaphors We Live By.* Chicago: University of Chicago Press, 1980.

Lane, Edward William. *Arabic-English Lexicon.* 8 vols. London and Edinburgh: Williams and Norgate, 1863.

Latham, J. D. "The Beginnings of Arabic Prose Literature: The Epistolary Genre." In *Arabic Literature to the End of the Umayyad Period,* ed. A. F. L. Beeston et al., 154–79. Cambridge: Cambridge University Press, 1983.

Lecomte, Gérard. "L'introduction du Kitāb adab al-kātib d'Ibn Qutayba." In *Mélanges Louis Massignon,* vol. 3, ed. L'Institut d'études islamiques de l'Université de Paris and l'Institut français de Damas, 47–65. Damascus: Institut Français de Damas, 1957.

Levin, Benjamin. "Qadish 'atiq miyemei ha-geonim." *Ginze Kedem* 2 (1923): 46–48.

Levin, Israel. *Avraham Ibn Ezra: Ḥayyav ve-shirato.* Tel Aviv: Ha-Qibbuṣ ha-Me'uḥad, 1969.

Levin, Israel. *Keter malkhut le-rabi Shelomoh Ibn Gabirol.* Ed. Yisrael Levin. Tel Aviv: Tel Aviv University Press, 2005.

Levin, Israel. *Me'il Tashbeṣ: Ha-sugim ha-shonim shel shirat ha-ḥol ha-'ivrit be-Sefarad.* 3 vols. Tel Aviv: Ha-Qibbuṣ ha-Me'uḥad, 1995.

Lida, Maria Rosa. "La hyperbole sagrada en la poesía castellana del siglo XV." *Revista de Filología Hispánica* 8 (1946): 121–30.

Linder, Amnon. "'The Jews Too Were Not Absent . . . Carrying Moses's Law on Their Shoulders': The Ritual Encounter of Pope and Jews from the Middle Ages to Modern Times." *JQR* 99, no. 3 (2009): 323–95.

López-Morillas, Consuelo. "Language." In *The Literature of al-Andalus*, ed. María Rosa Menocal, Raymond P. Scheindlin, and Michael Sells, 33–59. Cambridge: Cambridge University Press, 2000.

Lorberbaum, Yair. *Disempowered King: Monarchy in Classical Jewish Literature.* London: Bloomsbury, 2011.

Mack, Burton L. *Wisdom and the Hebrew Epic: Ben Sira's Hymn in Praise of the Fathers.* Chicago: University of Chicago Press, 1985.

Madelung, Wilferd. "Das Imamat in der frühen ismailitischen Lehre." *Islam* 37, nos. 1–3 (1961): 43–135.

Mahdi, Muhsin. "Kitāb al-shiʿr." *Shiʿr* 3 (1959): 90–95.

Mahdjoub, Mohammad-Dja'far. "The Evolution of Popular Eulogy of the Imams Among the Shiʿa." In *Authority and Political Culture in Shiʿism*, ed. Said Amir Arjomand, 54–79. Albany: SUNY Press, 1988.

Maimonides. See Ben Maimon, Mosheh.

Mallette, Karla. *The Kingdom of Sicily 1100–1250: A Literary History.* Philadelphia: University of Pennsylvania Press, 2005.

Mann, Jacob. *The Jews in Egypt and in Palestine Under the Fāṭimid Caliphs: A Contribution to Their Political and Communal History Based Chiefly on Genizah Material Hitherto Unpublished.* 2 vols. Oxford: Oxford University Press, 1920.

Mann, Jacob. *Texts and Studies in Jewish History and Literature: Ḳaraitica*. Vol. 1. Reprint. New York: Ktav, 1972.

Margoliouth, David Samuel, ed. *Dīwān shiʿr Abī al-Fatḥ Muḥammad Ibn ʿUbayd ʿAllāh Ibn ʿAbd Allāh al-maʿrūf bi-Sibṭ Ibn al-Taʿāwīdhī.* Miṣr: Maṭbaʿat al-Muqtaṭaf, 1903.

Marin, Louis. *Portrait of the King.* Trans. Martha M. Houle. Minneapolis: University of Minnesota Press, 1988.

Marsham, Andrew. *Rituals of Islamic Monarchy: Accession and Succession in the First Muslim Empire.* Edinburgh: Edinburgh University Press, 2009.

Matar, Nabil. "Alfārābī on Imagination: With a Translation of His Treatise on Poetry." *College Literature* 23, no. 1 (1996): 100–110.

Matheson, Craig. "Weber and the Classification of Forms of Legitimacy." *British Journal of Sociology* 38, no. 2 (1987): 199–215.

Matt, Daniel. *Zohar: The Pritzker Editions* (Book 9). Palo Alto, Calif.: Stanford University Press, 2016.

Mauss, Marcel. *The Gift: The Form and Reason for Exchange in Archaic Societies.* Trans. W. D. Halls. Reprint. New York: W. W. Norton, 1990.

McFadden, K. "Hyperbole." In *Princeton Encyclopedia of Poetry and Poetics*, ed. Roland Greene, Stephen Cushman, and Clare Cavanagh, 648. Princeton, N.J.: Princeton University Press, 2012.

Meacham-Yoreh, Tirzah, ed., and Miriam Frenkel, trans. *The Book of Maturity by Rav Shemuel Ben Ḥofni Gaon and the Book of Years by Rav Yehudah Ha-Kohen Rosh Ha-Seder* (Hebrew). Jerusalem: Yad ha-Rav Nisim, 1999.

Meisami, Julie Scott. "Literary Criticism, Medieval." In *Encyclopedia of Arabic Literature*, ed. Julie Scott Meisami and Paul Starkey, 2:472–74. London: Routledge, 1998.

Mezliś, Yiṣḥaq. *Shirat ha-maor.* Jerusalem: R. Mas, 1984.

Melchert, Christoph. "The Piety of the Hadith Folk." *International Journal of Middle Eastern Studies* 34, no. 3 (2002): 425–39.

Merquoir, J. G. *Rousseau and Weber: Two Studies in the Theory of Legitimacy.* London: Routledge and Kegan Paul, 1980.

Mirkin, Mosheh Aryeh, ed. *Midrash rabbah.* 11 vols. Tel Aviv: Yavneh, 1959.

Moin, A. Azfar. *The Millennial Sovereign: Sacred Kingship and Sainthood in Islam.* New York: Columbia University Press, 2012.

Motzkin, Aryeh Leo. "The Arabic Correspondence of Judge Elijah and His Family." Ph.D. diss., University of Pennsylvania, 1965.

Motzkin, Aryeh Leo. "A Thirteenth-Century Jewish Teacher in Cairo." *Journal of Semitic Studies* 21 (1970): 49–64.

Mottahedeh, Roy. *Loyalty and Leadership in an Early Islamic Society.* London: I. B. Tauris, 2001.

Münz-Manor, Ophir. "'As the Apple Among Fruits, So the Priest When He Emerges': Poetic Similies in Preclassical Poems of the 'How Lovely' Genre" (Hebrew). *Ginzei Qedem* 5 (2009): 165–88.

Naaman, Erez. "*Sariqa* in Practice: The Case of Al-Ṣāḥib Ibn 'Abbād." *Middle Eastern Literatures* 14, no. 3 (2011): 271–85.

Najā, Ashraf Maḥmūd. *Qaṣīdat al-madīḥ fī'l-Andalus: 'Aṣr al-ṭawā'if: Dirāsah fannīyah.* Alexandria: Dār al-Ma'rifah al-Jāmī'iyyah, 1997.

Nemoy, Leon. *Karaite Anthology: Excerpts from the Early Literature.* New Haven, Conn.: Yale University Press, 1952.

Nesbitt, J. W. *Catalogue of Byzantine Seals at Dumbarton Oaks and in the Fogg Museum of Art.* Vol. 6, *Emperors, Patriarchs of Constantinople, Addenda.* Washington, D.C.: Dumbarton Oaks, 2009.

Neubauer, Adolph. *Medieval Jewish Chronicles.* 2 vols. Oxford: Clarendon Press, 1887–95.

Neusner, Jacob, trans. *The Tosefta.* Vol. 4, *Eduyot.* Atlanta: Scholars Press, 1999.

Newman, Andrew J. "Madjlis." In *Encyclopaedia of Islam*, 2nd ed., ed. P. Bearman et al. Brill Online, 2014. http://referenceworks.brillonline.com/entries/encyclopaedia-of-islam-2/mad-j-lis-COM_0606.

Orfali, Bilal. "In Defense of the Use of Qur'ān in Adab: Ibn Abī l-Luṭf's Raf' al-iltibās 'an munkir al-iqtibās." In *The Heritage of Arabo-Islamic Learning*, ed. Maurice Pomerantz and Aram Shahim, 498–527. Leiden: E. J. Brill, 2015.

Orfali, Bilal. "The Works of Abū Manṣūr al-Tha'ālibī (350–429/961–1039)." *Journal of Arabic Literature* 40, no. 3 (2009): 273–318.

Orfali, Bilal, and Maurice Pomerantz. "'I See a Distant Fire': Al-Tha'ālibī's *Kitāb al-Iqtibās min al-Qur'ān al-Karīm.*" In *Qur'an and Adab: The Shaping of Literary Traditions in Classical Islam*, ed. Nuha Alshaar. Oxford: Oxford University Press, forthcoming.

Pagis, Dan. *Ha-shir davur 'al ofnav: Meḥqarim u-masot ba-shirah ha-'ivrit shel yemei ha-beinayyim.* Ed. Ezra Fleischer. Jerusalem: Magnes, 1993.

Pagis, Dan. *Hebrew Poetry of the Middle Ages and the Renaissance.* Berkeley: University of California Press, 1991.

Pagis, Dan. *Shirat ha-ḥol ve-torat ha-shir le-Mosheh Ibn Ezra u-venei doro.* Jerusalem: Bialik, 1970.

Pagis, Dan. "Shirei temunah 'ivriyyim ve-'od ṣurot melakhutiot." *Hasifrut* 7 (1977): 13–27.

Pagis, Dan. "Shirei yayyin me-lifnei tequfat Sefarad." In *Sefer Dov Sadan: Qoveṣ meḥqarim, mugashim be-meliat lo shiv'im ve-ḥamesh shanah,* ed. Samuel Werses, Nathan Rotenstreich, and Chone Shmeruk, 245–55. Tel Aviv: Ha-Qibbuṣ ha-Me'uḥad, 1977.

Patai, Yosef. "Shirei ḥol shel Shelomoh Bonafed." *Mi-ṣefune ha-shirah,* 67–85. Jerusalem: R. Mas, 1939.

Pedersen, Johannes. *Der Eid bei den Semiten: In seinem Verhältnis zu verwandten Erscheinungen sowie die Stellung des Eides im Islam.* Strassburg: K. J. Trübner, 1914.

Penslar, Derek. *Jews and the Military: A History.* Princeton, N.J.: Princeton University Press, 2014.

Perry, Theodore A. *The Moral Proverbs of Santob de Carrión: Jewish Wisdom in Christian Spain.* Princeton, N.J.: Princeton University Press, 1987.

Prats, Arturo. "A Hebrew Poetry Contest in Early-Fifteenth-Century Zaragoza." *Journal of Medieval Iberian Studies* 6, no. 2 (2014): 214–36.

Press, Alan R., ed. and trans. *Anthology of Troubadour Lyric Poetry.* Austin: University of Texas Press, 1971.

Qutbuddin, Tahera. *Al-Mu'ayyad al-Shīrāzī and Fatimid Da'wa Poetry: A Case of Commitment in Classical Arabic Literature.* Leiden: E. J. Brill, 2005.

Rajak, Tessa. *The Jewish Dialogue with Greece and Rome: Studies in Cultural and Social Interaction.* Leiden: E. J. Brill, 2001.

Ratzhaby, Yehudah. *Moṭivim she'ulim be-sifrut Yisra'el.* Ramat Gan: Bar-Ilan University, 2006.

Ratzhaby, Yehudah. "Shirah 'aravit be-fi yehudim be-Andalusiya." In *Sefer Yisra'el Levin,* ed. Reuven Tzur and Tova Rosen, 1:329–50. Tel Aviv: Makhon Katz, 1994.

Ratzhaby, Yehudah. "Shnei shirim sefardiyyim me-oṣar ha-geniza." *Moznaim* 66, no. 6 (1992): 10–13.

Ray, Jonathan. *The Sephardic Frontier: The Reconquista and the Jewish Community in Medieval Iberia.* Ithaca, N.Y.: Cornell University Press, 2006.

Rees, Roger. *Layers of Loyalty in Latin Panegyric.* Oxford: Oxford University Press, 2002.

Revel, Dov. "Iggeret rav Sa'adia Gaon." *Devir* 1 (1923): 181–88, with addendum by Y. N. Epstein, 189–90.

Rippin, A. "Review of: *God's Caliph: Religious Authority in the First Centuries of Islam* by Patricia Crone, Martin Hinds." *BSOAS* 51, no. 2 (1988): 328–29.

Robinson, Cynthia. *In Praise of Song: The Making of Courtly Culture in Al-Andalus and Provence, 1005–1134 A.D.* Leiden: E. J. Brill, 2002.

Robles, Santiaga Benavente, and Ángel Sáenz-Badillos, eds. *Tĕšuḇot de los discípulos de Mĕnaḥem contra Dunaš Ben Labraṭ.* Granada: Universidad de Granada, 1986.

Roche, Paul. *Pliny's Praise: The Panegyricus in the Roman World.* Cambridge: Cambridge University Press, 2011.

Rosenblatt, Samuel. "The Relations Between Jewish and Muslim Laws Concerning Oaths and Vows." *PAAJR* 7 (1935–36): 229–43.

Rosenthal, Norman, et al. *Citizens and Kings: Portraits in the Age of Revolution 1760–1830.* London: Royal Academy of Arts, 2007.

Roth, Cecil. "Ecclesiasticus in the Synagogue Service." *Journal of Biblical Literature* 71, no. 3 (1952): 171–78.

Roth, Norman. *Jews, Visigoths, and Muslims in Medieval Spain.* Leiden: Brill, 1994.

Rowland, Jon Thomas. *Faint Praise and Civil Leer: The "Decline" of Eighteenth-Century Panegyric.* Newark: University of Delaware Press, 1994.

Russell, Donald. "The Panegyrists and Their Teachers." In *The Role of Panegyric in Late Antiquity*, ed. Mary Whitby, 17–52. Leiden: E. J. Brill, 1998.

Rustow, Marina. "Formal and Informal Patronage Among Jews in the Islamic East: Evidence from the Cairo Geniza." *Al-Qantara* 29, no. 2 (2008): 341–82.

Rustow, Marina. "The Genizah and Jewish Communal History." In *From a Sacred Source: Genizah Studies in Honor of Stefan C. Reif*, ed. Ben Outhweite and Siam Bhayro, 289–317. Leiden: E. J. Brill, 2014.

Rustow, Marina. *Heresy and the Politics of Community: The Jews of the Fatimid Caliphate.* Ithaca, N.Y.: Cornell University Press, 2008.

Rustow, Marina. "The Legal Status of Ḍimmīs in the Fatimid East: A View from the Palace in Cairo." In *The Legal Status of Ḍimmīs in the Islamic West*, ed. Maribel Fierro and John Tolan, 307–32. Turnhout: Brepols, 2013.

Rustow, Marina. "Patronage in the Context of Solidarity and Reciprocity." In *Patronage, Production, and Transmission of Texts in Medieval and Early Modern Jewish Cultures*, ed. Esperanza Alfonso and Jonathan Decter, 13–44. Turnhout: Brepols, 2014.

Sa'adia Gaon. See Ben Yosef, Sa'adia.

Sadan, Yosef. "Rabbi Judah al-Ḥarīzī as Cultural Crossroads: An Arabic Biography of a Jewish Artist in the Eyes of an Orientalist" (Hebrew). *Pe'amim* 68 (1996): 16–67.

Sáenz-Badillos, Angel. "Hebrew Invective Poetry: The Debate Between Todros Abulafia and Phinehas Halevi." *Prooftexts* 16, no. 1 (1996): 49–73.

Sáenz-Badillos, Angel. "The Literary World of Shelomoh Bonafed." In *Studies in Medieval Jewish Poetry: A Message upon the Garden*, ed. Alessandro Guetta and Masha Itzhaki, 167–83. Leiden: E. J. Brill, 2009.

Sáenz-Badillos, Angel. "Shelomoh Bonafed at the Crossroads of Hebrew and Romance Cultures." In *Encuentros y Desencuentros: Spanish-Jewish Cultural Interaction Throughout History*, ed. Carlos Carrete Parrondo and Aviva Doron, 343–79. Tel Aviv: Tel Aviv University Press, 2000.

Safran, Bezalel. "Bahya Ibn Paquda's Attitude Toward the Courtier Class." In *Studies in Medieval Jewish History and Literature*, ed. Isadore Twersky, 154–96. Cambridge, Mass.: Harvard University Press, 1979.

Safran, Janina. "The Command of the Faithful in al-Andalus: A Study in the Articulation of Caliphal Legitimacy." *IJMES* 30, no. 2 (1998): 183–98.

Safran, Janina. *The Second Umayyad Caliphate: The Articulation of Legitimacy in al-Andalus.* Cambridge, Mass.: Harvard University Press, 2000.

Sanders, Paula. *Ritual, Politics, and the City in Fatimid Cairo.* Albany: SUNY Press, 1994.

Schechter, Solomon. "Genizah Specimens." *JQR* 12, no. 1 (1900): 112–13.

Schechter, Solomon. *Saadyana: Geniza Fragments of Writings of R. Saadya Gaon and Others*. 3 vols. Cambridge: Deighton and Bell, 1903.

Scheiber, Alexander. "Panegyrics in Honour of a Baghdad Dignitary from the Kaufmann Geniza." *Acta Orientalia Academiae Scientiarum Hungaricae* 3 (1953): 107–33.

Scheiber, Alexander. "Two Additional Poems of Praise in Honor of Abraham of Baghdad" (Hebrew). *Zion* 30, nos. 3–4 (1965): 123–27.

Scheiber, Sándor. "Introduction." In *Codex Maimuni: Moses Maimonides' Code of Law*, ed. Sándor Scheiber et al., 11–24. Budapest: Corvina, 1984.

Scheindlin, Raymond P. *The Gazelle: Medieval Hebrew Poems on God, Israel, and the Soul* Philadelphia: Jewish Publication Society, 1991.

Scheindlin, Raymond P. "The Hebrew Qasida in Spain." In *Qasida Poetry in Islamic Asia and Africa*, ed. Stefan Sperl and Christopher Shackle, 121–36. Leiden: E. J. Brill, 1996.

Scheindlin, Raymond P. "The Misogynist." In *Rabbinic Fantasies*, ed. David Stern and Mark Jay Mirsky, 269–94. New York: Jewish Publication Society, 1990.

Scheindlin, Raymond P. "Poet and Patron: Ibn Gabirol's Poem of the Palace and Its Gardens." *Prooftexts* 16, no. 1 (1996): 31–47.

Scheindlin, Raymond P. "Rabbi Moshe Ibn Ezra on the Legitimacy of Poetry." *Medievalia et Humanistica: Studies in Medieval and Renaissance Culture* 7 (1976): 101–15.

Scheindlin, Raymond P. "Secular Hebrew Poetry in Fifteenth-Century Spain." In *Crisis and Creativity in the Sephardic World 1391–1648*, ed. Benjamin R. Gampel, 25–37. New York: Columbia University Press, 1997.

Scheindlin, Raymond P. *The Song of the Distant Dove: Judah Halevi's Pilgrimage*. Oxford: Oxford University Press, 2007.

Scheindlin, Raymond P. *Wine, Women, and Death: Medieval Hebrew Poems on the Good Life*. Philadelphia: Jewish Publication Society, 1986.

Schimmel, Annemarie. *Mystical Dimensions of Islam*. Chapel Hill: University of North Carolina Press, 1975.

Schirmann, Ḥayyim. "The Function of the Poet in Medieval Spain." *JSS* 16, no. 3 (1954): 235–52.

Schirmann, Ḥayyim. "Ha-meshorerim benei doram shel Mosheh Ibn Ezra vi-Yehudah ha-Levi." *Yedi'ot ha-makhon le-ḥeqer ha-shirah ha-'ivrit* 2 (1936): 119–94.

Schirmann, Ḥayyim. *Ha-shirah ha-'ivrit bi-Sefarad u-be-Provans*. 2 vols. Tel Aviv: Dvir; Jerusalem: Mosad Bialik, 1954–60.

Schirmann, Ḥayyim. "Samuel Hanaggid: The Man, the Soldier, the Politician." *JSS* 13, no. 2 (1951): 99–126.

Schirmann, Ḥayyim. *Shirim ḥadashim min ha-genizah*. Jerusalem: Ha-Aqademia ha-Le'umit ha-Yisra'elit le-Mada'im, 1965.

Schirmann, Ḥayyim. *Toledot ha-shirah ha-'ivrit bi-Sefarad ha-muslemit*, ed. Ezra Fleischer. Jerusalem: Magnes Press, 1995.

Schirmann, Ḥayyim. *Toledot ha-shirah ha-'ivrit bi-Sefarad ha-noṣrit u-ve-darom Ṣarfat*. Jerusalem: Magnes, 1997.

Schlossberg, Eliezer. "A Booklet on the Names of the Lord and His Attributes Attributed to Rav Shemuel Ben Ḥofni Gaon" (Hebrew). *Da'at* 67 (2009): 5–38.

Schmitt, Carl. *Political Theology: Four Chapters on the Concept of Sovereignty*, trans. G. Schwab. Chicago: University of Chicago Press, 2005.

Schwartz, Seth. *Were the Jews a Mediterranean Society? Reciprocity and Solidarity in Ancient Judaism*. Princeton, N.J.: Princeton University Press, 2010.

Scott, James. *Domination and the Arts of Resistance: Hidden Transcripts*. New Haven, Conn.: Yale University Press, 1990.

Seidman, Naomi. *Faithful Renderings: Jewish-Christian Difference and the Politics of Translation*. Chicago: University of Chicago Press, 2006.

Septimus, Bernard. "Piety and Power in Thirteenth-Century Catalonia." In *Studies in Medieval Jewish History and Literature*, ed. Isadore Twersky, 197–230. Cambridge, Mass.: Harvard University Press, 1979.

Sharlet, Jocelyn. *Patronage and Poetry in the Islamic World: Social Mobility and Status in the Middle East and Central Asia*. London: I. B. Tauris, 2011.

Shepard, Sanford. *Shem Tov: His World and His Words*. Miami: Ediciones Universal, 1978.

Silverstein, Adam. "Jews and the News: The Interaction of Private and Official Communication Networks in Jewish History." In *Highways, Byways, and Road Systems in the Pre-Modern World*, ed. Susan E. Alcock, John Bodel, and Richard J. A. Talbert, 265–75. West Sussex: Wiley-Blackwell, 2005.

Silverstein, Adam. *Postal Systems in the Pre-Modern Islamic World*. Cambridge: Cambridge University Press, 2007.

Simonsohn, Shlomo. *The Jews in Sicily*. 14 vols. Leiden: E. J. Brill, 1997.

Smoor, P. "'The Master of the Century': Fatimid Poets in Cairo." In *Egypt and Syria in the Fatimid, Ayyubid and Mamluk Eras I*, ed. U. Vermeulen and D. De Smet, 139–62. Leuven: Peeters, 1995.

Sola-Solé, J. M. *Corpus de Poesía Mozárabe (Las Hargas andalusies)*. Barcelona: Ediciones Hispam, 1973.

Sperl, Stefan. "Islamic Kingship and Arabic Panegyric Poetry in the Early Ninth Century." *JAL* 8 (1977): 20–35.

Stein, Leopold. *Untersuchungen über die Proverbios morales von Santob de Carrión*. Berlin: Mayer & Müller, 1900.

Stern, David. *Parables in Midrash: Narrative and Exegesis in Rabbinic Literature*. Cambridge, Mass.: Harvard University Press, 1991.

Stern, Samuel Miklos. "Heterodox Isma'ilism at the Time of al-Mu'izz." *BSOAS* 17 (1955): 10–33. Repr. in Stern, *Studies in Early Ismā'īlism*, 257–88. Jerusalem: Magnes Press, 1983.

Stern, Samuel Miklos. *Hispano-Arabic Strophic Poetry*, ed. L. P. Harvey. Oxford: Clarendon Press, 1974.

Stern, Samuel Miklos. "Ibn al-Samḥ." *Journal of the Royal Asiatic Society* 88, nos. 1–2 (1956): 31–44.

Stern, Samuel Miklos. "Petitions from the Ayyūbid Period." *BSOAS* 27, no. 1 (1964): 1–32

Stern, Samuel Miklos. "Petitions from the Mamlūk Period." *BSOAS* 29, no. 2 (1966): 233–76.

Stern, Samuel Miklos. *Studies in Early Ismāʿīlism*. Jerusalem: Magnes Press, 1983.

Stern, Samuel Miklos. "Three Petitions of the Fāṭimid Period." *Oriens* 15 (1962): 172–209.

Stern, Samuel Miklos. "A Twelfth-Century Circle of Hebrew Poets in Sicily." *JJS* 5 (1954): 60–79, 110–13.

Stern, Selma. *The Court Jew: A Contribution to the History of the Period of Absolutism in Central Europe*. Trans. Ralph Weiman. Philadelphia: Jewish Publication Society, 1950.

Stetkevych, Jaroslav. "Arabic Poetry and Assorted Poetics." In *Islamic Studies: A Tradition and Its Problems*, ed. M. H. Kerr, 103–23. Malibu, Calif.: Undena Publications, 1980.

Stetkevych, Suzanne Pinckney. *The Mantle Odes: Arabic Praise Poems to the Prophet Muhammad*. Bloomington: Indiana University Press, 2010.

Stetkevych, Suzanne Pinckney. *The Poetics of Islamic Legitimacy: Myth, Gender and Ceremony in the Classical Arabic Ode*. Bloomington: Indiana University Press, 2002.

Stillman, Norman A. *The Jews of Arab Lands*. Philadelphia: Jewish Publication Society, 1979.

Strenki, Ivan. *Theology and the First Theory of Sacrifice*. Leiden: E. J. Brill, 2003.

Stroumsa, Sarah. *Maimonides in His World: Portrait of a Mediterranean Thinker*. Princeton, N.J.: Princeton University Press, 2009.

Stroumsa, Sarah. "A Note on Maimonides' Attitude to Joseph Ibn Ṣadiq" (Hebrew). In *Shlomo Pines Jubilee Volume*. Part 2, *Jerusalem Studies in Jewish Thought* 8 (1990): 210–15.

Swartz, Michael D., and Yosef Yahalom. *Avodah: Ancient Poems for Yom Kippur*. University Park: Pennsylvania State University Press, 2005.

Sysling, Harry. "Laments at the Departure of a Sage: Funeral Songs for Great Scholars as Recorded in Rabbinic Literature." In *Studies in Hebrew Literature and Jewish Culture: Presented to Albert van der Heide on the Occasion of His Sixty-Fifth Birthday*, ed. Martin F. J. Baasten and Reinier Munk, 81–102. Dordrecht: Springer, 2007.

Talmage, Frank. "The Francesc de Sant Jordi-Solomon Bonafed Letters." In *Studies in Medieval Jewish History and Literature*, ed. Isadore Twersky, 337–64. Cambridge, Mass.: Harvard University Press, 1979.

Tayan, E. "Bayʿa." In *Encyclopaedia of Islam*, 2nd ed., ed. P. Bearman et al. Brill Online, 2014. http://referenceworks.brillonline.com/entries/encyclopaedia-of-islam-2/baya-COM_0107.

Tobi, Yosef. *Between Hebrew and Arabic Poetry: Studies in Spanish Medieval Hebrew Poetry*. Leiden: E. J. Brill, 2010.

Tobi, Yosef. "Preliminary Study in Ḥilyat al-Muḥāḍara by Abū ʿAlī Muḥammad al-Ḥātimī: The 'Lost' Source of Moše Ibn Ezra for His Kitāb al-Muḥāḍara wa-al-Mudhākara." In *Between Hebrew and Arabic Poetry: Studies in Spanish Medieval Hebrew Poetry*, 355–68. Leiden: E. J. Brill, 2010.

Turner, Victor. *Dramas, Fields, and Metaphors: Symbolic Action in Human Society*. Ithaca, N.Y.: Cornell University Press, 1974.

Udah, Tsabih. *Ha-mikhtavim ha-ʿaraviyim shel ha-soḥarim ha-yehudim bi-genizat Qahir ba-meʾah ha-aḥat-ʿesreh*. Tel Aviv: Tel Aviv University, 1992.

Van Bekkum, Wout. *The Secular Poetry of El'azar Ben Ya'aqov ha-Bavli.* Leiden: E. J. Brill, 2007.

Van Gelder, G. J. H. "Forbidden Firebrands: Frivolous *Iqtibās* (Quotation from the *Qur'ān*) According to Medieval Arab Critics." *Quaderni di Studi Arabi* 20/21 (2002–3): 3–16.

Van Gelder, G. J. H., and Marle Hammond, eds. *Takhyīl: The Imaginary in Classical Arabic Poetics.* Cambridge, Mass.: Gibb Memorial Trust, 2009.

Vardi, Tirza. "'Adat ha-nognim be-Saragosa: Shirat ha-ḥol." Ph.D. diss., Hebrew University, 1996.

Vardi, Tirza. "A Wedding in Agramont: The Wedding Poetry of Solomon Bonafed" (Hebrew). *Meḥqarei Yerushalayim be-Sifrut 'Ivrit* 14 (1993): 169–91.

Villanueva, Francisco Márquez. *El Concepto Cultural Alfonsí.* Madrid: Editorial Mapfre, 1994.

Wacks, David A. *Double Diaspora in Sephardic Literature: Jewish Cultural Production Before and After 1492.* Bloomington: Indiana University Press, 2015.

Weber, Max. "Social Psychology of the World Religions." In *Max Weber: Essays in Sociology,* ed. H. H. Gerth and C. W. Mills, 267–301. London: Routledge and Kegan Paul, 1947.

Weber, Max. *The Theory of Social and Economic Organization.* Trans. A. M. Henderson and Talcott Parsons, ed. Talcott Parsons. New York: Free Press, 1964.

Weinberger, Leon. *Twilight of a Golden Age: Selected Poems of Abraham Ibn Ezra.* Tuscaloosa: University of Alabama Press, 1997.

Weiss, Yosef. "Tarbuṭ ḥaṣranit ve-shirah ḥaṣranit." *WCJS* 1 (1952): 396–403.

Weitzmann, Steven. "Mediterranean Exchanges: A Response to Seth Schwartz's *Were the Jews a Mediterranean Society?*." *JQR* 102, no. 4 (2012): 491–512.

Wensinck, A. J., and C. E. Bosworth. "Lawḥ." In *Encyclopaedia of Islam,* 2nd ed., ed. P. Bearman et al. Brill Online, 2014. http://referenceworks.brillonline.com/entries/encyclopaedia-of-islam-2/lawh-COM_0576.

Whitby, Mary, ed. *The Propaganda of Power: The Role of Panegyric in Late Antiquity.* Leiden: E. J. Brill, 1998.

Yahalom, Yosef. "Arabic and Hebrew as Poetic Languages Within Jewish and Muslim Society: Judah Alḥarizi Between East and West" (Hebrew). *Leshonenu* 74 (2012): 305–21.

Yahalom, Yosef. "Redacción y reelaboración: Entre el original y la reelaboración en la creación literaria de R. Judá Al-Ḥarizi." *Iberia Judaica* 5 (2013): 173–94.

Yahalom, Yosef. "The Temple and the City in Liturgical Hebrew Poetry." In *The History of Jerusalem: The Early Muslim Period, 638–1099,* ed. Joshua Prawer and Haggai Ben-Shammai, 270–94. New York: New York University Press, 1996.

Yovhannēs V Drasxanakertc'i. *History of Armenia.* Trans. Krikor H. Maksoudian. Atlanta: Scholars Press, 1987.

Yuval, Israel. *Two Nations in Your Womb: Perceptions of Jews and Christians in Late Antiquity.* Berkeley: University of California Press, 2006.

Zackin, Jane Robin. "A Jew and His Milieu: Allegory, Polemic, and Jewish Thought in Sem Tob's *Proverbios Morales* and *Ma'aseh Harav.*" Ph.D. diss., University of Texas, 2008.

Zemke, John. *Critical Approaches to the Proverbios Morales of Shem Tov of Carrión: An Annotated Bibliography.* Newark, Del.: Juan de La Cuesta Hispanic Monographs, 1997.

Zonta, Mauro. *La "Classificazione delle Scienze" di al-Fārābī nella Tradizione Ebraica: Edizione critica e traduzione annotata della versione ebraica di Qalonymos ben Qalonymos ben Me'ir.* Turin: Università degli Studi di Venezia, 1992.

GENERAL INDEX

Page numbers in italics refer to illustrations.

Geertz, Clifford, 34
generosity, 98–101
geography, representation of, 23–26, 128–30, 139
geonim: bestowal of titles by, 45; defined, 6; humility as trait of, 96; maintenance of relationships as chief function of, 21, 31, 40, 72, 74–75, 86; reputation of, 14; roles of, 72. *See also* academies
Gerona school, 228–32
al-Ghaḍā'irī, Abū al-Riḍā, 106
al-Ghazzālī, 187; *Iḥyā' 'ulūm al-dīn*, 145
al-ghulū (hyperbole), 166–67, 171, 174, 196
gift culture, 26, 67–89; of the academies, 71–76; in al-Andalus, 78–80; biblical terminology associated with, 298n55; dynamic quality of exchange in, 69; embedded vs. disembedded exchange in, 69–70, 86, 155–57, 296n8; in Islamic East, 76–78; panegyrics as component of, 69; relationship maintenance as purpose of, 68; sacrificial language and, 84–89
Ginzberg, Louis, 3
God: contemporary associations of biblical praises for, 176–78; ethics of praise in relation to, 150–54; generosity as trait of, 98; gift exchange and, 84–89; names appropriate to, in Islam, 186–87; names of, in Judaism, 193–95, 326n64; political rulers likened to, 178–81, 183–92, 196–205; praise of, 15, 17–18, 28; references to, in interreligious panegyrics, 243–45, 248, 250, 252, 254–56, 258, 265, 268, 270, 274–75; trustworthiness as trait of, 111. *See also* political theology
God's caliph (*khalīfat allah*), 179, 185
Goitein, S. D., 3, 24–25, 39, 45, 81, 84, 86, 122
ha-Gorni, Yiṣḥaq, 225–26, 242
Granada, massacre of the Jews in (1066), 63, 65, 98, 295n137
Greenblatt, Stephen, 180–81
Greenstone, Julius, 252, 257
Gross, Avraham, 238
Gruendler, Beatrice, 9, 69, 80, 174–75
Guadalajara, 136–37, 139
guzma. See *havai*; hyperbole

habitus, 14, 213, 267, 270
Hai Ben Sherirah Gaon, 3, 11, 22, 30–32, 49, 50, 71, 74, 85, 86, 99–100, 117, 129–30, 158
Halevi, Yehudah, 14, 22, 24, 25, 27, 57, 60–62, 78–80, 97, 100, 102, 104–5, 110, 112–17, 121, 130–41, 151–54, 158, 196–97, 200–201, 203–4, 214, 236; "Clear a road and pay honor before our king!," 130–33; "Ereṣ keyaldah haytah yoneqet," 1; "Grace, grace," 138–40; *Kuzari*, 151–53; *Treatise on Hebrew Meters*, 151; "When the people's chiefs assemble," 137
hand gestures, 37, 102, 286n23
al-Ḥarīrī, 224
al-Ḥarīzī, Yehudah, 25, 27, 97, 141–44, 155, 158, 208, 225, 259–64; *Book of Taḥkemoni*, 142, 263; "Iggeret leshon ha-zahav," 142; *Kitāb al-durar*, 262, 263
al-Ḥasan al-Baṣrī, 113
al-Ḥātimī, *Ḥilyat al-muḥāḍara*, 165
havai (hyperbole), 160–61, 318n4, 320n37. *See also* hyperbole
Hebrew language: Judeo-Arabic compared to, 47–48; status of, 39, 43, 268
Herakleios, 250
al-Ḥillī, Ṣafī al-Dīn, 165, 188
Hinds, Martin, 185
Hishām II, 102
Hispano-Romance language, 131–33, 137
al-Hītī, 'Amram, 97
Ḥizqiyah, Rabbi, 18
Hodgson, Marshall, 95
Horden, Peregrine, 23, 25
Hubert, Henri, 87

INDEX OF GENIZA MANUSCRIPTS

* indicates unpublished. Page numbers in italics refer to illustrations.

CAMBRIDGE

GENEVA

NEW YORK

OXFORD

ACKNOWLEDGMENTS

This project could not have been completed without essential collegial, institutional, and personal support. Since this is a book about panegyric, I thought it fitting to gather scattered bits of praise from the words of the wise דָּבָר דָּבֻר
עַל־אָפְנָיו.

I have enjoyed the kindness of all of my colleagues in the Department of Near Eastern and Judaic Studies at Brandeis University. In particular, I wish to thank those who have shown a special interest in this project or been significant in other ways (not all are at Brandeis presently): Tzvi Abusch מְבַקֵּשׁ
כָּל־עֲצוֹתָיו כְּשׁוֹאֵל Marc Brettler ,דָּת רְאֵה לִבּוֹ אֵרוֹן לָהּ דְּרָשׁ־לְךָ מִלְּשׁוֹנוֹ מִפְּתְחוֹתָיו
תִּמְצָא חֶסֶד וּמִדּוֹת טוֹבוֹת וְעִנְיָן טוֹב עָלֶיהָ לְהַרְבּוֹת Bernadette Brooten ,בָּאוּרִים,
David Ellenson הַבֵּט לְשׁוֹן קֹדֶשׁ וְשׁוּר כִּי לֹא יִתְקַבְּצוּ תוֹכוֹ שְׁנֵי נָחִים, Carl Sharif el-
Tobgui وبات على النار شريف و الندى رضيعي لبان ثدي أم, Sylvia Barack Fishman כֶּתֶר תֹּם
לוּחוֹת לְבָבָהּ כְּלוּחוֹת בְּרִית הֵם וְאַךְ הֵם ChaeRan Freeze ,עַל־רֹאשָׁהּ יְקָרָה הִיא מִפְּנִינִים
רָבִיד לְצַוָּאר תֹּם וְלִימִין הַיְקָר צָמִיד וְלִשְׂמֹאל Sylvia Fuks Fried ,בְּאֶצְבַּע אֱלֹהִים כְּתוּבִים
כְּמַלְאָךְ בִּקְדֻשָּׁה יוֹשֵׁב תַּלְמוּד וְאַגָּדוֹת בְּחָכְמָה Reuven Kimelman ,הָאֱמֶת חוֹתֶמֶת
לְפָאֵר וּלְקַלֵּס לְשַׁבֵּחַ Jonathan Sarna ,בּוֹר סוּד וּמַעְיָן מִתְגַּבֵּר Yehudah Mirsky ,מְיֻשָּׁב
רוּחַ Ilana Szobel ,הַשָּׂר בְּךָ יוֹשֶׁר וְאֵין אִתְּךָ עָוֶל וְכָל חֶסֶד בְּךָ נִמְצָא Ilan Troen ,וּלְהַשְׁבִּיחַ
כְּפִיר דֵּעָה Eugene Sheppard ,נְדִיבָה שְׁאֵלִים תַּעֲנִיק וְיָד יַעַצְרוּ עָבִים וְהִיא מַגְשֶׁמֶת
מִקְדַּשׁ חֲסָדִים כּוֹנְנוּ יָדָיו עֲלֵי אַדְנֵי תְהִלּוֹת עַל־ and David Wright ,וּמוֹעֵצָה וְשַׁחַל תְּבוּנָה
תְּהוֹם הִטְבִּיעַ.

I especially wish to thank friend-colleagues who were generous enough to offer general insights into the project or comments on sections of the work or the entire manuscript: Esperanza Alfonso כִּמְנוֹרָה וְזָהָב כֻּלָּהּ גֻּלָּה עַל רֹאשָׁהּ לְשֵׁם
וּתְהִלָּה Arnold Franklin ,וְהוּא רָם בְּעֵין כֹּל וְשָׁפָל בְּעֵינָיו וְיָחִיד וְרַבִּים הֲלָכָה כְּרַבִּים Ra'anan
Boustan יְלָדוּנוּ בְּנוֹת יָמִים פְּרָדִים וּבַת אַהֲבָה יְלָדַתְנוּ תְאוֹמִים Ross Brann עֵקֶב דְּרָכֶיךָ
לו אעארני אלחרירי פצאחתה ובדיע Luis Girón ,אֲשֶׁר יָשְׁרוּ אד' ג'א פתח אללה ואלנצר
גְּבִירָה מִיּוֹם הֱיוֹתֵךְ חָכְמָה Tova Rosen ,אלזמאן בלאגתה למא קדרת עלי וצף ג'ז מן מעאליה
חַף תּוֹרָתוֹ כָּל־יוֹם תּוֹסִיף גַּם־עַנְוָתוֹ כֵּן Jonathan Ray ,לְבַד הָיְתָה רְעוּתֵךְ הִיא אַתְּ וְאַתְּ הִיא
הִיא הָאֱמוּנָה תּוֹךְ נְוֵה צֶדֶק וְשַׁד הַתֹּם עֲלֵי־חֵיק הָאֱמֶת יוֹנֶקֶת Maud Kozodoy ,נוֹסֶפֶת,

Eitan Fishbane נַשְׁרָא רַבְרְבָא וּבוּצִינָא קְדִישָׁא, Susannah Heschel הַגְּבֶרֶת הַנֶּהֱדֶרֶת אֲשֶׁר כְּזוֹהַר הַחָכְמָה זוֹהֶרֶת, Raymond Scheindlin חָבֵר לְשׁוֹן עֵבֶר וּפִי עֵפֶר וְעֵיפָה, Jocelyn Sharlet غيث الورى نجم السرى نار القرى, Adena Tanenbaum קָשַׁר כֶּתֶר בֵּין עַל־רֹאשָׁהּ וַיָּשֶׂם תֹּם לָהּ מִצְנֶפֶת, and Ryan Szpiech וְאִם אַתָּה גְּדוֹלוֹת לֹא תְבַקֵּשׁ אֱלֹהִים עִתְּדָךְ לִנְתוֹץ וְלִבְנוֹת. For all of them, I am most grateful.

عصابة جاورت أدابهم أدبي فهم وإن فرقوا في الأرض جيراني.

Of scholars I never met, I note that the work of the highly eclectic and erudite Samuel Miklos Stern (1920–69) was waiting along every corridor I went—Fatimid petitions, Romance *kharjas*, Jewish Neoplatonism, the Hebrew poetry of Sicily, Arabic literature by Jewish authors, and the Arabic version of Aristotle's *Poetics.* He died when he was just a few years older than I am now. I only wish to acknowledge his rare gift for spotting interesting subjects and his extraordinary contribution.

Sections of this book were presented at various conferences and invited lectures. The feedback I received from participants at these venues, far too many to name, was invaluable: the Katz Center for Advanced Jewish Studies at the University of Pennsylvania; Brown University; Dartmouth College; Harvard University; the Jewish Theological Seminary of America; the Institute for Advanced Study, Princeton; the Tauber Institute for the Study of European Jewry, Brandeis University; Columbia University; the University of California Los Angeles; the University of Southern California; the University of California, Davis; the Association for Jewish Studies; the Medieval Hebrew Poetry Colloquium; and the Mediterranean Seminar.

Research and indexing were supported by grants from the European Research Council ("Inteleg: The Intellectual and Material Legacies of Late Medieval Sephardic Judaism"), the Tauber Institute for the Study of European Jewry at Brandeis University, and the Theodore and Jane Norman Fund for Faculty Research at Brandeis.

A number of students assisted with research, bibliography compilation, and editing: Aviv Ben-Or, Lucia Finotto, Allyson Gonzalez, Mostafa Hussein, Benjamin Notis, and Benjamin Steiner. צִבְיֵי עֲפָרִים וּמִשְׂכְּלָם הֲלֹא אִלְּפוּ עָרְמָה פְּתָאִים וּבָם חָכְמוּ חֲכָמֵינוּ.

Parts of Chapter 4 are from my chapter "Mediterranean Regionalism in Hebrew Panegyric Poetry," in *Regional Identities and Cultures of Medieval Jews*, ed. Talya Fishman and Ephraim Kanarfogel (Liverpool: Littman Library of Jewish Civilization in association with Liverpool University Press, 2018). They are reproduced here by permission.

I don't believe that a single page of this book was not written or edited while I sat at Café Fixe (Brookline, Massachusetts). I wish to thank the regulars, especially Monique Hamze, Charles Kaner, Yoav Mehozay, and Moshe Sofer, for leaving me to work when I wished but also for being available for much needed human interaction. القهوة أخت الوقت.

My family and friends have been an enduring source of love, support, and encouragement: my parents, David Decter אִישׁ אֶחָד וְיִקָּרֵא קְהִלָּה and Carole Decter אֵם הַיְּקָר תַּמָּה כְבוּדָה כְּמוֹ שֶׁמֶשׁ בְּדוֹרָךְ; my brother and sister-in-law, Adam and Margie, and my three wonderful nephews, Noah, Jacob, and Zack; my in-laws from Chicago—Debra, Mia and Megan, Gideon, Noa, and Grandma Marilyn Horberg; and in Nashville, Bonnie, Doug, and Reshmi. Back in Boston, I am grateful for the entire extended clan; in particular, my cousins Philip, Jennifer, and Emmett Wickham Decter have provided much warmth, fun, and counsel. I am also thankful for good friends (in addition to those included above) who are basically family: Edna Friedberg and Stig Tromer, Stuart and Wiebke Light, and Gavriel Speyer.

מְסַכְתֶּם לִי אֲהָבוֹת עִם נְדָבוֹת וְנַפְשִׁי בַּעֲסִיסֵיהֶן שְׁכוּרָה.

Most profoundly, I thank my wife Nikki, who, to quote one of the desert fathers, has "suffered with me."

שֵׂכֶל תַּעְטֶה כְּרִקְמָה וְיֹפִי תַּעְדֶּה כְּחֶלְיָה מַתָּן אִמְרֵי שֶׁפֶר וְלִבּוֹת תְּנַהֵג בַּשְּׁבִיָּה רְשָׁפֶיהָ רִשְׁפֵּי אֵשׁ שַׁלְהֶבֶתְיָה.

Our two beautiful and wondrous daughters, Lila Ya'el and Ariel Paz, are the greatest gifts life could bring. My gratitude for all of their love is immeasurable.

יַעֲלַת חֵן יַלְדָּה נֶחְמָדָה יְקָרָה הִיא מִפְּנִינִים כָּל הַמִּשְׁפָּחָה בָּהּ דְגוּלִים מַתְּנַת אֵל שׁוֹכֵן מְעוֹנִים.